YALE ORIENTAL SERIES
CUNEIFORM TEXTS
VOLUME XXIV

YALE ORIENTAL SERIES • CUNEIFORM TEXTS VOL. XXIV

LATE BABYLONIAN ADMINISTRATIVE AND LEGAL TEXTS, CONCERNING CRAFTSMEN, FROM THE EANNA ARCHIVE

BY

YUVAL LEVAVI AND ELIZABETH E. PAYNE

Yale UNIVERSITY PRESS

NEW HAVEN AND LONDON

Published with assistance from the Yale Babylonian Collection and the Alexander Kohut Memorial Fund.

Yale University Press books may be purchased in quantity for educational, business, or promotional use. For information, please e-mail sales.press@yale.edu (U.S. office) or sales@yaleup.co.uk (U.K. office).

Designed by Klaus Wagensonner. Set in Palatino type by Klaus Wagensonner.

Printed in the United States of America.

Library of Congress Control Number: 2024933537
ISBN 978-0-300-27190-4 (hardcover: alk. paper)

A catalogue record for this book is available from the British Library.

This paper meets the requirements of ANSI/NISO Z39.48-1992 (Permanence of Paper).

10 9 8 7 6 5 4 3 2 1

CONTENTS

Foreword *vii*

Preface *ix*

Abbreviations *xi*

Introduction 1
- On the Present Volume 1
- Chronological Distribution 1
- Arrangement of Texts in This Volume 1
- Typology of Texts 2
- Seal Impressions 5
- Translation and Conventions 5

Catalogue 7

Concordance of Museum Numbers 23

Text Editions 35

Indices 241
- Personal Names 241
- Akkadian Words 270
- Month Names 291
- Temples 291
- Divine Names 291
- Geographical Names and Toponyms 291
- Texts 292

Bibliography 297

Plates 303

FOREWORD

The first volume of the Yale Oriental Series: Babylonian Texts—*Miscellaneous Inscriptions in the Yale Babylonian Collection*—was published in 1915 by Albert T. Clay. For more than a century, the standard format for volumes in the series has been a short introduction, followed by a text catalogue, sometimes with selected (partial) editions, indices, and plates with hand copies.

Beginning with the present volume, Yuval Levavi and Elizabeth E. Payne's volume *Late Babylonian Administrative and Legal Texts, Concerning Craftsmen, from the Eanna Archive*, the format of the series will see some changes, which we hope will enhance its usefulness. Most importantly, volumes will from now on include full editions of all published texts, with transliterations, translations, and commentaries. This will make the texts much more accessible to audiences beyond a slim circle of specialists. Moreover, one year after their publication in print, eBook versions of new volumes will be made available for free. Finally, the title of the series will change to Yale Oriental Series: Cuneiform Texts.

Over the past years, the Yale Babylonian Collection has seen some changes as well. Most importantly, it is now part of the Division of Anthropology of the Yale Peabody Museum. But it remains a distinct collection housed in Yale's Sterling Memorial Library and continues to carry out its central mission: to safeguard and study the cuneiform tablets, seals, and other ancient artifacts that it holds.

The Yale Babylonian Collection Publication Committee
Eckart Frahm, Agnete Wisti Lassen, Klaus Wagensonner

PREFACE

The texts presented here are published with the kind permission of Agnete Wisti Lassen, associate curator of the Yale Babylonian Collection. The project was first initiated by Elizabeth E. Payne with the support of Benjamin R. Foster, former curator of the Yale Babylonian Collection, Eckart Frahm, professor of Assyriology at Yale University, and Ulla Kasten, former associate curator of the collection. The work of Y. Levavi was conducted under the auspices of the project *"The Material Culture of Babylonia in the First Millennium BC"* funded by the ANR and the Austrian Science Fund (FWF), I 3927-G25. A special thanks is owed to Michael Jursa, without whose support and numerous suggestions the completion of this volume would not have been possible. Further thanks are extended to Klaus Wagensonner from the Yale Babylonian Collection for supplying us with quality images of the tablets as well as for his ample and thoughtful help during the work on the manuscript. We would also like to thank the following friends and colleagues who lent their hand along the way: Rasmus Aarslev, Rosaura Cauchi, Johannes Hackl, Louise Quillien, Zachary Rubin, Ran Zadok, and Shana Zaia.

ABBREVIATIONS

AfO	*Archiv für Orientforschung*
AHw	W. von Soden, *Akkadisches Handwörterbuch* (1965–1981)
AnOr	*Analecta Orientalia*
AOAT	Alter Orient und Altes Testament
AoF	*Altorientalische Forschungen*
API	E. Herzfeld, *Altpersische Inschriften*. Berlin: Reimer, 1938
ArOr	*Archiv orientálni*
ARRIM	*Annual Review of the Royal Inscriptions of Mesopotamia Project*
AUWE	Ausgrabungen in Uruk-Warka, Endberichte
BaM	*Baghdader Mitteilungen*
BC	new siglum of cuneiform texts housed in the Yale Babylonian Collection (see also GCBC, NBC, NCBT, and YBC)
BE	The Babylonian Expedition of the University of Pennsylvania
BIN	Babylonian Inscriptions in the Collection of James B. Nies
BiOr	*Bibliotheca Orientalis*
BM	siglum of cuneiform texts housed in the British Museum, London
BRM	Babylonian Records in the Library of J. Pierpont Morgan
CAD	*Chicago Assyrian Dictionary*
Camb	J. N. Strassmaier, *Inschriften von Cambyses, König von Babylon*. Leipzig: Pfeiffer, 1890
CDA	*Concise Dictionary of Akkadian*

CDLI	Cuneiform Digital Library Initiative (https://cdli.mpiwg-berlin.mpg.de)
CM	Cuneiform Monographs
CT	Cuneiform Texts from Babylonian Tablets in the British Museum
Cyr	J. N. Strassmaier, *Inschriften von Cyrus, König von Babylon*. Leipzig: Pfeiffer, 1890
Dar	J. N. Strassmaier, *Inschriften von Darius, König von Babylon*. Leipzig: Pfeiffer, 1897
Eames	siglum of cuneiform texts housed in the New York Public Library, New York City
Ehrenberg, AUWE 18	E. Ehrenberg, *Uruk. Late Babylonian Seal Impressions on Eanna-Tablets* (AUWE 18). Mainz: von Zabern, 1999
EPHE	texts published in J.-M. Durand, *Documents cunéiformes de la IVe section de l'École pratique des Hautes Études*. Geneva and Paris: Librairie Droz, 1982
FLP	siglum of cuneiform texts housed in the Free Library of Philadelphia, Philadelphia
GAG	Grundriß der akkadischen Grammatik
GC	Goucher College Cuneiform Inscriptions
GCBC	siglum of cuneiform texts in the Goucher College Babylonian Collection (Yale University)
GMTR	Guides to the Mesopotamian Textual Record
JSOR	*Journal of the Society of Oriental Research*
JTVI	*Journal of the Transactions of the Victoria Institute*
Iraq 59	texts published in M. Jursa, "Neu- und spätbabylonische Texte aus den Sammlungen der Birmingham Museums and Art Gallery," *Iraq* 59 (1997): 97–174
MR	texts published in C. Waerzeggers, *Marduk-rēmanni: Local Networks and Imperial Politics in Achaemenid Babylonia* (OLA 233). Leuven: Peeters, 2014
N.A.B.U.	*Nouvelles Assyriologiques Brèves et Utilitaires*
NBC	siglum for tablets in the Nies Babylonian Collection (Yale University)
NBDMich	E. W. Moore, *Neo-Babylonian Documents in the University of Michigan Collection*. Ann Arbor: University of Michigan Press, 1939

Nbk	J. N. Strassmaier, *Inschriften von Nabuchodonosor, König von Babylon*. Leipzig: Pfeiffer, 1889
Nbn	J. N. Strassmaier, *Inschriften von Nabonidus, König von Babylon*. Leipzig: Pfeiffer, 1889
NCBT	siglum for tablets in the Newell Collection of Babylonian Tablets (Yale University)
NINO	Nederlands Instituut Voor Het Nabije Oosten
OECT	Oxford Editions of Cuneiform Texts
OLA	Orientalia Lovaniensia Analecta
OrAn	*Oriens antiquus. Rivista del Centro per l'antichità e la storia dell'arte del Vicino Oriente*
PTS	siglum for tablets in the collections of the Princeton Theological Seminary
RA	*Revue d'Assyriologie et d'Archéologie Orientale*
RGTC 8	R. Zadok, *Geographical Names According to New- and Late-Babylonian Texts* (RGTC 8). Wiesbaden: Reichert, 1985
RLA	Reallexikon der Assyriologie
SAA	State Archives of Assyria
Sack CD	R. H. Sack, *Cuneiform Documents from the Chaldean and Persian Periods.* Selinsgrove: Susquehanna University Press and London and Toronto: Associated University Presses, 1994
SBTU	Spätbabylonische Texte aus Uruk
TCL	Textes cunéiformes du Louvre
UCP	University of California Publications in Semitic Philology
UF	Ugarit-Forschungen. Internationales Jahrbuch für die Altertumskunde Syrien-Palästinas
VAB	Vorderasiatische Bibliothek
VS	Vorderasiatische Schriftdenkmäler der Königlichen Museen zu Berlin
YBC	siglum for tablets in the` Yale Babylonian Collection (Yale University)
YOS	Yale Oriental Series, Babylonian Texts
ZA	*Zeitschrift für Assyriologie und Vorderasiatische Archäologie*

Babylonian dates are given as "day . month (in capital Roman numerals) . regnal year" followed by the king's name. Accession years are expressed as "0a RN." In the translations, dates are spelled out. The rulers' names are abbreviated as follows:

Am	Amīl-Marduk
Camb	Cambyses
Cyr	Cyrus
Dar	Darius
Kan	Kandalānu
Nbk	Nebuchadnezzar
Nbn	Nabonidus
Ner	Neriglissar
Npl	Nabopolassar

Three-part filiations are rendered as: personal name/father's name//family name.

⸢ ⸣	partially preserved signs
*	reading improved by collation
[ ]	broken and/or restored signs and passages
{ }	erased by the scribe
< >	omitted signs in the cuneiform text
<< >>	redundant signs in the cuneiform text
!	emended sign
?	uncertain reading of a sign
o	sign written over previous sign
DN	divine name
eras.	erasure
GN	geographical name
Le.E.	left edge of a tablet
Lo.E.	lower edge of a tablet
Obv.	obverse of a tablet
Pl.	plural
PN	personal name
Rev.	reverse of a tablet
Sg.	singular
T.	Text
Up.E.	upper edge of a tablet

The handcopies on Plates I–LXXXVIII are printed 120% of the original size.
The photos on Plate LXXXIX are printed 200% of the original size.

INTRODUCTION

On the Present Volume

The 315 texts in this volume were assembled by E. E. Payne as part of her study of the craftsmen, textile and metal workers in the Eanna temple during the Neo-Babylonian Period.[1] This forms the common thread for most texts in this volume, either in the form of subject matter or prosopography.[2] In the course of 2004–2008, E. E. Payne prepared hand-copies, preliminary transliterations, and translations of most of the texts. This draft was then shelved for about twelve years, until the spring of 2019, when Y. Levavi took over the manuscript. His work included a review and update of the editions, the translation of the remaining untranslated texts, collating and, when necessary, emending the hand-copies, and adding commentary, prosopography, indices, and the introduction. Regarding hand-copies, 314 were prepared by E. E. Payne, while Y. Levavi is responsible for **No. 281**, as well as for minor corrections and improvements in about twenty additional copies.

Previous YOS volumes traditionally focused on presenting autographed copies of the tablets from the Yale Babylonian Collection (alongside indices and a catalog). The present volume, however, includes full text editions: transliterations, translations, and essential commentary. This will allow scholars of various levels and backgrounds easier access to primary sources. Note, however, that due to space and format limitations, both philological and (even more so) prosopographical commentary are kept to a minimum. The latter is restricted to the context of dating the tablets.

Chronological Distribution

Of the 315 tablets, 204 are dated at least by year (including reconstructions) (**Fig. 1**). The earliest text in the corpus, **No. 33**, is dated to 14 Kan (635 BCE) and the latest, **No. 215**, was written in 4 Camb (526 BCE). Yet the chronological distribution of the (dateable) texts is highly uneven, with the vast majority of dateable texts dated to the reign of Nebuchadnezzar (177/204, 86%), especially from year 12 (593 BCE) onwards. An additional eighty tablets can only be roughly dated based on prosopography, with the following distribution: Kan–Npl, 5/80 (6.25%); Npl–early Nbk, 30/80 (37.5%); Nbk (mostly mid-reign), 21/80 (26.25%); late Nbk–early Persian, 19/80 (23.75%); Cyr–Camb, 5/80 (6.25%). Thirty-one tablets cannot be dated.

Arrangement of Texts in This Volume

The texts are arranged in clusters, first based on subject matter (mainly source material), with typology serving as a secondary criterion. Naturally, these criteria, especially the former, are not mutually exclusive: many texts deal with multiple items/source materials (e.g., gold, iron, textiles, etc.), and

1 See Payne 2007.

2 Note, however, that editions of some texts that at some point were deemed either less or not relevant to Payne's study (2007) were not omitted from the present volume.

could thus be placed in several different clusters. The first four clusters concern metals: gold (**Nos. 1–44**), silver (as source material, **Nos. 45–56**), bronze (**Nos. 57–71**), and iron (**Nos. 72–140**).[3] These are followed by clusters of stones (**Nos. 141–143**), textiles (**Nos. 144–167**), wool (**Nos. 168–183**), goat hair (**Nos. 184–185**), and dyes (**Nos. 186–188**). The texts in the next two clusters deal mostly with salaries and other transactions in silver (**Nos. 189–214**) and barley (**Nos. 215–234**). There follow several small clusters that focus on various commodities: beer (**Nos. 235–241**), dates (**Nos. 242–248**), flour (**Nos. 249–251**), reeds (**Nos. 252–260**), hides (**Nos. 261–271**), oil (**Nos. 272–274**), wax (**Nos. 275–276**), honey (**No. 277**), sesame (**No. 278**), wood (**No. 279**), and salt (**No. 280**). Animal husbandry is at the focus of the next cluster (**Nos. 281–287**), followed by personnel lists (**Nos. 288–299**), general cult (**Nos. 300–301**), and miscellanea (**Nos. 302–310**). The last cluster contains five legal texts (**Nos. 311–315**).[4] It is important to stress again that many materials, commodities, and items are referred to in more than just one specific cluster. For a full list of attestations, the reader should consult the index.

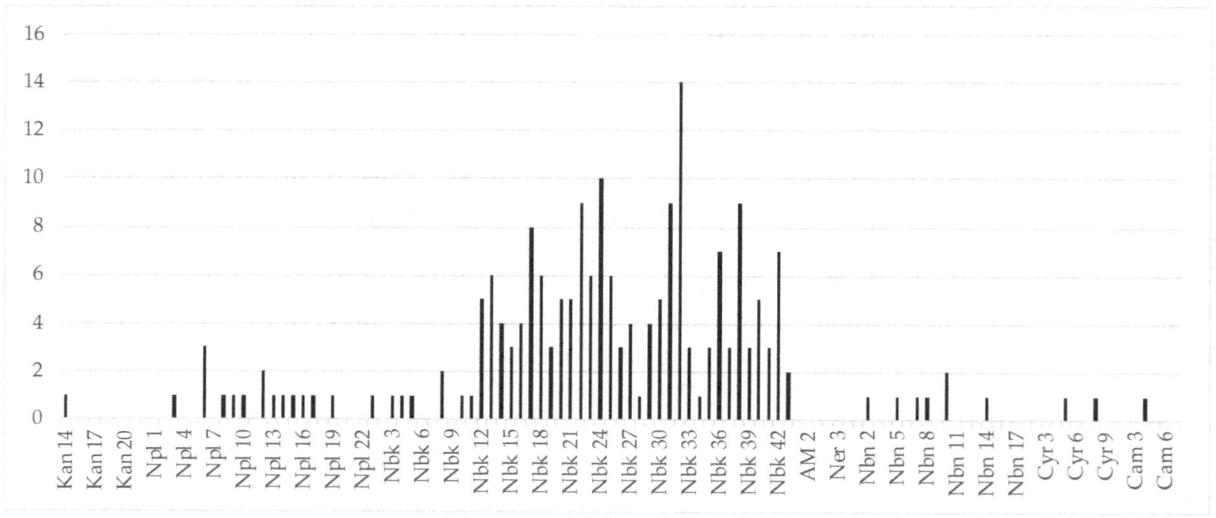

Fig. 1 Chronological distribution of (dateable) texts

Typology of Texts

Apart from the seven (witnessed) legal records (**Nos. 71, 232, 311–315**), all texts in this volume may be classified as administrative notes and lists.[5] In the catalogue below, an attempt has been made for a typological standardization, based on both functional and formal aspects of the administrative sources. Vague generic headings were avoided when possible, though in some cases the lack of context or fragmentary state compelled us to resort to headings with less heuristic value. Among these we might include several texts in the "accounting inventory" group as well as "personnel lists";

[3] Within the iron cluster, the dossier of the blacksmith Nabû-zēru-iddin is presented first (**Nos. 72–94**), followed by the texts featuring his son, Mušēzib-Bēl (**Nos. 95–102**).

[4] Note that **Nos. 71** and **232** are witnessed texts as well, though they are included in different clusters.

[5] A definition and differentiation between these two terms, notes and lists, is elusive, and must be based on flexible quantitative guidelines. As a rule of thumb, we may say that a note contains 1–3 items, beyond which we may talk of a list. One may think of the following modern example: "(buy) milk and cat food" is a note while "milk, cat food, wine, diapers, broccoli, and garlic" is a shopping list.

see below. In the following we first present the main three text types (accompanied by examples), which is followed by a short description of additional typologies used in this volume.

***ina pāni* note/list** is the most common text type in the corpus: 100 cases (some are combined with other types). The basic core formula, "x *ina pāni* PN," is translated as "x is at the disposal of PN." Such *ina pāni* clauses can be used in various contexts and in combination with several other key phrases and typologies. A text is considered to be an *ina pāni* note/list in cases in which this phrase is the main/focal point. **No. 59** is an example of a simple, short *ina pāni* note:

59. NCBT 922

Copy: Plate XVI
Date: 14.VI.31 Nbk
Summary: *ina pāni* note: bronze

Obv. ⸢1 MA⸣.NA 50 GIN$_2$ ZABAR
⸢*a-na dul*⸣*-lu ina pa-ni*
^{I}⸢*lib*⸣*-luṭ* ^{lu_2}SIMUG
(blank)
Rev. ^{iti}KIN UD.14.KAM MU.31.KAM
^{d}AG-NIG$_2$.⸢DU-URU$_3$ LUGAL⸣ TIN.TIR$^{!ki}$

1 mina 50 shekels of bronze are at the disposal of Libluṭ, the smith, for work.
Month VI, day 14, year 31 of Nebuchadnezzar, king of Babylon.

***maḫir* receipt** is the second most common text type, with 75 cases (some are combined with other types). The basic core formula, "x PN *maḫir*," is translated as "x was received from PN." In the context of the Eanna archive, these texts are always written from the temple perspective, and Eanna is the unmentioned receiver in all cases.[6] Like in the case of *ina pāni* above, the *maḫir* clause can be incorporated alongside other formulae, and in various combinations. A text is considered to be a *maḫir* receipt in cases in which the pertinent clause is the main/focal point. **No. 268** is an example of a simple, short *maḫir* receipt:

268. NCBT 727

Copy: Plate LXVIII
Date: 29.XII.22 Nbk
Summary: *maḫir* receipt: hides

Obv. 10 ^{kuš}*ṣal-la*^{me}
^{I}NUMUN-*u$_2$-tu* A ^{Id}UTU-SU
^{lu_2}*ṣa-rip* ^{kuš}*du-šu-u$_2$*
IGI^{ir}
Rev. (blank)

6 On the use of *maḫāru* in contemporary archival sources, see Jursa 2005, 46–7.

^{iti}ŠE UD.29.KAM ⸢MU⸣.22.KAM
⸢^{d}AG⸣-NIG$_2$.DU-URU$_3$ LUGAL TIN.TIR^{ki}

Ten tanned hides were received from Zērūtu, son of Šamaš-erība, the leather dyer. Month XII, day 29, year 22 of Nebuchadnezzar, king of Babylon.

withdrawal (*našû*) notes/lists record items that have been taken away by temple personnel. In the catalogue, 51 texts are defined as withdrawal (*našû*) notes. Many of them record multiple transactions of various kinds. The verb *našû* is most often written with the logogram GIŠ (often with phonetic complements), though syllabic spellings are found too: Sg. *it-ta-ši* (e.g., **No. 181**: 4), and Pl. *it-ta-šu$_2$-u* (e.g., **No. 201**: 11). **No. 270** is an example of a simple, short withdrawal (*našû*) note:

270. NCBT 122

Copy: Plate LXVIII
Date: 21.IX.21 Nbk
Summary: withdrawal (*našû*) note: hides

Obv. 13° KUŠ° ^{meš} *ša$_2$*$^{?!}$ ⸢6⸣ UDU.NITA$_2$^{me}
ku-⸢mi°⸣ 2° ŠUK°.ḪI.A^{meš} *ša$_2$*
^{iti}⸢AB$^{?}$ ^{I}⸣^{d}EN-E ^{lu_2}UŠ$^{!}$.BAR GIŠ
{one line erased}
Rev. (blank)
^{iti}GAN UD.21.KAM MU.21.KAM
^{d}AG-NIG$_2$.DU-URU$_3$ LUGAL TIN.TIR^{ki}

Bēl-iqbi, the weaver, withdrew thirteen hides of six sheep instead of two salaries of month X. Month IX, day 21, year 21 of Nebuchadnezzar, king of Babylon.

issue (*nadin*) note/list, which is used in 23 cases (some combined with additional types), is a rather straightforward description of both content and function. The verb *nadānu* is written either syllabically or logographically (SUM), and in various grammatical forms. Longer lists may contain headings; e.g., **Nos. 189** and **190**. **No. 191** is an example of a simple, short issue (*nadin*) note:

191. NCBT 434

Copy: Plate XLVIII
Date: 21.X.12 Nbk
Summary: issue (*nadin*) note: silver

Obv. 1 GIN$_2$ KU$_3$.BABBAR *a-na*
^{giš}DA *a-na* ^{I}*na-din*
A ^{Id}AMAR.UTU-GI *na-din*
Rev. (blank)
^{iti}AB ⸢UD⸣.21.KAM MU.12.KAM

⸢^{d}AG⸣-NIG$_{2}$.DU-URU$_{3}$
⸢LUGAL⸣ TIN.TIR⸢^{ki}⸣

1 shekel of silver was given to Nādinu, son of Marduk-ušallim, for a writing board. Month X, day 21, year 12 of Nebuchadnezzar, king of Babylon.

Inventory note/list, though relatively generic as a typological term, is nonetheless used for 15 texts.[7] These texts lack an operative clause regarding transactions or movements of items, and present a static image. The context of these texts often eludes us, though some texts do contain explanatory headings or statements regarding the whereabouts of the listed items. In essence, an inventory note/list may be seen as an administration-internal *ina pāni* note.

Accounting note/inventory is used for a variety of inventory entries that "surpass" the simple inventorial note, altogether 42 texts. That is, a text of this category contains additional information regarding origin and/or destination of a commodity, and/or more elaborate calculations (compared to a simple inventory note). With this text type, we prefer "accounting inventory" over "accounting list," since some of these texts present greater complexity than a straightforward list. Thus, some accounting inventories may contain *ina pāni*, *maḫir*, or *nadin* clauses as part of a wider-ranging accounting procedure.

Other typologies used are straightforward and require no further commentary. Delivery (*šūbulu*) notes are records of outgoing shipments (7 cases). Payment (*apil/eṭir*) note refers to records of various allocations (gold, silver, and barley) paid for service to the temple (7 cases). Personnel list is a straightforward description of content (10 texts). Among the few legal documents included in this volume, we find records of interrogation/testimony, summons guarantees, promissory notes,[8] and a work contract.

Seal Impressions

Three tablets in the corpus contain seal impressions (see Plate LXXXIX). All of these were included in Ehrenberg 1999:

Ehrenberg, AUWE 18	YOS 24	Description
97	No. 237	short-haired worshipper in front of a symbol
14	No. 239	double lion-headed standard under an eight-pointed star, with lifted forearm to its right. The seal is probably the same as the one imprinted by Bēl-nādin-apli on GC 2, 389 (Ehrenberg 1999, 49).[9]
17	No. 240	same as No. 239

Translation and Conventions

All texts in this volume were written in the Late Babylonian dialect on clay tablets. As may be expected from a product of a temple's bureaucratic system, the language is generally "dry," relies heavily on administrative stock phrases, and is packed with technical terminology. In translating

7 These do not include "accounting inventories," on which see below.

8 Note **No. 106**, which contains no witnesses.

9 The seal on GC 2, 389 is Ehrenberg 1999, No. 18; note the typo GCCI 2, 39, and the omission of the 8.

administrative stock phrases, we favor functionality and clarity over literality and grammatical accuracy; note the following examples: *ina pāni* PN ("at the disposal of PN"), *ina muḫḫi* PN ("owed by PN"), *ina qāt* PN ("via PN"), PN *maḫir* ("received from PN").

Translating specific technical terminology, especially (official) titles, professions, and objects (tools, vessels, etc.), is more complicated. In line with the overall intention to make these sources as accessible as possible, Akkadian terminology is left untranslated only in one of three cases. First, unclear terms, whether we know the general semantic sphere or not, are not (and cannot be) translated into English. In these cases, we may or may not present a conjectured form, depending on the context and readability of the lemma. Second, terms are left in the original form when no simple English parallel is available, and in particular, none that does not require further elaboration and/or does not carry further (unwanted) connotations. Among these cases we may mention terms denoting functionaries such as, e.g., the *šatammu*, *qīpu*, and *rab sikkati*. Third, cases of multiple Akkadian terms for which no distinction can be made in English are left untranslated. Note, for example, the following Akkadian words for different bowls: *makkasu*, *šappu*, and *kallu*; these are translated as *makkasu*-bowl, *šappu*-bowl, and *kallu*-bowl, respectively.

Translations are kept as consistent and clear as possible. Context, however, may force us to employ several English translations of a single Akkadian word. Thus, for example, *kurummatu* is translated in most cases as "salaries," and not, as often found in the literature, as "rations."[10] The latter, however, is used in context for which "salaries" cannot be maintained; e.g., *kurummatu ša šarri*, as well the *kurummatu* of the captive women in **No. 222**, and the *kurummatu* for the wildcats in **No. 233**.

Numbers are in general given in numerals when ocurring with measurements; otherwise, they are spelled out; thus "2 shekels (of silver)," but "two sheep." When unspecified or broken objects are counted, numerals are used. Triple-digit numbers (and higher) are given in numerals, with a few exceptions for the sake of consistency within a single text. Fractions of minas, when combined with shekels, are given in shekels; e.g., ⅓ (MA.NA) 6 GIN_2 is rendered as 26 shekels. Notation of capacity measurements follows the standard practice in first millennium Babylonia scholarship: 1;2.3.4 = 1 *kurru*, 2 *pānu*, 3 *sūtu*, 4 *qû*.[11]

For the rendering of personal names, see the introductory remarks to the personal name index.

[10] The semantic difference between the two English terms is especially important in the context of temple administration; see Jursa 2010, 672–3.

[11] These, however, are spelled out in cases of a single measurement; thus "1 kor" rather then 1;0.0.0.

CATALOGUE

No.	*Museum No.*	*Date*	*Measurements (in mm)*	*Summary*	*Plate*
1	NCBT 1121	07.XI.37 Nbk	27 × 43 × 15	*ina pāni* note: gold	I
2	NCBT 1227	undated (Kan–Npl)	40 × 61 × 20	*ina pāni* note: gold	I
3	NCBT 792	30.XI.37 Nbk	34 × 51 × 19	*ina pāni* note: gold	I
4	YBC 9031	08.[×].0a [Ner–Nbn]	30 × 43 × 16	*ina pāni* note: gold	I
5	YBC 9039	21.XIIb.10(+) Npl	30 × 44 × 16	*ina pāni* note: gold	II
6	YBC 9414	25.III.29 Nbk	26 × 35 × 15	*ina pāni* note: gold	II
7	YBC 9516	17.VI.30 Nbk	31 × 47 × 16	*ina pāni* note: gold	II
8	YBC 9590	24.VI.31 Nbk	28 × 40 × 17	*ina pāni* note: gold	II
9	NBC 9820	02.[×.× Nbk–Nbn]	17 × 34 × 14	*ina pāni* note: gold	III
10	NCBT 410	22?.[×].17? [Npl]	27 × 41 × 17	*ina pāni* note: gold	III
11	NCBT 974	07.II.03 (Npl)	27 × 39 × 18	*ina pāni* note + *maḫir* receipt: gold	III
12	NCBT 568	23.X.08 --	29 × 47 × 19	*ina pāni* note + *maḫir* receipt: gold and silver	III
13	NCBT 653	undated (Kan–Npl)	41 × 74 × 23	*ina pāni* note + weighing: gold	IV
14	YBC 9436	01.V.32 Nbk	30 × 42 × 16	*ina pāni* note: crown of Nanāya	IV
15	NCBT 500	undated	37 × 53 × 20	unfinished *ina pāni* note: gold	IV
16	NCBT 462	13.IV.16 (Kan–Npl)	29 × 40 × 15	*maḫir* receipt + payment (*eṭir*) note: gold	IV
17	YBC 11495	14.IV.15 (Npl)	27 × 40 × 16	*maḫir* receipt: gold	V

No.	*Museum No.*	*Date*	*Measurements (in mm)*	*Summary*	*Plate*
18	NBC 4815	[...Npl/Nbk]	67 × 41 × 22	*maḫir* receipt: gold and silver + *ina pāni* clause	V
19	NCBT 1157	--.--.13 (Nbk)	40 × 57 × 18	payment (*eṭir*) note: gold	V
20	NCBT 442	01.VI.12 (Npl)	26 × 37 × 14	payment (*eṭir*) note: gold	V
21	YBC 9447	[×.×.×] Nbk	85 × 54 × 24	inventory list: cultic ornaments	VI
22	NCBT 503	undated	43 × 59 × 23	accounting inventory: gold	VI
23	YBC 8798	19.III.30 Nbk	27 × 37 × 15	accounting note: gold	VII
24	YBC 9204	01.XII.17 Nbk	59 × 34 × 17	inventory list: gold items	VII
25	YBC 9235	18.VIII.32 Nbk	34 × 48 × 18	accounting + withdrawal (*našû*) note: gold and cress	VII
26	NCBT 734	22.XI.22 Nbk	28 × 39 × 16	issue (*nadin*) note: gold	VII
27	NCBT 604	14?.VI.12 [Npl]	38 × 42 × 18	accounting inventory: gold	VIII
28	NCBT 622	undated	36 × 62 × 24	accounting note: silver and gold	VIII
29	YBC 9326	29.III.29 Nbk	43 × 58 × 17	accounting inventory: gold	VIII
30	NCBT 527	undated (Npl)	45 × 77 × 21	accounting inventory: gold for silver	IX
31	NBC 4624	16.V.06 (Npl)	26 × 39 × 17	*ina pāni* list	IX
32	NCBT 508	02.VIII.-- --	36 × 56 × 19	*ina pāni* note: gold and beads	IX
33	NCBT 368	09.IV.14 Kan	38 × 66 × 19	*maḫir* receipt (+ *ina pāni* clause): red gold and bronze	X
34	YBC 9240	27.XI.25 Nbk	37 × 50 × 16	*ina pāni* note (no PN): gold ornaments	X
35	NCBT 988	21.VII.08 (Npl–Nbk)	27 × 51 × 14	*ina pāni* note: gold	X
36	NCBT 296	19.II.33 Nbk	25 × 39 × 15	*ina pāni* note: gold	X
37	NCBT 1187	20.×.13 --	30 × 43 × 17	*ina pāni* note: ornaments	XI
38	NCBT 559	25.XI.14 (Npl)	34 × 47 × 17	*maḫir* receipt: gold ornaments	XI
39	NCBT 956	28.XI.33 Nbk	34 × 50 × 17	*maḫir* receipt: gold ornaments	XI

No.	Museum No.	Date	Measurements (in mm)	Summary	Plate
40	NCBT 1008	14.II.38 Nbk	39 × 53 × 19	inventory list: gold ornaments	XI
41	YBC 11486	01.V.27 Nbk	26 × 36 × 14	inventory note: gold ornaments	XII
42	YBC 3438	14.II.31 Nbk	34 × 46 × 15	inventory note: gold ornaments	XII
43	YBC 9638	04(+)II?.33 Nbk	32 × 44 × 17	inventory note: gold ornaments	XII
44	YBC 8818	01.I.26 Nbk	36 × 45 × 18	inventory note: gold ornaments	XII
45	NBC 4638	11.XI.24 Nbk	29 × 40 × 15	delivery (*šūbulu*) note: silver	XIII
46	NCBT 794	20.IV.04 --	38 × 59 × 19	*ina pāni* note: silver	XIII
47	NCBT 536	undated (Nbk)	37 × 62 × 20	*ina pāni* note: silver (undated)	XIII
48	NBC 4672	03.I.12 (Npl–Nbk)	29 × 47 × 17	*ina pāni* note: white silver	XIII
49	NCBT 755	05.IX.37 Nbk	30 × 40 × 14	accounting inventory: silver	XIV
50	NCBT 357	02.XII.31 Nbk	72 × 42 × 22	inventory list: divine silver items	XIV
51	NCBT 1246	01(+).III?.03(+) --	61 × 40 × 20	inventory list: varia	XV
52	YBC 9393	30.II.40? Nbk	24 × 32 × 13	issue (*nadin*) note: silver	XIV
53	GCBC 636	[×].IX?.5 Nbn	23 × 32 × 15	*maḫir* receipt: silver	XV
54	YBC 9178	05.VII.03? Nbk	34 × 49 × 16	*maḫir* receipt: gold and silver items	XV
55	NCBT 147	26.XI.17 Nbk	28 × 40 × 15	withdrawal (*našû*) + delivery (*šūbulu*) note: silver	XVI
56	NCBT 468	26.XI.17 Nbk	28 × 42 × 16	withdrawal (*našû*) note: silver	XVI
57	NCBT 265	18.XI.36 Nbk	25 × 37 × 14	[*ina pāni*] note: cooking pot	XVI
58	NCBT 735	12.VIII.20 Nbk	24 × 34 × 15	*ina pāni* note: bronze	XVI
59	NCBT 922	14.VI.31 Nbk	24 × 36 × 14	*ina pāni* note: bronze	XVI
60	YBC 11278	24.XI.07 (Npl–Nbk)	16 × 25 × 12	*ina pāni* note: bronze	XVII
61	NBC 4560	23.XI.06 --	23 × 38 × 14	*ina pāni* note: bronze	XVII

No.	*Museum No.*	*Date*	*Measurements (in mm)*	*Summary*	*Plate*
62	NCBT 325	23.I.42 Nbk	27 × 37 × 14	*ina pāni* note: bronze	XVII
63	YBC 9442	28.VI.27 Nbk	26 × 35 × 13	*ina pāni* note: bronze bowl	XVII
64	NCBT 912	20.IV.14 N[pl/bk]	29 × 39 × 14	*ina pāni* note: copper	XVII
65	YBC 9237	27.XII.33 Nbk	35 × 47 × 17	issue (*nadin*) note: a bronze vessel	XVII
66	NCBT 443	16?.IX.09 --	27 × 41 × 16	*maḫir* receipt: bowl?/grain?	XVIII
67	YBC 16193	11?.II.36 Nbk	34 × 45 × 17	*maḫir* receipt: bronze	XVIII
68	NCBT 80	13.IV.39 Nbk	24 × 36 × 14	*maḫir* receipt: bronze vessel	XVIII
69	NCBT 828	23.VI.22 Nbk	31 × 44 × 16	*maḫir* receipt: bronze vessel	XVIII
70	YBC 9380	14.III.22 Nbk	28 × 39 × 15	*maḫir* receipt: iron	XVIII
71	YBC 9172	25.XII.36 Nbk	36 × 50 × 17	promissory note: bronze	XIX
72	NCBT 982	18.VI.-- (Npl/Nbk)	29 × 40 × 15	*ina pāni* note: iron	XIX
73	GCBC 346	22.[×.×] Nbk	22 × 36 × 14	*ina pāni* note: iron	XIX
74	GCBC 602	[×].II.12 N[pl/bk]	29 × 46 × 17	*ina pāni* note: iron	XIX
75	NCBT 1040	14.VI.09 (Npl/Nbk)	25 × 36 × 15	*maḫir* receipt + *ina pāni* note: iron	XX
76	NCBT 1130	09.I.07 (Npl/Nbk)	22 × 38 × 16	*maḫir* receipt + *ina pāni* note: iron	XX
77	NCBT 204	27.XI.19 Npl	31 × 39 × 17	*maḫir* receipt + *ina pāni* note: iron tools	XX
78	NCBT 805	29.IV.13 (Npl/Nbk)	31 × 47 × 18	*maḫir* receipt + *ina pāni* note: iron tools	XX
79	NCBT 464	22.VII.14 (Npl/Nbk)	25 × 41 × 15	*maḫir* receipt + issue (*nadin*) note: silver	XX
80	NBC 4550	01.X.11 (Npl/Nbk)	22 × 32 × 13	*maḫir* receipt: iron	XXI
81	NCBT 1188	06.III.19 (Npl/Nbk)	27 × 39 × 15	*maḫir* receipt: iron	XXI
82	NCBT 1190	28.VIII.13 (Npl/Nbk)	27 × 39 × 14	*maḫir* receipt: iron	XXI
83	YBC 9035	22.VII.14 (Npl/Nbk)	29 × 45 × 17	*maḫir* receipt: iron	XXI

No.	*Museum No.*	*Date*	*Measurements (in mm)*	*Summary*	*Plate*
84	NCBT 465	26.XII.13 (Npl/Nbk)	27 × 38 × 14	*maḫir* receipt: iron	XXI
85	NCBT 937	29.II.-- (Npl/Nbk)	29 × 43 × 16	*maḫir* receipt: iron objects	XXI
86	NBC 4561	18.XII.04 (Npl/Nbk)	26 × 36 × 16	*maḫir* receipt: iron tools	XXII
87	NCBT 1110	24.VII.13 (Npl/Nbk)	25 × 36 × 15	*maḫir* receipt: iron tools	XXII
88	NCBT 450	28.V.16 (Npl)	25 × 31 × 15	*maḫir* receipt: iron tools	XXII
89	NCBT 453	25.XI.11 (Npl/Nbk)	26 × 42 × 14	*maḫir* receipt: iron tools	XXII
90	NCBT 616	15.VI?.02 (Npl/Nbk)	27 × 36 × 17	*maḫir* receipt: iron tools	XXII
91	NCBT 737	24.III.16 (Npl/Nbk)	26 × 37 × 15	*maḫir* receipt: iron tools	XXIII
92	NCBT 770	05.XII.05(+) Nbk	30 × 42 × 17	*maḫir* receipt: iron tools	XXIII
93	YBC 9046	23.VI.09 (Npl/Nbk)	30 × 46 × 17	*maḫir* receipt: iron tools	XXIII
94	NCBT 439	16.I.10 (Npl/Nbk)	28 × 39 × 16	*ina pāni* note: quivers	XXIII
95	YBC 11492	18.II.18 Nbk	23 × 30 × 12	*ina pāni* note: iron	XXIII
96	YBC 8809	13.VI.24 Nbk	26 × 38 × 14	*ina pāni* note: iron	XXIV
97	NCBT 429	06.I.22 Nbk	28 × 39 × 14	*maḫir* receipt (+ *ina pāni* clause): iron sickles	XXIV
98	YBC 9621	13.II.32 Nbk	27 × 38 × 17	*maḫir* receipt: iron	XXIV
99	NCBT 274	13.VIII.[×] Nbk	31 × 45 × 18	*maḫir* receipt: iron	XXIV
100	YBC 9521	28.X.[×] Nbk	29 × 46 × 17	*maḫir* receipt: iron + *ina pāni* note	XXIV
101	YBC 6894	07.XI.32 Nbk	22 × 33 × 13	*maḫir* receipt: iron tools	XXV
102	YBC 9417	10?.II.25 Nbk	25 × 38 × 14	*maḫir* receipt: iron tools	XXV
103	NCBT 757	11.II.14 Nbk	28 × 44 × 16	withdrawal (*našû*) + delivery (*šūbulu*) note: silver and iron	XXV
104	NCBT 716	23.X.23 Nbk	23 × 36 × 16	account balance: iron	XXV
105	NCBT 504	16.X.-- (Npl/Nbk)	35 × 58 × 24	accounting inventory: iron (and silver?)	XXV

No.	*Museum No.*	*Date*	*Measurements (in mm)*	*Summary*	*Plate*
106	YBC 9271	--.VI.33 Nbk	33 × 46 × 16	promissory note: silver (no witnesses)	XXVI
107	NCBT 1235	undated (Nbk)	28 × 47 × 16	*ina pāni* note: (multiple) iron tools	XXVI
108	YBC 11288	13.I.23 (Nbk)	22 × 33 × 11	*ina pāni* note: a rope and an axe	XXVI
109	YBC 11658	09.III.43 (Nbk)	19 × 25 × 15	*ina pāni* note: iron	XXVI
110	YBC 8796	27.XII.15 Nbk	25 × 39 × 15	*ina pāni* note: iron	XXVI
111	YBC 8804	[×.×.× RN]	29 × 40 × 17	*ina pāni* note: iron	XXVI
112	NBC 4625	23.XIIb.42 Nbk	30 × 44 × 14	*ina pāni* note: iron bowl	XXVII
113	NCBT 416	06.IV.38 (Nbk)	24 × 38 × 15	*ina pāni* note: iron spades	XXVII
114	NCBT 263	01.IX.22 Nbk	23 × 34 × 15	*ina pāni* note: iron sickles	XXVII
115	NCBT 78	03.I.23 Nbk	26 × 36 × 12	*ina pāni* note: iron tool	XXVII
116	NCBT 1019	22.[×.×] --	31 × 45 × 19	*ina pāni* note: iron tools	XXVII
117	NCBT 1098	14.VII.14 Nbk	32 × 45 × 18	*ina pāni* note: iron tools	XXVIII
118	NCBT 71	17.XII.36 Nbk	29 × 44 × 15	*ina pāni* note: iron tools	XXVIII
119	NCBT 942	02.I.20 (Nbk)	27 × 38 × 15	*ina pāni* note: iron tools	XXVIII
120	NCBT 971	11?.X.03 -- (early Achaemenid)	27 × 39 × 17	*ina pāni* note: iron tools	XXVIII
121	YBC 9641	09.II.41 (Nbk)	23 × 36 × 15	*ina pāni* note: iron tools	XXVIII
122	NCBT 478	15.VII.02 (Cyr–Camb)	29 × 39 × 17	*ina pāni* note: iron tools	XXIX
123	YBC 11305	undated	31 × 44 × 16	inventory list: varia	XXIX
124	YBC 16018	22.XI.18 --	25 × 33 × 15	*maḫir* receipt (+ *ina pāni* note?): iron	XXIX
125	NCBT 1036	25.IV.08 (Npl)	25 × 34 × 15	*maḫir* receipt + *ina pāni* note: iron	XXIX
126	NBC 4694	07.IX.32 Nbk	28 × 41 × 16	*maḫir* receipt + *ina pāni* note: iron	XXIX
127	NBC 4541	03.VIII.14 --	32 × 47 × 15	*maḫir* receipt + *ina pāni* note: iron tools	XXX

No.	*Museum No.*	*Date*	*Measurements (in mm)*	*Summary*	*Plate*
128	NCBT 791	13.X.09 (Npl)	37 × 55 × 20	*maḫir* receipt + *ina pāni* note: iron tools	XXX
129	YBC 9136	26?.II.29 Nbk	33 × 56 × 17	*maḫir* receipt + *ina pāni* note: iron tools	XXX
130	NCBT 966	21.XI.-- (Kan–Npl)	41 × 61 × 19	*maḫir receip*t: iron items + accounting note	XXX
131	NCBT 972	02.VIII.07 --	23 × 35 × 13	*maḫir* receipt: iron items + accounting note	XXXI
132	NCBT 721	13.IV.19 Nbk	27 × 41 × 15	*maḫir* receipt: iron tools	XXXI
133	NCBT 752	02.III.18 Nbk	30 × 43 × 17	*maḫir* receipt: iron tools	XXXI
134	YBC 9068	05.IX.14 Nbk	24 × 31 × 15	*maḫir* receipt: iron tools	XXXI
135	YBC 9293	15.XI.32 Nbk	30 × 45 × 18	*maḫir* receipt: iron items	XXXI
136	YBC 9428	13.VI.19 Nbk	27 × 43 × 15	*maḫir* receipt: iron tools	XXXII
137	YBC 9423	04.VIII.27 Nbk	27 × 41 × 15	accounting note: iron tools from *iškaru*	XXXII
138	YBC 3989	--.--.17 Nbk	54 × 86 × 20	tabulated account: iron	XXXII–XXXIII
139	+YBC 9274	17.V.25 Nbk	31 × 49 × 17	withdrawal (*našû*) note: iron tools	XXXIII
140	NCBT 417	01(+).I.08 Nbn	27 × 43 × 16	*ina pāni* note: spades	XXXIII
141	YBC 9209	13?.XII.10 Nbk	37 × 53 × 18	*ina pāni* + withdrawal (*našû*) notes: silver	XXXIV
142	NCBT 135	21.II.16 Nbk	22 × 34 × 12	*ina pāni* note: stones	XXXIV
143	YBC 3990	--.XII.12 --	107 × 66 × 26	accounting inventory: multiple items	XXXV
144	NBC 4692	11.IX.18 Nbk	27 × 41 × 17	accounting inventory: textiles	XXXIV
145	NCBT 597	[×].XI.16 --	31 × 48 × 18	*ina pāni* note: garments	XXXIV
146	NBC 4563	31.XII.17 -- (Npl/Nbk)	25 × 37 × 14	*ina pāni* note: textile	XXXIV
147	NCBT 706	25.III.40 Nbk	23 × 30 × 14	accounting note: textile	XXXV
148	NBC 4750	14.II.31 Nbk	63 × 40 × 18	inventory list: cultic garments	XXXV
149	YBC 9582	09.IV.24 Nbk	28 × 41 × 16	*maḫir* receipt: cloth	XXXVI

No.	*Museum No.*	*Date*	*Measurements (in mm)*	*Summary*	*Plate*
150	YBC 9636	19.XII.09 (Npl/Nbk)	26 × 33 × 14	*maḫir* receipt: cloth	XXXV
151	YBC 3464	(×+)9.--.12 (Nbk)	32 × 51 × 19	*maḫir* receipt: garments	XXXVI
152	YBC 9457	05.II.23 Nbk	33 × 46 × 18	*maḫir* receipt: silver	XXXVI
153	NBC 4652	15.II.25 Nbk	32 × 49 × 16	*maḫir* receipt: textile	XXXVI
154	NBC 4934	03(+).VII.10 Nbn	50 × 70 × 21	*maḫir* receipt: textile	XXXVII
155	NCBT 90	25.IX.24 Nbk	26 × 39 × 13	*maḫir* receipt: textile	XXXVI
156	NCBT 240	30.XI.41 Nbk	24 × 35 × 14	*maḫir* receipt: yarn	XXXVII
157	NCBT 1069	--.XII.09 --	66 × 39 × 19	withdrawal (*našû*) + *ina pāni* list: garments	XXXVII
158	NBC 8363	15.I.27 Nbk	26 × 39 × 15	withdrawal (*našû*) note: garments	XXXVIII
159	NCBT 856	24.III.39 Nbk	39 × 61 × 19	withdrawal (*našû*) note: garments	XXXVIII
160	NCBT 826	09.XI.18 Nbk	25 × 35 × 16	accounting note: garment	XXXVIII
161	YBC 4808	undated (Nbk)	24 × 34 × 15	withdrawal (*našû*) note: garments	XXXVIII
162	YBC 9533	12.IV.36 Nbk	29 × 38 × 14	withdrawal (*našû*) note: garments and wool	XXXIX
163	NBC 8350	11.I.13(+) (Nbk)	33 × 45 × 17	*ina pāni* note: linen	XXXIX
164	NCBT 146	26.V.25 Nbk	25 × 33 × 16	*ina pāni* note: linen	XXXIX
165	NCBT 242	11.V.25 Nbk	25 × 30 × 13	*ina pāni* note: linen	XXXIX
166	YBC 9470	13.VI.24 Nbk	32 × 45 × 15	*ina pāni* note: linen	XXXIX
167	YBC 9385	01.XII.31+ Nbk	29 × 44 × 15	*maḫir* receipt: linen	XL
168	NBC 4920	05.×.05 Cyr	97 × 57 × 21	issue (*nadin*) list: wool	XL–XLI
169	NBC 4679	25.I.-- (Nbk–Nbn)	33 × 47 × 19	issue (*nadin*) note: silver	XL
170	NCBT 1057	undated (Npl–Nbk)	52 × 70 × 21	accounting inventory: wool for silver	XL–XLI
171	YBC 9368	13.I.26 Nbk	30 × 46 × 16	*ina pāni* note + withdrawal (*našû*) note: wool	XLI

No.	*Museum No.*	*Date*	*Measurements (in mm)*	*Summary*	*Plate*
172	NCBT 710	25.I.13 Nbk	27 × 38 × 15	*ina pāni* note: wool	XLI
173	YBC 9411	24.XIIb.[×] Nbk	30 × 42 × 15	*ina pāni* note: wool	XLII
174	NCBT 641	19.IV.38 Nbk	45 × 70 × 17	accounting inventory: textiles	XLII–XLIII
175	NBC 4707	13.VIII.38? Nbk	26 × 39 × 15	accounting inventory: silver	XLII
176	NCBT 632	13.II.14 (Nbn)	93 × 67 × 20	issue (*nadin*) list + *maḫir* receipt: textiles	XLII–XLIII
177	NCBT 758	03.XIIb.42 Nbk	29 × 40 × 16	*maḫir* receipt + *ina pāni* note: wool	XLIII
178	YBC 3512	[... *Nbk*]	44 × 72 × 23	*maḫir* receipt: garments	XLIV
179	NBC 4645	19.III.04 (Nbk)	52 × 37 × 18	*maḫir* receipt (with heading): silver	XLIV
180	YBC 11471	11(+).III.× Nbk	38 × 44 × 19	withdrawal (*našû*) note(?) + *maḫir* receipt(?): wool	XLIV
181	NBC 4765	21.II.31 Nbk	39 × 58 × 17	withdrawal (*našû*) note: wool	XLV
182	YBC 9494	29.IV.24 Nbk	24 × 32 × 14	withdrawal (*našû*) note: wool	XLIV
183	YBC 9510	04.II.11 Nbk	28 × 34 × 15	withdrawal (*našû*) note: wool	XLV
184	YBC 9574	20.X.33 Nbk	30 × 43 × 14	*ina pāni* note: hair + withdrawal (*našû*): silver	XLV
185	NCBT 477	07.V.19 Nbk	27 × 41 × 17	withdrawal (*našû*) note: goat hair	XLV
186	YBC 9547	29.III.24 Nbk	30 × 45 × 16	*ina pāni* note: alum and dye	XLVI
187	YBC 9431	29.XI.23 Nbk	29 × 43 × 15	*ina pāni* note: dye	XLVI
188	YBC 9540	19.V.24 Nbk	27 × 37 × 14	*ina pāni* note: dye	XLVI
189	YBC 11613	06.VI.08 Cyr	81 × 54 × 26	issue (*nadin*) list: wheat	XLVI
190	YBC 4165	undated (Nbk)	109 × 69 × 30	issue (*nadin*) list: grain	XLVII
191	NCBT 434	21.X.12 Nbk	29 × 39 × 16	issue (*nadin*) note: silver	XLVIII
192	NCBT 1100	undated (Nbk)	28 × 39 × 16	payment (*apil*) note: salaries	XLVIII
193	NCBT 1318	undated (Nbk)	94 × 55 × 25	summary withdrawal (*našû*) list: salaries	XLVIII

No.	*Museum No.*	*Date*	*Measurements (in mm)*	*Summary*	*Plate*
194	YBC 11652	08.[×].13 Nbk	33 × 44 × 16	withdrawal (*našû*) list: salaries	XLIX
195	YBC 9328	06.II.12 Nbk	34 × 48 × 21	accounting note: salaries	XLIX
196	YBC 9330	01(+).III.21 (Nbk)	35 × 58 × 17	withdrawal (*našû*) list: salaries	XLIX
197	YBC 11491	15.VII?.05 (Camb)	30 × 37 × 16	accounting note: salaries	L
198	NBC 4919	undated	87 × 57 × 17	withdrawal (*našû*) list: salaries	L
199	YBC 6859	18.XI.28 Nbk	36 × 53 × 18	withdrawal (*našû*) list: silver	XLIX
200	NBC 4557	17.X.06 (Npl/Nbk)?	29 × 36 × 18	payment (*apil*) + withdrawal (*našû*) note: salaries	L
201	NCBT 95	2(+).VIII.30(+) Nbk	29 × 42 × 15	withdrawal (*našû*) note: salaries	LI
202	NCBT 948	undated (Nbk)	55 × 40 × 20	accounting inventory: (outgoing) silver	LI
203	NBC 4774	09.III.19 --	38 × 59 × 19	accounting inventory: salaries	LI
204	NCBT 162	03.V.31 Nbk	23 × 33 × 14	issue (*nadin*) note: silver	LII
205	GCBC 84	15.XI.32 Nbk	24 × 34 × 13	withdrawal (*našû*) note: silver	LII
206	NCBT 243	14.X.17 Nbk	24 × 35 × 14	withdrawal (*našû*) note: silver	LII
207	NCBT 961	12.XI.32 Nbk	28 × 40 × 17	withdrawal (*našû*) note: silver	LII
208	NCBT 471	01.XIIb.17(+) Nbk	24 × 35 × 14	withdrawal (*našû*) note: silver + issue (*nadin*) note: barley	LII
209	NCBT 1176	10.II.18 Nbk	31 × 45 × 17	withdrawal (*našû*) note: silver	LIII
210	NCBT 148	01.I.13 Nbk	28 × 43 × 14	accounting note: (outgoing) silver	LIII
211	NBC 4623	06.VIII.32 Nbk	30 × 41 × 17	issue (*nadin*) note: silver	LIII
212	NBC 4779	undated (late Nbk–Camb)	62 × 42 × 18	inventory list: silver credits	LIII
213	NCBT 529	undated (Nbk)	71 × 48 × 25	accounting inventory: silver, gold, wool	LIV
214	NBC 4780	10(+).X.01(+) [Nbn–Camb]	41 × 58 × 22	withdrawal (*našû*) note: multiple items	LIV

No.	*Museum No.*	*Date*	*Measurements (in mm)*	*Summary*	*Plate*
215	YBC 11443	--.IV.04 Camb	69 × 58 × 26	issue (*nadin*) list: salaries (barley)	LV
216	YBC 11938	02.II.02 Nbn	45 × 46 × 17	*ina pāni* note: barley	LIV
217	NCBT 643	10.IX.33 Nbk	65 × 42 × 18	issue (*nadin*) list: barley	LV
218	NBC 4567	07.V.12 --	21 × 41 × 14	*maḫir* receipt: barley	LVI
219	NBC 4710	03.VI.21 --	30 × 45 × 16	payment (*apil*) note: barley	LVI
220	YBC 9491	04.XII.13 Nbk	24 × 32 × 14	payment (*eṭir*) note: barley	LVI
221	NCBT 680	05.IX.0a [AM–Nbn]	46 × 72 × 21	personnel list + accounting note	LVI
222	NBC 4732	04.X.38 Nbk	33 × 52 × 17	withdrawal (*našû*) note: barley	LVII
223	NCBT 139	21.VII.<×> Nbk	24 × 33 × 14	withdrawal (*našû*) note: barley	LVII
224	NCBT 197	23.II.15 Nbk	28 × 40 × 17	withdrawal (*našû*) note: barley	LVII
225	NCBT 82	03.X.21 Nbk	27 × 43 × 15	withdrawal (*našû*) note: barley	LVII
226	NCBT 950	29.I.32 Nbk	39 × 53 × 20	withdrawal (*našû*) note: barley	LVIII
227	NBC 4773	20.VI.14 Nbk	40 × 57 × 22	withdrawal (*našû*) note: *irbu*	LVIII
228	NCBT 495	15[?].XI.12 Nbk	22 × 32 × 15	withdrawal (*našû*) note: silver	LVIII
229	YBC 3513	14.IX.18 Nbk	41 × 62 × 20	withdrawal (*našû*) list: dates and barley	LIX
230	NCBT 1165	undated (ca. 30 Nbk)	36 × 50 × 16	accounting inventory: barley	LIX
231	NBC 4613	22.III.32 Nbk	31 × 44 × 16	accounting inventory: barley	LVIII
232	YBC 6863	23.IX.24 Nbk	37 × 53 × 16	promissory note: barley	LIX
233	YBC 8838	26.II.08(+) Nbk	30 × 43 × 18	withdrawal (*našû*) note: barley	LIX
234	NBC 4637	04.VI.30 Nbk	32 × 45 × 17	withdrawal (*našû*) note: barley	LX
235	YBC 9557	×.IX.26 Nbk	28 × 42 × 15	delivery (*šūbulu*) note: silver + withdrawal (*našû*): beer	LX
236	NCBT 1115	15.IV.10 N[bn]	27 × 36 × 15	*maḫir* receipt: beer	LX

No.	*Museum No.*	*Date*	*Measurements (in mm)*	*Summary*	*Plate*
237	NCBT 1127	26.VIII.38 (Nbk)	24 × 32 × 12	*maḫir* receipt: beer	LX
238	NCBT 251	17.XIIb.36 Nbk	25 × 34 × 13	*maḫir* receipt: beer	LX
239	NCBT 258	06.III.38 Nbk	25 × 31 × 14	*maḫir* receipt: beer	LXI
240	NCBT 913	15.XI.-- (late Nbk)	23 × 33 × 14	*maḫir* receipt: beer	LXI
241	NCBT 97	26.III.16 Nbk	33 × 47 × 15	withdrawal (*našû*) and issue (*nadin*) note: silver	LXI
242	NCBT 663	17.I.35 Nbk	66 × 43 × 23	accounting inventory: barley and dates	LXII
243	NBC 4653	--.VI.32 Nbk	36 × 50 × 17	*ina pāni* note: multiple entries (*imittu*)	LXI
244	NCBT 170	28.IV.42 Nbk	40 × 54 × 18	issue (*nadin*) list: dates and barley	LXII
245	NCBT 631	16.X.32? Nbk	96 × 67 × 26	issue (*nadin+našû*) note: salaries in dates	LXIII
246	NCBT 667	28.III.40 Nbk	43 × 64 × 18	*maḫir* receipt: dates	LXII
247	YBC 9141	11.IV?.20 Nbk	39 × 56 × 18	withdrawal (*našû*) account: dates	LXIV
248	YBC 9315	18.IX.38? Nbk	34 × 47 × 17	withdrawal (*našû*) note: dates	LXIV
249	NCBT 81	--.III.40 Nbk	29 × 40 × 17	accounting note: flour	LXIV
250	NCBT 1023	19.IX.34 Nbk	29 × 40 × 16	*ina pāni* note: barley	LXIV
251	NCBT 812	22.XII.41 Nbk	23 × 30 × 14	*maḫir* receipt: (barley)?	LXIV
252	NCBT 166	11.II.22 Nbk	31 × 47 × 18	issue (*nadin*) note: silver	LXV
253	NCBT 92	11.X.16 Nbk	24 × 37 × 14	delivery (*šūbulu*) note: silver	LXV
254	NCBT 473	06.X16 Nbk	26 × 36 × 16	delivery (*šūbulu*) note: silver + issue (*nadin*) note: reed	LXV
255	NCBT 901	undated (mid-Nbk)	27 × 36 × 17	accounting note: reed items	LXV
256	YBC 7372	undated	32 × 46 × 15	accounting inventory: reeds	LXVI
257	NCBT 891	26.VIII.22 Nbk	48 × 32 × 16	*ina pāni* note: reed mats	LXVI
258	NCBT 747	03.V.12 Nbk	24 × 33 × 16	*ina pāni* note: silver and reed	LXVI

No.	*Museum No.*	*Date*	*Measurements (in mm)*	*Summary*	*Plate*
259	YBC 8783	09.V.17 Nbk	24 × 30 × 12	issue (*nadin*) note: barley	LXVI
260	NCBT 140	03.III.17 Nbk	22 × 31 × 11	*maḫir* receipt: reed mats	LXVI
261	NCBT 808	15.VII.31 Nbk	31 × 44 × 15	*ina pāni* note: goats and hides	LXVII
262	NCBT 838	08.IV.08 Nbk	33 × 44 × 16	*ina pāni* note: leather	LXVII
263	NCBT 444	14(+).X.-- --	23 × 33 × 14	inventory note: hides and sinews	LXVII
264	NCBT 431	13.*IX*.20(+) Nbk	25 × 34 × 15	issue (*nadin*) note: hides	LXVII
265	NCBT 1033	[×].VIII.06 [Nbn/Cyr]	22 × 28 × 13	*maḫir* receipt: hides	LXVII
266	NCBT 127	21.I.35 Nbk	25 × 35 × 13	*maḫir* receipt: hides	LXVIII
267	NCBT 152	28.I.43 Nbk	25 × 35 × 13	*maḫir* receipt: hides	LXVIII
268	NCBT 727	29.XII.22 Nbk	27 × 38 × 16	*maḫir* receipt: hides	LXVIII
269	NCBT 709	21.VII.42 Nbk	25 × 35 × 14	*maḫir* receipt: various tools	LXVIII
270	NCBT 122	21.IX.21 Nbk	27 × 35 × 16	withdrawal (*našû*) note: hides	LXVIII
271	NCBT 843	19.IX.38 Nbk	32 × 44 × 17	withdrawal (*našû*) note: iron tools	LXIX
272	YBC 9539	01.VIII.31 Nbk	32 × 44 × 17	delivery (*šūbulu*) note: silver + issue (*nadi*n) note: oil	LXIX
273	NCBT 797	23.XI.0a Nbk	39 × 56 × 22	accounting inventory: oil	LXIX
274	NCBT 762	28.VI.42 Nbk	28 × 38 × 15	withdrawal (*našû*) note: oil	LXIX
275	NBC 4532	21.I.19 -- (Npl–Nbk)	25 × 36 × 15	*ina pāni* note: wax	LXX
276	NCBT 895	undated	69 × 54 × 25	inventory note (unclear)	LXX
277	NCBT 564	01.I[?].36 Nbk	37 × 50 × 18	withdrawal (*našû*) note: honey	LXX
278	NCBT 817	20.XII.41 Nbk	25 × 36 × 16	withdrawal (*našû*) note: sesame	LXX
279	NCBT 1105	20.VII.-- --	31 × 44 × 18	*ina pāni* note: wood + (unrelated)[?] tallies	LXXI
280	YBC 9536	30.XII.32 Nbk	30 × 44 × 17	*maḫir* receipt: silver + *ina pāni* note	LXXI

No.	*Museum No.*	*Date*	*Measurements (in mm)*	*Summary*	*Plate*
281	YBC 16253	undated (mid Nbk–mid Nbn)	60 × 41 × 21	accounting inventory: livestock	LXXI
282	YBC 6926	undated (late Nbk–Camb)	108 × 66 × 25	accounting inventory: animals (and by-products)	LXXII
283	NCBT 479	17.XII.14 (Nbn/Dar)	26 × 40 × 14	*maḫir* receipt: ducks + allocation of sheep	LXXIII
284	NCBT 760	17.XII.21 Nbk	30 × 42 × 16	*maḫir* receipt: sheep	LXXIII
285	NBC 4602	undated (Nbn–Cyr)	77 × 51 × 21	accounting inventory: sheep and iron	LXXIII
286	NCBT 702	undated (Camb)	93 × 59 × 22	accounting inventory: varia	LXXIV
287	NBC 4693	04.V.27 Nbk	31 × 42 × 16	witnessed accounting note: silver	LXXV
288	NCBT 780	undated	47 × 32 × 16	personnel list	LXXIV
289	NCBT 671	undated	67 × 41 × 22	note regarding a shearing commitment	LXXIV
290	NCBT 488	12.IX.06 (Npl)	27 × 47 × 16	note regarding serfs + *ina pāni* note: iron	LXXV
291	NCBT 1006	undated	38 × 54 × 19	personnel list	LXXV
292	NCBT 1024	undated	31 × 44 × 17	personnel list	LXXV
293	NCBT 1189	undated	27 × 40 × 15	personnel list	LXXVIII
294	YBC 11085	[×.×].07 [Nbn]	66 × 44 × 22	personnel list	LXXVIII
295	YBC 6846	undated (Nbn)	47 × 25 × 12	personnel list	LXXVIII
296	YBC 9027	19.V.[× Nbn]	130 × 62 × 26	personnel list	LXXVI–LXXVII
297	YBC 9268	11.VIII.22 Nbk	57 × 37 × 21	personnel list	LXXIX
298	NBC 4864	undated (late Nbk–Cyr)	74 × 47 × 20	personnel list	LXXIX
299	YBC 15720	undated (early Nbk)	110 × 65 × 33	tabulated accounting inventory	LXXX
300	NCBT 1031	24.V.21 (Nbk)	28 × 39 × 16	*ina pāni* note(?): unclear	LXXIX
301	NBC 4606	*11*.I.[×] Nbk	88 × 52 × 24	inventory list: chariot equipment	LXXXI
302	YBC 9273	12.VI.[×] Nbk	33 × 45 × 18	account settlement: silver	LXXXI

No.	*Museum No.*	*Date*	*Measurements (in mm)*	*Summary*	*Plate*
303	NBC 4859	undated (Nbn)	130 × 78 × 27	accounting inventory: multiple items	LXXXII
304	NBC 4891	undated (9? Cyr–Camb)	117 × 66 × 24	accounting inventory: multiple items	LXXXIII
305	YBC 3529	undated (Nbn–Cyr)	59 × 73 × 23	*ina pāni* list: various items	LXXXIV
306	GCBC 705	undated (ca. late Nbk)	24 × 31 × 14	*ina pāni* note: (not specified)	LXXXIV
307	NCBT 1154	undated (late Nbk–Nbn)	56 × 37 × 16	*maḫir* receipt: multiple complex entries	LXXXV
308	NBC 4597	undated (late Nbk–Camb)	97 × 71 × 26	accounting inventory: varia	LXXXV–LXXXVI
309	NBC 4627	26.[×].13 [Npl]	33 × 45 × 18	payment (*eṭir*) note: silver	LXXXVI
310	NCBT 1016	12.I.23 Nbk	32 × 51 × 18	withdrawal and delivery note	LXXXVI
311	YBC 9223	*18*.IX.*39* Nbk	36 × 49 × 17	record of interrogation	LXXXVII
312	YBC 9155	12.VI.42 Nbk	40 × 55 × 17	record of a testimony	LXXXVII
313	YBC 7391	[×.×.×] Nbn	44 × 57 × 20	summons guarantee	LXXXVII
314	YBC 9179	10.VIII.35 Nbk	43 × 59 × 20	summons guarantee	LXXXVIII
315	YBC 3715	06.X.40 Nbk	38 × 53 × 19	work contract: laundry	LXXXVIII

CONCORDANCE OF MUSEUM NUMBERS

Museum No.	*BC No.*	*No.*
GCBC 84	BC.033701	205
GCBC 346	BC.033963	73
GCBC 602	BC.034219	74
GCBC 636	BC.034253	53
GCBC 705	BC.034322	306
NBC 4532	BC.007508	275
NBC 4541	BC.007517	127
NBC 4550	BC.007526	80
NBC 4557	BC.007533	200
NBC 4560	BC.007536	61
NBC 4561	BC.007537	86
NBC 4563	BC.007539	146
NBC 4567	BC.007543	218
NBC 4597	BC.007573	308
NBC 4602	BC.007578	285
NBC 4606	BC.007582	301
NBC 4613	BC.007589	231
NBC 4623	BC.007599	211
NBC 4624	BC.007600	31
NBC 4625	BC.007601	112
NBC 4627	BC.007603	309
NBC 4637	BC.007613	234
NBC 4638	BC.007614	45
NBC 4645	BC.007621	179
NBC 4652	BC.007628	153
NBC 4653	BC.007629	243
NBC 4672	BC.007648	48
NBC 4679	BC.007655	169
NBC 4692	BC.007668	144
NBC 4693	BC.007669	287
NBC 4694	BC.007670	126
NBC 4707	BC.007684	175
NBC 4710	BC.007687	219
NBC 4732	BC.007710	222
NBC 4750	BC.007728	148
NBC 4765	BC.007744	181
NBC 4773	BC.007752	227
NBC 4774	BC.007753	203
NBC 4779	BC.007758	212
NBC 4780	BC.007759	214
NBC 4815	BC.007794	18
NBC 4859	BC.007838	303
NBC 4864	BC.007843	298
NBC 4891	BC.007870	304
NBC 4919	BC.007898	198
NBC 4920	BC.007899	168
NBC 4934	BC.007913	154
NBC 8350	BC.011346	163
NBC 8363	BC.011359	158
NBC 9820	BC.012789	9
NCBT 71	BC.034616	118
NCBT 78	BC.034623	115
NCBT 80	BC.034625	68
NCBT 81	BC.034626	249
NCBT 82	BC.034627	225
NCBT 90	BC.034635	155
NCBT 92	BC.034637	253
NCBT 95	BC.034640	201
NCBT 97	BC.034642	241
NCBT 122	BC.034667	270
NCBT 127	BC.034672	266
NCBT 135	BC.034680	142
NCBT 139	BC.034684	223
NCBT 140	BC.034685	260
NCBT 146	BC.034691	164
NCBT 147	BC.034692	55
NCBT 148	BC.034693	210
NCBT 152	BC.034697	267
NCBT 162	BC.034707	204
NCBT 166	BC.034711	252

Museum No.	*BC No.*	*No.*	*Museum No.*	*BC No.*	*No.*
NCBT 170	BC.034715	244	NCBT 559	BC.035104	38
NCBT 197	BC.034742	224	NCBT 564	BC.035109	277
NCBT 204	BC.034749	77	NCBT 568	BC.035113	12
NCBT 240	BC.034785	156	NCBT 597	BC.035142	145
NCBT 242	BC.034787	165	NCBT 604	BC.035149	27
NCBT 243	BC.034788	206	NCBT 616	BC.035161	90
NCBT 251	BC.034796	238	NCBT 622	BC.035167	28
NCBT 258	BC.034803	239	NCBT 631	BC.035176	245
NCBT 263	BC.034808	114	NCBT 632	BC.035177	176
NCBT 265	BC.034810	57	NCBT 641	BC.035186	174
NCBT 274	BC.034819	99	NCBT 643	BC.035188	217
NCBT 296	BC.034841	36	NCBT 653	BC.035198	13
NCBT 325	BC.034870	62	NCBT 663	BC.035208	242
NCBT 357	BC.034902	50	NCBT 667	BC.035212	246
NCBT 368	BC.034913	33	NCBT 671	BC.035216	289
NCBT 410	BC.034955	10	NCBT 680	BC.035225	221
NCBT 416	BC.034961	113	NCBT 702	BC.035247	286
NCBT 417	BC.034962	140	NCBT 706	BC.035251	147
NCBT 429	BC.034974	97	NCBT 709	BC.035254	269
NCBT 431	BC.034976	264	NCBT 710	BC.035255	172
NCBT 434	BC.034979	191	NCBT 716	BC.035261	104
NCBT 439	BC.034984	94	NCBT 721	BC.035266	132
NCBT 442	BC.034987	20	NCBT 727	BC.035272	268
NCBT 443	BC.034988	66	NCBT 734	BC.035279	26
NCBT 444	BC.034989	263	NCBT 735	BC.035280	58
NCBT 450	BC.034995	88	NCBT 737	BC.035282	91
NCBT 453	BC.034998	89	NCBT 747	BC.035292	258
NCBT 462	BC.035007	16	NCBT 752	BC.035297	133
NCBT 464	BC.035009	79	NCBT 755	BC.035300	49
NCBT 465	BC.035010	84	NCBT 757	BC.035302	103
NCBT 468	BC.035013	56	NCBT 758	BC.035303	177
NCBT 471	BC.035016	208	NCBT 760	BC.035305	284
NCBT 473	BC.035018	254	NCBT 762	BC.035307	274
NCBT 477	BC.035022	185	NCBT 770	BC.035315	92
NCBT 478	BC.035023	122	NCBT 780	BC.035325	288
NCBT 479	BC.035024	283	NCBT 791	BC.035336	128
NCBT 488	BC.035033	290	NCBT 792	BC.035337	3
NCBT 495	BC.035040	228	NCBT 794	BC.035339	46
NCBT 500	BC.035045	15	NCBT 797	BC.035342	273
NCBT 503	BC.035048	22	NCBT 805	BC.035350	78
NCBT 504	BC.035049	105	NCBT 808	BC.035353	261
NCBT 508	BC.035053	32	NCBT 812	BC.035357	251
NCBT 527	BC.035072	30	NCBT 817	BC.035362	278
NCBT 529	BC.035074	213	NCBT 826	BC.035371	160
NCBT 536	BC.035081	47	NCBT 828	BC.035373	69

Museum No.	*BC No.*	*No.*	*Museum No.*	*BC No.*	*No.*
NCBT 838	BC.035383	262	NCBT 1187	BC.035732	37
NCBT 843	BC.035388	271	NCBT 1188	BC.035733	81
NCBT 856	BC.035401	159	NCBT 1189	BC.035734	293
NCBT 891	BC.035436	257	NCBT 1190	BC.035735	82
NCBT 895	BC.035440	276	NCBT 1227	BC.035772	2
NCBT 901	BC.035446	255	NCBT 1235	BC.035780	107
NCBT 912	BC.035457	64	NCBT 1246	BC.035791	51
NCBT 913	BC.035458	240	NCBT 1318	BC.035863	193
NCBT 922	BC.035467	59			
NCBT 937	BC.035482	85	YBC 3438	BC.017504	42
NCBT 942	BC.035487	119	YBC 3464	BC.017530	151
NCBT 948	BC.035493	202	YBC 3512	BC.017577	178
NCBT 950	BC.035495	226	YBC 3513	BC.017578	229
NCBT 956	BC.035501	39	YBC 3529	BC.017594	305
NCBT 961	BC.035506	207	YBC 3715	BC.017780	315
NCBT 966	BC.035511	130	YBC 3989	BC.018054	138
NCBT 971	BC.035516	120	YBC 3990	BC.018055	143
NCBT 972	BC.035517	131	YBC 4165	BC.018230	190
NCBT 974	BC.035519	11	YBC 4808	BC.018872	161
NCBT 982	BC.035527	72	YBC 6846	BC.020912	295
NCBT 988	BC.035533	35	YBC 6859	BC.020925	199
NCBT 1006	BC.035551	291	YBC 6863	BC.020929	232
NCBT 1008	BC.035553	40	YBC 6894	BC.020960	101
NCBT 1016	BC.035561	310	YBC 6926	BC.020992	282
NCBT 1019	BC.035564	116	YBC 7372	BC.021437	256
NCBT 1023	BC.035568	250	YBC 7391	BC.021456	313
NCBT 1024	BC.035569	292	YBC 8783	BC.022842	259
NCBT 1031	BC.035576	300	YBC 8796	BC.022855	110
NCBT 1033	BC.035578	265	YBC 8798	BC.022857	23
NCBT 1036	BC.035581	125	YBC 8804	BC.022863	111
NCBT 1040	BC.035585	75	YBC 8809	BC.022868	96
NCBT 1057	BC.035602	170	YBC 8818	BC.022877	44
NCBT 1069	BC.035614	157	YBC 8838	BC.022897	233
NCBT 1098	BC.035643	117	YBC 9027	BC.023082	296
NCBT 1100	BC.035645	192	YBC 9031	BC.023086	4
NCBT 1105	BC.035650	279	YBC 9035	BC.023090	83
NCBT 1110	BC.035655	87	YBC 9039	BC.023094	5
NCBT 1115	BC.035660	236	YBC 9046	BC.023101	93
NCBT 1121	BC.035666	1	YBC 9068	BC.023123	134
NCBT 1127	BC.035672	237	YBC 9136	BC.023191	129
NCBT 1130	BC.035675	76	YBC 9141	BC.023196	247
NCBT 1154	BC.035699	307	YBC 9155	BC.023210	312
NCBT 1157	BC.035702	19	YBC 9172	BC.023227	71
NCBT 1165	BC.035710	230	YBC 9178	BC.023233	54
NCBT 1176	BC.035721	209	YBC 9179	BC.023234	314

Museum No.	*BC No.*	*No.*	*Museum No.*	*BC No.*	*No.*
YBC 9204	BC.023259	24	YBC 9516	BC.023571	7
YBC 9209	BC.023264	141	YBC 9521	BC.023576	100
YBC 9223	BC.023278	311	YBC 9533	BC.023588	162
YBC 9235	BC.023290	25	YBC 9536	BC.023591	280
YBC 9237	BC.023292	65	YBC 9539	BC.023594	272
YBC 9240	BC.023295	34	YBC 9540	BC.023595	188
YBC 9268	BC.023323	297	YBC 9547	BC.023602	186
YBC 9271	BC.023326	106	YBC 9557	BC.023612	235
YBC 9273	BC.023328	302	YBC 9574	BC.023629	184
YBC 9274	BC.023329	139	YBC 9582	BC.023637	149
YBC 9293	BC.023348	135	YBC 9590	BC.023645	8
YBC 9315	BC.023370	248	YBC 9621	BC.023676	98
YBC 9326	BC.023381	29	YBC 9636	BC.023691	150
YBC 9328	BC.023383	195	YBC 9638	BC.023693	43
YBC 9330	BC.023385	196	YBC 9641	BC.023696	121
YBC 9368	BC.023423	171	YBC 11085	BC.024879	294
YBC 9380	BC.023435	70	YBC 11278	BC.025072	60
YBC 9385	BC.023440	167	YBC 11288	BC.025082	108
YBC 9393	BC.023448	52	YBC 11305	BC.025099	123
YBC 9411	BC.023466	173	YBC 11443	BC.025237	215
YBC 9414	BC.023469	6	YBC 11471	BC.025265	180
YBC 9417	BC.023472	102	YBC 11486	BC.025279	41
YBC 9423	BC.023478	137	YBC 11491	BC.025284	197
YBC 9428	BC.023483	136	YBC 11492	BC.025285	95
YBC 9431	BC.023486	187	YBC 11495	BC.025288	17
YBC 9436	BC.023491	14	YBC 11613	BC.025408	189
YBC 9442	BC.023497	63	YBC 11652	BC.025447	194
YBC 9447	BC.023502	21	YBC 11658	BC.025454	109
YBC 9457	BC.023512	152	YBC 11938	BC.025734	216
YBC 9470	BC.023525	166	YBC 15720	BC.028982	299
YBC 9491	BC.023546	220	YBC 16018	BC.029282	124
YBC 9494	BC.023549	182	YBC 16193	BC.029452	67
YBC 9510	BC.023565	183	YBC 16253	BC.029511	281

BC No.	*Museum No.*	*No.*	*BC No.*	*Museum No.*	*No.*
BC.007508	NBC 4532	275	BC.017504	YBC 3438	42
BC.007517	NBC 4541	127	BC.017530	YBC 3464	151
BC.007526	NBC 4550	80	BC.017577	YBC 3512	178
BC.007533	NBC 4557	200	BC.017578	YBC 3513	229
BC.007536	NBC 4560	61	BC.017594	YBC 3529	305
BC.007537	NBC 4561	86	BC.017780	YBC 3715	315
BC.007539	NBC 4563	146	BC.018054	YBC 3989	138
BC.007543	NBC 4567	218	BC.018055	YBC 3990	143
BC.007573	NBC 4597	308	BC.018230	YBC 4165	190
BC.007578	NBC 4602	285	BC.018872	YBC 4808	161
BC.007582	NBC 4606	301	BC.020912	YBC 6846	295
BC.007589	NBC 4613	231	BC.020925	YBC 6859	199
BC.007599	NBC 4623	211	BC.020929	YBC 6863	232
BC.007600	NBC 4624	31	BC.020960	YBC 6894	101
BC.007601	NBC 4625	112	BC.020992	YBC 6926	282
BC.007603	NBC 4627	309	BC.021437	YBC 7372	256
BC.007613	NBC 4637	234	BC.021456	YBC 7391	313
BC.007614	NBC 4638	45	BC.022842	YBC 8783	259
BC.007621	NBC 4645	179	BC.022855	YBC 8796	110
BC.007628	NBC 4652	153	BC.022857	YBC 8798	23
BC.007629	NBC 4653	243	BC.022863	YBC 8804	111
BC.007648	NBC 4672	48	BC.022868	YBC 8809	96
BC.007655	NBC 4679	169	BC.022877	YBC 8818	44
BC.007668	NBC 4692	144	BC.022897	YBC 8838	233
BC.007669	NBC 4693	287	BC.023082	YBC 9027	296
BC.007670	NBC 4694	126	BC.023086	YBC 9031	4
BC.007684	NBC 4707	175	BC.023090	YBC 9035	83
BC.007687	NBC 4710	219	BC.023094	YBC 9039	5
BC.007710	NBC 4732	222	BC.023101	YBC 9046	93
BC.007728	NBC 4750	148	BC.023123	YBC 9068	134
BC.007744	NBC 4765	181	BC.023191	YBC 9136	129
BC.007752	NBC 4773	227	BC.023196	YBC 9141	247
BC.007753	NBC 4774	203	BC.023210	YBC 9155	312
BC.007758	NBC 4779	212	BC.023227	YBC 9172	71
BC.007759	NBC 4780	214	BC.023233	YBC 9178	54
BC.007794	NBC 4815	18	BC.023234	YBC 9179	314
BC.007838	NBC 4859	303	BC.023259	YBC 9204	24
BC.007843	NBC 4864	298	BC.023264	YBC 9209	141
BC.007870	NBC 4891	304	BC.023278	YBC 9223	311
BC.007898	NBC 4919	198	BC.023290	YBC 9235	25
BC.007899	NBC 4920	168	BC.023292	YBC 9237	65
BC.007913	NBC 4934	154	BC.023295	YBC 9240	34
BC.011346	NBC 8350	163	BC.023323	YBC 9268	297
BC.011359	NBC 8363	158	BC.023326	YBC 9271	106
BC.012789	NBC 9820	9	BC.023328	YBC 9273	302

BC No.	*Museum No.*	*No.*	*BC No.*	*Museum No.*	*No.*
BC.023329	YBC 9274	139	BC.025279	YBC 11486	41
BC.023348	YBC 9293	135	BC.025284	YBC 11491	197
BC.023370	YBC 9315	248	BC.025285	YBC 11492	95
BC.023381	YBC 9326	29	BC.025288	YBC 11495	17
BC.023383	YBC 9328	195	BC.025408	YBC 11613	189
BC.023385	YBC 9330	196	BC.025447	YBC 11652	194
BC.023423	YBC 9368	171	BC.025454	YBC 11658	109
BC.023435	YBC 9380	70	BC.025734	YBC 11938	216
BC.023440	YBC 9385	167	BC.028982	YBC 15720	299
BC.023448	YBC 9393	52	BC.029282	YBC 16018	124
BC.023466	YBC 9411	173	BC.029452	YBC 16193	67
BC.023469	YBC 9414	6	BC.029511	YBC 16253	281
BC.023472	YBC 9417	102	BC.033701	GCBC 84	205
BC.023478	YBC 9423	137	BC.033963	GCBC 346	73
BC.023483	YBC 9428	136	BC.034219	GCBC 602	74
BC.023486	YBC 9431	187	BC.034253	GCBC 636	53
BC.023491	YBC 9436	14	BC.034322	GCBC 705	306
BC.023497	YBC 9442	63	BC.034616	NCBT 71	118
BC.023502	YBC 9447	21	BC.034623	NCBT 78	115
BC.023512	YBC 9457	152	BC.034625	NCBT 80	68
BC.023525	YBC 9470	166	BC.034626	NCBT 81	249
BC.023546	YBC 9491	220	BC.034627	NCBT 82	225
BC.023549	YBC 9494	182	BC.034635	NCBT 90	155
BC.023565	YBC 9510	183	BC.034637	NCBT 92	253
BC.023571	YBC 9516	7	BC.034640	NCBT 95	201
BC.023576	YBC 9521	100	BC.034642	NCBT 97	241
BC.023588	YBC 9533	162	BC.034667	NCBT 122	270
BC.023591	YBC 9536	280	BC.034672	NCBT 127	266
BC.023594	YBC 9539	272	BC.034680	NCBT 135	142
BC.023595	YBC 9540	188	BC.034684	NCBT 139	223
BC.023602	YBC 9547	186	BC.034685	NCBT 140	260
BC.023612	YBC 9557	235	BC.034691	NCBT 146	164
BC.023629	YBC 9574	184	BC.034692	NCBT 147	55
BC.023637	YBC 9582	149	BC.034693	NCBT 148	210
BC.023645	YBC 9590	8	BC.034697	NCBT 152	267
BC.023676	YBC 9621	98	BC.034707	NCBT 162	204
BC.023691	YBC 9636	150	BC.034711	NCBT 166	252
BC.023693	YBC 9638	43	BC.034715	NCBT 170	244
BC.023696	YBC 9641	121	BC.034742	NCBT 197	224
BC.024879	YBC 11085	294	BC.034749	NCBT 204	77
BC.025072	YBC 11278	60	BC.034785	NCBT 240	156
BC.025082	YBC 11288	108	BC.034787	NCBT 242	165
BC.025099	YBC 11305	123	BC.034788	NCBT 243	206
BC.025237	YBC 11443	215	BC.034796	NCBT 251	238
BC.025265	YBC 11471	180	BC.034803	NCBT 258	239

BC No.	*Museum No.*	*No.*	*BC No.*	*Museum No.*	*No.*
BC.034808	NCBT 263	114	BC.035177	NCBT 632	176
BC.034810	NCBT 265	57	BC.035186	NCBT 641	174
BC.034819	NCBT 274	99	BC.035188	NCBT 643	217
BC.034841	NCBT 296	36	BC.035198	NCBT 653	13
BC.034870	NCBT 325	62	BC.035208	NCBT 663	242
BC.034902	NCBT 357	50	BC.035212	NCBT 667	246
BC.034913	NCBT 368	33	BC.035216	NCBT 671	289
BC.034955	NCBT 410	10	BC.035225	NCBT 680	221
BC.034961	NCBT 416	113	BC.035247	NCBT 702	286
BC.034962	NCBT 417	140	BC.035251	NCBT 706	147
BC.034974	NCBT 429	97	BC.035254	NCBT 709	269
BC.034976	NCBT 431	264	BC.035255	NCBT 710	172
BC.034979	NCBT 434	191	BC.035261	NCBT 716	104
BC.034984	NCBT 439	94	BC.035266	NCBT 721	132
BC.034987	NCBT 442	20	BC.035272	NCBT 727	268
BC.034988	NCBT 443	66	BC.035279	NCBT 734	26
BC.034989	NCBT 444	263	BC.035280	NCBT 735	58
BC.034995	NCBT 450	88	BC.035282	NCBT 737	91
BC.034998	NCBT 453	89	BC.035292	NCBT 747	258
BC.035007	NCBT 462	16	BC.035297	NCBT 752	133
BC.035009	NCBT 464	79	BC.035300	NCBT 755	49
BC.035010	NCBT 465	84	BC.035302	NCBT 757	103
BC.035013	NCBT 468	56	BC.035303	NCBT 758	177
BC.035016	NCBT 471	208	BC.035305	NCBT 760	284
BC.035018	NCBT 473	254	BC.035307	NCBT 762	274
BC.035022	NCBT 477	185	BC.035315	NCBT 770	92
BC.035023	NCBT 478	122	BC.035325	NCBT 780	288
BC.035024	NCBT 479	283	BC.035336	NCBT 791	128
BC.035033	NCBT 488	290	BC.035337	NCBT 792	3
BC.035040	NCBT 495	228	BC.035339	NCBT 794	46
BC.035045	NCBT 500	15	BC.035342	NCBT 797	273
BC.035048	NCBT 503	22	BC.035350	NCBT 805	78
BC.035049	NCBT 504	105	BC.035353	NCBT 808	261
BC.035053	NCBT 508	32	BC.035357	NCBT 812	251
BC.035072	NCBT 527	30	BC.035362	NCBT 817	278
BC.035074	NCBT 529	213	BC.035371	NCBT 826	160
BC.035081	NCBT 536	47	BC.035373	NCBT 828	69
BC.035104	NCBT 559	38	BC.035383	NCBT 838	262
BC.035109	NCBT 564	277	BC.035388	NCBT 843	271
BC.035113	NCBT 568	12	BC.035401	NCBT 856	159
BC.035142	NCBT 597	145	BC.035436	NCBT 891	257
BC.035149	NCBT 604	27	BC.035440	NCBT 895	276
BC.035161	NCBT 616	90	BC.035446	NCBT 901	255
BC.035167	NCBT 622	28	BC.035457	NCBT 912	64
BC.035176	NCBT 631	245	BC.035458	NCBT 913	240

BC No.	*Museum No.*	*No.*	*BC No.*	*Museum No.*	*No.*
BC.035467	NCBT 922	59	BC.035602	NCBT 1057	170
BC.035482	NCBT 937	85	BC.035614	NCBT 1069	157
BC.035487	NCBT 942	119	BC.035643	NCBT 1098	117
BC.035493	NCBT 948	202	BC.035645	NCBT 1100	192
BC.035495	NCBT 950	226	BC.035650	NCBT 1105	279
BC.035501	NCBT 956	39	BC.035655	NCBT 1110	87
BC.035506	NCBT 961	207	BC.035660	NCBT 1115	236
BC.035511	NCBT 966	130	BC.035666	NCBT 1121	1
BC.035516	NCBT 971	120	BC.035672	NCBT 1127	237
BC.035517	NCBT 972	131	BC.035675	NCBT 1130	76
BC.035519	NCBT 974	11	BC.035699	NCBT 1154	307
BC.035527	NCBT 982	72	BC.035702	NCBT 1157	19
BC.035533	NCBT 988	35	BC.035710	NCBT 1165	230
BC.035551	NCBT 1006	291	BC.035721	NCBT 1176	209
BC.035553	NCBT 1008	40	BC.035732	NCBT 1187	37
BC.035561	NCBT 1016	310	BC.035733	NCBT 1188	81
BC.035564	NCBT 1019	116	BC.035734	NCBT 1189	293
BC.035568	NCBT 1023	250	BC.035735	NCBT 1190	82
BC.035569	NCBT 1024	292	BC.035772	NCBT 1227	2
BC.035576	NCBT 1031	300	BC.035780	NCBT 1235	107
BC.035578	NCBT 1033	265	BC.035791	NCBT 1246	51
BC.035581	NCBT 1036	125	BC.035863	NCBT 1318	193
BC.035585	NCBT 1040	75			

Museum No.	*BC No.*	*CDLI No.*	*Museum No.*	*BC No.*	*CDLI No.*
GCBC 84	BC.033701	P293986	NBC 4624	BC.007600	P297643
GCBC 346	BC.033963	P294245	NBC 4625	BC.007601	P297644
GCBC 602	BC.034219	P294501	NBC 4627	BC.007603	P297646
GCBC 636	BC.034253	P294535	NBC 4637	BC.007613	P297656
GCBC 705	BC.034322	P294604	NBC 4638	BC.007614	P297657
			NBC 4645	BC.007621	P297664
NBC 4532	BC.007508	P297551	NBC 4652	BC.007628	P297671
NBC 4541	BC.007517	P297560	NBC 4653	BC.007629	P297672
NBC 4550	BC.007526	P297569	NBC 4672	BC.007648	P297691
NBC 4557	BC.007533	P297576	NBC 4679	BC.007655	P297698
NBC 4560	BC.007536	P297579	NBC 4692	BC.007668	P297711
NBC 4561	BC.007537	P297580	NBC 4693	BC.007669	P297712
NBC 4563	BC.007539	P297582	NBC 4694	BC.007670	P297713
NBC 4567	BC.007543	P297586	NBC 4707	BC.007684	P297727
NBC 4597	BC.007573	P297616	NBC 4710	BC.007687	P297730
NBC 4602	BC.007578	P297621	NBC 4732	BC.007710	P297753
NBC 4606	BC.007582	P297625	NBC 4750	BC.007728	P297771
NBC 4613	BC.007589	P297632	NBC 4765	BC.007744	P297787
NBC 4623	BC.007599	P297642	NBC 4773	BC.007752	P297795

Museum No.	*BC No.*	*CDLI No.*	*Museum No.*	*BC No.*	*CDLI No.*
NBC 4774	BC.007753	P297796	NCBT 296	BC.034841	P302349
NBC 4779	BC.007758	P297801	NCBT 325	BC.034870	P302378
NBC 4780	BC.007759	P297802	NCBT 357	BC.034902	P302410
NBC 4815	BC.007794	P297837	NCBT 368	BC.034913	P302421
NBC 4859	BC.007838	P297881	NCBT 410	BC.034955	P302463
NBC 4864	BC.007843	P297886	NCBT 416	BC.034961	P302469
NBC 4891	BC.007870	P297913	NCBT 417	BC.034962	P302470
NBC 4919	BC.007898	P297941	NCBT 429	BC.034974	P302482
NBC 4920	BC.007899	P297942	NCBT 431	BC.034976	P302484
NBC 4934	BC.007913	P297956	NCBT 434	BC.034979	P302487
NBC 8350	BC.011346	P299710	NCBT 439	BC.034984	P302492
NBC 8363	BC.011359	P299723	NCBT 442	BC.034987	P302495
NBC 9820	BC.012789	P300927	NCBT 443	BC.034988	P302496
			NCBT 444	BC.034989	P302497
NCBT 71	BC.034616	P302124	NCBT 450	BC.034995	P302503
NCBT 78	BC.034623	P302131	NCBT 453	BC.034998	P302506
NCBT 80	BC.034625	P302133	NCBT 462	BC.035007	P302515
NCBT 81	BC.034626	P302134	NCBT 464	BC.035009	P302517
NCBT 82	BC.034627	P302135	NCBT 465	BC.035010	P302518
NCBT 90	BC.034635	P302143	NCBT 468	BC.035013	P302521
NCBT 92	BC.034637	P302145	NCBT 471	BC.035016	P302524
NCBT 95	BC.034640	P302148	NCBT 473	BC.035018	P302526
NCBT 97	BC.034642	P302150	NCBT 477	BC.035022	P302530
NCBT 122	BC.034667	P302175	NCBT 478	BC.035023	P302531
NCBT 127	BC.034672	P302180	NCBT 479	BC.035024	P302532
NCBT 135	BC.034680	P302188	NCBT 488	BC.035033	P302541
NCBT 139	BC.034684	P302192	NCBT 495	BC.035040	P302548
NCBT 140	BC.034685	P302193	NCBT 500	BC.035045	P302553
NCBT 146	BC.034691	P302199	NCBT 503	BC.035048	P302556
NCBT 147	BC.034692	P302200	NCBT 504	BC.035049	P302557
NCBT 148	BC.034693	P302201	NCBT 508	BC.035053	P302561
NCBT 152	BC.034697	P302205	NCBT 527	BC.035072	P302580
NCBT 162	BC.034707	P302215	NCBT 529	BC.035074	P302582
NCBT 166	BC.034711	P302219	NCBT 536	BC.035081	P302589
NCBT 170	BC.034715	P302223	NCBT 559	BC.035104	P302612
NCBT 197	BC.034742	P302250	NCBT 564	BC.035109	P302617
NCBT 204	BC.034749	P302257	NCBT 568	BC.035113	P302621
NCBT 240	BC.034785	P302293	NCBT 597	BC.035142	P302650
NCBT 242	BC.034787	P302295	NCBT 604	BC.035149	P302657
NCBT 243	BC.034788	P302296	NCBT 616	BC.035161	P302669
NCBT 251	BC.034796	P302304	NCBT 622	BC.035167	P302675
NCBT 258	BC.034803	P302311	NCBT 631	BC.035176	P302684
NCBT 263	BC.034808	P302316	NCBT 632	BC.035177	P302685
NCBT 265	BC.034810	P302318	NCBT 641	BC.035186	P302694
NCBT 274	BC.034819	P302327	NCBT 643	BC.035188	P302696

Museum No.	*BC No.*	*CDLI No.*	*Museum No.*	*BC No.*	*CDLI No.*
NCBT 653	BC.035198	P302706	NCBT 948	BC.035493	P303001
NCBT 663	BC.035208	P302716	NCBT 950	BC.035495	P303003
NCBT 667	BC.035212	P302720	NCBT 956	BC.035501	P303009
NCBT 671	BC.035216	P302724	NCBT 961	BC.035506	P303014
NCBT 680	BC.035225	P302733	NCBT 966	BC.035511	P303019
NCBT 702	BC.035247	P302755	NCBT 971	BC.035516	P303024
NCBT 706	BC.035251	P302759	NCBT 972	BC.035517	P303025
NCBT 709	BC.035254	P302762	NCBT 974	BC.035519	P303027
NCBT 710	BC.035255	P302763	NCBT 982	BC.035527	P303035
NCBT 716	BC.035261	P302769	NCBT 988	BC.035533	P303041
NCBT 721	BC.035266	P302774	NCBT 1006	BC.035551	P303059
NCBT 727	BC.035272	P302780	NCBT 1008	BC.035553	P303061
NCBT 734	BC.035279	P302787	NCBT 1016	BC.035561	P303069
NCBT 735	BC.035280	P302788	NCBT 1019	BC.035564	P303072
NCBT 737	BC.035282	P302790	NCBT 1023	BC.035568	P303076
NCBT 747	BC.035292	P302800	NCBT 1024	BC.035569	P303077
NCBT 752	BC.035297	P302805	NCBT 1031	BC.035576	P303084
NCBT 755	BC.035300	P302808	NCBT 1033	BC.035578	P303086
NCBT 757	BC.035302	P302810	NCBT 1036	BC.035581	P303089
NCBT 758	BC.035303	P302811	NCBT 1040	BC.035585	P303093
NCBT 760	BC.035305	P302813	NCBT 1057	BC.035602	P303110
NCBT 762	BC.035307	P302815	NCBT 1069	BC.035614	P303122
NCBT 770	BC.035315	P302823	NCBT 1098	BC.035643	P303151
NCBT 780	BC.035325	P302833	NCBT 1100	BC.035645	P303153
NCBT 791	BC.035336	P302844	NCBT 1105	BC.035650	P303158
NCBT 792	BC.035337	P302845	NCBT 1110	BC.035655	P303163
NCBT 794	BC.035339	P302847	NCBT 1115	BC.035660	P303168
NCBT 797	BC.035342	P302850	NCBT 1121	BC.035666	P303174
NCBT 805	BC.035350	P302858	NCBT 1127	BC.035672	P303180
NCBT 808	BC.035353	P302861	NCBT 1130	BC.035675	P303183
NCBT 812	BC.035357	P302865	NCBT 1154	BC.035699	P303207
NCBT 817	BC.035362	P302870	NCBT 1157	BC.035702	P303210
NCBT 826	BC.035371	P302879	NCBT 1165	BC.035710	P303218
NCBT 828	BC.035373	P302881	NCBT 1176	BC.035721	P303229
NCBT 838	BC.035383	P302891	NCBT 1187	BC.035732	P303240
NCBT 843	BC.035388	P302896	NCBT 1188	BC.035733	P303241
NCBT 856	BC.035401	P302909	NCBT 1189	BC.035734	P303242
NCBT 891	BC.035436	P302944	NCBT 1190	BC.035735	P303243
NCBT 895	BC.035440	P302948	NCBT 1227	BC.035772	P303280
NCBT 901	BC.035446	P302954	NCBT 1235	BC.035780	P303288
NCBT 912	BC.035457	P302965	NCBT 1246	BC.035791	P303299
NCBT 913	BC.035458	P302966	NCBT 1318	BC.035863	P303371
NCBT 922	BC.035467	P302975			
NCBT 937	BC.035482	P302990	YBC 3438	BC.017504	P304874
NCBT 942	BC.035487	P302995	YBC 3464	BC.017530	P304900

Museum No.	*BC No.*	*CDLI No.*	*Museum No.*	*BC No.*	*CDLI No.*
YBC 3512	BC.017577	P304944	YBC 9315	BC.023370	P310037
YBC 3513	BC.017578	P505879	YBC 9326	BC.023381	P310048
YBC 3529	BC.017594	P304960	YBC 9328	BC.023383	P310050
YBC 3715	BC.017780	P305073	YBC 9330	BC.023385	P310052
YBC 3989	BC.018054	P305301	YBC 9368	BC.023423	P310090
YBC 3990	BC.018055	P305302	YBC 9380	BC.023435	P310102
YBC 4165	BC.018230	P305477	YBC 9385	BC.023440	P310107
YBC 4808	BC.018872	P305953	YBC 9393	BC.023448	P310115
YBC 6846	BC.020912	P307861	YBC 9411	BC.023466	P310133
YBC 6859	BC.020925	P307874	YBC 9414	BC.023469	P310136
YBC 6863	BC.020929	P307878	YBC 9417	BC.023472	P310139
YBC 6894	BC.020960	P307910	YBC 9423	BC.023478	P310145
YBC 6926	BC.020992	P307940	YBC 9428	BC.023483	P310150
YBC 7372	BC.021437	P308316	YBC 9431	BC.023486	P310153
YBC 7391	BC.021456	P308335	YBC 9436	BC.023491	P310158
YBC 8783	BC.022842	P505898	YBC 9442	BC.023497	P310164
YBC 8796	BC.022855	P505903	YBC 9447	BC.023502	P310169
YBC 8798	BC.022857	P505919	YBC 9457	BC.023512	P310179
YBC 8804	BC.022863	P505927	YBC 9470	BC.023525	P310192
YBC 8809	BC.022868	P505906	YBC 9491	BC.023546	P310213
YBC 8818	BC.022877	P505907	YBC 9494	BC.023549	P310216
YBC 8838	BC.022897	P505925	YBC 9510	BC.023565	P310232
YBC 9027	BC.023082	P309759	YBC 9516	BC.023571	P310238
YBC 9031	BC.023086	P309763	YBC 9521	BC.023576	P310243
YBC 9035	BC.023090	P309767	YBC 9533	BC.023588	P310255
YBC 9039	BC.023094	P309771	YBC 9536	BC.023591	P310258
YBC 9046	BC.023101	P309778	YBC 9539	BC.023594	P505886
YBC 9068	BC.023123	P309800	YBC 9540	BC.023595	P310261
YBC 9136	BC.023191	P309858	YBC 9547	BC.023602	P310268
YBC 9141	BC.023196	P309863	YBC 9557	BC.023612	P505892
YBC 9155	BC.023210	P309877	YBC 9574	BC.023629	P310287
YBC 9172	BC.023227	P309894	YBC 9582	BC.023637	P310295
YBC 9178	BC.023233	P309900	YBC 9590	BC.023645	P310303
YBC 9179	BC.023234	P309901	YBC 9621	BC.023676	P310334
YBC 9204	BC.023259	P309926	YBC 9636	BC.023691	P310349
YBC 9209	BC.023264	P309931	YBC 9638	BC.023693	P310351
YBC 9223	BC.023278	P309945	YBC 9641	BC.023696	P310354
YBC 9235	BC.023290	P309957	YBC 11085	BC.024879	P311357
YBC 9237	BC.023292	P309959	YBC 11278	BC.025072	P311454
YBC 9240	BC.023295	P309962	YBC 11288	BC.025082	P311464
YBC 9268	BC.023323	P309990	YBC 11305	BC.025099	P311481
YBC 9271	BC.023326	P309993	YBC 11443	BC.025237	P311614
YBC 9273	BC.023328	P309995	YBC 11471	BC.025265	P311641
YBC 9274	BC.023329	P309996	YBC 11486	BC.025279	P311655
YBC 9293	BC.023348	P310015	YBC 11491	BC.025284	P311660

Museum No.	*BC No.*	*CDLI No.*
YBC 11492	BC.025285	P311661
YBC 11495	BC.025288	P311664
YBC 11613	BC.025408	P311774
YBC 11652	BC.025447	P311813
YBC 11658	BC.025454	P311820
YBC 11938	BC.025734	P311908
YBC 15720	BC.028982	P312739
YBC 16018	BC.029282	P312783
YBC 16193	BC.029452	P312822
YBC 16253	BC.029511	P505896

TEXT EDITIONS

1. NCBT 1121

Copy: Plate I
Date: 07.XI.37 Nbk
Summary: *ina pāni* note: gold

Obv. 4 ⸢GIN$_2$ *bit-qa* KU$_3$.GI⸣ *ina* KU$_3$.GI *ir-bi ša*$_2$ LU[GA]L
a-na bat-qa ša$_2$ *šu-kut-ti* KU$_3$.GI
ša$_2$ ^{d}GAŠAN *ša*$_2$ UNUG^{ki} *u bat-qa*
ša$_2$ *nu-ur*$_2$*-<mu>-u*$_2$ *ša*$_2$ $^{d⸢}$GIGIR⸣
⸢*u* UR$^{!}$.MAḪ$^{me○?}$ *ša*$_2$⸣ ^{d}GAŠAN *ša*$_2$ SAG
⸢*ina* IGI⸣ ^{Id}INNIN-MU-⸢DU$_3$ *u*⸣ ^{Id}EN-DU$_3$
Lo.E. ^{lu2}KU$_3$.DIM^{me}
Rev. (blank)
⸢^{iti}ZIZ$_2$⸣ UD.7.KAM
⸢MU⸣.37.KAM
⸢^{d}AG⸣-NIG$_2$.DU-URU$_3$ LUGAL TIN.TIR$^{⸢ki⸣}$

4 ⅛ shekels of gold, from the gold income from the king, for the repair of the gold jewelry of the Lady-of-Uruk and for the repair of the pomegranate (beads) of the divine chariot and the lion (ornament) of Bēltu-ša-Rēš, are at the disposal of Ištar-šumu-ibni and Bēl-ibni, the goldsmiths.
Month XI, day 7, year 37 of Nebuchadnezzar, king of Babylon.

5 The same two goldsmiths receive gold for the repair of the lions of the *lubār mēṭi*-headdress of Bēltu-ša-Rēš in **No. 4**: 2–3. The present lion ornaments were probably of the same garment; cf. UR.MAḪ *ša*$_2$ TUG$_2$.ḪI.A $^{d.giš}$KU.AN *ša*$_2$ ^{d}GAŠAN *ša*$_2$ SAG (NCBT 1251), 15 UR.MAḪ KU$_3$.GI *ša*$_2$ ^{tug2}*lu-bar me-ṭu ša*$_2$ ^{d}GAŠAN *ša*$_2$ SAG (PTS 2927), 25 UR.MAḪ^{meš} TUR^{m}[^{eš}] *ša*$_2$ TUG$_2$.ḪI.A *me-ṭu ša*$_2$ ^{d}GAŠAN *ša*$_2$ SAG (NCBT 557: 9), and Beaulieu 2003, 220–1. See also YOS 6, 3 and Sack CD, 6, in which the two are working on the *urmaḫlullû* (lion-centaur); see Beaulieu 2003, 367.

2. NCBT 1227

Copy: Plate I
Date: undated (Kan–Npl)
Summary: *ina pāni* note: gold

Obv. [(×)]8 GIN$_2$ 4^{tu2} KU$_3$.G[I (×)] ⸢*e*$^{?}$⸣*-lat*$^{?}$ KU$_3$.GI *ša*$_2$ GABA KU$_3$.GI
(blank)

⸢*ša*$_2$⸣ ^{d}15 *ina* ⸢IGI ^{I}*ša*$_2$-*du*⸣-*nu*
(blank)
[ ] ^{na_4}KIŠIB^{me} KU$_3$.GI *ša*$_2$ GABA KU$_3$.GI
[ ] ⸢×⸣ ^{na_4}KIŠIB^{me} *a*$_4$
[s]um$^{?}$ ⸢ME KU$_3$.GI⸣
Rev. (uninscribed)

8(+) ¼ shekels of gold (...), *apart from* the gold of the gold breast (ornament) of Ištar, are at the disposal of Šadûnu; [...] gold cylinder seal (shaped beads) for the gold breast (ornament) ... these cylinder seal (shaped beads) [...] ... gold.

2 Šadûnu, a goldsmith (*kutimmu*), was active from the final years of Kandalānu (**No. 33**, 14 Kan) throughout the reign of Nabopolassar (e.g., PTS 2208, 20 Npl); see Payne 2007, 253–4.

3. NCBT 792

Copy: Plate I
Date: 30.XI.37 Nbk
Summary: *ina pāni* note: gold

Several spots of weave impressions are noted on the reverse.

Obv. 1 MA.NA 4 GIN$_2$ 4^{tu_2} KU$_3$.GI
a-na bat-qa ša$_2$ ^{giš}KI.TUŠ
ša$_2$ ^{d}GAŠAN *ša*$_2$ UNUG^{ki}
ina IGI ^{Id}15-MU-DU$_3$
u ^{Id}EN-DU$_3$ ^{lu_2}KU$_3$.DI[M]⸢^{me}⸣
Rev. (blank)
^{iti}ZIZ$_2$ ⸢UD.30⸣.KAM MU.37.KAM
^{d}AG-NIG$_2$.DU-URU$_3$ LUGAL TIN.⸢TIR⸣^{ki}

1 mina 4 ¼ shekels of gold for the repair of the pedestal of the Lady-of-Uruk is at the disposal of Ištar-šumu-ibni and Bēl-ibni, the goldsmiths.
Month XI, day 30, year 37 of Nebuchadnezzar, king of Babylon.

4. YBC 9031

Copy: Plate I
Date: 08.[×].0a [Ner–Nbn]
Summary: *ina pāni* note: gold

Obv. [6 ½ GIN$_2$] KU$_3$.GI
[*a-na* × UR.MA]Ḫ KU$_3$.GI^{me}
[*ša*$_2$] ⸢^{tug_2}*lu*⸣-*bar* ^{giš}KU.AN *ša*$_2$ ^{d}GAŠAN *ša*$_2$ SAG
1 GIN$_2$ 3.IGI.4.GAL$_2$.LA^{me} *ḫum-muš* KU$_3$.GI
ul-tu ^{giš}*šad-du ša*$_2$ *bat-qa*
Rev. PAP 8 ½ GIN$_2$ *gi-ru-u*$_2$ LA$_2$-*ṭi* KU$_3$.GI
a-na bat-qu ina IGI
⸢^{Id}INNIN⸣-MU-DU$_3$ *u* ^{Id}EN-DU$_3$

[^{lu_2}K]U$_3$.DIM^{me}
[^{iti}×] ⸢UD⸣.8.KAM MU.SAG.NAM.LUGAL.LA
[... LU]GAL TIN.TIR^{ki}

[6 ½ shekels of] gold [for ×] gold [lio]n (ornaments) [of] the *lubār mēṭi*-headdress of Bēltu-ša-Rēš; 1 $^{19}/_{20}$ shekels of gold from the repair box; total of 8 $^{11}/_{24}$ shekels of gold for repairs are at the disposal of Ištar-šumu-ibni and Bēl-ibni, the [gold]smiths.
[Month ×], day 8, year 0a of [RN], king of Babylon.

3 For the divine headdress *lubār mēṭi* (*miṭṭu*), see Beaulieu 2003, 220–1; Zawadzki 2006, 128–9; and Quillien 2022, 525. For the *mēṭu*-mace, without *lubāru*, see, e.g., **No. 51**: 14; **No. 301**: 6′.

8 The goldsmiths Ištar-šumu-ibni and Bēl-ibni are often attested alongside each other from the last third of Nebuchadnezzar's reign (e.g., **No. 245**, 32$^?$ Nbk) until the mid-reign of Nabonidus (e.g., YOS 6, 121, 8 Nbn); see Payne 2007, 235–7, 240–1, respectively. The tablet should thus be dated to the accession year of Neriglissar, Amīl-Marduk, or Nabonidus.

5. YBC 9039

Copy: Plate II
Date: 21.XIIb.10(+) Npl
Summary: *ina pāni* note: gold

Obv. ⸢½⸣ MA.⸢NA⸣ 5 <GIN$_2$> KU$_3$.GI SA$_5$ TA
^{giš}*šad-du ša*$_2$ *bat-qu ša*$_2$ E$_2$ ^{d}URU$_3$-INIM-⸢*su*⸣
⸢*a*$^!$⸣-*na gu*$_2$-*ḫal-ṣu ša*$_2$ ^{na_4}KIŠIB^{m}[$^{e(š)}$]
ša$_2$ ^{d}15 *ina* IGI ^{I}*re-mut* ⸢*u*$_3$⸣
^{I}KI-^{d}AMAR.UTU-TIN A^{me} *ša*$_2$ ^{Id}EN-Š[EŠ-MU]
2 GIN$_2$ KU$_3$.GI 2⸢^{ta}⸣ *kam*-⸢×⸣ [ ]
Lo.E. *ša*$_2$ ^{d}UNUG^{ki}-*a-ti* [ ]
^{I}*re-mut im-m*[*a*$^?$-×]
Rev. {GIN$_2$$^?$}
4 GIN$_2$ KU$_3$.BABBAR 1^{en} *ša*$_2$ ^{giš}IG *ša*$_2$$^?$ ⸢^{d}15$^?$⸣
[(×)] *ši*-⸢*bir*⸣ *a-na bat-qu ina*$^!$ IGI ^{I}⸢*re-mut*⸣
⸢^{iti}DIRI⸣.ŠE UD.21.KAM
[MU.(×+)]10.KAM ⸢^{d}AG⸣-A-PAP
Up.E. [LUGAL] ⸢E⸣^{ki}

35 <shekels> of red gold from the repair box of the Uṣur-amāssu temple, for the wire of the cylinder seal (shaped beads) of Ištar, are at the disposal of Rēmūtu and Itti-Marduk-balāṭu, sons of Bēl-a[ḫu-iddin].
2 shekels of gold (for) two *kam*[...] of Urkayītu [...] Rēmūtu ... 4 shekels of silver, one *of* the *door of* (*temple*/*cella of*) *Ištar*, the *staff*, for repairs, is at the disposal of Rēmūtu.
Month XIIb, day 21, [Year] 10(+) of Nabopolassar, [king of] Babylon.

10 *ši-bir* is taken here for *šibirru*, although the context can certainly support a form of *šibru*, "broken," thus in need of repairs.

6. YBC 9414

Copy: Plate II
Date: 25.III.29 Nbk
Summary: *ina pāni* note: gold

Obv. 11 2ta ŠU$^{II.me}$ KU$_3$°.GI°
bat-qa ša$_2$ *ul-tu* e$_2$
^{d}IGI.DU *u*$_2$*-ri-di*
a-na dul-lu
ina IGI ^{I}*na-din*
Lo.E. *u* ^{Id}AG-MU-DU
^{lu_2}KU$_3$.DIM^{me}
Rev. (blank)
^{iti}SIG$_4$ UD.25.KAM
MU.29.KAM
^{d}AG-NIG$_2$.DU-URU$_3$
LUGAL TIN.TIR^{ki}

11 ⅔ (shekels) of gold (for) repairs, which was removed from the ^{d}IGI.DU temple, are at the disposal of Nādinu and Nabû-šumu-ukīn, the goldsmiths, for work.
Month III, day 25, year 29 of Nebuchadnezzar, king of Babylon.

3 For the problems of the reading of ^{d}IGI.DU see Beaulieu 2003, 282.

7. YBC 9516

Copy: Plate II
Date: 17.VI.30 Nbk
Summary: *ina pāni* note: gold

Obv. 9 GIN$_2$ *ḫum-mu-šu*$_2$ KU$_3$.GI
3-ta mu-še-zib-e-ti ša$_2$ ⸢AGA KU$_3$⸣.[GI]
⸢*1-en*⸣ IGI.BAR-*ni*? KU$_3$.GI *a-na bat-*⸢*qu*⸣
[*ina*] ⸢IGI⸣ ^{I}*na-din* ⸢A ^{I}*mar-duk u*⸣
[^{I}]⸢^{d}AG⸣-MU-⸢DU A ^{Id}U.GUR-TIN⸣[^{iṭ}]
Rev. (blank)
^{iti}KIN UD.17.KAM MU.30.KAM
^{d}AG-NIG$_2$.DU-URU$_3$ LUGAL TIN.TIR⸢^{ki}⸣

9 ⅕ shekels of gold (for) three *cover-(plates)* of the gold crown (and) one gold ... for repairs are at the disposal of Nādinu, son of Marduk, (and) Nabû-šumu-ukīn, son of Nergal-uballiṭ.
Month VI, day 17, year 30 of Nebuchadnezzar, king of Babylon.

2 "*Cover-(plates)*" for *mušēzibētu* is suggested based on the phrase *mušēzib qātē*, "cover, protector" (of furniture); see CAD M/II, 369, s.v. *mušēzibu* 2., for examples.

3 The meaning of IGI.BAR-*ni*? is unclear. Readings and forms of *naplastu* or *palāsu* do not seem to fit. The last sign (NI) may alternatively be *du*$_3$ or *ir*.

8. YBC 9590

Copy: Plate II
Date: 24.VI.31 Nbk
Summary: *ina pāni* note: gold

The tablet's surface is badly abraded. For lines 1–3 see Beaulieu 2003, 243.

Obv. [× GI]N$_2$ ⸢*gi*⸣-*ru-u*$_2$ ⸢KU$_3$.GI⸣
a-na bat-qu <<*ša*$_2$>> *ša*$_2$ *ku-ma-ra-a-ta*$^{⸢meš?⸣}$
ša$_2$ ^{d}URU$_3$-INIM-*su ina pa-ni*
^{I}*na-din u* ^{Id}AG-MU-DU ^{lu_2}KU$_3$.D[IM^{me}]
ina ⸢KI⸣.LA$_2$ *ša*$_2$ AN.BAR *ina* KA$_2$ *ša*$_2$ *bi-ir-ṣ*[*i*]
KU$_3$.GI *ḫi-i-ṭu*
Rev. (blank)
^{iti}KIN UD.24.KAM MU.31.K[AM]
^{d}AG-NIG$_2$.DU-URU$_3$ LUGAL TIN.TIR^{k}[^{i}]

[×] $\frac{1}{24}$ shekels of gold for the repair of the frame(d ornaments) of Uṣur-amāssu are at the disposal of Nādinu and Nabû-šumu-ukīn, the goldsm[iths]. The gold was weighed according to the iron weight at the *Birṣu* gate.
Month VI, day 24, year 31 of Nebuchadnezzar, king of Babylon.

5 KA$_2$ *ša*$_2$ *bi-ir-ṣ*[*i*]; the *Birṣu* gate is unknown, and the phrase and its meaning are unclear. If the word is indeed *birṣu*, then it might be related to illumination; perhaps in respect to cardinal directions? Ran Zadok (personal communication) raised the possible derivation from B-R-Ṣ; cf. Aramaic ברצ(א), "perforation." A third option would be to read KA$_2$ NIG$_2$.GA$^{!(T.\ bi)}$ × ×.

9. NBC 9820

Copy: Plate III
Date: 02.[×.× Nbk–Nbn]
Summary: *ina pāni* note: gold

For the chronological horizon of the goldsmiths Bēl-ibni and Ištar-šumu-ibni, see comment to **No. 4**, line 8.

Obv. [21 ½ GIN$_2$ *gi-ru-u*$_2$ KU$_3$.GI *ša*$_2$ ^{Id}EN-*ib-ni*]
u ^{Id}INNIN-M[U]-DU$_3$ ^{lu_2}⸢KU$_3$.DIM⸣^{m}[^{eš}]
ina UD[UN *k*]*i-i šak-nu*
3 ⸢GIN$_2$ *gi*⸣-*ru-u*$_2$ KU$_3$.GI
ina UDUN *in-da-ṭu*
Lo.E. *re-e-ḫi* 18 ½ GIN$_2$ KU$_3$.G[I]
Rev. *a-na* [(×)] ⸢*dul-lu*⸣
in[*a* IGI]-*šu*$_2$-*nu*
^{it}[^{i}×] ⸢UD⸣.2.KAM MU.[×.KA]M
[... LUGAL TIN.TIR^{ki}]

[21 $\frac{13}{24}$ shekels of gold of Bēl-ibni] and Ištar-šumu-ibni, the goldsmiths: when put in the

kiln, 3 1/24 shekels of gold were lost in the kiln; the balance, 18 ½ shekels of gold, is at their [disposal] for (…) work.
[Month ×], day 2, [year × of RN, king of Babylon].

10. NCBT 410

Copy: Plate III
Date: 22?.[×].17? [Npl]
Summary: *ina pāni* note: gold

For Šadûnu, a goldsmith, see **No. 2**. Gimillu might be identified as the jeweler (*kabšarru*) attested, e.g., in GC 2, 45, 9 Npl; see Payne 2007, 266 (not mentioning the present text).

Obv. [2+] 1 ⌜MA⌝.NA 5 GIN$_2$ KU$_3$.G[I] *na-⌜al-ṭar⌝* IGI^{u}
13 GIN$_2$ 4^{tu_2} *a-di-⌜i⌝ ša$_2$ ^{I}gi-mil-l[u]*
6 GIN$_2$ *na-al-ṭar ša$_2$ iš-šu$_2$*
PAP ⌜3⌝ MA.NA ⅓ 4 GIN$_2$ KU$_3$.⌜GI⌝
a-na AŠ$^{!}$.ME KU$_3$.GI^{meš}
Lo.E. 11 GIN$_2$ KU$_3$.⌜GI⌝ SA$_5$
⌜a⌝-na ḫu-⌜bu?⌝-ša$_2$-nu
ina pa-[n]i $^{I!}$ša$_2$-du-ni
Rev. PAP.PAP 3 ⌜½ MA⌝.NA 5 GIN$_2$ KU$_3$.GI
⌜a⌝-na bat-qa ⌜ša$_2$ šu⌝-kut-ti KU$_3$.GI
[ša$_2$] ⌜^{d}⌝na-na-a i[na IG]I *^{I}ša$_2$-du-ni*
[ITI].⌜× UD⌝.22?.KAM MU.17?.KAM
[^{d}AG-A-URU$_3$? LUGAL TIN.TIR^{k}]^{i} *uṭ-ṭur*

[2+]1 minas 5 shekels of *nalṭar*-gold were received, (as well as) 13 ¼ shekels, including that of Gimillu; 6 shekels of *nalṭar*(-gold) that he withdrew (already): a total of 3 minas 24 shekels of gold for the gold sun-disk.
11 shekels of red gold for the *ḫubšu*-objects are at the disposal of Šadûnu.
A grand total (of) 3 minas 35 shekels of gold for the repairs of the gold jewelry of Nanāya are at the disposal of Šadûnu.
[Month ×], day 22?, year 17? of [*Nabopolassar*, king of Babylo]n. It was paid in full.

4 A quarter of a shekel is missing in the summary.

5 The three small traces above the AŠ sign were perhaps meant as a DINGIR.

7 *ḫu-⌜bu?⌝-ša$_2$-nu* may be a plural form of *ḫubšu*, an unclear cultic object. Cf. possibly *ḫu-bu-šu$_2$* (Nbn 1097: 4), translated by the CAD as "defective" (CAD Ḫ, 214, s.v. *ḫubšu* 2). An alternative reading would be *ḫu-še-⌜e?⌝-nu*, possibly a plural form of *ḫušû*, a metal plate. The designation of jewelry in the grand total seem to favor the former.

13 If read correctly (the loss of the first half of the line renders the interpretation of the second half somewhat conjectural), this D form of *eṭēru* may be a scribal note confirming actual payment. Alternatives: *⌜šu$_2$⌝-uṭ-ṭur* is improbable due for orthographic reasons (word-initial *šu$_2$* is unexpected); a form of *paṭāru* is not favored by the remaining traces of the sign preceding UD.

11. NCBT 974

Copy: Plate III
Date: 07.II.03 (Npl)
Summary: *ina pāni* note + *maḫir* receipt: gold

For Šadûnu, a goldsmith, see **No. 2**. Bēl-aḫu-iddin, a goldsmith as well, is attested during the reign of Nabopolassar; see Payne 2007, 234–5.

Obv.	⸢⅓ GIN$_2$⸣ 4$^{\textit{tu}_2}$ KU$_3$.GI
	a-na E$_2$ ^{giš}*tal*$^{\text{!(T. \textit{ḫu})}}$-⸢*la*⸣
	ina IGI ^{Id}EN-ŠEŠ-MU
	8 ½ GIN$_2$ ⸢KU$_3$.GI⸣
	⸢2⸣ *ga-ap-pi*
Lo.E.	3 *še-pu-ṭu*
Rev.	22 *a-a-ru ša*$_2$ KA$_2$ *tam-*⸢*le*$^?$*-e*$^{?!}$⸣
	^{I}*ša*$_2$-⸢*du-ni*⸣ IGI$^{\textit{ir}}$
	^{iti}GU$_4$ UD.7.KAM
	MU.3.KAM

20 ¼ shekels of gold for the (gold plated) pole *base* are at the disposal of Bēl-aḫu-iddin.
8 ½ shekels of gold (in the form of) two quills, three *šepūṭus*$^?$, twenty-two inlaid rosettes with *opening* were received from Šadûnu.
Month II, day 7, year 3.

2 To the best of our knowledge this is the only attestation of *bīt talli*. One may speculate that the text refers to the base on which the *tallu* was fixed. On the *tallu* and its various uses in the temple, see Gordin 2020. An interesting parallel may be the *manditu ša talli* attested in YOS 19, 246: 1–2, 8, which seem to have been written 15 days after the present text (Month II, day 22, year 3); both date formulae do not mention a royal name.

6 *še-pu-ṭu* unclear; possibly related to *šu-b/pu-u*$_2$*-ṭu* in YBC 11390: 4 (Beaulieu 2003, 232–5).

7 *a-a-ru ša*$_2$ KA$_2$ *tam-*⸢*le*$^?$*-e*$^{?!}$⸣; for inlaid rosettes cf. 11 *a-a-ri* KU$_3$.GI *ša*$_2$ *tam-le-e* "11 inlaid rosettes of gold" (NBC 4894: 63; see also 30 rosettes in l. 69, translation Beaulieu 2003, 143–5). For *bābu* (KA$_2$) in this context, cf. 5 GIN$_2$ KU$_3$.⸢GI⸣ 44 *a-a-ru ša*$_2$ KA$_2$ ⸢IGI$^?$*-u*$_2$$^?$⸣ "5 shekels of gold (for) 44 rosettes (for) the front(?) opening" (YBC 11390: 18, translation Beaulieu 2003, 232–5); (16 *sūtu* of gold for) *a-a-ri* KA$_2$ KU$_3$.GI [*ša*$_2$ ^{d}*n*]*a-na-a* "the golden rosette with opening(?) [belonging to N]anāya" (NBC 4577: 18, translation Beaulieu 2003, 198). A similar phrase is probably attested in **No. 16**: 1, ⸢*a-a*$^!$⸣*-ri* KA$_2$ *tam-*UD^{me}; see there for the difficulties with this reading.

12. NCBT 568

Copy: Plate III
Date: 23.X.08 --
Summary: *ina pāni* note + *maḫir* receipt: gold and silver

Uk(k)umu is attested here and in **No. 32**; see comment there. The tablet cannot be dated.

Obv.	4 ⸢MA⸣.NA KU$_3$.⸢GI <<KU$_3$⸣.GI>> SA$_5$
	a-na 1 ⸢SAG$^?$ × *ša*$_2$$^?$ *ma*⸣*-ak-*⸢*ka-su*⸣

ina IGI ^{I}*u*$_2$-*ku-mu* ^{iti}AB
UD.23.KAM MU.8.KAM
{6$^?$}
Rev. (blank)
6 MA.NA 16 ½° GIN$_2$ KU$_3$.BABBAR *ša*$_2$ SIK$_2$.ḪI.A
31 GUN 9 MA.NA KU$_3$.BABBAR IGI^{ir}
^{iti}AB UD.23.KAM

4 minas of red gold for one ... *of* the *makkasu*-bowl are at the disposal of Uk(k)umu; Month X, day 23, year 8. 6 minas 16 ½ shekels of silver for wool (weighing) 31 talents 9 minas; the silver was received (from Uk(k)umu$^?$).
Month X, day 23.

2 *šakru*, "handle" of a bowl, is known from MB and EA texts (CAD Š/I, 192). There seems to be, however, a bit too much space for *šak-ru*, and it is perhaps better to read, "one × (and) two bowls." With regard to the large amount of gold, note the reference in CAD to a *makkasu* bowl weighing 142 ½ shekels of gold (1882-09-18, 284e: 2). We have not seen the text.

5 It seems that the scribe was about to write down the "6 MA.NA," but then decided to write it all together on the reverse.

6–7 The conversion rate is 1 shekel of silver per ca. 5 minas of wool. These prices are known from the mid reign of Nebuchadnezzar but also from Neriglissar and Nabonidus; see Kleber 2010, 604.

13. NCBT 653

Copy: Plate IV, photograph of Up. E. on Plate LXXXIX
Date: undated (Kan–Npl)
Summary: *ina pāni* note + weighing: gold

The smith Nabû-zēru-ibni is attested from the reign of Kandalānu (EPHE 609, 10+ Kan) to Nabopolassar (e.g, GC 2, 54, 10 Npl); see Payne 2007, 317.

Obv. ⸢12⸣ MA.NA KU$_3$.GI 1^{en} *ḫa-a-ṭu*
⸢11⸣ ⅚ MA.NA 5 GIN$_2$ 2°-*u*$_2$ <*ḫa*>-*a-ṭu*
[PAP] 23 ⅚ MA.NA 5 GIN$_2$ KU$_3$.GI
[*a*]-⸢*na pi*⸣-*da-ni i-na* IGI
⸢^{Id}AG-NUMUN⸣-*ib-ni* ^{lu_2}SIMUG
[× M]A.⸢NA⸣ 5 GIN$_2$ KU$_3$.GI *ša*$_2$ *šu-kut-ti*$^!$
[*a-na*] ⸢*pi-da*⸣-*nu ina* IGI ^{Id}AG-NUMUN-DU$_3$
Lo.E. [ ] ⸢× ×⸣ *ša*$_2$ UGU GIŠ.ŠU$_2$.A 5 *ma-nu-u*$_2$
[ ] ⸢ZABAR⸣ 1 MA.NA *ša*$_2$ ^{na_4}KUR-*ni*
Rev. [ ] ⸢*a*⸣-*na* KU$_3$.GI *ḫi-i-ṭi*
[× M]A.NA 1^{en} <KI>.LA$_2$ 5 GIN$_2$ LA$_2$
⸢6$^?$⸣ MA.NA 2^{u_2} 15 GIN$_2$
⸢6$^?$⸣ MA.NA *šal-šu* 10 GIN$_2$
⸢5$^?$⸣ MA.NA 4^{u} 11 GIN$_2$
⸢2$^?$⸣ MA.NA 50 GIN$_2$ 5^{šu_2}
(markings on Up.E.)

12 minas of gold, the first installment, 11 minas 55 shekels, the second installment—[a total of] 23 minas 55 shekels of gold—are at the disposal of Nabû-zēru-ibni, the smith, for assaying.
[×] mina(s) 5 shekels of gold from/for jewelry are at the disposal of Nabû-zēru-ibni, [for] assaying; [...] that is on the stool, *counted/weighed* five (times) ... [... bro]nze (and) 1 mina of hematite [...] weighed for gold: [×] mina(s), the first weighing,—missing 5 shekels; *6* minas, the second—(missing) 15 shekels; *6* minas, the third—(missing) 10 shekels; *5* minas, the fourth—(missing) 11 shekels; [(×+)] 2 minas 50 shekels, the fifth ...

14. YBC 9436

Copy: Plate IV
Date: 01.V.32 Nbk
Summary: *ina pāni* note: crown of Nanāya

Obv. 9 *in-bi* KU$_3$.GI^{me}
ša$_2$ *ku-lu-lu* KU$_3$.GI
ša$_2$ ^{d}*na-na-a*
ma-ṭu-u$_2$
ku-lu-lu ša$_2$ ^{d}*na-na-a*
Lo.E. ⸢*a*⸣*-na bat-qu*
Rev. *ina* IGI ⸢^{lu_2}KAB.SAR⸣^{me}
u ^{lu_2}⸢KU$_3$.DIM⸣^{me}
^{iti}NE UD.1.KAM
MU.32.KAM
^{d}AG-NIG$_2$.DU-URU$_3$
LUGAL TIN.TIR^{ki}

Nine gold fruit(-shaped jewels) of the gold crown of Nanāya are missing.
The crown of Nanāya is at the disposal of the jewelers and the goldsmiths for repair.
Month V, day 1, year 32 of Nebuchadnezzar, king of Babylon.

7 Note that the crown of Nanāya is not entrusted to a single jeweler, but to a collective of jewelers. In similar cases, e.g., **No. 34** (goldsmiths) and **No. 145** (broken, garments related), such an arrangement seems to be due to the large quantity of items involved. In the present case, however, it may be owed to the importance of the item, the crown of Nanāya. Having said that, it must also be noted that the crown was probably a massive, heavy object by itself. On the divine crowns, see Beaulieu forthcoming.

15. NCBT 500

Copy: Plate XVI
Date: undated
Summary: unfinished *ina pāni* note: gold

Obv. [× (×) *-d*]*a-a-ta ša*$_2$ 4 ⸢*šap*⸣*-pe-e*^{me} KU$_3$.GI
[× (×) ⅔ GIN$_2$] KU$_3$.GI *ḫa-a-ṭu* ⅓ 3$^{?!}$ ½ GIN$_2$ KU$_3$.GI
[TA$^?$ E$^{?k}$]^{i} *nu-uš-tar-du*
[(ø)] PAP 1 MA.NA 3 ½ GIN$_2$ KU$_3$.⸢GI⸣

[*ina*] *šu-qul-tu*$_2$ *ša*$_2$ AN.BAR
ina IGI (blank)
Rev. (uninscribed)

... of/for four *šappu*-bowls of gold, [*40 shekels*] of gold, stock; 23 ½ shekels of gold we have sent/led down/away [*from Babyl*]*on*; total of 1 mina 3 ½ shekels of gold [according to] the iron weight standard is at the disposal of (blank).

3 An alternative reconstruction may be [*ana*] ⸢E$_2$⸣ *nu-uš-tar-du*, "we sent down [*to the tem*]*ple*." Regardless of the restoration of the broken signs, if the verbal form is indeed 1st person Pl. perfect Š of *arādu*, or alternatively of *redû*, then it is a rare use of the 1st person in administrative texts. In administrative context, apart from epistolography, this is known mainly from (the somewhat ill-defined) memoranda.[1] The missing name at the end of line 6 suggest that the text was in fact "unfinished." That, in addition to the lack of date, may point to the tablet as being some sort of a draft (for personal use?).

16. NCBT 462

Copy: Plate IV
Date: 13.IV.16 (Kan–Npl)
Summary: *maḫir* receipt + payment (*eṭir*) note: gold

If the restoration of the name Šadûnu is correct, then the chronological horizon of the tablet would be Kan–Npl; see comment to **No. 2**. The traces in line 3, however, may be of du$_3$, in which case DN-(šumu/zēru)-ibni should be restored; see, e.g., the note regarding Nabû-zēru-ibni in **No. 13**.

Obv. [× M]A.NA KU$_3$.GI ⸢*a-a*$^!$⸣*-ri* KA$_2$ *tam*-UD^{me}
[*ša*$_2$ *a-na*] *pit*$_2$*-qu na-ad-da-ti*^{me}
[^{I}*ša*$_2$$^?$*-du*$^?$*-n*]*i*$^?$ IGI^{ir}
[× × KU$_3$$^?$].⸢BABBAR$^?$⸣ *ša*$_2$ *a-na* UGU
[*pi*]-⸢*ti*⸣*-iq e-ṭir*
Lo.E. ⸢^{iti}⸣ŠU UD.13.KAM
MU.⸢16⸣.KAM
Rev. (uninscribed)

[× m]inas of gold, *inlaid rosettes with opening*, [which was] *given* for the purpose of smelting, were received from [*Šadûn*]*u*. He was paid [× si]lver, which was for the [sme]lting.
Month IV, day 13, year 16.

1 ⸢*a-a*$^!$⸣*-ri* KA$_2$ *tam*-UD^{me}: The clear sequence ⸢*a-a*$^!$⸣*-ri* KA$_2$ *tam-* must be related to *a-a-ru ša*$_2$ $^{na_4?!(T.\ ka_2)}$*tam*-⸢*le*$^?$*-e*$^{?!}$⸣ (**No. 11**: 7, see comment there), though the final two signs cannot be reconciled. We reject the reading UD.UD (DADAG), Akk. *ebbu*, "pure, shining, polished" etc., which may be said of gold (Beaulieu 2003, 381) or precious stones, though it is not at all common in Neo-Babylonian sources (CAD N/I, 2).

2 The word *na-ad-da-ti*^{me} remains difficult and unclear. It may be taken as an unexpected/faulty feminine stative form for *nadnat* with the ^{me} determinative to indicate the plural, as is cautiously

[1] For memoranda (Akk. *taḫsistu*), see Jursa 2004a, 153–4; Levavi 2018, 36.

translated, but there is no clear feminine noun to which it may refer. Omitting the restored [*ša*$_2$ …] at the head of the line and understanding *na-ad-da-ti*^{me} as a qualifier of the smelting process does not work well in the context.

17. YBC 11495

Copy: Plate V
Date: 14.IV.15 (Npl)
Summary: *maḫir* receipt: gold

The two goldsmiths, Rēmūtu and Itti-Marduk-balāṭu, were brothers. Rēmūtu is attested from 7 Npl (YBC 3455) to 1 Nbk (YOS 17, 245), while Itti-Marduk-balāṭu is attested until 20 Npl (**No. 5**); see Payne 2007, 242, 252–3, respectively.

Obv. [× GIN$_2$ (×)] *gi-re-e* KU$_3$.GI
[ ] KU$_3$.GI 2 IGI MAŠ.DA$_3$ KU$_3$.GI
[KU$_3^?$.G]I$^?$ *ša*$_2^?$ *pa-ni* MAŠ.DA$_3$ KU$_3$.GI
[ ] ⸢×⸣ KU$_3$.GI *ša*$_2$ *tup*$^!$-*kat*$_2$ KU$_3$.GI
[*ša*$_2$] ⸢^{d}*na*⸣-*na-a* ^{I}*re-mut*
Lo.E. *u* ^{I}KI-⸢^{d}⸣ŠU$_2$-TIN$^!$
maḫ-ru-⸢ʾ*u*⸣
Rev. (blank)
^{iti}ŠU$^!$ UD.14.KAM
MU.15.KAM

[× +] ⸢×/24⸣ shekel(s) of gold […] gold, two golden gazelle faces […*gol*]*d of* a golden gazelle face […] gold for kidney-shaped gold beads [of] Nanāya, were received by Rēmūtu and Itti-Marduk-balāṭu.
Month IV, day 14, year 15.

2, 3 For gazelle face ornaments of gold see Beaulieu 2003, 387; and cf. YBC 11649 (Beaulieu 2003, 150).

18. NBC 4815

Copy: Plate V
Date: [… Npl/Nbk]
Summary: *maḫir* receipt: gold and silver + *ina pāni* clause

Neither of the two protagonists can be identified. Both silver-to-gold conversions (ll. 3–4, 7–8) are at the rate of 1 shekel of gold for ca. 8 shekels of silver. For the price of gold during the sixth century see Kleber 2020, 28–30.

Obv. 12 GIN$_2$ 3 *re-ba-a*-⸢*ta*⸣ KU$_3$.GI 1^{en} *ḫa-a-ṭu*
a-na 2 MA.NA 14 GIN$_2$ *bit-qa* LA$_2$°-*ṭi* KU$_3$.BABBAR° IGI$^{\circ ir}$
6 {½} GIN$_2$ *gi-ru-u*$_2$ KU$_3$.GI
a-na ⅔ MA.<NA> 8 ½ GIN$_2$ KU$_3$.BABBAR IGI^{ir}
PAP 19 GIN$_2$ *ḫum-mu-šu*$_2$ LA$_2$-*ṭi* KU$_3$.GI
ina ŠU^{II} ^{Id}AG-ŠEŠ-KAM ⸢A⸣-*šu*$_2$ *ša*$_2$ ^{I}ZALAG$_2$-<*e*>-*a* IGI^{ir}
9 GIN$_2$ *ḫum*-⸢*mu-šu*$_2$ LA$_2$-*ṭi*⸣ KU$_3$.GI ⸢*ina* IGI-*šu*$_2$⸣

⸢*a-na*⸣ 1 MA.NA 10 ⸢GIN$_2$ 4$^{tu_2!}$ ⸢*bit*$^?$-*qi*$_2^?$ <<KU$_3^?$>>⸣ KU$_3$.BABBAR
[*ina* ŠU^{II}] ⸢^{I}INNIN$^{!?}$.NA⸣-NUMUN-[×]
[A-*šu*$_2$ *ša*$_2$ ^{I}]^{d}EN-PAP IGI$^{⸢ir⸣}$
[ ] ⸢× × ×⸣ [ ]
(remainder of Obv. broken)
Rev. (beginning of Rev. broken)
[ ]
[^{d}AG-×-UR]U$_3$ LUGAL TIN.TIR^{ki}

12 ¾ shekels of gold, the first instalment for 2 minas 13 ⅞ shekels of silver, were received; 6 1/24 shekels of gold for 48 ½ shekels of silver were received; a total of 18 ⅘ shekels of gold were received from Nabû-aḫu-ēreš, son of Nūrea; 8 ⅘ shekels of gold are (still) at his disposal. He received (it) for 1 mina 10 ⅜ shekels of silver from Innin$^?$-zēru-[×, son of] Bēl-nāṣir. ... (remainder illegible).
[…]
[Month ×, day ×, year × of Nabû-×-uṣu]r king of Babylon.

5 The total of 18 ⅘ approximates, but does not perfectly match, the actual total weight of gold, namely 18 19/24 shekels: it is one *girû* off.

19. NCBT 1157

Copy: Plate V
Date: –.–.13 (Nbk)
Summary: payment (*eṭir*) note: gold

Obv. 33 KU$_3$.GI
ša$_2$ *ina* ŠU^{II} ^{Id}AG-SUR-ZI^{me}
^{Id}AG-ŠEŠ^{me}-TIN
u ^{I}ŠEŠ-MU-^{d}AMAR.UTU
ša$_2$ MU.13.KAM SUR$^{!(T.\ pad)}$
Rev. (uninscribed)

33 gold (blank), via Nabû-ēṭir-napšāti, *were paid to* Nabû-aḫḫē-bulliṭ, and Aḫu-iddin-Marduk *for* year 13.

1 Either a measurement or an object is clearly missing.

4 Aḫu-iddin-Marduk is an uncommon name. Apart from **No. 174**: 8, in which we find Nabû-mukīn-apli / Aḫu-iddin-Marduk, the only other known attestation is from the letter YOS 21, 78 (= SbB 2, 54), as having a *bīt ritti*. Interestingly, the writer of the letter is Nabû-ēṭir-napšāti (deputy of the Sealand). If either of these attestations refers to our Aḫu-iddin-Marduk, it would date the present text to the reign of Nebuchadnezzar. Having said that, there is no clear indicator connecting either of the texts to each other.

20. NCBT 442

Copy: Plate V
Date: 01.VI.12 (Npl)
Summary: payment (*eṭir*) note: gold

For the goldsmith Itti-Marduk-balāṭu (l. 5), see **No. 17**.

Obv. 2 GIN$_2$ ⸢2⸣ *ḫum-mu-šu*$_2$ LA$_2$ KU$_3$.GI
a-na bat-qu ša$_2$ KI.GAL
ša$_2$ ^{d}*aš*$_2$-⸢*ka*⸣-*i*?-*ti*
4 *ku-um ana ku-um*
Lo.E. ^{I}KI-^{d}AMAR.UTU-<TIN> *e-ṭer*
Rev. (blank)
^{iti}⸢KIN⸣ UD.1.K[AM]
MU.12.KAM

Itti-Marduk-<balāṭu> was paid 1 ⅗ shekel of gold for the repair of the pedestal of Urkayītu, "one for the other." Month VI, day 1, year 12.

1 1 ⅗; lit. 2 shekels minus 2 fifths.
4 Additional cases of the relatively rare phrase *kūm ana kūm* ("one for one / the other") are found in, e.g., GC 2, 51: 4, Nbk 40: 8; see CAD K, 531, s.v. *kūm* e.

21. YBC 9447

Copy: Plate VI
Date: [×.×.×] Nbk
Summary: inventory list: cultic ornaments

Obv. [*šukutti*? *ša*$_2$? DN?]
[ ]
[MU.×.KAM] ^{d}AG-NIG$_2$.DU-URU$_3$ LUGAL TI[N.TIR^{ki}]

[KU$_3$.GI *ša*$_2$ *k*]*u-lu-lu* KU$_3$.GI 2 *ša*$_2$ *ku-ma-r*[*i* ...]
[*du-di*]-*it-ti a-ḫa-meš ṣab-ta* [(...)]
[ ] × UL.GA^{meš} *ina gu*$_2$-*ḫal*-⸢*ṣu*⸣ K[U$_3$.GI]
[K]U$_3$.GI *ša*$_2$ 4ta *a-gur-ru sa-ma-ḫal-li-šu*$_2$ [(...)]
[ ] bit tu$_2$ aš *ša*$_2$ *man-di-tu*$_4$ KU$_3$.GI *ina* 4 *gu*$_2$-*ḫal-ṣ*[*u*]
[K]U$_3$.GI *ša*$_2$ *zi-i-mu ina lib*$_3$-*bi* 20 la ar [...]
[ ] (blank) 1 MUL BAL ⸢×⸣ [...]
[ ] ⸢×⸣ $^{na_4.im}$DUB *la mit-ḫar-ru ša*$_2$ *man-di-t*[*u*$_4$]
[(+)]25 NA$_4$ KU$_3$.GI 28 ^{na_4}*tuk-pi-tu*$_4$ 3 ^{na_4}⸢×⸣ [ ]
[ ] ⸢× ^{na_4}⸣ZA.GIN$_3$ 2 ^{na_4}*sag-gil-mud ina* GU$_2$ GADA ⸢×⸣ [...]
[ ] KU$_3$.GI 98 $^{na_4.im}$DUB *la mit-ḫar-r*[*u*]
[ ] ⸢×⸣ KU$_3$.gi 6 *ka-su-su-e* (blank) [ ]
[ ] ⸢GABA⸣^{meš} KU$_3$.GI 7ta *a-gur-ru ša*$_2$ ⸢$^{giš?}$×⸣ [...]
[GA]BA^{meš} KU$_3$.GI *ša*$_2$ di ik lu *ša*$_2$ ⸢×⸣ [ ]
[ ] ⸢×⸣ ḫu PAP *šu-kut-ti* KU$_3$.GI ⸢*ša*$_2$⸣ [...]

[KU$_3$].GI *taš-kis* KU$_3$.GI *ša$_2$-lam* š[u$^?$]

[KU$_3$.G]I *ša$_2$* 4^{u_2} *ša$_2$-lam* 2 [ ]

[KU$_3$.G]I *ša$_2$* 4⌜$^{u_2?}$ *it*⌝-*t*[*i*]

[ ] ⌜× × × × × ×⌝ [ ]

(remainder of Obv. broken)

Rev. [ ] mu [ ]

[ ] ⌜× E$_2^?$ *ia* × ×⌝ [ ]

[ ] ⌜30/eš⌝ [ ]

[ ]

[ ]

[K]U$_3$.GI ⌜45 × ×⌝ [ ]

[ ] KU$_3$.GI 75 ⌜*nu-ur*⌝-[*mu*$^?$-*u$_2$*]

[ ] ⌜KU$_3$.GI⌝ 52 ⌜× ×⌝^{meš} [ ]

[ ] ⌜× KU$_3$.GI 40 × × ŠU$^{II.meš}$⌝ [ ]

[ ] (blank) ⌜×*tu$_2$*$^?$ 3$^?$⌝ [ ]

[ ] KU$_3$.G[I (×+)] 7 ⌜*ka-su-su* ×⌝[ ]

[*nu*]-*ur-mu*-⌜*u$_2$*⌝ KU$_3$.GI *ša$_2$* ⌜*qa*$^?$⌝-*an* [ ]

[ ] ⌜^{gada}⌝*šal-ḫu* (blank) [( )]

[ ] *lu ša$_2$*-⌜*lam*⌝ 21 ⌜ŠU$^{?II?}$⌝ KU$_3$.⌜GI *it-ti*⌝ [ ]

[^{n}]$^{a_4.im}$DUB ^{na_4}⌜ZA⌝.[GIN$_3$] ⌜*ša$_2$ man-di-ti* KU$_3$⌝.[GI]

[ ] ⌜*sur* × × × ×⌝ KU$_3$.⌜GI *lu*⌝ [ ]

[ ] ⌜UD MIN UL.GA^{meš} KU$_3$.GI × ×⌝ [ ]

[ ] ⌜× KU$_3$.GI *lu* × ×⌝ LAGAB

[*Gold jewelry of DNs that …; year* × of] Nebuchadnezzar, king of Ba[bylon]:
[… of gold for the] golden crown, two for the gold frame(d ornaments), […, … gold fib]ulas fastened together [……] … from the gold wire, [… …] gold of four *agurru*-ornaments of its *hooks* [… …] … of gold mounting in four wires, […] of golden appearance, twenty of which are not … [ ] one star … […].
[…] … inscribed stones of various sizes of the mountings […] twenty-five(+) gold beads, twenty(+)-eight kidney-shaped beads, three [… …] lapis lazuli, two (of) *saggilmud*-stone from the *linen* necklace [… …] of gold, ninety-eight inscribed stones of various sizes […] of gold, six falcon (figurines) […] gold breast (ornament), seven *agurru*-ornaments of … […] gold breast (ornament) of … of … […] … total of gold jewelry of [DN].
[…] *tarkisu*-ornament of gold … [… …] gold *of the* four(th) … two [… …] gold of the four(th) … [ ] […]
[] … [ ] … [ ] gold, forty-five … [… …] gold, seventy-five *pomegr*[*anete* (*shaped beads*) …] gold, fifty-two …[… …] gold, forty … *hands* […] … *three* […] gold, seven falcon (figurines) [… *pom*]*egranete* (*shaped beads*) of gold from […] linen *šalḫu*-cloth [(…)].
[…] …, twenty-one *hands* of gold with […] inscribed stones of lapis lazuli (with) mounting of gold […] … gold … [ ] …

7′ *Sa-ma-ḫal-li-šu$_2$*; possibly a by-form of *sanḫu*? Cf. *sa-ma-ḫal* (**No. 38**: 1), and see note there.

11′ Also 14′, 15′: $^{na_4.im}$DUB …; cf. ^{na_4}KIŠIB *la mit-ḫar man-di-ti* KU$_3$.GI (*ArOr* 33, 22: 7). For an "inscribed NA$_4$," cf ^{na_4}*ṭup-pi*/DUB ZA.GIN$_3$ in BM 74586: 2, 6 (Waerzeggers, MR 79).

19′ Also 20′, 14″: *ša$_2$-lam* is unclear in this context. The three clear attestations with the same spelling exclude emendations such as ($^{\text{tug}_2}$)NIG$_2$.LAM$_2$, for *lamḫuššu*, for example.

22. NCBT 503

Copy: Plate VI
Date: undated
Summary: accounting inventory: gold

Obv. [ ]
[×] ⸢MA⸣.NA [ ]
[+]⸢1⸣ MA.NA 55 ⸢GIN$_2$⸣
⸢5⸣ ⅔ MA.NA 5
5 ⅚ MA.NA
Lo.E. 4 ½ MA.NA 5
Rev. 4 ⅚ MA.NA 8
6 MA.NA
7 MA.NA 55
[PAP]? 53 ⸢MA⸣.NA ⅓ 8 GIN$_2$
[× MA.N]A 11 GIN$_2$ KU$_3$.GI *ba-ab-ti*
Up.E. [× MA].⸢NA 13⸣ [(+)] ⸢GIN$_2$⸣ KU$_3$.GI
[ ]-⸢×-*da*⸣-*nu* {eras.}

[…, ×] mina(s) […], 1(+) mina(s) 55 shekels, 5 ⅔ minas 5 (shekels), 5 ⅚ minas, 4 ½ minas 5 (shekels), 4 ⅚ minas 8 (shekels), 6 minas, 7 minas 55 (shekels); [*total of*] 53 minas 28 shekels, [× min]a(s) 11 shekels of gold, is part of [× min]as 13+ shekels of gold […] …

11 For *bābtu* see commentary to **No. 97**: 5.

23. YBC 8798

Copy: Plate VII
Date: 19.III.30 Nbk
Summary: accounting note: gold

Obv. 5 ½ GIN$_2$ 1 *gi-ru-u$_2$* KU$_3$.GI
ir-bi ša$_2$ ^{Id}INNIN-*na*°-⸢*din*-IBILA⸣
A-*šu$_2$ ša$_2$* ^{Id}AG-ŠEŠ-[×]
^{iti}SIG$_4$° UD.20.1.LA$_2$.⸢KAM⸣
MU.30.KAM
Rev. ^{d}AG-NIG$_2$.⸢DU-URU$_3$⸣
LUGAL ⸢TIN.TIR^{ki}⸣

5 $^{13}/_{24}$ shekels of gold, the income from Ištar-nādin-apli, son of Nabû-aḫu-[×].
Month III, day 19, year 30 of Nebuchadnezzar, king of Babylon.

2 ^{Id}INNIN-*na*°-⸢*din*-IBILA⸣ may alternatively be read ^{Id}INNIN-DU°-⸢IBILA⸣ for Ištar-mukīn-apli.

24. YBC 9204

Copy: Plate VII
Date: 01.XII.17 Nbk
Summary: inventory list: gold items

Obv. 3 AŠ.ME KU$_3$.GI *ḫab-⸢ṣu⸣-tu*
1 GU$_2$ *ša*$_2$ ^{na_4}KIŠIB^{me}
la mit-ḫar
31 *a-a-ri* KU$_3$.⸢GI⸣
ša$_2$ *sa-a-du*
PAP *šu-kut-ti* KU$_3$.GI
⸢*ša*$_2$⸣ ^{d}GAŠAN *ša*$_2$ UNUG^{ki}
ša$_2$ *ina* ^{giš}*šad-du ša*$_2$ *bat-⸢qa⸣*
Rev. (blank)
^{iti}ŠE UD.1.KAM MU.17.KAM
^{d}AG-NIG$_2$.DU-URU$_3$
LUGAL TIN.TIR^{ki}

Three lustrous gold sun-disks, one necklace of cylinder seal (shaped beads) of various sizes, (and) thirty-one rosettes of *sādu*-gold; the total gold jewelry of the Lady-of-Uruk that is in the repair box.
Month XII, day 1, year 17 of Nebuchadnezzar, king of Babylon.

4–5 The meaning of *ša sādu* as qualifier of gold is unclear.

25. YBC 9235

Copy: Plate VII
Date: 18.VIII.32 Nbk
Summary: accounting + withdrawal (*našû*) note: gold and cress

Obv. ½ MA.NA 2 GIN$_2$ 2⸢*ta*⸣ ŠU$^{II.meš}$ KU$_3$.GI
ir-bi ša$_2$ UN^{meš} *ša*$_2$ ⸢*ul*⸣*-tu* ^{iti}ŠU
a-di ^{iti}APIN *ina* ŠU^{II} ^{Id}AG-MU-GIŠ
A ^{lu_2}E$_2$.BAR-^{d}*za-ri-qu*
⸢*u*$_3$⸣ ^{Id}AG-SUR-ZI^{meš}
[A-*šu*$_2$ *ša*$_2$] ⸢^{I}⸣^{d}EN-BA^{ša_2} A ^{Id}EN-A-URU$_3$
[*a-na n*]*a-da-nu a-na* KU$_3$.BABBAR
Lo.E. [*a-na*] ⸢E$_2$.SAG.IL$_2$⸣
Rev. [*šap-ru* 3 SILA$_3$] I$_3$.GIŠ
3 ⸢SILA$_3$ MUN.ḪI.A 3 SILA$_3$ *saḫ*⸣*-le-e*
a-na ⸢*ṣi-di-ti-šu*$_2$*-nu*⸣ *it-ta-šu*$_2$*-u*$_2$
^{iti}APIN UD.18.KAM MU.32.KAM
^{d}AG-NIG$_2$.DU-URU$_3$ LUGAL TIN.TIR^{ki}

32 ⅔ shekels of gold, the income from (various) people for months IV–VIII [were sent to] Esangil via Nabû-šumu-līšir, descendant of Šangû-Zāriqu and Nabû-ēṭir-napšāti, son of Bēl-iqīša, descendant of Bēl-aplu-uṣur, [for the purpose of being s]old for silver. They

withdrew [3 *qû*] of oil, 3 *qû* of salt, 3 *qû* of cress as their (travel) provisions.
Month VIII, day 18, year 32 of Nebuchadnezzar, king of Babylon.

9 Although we are unaware of exact parallels of gold shipments to be sold, there is evidence for the temple liquidating its gold for various purposes; see Zaia 2021 and her discussion of YOS 17, 390.

26. NCBT 734

Copy: Plate VII
Date: 22.XI.22 Nbk
Summary: issue (*nadin*) note: gold

Obv. 5 GIN$_2$ KU$_3$.GI *ina* KU$_3$.⸢GI *ša*$_2$ ×⸣ [× (×)]
a-na bat-qa ša$_2$ *šu-kut-*⸢*ti*⸣
a-na ^{I}*ba-la-ṭu* A-*šu*$_2$ *ša*$_2$
^{I}*ina*-SUḪ$_3$-SUR *u* ^{lu2}*um-man-ni*
ša$_2$ E$_2$.SAG.IL$_2$ *na-din*
Rev. (blank)
^{iti}ZIZ$_2$ UD.22.KAM MU.22.KAM
^{d}AG-NIG$_2$.DU-URU$_3$ LUGAL TIN.⸢TIR^{ki}⸣

5 shekels of gold from the gold of ... for the repair of jewelry were given to Balāṭu, son of Ina-tēšî-ēṭir, and the craftsmen of Esagil.
Month XI, day 22, year 22 of Nebuchadnezzar, king of Babylon.

27. NCBT 604

Copy: Plate VIII
Date: 14$^{?}$.VI.12 [Npl]
Summary: accounting inventory: gold

Nabû-nāṣir, a goldsmith, is attested during the reign of Nabopolassar; see Payne 2007, 248–9. For Rēmūtu see **No. 17.** For Šadûnu see **No. 2**.

Obv. 3 MA.NA ⅓ GIN$_2$ KU$_3$.GI 3 *man-d*[*a*$^{?}$*-a*$^{?}$*-ta*$^{?}$]
ša$_2$ ^{d}URU$_3$-INIM-*su ina lib*$_3$-⸢*bi* 3⸣ [ ]
^{I}*ša*$_2$*-du-nu ma-ḫir* [ ]
{eras.} *re-*⸢*e*⸣*-ḫi* 1 ⸢MA.NA ⅓$^{?}$⸣ G[IN$^{?}$]
2 MA.NA 18° GIN$_2$ ⸢KU$_3$.GI 2$^{?}$⸣ [ ]
šu-uḫ-ḫu-tu ina lib$_3$*-bi* ⸢1$^{?}$ $^{giš?}$× (×)⸣ [ ]
^{I}[^{d}A]G-PAP *u* ^{I}*re-mut* [IGI$^{u?}$]
Rev. 1 MA.NA ⅔$^{?}$° 2$^{?}$ GIN$_2$° ⸢KU$_3$.GI⸣ [ ]
1 MA°.NA KU$_3$.GI ⸢*u*$_3$$^{?}$⸣ [ ]
ša$_2$ *ina* ^{iti}ŠU *ša*$_2$ MU.12.KAM [ ]
{eras.} $^{lu2?}$2 *ša*$_2$ A {eras.} ⅓ ⸢3⸣ GIN$_2$ ⸢$^{I?}$×⸣ [ ]
⸢*ša*$_2$⸣ *kal-za*$^{!}$*-a-tu*$_2$$^{!}$ *ina lib*$_3$*-bi* 3° MA.[NA]
a°*-di* KU$_3$.GI 1 ½ MA.NA 6 GI[N$_2$]
ša$_2$$^{!?}$ ^{Id}AG-PAP *u* ^{I}*re-mut ana*$^{?}$ *bat*$^{?}$-[*qu*$^{?}$]
ir-ru-bu-ma it-ti-šu$_2$*-nu* NU ⸢LAT$^{?}$⸣ [ ]

KA$_2$$^!$-*ti-i* ⌜7(+$^?$)⌝ ½ MA.NA 2 GI[N$_2$]
(tiny line) *ina* IGI-*šu*$_2$-*nu* [( )]

Up.E. ^{iti}KIN UD.14$^?$.KAM MU.12.KA[M]
LUGAL TIN.⌜TIR⌝^{ki} [ ]

3 minas 20 shekels of gold (for) three … […] of Uṣur-amāssu, thereof three […], were received from Šadûnu. […] the balance (is) 1 mina *20 she*[*kels* (…)]
2 minas 18 shekels of gold, *2* […] (for$^?$) *cleaning*, thereof *1* … [… *received from*] Nabû-nāṣir and Rēmūtu.
1 mina *42* shekels of gold […] 1 mina gold *and* […] that in month IV of year 12 […] *deputy of the Sealand*, 23 shekels … [ ] that was stored, thereof 3 mi[nas …] including the gold, 1 mina 36 sheke[ls …] that Nabû-nāṣir and Rēmūtu, for the repa[ir … *said* …] they will enter, and with them, … [ ], (which is) part of the 7(+) minas 32 shek[els …] at their disposal.
Month VI, day 14$^?$, year 12 of [RN], king of Babylon.

1 The spelling *man-da-a-ta* for *mandītu*, mounting, is attested in BIN 1, 132: 1. Note, however, that the large amount of gold seems too much for just three mountings.

6 Note that *šu-uḫ-ḫu-tu*, as a D stem of *šaḫātu*, to clean / wash, is unknown in this meaning.

8 ⅔ 2 Could also be read ⅓ 3.

11 The spelling of ^{lu_2}2 *ša*$_2$ A for *šanû ša tâmti*, deputy of the Sealand is unexpected, and the reading must remain uncertain.

16 For *bābtu* see commentary to **No. 97**: 5. The significance, if any of the spelling KA$_2$-*ti-i* (rather than KA$_2$-*ti* or *ba-ab-ti*), is unclear; see also UCP 9/1 I, 10: 1, 5 and possibly UCP 9/1 II, 59: 7 ([KA$_2$$^?$]-*ti-i*], 13 (KA$_2$-*ti*-[(*i*)]).

28. NCBT 622

Copy: Plate VIII
Date: undated[2]
Summary: accounting note: silver and gold

To the best of our knowledge, Nergal-ēṭir / Iddin-Ištar is unattested elsewhere and there is no secure identification for Nabû-aḫḫē-iddin; the tablet cannot be securely dated. The possibility, however, that the present Nabû-aḫḫē-iddin was in fact the *šatammu* (in office: 4–19 Nbk; on his career see Levavi 2014; Levavi 2018, 134–40 and *passim*; Levavi 2020; Jursa and Gordin 2018) should be discussed here. Nabû-aḫḫē-iddin's career seem to have ended in his removal from office and later the confiscation of his property (see Jursa and Gordin 2018). If our Nabû-aḫḫē-iddin is indeed the fallen *šatammu*, then it may be speculated that the present text relates to assessing his assets in this context. It must be stressed that this is highly speculative. The ubiquity of the name and the lack of additional affiliation prevent any proper identification.

Obv. [(1+)$^?$] 2 ⅔ MA.NA 1 ½ GIN$_2$ KU$_3$.BABBAR ŠAM$_2$° 17 GIN$_2$ KU$_3$.GI
ša$_2$ ^{Id}AG-ŠEŠ^{meš}-SUM.NA
7 MA.NA 50 GIN$_2$ ŠAM$_2$ 50 GIN$_2$ ½ GIN$_2$ LA$_2$-*ṭi* KU$_3$.⌜GI⌝
ša$_2$ ^{Id}U.GUR-SUR A ^{I}MU-^{d}INNIN$^!$
Rev. (uninscribed)

2 See discussion below for the possibility of dating the text to the second half of Nebuchadnezzar's reign.

2 (or 3) minas 41 ½ shekels of silver is the price of 17 shekels of gold of Nabû-aḫḫē-iddin.
7 minas 50 shekels is the price of 49 ½ shekels of gold of Nergal-ēṭir, son of Iddin-Ištar.

2 An additional wedge could have theoretically been placed at the head of l. 2, making it 3 rather than 2 (minas of silver). However, assuming that the silver-to-gold rate is the same as in l. 3 (see below), 2 minas 41 ½ shekels of silver for 17 shekels of gold would indeed fit a 1:9.5 conversion rate.

3 The 7 minas 50 shekels of silver for 49 ½ shekels of gold represents a conversion rate of 1:9.5 silver to gold.

29. YBC 9326

Copy: Plate VIII
Date: 29.III.29 Nbk
Summary: accounting inventory: gold

Obv. ⸢1⸣ MA.NA KU$_3$.GI *ina*$^{!(T.\ ana)}$ UDUN$^{!(T.\ diš.mu)}$ LAGAB *šak-nu ir-bi ša*$_2$ LUGAL
ša$_2$ ^{iti}ŠE MU.28.KAM
2 MA.NA 1 ½ GIN$_2$ KU$_3$.GI *ir-bi ša*$_2$ UN^{me}
⸢PAP⸣ 3 MA.NA 1 ½ GIN$_2$ KU$_3$.GI ⸢*ša*$_2$ *ina*⸣ UDUN *šak-nu*
[ ] ⅚ MA.NA 2 ⅓$^?$ GIN$_2$ *ḫum-mu-šu*$_2$ KU$_3$.GI
[*ina*$^?$] ⸢UDUN⸣ *in-da-aṭ a-na* 2 MA.NA 18 GIN$_2$
[×] ⸢GIN$_2$ *gir*$_2$⸣*-u*$_2$ KU$_3$.GI *it-tur*
[(×+)] ⸢2⸣ ½ GIN$_2$ KU$_3$.GI *ul-tu*
[^{giš}*šad-da ša*$_2$ *bat-q*]*a ša*$_2$ E$_2$ ^{d}URU$_3$-INIM-*su*
[ ] 4^{tu_2} *bit-qa ḫal-lu-ru*
Lo.E. [*ul-t*]*u* $^{<giš>}$*šad-da*$^!$ *ša*$_2$ *ba*[*t*]*-qa*
[^{d}ME.ME$^?$] ⸢*u*⸣ ^{d}IGI.DU
Rev. [(×+)] ⸢26 ½$^?$⸣ GIN$_2$ *ḫum-mu-šu*$_2$
[ ] ⸢*ḫal-lu*⸣*-ru* KU$_3$.GI *ša*$_2$ *ul-tu* UD.20.KAM
⸢*ša*$_2$ ^{iti}⸣SIG$_4$ MU.29.KAM *a-di* UD.29.KAM
ša$_2$ ^{iti}SIG$_4$ *a-na dul-lu a-na* ^{I}*na-din*
u ^{Id}AG-MU-DU ^{lu_2}KU$_3$.DIM^{me} *na-dan*
⸢^{iti}⸣SIG$_4$ UD.28.KAM MU.29.KAM
^{d}AG-NIG$_2$.DU-URU$_3$ LUGAL TIN.TIR^{ki}
{eras.}

1 mina gold, to be placed in the kiln, is the income from the king for month XII, day 28.
2 minas 1 ½ shekels of gold is the income from the people; a total of 3 minas 1 ½ shekels of gold which was put into the kiln.
[×+] 52 ⅓$^?$ shekels + ⅕ (shekels) of gold was lost [in] the kiln; for 2 minas, 18 shekels [...] $\frac{1}{24}$ shekels of gold were returned. [×+] 2 ½ shekels of gold from the [repair bo]x of the Uṣur-amāssu temple [...] ¼, ⅛, ⅒ [...] from the repair box [of *Gula*] and ^{d}IGI.DU, [×+]26 ½$^?$ shekels + ⅕ [...] ⅒ [shekels of] gold, which was given to Nādinu and Nabû-šumu-ukīn, the goldsmiths, for work from month III, day 20, year 29, to month III, day 29, (year 29).
Month III, day 28, year 29 of Nebuchadnezzar, king of Babylon.

1 The meaning of LAGAB is unclear. In fact, it is the multiple readings and meanings that make it uncertain. LAGAB may be read as NIGIN$_2$, for forms of either *paḫāru* (gathered in the kiln) or *saḫāru* (put back in the kiln). At the same time, it is difficult to disregard the reading LAGAB×NIG$_2$/IM for *tinūru* (oven).

12 The restoration of Gula's name is based on multiple joined attestations in similar administrative contexts; for example, AUWE 5, 81: 12; *ARRIM* 7, 47: 4; NCBT 1178: 5–6; and see the note made in Beaulieu 2003, 81 (point no. 3).

30. NCBT 527

Copy: Plate IX
Date: undated (Npl)
Summary: accounting inventory: gold for silver

For the goldsmith Nabû-nāṣir (l. 3), see **No. 27**.

Obv. 15 ⌈GIN$_2$⌉ 4!-⌈*tu*$_2$⌉ KU$_3$.GI *ša*$_2$ ^{I}NUMUN-*ia*$_2$ 2 ⅚ MA.NA 8 ⌈GIN$_2$⌉ 4⌈^{tu_2} KU$_3$.BABBAR⌉
⌈½⌉ MA.NA ⌈4⌉-*tu*$_2$ *ša*$_2$ ^{I}NUMUN-*ia*$_2$ 5 [M]A.⌈NA ⅓ 7⌉ GIN$_2$ 4^{tu_2} KU$_3$.BABBAR
⅚ MA.NA 7 GIN$_2$ 4^{tu_2} ⌈*ša*$_2$ $^{I⌉d}$AG-PAP 8 ⅚ MA.NA
1 ½ MA.NA 5 GIN$_2$ *ša*$_2$ ^{I}*ba-laṭ-su*! 17 MA.⌈NA ⅓⌉ 4 GIN$_2$
10 GIN$_2$ 4^{tu_2} LA$_2$-*ṭi* *ša*$_2$ ^{Id}EN-PAP^{me}-SU 1 ⅚ MA.NA 7! GIN$_2$ 4^{tu_2}
(blank)

{5… … 3}
Rev. (blank)
2 ⅚ 8 GIN$_2$
5 ⅓ 7
8 ⅚
17 ⅓ 5
1 ⅚ 7 4⌈^{tu_2}⌉

15 ¼ shekels of gold of Zēria (for?) 2 minas 58 ¼ shekels of silver; 30 ¼ shekels (of gold) of Zēria (for?) 5 minas 27 ¼ shekels of silver; 57 ¼ shekels (of gold) of Nabû-nāṣir (for?) 8 ⅚ minas (of silver); 1 mina 35 shekels (of gold) of Balāssu (for?) 17 minas 24? shekels (of silver); 10 shekels, minus ¼ (shekel, of gold) of Bēl-aḫḫē-erība (for?) 1 mina 57 ¼ (shekels of silver). (Corresponding tallies of silver on the reverse)

1–5 The five silver-to-gold conversions listed in the text do not reflect a singular rate: 1:ca. 11 ⅔ (l. 1), 1:10⅘ (l. 2), 1:8⅖ (l. 3), 1:11 (l. 4),1:12 (l. 5). The differences cannot be explained simply by the scale of the specific transaction, and other (unknown) aspects must have influenced the price, e.g., quality of the metals and the location of transaction. For the price of gold during the sixth century see Kleber 2020, 28–30.

6–10 The tallies on the reverse of the tablet correspond to the silver mentioned in the entries on the obverse, with the minas and shekels represented in the two columns. Fractions of shekels are inconsistently provided, and l. 9 lists one shekel more than is given on the obverse.

31. NBC 4624

Copy: Plate IX
Date: 16.V.06 (Npl)
Summary: *ina pāni* list

All identified protagonists are attested during the reign of Nabopolassar: for Bēl-aḫu-iddin see **No. 11**, for Itti-Marduk-balāṭu see **No. 17**, for Nabû-zēru-ibni see **No. 13**, for Rēmūtu see **No. 17**, and for Šadûnu see **No. 2**.

Obv. ⸢⅔$^?$⸣ 4 GIN$_2$ ZABAR ⸢*e*$^{!?}$⸣-*l*[*at*$^?$]
⸢⅚ MA⸣.NA *ša*$_2$ ^{Id}AMAR.UTU-GAR-M[U]
⸢*id-da*⸣-*aš-šu*$_2$ *ba-ab-*⸢*ti*⸣
1 MA.NA ⸢4⸣ GIN$_2$ ZAB[AR]
Lo.E. *a-na* SAG SIG KUR ⸢*tu*$_4$⸣
Rev. ^{I}⸢^{d}AG⸣-NUMUN-DU$_3$ ^{lu_2}⸢SIMUG⸣ [(ZABAR)]
^{iti}NE ⸢UD⸣.16.KAM ⸢MU.6⸣.[KAM]
10 MA.NA ⅓ 5 ⸢GIN$_2$ 3$^?$ *gi*$^?$⸣-[*ru*$^?$-*u*$_2$$^?$ (KU$_3$.GI)]
ina IGI ^{I}*re-mut u* ⸢^{I}KI-^{d}⸣AM[AR.UTU-TIN]
⸢DUMU^{me} *ša*$_2$$^!$ ^{Id}EN-ŠEŠ-MU⸣ [(^{lu_2}KU$_3$.TIM)$^?$]
Up.E. 10 MA.NA 5 GIN$_2$ ⸢4$^{!?}$-*tu*$_2$ KU$_3$.GI⸣
ina IGI ^{I}*ša*$_2$-*du-nu* ⸢$^{lu_2?}$KU$_3$$^?$⸣.[TIM$^?$]

44 shekels of bronze, *apart from the* 50 shekels that Marduk-šākin-š[umi] gave him, is part of the 1 mina 4 shekels of bronze for *the top of* … (*is at the disposal of*) Nabû-zēru-ibni, the [(bronze)]smith; Month V, day 16, year 6. 10 minas 25 shekels *and 3 gīr*[*us* (of gold)] are at the disposal of Rēmūtu and Itti-Mar[duk-balāṭu], sons of Bēl-aḫu-iddin, [(the goldsmiths)]. 10 minas 5 ¼ shekels of gold are at the disposal of Šadûnu, the *goldsmith.*

1 The first fraction might be ⅓ rather than ⅔.
The reading ⸢*e*$^{?}$⸣-*l*[*at*$^?$] is highly questionable.
3 For *bābtu* see commentary to **No. 97**: 5.
5 The sequence SAG SIG KUR ⸢*tu*$_4$⸣ is unclear; the reading of the signs is quite certain. SIG KUR could be read syllabically as *sik-kur* for *sikkūru*, a "bar" or a "bolt." Moreover, the word can also be written ^{giš}SAG.KUL, and so a combined spelling such as SAG^{sik}-*kur* may be envisioned. Still, however, the final -*tu*$_4$ does not work with *sikkūru*, whatever spelling one may reconstruct.

32. NCBT 508

Copy: Plate IX
Date: 02.VIII.-- --
Summary: *ina pāni* note: gold and beads

The uncommon name Uk(k)umu is attested in **No. 12** and the two must be the same individual. That being said, prosopography does not allow for the dating of the tablet.[3]

[3] A certain Uk(k)umu is attested as the father of Nabû-ēṭir in a house purchase from Uruk, BM 108858, dated to 16 Kan. Also attested in the text is a certain Nergal-iddin, whose father's name is Kalbi (possibly Kalbi-ilāni). This is of course not sufficient for an identification of our two protagonists.

Obv. 2 GIN$_2$ KU$_3$.GI ⸢*u*$_3$ ^{na_4}⸣K[IŠIB]
ša ^{na_4}AŠ.GI$_3$.GI$_3$ {AŠ GI$_3$}
šul-ma-nu ša$_2$ ^{I}*na-di-nu*
DUMU-*šu*$_2$ *ša*$_2$ ^{I}UR-DINGIR^{meš}
ina IGI ^{I}*u*$_2$*-ku-mu* A ^{I}*im-ba-a*
^{iti}APIN UD.2.KAM
Le.E. ME

2 shekels of gold and cylinder seal (shaped)-bead of *ašgikû*-stone, the *šulmānu*-offering of Nādinu, son of Kalbi-ilāni, is at the disposal of Uk(k)umu, son of Imbāya.
Month VIII, day 2. . . .

5 Zadok (2003: 484 n. 12) assumes the name is non-Semitic (rather than West Semitic "black").
7 The two wedges on the left edge are unclear; they may represent the number 100, a kind of a "check" notation, or perhaps an irrelvant, random mark.

33. NCBT 368

Copy: Plate X
Date: 09.IV.14 Kan
Summary: *maḫir* receipt (+ *ina pāni* clause): red gold and bronze[4]

Obv. 13 MA.NA ⅓ 5 GIN$_2$ KU$_3$.GI SA$_5$ NIG$_2$.NA *ša*$_2$ ^{I}*šad-*⸢*u*$_2$*-ni*⸣
⅓ 6 ½ GIN$_2$ ZABAR 2^{u_2} ŠEN *ba-ba*$^{?!(T.\ la)}$*-nu-*<*u*$^{?}$>
⸢PAP⸣.PAP 13 MA.NA 51 ½ GIN$_2$ KU$_3$.GI SA$_5$ *a-di* ZABAR
ina lib$_3$*-bi* 7 MA.NA 15 ½ GIN$_2$ 3 *ta-ri-ka-a-ta*
ša$_2$ *la-a-ni* 5 MA.NA ⅓ 6 GIN$_2$ KU$_3$.GI
kal-la u$_3$ *ku-us-bir-ti*
a-di-i$^{!}$ ⸢ZABAR 7⸣ GIN$_2$ *kit-ti*
⸢PAP⸣ 12 ⅔$^{!(T.\ 5/6)}$ MA.NA 8 GIN$_2$ KU$_3$.GI {eras.} SA$_5$
Lo.E. *a-di-i* ZABAR *ḫa-a-ṭu ša*$_2$ NIG$_2$.NA
u$_3$ 1 MA.NA *te-ḫir-ti*
Rev. PAP.PAP 13 ⅔$^{!(T.\ 5/6)}$ MA.NA 8 ½ GIN$_2$ KU$_3$.GI
^{I}*ša*$_2$*-du-ni* IGI^{ir} 3 GIN$_2$ *re-e-ḫi*
^{iti}ŠU UD.9.KAM MU.14.KAM
kan-da-la-nu LUGAL TIN.TIR^{ki}

13 minas 25 shekels of red gold (from) the censer of Šadûnu and 26 ½ shekels of bronze (from) a second cauldron *of top quality*—a total of 13 minas 51 ½ shekels of red gold, including the bronze. From this, 7 minas 15 ½ shekels were used for the three *tariktu-ornaments* of the body (of the censer), 5 minas 26 shekels of gold were used for the *kallu*-bowl and the *cover / base*, including 7 shekels of bronze for the *kittu*-bowl. A total of 12 minas 4'8 shekels of red gold, including the bronze, is the weight of the censer and 1 mina is the remainder.
A grand total of 13 minas 4'8 ½ shekels of gold was received from Šadûnu. The balance is 3 shekels.
Month IV, day 9, year 14 of Kandalānu king of Babylon.

---

4 A previous edition is included in Payne 2007, 68.

4 The exact nature of the *tariktu* is unclear. Some were made of precious metals, attested at times alongside *ayaru* and *tenšû*, e.g., TCL 12, 101, Nbn 591. These appear to be ornamental. In other cases, however, we find *tariktu* of bronze and even iron, weighing up to two kg.; e.g., Nbn 2232, Nbn 118.

6 For *kusibirītu* as a base, or possibly a cover, see Jursa 2006–2008, 225.

34. YBC 9240

Copy: Plate X
Date: 27.XI.25 Nbk
Summary: *ina pāni* note (no PN): gold ornaments

Obv. ⸢1⸣ LIM 1 ME MUL KU$_3$.GI
u$_3$ ḫa-še-e KU$_3$.GI
⸢*ša$_2$*⸣ UGU ^{tug_2}BAR.DUL$_8$ *ša$_2$*
^{d}GAŠAN *ša$_2$* UNUG^{ki}
[*i*]*na* IGI ^{lu_2}KU$_3$.DIM^{meš}
[(×)] ⸢36⸣ *šu-ub-bu-ru-tu*
[*ina*] ⸢*nak*⸣*-ma-ru*
Lo.E. [ ] *ša$_2$ a-*⸢*a*⸣*-ri* KU$_3$.GI
Rev. [× (×+)] 2 *te-en-ši-ia* KU$_3$.GI
[*ša$_2$* U]GU ^{tug_2}BAR.DUL$_8$ *ša$_2$*
^{d}*na-na-a ina* IGI ^{lu_2}KU$_3$.DIM^{meš}
ina ⸢*lib$_3$-bi*⸣ 1 *a-a-*⸢*ri* KU$_3$.GI⸣
1-*en ten-šu-u$_2$* ⸢KU$_3$.GI⸣ 1 GIN$_2$ *šal-šu$_2$ ḫal-lu-ru*
KI.LA$_2$.BI-*šu$_2$-nu ina* IGI ⸢^{lu_2}KU$_3$.DIM⸣^{me}
(tiny inserted line) *a-na bat-qu* [( )]
Up.E. [^{it}]^{i}ZIZ$_2$ UD.27.KAM ⸢MU⸣.25.KAM
^{d}AG-NIG$_2$.DU-URU$_3$ ⸢LUGAL TIN.TIR⸣^{ki}

1,100 gold stars and gold *ḫašû*-ornaments from the *kusītu*-garment of the Lady-of-Uruk are at the disposal of the goldsmiths; (×+)36 broken ones are [in] *nakmaru*-baskets; ... of gold rosettes ... (×+)2 gold squares from the *kusītu*-garment of Nanāya are at the disposal of the goldsmiths. Thereof 1 gold rosette (and) 1 gold square—1 $^{13}/_{30}$ shekels is their weight—are at the disposal of the goldsmiths, for repairs (...).
Month XI, day 27, year 25 of Nebuchadnezzar, king of Babylon.

35. NCBT 988

Copy: Plate X
Date: 21.VII.08 (Npl–Nbk)
Summary: *ina pāni* note: gold

For Rēmūtu (l. 4), see **No. 17**.

Obv. ⸢79 *su*⸣*-u$_2$-ta-a-ta* ⸢KU$_3$.GI⸣
ša$_2$ ⸢GABA⸣ *ša$_2$* ^{d}KAŠ.⸢NAM⸣:DIN
a-na ša$_2$-pe-e ša$_2$ GABA^{me}
ina IGI ^{I}*re-mut* ^{lu_2}KU$_3$.DIM

Lo.E. ^{iti}DU$_6$ UD.21.⸢KAM⸣
6 MU.8.KAM
Rev. (uninscribed)

Seventy-nine gold *sūtu*-attachments of the breast (ornament) of Kurunnītu for embroidering the breast (ornaments) are at the disposal of Rēmūtu, the goldsmith.
Month VII, day 21, year 8.

3 For *šapû*, to embroider, see Quillien 2022, 430–1.

36. NCBT 296

Copy: Plate X
Date: 19.II.33 Nbk
Summary: *ina pāni* note: gold

Obv. 15 GIN$_2$ KU$_3$.GI *a-na*
bat-qa ša$_2$ *šu-kut-ti*
ina IGI ⸢^{Id}15-MU⸣-DU$_3$
⸢*u* ^{Id}⸣E[N-DU$_3$ ^{lu_2}KU$_3$.DIM^{meš}]
Rev. (blank)
⸢^{iti}GU$_4$ UD.20⸣.1.LA$_2$.KAM
MU.33.KAM ^{d}AG-NIG$_2$.DU-URU$_3$
LUGAL TIN.TIR^{ki}

15 shekels of gold for the repair of jewelry are at the disposal of Ištar-šumu-ibni and Bēl-[ibni, the goldsmiths].
Month II, day 19, year 33 of Nebuchadnezzar, king of Babylon.

37. NCBT 1187

Copy: Plate XI
Date: 20.×.13 --
Summary: *ina pāni* note: ornaments

None of the women can be identified and the text cannot be dated.

Obv. ⸢2(+)⸣ ME 11 *ḫar-ḫar-ru* KU$_3$.GI *en* ⸢× ×⸣
52 ^{na_4}*sag-gil*$^{!}$*-mud*
ina IGI ^{f}*ku-pi-ti*
^{f}*šam-ḫat u* ^{f}DU$_3$-*tu*$_2$-<E$_2$>.SAG.IL$_2$
a-na ^{giš}*pi-ša*$_2$*-an-ni*
Rev. (blank)
⸢^{iti}×⸣ UD.20.⸢KAM⸣
[M]U.13.⸢KAM⸣

Two-hundred and eleven gold (rings of a) chain ..., fifty-two *saggilmud*-stones at the disposal of ^{f}Kupīti, ^{f}Šamḫat and ^{f}Bānītu-<E>sagil for the *pišannu*-box.
Month ×, day 20, year 13.

5 The *pišannu*—a wooden box that housed divine jewelry, adorned with linen, wool, and silver—is discussed in Popova and Quillien 2021.

38. NCBT 559

Copy: Plate XI
Date: 25.XI.14 (Npl)
Summary: *maḫir* receipt: gold ornaments

Obv. 17 ½ GIN$_2$ KU$_3$.GI *sa-ma-ḫal*$^{(sic)}$ KU$_3$.GI
⸢*ša*$_2$⸣ GABA *a-ḫa-nu* KU$_3$.GI *ša*$_2$ ^{d}KAŠ.DIN.NAM
3 *ar*$_2$*-zal-lu*$_4$ KU$_3$.GI 3 *a-gur-ru* KU$_3$.G[I]
51 *ḫar-ḫar-*<*ru*> KU$_3$.GI 27 NUMUN UKUŠ$_2$ KU$_3$.⸢GI⸣
40 *sa-an-*<*ḫa*> KU$_3$.GI GAL^{me} 50 TUR^{me}
⸢^{Id}AG-PAP$^{?}$⸣ IGI^{ir}
Rev. (blank)
^{iti}ZIZ$_2$ UD.25.KAM MU.14.KAM

17 ½ shekels of gold (in the form of) gold *hooks* of the "winged" gold breast-ornament of Kurunnītu, three gold *arzallu*-jewels, three gold *agurru*-ornaments, fifty-one gold (rings of a) chain, twenty-seven gold melon seed(-shaped bead)s, forty large gold hooks, and fifty small ones, were received from Nabû-nāṣir.
Month XI, day 25, year 14.

1 *sa-ma-ḫal* is unclear. It is taken as a form of *sanḫu* due to the multiple attestations of *sanḫu* alongside *irtu* (GABA) as in the present text; for example, Nbn 190, GC 2, 261. For the spelling, cf. possibly *sa-ma-ḫal-li-šu*$_2$ (**No. 21**: 7′). The fact that the scribe uses the expected spelling in l. 5 further complicates this peculiar spelling.

6 For Nabû-nāṣir, see **No. 27**.

39. NCBT 956

Copy: Plate XI
Date: 28.XI.33 Nbk
Summary: *maḫir* receipt: gold ornaments

Obv. 2 GIN$_2$ *šal-šu*$_2$ 1 GIN$_2$ KU$_3$.GI 55 ^{giš}BAN$_2$^{meš}
ša$_2$ GU$_2$ *ša*$_2$ IGI ŠU$^{II.meš}$ *ša*$_2$ ^{d}*na-na-a*
5 MUL^{meš} *ša*$_2$ *ina* 1 ME *ša*$_2$ ^{d}GAŠAN *ša*$_2$ UNUG^{ki}
1 *kur-ṣu-u*$_2$ *ša*$_2$ GU$_2$ ^{na4}*nu-ur*$_2$*-mu-u*$_2$
⸢^{na4}⸣BABBAR.DIL *ša*$_2$ ^{d}*na-na-a*
1 *su-u*$_2$*-tu* *ša*$_2$ GABA KU$_3$.GI *ša*$_2$ *bi-rit* ⸢ŠU^{II}⸣$^{.me}$
ša$_2$ ^{d}*na-na-a* ^{I}*na-din*
Lo.E. *u* ^{Id}AG-MU-DU ^{lu2}KU$_3$.DIM^{me}
maḫ-ru
Rev. (blank)
^{iti}ZIZ$_2$ UD.28.KAM MU.33.KAM
^{d}AG-NIG$_2$.DU-URU$_3$ LUGAL TIN.TIR^{ki}

2 ⅓ shekels of gold (in the form of) fifty-five *sūtu*-attachments for the necklace in front of the hands of Nanāya; five stars that are from the one-hundred (stars) of the Lady-of-Uruk; one link for the necklace of pomegranate (beads) of *pappardilu*-stone of Nanāya; one *sūtu*-attachment for the gold breast (ornament) between the hands of Nanāya; (all these) were received from Nādinu and Nabû-šumu-ukīn, the goldsmiths.
Month XI, day 28, year 33 of Nebuchadnezzar, king of Babylon.

5 For *irtu ša birīt qātē*, see Beaulieu 2003, 382.

40. NCBT 1008

Copy: Plate XI
Date: 14.II.38 Nbk
Summary: inventory list: gold ornaments

Obv. ⸢7⸣ ME 59 {eras.} MUL$^!$ ⸢KU$_3$.GI⸣
⸢*u*$_3$⸣ *ḫa-še-e ša*$_2$ U[GU] ⸢^{tug_2}BAR.DUL$_8$⸣
(tiny line) *ša*$_2$ ^{d}GAŠAN ⸢*ša*$_2$⸣ [UNUG^{ki}]
ina nak-ma-ru ⸢4 ME 14$^?$⸣
MUL KU$_3$.GI *u*$_3$ *ḫa-še-*⸢*e*⸣
a-na bat-qu ina E$_2$ ^{lu_2}⸢*um-man*⸣*-nu*
⸢7⸣ ME 6 *a-a-ri* KU$_3$. [GI]
Lo.E. ⸢7 ME 6 *te*⸣*-en-*⸢*ši-ia*⸣ [(×)]
Rev. PAP 1 *lim* 4 ME ⸢12 *a-a-ri* KU$_3$⸣.[GI]
(tiny line) *u*$_3$ *te-*⸢*en-ši-ia*⸣
ša$_2$ UGU ^{tug_2}BAR-⸢DUL$_8$⸣ *ša*$_2$ ^{d}⸢*na-na-a*⸣
ina nak-ma-ru
^{iti}GU$_4$ UD.14.KAM MU.38.KAM
^{d}AG-NIG$_2$.⸢DU-URU$_3$ LUGAL TIN.TIR^{ki}⸣

759 gold stars and *ḫašû*-ornaments from the *kusītu*-garment of the Lady-of-[Uruk] are in the *nakmaru*-basket; 414 gold stars and *ḫašû*-ornaments for repairs are in the craftsmen's workshop; 706 gold rosettes and 706 [gold] squares, a total of 1,412 gold rosettes and squares from the *kusītu*-garment of Nanāya are in the *nakmaru*-basket.
Month II, day 14, year 38 of Nebuchadnezzar, king of Babylon.

41. YBC 11486

Copy: Plate XII
Date: 01.V.27 Nbk
Summary: inventory list: gold ornaments

Obv. [7/8] ⸢ME 6 *a-a-ri*⸣ [(KU$_3$.GI)]
[8/7] ⸢ME 6 *te*⸣-[*en-ši-ia*]
⸢PAP 1 *lim* 5$^?$ ME 12⸣
4 ⸢*ša*$_2$ *ul-tu* UGU⸣
Lo.E. ⸢^{d}*na-na*⸣*-a*
Rev. ⸢*u*$_2$⸣*-ri-du-nu*
⸢^{iti}NE UD.1.KAM⸣

⸢MU.27.KAM⸣
⸢^{d}AG-NIG$_2$⸣.[DU-KAM LUGAL TIN.TIR^{ki}]

[Seven/eight]-hundred and six [(gold)] rosettes and [eight/seven]-hundred and six (gold) squares; a total of 1,512 that were removed from (the garments of) Nanāya.
Month V, day 1, year 27 of Nebuchad[nezzar, king of Babylon].

3 Given the eroded surface, we left the reading of the total as it is visible on the tablet, but equal numbers of rosettes and squares (so 706+706 or 806+806, rather than 706+806) are more likely; see, e g., **Nos. 40** and **42**.

42. YBC 3438

Copy: Plate XII
Date: 14.II.31 Nbk
Summary: inventory note: gold ornaments

Obv. 5 ⸢ME⸣ 52 ⸢MUL⸣^{me} KU$_3$.GI
5 ME 53 ⸢*ḫa*⸣-[*še-e* KU$_3$.G]I
PAP 1 *lim* ⸢1 ME 5 MUL^{me}⸣
u ⸢*ḫa*⸣-[*še-e ša*$_2$ UGU ^{tug2}BAR.D]UL$_8$
(tiny line) ⸢*ša*$_2$ ^{d}⸣[GAŠAN *ša*$_2$ UNUG^{ki} *rak-su* × × K]U$_3$.GI
⸢*ina* UGU ^{tug2}BAR.DUL$_8$ *ša*$_2$ ^{d}⸣[GAŠAN$^?$ *ša*$_2$$^?$ UNUG$^{ki?}$] ⸢×⸣-*lu*
7 ME 6 *a-a-*⸢*ri*⸣ [KU$_3$.GI]
⸢7⸣ ME 6 *t*[*e-en-ši-ia* KU$_3$.GI]
Lo.E. ⸢PAP⸣ 1 *lim* 4 ME$^{!(T. ša_2)}$ 12 *ša*$_2$ UG[U]
Rev. ^{tug2}BAR.DUL$_8$ *ša*$_2$ ^{d}*na-na-a rak*$^{!(T. gu)}$*-su*
(blank)
^{iti}GU$_4$ UD.14.KAM MU.31.KAM
^{d}AG-NIG$_2$.DU-URU$_3$ LUGAL TIN.TIR^{ki}

552 gold stars and 553 gold *ḫa*[*šû*-ornaments], a total of 1,105 [gold] stars and *ḫa*[*šû*-ornaments, attached to the *kus*]*ītu*-garment of the [Lady-of Uruk …] of gold for the *kusītu*-garment of [the *Lady-of Uruk* … g]old. 706 [gold] rosettes … and 706 [gold] sq[uares], a total of 1,412 that were attached to the *kusītu*-garment of Nanāya.
Month II, day 14, year 31 of Nebuchadnezzar, king of Babylon.

4–6 It is difficult to connect the beginning of the lines to their respective ends at the right of the break. The reconstruction presented above is conjectural.

43. YBC 9638

Copy: Plate XII
Date: 04(+)II$^?$.33 Nbk
Summary: inventory note: gold ornaments

Obv. 1 LIM 1 ME 73 MUL KU$_3$.GI^{me}
u$_3$ *ḫa-še-e*
ša$_2$ UGU ⸢^{tug2}BAR⸣.DUL$_8$

ša$_2$ ˹^{d}GAŠAN˺ [*ša*$_2$] ˹UNUG˺^{ki}
1 *lim* ˹4 ME˺ 13 ˹*a-a*˺-*ri* KU$_3$.GI
u$_3$ ˹*te-en-ši*˺-*ia* ˹KU$_3$.GI˺
Lo.E. *ša*$_2$ UGU ^{tug_2}BAR.DUL$_8$
Rev. *š*[*a*$_2$ ^{d}*na-n*]*a-a*
[ITI].˹GU$_4$$^?$ UD.(×)4˺.KAM
[MU].33.KAM
[^{d}A]G-NIG$_2$.DU-URU$_3$
LUGAL TIN.TIR^{ki}

1,173 gold stars and *ḫašû*-ornaments from the *kusītu*-garment of the Lady-of-Uruk; 1,413 gold rosettes and gold squares of the *kusītu*-garment of [Nan]āya.
Month II$^?$, day 4(+), year 33 of Nebuchadnezzar, king of Babylon.

5 Although only three wedges are visible, several attestations of 1,412 rosettes (**Nos. 40**, **44**, for example) point to the reading 4 ME.

10 [MU].33.KAM; pace Beaulieu (2003, 25), who dates the tablet to year 36.

44. YBC 8818

Copy: Plate XII
Date: 01.I.26 Nbk
Summary: inventory note: gold ornaments

Obv. [6] ˹ME˺ 95 *a-a-ri* KU$_3$.˹GI˺
[6] ME 96 *te-en-ši-ia*$_2$
[PAP] ˹1 LIM˺ 3 ME 91 ˹TA *muḫ-ḫi*˺
[^{tug_2}]˹BAR˺.<DUL$_8$> *ša*$_2$ ^{d}*na-na-a*
[*ina nak-ma*]-*ru* {eras.}
[(×) *a-a-ri*] ˹*u*˺ *te-en*-˹*ši-ia*$_2$˺
[*ina nak*]-˹*ma*˺-*ri*
Lo.E. ˹PAP$^{!?(T. pa?)}$˺ 1 ˹LIM˺ 4 ME 12
Rev. [*a-a*]-˹*ri*˺ KU$_3$.GI *te-en-ši-ia*$_2$
[× ×] ˹×˺ AM-RI *ina nak-ma-ri*
(blank)
[ITI].˹BARA$_2$$^?$ UD˺.1.KAM MU.26.KAM
[^{d}AG-NI]G$_2$.DU-URU$_3$ LUGAL TIN.TIR^{ki}

[6]95 gold rosettes and [6]96 squares; a total of 1,391 that are from the *kusītu*-garment of Nanāya, [are in the *nakm*]*aru*-basket.
[× rosettes] and squares [in the *nakm*]*aru*-basket; *total of* 1,412 gold rosettes and squares … in the *nakmaru*-basket.
Month I, day 1, year 26 of Nebuchadnezzar, king of Babylon.

45. NBC 4638

Copy: Plate XIII
Date: 11.XI.24 Nbk
Summary: delivery (*šūbulu*) note: silver

Obv. 11 GIN$_2$ KU$_3$.BABBAR *a-na bat-qu*
ša$_2$ *šu-us-su-lu ša*$_2$ ^{lu_2}ŠU.KU$_6$
ina ŠU^{II} ^{I}*ba°-laṭ-su*
A-*šu*$_2$ *ša*$_2$ ^{I}*šu-ma-a* A ^{I}*na-ba-a-a*
a-na ^{I}*na-din*
u ^{Id}AG-MU-DU
^{lu_2}KU$_3$.DIM^{meš}
Lo.E. *šu-bu-ul*
Rev. ^{iti}ZIZ$_2$ UD.11.KAM
MU.24.KAM ^{d}AG-NIG$_2$.DU-URU$_3$
LUGAL TIN.TIR^{ki}

11 shekels of silver were delivered to Nādinu and Nabû-šumu-ukīn, the goldsmiths, by Balāssu, son of Šumāya, descendant of Nabāya for the repair of the fishermen chest.
Month XI, day 11, year 24 of Nebuchadnezzar, king of Babylon.

46. NCBT 794

Copy: Plate XIII
Date: 20.IV.04 --
Summary: *ina pāni* note: silver

Obv. ⸢11⸣ [(×)] MA.NA KU$_3$.BABBAR *a-na ša*$_2$*-ka-nu*
ina UDUN *ina* IGI ^{I}I-^{d}15
(blank)
Rev. (blank)
^{iti}ŠU UD.20.⸢KAM⸣ MU.4.KAM

11(+) minas of silver to be placed in the kiln are at the disposal of Naʾid-Ištar.
Month IV, day 20, year 4.

47. NCBT 536

Copy: Plate XIII
Date: undated (*Nbk*)
Summary: *ina pāni* note: silver

The lack of a family name for any of the three individuals makes a positive identification problematic. Nabû-aḫḫē-bulliṭ/Marduk-zēru-ibni might be from the Aḫu-ibni family, attested from 17 Npl (YBC 3808) to 34 Nbk (FLP 1545). Bēl-aḫḫē-iddin/Nabû-zēru-ibni might be the individual by that name (no family name) attested in BIN 1, 127 (15 Nbk). In light of this, we tentatively suggest dating the tablet to the reign of Nebuchadnezzar.

Note the unique orthography of A-*šu*$_2$ *ša*$_2$, which is written as a ligature. The fact that the scribe repeats the same sign twice suggests that this should not be seen as a simple scribal error.

Obv. 57 ½ GIN$_2$ KU$_3$.BABBAR *ina* IGI ^{Id}AG-ŠEŠ^{me}-TIN
A+*šu*$_2$+*ša*$_2^!$ ^{Id}AMAR.UTU-NUMUN-DU$_3$
57 ½ GIN$_2$ *ina* IGI ^{Id}EN-ŠEŠ^{me}-MU A+*šu*$_2$+*ša*$_2^!$ ^{Id}AG-NUMUN-DU$_3$
½ MA.NA 1 GIN$_2$ 4^{tu_2} LA$_2$ ⸢*ina* IGI⸣ ^{Id}EN-ŠEŠ^{me}-SU
5 A+*šu*$_2$+*ša*$_2^!$ ^{I}*mar-duk-a*
PAP 2 MA.NA 14$^{!(sic)}$ GIN$_2$ 4^{tu_2} LA$_2$-*ṭi*
Rev. (uninscribed)

57 ½ shekels of silver are at the disposal of Nabû-aḫḫē-bulliṭ, son of Marduk-zēru-ibni;
57 ½ shekels (of silver) are at the disposal of Bēl-aḫḫē-iddin, son of Nabû-zēru-ibni;
31 shekels, minus ¼ (shekel), are at the disposal of Bēl-aḫḫē-erība, son of Marduka;
a total of 2 mina 14$^!$ shekels, minus ¼ (shekel of silver).

6 The sums listed in text add up to 2 minas 25 ¾ shekels, which is 12 shekels off from the 2 minas 13 ¾ shekels calculated by the scribe.

48. NBC 4672

Copy: Plate XIII
Date: 03.I.12 (Npl–Nbk)
Summary: *ina pāni* note: white silver

Marduka / Nabû-zēru-ibni is attested from 3$^?$ Npl (PTS 2385) to 3$^?$ Nbk (**No. 54**); see Payne 2007, 314.

Obv. 3 MA.NA ⅓ 3 GIN$_2$ KU$_3$.BABBAR BABBAR-*u*$_2$
a-na 2 *šap-pe-e* KU$_3$.BABBAR *ina* IGI
^{I}*mar-duk*-<*a*> A-*šu*$_2$ *ša*$_2$ ^{Id}AG-NUMUN-DU$_3$
4 ^{lu_2}SIMUG ZABAR ^{iti}BARA$_2$
Lo.E. ⸢UD⸣.3.KAM MU.12.KAM
Rev. *ina* ŠA$_3$ 3 MA.NA ⅓ 7 GIN$_2$ KU$_3$.BABBAR
ša$_2$ ^{lu_2}ŠA$_3$.TAM *a-na šap-pe-e*
a-ga-a id-da-aš$_2$-*šu*$_2$
9 2 ½ GIN$_2$ *in-da-ṭu* 1 ½ GIN$_2$
Up.E. *kal-za*$^!$-*ta*

3 minas 23 shekels of white silver for two silver *šappu*-bowls are at the disposal of Marduka, son of Nabû-zēru-ibni, the bronzesmith. Month I, day 3, year 12. From the 3 minas 27 shekels of silver that the *šatammu* gave to him for these *šappu*-bowls, 2 ½ shekels were lost, 1 ½ shekels are *stored*.

10 *kal-za*$^!$-*ta*; taken here as a stative of *kanāzu*, to store; see also **No. 27**: 12 and NCBT 885: 5, edited in Payne 2007, 65, with note there.

49. NCBT 755

Copy: Plate XIV
Date: 05.IX.37 Nbk
Summary: accounting inventory: silver

Obv. 15 GIN$_2$ KU$_3$.BABBAR *a-na u$_2$-*⸢×⸣-[ ]
9 ½ GIN$_2$ *bit-qa* ⸢KU$_3$⸣.[BABBAR]
a-na bat-qa ša$_2$ qaq-qar-a-nu
PAP ⅓ 4° ½ GIN$_2$ *bit-qa* KU$_3$.BABBAR
a-na bat-qa ša$_2$ NIG$_2$.NA KU$_3$.BABBAR
ša$_2$ ^{d}gu-la ša$_2$ KISAL$^{!}$
Lo.E. ⸢*ṣa*⸣*-bit* 6 ½ GIN$_2$ KU$_3$.BABBAR
Rev. *te-*⸢*ḫir*⸣*-ti ša$_2$ kal-lu*
ša$_2$ nig$_2$-na-qu a-na NIG$_2$.GA.
it-ta$^{!}$-aḫ-si
(blank)
^{iti}GAN UD.5.KAM
MU.37.KAM
Up.E. ^{d}AG-NIG$_2$.DU-URU$_3$
LUGAL TIN.TIR^{k}[^{i}]
Le.E. {eras.}

15 shekels of silver for the …, 9 ½ shekels of ⅛ alloy silver for the repairing of a *plate*; total of 24 ½ shekels of ⅛ alloy silver *are held* for the repairing of the silver censer of Gula of the courtyard.
6 ½ shekels, the remainder of the *kallu*-bowl of the censer, returned to the temple stores.
Month IX, day 5, year 37 of Nebuchadnezzar, king of Babylon.

3 The meaning of *qaqqaru* in the present context, i.e., made out of silver, is difficult. AHw translates the Middle Assyrian attestation *qaqqar šēḫāti* (Or 21, 130, 137) as "Boden (eines) Räuchergefäßes" (AHw, 901b, meanings 12c.). Given that repairs concern Gula of the courtyard, the *qaqqaru* might have been a plate or a kind of a tray on which the censer would be placed.

50. NCBT 357

Copy: Plate XIV
Date: 02.XII.31 Nbk
Summary: inventory list: divine silver items

Obv. ⸢8⸣ *pi-in-ga* KU$_3$.BABBAR
10 *ḫar-gul-lu$_4$* KU$_3$.BABBAR
40 *ḫa-an-du-uḫ-ḫu* KU$_3$.BABBAR
ina lib$_3$-bi 1 MU.⸢29$^{?}$⸣.KAM *ḫa-liq*
ša$_2$ ^{d}GAŠAN *ša$_2$* UNUG$^{⸢ki⸣}$
⸢2⸣ *pi-in-ga* KU$_3$.BABBAR
4 *ḫar-gul-lu$_4$* KU$_3$.BABBAR
(tiny line) 12 *ḫa-an-du-*⸢*uḫ*⸣*-ḫu*$^{!(T. ri)}$ KU$_3$.BABBAR
ša$_2$ ^{d}na-na-a

2 *pi-in-gu* KU$_3$.BABBAR
4 *ḫar-gul-lu$_4$* KU$_3$.BABBAR
12 *ḫa-an-du-uḫ-ḫu* KU$_3$.BABBAR
ša$_2$ ^{d}GAŠAN *ša$_2$* SAG
4 *pi-in-ga* KU$_3$.BABBAR
⸢4⸣ *ḫar-gul-lu$_4$* KU$_3$.BABBAR
Lo.E. ⸢16⸣ *ḫa-an-du-*⸢*uḫ-ḫu*⸣ <KU$_3$.BABBAR>
⸢*ša$_2$*⸣ ^{d}*a-da-pi*
Rev. (blank)
^{iti}ŠE UD.2.KAM MU.31.KAM
^{d}AG-NIG$_2$.DU-URU$_3$
LUGAL TIN.TIR^{ki}

Eight silver knobs, ten silver locks, forty silver lock parts, one of which is missing from year 29, of Bēltu-ša-Uruk. Two silver knobs, four silver locks, twelve silver lock parts, of Nanāya. Two silver knobs, four silver locks, twelve silver lock parts, of Bēltu-ša-rēši. Four silver knobs, four silver locks, sixteen silver lock parts, of Adapa.
Month XII, day 2, year 31 of Nebuchadnezzar, king of Babylon.

1–3 For the translation of *pingu* (knob, ll. 1, 6, 10, 14), *ḫargullu* (lock, ll. 2, 7, 11, 15), and *ḫandūḫu* (part of a lock, ll. 3, 8, 12, 16), as part of door-locking mechanisms, see Beaulieu 2003, 12.

51. NCBT 1246

Copy: Plate XV
Date: 01(+).III$^{?}$.03(+) --
Summary: inventory list: varia

Up.E. ⸢23$^{?}$⸣(+)
[ ] ⸢×⸣
Obv. [ ] ⸢GAL⸣ KU$_3$.BABBAR ^{iti}S[IG$_4$]$^{?}$
⸢UD.1[(+)].⸢KAM MU.3⸣[(+)].KAM⸣

---

1 *nig$_2$-nak la-ba-nu* KU$_3$.BABBAR
1 *a-a-ri-i-tu$_4$* KU$_3$.BABBAR
3 ⸢*ša$_2$*⸣*-a-ri(-)i-še-eṭ-ṭu* KU$_3$.BABBAR
2 ^{na4}⸢*ḫi-in-ša$_2$*⸣*-nu ša$_2$* ^{na4}GIŠ.NU$_{11}$.GAL
3 *ša$_2$* ^{na4}ZA.GIN$_3$
1 *ša$_2$* ^{na4}BABBAR.DIL
1 *ša$_2$* ^{na4}UGU.AŠ.GI$_3$.GI$_3$
2-*ta* GIR$_2$ AN.BAR⸢^{me} *ša$_2$*⸣ KU$_3$.BABBAR *u* KU$_3$.GI
1 *ad-du* AN.<BAR> KU$_3$.BABBAR *u* KU$_3$.GI
4 *me-ṭa-nu* AN.BAR *u* KU$_3$.GI
2 *tu-ḫul$^{?}$-la-nu* KU$_3$.BABBAR
1 NIG$_2$.GAL$_2$.LA AN.BAR
Lo.E. 1 *kal-la* ⸢× *nu tu$_2$ nu u$_2$* × × KU$_3$.BABBAR⸣
NU 2 PA A TA KUŠ.ḪI.A
u KU$_3$.BABBAR

Rev. 1 *ša*$_2$ *ḫu-na-qa-nu* KUŠ.ḪI.A
u KU$_3$.BABBAR
2 PI ŠIM *pa-na-nu* KUŠ.ḪI.A
u$_3$ KU$_3$.BABBAR *a-*⸢*di*⸣ 4 GIN$_2$[!] ×.ME KU$_3$.BABBAR
2 ^{giš}BAN^{me} KU$_3$.BABBAR 1^{en} *si-gi-ir-ru*
KU$_3$.BABBAR *u* KU$_3$.GI
⸢1-*en*⸣ *man-za-za ša*$_2$ *si-gi-ir-ru* KU$_3$.BABBAR
50 *a-a-*⸢*ri*⸣ KU$_3$.BABBAR TUR^{meš}
10 *a-a-ri* ⸢KU$_3$.BABBAR GAL^{meš}⸣
(blank)
½$^?$ SILA$_3$ I$_3$.GIŠ ⸢*a*⸣-*na* ⸢^{giš}MAR⸣

23 … […] … silver, Month III, day 1(+), year 3(+): One silver frankincense censer, one silver cowrie, three silver *šāri*$^?$ *išiṭṭi*$^?$, two *ḫinšu*s of alabaster, three of lapis lazuli, one of *pappardilu*-stone, one of *ašgikû*-stone, two iron daggers with silver and gold (ornaments), one iron *throwing-stick* with silver and gold (ornaments), four *mēṭu*-maces of iron and gold, two silver *tuḫullu*$^?$, one iron sickle, one *kallu*-bowl … of silver, … 2 … of leather and silver, one for the (horse) collar of leather and silver, 2 … of leather and silver, including 4 shekels … of silver, two silver bows, one *sigirru* (vessel$^?$) of silver and gold, one silver stand of a *sigirru* (vessel$^?$), fifty small silver rosettes, ten large silver rosettes, one ½ *qû* of oil for a spade.

1 ⸢23$^?$⸣ may actually be [KU$_3$].⸢GI⸣
3 ^{iti}S[IG$_4$] could also be ^{iti}Š[E].
5 To the best of our knowledge this is the only attestation of the form *la-ba-nu*, for *labānu* clearly related to Aram. לבונא/ה (Heb. לבונה), frankincense, rather than *labanātu*, attested in medical context (BRM 4, 32: 15, RA 53 8: 37).
7 For *šāri*$^?$ *išiṭṭi*$^?$ see glossary.
12 The iron daggers were probably decorated with silver and gold; cf. **No. 301**: 5′.
14 Cf. *me-ṭu*^{meš} (**No. 301**: 5′).
15 *Tuḫullu*, if read correctly, is unknown.
18 NU 2 PA A TA; unclear.
20 For *ḫunāqi* see glossary.
22 2 PI ŠIM *pa-na-nu*; unclear.
24, 26 The form *si-gi-ir-ru* is unknown. The fact that the *si-gi-ir-ru* has a stand, points to it being a kind of a vessel, a composite item of gold and silver. The shape and / or function of the vessel might be derived from the root *sgr*, with the basic meaning "(to) (en)close."[5]

52. YBC 9393

Copy: Plate XIV
Date: 30.II. 40$^?$ Nbk
Summary: issue (*nadin*) note: silver

Obv. 1 GIN$_2$ KU$_3$.BABBAR *a-na bat-q*[*u*]
ša$_2$ *na-ṭi-il-ti* KU$_3$.BABBAR

5 Kleber has shown that the CAD's *sekēru* B (CAD S, 213), "(to) heat," should not be separated from *sekēru* A (p. 210, "close / dam"), and *sekēru* in these cases means "to purify (gold)" (by means of cementation); Kleber 2016b.

a-na ^{Id}INNIN-MU-DU$_3$
^{lu2}KU$_3$.DIM *na-din*

Rev. (blank)

^{iti}GU$_4$ UD.30.KAM MU.4[0$^?$.KAM]
^{d}AG-NIG$_2$.DU-URU$_3$
LUGAL TIN.TIR^{ki}

1 shekel of silver for the repair of (a) silver *ladle* was given to Ištar-šumu-ibni, the goldsmith. Month II, day 30, year 40$^?$ of Nebuchadnezzar, king of Babylon.

2 The word *naṭiltu* is unknown, and *na-ṭi-il-ti* must stand for *nāṭilu*, which CDA (p. 247) sees as a loan from Arm *nṭl*, "ladle"; note that the AHw has only "sehend" for *nāṭilu*. The CAD (N/II, 129) derives *nāṭilu* from Akkadian *naṭalu* as well, but takes it as a "grate," a sort of a filter, in the sense of "to look through."

53. GCBC 636

Copy: Plate XV
Date: [×].IX$^?$.5 Nbn
Summary: *maḫir* receipt: silver

For the goldsmiths Bēl-ibni and Ištar-šumu-ibni see **No. 4**.

Obv. [×] ⸢GIN$_2$ KU$_3$.BABBAR *a*⸣-[*na* ×] ⸢×⸣
[× ×]⸢^{d}⸣*na-n*[*a-a* × × ×]
⸢*ša*$_2$ ^{d}URU$_3$-<INIM>$^?$-*su*$^{!?(T. dumu)}$ *ša*$_2$⸣ DIN[GIR × ×]
(tiny line) ⸢3 1 ½ ×⸣ [(×)]
^{Id}EN-DU$_3$ *u* $^{Id!}$15-MU-DU$_3$
^{lu2}KU$_3$.DIM^{meš} IGI^{ir}

Rev. (blank)

[^{iti}GA]N$^?$ UD.[×.KAM]
⸢MU.5⸣.KAM ^{d}A[G-I]

Up.E. ⸢LUGAL TIN.TIR^{ki}⸣

× shekels of silver f[or the … of] Nan[āya …] of *Uṣur-amāssu*, …, were received from Bēl-ibni and Ištar-šumu-ibni, the goldsmiths.
Month IX$^?$, day [×], year 5 of Nab[onidus] king of Babylon.

54. YBC 9178

Copy: Plate XV
Date: 05.VII.03$^?$ Nbk
Summary: *maḫir* receipt: gold and silver items

Obv. 4 MA.⸢NA 5$^?$4⸣ GIN$_2$ KU$_3$.BABBAR *la-a-nu ša*$_2$ *ki-šuk-ku* KU$_3$.BABBAR
ša$_2$ IGI ^{d}GAŠAN-TIN *i-na* 5 *ma-nu-u ša*$_2$ ⸢ZABAR⸣
KI.LA$_2$ *ša*$_2$ AN.BAR *a-na*$^!$ IGI KU$_3$.BABBAR <*ul*>-*tu ḫa-a-ṭu*
ša$_2$ ^{Id}EN-DU$_3$ A-*šu*$_2$ *ša*$_2$ ^{Id}AG-NUMUN-DU$_3$ ^{I}*mar-duk-a*
u ^{I}*šu-la-a* ŠEŠ^{me}-*šu*$_2$ IGI^{u2}

---

1 MA.NA 15 GIN$_2$ KU$_3$.BABBAR *ki-rit-ti* KU$_3$.BABBAR
ša$_2$ šul-sul KU$_3$.BABBAR *ša$_2$* ^{lu_2}ŠU.KU$_6$
Lo.E. *ša$_2$* IGI ^{d}15 *i-na* 1 *ma-ne$_2$-e* ^{na_4}˹*šad-da*˺-[*nu*]
KI.LA$_2$ AN.BAR
Rev. 2 MA.NA ˹17$^!$ GIN$_2$ KU$_3$.BABBAR × × (×)˺
u$_3$ ku-us-˹*i-bir-ri-*(×)-*ti* KU$_3$.BABBAR˺
ša$_2$ ki-šuk ˹*ša$_2$* ^{d}GAŠAN-TIN *i-na* 2$^?$ *ma-nu-u*˺ *ša$_2$* ZABAR
˹KI˺.LA$_2$ *ša$_2$* AN.˹BAR ^{I}*mar-duk*˺-*a*
u ^{I}*šu-*˹*la-a* A$^{\langle me\rangle}$ *ša$_2$* ^{Id}AG˺-NUMUN-DU$_3$
IGI˹^{u_2}˺
Up.E. ^{iti}DU$_6$ UD.5°.KAM MU.3$^?$.KAM
^{d}AG$^!$-NIG$_2$.DU-URU$_3$ LUGAL E^{ki}

4 minas 54 shekels of silver (in the form of) the body of the silver grate that is before Bēlet-balāṭi. (It was weighed) against a 5 mina (weight) of bronze, (with smaller) weights of iron (added to balance) the silver. It is from the stock of Bēl-ibni, son of Nabû-zēru-ibni, (and) was received from Marduka and Šulāya, his brothers.
1 mina 15 shekels of silver (in the form of) a silver *kirītu*-ornament of the silver fishermen chest that is before Ištar; (weighed) according to the 1 mina hematite weight and (balanced with) weights of iron.
2 minas 17 shekels of silver (in the form of) ... and silver *cover/base* of the grate of Bēlet-balāṭi; (weighed) according to the 2$^?$ minas (weight) of bronze, (balanced with) weights of iron; (this amount) was received from Marduka and Šulāya, sons of Nabû-zēru-ibni.
Month VII, day 5, year 3$^?$ of Nebuchadnezzar, king of Babylon.

16 The year may be read 4 (rather than 3).

55. NCBT 147

Copy: Plate XVI
Date: 26.XI.17 Nbk
Summary: withdrawal (*našû*) + delivery (*šūbulu*) note: silver

For the problem of identifying Bēlšunu as the *bēl piqitti* in this context, as well as in **No. 56**, see note there.

Obv. 18 ½ GIN$_2$ KU$_3$.BABBAR *ša$_2$*
^{I}EN-*šu$_2$-nu* GIŠ˹^{u_2}˺
3 ½ ˹GIN$_2$˺ *ša$_2$* ^{I}IR$_3$-^{d}INNIN.NA
A ^{I}GI-^{d}˹AMAR.UTU˺ GIŠ^{u_2}
PAP ⅓ 2 GIN$_2$ KU$_3$.˹BABBAR˺ *a-*˹*na*˺
bat-qa ša$_2$ ak-kul-˹*lat*˺
Lo.E. *a-na* ^{I}SUM.NA˹-*a* A-*šu$_2$*˺
˹*ša$_2$*˺ ^{I}*ne$_2$-e-šu$_2$ šu-bul*
Rev. 1 GIN$_2$ *ina* ŠUK-*šu$_2$-nu*
^{I}IR$_3$-^{d}INNIN.NA <<×>> *u*
^{I}KI-E$_2$.AN.<NA>-*b*[*u-d*]*i-ia$_2$* ˹GIŠ˺[^{u_2}]

(blank)
^{iti}ZIZ$_2$ UD.26.KAM
MU.17.KAM ^{d}AG-NIG$_2$.DU-URU$_3$
Up.E. LUGAL TIN.⸢TIR⸣^{ki}

18 ½ shekels of silver that Bēlšunu withdrew and 3 ½ shekels that Arad-Innin, son of Mušallim-Marduk, withdrew; a total of 22 shekels of silver for the repair of the *mattock* were delivered to Iddināya, son of Nēšu. Arad-Innin and Itti-Eanna-būdia withdrew 1 shekel for their salaries.
Month XI, day 26, year 17 of Nebuchadnezzar, king of Babylon.

5–8 For *akkullu(attu)*, see glossary. In **No. 56**, written on the same day, Bēlšunu (along with Ša-Nabû-šū) withdraws 18 ½ shekels of silver for the repair of the same object. Occam's razor suggests these are the same 18 ½ shekels mentioned here, though the reason for the duplication is unclear.

56. NCBT 468

Copy: Plate XVI
Date: 26.XI.17 Nbk
Summary: withdrawal (*našû*) note: silver

See **No. 55**, which records an identical transaction.

Obv. 18 ½ GIN$_2$ ⸢KU$_3$⸣.BABBAR *a-*⸢*na*⸣
bat-qa ⸢*ša*$_2$ *ak*$^?$⸣*-kul-*⸢*lat*⸣
^{I}⸢EN⸣-*šu*$_2$*-nu* ^{lu_2}EN ⸢*pi*⸣*-qit-*⸢*tu*$_2$⸣
[A] ⸢^{I}⸣*ša*$_2$-^{d}AG-*šu-u*$_2$ GIŠ[(^{u_2})]
Rev. (blank)
⸢^{iti}ZIZ$_2$⸣ UD.26.KAM
⸢MU.17.KAM⸣ ^{d}AG-NIG$_2$.⸢DU-URU$_3$⸣
⸢LUGAL TIN⸣.[TI]R⸢^{ki}⸣

Bēlšunu, the commissioner, [*son of*] Ša-Nabû-šū withdrew 18 ½ shekels of silver for the repair of the *mattock*.
Month XI, day 26, year 17 of Nebuchadnezzar, king of Babylon.

2 For *akkullu(attu)*, see glossary.

3–4 The relations between Bēlšunu, the *bēl piqitti*, and Ša-Nabû-šū are not entirely clear. There are three main ways in which we may read these lines: 1) Bēlšunu, the *bēl piqitti*, [and] Ša-Nabû-šū; 2) Bēlšunu, the *bēl piqitti* [of] Ša-Nabû-šū; 3) Bēlšunu, the *bēl piqitti*, [son of] Ša-Nabû-šū.[6] The latter is preferred here given that Bēlšunu/Ša-Nabû-šū is known from YOS 17, 220 (17 Nbk), and see also Bēlšunu/Ša-Nabû-šū//Egibi in BM 114461 (25 Nbk). Another individual that should be mentioned here is Nabû-bēlšunu/Nabû-šumu-ukīn who was in charge of Eanna's work in the North Palace project, bearing the title *bēl piqitti* (*ša eanna ša muḫḫi dulli ša ekalli*); see Kleber 2008, 160, note 456.[7] If

[6] One may also read, "Bēlšunu, the *bēl piqitti*, [and] Ša-Nabû-šū," as three individuals, though this seems less likely.

[7] The North Palace project is first attested in 19 Nbk (see Kleber 2008, 159). While it is clear that the project started earlier (ibid), the use of the *bēl piqitti* in the Eanna archive at this early stage would be surprising (though certainly not impossible).

Bēlšunu is indeed to be identified as Nabû-bēlšunu, then Ša-Nabû-šū was not his father, and the text lists two separate individuals who withdrew the silver.

57. NCBT 265

Copy: Plate XVI
Date: 18.XI.36 Nbk
Summary: [*ina pāni*] note: cooking pot

Obv. [1]$^?$ *mu-šaḫ-ḫi-in-nu* ⸢ZABAR⸣
[*ša*$_2$] ⸢3⸣ *ne*$_2$*-sip*^{meš}
[*a*]-⸢*na qu-li*⸣*-i ša*$_2$ I$_3$.GIŠ
[*ša*$_2$] ⸢E$_2$ *ḫi-il-ṣu*⸣
5 [*ina* IGI] ⸢^{Id}AG-*mu-še-*<<*ti*>>*-tiq*$_2$⸣-[UD.D]A
Lo.E. [A] ⸢I⸣ A-*a*
Rev. (blank)
^{iti}ZIZ$_2$ UD.18.KAM
MU.36.KAM
9 ^{d}AG-NIG$_2$.DU-URU$_3$
Up.E. [LUG]AL TIN.TIR^{ki}

[*One*] bronze cooking pot [of] three *nēsepu*-containers for *cooking/roasting* the oil [of] the *bīt ḫilṣi* [are at the disposal of] Nabû-mušētiq-uddê, [son of] Aplāya.
Month XI, day 18, year 36 of Nebuchadnezzar, king of Babylon.

1 For the *mušaḫḫinu* cooking pot, see Levavi forthcoming.

3–4 The "cooking / roasting" of the oil was most probably in the context of cooking resinous substances (in the oils) in the process of perfume production; see Jursa 2004b. The production of aromatic ointment / liquid in the *bīt ḫilṣi* may also have had medicinal purposes; see Joannès 2006.

5 Nabû-mušētiq-uddê / Aplāya is attested as the *šangû* of the *bīt ḫilṣi* in NCBT 682 (20 Nbk); see also YOS 17, 176 (17 Nbk), NCBT 903 (32 Nbk), NCBT 245 (38 Nbk), YBC 11898 (1 Ner) for his activity in the *bīt ḫilṣi*.

58. NCBT 735

Copy: Plate XVI
Date: 12.VIII.20 Nbk
Summary: *ina pāni* note: bronze

The tablet's surface is badly abraded.

Obv. ⸢4 ⅔ MA.NA ZABAR⸣
⸢*a-na ma-ḫi-ṣu*⸣
⸢*ina* IGI ^{I}*lib-luṭ*⸣
4 ⸢A ^{Id}*na-na-a*-MU⸣
Lo.E. ⸢^{lu2}SIMUG⸣ ZABAR
Rev. (blank)
^{iti}APIN UD.12.KAM
MU.20.KAM ^{d}AG-NIG$_2$.DU-URU$_3$

LUGAL TIN.⸢TIR^{ki}⸣

4 ⅔ minas of bronze for a *mallet* is at the disposal of Libluṭ, son of Nanāya-iddin, the bronzesmith.
Month VIII, day 12, year 20 of Nebuchadnezzar, king of Babylon.

2 For *māḫiṣu*, a *mallet*(?), see glossary.

59. NCBT 922

Copy: Plate XVI
Date: 14.VI.31 Nbk
Summary: *ina pāni* note: bronze

For the edition of the text see page 3 in the introduction.

60. YBC 11278

Copy: Plate XVII
Date: 24.XI.07 (Npl–Nbk)
Summary: *ina pāni* note: bronze

The bronzesmith Bēl-ibni / Nabû-zēru-ibni is attested from 7 Npl (NCBT 885, edited in Payne 2007, 65) to 11 Nbk (YOS 17, 333); see Payne 2007, 300–1.

Obv. 1 MA.NA ⸢ZABAR⸣
a-na ⸢*ar*$_2$-*ṣa*⸣-*a-bat-tu*$_4$
ina IGI ^{Id}EN-*ib-ni*
Lo.E. ⸢A-*šu*$_2$ *ša*$_2$⸣ $^{I⸢d}$AG⸣-NUMUN-DU$_3$
Rev. ^{lu_2}⸢SIMUG ZABAR⸣
6 ⸢^{iti}GAN UD.24.KAM⸣
MU.7.⸢KAM⸣

1 mina of bronze for *arṣabu*-tools is at the disposal of Bēl-ibni, son of Nabû-zēru-ibni, the bronzesmith.
Month XI, day 24, year 7.

2 The *arṣabu / attu* is an unidentified agricultural implement; see also YOS 6, 218: 46, 47, Camb 18: 8.

61. NBC 4560

Copy: Plate XVII
Date: 23.XI.06 --
Summary: *ina pāni* note: bronze

No other attestations of the bronzesmith Balāssu are known to us.

Obv. ⅚ MA.NA 3 GIN$_2$ ZABAR
a$^!$-*na bat-qa ša*$_2$ ŠEN URUDU
ša$_2$ E$_2$ ^{d}⸢URU$_3$⸣-INIM-*su*

ina ⸢IGI⸣ ^{I}TIN^{su} ^{lu_2}SIMUG ZABAR
Lo.E. ^{iti}ZIZ$_2$ UD.23.KAM MU.6.KAM
Rev. (uninscribed)

53 shekels of bronze for repairing the copper cauldron of the Uṣur-amāssu temple are at the disposal of Balāssu, the bronzesmith.
Month XI, day 23, year 6.

62. NCBT 325

Copy: Plate XVII
Date: 23.I.42 Nbk
Summary: *ina pāni* note: bronze

Obv. 2 ⸢½⸣ MA.NA 8 GIN$_2$
⸢ZABAR⸣ *a-na bat-qa*
ša$_2$ mu-šaḫ-ḫi-nu
ša$_2$ E$_2$ ^{lu_2}UŠ.BAR^{me}
ina IGI ^{I}IR$_3$-^{d}INNIN.NA
Lo.E. ^{lu_2}SIMUG
Rev. (blank)
⸢^{iti}⸣BARA$_2$ UD.23.KAM
MU.42.KAM ^{d}AG-NIG$_2$.⸢DU⸣-URU$_3$
LUGAL TIN.TIR^{k}[^{i}]

2 minas 38 shekels of bronze for the repair of the cooking pot of the weavers' workshop are at the disposal of Arad-Innin, the (bronze) smith.
Month I, day 23, year 42 of Nebuchadnezzar, king of Babylon.

63. YBC 9442

Copy: Plate XVII
Date: 28.VI.27 Nbk
Summary: *ina pāni* note: bronze bowl

Obv. ⸢*1-et*⸣ *qa-bu-ut-tu$_2$* ZABAR
a-na nap-⸢*ta*⸣*-nu*
ša$_2$ E$_2$ ^{d}IDIM
ina IGI ^{Id}AG-NUMUN-BA^{ša_2}
ša$_2$ ŠUK.ḪI.A LUGAL
Rev. (blank)
^{iti}KIN UD.28.KAM
MU.27.KAM
^{d}AG-NIG$_2$.DU-URU$_3$
Up.E. LUGAL ⸢TIN⸣.TIR^{ki}

One bronze *qabūtu*-bowl for the *naptanu*-meal of the Ea temple is at the disposal of Nabû-zēru-iqīša, (who is in charge) of the royal rations.
Month VI, day 28, year 27 of Nebuchadnezzar, king of Babylon.

64. NCBT 912

Copy: Plate XVII
Date: 20.IV.14 N[pl/bk]
Summary: *ina pāni* note: copper

Obv. 8 MA.NA *e-⸢ri⸣*
⸢a⸣-na dul-lu ina ⸢IGI⸣
^{I}⸢IR$_3$⸣-^{d}*gu-la*
7 ⅚ MA.NA
Rev. *ina* IGI
^{I}DUG$_3$.GA-IM-^{d}INNIN
^{iti}ŠU UD.20.⸢KAM⸣
MU.14.KAM ^{d}A[G-...]
LUGAL TIN.TI[R^{ki}]

8 minas of copper for work are at the disposal of Arad-Gula.
7 ⅚ minas are at the disposal of Ṭāb-šār-Ištar.
Month IV, day 20, year 14 of Nabû-[…], king of Babylon.

65. YBC 9237

Copy: Plate XVII
Date: 27.XII.33 Nbk
Summary: issue (*nadin*) note: a bronze vessel

Obv. 1-*et* ^{giš}BAN$_2$ ZABAR
ša$_2$ a-na me-e ⸢ŠU^{II}⸣ *a-na*
⸢E$_2$⸣ ^{d}*gu-la* SUM.NA^{ti}
^{I}⸢^{d}AG-DU-IBILA⸣ *a-na* E$_2$ *ka-re-e*
⸢IGI^{ir} *a-na*⸣ E$_2$ ^{lu_2}MUḪALDIM^{meš}
ša$_2$ E$_2$.AN.NA SUM.NA^{at}
Lo.E. *k[i]-⸢ir⸣-ri* ZABAR *eš-šu$_2$*
Rev. *⸢ku-um! a-na⸣* E$_2$ ^{d}*gu-la*
a-na me-e ŠU^{II} *na-din*
(blank)
^{iti}ŠE UD.27.KAM MU.33.KAM
^{d}AG-NIG$_2$.DU-URU$_3$ LUGAL TIN.TIR^{ki}

One bronze *sūtu*(-bowl), which had been given to the Gula temple for the hand(-washing) water, has been received from Nabû-mukīn-apli for the depot; it was given to the bakery of Eanna. A new bronze *kirru*-vessel has been given instead to the Gula temple for the hand(-washing) water.
Month XII, day 27, year 33 of Nebuchadnezzar, king of Babylon.

4–6 The phrasing of these lines suggests that the bakery (E$_2$ ^{lu_2}MUḪALDIM^{meš}) may have been part of the depot (*bīt karê*) (Kleber 2005, 310).

66. NCBT 443

Copy: Plate XVIII
Date: 16$^{?}$.IX.09 --
Summary: *maḫir* receipt: bowl$^{?}$/grain$^{?}$

Obv. 1 BAN$_2$ *ina* ^{giš}BAN$_2$ ZABAR
^{I}LU$_2$-^{d}*na-na-a ma-ḫir*
^{iti}GAN UD.16$^{°?}$.KAM MU.9.KAM
Rev. (uninscribed)

1 *sūtu* (of x, measured) in the bronze *sūtu*-bowl was received from Amīl-Nanāya.
Month IX, day 16$^{?}$, year 9.

67. YBC 16193

Copy: Plate XVIII
Date: 11$^{?}$.II.36 Nbk
Summary: *maḫir* receipt: bronze

Obv. 1 *mu-šaḫ-ḫi-nu* ⸢ZABAR⸣
4 MA.NA 10 GIN$_2$ *ḫa-a-ṭu*
a-na 6 MA.NA 15 GIN$_2$
ZABAR *ḫu-še-e*
⸢*a*⸣-*na* ^{I}*ina*-SUḪ$_3$-SUR
Lo.E. A ^{I}MU-URU$_3$ *na-din*
Rev. ZABAR *ḫu-še-e*
ma-ḫi-ir
(blank)
^{iti}GU$_4$ UD.11$^{?}$.KAM MU.36.KAM
^{d}AG-NIG$_2$.DU-URU$_3$ LUGAL TIN.TIR$^{⸢ki⸣}$

One bronze cooking pot (and bronze) stock of 4 minas 10 shekels were given to Ina-tēšî-ēṭir, son of Šumu-uṣur, for scrap bronze of 6 minas 15 shekels. The scrap bronze was received from him.
Month II, day 11$^{?}$, year 36 of Nebuchadnezzar, king of Babylon.

3–4 The 6 minas and 15 shekels of scrap (*ḫušê*) bronze was probably the combined weight of the cooking pot and the stock (*ḫaṭû*) bronze given to the smith. Those were perhaps smelted, but in any case, were returned to the temple together, possibly as one ingot.

9 11$^{?}$ may be read 1° (over an erased 10).

68. NCBT 80

Copy: Plate XVIII
Date: 13.IV.39 Nbk
Summary: *maḫir* receipt: bronze vessel

Obv. 23 MA.⸢NA⸣ ZABAR ⸢*gam*⸣-*mar*
1 ŠEN ZABAR
^{Id}U.GUR-TIN^{it}

	A ^{I}*šu-ma-a* IGI^{ir}
5	^{iti}ŠU UD.13.KAM
Lo.E.	MU.39.<KAM>
Rev.	⸢^{d}AG⸣-NIG$_2$.DU-URU$_3$
	LUGAL TIN.TIR^{ki}

23 minas of processed bronze (in the form of) one bronze cauldron were received from Nergal-uballiṭ, son of Šumāya.
Month IV, day 13, year 39 of Nebuchadnezzar, king of Babylon.

69. NCBT 828

Copy: Plate XVIII
Date: 23.VI.22 Nbk
Summary: *maḫir* receipt: bronze vessel[8]

Obv.	6 MA.NA 15 GIN$_2$ ZABAR *gam-ru*
	1 *ki-ir-ri* ZABAR
	ša$_2$ E$_2$ *ḫi-il*$^{!}$*-ṣu*
	^{I}*lib-luṭ* A ^{Id}*na-na-a*-MU
Lo.E.	^{lu2}SIMUG ZABAR
6	IGI^{ir}
Rev.	(blank)
	^{iti}KIN UD.23.KAM
	MU.22.KAM ^{d}AG-NIG$_2$.DU-URU$_3$
	LUGAL TIN.TIR^{ki}

6 minas 15 shekels of processed bronze (in the form of) one bronze *kirru*-vessel for the *bīt ḫilṣi* were received from Libluṭ, son of Nanāya-iddin, the bronzesmith.
Month VI, day 23, year 22 of Nebuchadnezzar, king of Babylon.

70. YBC 9380

Copy: Plate XVIII
Date: 14.III.22 Nbk
Summary: *maḫir* receipt: iron

Obv.	⸢4$^{?}$ ½ MA⸣.NA ZABAR *gam-r*[*i* (×)]
	[×] ⸢*lab-ba-nu*⸣ *ša*$_2$ *ku*$^{?}$ *la*$_2^{?}$ ⸢×⸣ [...]
	⸢*ša*$_2$ *a-na* ^{d}UTU SUM^{nu}⸣
	⸢^{I}*lib-luṭ* A ^{Id}*na*⸣-*n*[*a-a*-MU]
5	⸢^{Id}INNIN.NA⸣-NUMUN-TIL A ^{Id}E[N-DU$_3$]
	[^{I}]⸢*ba*⸣-*bi-ia* A ^{I}⸢^{d}⸣[AMAR.UTU-KAM]
Lo.E.	^{Id}ŠU$_2$-MU-PAP
Rev.	⸢A ^{I}⸣<KAR>-^{d}ŠU$_2$ [×(×)]
	^{lu2}SIMUG^{me} I[GI^{u2}]
	(blank)

[8] A previous edition is included in Payne 2007, 281.

^{iti}SIG$_4$ UD.14.[KAM]
MU.22.KAM
^{d}AG-NIG$_2$.⸢DU⸣-UR[U$_3$]
Up.E. LUGAL ⸢TIN.TIR⸣^{ki}

4 ½ minas of processed bronze (in the form of) [x] …, which were given to Šamaš, were received from Libluṭ, son of Nan[āya-iddin], Innin-zēru-šubši, son of Bē[l-ibni], Bābia, son of [Marduk-ēreš], (and) Marduk-šumu-uṣur, son of <Mušēzib>-Marduk, the smiths. Month III, day 14, year 22 of Nebuchadnezzar, king of Babylon.

2 Though the reading *lab-ba-nu* seems reasonable, *labbānu* is not the expected Pl. form of *labbu*, and this reading remains highly uncertain. The reading of *ku* as ^{tug_2} is difficult given that we would not expect bronze attachments to a garment. The reading *ma*$^{!}$*-gar*$^{!}$*-r*[*i*] could be suggested as well: a bronze *labbānu* of a wheel.

8 Marduk-šumu-uṣur's father must be Mušēzib-Marduk; see Payne 2007, 313 n. 475.

71. YBC 9172

Copy: Plate XIX
Date: 25.XII.36 Nbk
Summary: promissory note: bronze

Obv. [(×+)] ⸢1 MA.NA⸣ ⅓ 2 GIN$_2$ ZABAR
⸢*re-eḫ-ti*⸣ 5 MA.NA *šu-qul-ti*
⸢NIG$_2$.GA ^{d}GAŠAN *ša*$_2$⸣ UNUG^{ki} *u* ^{d}*na-na-a*
(tiny line) *ina mu*[*ḫ-ḫ*]*i* ^{I}*ṣil-la-a* A-*šu*$_2$ <×>
⸢*ša*$_2$⸣ ^{I}LU$_2$-⸢^{d}*na-na-a*⸣ *u* ^{Id}*a-nu*$_3$-MU-DU$_3$
A-*šu*$_2$ *ša*$_2$ ^{I}NUMUN-⸢*ia*⸣ *ina* ^{iti}GU$_4$
i-nam-di-nu
u$_2$*-il*$_3$*-ti*$_3$ *ša*$_2$ 5 MA.NA
⸢ZABAR⸣ *ša*$_2$ *ina muḫ-ḫi-šu*$_2$*-n*[*u*]
Lo.E. *ḫi-pa-a-ta*
Rev. ^{lu_2}*mu-kin-nu* ^{Id}INNIN.NA-NUMUN-TIL
A-*šu*$_2$ ⸢*ša*$_2$ ^{I}⸣*ba-laṭ-su*
⸢^{I}DU$_3$-*ia* A⸣-*šu*$_2$ *ša*$_2$ ^{Id}AG-TIN^{su}-E
⸢*u* ^{lu_2}⸣UMBISAG ^{Id}AG-DU$_3$-ŠEŠ
⸢A-*šu*$_2$ *ša*$_2$ ^{I}DU$_3$⸣-*ia*$^{!sic.}$ UNUG^{ki}
⸢^{iti}ŠE UD.25⸣.KAM
Up.E. ⸢MU.36.KAM ^{d}AG-NIG$_2$.DU⸣-[URU$_3$]
⸢LUGAL TIN.TIR^{ki}⸣

1(+) mina(s) 22 shekels of bronze, the remainder of the weighed 5 minas, property of the Lady-of-Uruk and Nanāya, is owed by Ṣillāya, son of Amīl-Nanāya, and Anu-šumu-ibni, son of Zēria. They will repay it by month II. The promissory note for the 5 minas of bronze owed by them is void (lit. broken).
Witnesses: Innin-zēru-šubši, son of Balāssu; Bānia, son of Nabû-balāssu-iqbi, and the scribe Nabû-bān-aḫi, son of Ibnāya. Uruk. Month XII, day 25, year 36 of Nebuchadnezzar, king of Babylon.

72. NCBT 982

Copy: Plate XIX
Date: 18.VI.-- (Npl/Nbk)
Summary: *ina pāni* note: iron

Nabû-zēru-iddin, the most prominent smith in the present corpus, is attested from 1 Npl (YBC 11273) to 14 Nbk (YOS 17, 362); see Payne 2007, 317–21.

Obv. 10 ½ MA.NA AN.BAR
a-na ma-ag-ga-nu
ina IGI ^{Id}AG-NUMUN-MU
Rev. (blank)
⸢^{iti}KIN⸣ UD.18.KAM

10 ½ minas of iron for … are at the disposal of Nabû-zēru-iddin.
Month VI, day 18.

2 The reading *ma-ag-ga-nu* is quite clear, except for the *nu* sign, which may be said to look more like a PAP. Being made of iron, one may think of a "shield" (Heb. And Aram. מגן). The form *magannu*, however, would be unexpected; c.f. *maginnu*, indeed, a "(head) shield" (CAD M/II, 44, AHw, 576), VAB 3, 89: 18, API No. 24: 26, referring to Greek soldiers. The reading *ma-aq-qa$_2$-nu* for *maqqû*-bowls is rejected, given that the reading *qa$_2$* (for GA) is unlikely in Late Babylonian texts, as well as the fact that the bowl would not be of iron.

73. GCBC 346

Copy: Plate XIX
Date: 22.[×.×] Nbk
Summary: *ina pāni* note: iron

Obv. [×] ⸢MA.NA⸣ AN.BAR
[*ina* IG]I ^{T}[^{d}AG-NUM]UN-MU
⸢^{lu2}SIMUG⸣ [(×) ^{iti}×]
Lo.E. ⸢UD⸣.22.[KAM]
Rev. ⸢MU⸣.[×].⸢KAM ^{d}AG-NIG$_2$.DU-URU$_3$⸣
6 [LUGAL] ⸢TIN.TIR⸣^{ki}

[×] mina(s) of iron is/are at the disposal of [Nabû-zē]ru-iddin, the smith.
[Month ×], day 22, [year ×] of Nebuchadnezzar, king of Babylon.

74. GCBC 602

Copy: Plate XIX
Date: [×].II.12 N[pl/bk]
Summary: *ina pāni* note: iron

For Nabû-zēru-iddin (l. 3), the smith, see **No. 72.**

Obv. ⸢17⸣ MA.NA ⸢11(+)⸣ [GIN$_2$] ⸢AN.BAR⸣

	a-na ⸢×⸣ [× × ×] ⸢AN.BAR⸣
	[(×) *ina* IGI] ⸢^{Id}⸣[AG]-⸢NUMUN-MU⸣
	[^{iti}]GU$_4$ UD.[×.KA]M
Lo.E.	[M]U.⸢12⸣.K[AM] ^{d}A[G-×]
	⸢LUGAL⸣ [TIN.TIR^{ki}]
Rev.	(uninscribed)

17 minas *11* shekels of iron for the (making of) an iron … [are at the disposal of] Nabû-zēru-iddin.
Month II, day [×], year 12 of N[abopolassar] / N[ebuchadnezzar)] king of [Babylon].

75. NCBT 1040

Copy:	Plate XX
Date:	14.VI.09 (Npl / Nbk)
Summary:	*maḫir* receipt + *ina pāni* note: iron

For Nabû-zēru-iddin (l. 4), the smith, see **No. 72**.

Obv.	3 ⸢MA.NA 53⸣ GIN$_2$ AN.BAR
	2 MAR AN.BAR^{meš} *u*$_3$
	na-aš$_2$*-ḫe-ep-ti ša*$_2$ E$_2$ ⸢*pa-pa*⸣*-ḫi*
	^{Id}AG-NUMUN-MU IGI^{ir}
Rev.	^{iti}KIN UD.14.KAM MU.9.KAM$^{!}$
	(blank)
	2-ta MAR ⸢AN⸣.BAR^{me}
	ina IGI ^{I}*re-mut* A ^{I}*m / ba-bi-a*$^{?}$*-p/bu* ^{lu_2}[×]

3 minas 53 shekels of iron (in the form of) two iron spades and (a) shovel(s) for the cella were received from Nabû-zēru-iddin;
Month VI, day 14, year 9. (The) two iron spades are at the disposal of Rēmūtu, son of …, the […].

76. NCBT 1130

Copy:	Plate XX
Date:	09.I.07 (Npl / Nbk)
Summary:	*maḫir* receipt + *ina pāni* note: iron

For Nabû-zēru-iddin (l. 3), the smith, see **No. 72**.

(Le.E. ↓)	
Obv.	9 ⅚ MA.NA 5 ½ GIN$_2$ AN.BAR
	na-aṣ-ba-ra-na ša$_2$ ^{giš}IG^{meš}
	u$_3$ *sik-ka-a-ta* ^{Id}AG-NUMUN-MU IGI^{ir}
	^{iti}BARA$_2$ UD.9.KAM MU.7.KAM
Rev.	1 MA.NA 10 GIN$_2$ AN.BAR *re-ḫe-et*
	ma-ḫi-ṣu ina IGI ^{Id}AG-NUMUN-MU

9 ⅚ minas 5 ½ shekels of iron (in the form of) two mountings for doors and pegs were received from Nabû-zēru-iddin. Month I, day 9, year 7.
1 mina 10 shekels of iron, the remainder of the *mallet* is at the disposal of Nabû-zēru-iddin.

6 For *māḫiṣu*, a *mallet*(?), see glossary.

77. NCBT 204

Copy: Plate XX
Date: 27.XI.19 Npl
Summary: *maḫir* receipt + *ina pāni* note: iron tools

Obv. 5 MA.NA 13 GIN$_2$ AN.BAR
1-*en e-su-u*$_2$ AN.BAR
^{Id}AG-NUMUN-MU
^{lu_2}SIMUG$^!$ AN.BAR
IGI^{ir}
Lo.E. *ina* IGI ^{I}*mar-duk-a*
Rev. A ^{Id}AG-NUMUN-DU$_3$
(blank)
^{iti}ZIZ$_2$ UD.27.KAM
MU.19.KAM ^{d}AG-A-URU$_3$
LUGAL TIN.TIR^{ki}

5 minas 13 shekels of iron (in the form of) one iron *esû* were received from Nabû-zēru-iddin, the blacksmith. (They are now) at the disposal of Marduka, son of Nabû-zēru-ibni. Month XI, day 27, year 19 of Nabopolassar king of Babylon.

2 This is the only attestation of the *esû* tool known to us, and its exact function remains unclear. It is difficult to connect this clearly iron tool to *esû / asû*, attested in lexical lists as a wooden part of a loom; see CAD E, 328, s.v. *esū* A.

78. NCBT 805

Copy: Plate XX
Date: 29.IV.13 (Npl/Nbk)
Summary: *maḫir* receipt + *ina pāni* note: iron tools[9]

For Nabû-zēru-iddin (l. 3) see **No. 72**. Taqīš-Gula is attested from 18 Npl (PTS 2813) to 9 Nbk (PTS 2406); see Payne 2007, 276.

Obv. 9 MA.NA ⅓ GIN$_2$ AN.BAR *gam-mar*
7 MAR^{me} AN.BAR 4 *u-ra-<ke>-e* AN.BAR
^{Id}AG-⌜NUMUN-MU IGI^{ir}⌝
4 *u*$_2$-⌜*ra*⌝-*ak ina* IGI ^{I}*ta-qiš*$_2$-^{d}*gu-la*
u $^{I⌜d}$AG⌝-MU
Rev. (blank)

[9] A previous edition is included in Payne 2007, 259.

^{iti}ŠU UD.29.KAM MU.13.KAM

9 minas 20 shekels of processed iron (in the form of) seven iron spades (and) four iron *urāku*-chisels were received from Nabû-zēru-iddin; the four iron *urāku*-chisels are at the disposal of Taqīš-Gula and Nabû-iddin.
Month IV, day 29, year 13.

79. NCBT 464

Copy: Plate XX
Date: 22.VII.14 (Npl/Nbk)
Summary: *maḫir* receipt + issue (*nadin*) note: silver[10]

For Nabû-zēru-iddin (l. 2), the smith, see **No. 72**.

Obv. 1 MA.NA ⅓ 5 GIN$_2$ 1^{en} *pa-a-šu*$_2$ AN.BAR
^{Id}AG-NUMUN-MU IGI^{ir}
a-na ^{Id}AG-ŠEŠ-MU ^{lu_2}NAGAR *na-din*
(blank)
^{iti}DU$_6$ UD.22.KAM MU.14.KAM
Rev. (uninscribed)

1 mina 25 shekels (in the form of) one iron *pāšu*-axe were received from Nabû-zēru-iddin; (the axe) was given to Nabû-aḫu-iddin, the carpenter.
Month VII, day 22, year 14.

80. NBC 4550

Copy: Plate XXI
Date: 01.X.11 (Npl/Nbk)
Summary: *maḫir* receipt: iron

For Nabû-zēru-iddin (l. 4), the smith, see **No. 72**.

Obv. 1 MA.NA ⸢8 GIN$_2$⸣ AN.BAR
3 ⸢*ḫa*⸣-*ṭa-a-ta* AN.BAR
ša$_2$ ⸢*ši-in*⸣-*du* *ša*$_2$ AB$_2$.GU$_4$.ḪI.A
^{Id}AG-NUMUN-MU IGI^{ir}
Rev. (blank)
⸢^{iti}AB UD.1.KAM⸣
⸢MU.11.KAM⸣

1 mina 8 shekels of iron (in the form of) three iron rods of the cattle branding iron were received from Nabû-zēru-iddin.
Month X, day 1, year 11.

2–3 ⸢*ḫa*⸣-*ṭa-a-ta*, Pl. of *ḫaṭṭu*, "scepter, stick"; in the present case, these are the rods of the branding iron.

10 A previous edition is included in Payne 2007, 84.

81. NCBT 1188

Copy: Plate XXI
Date: 06.III.19 (Npl/Nbk)
Summary: *maḫir* receipt: iron

For Nabû-zēru-iddin (l. 2), the smith, see **No. 72**.

Obv. 17 GIN$_2$ AN.BAR *gam-ru*
^{Id}AG-NUMUN-MU
IGI^{ir}
Rev. (blank)
^{iti}SIG$_4$ UD.6.KAM
MU.19.KAM

17 shekels of processed iron were received from Nabû-zēru-iddin.
Month III, day 6, year 19.

1–3 Note that it is unusual for a receipt for processed (*gamru*) iron not to list the actual iron items/tools.

82. NCBT 1190

Copy: Plate XXI
Date: 28.VIII.13 (Npl/Nbk)
Summary: *maḫir* receipt: iron

For Nabû-zēru-iddin (l. 2), the smith, see **No. 72**.

Obv. ⸢7 MA.NA ⅓ GIN$_2$ AN.BAR⸣
⸢5 MAR^{me} AN.BAR ^{Id}AG-NUMUN-MU IGI^{ir}⸣
⸢1-*en* ×⸣ [ ]-*nu*
⸢*ša*$_2$ *a-na* 1 ^{giš}×⸣ [(^{I})×]-⸢SUM/ZALAG$_2$?⸣
⸢IGI^{ir}⸣
Rev. (blank)
^{iti}APIN UD.28.KAM
MU.13.KAM

7 ⅓ minas of iron (in the form of) five iron spades were received from Nabû-zēru-iddin.
One … was received … for ...
Month VIII, day 28, year 13.

83. YBC 9035

Copy: Plate XXI
Date: 22.VII.14 (Npl/Nbk)
Summary: *maḫir* receipt: iron

For Nabû-zēru-iddin (l. 2), the smith, see **No. 72**.

Obv. 1 MA.NA ⅓ 5 GIN$_2$ *pa-a°-šu$_2$* AN°.BAR
$^{\text{I}\circ\text{d}}$AG°-NUMUN-MU° IGI^{ir}
(blank)
^{iti}DU$_6$ UD.22.KAM
Lo.E. MU.14.KAM
Rev. (uninscribed)

1 mina 25 shekels (of iron, in the form of) an iron *pāšu*-axe, were received from Nabû-zēru-iddin.
Month VII, day 22, year 14.

84. NCBT 465

Copy: Plate XXI
Date: 26.XII.13 (Npl/Nbk)
Summary: *maḫir* receipt: iron

For Nabû-zēru-iddin (l. 6), the smith, see **No. 72**.

Obv. ⸢1 MA⸣.NA 2 ⸢GIN$_2$⸣ AN.⸢BAR⸣
⸢*a-na*⸣ *šu*$^!$-⸢*u$_2$*⸣-*re-e*
⸢*ša$_2$*⸣ 2ta ⸢MAR⸣ 4 ^{giš}[ ]
⸢× ×⸣ 4 *na*-⸢*aṣ-ṣa*⸣-[*ar-tu*]
⸢*ša$_2$*$^?$⸣ *a-na* ^{I}⸢×⸣[ ]
^{Id}AG-NUMUN-MU [($^{\text{lu}_2}$SIMUG) IGI^{ir}]
Rev. (blank)
⸢^{iti}⸣ŠE UD.26$^?$.KAM
MU.13.KAM

1 mina 2 shekels of iron for *šūrû*-tools for two spades, four [...] ... four *storage jars* for [PN, were received from] Nabû-zēru-iddin [(the smith)].
Month XII, day 26, year 13.

2 For the *šūrû*-tool see glossary.

4 Two meanings are known for *naṣṣaru* (*namṣaru*): a "storage jar" and a "sword/mace." Although the latter clearly fits better in the context, it is only the former that is possibly attested in contemporary texts; e.g., YOS 7, 42.

85. NCBT 937

Copy: Plate XXI
Date: 29.II.-- (Npl/Nbk)
Summary: *maḫir* receipt: iron objects

For Nabû-zēru-iddin (l. 4), the smith, see **No. 72**.

Obv. 2 ⅚ MA.NA AN.BAR
6 *sir$_2$-ra-pi* AN.BAR
⸢2-*ta*⸣ MUL$^{\text{me!(T. bar)}}$ AN.BAR
⸢^{I}⸣^{d}AG-NUMUN-MU IGI^{ir}

Rev. (blank)
5 ⸢^{iti}GU$_4$⸣ UD.29.KAM

2 5/6 minas of iron (in the form of) six iron shears (and) two iron stars were received from Nabû-zēru-iddin.
Month II, day 29.

3 The stars were probably used for the branding of animals (and humans?) with the star of Ištar; see Pearce 1996.

86. NBC 4550

Copy: Plate XXII
Date: 18.XII.04 (Npl/Nbk)
Summary: *maḫir* receipt: iron tools

For Nabû-zēru-iddin (l. 3), the smith, see **No. 72**.

Obv. 6 MA.NA AN.BAR
4 MAR AN.BAR^{me}
^{Id}AG-NUMUN-MU
^{lu_2}SIMUG AN.BAR IGI^{ir}
Rev. (blank)
5 ^{iti}ŠE UD.18.KAM
MU.4.KAM

6 minas of iron (in the form of) four iron spades were received from Nabû-zēru-iddin, the blacksmith.
Month XII, day 18, year 4.

87. NCBT 1110

Copy: Plate XXII
Date: 24.VII.13 (Npl/Nbk)
Summary: *maḫir* receipt: iron tools

For Nabû-zēru-iddin (l. 4), the smith, see **No. 72**.

Obv. 9 ⸢MA⸣.NA ⸢55 GIN$_2$⸣ AN.BAR
4 MAR^{me} AN.BAR
3 *kam-mat* AN.BAR
^{Id}AG-NUMUN-MU
Lo.E. IGI^{ir}
6 1 ½ MA.NA AN.BAR
Rev. 7 *šu-u$_2$-re-e*
14 *sik-kat* IGI^{ir}
(blank)
^{iti}DU$_6$ UD.24.KAM
10 MU.13.KAM

9 minas 55 shekels of iron (in the form of) four iron spades (and) three iron dowels were received from Nabû-zēru-iddin. 1 ½ minas of iron (in the form of) seven *šūrû*-tools (and) fourteen pegs were received (as well).
Month VII, day 24, year 13.

7 For the *šūrû*-tool, see glossary.

88. NCBT 450

Copy: Plate XXII
Date: 28.V.16 (Npl)
Summary: *maḫir* receipt: iron tools

For Nabû-zēru-iddin (l. 5), the smith, see **No. 72**.

Obv.	6 *šu*$^{!(\text{T. }ba)}$-*u*$_2$-*re-e* AN.BAR
	12 *sik-kat*$^!$ AN.BAR
	ša$_2$ MAR AN.BAR^{me}
	½ MA.NA AN.BAR
	⸢^{I}⸣^{d}AG-NUMUN-MU $^{\text{lu}_2}$⸢SIMUG⸣
Lo.E.	IGI^{ir}
Rev.	*ina* IGI ^{I}*ḫaš-di-ia*$_2$ $^{\text{lu}_2}$ENGAR
	(blank)
	^{iti}NE UD.⸢28⸣.KAM
	MU.⸢18⸣.KAM

Six iron *šūrû*-tools and twelve iron pegs for the iron spades, (at the weight of) 1 ½ mina of iron, were received from Nabû-zēru-iddin, the smith. (They are) at the disposal of Ḫašdia, the plowman.
Month V, day 28, year 18.

1 For the *šūrû*-tool, see glossary.

89. NCBT 453

Copy: Plate XXII
Date: 25.XI.11 (Npl/Nbk)
Summary: *maḫir* receipt: iron tools

For Nabû-zēru-iddin (l. 3), the smith, see **No. 72**.

Obv.	⅓ 4 ½ GIN$_2$ AN.BAR
	2 AN.BAR *ma*$^{?!}$-*kad-da-nu*
	^{Id}AG-NUMUN-MU $^{\text{lu}_2}$SIMUG
4	IGI^{ir}
Rev.	⸢^{iti}⸣ZIZ$_2$ UD.25.KAM MU.11.KAM

24 ½ shekels of iron (in the form of) two iron *spatulas* were received from Nabû-zēru-iddin, the smith.

Month XI, day 25, year 11.

2 If the reading *ma*$^{?!}$-*kad-da-nu* is correct, this would be the only non-lexical attestation of a *makaddu* tool in first millennium records. In lexical lists, *makaddu* is a kind of a spatula (cf. *kadādu*, "to rub"), though it is listed among wooden items; see AHw, 587.

90. NCBT 616

Copy: Plate XXII
Date: 15.VI$^{?}$.02 (Npl/Nbk)
Summary: *maḫir* receipt: iron tools

For Nabû-zēru-iddin (l. 8), the smith, see **No. 72**.

Obv. 1 MA.NA ⅓ GIN_2 AN.BAR *gam-ru*
1 *mu-ṣab-bi-it* AN.BAR
1 *ṣi*^{sic}-*ṣi-ib-ti* AN.BAR
1 *qup-pu-u*$_2$ AN.BAR
⸢1 *na*⸣-*al-pat* AN.BAR
Lo.E. [1$^{?}$ *n*]*a-at-kap* AN.BAR
⸢1 *ma*⸣-*ad-dar* AN.BAR
Rev. ^{I}⸢^{d}AG-NUMUN⸣-MU
⸢^{lu_2}⸣SIMUG AN.BAR IGI^{ir}
(blank)
⸢^{iti}⸣KIN$^{!?}$ UD.15.KAM
MU.2.KAM

1 mina 20 shekels of processed iron (in the form of) one iron ..., one (pair of) iron *fetters*, one iron knife, one iron *scraper*, [*one*] iron *a*]*wl*, and one iron *pickaxe* were received from Nabû-zēru-iddin, the blacksmith.
Month VI, day 15, year 2.

2 *mu-ṣab-bi-it* is unclear; see glossary.

3 *ṣi-ṣi-ib-ti* is translated here as *fetters*, which is taken as an unlikely and a peculiar scribal error for *ṣibtētu*.

4 The *quppû* knife is known only from SB texts; see CAD Q, 311, s.v. *quppû*. The present context, however, makes such a reading plausible.

5 For *nalpattu*, scraper$^{?}$, see glossary.

6 [*n*]*a-at-kap* is understood as a *mapras* form of **tkp*, "to pierce, puncture, stich," hence an "awl" or a similar pointed tool.

7 The suggested translation *pickaxe* for the otherwise unattested *ma-ad-dar*, is based on the WSem מעדר in the absence of a convincing Babylonian etymology. Note, however, that this would not be the expected form had this been a "new" WSem loanword.

10 The month name may be read $BARA_2$ (I).

91. NCBT 737

Copy: Plate XXIII
Date: 24.III.16 (Npl/Nbk)
Summary: *maḫir* receipt: iron tools

For Nabû-zēru-iddin (l. 4), the smith, see **No. 72**.

Obv. 6 AN.BAR *šu-re-e*^{me}
ša$_2$ $^{\text{giš!}}$⸢*rap-ša*$_2$⸣*-ta*
12 ½ GIN$_2^{!}$ *ḫa-a-ṭu*
Rev. ^{Id}AG-NUMUN-MU
IGI^{ir}
^{iti}SIG$_4$ UD.24.KAM
MU.⸢16⸣.KAM

Six iron *šūrû*-tools of the hoes (and) 12 ½ shekels in stock were received from Nabû-zēru-iddin. Month III, day 24, year 16.

1 For the *šūrû*-tool, see glossary.
3 The stock of 12 ½ shekels is probably remainder or unused material from the amount originally given to Nabû-zēru-iddin for the making of the spades.

92. NCBT 770

Copy: Plate XXIII
Date: 05.XII.05(+) Nbk
Summary: *maḫir* receipt: iron tools

The tablet's surface is badly abraded. For Nabû-zēru-iddin (l. 3), the smith, see **No. 72**.

Obv. 17 MA.NA ⅓ GIN$_2$ AN.BAR
14 *mar-rat* AN.BAR^{me}
^{Id}AG-NUMUN-MU
4 $^{\text{lu}_2}$⸢SIMUG⸣ AN.BAR
Lo.E. IGI^{ir}
Rev. (blank)
^{iti}ŠE UD.5.⸢KAM⸣
MU.⸢5(+×).KAM⸣
^{d}AG-⸢NIG$_2$.DU-URU$_3$⸣
LUGAL ⸢TIN.TIR^{ki}⸣

17 minas 20 shekels of iron (in the form of) fourteen iron spades were received from Nabû-zēru-iddin, the blacksmith.
Month XII, day 5, year 5(+) of Nebuchadnezzar, king of Babylon.

93. YBC 9046

Copy: Plate XXIII
Date: 23.VI.09 (Npl/Nbk)
Summary: *maḫir* receipt: iron tools

For Nabû-zēru-iddin (l. 4), the smith, see **No. 72**.

Obv. 5 MA.NA 6 ½$^{!}$ GIN$_2$ AN.BAR$^{!}$
2 MAR AN.BAR^{me} 1 *kam-mat* AN.BAR
1 *ap-pa-ti* AN.BAR
^{Id}AG-NUMUN-MU *ma-ḫir*
⌈^{iti}KIN UD.23⌉.KAM
Lo.E. MU.9.KAM
Rev. (strokes) | | | | |

5 minas 6 ½ shekels of iron (in the form of) two iron spades, one iron dowel, one iron tip, were received from Nabû-zēru-iddin.
Month VI, day 23, year 9. *I I I I I.*

7 The five strokes on the reverse cannot correspond to the four iron tools, and might stand for the 5 minas of iron, as a rough summary. See also GC 2, 304, in which the 14 strokes correspond to the 14 containers of oil recorded as received in the text. Alternatively, the five strokes may have very well been unrelated and random.

94. NCBT 439

Copy: Plate XXIII
Date: 16.I.10 (Npl/Nbk)
Summary: *ina pāni* note: quivers

For Nabû-zēru-iddin (l. 3), the smith, see **No. 72**.

Obv. 3 ^{kuš}*til-li*
rak-su-tu ina IGI
^{Id}AG-NUMUN-MU ^{lu_2}SIMUG
Rev. (blank)
^{iti}BARA$_2$ UD.16.KAM
MU.10.KAM

Three bundled quivers are at the disposal of Nabû-zēru-iddin, the smith.
Month I, day 16, year 10.

1 C.f. ^{kuš}*til-la rak-su-tu* (YOS 17, 316: 1); see also Kleber 2014, 437.

95. YBC 11492

Copy: Plate XXIII
Date: 18.II.18 Nbk
Summary: *ina pāni* note: iron

Obv. 22 MA.NA ⅓ GIN$_2$
AN.BAR *a-*⸢*na*⸣ *dul-lu*
ina pa-⸢*ni*⸣ ^{I}⸢KAR⸣-^{d}EN
A ^{I}⸢^{d}AG⸣-NUMUN-⸢MU⸣
Rev. (blank)
^{iti}GU$_4$ UD.18.KAM MU.18.KAM
^{d}AG-NIG$_2$.DU-URU$_3$ LUGAL TIN.TIR^{ki}

22 minas 20 shekels of iron for work are at the disposal of Mušēzib-Bēl, son of Nabû-zēru-iddin.
Month II, day 18, year 18 of Nebuchadnezzar, king of Babylon.

96. YBC 8809

Copy: Plate XXIV
Date: 13.VI.24 Nbk
Summary: *ina pāni* note: iron

Obv. 8 MA.NA 10 GIN$_2$ A[N.BAR]
a-na dul-lu ina I[GI]
^{I}*mu-še-zib-*^{d}EN
A ^{Id}AG-NUMUN-⸢MU⸣
Lo.E. ^{lu_2}SIMUG AN.BAR
Rev. (blank)
^{iti}KIN UD.13.KAM
MU.24.KAM ^{d}AG-⸢NIG$_2$.DU-URU$_3$⸣
LUGAL TIN.TIR^{k}[^{i}]

8 minas 10 shekels of iron are at the disposal of Mušēzib-Bēl, son of Nabû-zēru-iddin, the blacksmith, for work.
Month VI, day 13, year 24 of Nebuchadnezzar, king of Babylon.

97. NCBT 429

Copy: Plate XXIV
Date: 06.I.22 Nbk
Summary: *maḫir* receipt (+ *ina pāni* clause): iron sickles

Obv. 1 MA.NA 4 GIN$_2$ AN.BAR *gam-ru*
5 NIG$_2$.GAL$_2$.LA-*a-ti* AN.BAR
^{I}*mu-še-zib-*^{d}EN A ⸢^{Id}AG⸣-NUMUN-MU
IGI^{ir}
⸢KA$_2$⸣*-ti* 20 *a-na*
Rev. ⸢*e-ṣe*⸣*-du ša*$_2$ *ṣa-pi-ti*

ina IGI ^{Id}AG-MU-DU A-*šu*$_2$
ša$_2$ ^{Id}*na-na-a*-KAM
^{iti}BARA$_2$ UD.6.KAM MU.22.KAM
^{d}AG-NIG$_2$.DU-URU$_3$ LUGAL TIN.TIR^{ki}

1 mina 4 shekels of processed iron (in the form of) five iron sickles were received from Mušēzib-Bēl, son of Nabû-zēru-iddin. (It is now) part of twenty (sickles) for the harvest of the *ṣapitu*-reed (that) are at the disposal of Nabû-šumu-ukīn, son of Nanāya-ēreš.
Month I, day 6, year 22 of Nebuchadnezzar, king of Babylon.

5 The term *bābtu*, which is translated throughout this volume as "part," is elusive and requires clarification. The CAD assigns *bābtu* three meanings: (1) quarter, (2) outstanding staple/goods (to be delivered in the future), (3) loss/deficit (CAD B, 9–10, s.v. *babtu*).[11] M. Kozuh, in his work on animal husbandry, concludes that in the phrase "N_1 *babti* N_2 sheared/ counted/ delivered sheep," N_1 is the number of animals recorded on the tablet, while N_2 is the aggregated number, which include N_1 and similar figures from a specific period (a shearing season, a year, etc.). He refers to N_1 as the *bābtu*-number and to N_2 as the *bābtu*-total (Kozuh 2014, 55). Kozuh's reading works in the context of what he terms "scribal daybooks," but less so in the wider context. Importantly, while N_1 can indeed be seen as the "*bābtu*-number," N_2 cannot be thought of as the *bābtu*-total. Again, in the "N_1 *babti* N_2 x" formula found in the scribal daybooks N_2 is indeed *an* aggregated total, but it is specifically juxtaposed against the *bābtu*.

The *bābtu* may be translated in a number of ways, according to context, but its basic meaning is "part (of a whole)." Importantly, it is a tangible part.[12] This is not an accounting fiction like debt, credit, or a modeled figure, but an actual amount of staples or goods. It is used when the focus of the text is on this tangible part, rather than on the whole or on an outstanding part (debt) of the whole. Von Soden notes that the relationship between his *bābtu* I (Stadtviertel) and *bābtu* II (Handelsgut) is unclear (AHw, 95, s.v. *bābtu* II). Yet since *bābtu* is not simply "Handelsgut," but in fact is by definition part of a whole, the relation between the two meanings of *bābtu* becomes clear. Like the administrative *bābtu*, a district or a city quarter is part of a larger defined area, one that can be discussed both as part of that larger unit, but also on its own. An additional etymological connection that is clarified by our reading is that between *bābtu* and *bābu* (KA$_2$), in the sense of "installment." The latter too is a tangible portion, payment in this case, of a larger whole. In the present case, the five sickles, which were delivered to the temple by Mušēzib-Bēl, are now in the possession of Nabû-šumu-ukīn to be used for the chopping of reeds.

98. YBC 9621

Copy: Plate XXIV
Date: 13.II.32 Nbk
Summary: *maḫir* receipt: iron

Obv. 7 MA.NA AN.BAR *gam-ru*
30 *se-ra-pi*

---

11 Kozuh (2014, 55) is right in noting that although no NB references are listed under meaning 2, all of the examples listed in meaning 3 are translated according to meaning 2. The AHw's *bābtu* I (Torbereich, Stadtviertel) parallels the CAD's meaning 1 and *bābtu* II (Handelsgut) corresponds to meanings 2 and 3 in the CAD (AHw, 94–5).

12 In this respect, the CAD's specification in meaning 2 that it is an "amount of staples, finished goods or merchandise" is valid.

ša$_2$ gi-iz-zu
4 1 *mu-še-lu-u$_2$*
Lo.E. ⸢*ša$_2$* E$_2$ ^{lu_2}⸣LUNGA^{me}
Rev. ^{I}⸢KAR⸣-^{d}EN ⸢^{lu_2}⸣SIMUG
AN.BAR *ma*-⸢*ḫi*⸣-*ir*
^{iti}GU$_4$ UD.13.KAM
MU.32.KAM
^{d}AG-NIG$_2$.DU-URU$_3$
Up.E. LUGAL TIN.TIR⸢^{ki}⸣

7 minas of processed iron (in the form of) thirty shears for shearing (and) one door latch of the brewers' workshop were received from Mušēzib-Bēl, the blacksmith.
Month II, day 13, year 32 of Nebuchadnezzar, king of Babylon.

4 Of the several meanings of *mušēlû*, "part of a lock" (for a door/canal), fits the context best. The translation "door latch" is tentative and is based on the basic meaning of *elû*, "to lift/raise."

99. NCBT 274

Copy: Plate XXIV
Date: 13.VIII.[×] Nbk
Summary: *maḫir* receipt: iron

Obv. ⸢7⸣ MA.NA ⅓ GIN$_2$ AN.BAR
⸢*gam*⸣-*ru* 5 GIR$_2$ AN.BAR^{me}
ša$_2$ iš-kar ^{I}KAR-^{d}EN
A-*šu$_2$ ša$_2$* ^{Id}AG-NUMUN-MU
⸢*ma*⸣-*ḫi-ir*
Rev. (blank)
^{iti} APIN UD.13.KAM ⸢MU⸣.[×.K]AM
^{d}AG-NIG$_2$.DU-URU$_3$
LUGAL TIN.TIR^{ki}

7 minas 20 shekels of processed iron (in the form of) five iron daggers, which are (his) *iškāru*-obligation, were received from Mušēzib-Bēl, son of Nabû-zēru-iddin.
Month VIII, day 13, year [×] of Nebuchadnezzar, king of Babylon.

100. YBC 9521

Copy: Plate XXIV
Date: 28.X.[×] Nbk
Summary: *maḫir* receipt: iron + *ina pāni* note

Obv. 2 MA.NA 10 GIN$_2$ *gam-ru* 1^{et} GIR$_2$ AN.BAR
dul-lu$^{!}$ BABBAR-*u$_2$*
⸢52⸣ GIN$_2$ 1^{en} *ma-aq-qar* AN.BAR
PAP 3 MA.NA 2 GIN$_2$
⸢AN.BAR *gam-ru*⸣
Lo.E. ^{I}*mu-še-*[*zib*]-⸢^{d}EN⸣

Rev. ⸢A ^{Id}AG-NUMUN-MU⸣ [I]GI^{ir}
⸢*ma-aq-qar* AN.BAR *ina pa-ni*⸣
⸢I⸣^{d}AG-⸢ŠEŠ-MU $^{lu_2?}$SIMUG$^{?}$⸣
10 ^{iti}AB UD.28.[KAM MU.×.KAM]
^{d}AG-NIG$_2$.DU-⸢URU$_3$ LUGAL TIN.TIR^{ki}⸣

2 minas 10 shekels of processed (iron in the form of) one iron dagger (for) cleaning work and 52 shekels (in the form of) one iron *maqqāru*-chisel; a total of 3 minas 2 shekels of processed iron were received from Mušēzib-Bēl, son of Nabû-zēru-iddin. (*The*) iron *maqqāru*-chisel is at the disposal of Nabû-aḫu-iddin, the *smith*.
Month X, day 28, year [×] of Nebuchadnezzar, king of Babylon.

1–2 It is unclear how exactly the iron dagger relates to "white work," i.e., for cleaning. Perhaps a scraper-like tool is meant that would have a use particularly in leatherworking? Note that at more than one kg., this was a sizable tool.

101. YBC 6894

Copy: Plate XXV
Date: 07.XI.32 Nbk
Summary: *maḫir* receipt: iron tools

Obv. 4 ⅚ MA.NA AN.BAR
gam-ru
1 *na-aḫ-šip-ti*
4 ⸢*u*$_3$⸣ 1 *qul-mu-u*$_2$
Lo.E. ⸢I⸣KAR-^{d}EN
Rev. ⸢^{lu_2}SIMUG⸣ AN.BAR
ma-ḫi-ir
^{iti}⸢ZIZ$_2$⸣ UD.7.KAM
9 ⸢MU.32⸣.KAM
Up.E. ^{d}AG-NIG$_2$.DU-URU$_3$
LUGAL E^{ki}

4 ⅚ minas of processed iron (in the form of) one shovel and one *qulmû*-axe were received from Mušēzib-Bēl, the blacksmith.
Month XI, day 7, year 32 of Nebuchadnezzar, king of Babylon.

102. YBC 9417

Copy: Plate XXV
Date: 10$^{?}$.II.25 Nbk
Summary: *maḫir* receipt: iron

The tablet is unfired.

Obv. 3 ⅔° MA.NA° 5 GIN$_2$
AN.BAR *gam-ri* 2 ⸢ḪAR$^{?me}$⸣
ša$_2$ LUGAL ^{I}*mu*$^{!}$-*še-zib*-^{d}EN

⸢A ^{I}⸣^{d}AG-NUMUN-MU
⸢IGI⸣-*ir*
Rev. ^{iti}GU$_4$ UD.⸢10$^?$⸣.KAM
MU.25.KAM ^{d}AG-⸢NIG$_2$.DU-URU$_3$⸣
LUGAL TIN.TIR⸢^{ki}⸣

3 ⅔ minas 5 shekels of processed iron (in the form of) two *rings* of the king were received from Mušēzib-Bēl, son of Nabû-zēru-iddin.
Month II, Day 10$^?$, year 25 of Nebuchadnezzar, king of Babylon.

2 The reading of the damaged sign ḪAR$^?$ (*semeru*, "ring/shackles") is uncertain. Moreover, if the reading is correct, it is difficult to understand it in context, as "royal ring/shackles" seems to make little sense. One may suggest that the target of the shackles were omitted by mistake, e.g., (royal) slave/worker/official, etc.

103. NCBT 757

Copy: Plate XXV
Date: 11.II.14 Nbk
Summary: withdrawal (*našû*) + delivery (*šūbulu*) note: silver and iron

The tablet's surface is badly abraded. The text is probably part of the "early Tyre dossier"; see Kleber 2008, 144; Zaia 2021.

Obv. 10 MA.NA ⸢KU$_3$⸣.BABBAR *ša$_2$ ina* ŠU^{II} ^{I}*ši-rik-ti*
na-ša$_2$-a'
⸢5$^?$⸣ GUN 49 MA.NA 10 GIN$_2$ AN.BAR ⸢*gam-ru*⸣
4 *na-*⸢*aš$_2$*⸣*-ḫe-pe-*⸢*e*⸣*-ti*
⸢94⸣ *ḫa-*⸢*lil*⸣*-a-ni ina* ŠU^{II}
^{I}*nad-na-a* A ^{I}⸢*am*⸣*-me-ni-il$_3$*
^{I}⸢*šu-la-a*⸣ A ⸢^{I}IR$_3$⸣*-a*
Lo.E. *a-na* ^{lu_2}*qi$_2$-i-pi šu-bu-u*[*l*]
Rev. (blank)
⸢^{iti}GU$_4$⸣ UD.11.KAM MU.14.KAM
^{Id}AG-NIG$_2$.DU-URU$_3$
LUGAL TIN.TIR^{ki}

10 minas of silver that were brought by Širiktu (and) 5 talents 49 minas 10 shekels of processed iron (in the form of) four shovels and ninety-four *ḫālilu*-tools were delivered to the *qīpu* by Nadnāya, son of Ammēni-il, (and) Šulāya, son of Ardāya.
Month II, day 11, year 14 of Nebuchadnezzar, king of Babylon.

104. NCBT 716

Copy: Plate XXV
Date: 23.X.23 Nbk
Summary: account balance: iron[13]

Obv. NIG$_2$.KA$_9$ *ša*$_2$ AN.BAR
na-dan u ma-ḫar ma-la
a-na ^{I}IR$_3$-^{d}AG A-*šu*$_2$
ša$_2$ ^{I}*ša*$_2$-^{d}AG-*šu-u*$_2$ SUM^{mu}
it-ti ^{I}IR$_3$-^{d}AG
Lo.E. *ep*$_2$-*šu*$_2$-⌜*u*⌝
Rev. AN.⌜BAR⌝ *gam-ri* IGI^{ir}
i-di-šu$_2$ ⌜*e-ṭir*⌝
(blank)
^{iti}AB UD.23.KAM
MU.17.KAM ^{d}AG-NIG$_2$.DU-URU$_3$
Up.E. LUGAL TIN.TIR^{ki}
Le.E. {eras.}

The account of the iron (for) trade, as much as was given to Arad-Nabû, son of Ša-Nabû-šū, is settled with Arad-Nabû; the processed iron was received (from him and) his wages have been paid.
Month X, day 23, year 17 of Nebuchadnezzar, king of Babylon.

105. NCBT 504

Copy: Plate XXV
Date: 16.X.-- (Npl/Nbk)
Summary: accounting inventory: iron (and silver)

Three of the listed individuals can probably be identified elsewhere in the Eanna archive: Arad-Nanāya, the leatherworker (YOS 17, 233, 16 Nbk), Bēl-ana-mātišu/Nabû-ušallim (AUWE 5, 94, 16 Npl), and Nabû-šumu-ibni/Aḫḫēa (PTS 2550, 5 Nbk). The tablet was thus written during the reign of either Nabopolassar or Nebuchadnezzar.

Obv. 1 MAR AN.BAR *ina* IGI ^{I}ŠEŠ^{meš}-*ši*
1 ⌜*ba-ab-ti*⌝ 2$^{?}$ ^{Id}AG$^{!}$-NUMUN-DU$_3$ ⌜^{lu_2}⌝ENGAR
1 {eras.} ^{Id}AG-MU-DU$_3$ A ^{I}ŠEŠ^{me}-*e*-<*a*>
1 *ba-ab-ti* 2$^{?}$ ^{Id}*na-na-a*-KAM ⌜*u*$_3$⌝
1 *ina* IGI ^{Id}EN-*ana*-KUR-*šu*$_2$ A$^{!}$ ^{Id}AG-GI
1 *ina* ⌜IGI⌝ ^{Id}U.GUR-SUR
Lo.E. 1 *ina* IGI ^{I}ŠEŠ^{me}-*ša*$_2$-*a*
1 *ina* IGI ^{I}DUG$_3$.GA-UNUG^{ki}
Rev. ½ MA.NA ^{I}IR$_3$-^{d}*na-na-a* ^{lu_2}AŠGAB$^{!}$
^{f}*ana*-^{d}*na-na-a-ši-i* DAM-*su* ^{I}E$_2^{!}$.AN.NA$^{!}$-*li-pu*-PAP
$^{f!d}$*ba-ba*$_6$-*e-ṭe*-⌜*rat*⌝ DUMU^{me}-*šu*$_2$ *ina* ŠU^{II} ^{I}*ša*$_2$-*lam*

[13] A previous edition is included in Payne 2007, 51–2.

A-*šu*$_2$ *ša*$_2$ ^{I}⸢*nu*⸣-*uḫ-tim*$^{!}$-*mu* <^{lu2}>$^{?}$URU-<^{d}>GAŠAN-*ia*$_2$-*a-a* SUR$^{!}$-*ru-nu*
10 GIN$_2$ ^{I}DUG$_3$.GA-UNUG^{ki} ^{lu2}*šir*$_3$-*ku ana* ⸢UGU⸣
ti-ib-ni ^{iti}AB UD.16.KAM
Up.E. × (or scratches?)

One iron spade is at the disposal of Aḫḫēšu; one, out of (a total of) two, (*is at the disposal of*) Nabû-zēru-ibni, the plowman; one (*is at the disposal of*) Nabû-šumu-ibni, son of Aḫḫēa; one, out of (a total of) two, (*is at the disposal of*) Nanāya-ēreš *and* one is at the disposal of Bēl-ana-mātišu, son of Nabû-ušallim; one is at the disposal of Nergal-ēṭir; one is at the disposal of Aḫḫēšāya; one is at the disposal of Ṭāb-Uruk.
½ mina (for) Arad-Nanāya, the leatherworker, ^{f}Ana-Nanāya-šī, his wife, Eanna-līpi-uṣur (and) ^{f}Baba-eṭerat, his children, was paid by Šalam, son of *Nuḫtimmu*, from Āl-Bēltiya; 10 shekels (given to)$^{?}$ Ṭāb-Uruk, the temple serf, on account of straw.
Month X, day 16.

2, 4 For *bābtu* see commentary to **No. 97**: 5.

106. YBC 9271

Copy: Plate XXVI
Date: --.VI.33 Nbk
Summary: promissory note: silver (no witnesses)

Obv. 22 MA.NA AN.BAR *re-ḫe-et* KU$_3$.BABBAR
⸢*ra-šu-tu*⸣ *ša*$_2$ ^{I}NUMUN-*tu*$_2$ A-*šu*$_2$ *ša*$_2$ ^{Id}UTU-⸢SU⸣
ša$_2$ *ina* UGU ^{I}DU-^{d}AMAR.UTU A ^{I}*mu*-⸢*ra-nu*⸣
⸢*ina* UGU⸣ ^{I}AD-NU.ZU ^{lu2}*si*$^{?!}$-⸢*pir*⸣
(blank)
Rev. (blank)
^{iti}KIN MU.33.KAM ^{d}AG-NIG$_2$.DU-URU$_3$
⸢LUGAL⸣ TIN.TIR^{ki}

22 minas of iron, the remainder of silver, the credit of Zērūtu, son of Šamaš-erība, vis-à-vis Mukīn-Marduk, son of Murānu, is owed by Abu-ul-īde, the *alphabet scribe*.
Month VI, day --, year 33 of Nebuchadnezzar, king of Babylon.

107. NCBT 1235

Copy: Plate XXVI
Date: undated (*Nbk*)
Summary: *ina pāni* note: (multiple) iron tools

None of the listed individuals can be securely identified in additional texts. The only mentionable case is that of Ša-Nanāya-tašmēt. This relatively rare name is attested is attested between 11 Nbk (YOS 17, 334) and 30 Nbk (NBC 4711).

Obv. ^{giš}MAR AN.BAR *u* ^{giš}*rap-šu*$_2$ *ina* IGI ^{I}*ša*$_2$-^{d}*na*-⸢*na*⸣-*a-taš-met ša*$_2$ ^{Id}AG-MU-DU$_3$
^{giš}MAR AN.BAR *u* ^{giš}*rap-šu*$_2$ *ša*$_2$ ^{I}TIN^{su} ⸢A ^{I}⸣^{d}*na-na-a*-DU$_3$$^{!uš}$
ina IGI ^{I}SUM.NA-*a* A ^{I}*za-bi-da-a*

^{gi}[^{š}]MAR AN.BAR *ša*$_2$ ^{Id}UTU-DU$_3$^{uš} *ina* IGI ^{I}*ša*$_2$-^{d}*na*-<<*na*>>-*na-a-taš-met*
⸢^{giš}⸣MAR *ša*$_2$ ^{I}*tab-ne*$_2$*-e-a* *ina* IGI ^{I}*ša*$_2$-^{d}*na-na-a-*⸢*taš*⸣*-met*
^{giš}MAR *ša*$_2$ ^{Id}AG-MU-MU *ina* IGI ^{Id}*na-na-a-*⸢*šar*$^{?}$⸣*-di-nu*
^{giš}MAR *ša*$_2$ E$_2$.AN$^{\circ}$.NA *ša*$_2$ *ina* IGI ^{Id}AMAR.UTU-MU-⸢×⸣
(tiny line) *ina* IGI ^{I}*ša*$_2$-^{d}*n*[*a-na-a-taš-met*]
Lo.E. [^{gi}]^{š}MAR *ša*$_2$ E$_2$.AN.NA *ša*$_2$ *ina* IGI ^{I}⸢^{d}× ×⸣[(×) *ša*$_2$]
[^{l}]$^{\text{u}_2}$*qi*$_2$*-i-pi* ^{I}SUM.NA-*a* *it-ta-din*
Rev. ^{giš}MAR *ša*$_2$ E$_2$.AN.NA *ša*$_2$ *ina* IGI ^{Id}EN-NUMUN<-(×)$^{?}$>
ina IGI ^{I}*ša*$_2$-^{d}*na-na-a-taš-met*

An iron spade and a hoe are at the disposal of Ša-Nanāya-tašmēt on behalf of Nabû-šumu-ibni; an iron spade and a hoe of Balāssu, son of Nanāya-īpuš, are at the disposal of Iddināya, son of Zabidāya; an iron spade of Šamaš-īpuš is at the disposal of Ša-Nanāya-tašmēt; a spade of Tabnēa is at the disposal of Ša-Nanāya-tašmēt; a spade of Nabû-šumu-iddin is at the disposal of Nanāya-*šar-di-nu;* a spade of Eanna that was at the disposal of Marduk-šumu-× is (now) at the disposal of Ša-Na[nāya-tašmēt]; Iddināya gave a spade of Eanna that was at the disposal of … [… *of*] the *qīpu;* a spade of Eanna that was at the disposal of Bēl-zēri is (now) at the disposal of Ša-Nanāya-tašmēt.

6 The name ^{Id}*na-na-a-*⸢*šar*$^{?}$⸣*-di-nu* is unclear. On may also consider ^{Id}*na-na-a-*⸢MU/NUMUN-SI⸣. SA$_2$<<*nu*>>, or perhaps even ^{I}<*ša*$_2$>-^{d}*na-na-a-*⸢*taš*⸣<<*di*>>-*met*$^{!}$.

108. YBC 11288

Copy: Plate XXVI
Date: 13.I.23 (Nbk)
Summary: *ina pāni* note: a rope and an axe

Nanāya-ēreš/Ša-Nabû-šū (ll. 3–4) is to be identified with the decurion attested in YBC 9407 (17 Nbk).

Obv. 1 *aš*$_2$*-lu*
1 *qul-mu-u*$_2$ AN.⸢BAR⸣
ina IGI ^{Id}*na-na-a*-KAM
A ^{I}*ša*$_2$-^{d}AG-*šu*$_2$*-u*
Rev. (blank)
^{iti}BARA$_2$ UD.13.KAM
MU.23.KAM

One rope and one iron *qulmû*-axe are at the disposal of Nanāya-ēreš, son of Ša-Nabû-šū. Month I, day 13, year 23.

109. YBC 11658

Copy: Plate XXVI
Date: 09.III.43 (Nbk)
Summary: *ina pāni* note: iron

The tablet is unfired.

Obv. [× AN].⸢BAR⸣ *ir-bu* AN.BAR
ina IGI ^{I}⸢^{d}INNIN$^{?}$⸣-DU-A
A ^{I}NUMUN$^{?!}$-*tu*$_{2}$
Rev. (blank)
⸢^{iti}⸣SIG$_{4}$
⸢UD⸣.9.KAM
[M]U.43.KAM

[...], the income of iron, is at the disposal of Ištar-mukīn-apli, son of *Zērūtu*.
Month III, day 9, year 43.

1 The first preserved sign may alternatively be ½, part of a quantity notation.

110. YBC 8796
Copy: Plate XXVI
Date: 27.XII.15 Nbk
Summary: *ina pāni* note: iron

Obv. [×] ⸢MA.NA AN.BAR⸣ *a-na* MAR AN.BAR^{me} <<*ina*>>
u na-aš$_{2}$*-ḫi-pe-e-tu*$_{2}$ AN.BAR *ina* IGI
^{Id}EN-NIGIN^{ir} A ^{I}*na-din* ^{lu_2}SIMUG
(blank)
Rev. (blank)
^{iti}ŠE UD.27.KAM MU.15.KAM
^{d}AG-NIG$_{2}$.DU-URU$_{3}$ LUGAL TIN.TIR^{ki}

[×] mina(s) of iron for iron spades and shovels are at the disposal of Bēl-upaḫḫir, son of Nādinu, the smith.
Month XII, day 27, year 15 of Nebuchadnezzar, king of Babylon.

111. YBC 8804
Copy: Plate XXVI
Date: [×.×.× RN]
Summary: *ina pāni* note: iron

Obv. 40 MA.NA ⸢AN.BAR⸣
ina IGI ^{Id}*n*[*a-na-a*-KAM$^{?}$]
^{lu_2}SIMUG AN.[BAR]
Rev. (blank)
4 [...]
Up.E. ⸢LUGAL⸣ [TIN.TIR^{ki}]

40 minas of iron are at the disposal of Na[nāya-*ēreš*] the blacksmith.
[Month ×, day ×, year × of RN], king [of Babylon].

112. NBC 4625

Copy: Plate XXVII
Date: 23.XIIb.42 Nbk
Summary: *ina pāni* note: iron

Obv. 1 ^{giš}*kap-pu* AN.BAR
ina IGI ^{I}KI-E$_2$.AN.NA-*bu-di-ia*$_2$
^{lu_2}*ma/ba-la-a*
4 ^{iti}DIRI.ŠE.KIN.KUD
Lo.E. ⸢UD⸣.23.KAM
Rev. MU.42.KAM
^{d}AG-NIG$_2$.DU-URU$_3$
LUGAL TIN.TIR^{ki}

One iron *kappu*-bowl is at the disposal of Itti-Eanna-būdia, the ….
Month XIIb, day 23, year 42 of Nebuchadnezzar, king of Babylon.

3 The meaning of ^{lu_2}*ma/ba-la-a* is unknown. The reading of the signs is clear, and thus ^{lu_2}*ma-la-ḫu*$^{!}$ seems highly unlikely. A leatherworker named Itti-Eanna-būdia is attested in YOS 17, 362: 8 (14 Nbk). Thus, notwithstanding the chronological gap, one might read l. 3 as ^{lu_2}*aš*$_2^{!}$*-la-ku*$^{!}$.

113. NCBT 416

Copy: Plate XXVII
Date: 06.IV.38 (Nbk)
Summary: *ina pāni* note: iron spades

Obv. 2 ⸢^{giš}MAR⸣ AN.BAR^{meš}
ina IGI ^{Id}⸢AMAR.UTU-MU-DU$_3$⸣
⸢A ^{I}⸣TIN^{su} ⸢*a-na*⸣
⸢*dul-lu*⸣
Rev. (blank)
5 ^{iti}ŠU UD.6.⸢KAM⸣
MU.38.KAM

Two iron spades are at the disposal of Marduk-šumu-ibni, son of Balāssu, for work.
Month IV, day 6, year 38.

114. NCBT 263

Copy: Plate XXVII
Date: 01.IX.22 Nbk
Summary: *ina pāni* note: iron sickles

Obv. 5-*ta* NIG$_2$.GAL$_2$.LA AN.BAR
ina IGI ^{I}*tak-la-a-ta*
ša$_2$ *a-na* UGU *šam-mu*
šap-ru
(blank)

Rev. (blank)
^{iti}GAN UD.1.KAM MU.22.KAM
^{d}AG-NIG$_2$.DU-URU$_3$ LUGAL TIN.⸢TIR^{ki}⸣

Five iron sickles are at the disposal of Taklāta, who was sent for (cutting) grass.
Month IX, day 1, year 22 of Nebuchadnezzar, king of Babylon.

115. NCBT 78

Copy: Plate XXVII
Date: 03.I.23 Nbk
Summary: *ina pāni* note: iron tool

Obv. 1 *ṣip-te*$^{!(T. pi)}$*-ti* AN.BAR
ina pa-ni ^{I}*ba-la-ṭu*
⸢A⸣ ^{I}*šu-ma-a*
Rev. ^{iti}BARA$_2$ UD.3.KAM
MU.23.⸢KAM⸣
^{d}AG-NIG$_2$.DU-URU$_3$
LUGAL TIN.TIR^{ki}

One iron fetter is at the disposal of Balāṭu, son of Šumāya.
Month I, day 3, year 23 of Nebuchadnezzar, king of Babylon.

116. NCBT 1019

Copy: Plate XXVII
Date: 22.[×.×] --
Summary: *ina pāni* note: iron tools

Obv. ⸢20 ×⸣ [...] ⸢×⸣ AN.BAR
[ ] ⸢× ×⸣ AN.BAR
[P]A ḪA AK TI AN.BAR
[ ] ŠU$_2$ ME
[ ] × 1$^?$ GIR$^?$ *ina* IGI
Rev. ^{Id}EN-*iq-bi*
A-*šu*$_2$ *ša*$_2$ ^{I} BA^{ša_2}-*a*
^{Id}*na-na-a*-ŠEŠ-MU
⸢A⸣-*šu*$_2$ *ša*$_2$ ^{Id}EN-DU$_3$
^{iti}⸢×⸣ UD.22.KAM
Up.E. [MU.×.K]AM

... (five lines concerning iron, but too damaged to be translated) ... are at the disposal of Bēl-iqbi, son of Iqīša, (and) Nanāya-aḫu-iddin, son of Bēl-ibni.
Month ⸢×⸣, day 22, year [×].

117. NCBT 1098

Copy: Plate XXVIII
Date: 14.VII.14 Nbk
Summary: *ina pāni* note: iron tools

Obv. 11 ½ MA.NA AN.BAR *gam-ri*
1 MAR AN.BAR
2 *qul-lu-ma-a*$^{!}$*-ta*
1 *na-aš*$_{2}$*-ḫi-ip-ti*
5 *ina* IGI ^{I}*ba-ni-ia*$^{!}$ A ^{I}⌜^{d}EN-*re-man*⌝*-ni*
ša$_{2}$ *a-na* UGU *ku-pur*
a$^{!}$*-na* ^{uru}*i-ti šap-ri*
Lo.E. 12 ½ MA.NA ⌜AN.BAR⌝ *gam-ri*
9 1 MAR AN.BAR 1 *na-aš*$_{2}$*-ḫi-ip-tu*$_{2}$
Rev. 2 *qul-lu-ma-a-ta*
1 NIG$_{2}$.GAL$_{2}$.LA *ina* IGI
^{Id}AG-MU-KAM ^{lu2}MA$_{2}$.LAḪ$_{4}$
(blank)
^{iti}DU$_{6}$ UD.14.KAM MU.14.KAM
^{d}AG-NIG$_{2}$.DU-URU$_{3}$ ⌜LUGAL⌝ TIN.TIR^{ki}

11 ½ minas of processed iron (in the form of) one iron spade, two *qulmû*-axes and 1 shovel at the disposal of Bānia, son of Bēl-rēmanni, who was sent to Itu on account of bitumen.
12 ½ minas of processed iron (in the form of) one iron spade, two *qulmû*-axes, one shovel and one sickle, at the disposal of Nabû-šumu-ēreš, the boatman.
Month VII, day 14, year 14 of Nebuchadnezzar, king of Babylon.

118. NCBT 71

Copy: Plate XXVIII
Date: 17.XII.36 Nbk
Summary: *ina pāni* note: iron tools

Obv. 20 *se-ra-pi* ⌜AN.BAR^{me}⌝
ša$_{2}$ *gi-iz-zu*$^{!}$
[*ina*] IGI ^{Id}UTU-LUGAL-⌜*bul*⌝*-liṭ*
Lo.E. ⌜*ša*$_{2}$⌝ ^{lu2}*qi*$_{2}$*-i-pi*
Rev. ^{iti}ŠE UD.17.KAM
6 MU.36.KAM
^{d}AG-NIG$_{2}$.DU-URU$_{3}$
Up.E. LUGAL E⌜^{ki}⌝

Twenty iron shears for shearing are at the disposal of Šamaš-šarru-bulliṭ, (man) of the *qīpu*.
Month XII, day 17, year 36 of Nebuchadnezzar, king of Babylon.

3–4 The phrase *Šamaš-šarru-bulliṭ ša qīpi* is unclear and it seems that either the shearing or Šamaš-šarru-bulliṭ, or both, were under the responsibility of the *qīpu*. Thirty-five years later, a man by that name would be the *qīpu* of the Sealand (PTS 2130, 4 Cyr), but there is no reason to connect him to the present text.

119. NCBT 942

Copy: Plate XXVIII
Date: 02.I.20 (*Nbk*)
Summary: *ina pāni* note: iron tools

All known attestations of Nabû-šumu-ēreš / Zību come from undated tablets: NCBT 1208, NCBT 665, PTS 2446, GC 2, 307. Of these, NCBT 1208 can probably be dated to the reign of Nebuchadnezzar, based on prosopography.[14]

Obv. 2-*ta* MAR AN.BAR^{me}
ina IGI ^{Id}AG-MU-KAM
⸢A⸣-*šu*$_2$ ⸢*ša*$_2$⸣ ^{I}*zi-i-bu*
Rev. (blank)
^{iti}BARA$_2$ UD.2.KAM
MU.20{eras.}$^{?}$.KAM

Two iron spades are at the disposal of Nabû-šumu-ēreš, son of Zību.
Month I, day 2, year 20.

120. NCBT 971

Copy: Plate XXVIII
Date: 11$^{?}$.X.03 -- (*early Achaemenid*)
Summary: *ina pāni* note: iron tools

If Iddināya is the blacksmith attested in **No. 304**: 36′ (see Payne 2007, 321, s.v. Nadnāya), then the present text can be roughly dated to the early Achaemenid period as well.

Obv. 3 *qul-mu*$^{!(T.\ kur)}$ AN.BAR
ša$_2$ *ina* IGI ^{I}SUM.NA-*a*
A ^{I}*e-ṭir ina* IGI
^{Id}INNIN.NA-MU-URU$_3$
Lo.E. A ^{I}*ša*$_2$*-rid*
Rev. (blank)
^{iti}AB UD.11$^{\circ ?}$.KAM
MU.3.KAM

Three iron *qulmû*-axes that (were) at the disposal of Iddināya, son of Ēṭeru, (are now) at the disposal of Innin-šumu-uṣur, son of Šarīd.
Month X, day 11$^{?}$, year 3.

[14] Two men in NCBT 1208 are listed in at least one additional texts together, NCBT 650, dated to 15 Nbk.

121. YBC 9641

Copy: Plate XXVIII
Date: 09.II.41 (Nbk)
Summary: *ina pāni* note: iron tools

All twelve attestations of Rēmūtu / Nergal-iddin known to us from the Eanna archive fall between 17 Nbk (YBC 9407) and 39 Nbk (NBC 4837). Thus even though none of these is attested with a family name, it is reasonable to assume that most (if not all) should be identified with the present Rēmūtu / Nergal-iddin; note especially GC 1, 51 (36 Nbk) in which he has at his disposal an iron tool.

Obv. 4 NIG$_2$.GAL$_2$.LA AN.BAR
ina IGI ^{I}*re-mut* A ^{Id}U.GUR-MU
3 *ina* IGI ^{Id}EN-*tu-kul-*⌜*la*$^{!}$⌝*-tu-u*$_2$*-a*
u ^{I}*ana*-E$_2$-*šu*$_2$
Rev. (blank)
⌜^{iti}⌝GU$_4$ UD.9.KAM
MU.41.KAM

Four iron sickles are at the disposal of Rēmūtu, son of Nergal-iddin; three are at the disposal of Bēl-tuklātū᾿a and Ana-bītišu.
Month II, day 9, year 41.

122. NCBT 478

Copy: Plate XXIX
Date: 15.VII.02 (Cyr–Camb)
Summary: *ina pāni* note: iron tools

A bird-catcher by the name of Šamaš-iddin is attested in YOS 7, 69 (8 Cyr), and two are listed in TCL 13, 168 (5 Camb). Another attestation is found in GC 2, 273, written in the 16th year of an unknown king; probably 16 (Nbn), possibly 16 (Dar).

Obv. 3 *na-aš*$_2$*-ḫi-pe-e-ti* AN.BAR
5 *ḫa-lil* AN.BAR^{me}
a-na ḫi-⌜*ru-tu*⌝ *ša*$_2$ ID$_2$
ša$_2$ ^{garim}⌜E$_2$⌝ ^{d}30-*ka-*⌜*rab*⌝-ŠE.GA
ina IGI ^{I}LU$_2$-^{d}*na-na-a*
Lo.E. *u* ^{Id}*na-na-a*-ŠEŠ-MU
Rev. 3 MAR AN.BAR^{me}
ina IGI ^{Id}UTU-MU ^{lu2}MUŠEN.DU$_3$<<^{me}>>
u ina IGI ^{Id}UTU-SU A ^{I}KU$_4$-*šu*$_2$
^{iti}DU$_6$ UD.15.KAM
MU.2.KAM

Three iron shovels (and) five iron *ḫālilu*-tools, for the excavation of the canal of the irrigation district of Bīt-Sîn-karābu-šime, are at the disposal of Amīl-Nanāya and Nanāya-aḫu-iddin. Three iron spades are at the disposal of Šamaš-iddin, the bird-catcher, and at the disposal of Šamaš-erība, son of Erībšu.

Month VII, day 15, year 2.

4 Bīt-Sîn-karābu-šime is not listed by Zadok in RGTC 8. Note however the following attestations: YOS 7, 23, PTS 2309, and specifically *tamirtu ša Bīt-Sîn-karābu-šime* in YOS 21, 17: 17.

123. YBC 11305

Copy: Plate XXIX
Date: undated
Summary: inventory list: varia

The context and most of the content of this list are unclear. The scribe's handwriting can be described as rigid. The signs are straight and pressed hard against the clay. It is somewhat similar in appearance to tablets produced by modern students of Assyriology, experimenting with writing cuneiform; it lacks the natural flow of a skilled scribe.

Obv. AN.BAR *na-aš$_2$-ḫe-pe-<e-ti>*
1-et ^{tug_2}*da*$^?$*-ap-al-ti*
1-et ze-ri-in-nu-ut-ti ša$_2$ ḫu-ur-ra-ti
1-et ze-ri-in-nu-ut-ti$^!$ *ša$_2$ u$_2$-di-e*$^{!?(T. du)}$
ZABAR 8 *ri-sa*$^?$*-a-*⸢*ta*$^?$⸣
Lo.E. *1-en kak*$^?$*-ku*$^?$ *zu-um-bu*
1-en ^{giš}*ma-aš$_2$-ša$_2$-nu* GAL⸢$^{u_2?}$⸣
Rev. (uninscribed)

Iron shovels; one *dapastu*-cover; one *ze-ri-in-nu-ut-ti* for *madder*, one *ze-ri-in-nu-ut-ti* for bronze *equipment*, eight …, *fly* (*shaped*) *weapon*, one large set of tongs.

2 The *dapastu* was used to cover furniture, or possibly as a pillow; see Quillien 2022, 449–50.

3, 4 *ze-ri-in-nu-ut-ti* is unclear. The identical spelling in both lines suggests that this should be thought of as a simple scribal error. The fact that in both cases there is some uncertainty regarding the second part of the phrase makes the interpretation even more difficult: *ḫu-ur-ra-ti* is an unexpected spelling for *ḫurātu* (madder), and *u$_2$-di-e*$^{!?(T. du)}$ (equipment/tools) requires amending a scribal error. Additionally, even if both readings are correct, it is difficult to see how both would work in a parallel phrase.

124. YBC 16018

Copy: Plate XXIX
Date: 22.XI.18 --
Summary: *maḫir* receipt (+ *ina pāni* note$^?$): iron

Note the finger print above the date formula.

Obv. ⸢×⸣ 2 ½ M[A$^?$.NA$^?$ (×+)] 1 GIN$_2$ A[N-BAR]
a-na ⸢× × × ×⸣^{me}
⸢*ina* IGI ^{Id}EN/AG$^?$-×⸣
4 ^{lu_2}⸢SIMUG⸣ AN.BAR
Lo.E. IGI^{ir}
Rev. (finger print)

⸢^{iti}⸣ZIZ$_2$^{o} ⸢UD⸣.22.KAM
MU.18.KAM

× 2 ½ *m*[*inas* (×+)] *1 shekel*(*s*) of i[ron] for ..., which (was?) at the disposal of ... the blacksmith, was received (from him).
Month XI, day 22, year 18.

125. NCBT 1036

Copy: Plate XXIX
Date: 25.IV.08 (*Npl*)
Summary: *maḫir* receipt + *ina pāni* note: iron

Nanāya-ēreš is most probably the blacksmith attested in NCBT 1093 (20 Kan); see Payne 2007, 322–3. It is reasonable to assume that the eighth year in the present text should be attributed to Nabopolassar.

Obv. 1 MA.NA ⸢AN⸣.BAR
1-*en ṣib-te*!-*e-ti*
^{Id}*na-na-a*-KAM IGI^{ir}[⸢^{r}⸣]
4 *ina* IGI ^{Id}AG-G[I (×)]
Lo.E. ^{lu_2}SAG [LUGAL?]
Rev. (blank)
^{iti}ŠU UD.25.KAM
MU.8.KAM

1 mina of iron (in the form of) one fetter was received from Nanāya-ēreš. It is at the disposal of Nabû-ušallim, the *co*[*urtier*].
Month IV, day 25, year 8.

126. NBC 4694

Copy: Plate XXIX
Date: 07.IX.32 Nbk
Summary: *maḫir* receipt + *ina pāni* note: iron

Obv. 15 ⸢GIN$_2$ AN.BAR⸣
^{Id}EN-⸢DU$_3$^{uš}⸣ [× ×] ⸢×⸣ [(×)]
ma-ḫi-ir a-⸢*na dul-lu*⸣
ina IGI ^{I}KI-E$_2$.⸢AN.NA-*bu-di*⸣-<*ia*>
5 *ina lib$_3$-bi* 4 *a*-⸢*na*⸣
Lo.E. *u$_2$-re-e ina pa*-⸢*ni*⸣
^{I}*bi-bi-e-a*
Rev. (blank)
⸢^{iti}GAN⸣ UD.7.KAM MU.32.KAM
^{d}AG-⸢NIG$_2$⸣.DU-URU$_3$ LUGAL TIN.TIR^{ki}

15 shekels of iron were received from Bēl-īpuš …; they are at the disposal of Itti-Eanna-būdia for work. From these, 4 (shekels) for the stables are at the disposal of Bibēa.
Month IX, day 7, year 32 of Nebuchadnezzar, king of Babylon.

2 A blacksmith by the name of Bēl-īpuš/Ērišu is known from YOS 17, 310: 7 (^{I}⸢*e**-*ri**⸣-*ši* collated); note, however, that YOS 17, 310 was written almost 20 years earlier, in 6 Nbk.

3 For the uncommon sequence (*ma-ḫi-ir* +) *a-na dul-lu ina* IGI, see **No. 308**: 34′.

127. NBC 4541

Copy: Plate XXX
Date: 03.VIII.14 --
Summary: *maḫir* receipt + *ina pāni* note: iron tools

Obv. 12 MAR^{me} AN.BAR
^{I}*ta-ri-bi* IGI^{ir}
15 MAR^{me} AN.BAR *ina* IGI-*šu*$_2$
Rev. (blank)
^{iti}APIN UD.3.KAM
MU.14.KAM

Twelve iron spades were received from Tarību. Fifteen iron spades are (still) at his disposal. Month VIII, day 3, year 14.

2 A certain Tarību receives iron in a similar text, NCBT 259, which is dated to Month XI, day 9, year 14 Npl. If this is the same individual, then the present text should probably be dated to the 14th year of Nabopolassar as well.

128. NCBT 791

Copy: Plate XXX
Date: 13.X.09 (Npl)
Summary: *maḫir* receipt + *ina pāni* note: iron tools

For Šadûnu (l. 7), see **No. 2** and for Nanāya-ēreš (l. 5), see **No. 125**.

Obv. [×] ½ ⸢MA⸣.NA 5 GIN$_2$ AN.BAR
⸢5⸣ *mu-ṣib-bi-ta-nu* 12 *ak-kul-lat*$^{!(T.\ ša_2)}$-*ta*
na-aṣ-bar ap-pat$^{!(T.\ kur)}$ *kam-mat šu*$^{!}$-*ri-a*$^{!?(T.\ ša_2)}$-*nu*
šik-kat$_2^{!○}$ *ša*$_2^{!(T.\ 4)}$-*ḫi-il*$^{?}$ *u* $^{giš?!}$*gur-ra*
^{Id}*na-na-a*-KAM IGI^{ir} ^{iti}AB UD.⸢11⸣[(+).KA]M
3 *mu*-⸢*ṣib*⸣-*bi-ta-nu* 2ta *ak-kul-l*[*a-t*]*a*
ina IGI ^{I}⸢*ša*$_2$-*du*⸣-*ni* 2 *mu-ṣib-bi*-⸢*ta*⸣-[*nu*]
Lo.E. 10 *ak-kul-la*$^{!(T.\ na)}$-*a-ta ina* IGI ^{Id}EN-*iq-bi*
Rev. (blank)
^{iti}⸢AB⸣ UD.13.KAM MU.9.KAM
(textile/basket$^{?}$ impressions on reverse)

[×] mina(s) 35 shekels of iron (in the form of) five …, twelve mattocks, a (door) mounting, a tip, a dowel, *šūrû-tools*$^{?}$, a peg of a *bucket*, and a *GUR-RA*, were received from Nanāya-ēreš; Month X, day 11(+).
Five …, two mattocks are at the disposal of Šadûnu.
Two …, ten mattocks are at the disposal of Bēl-iqbi.

Month X, day 13, year 9.

2, 6, 7 *mu-ṣib-bi-ta-nu* is unclear; see glossary.
2, 6, 8 For *akkullu(attu)*, see glossary.
3 For the *šūrû*-tool, see glossary.
4 The unclear $^{giš?!}$*gur-ra* might be read ^{giš}*<it>-qur-ra*, a "spoon."

129. YBC 9136

Copy: Plate XXX
Date: 26$^?$.II.29 Nbk
Summary: *maḫir* receipt + *ina pāni* note: iron tools

Obv. 14 MA.NA AN.⸢BAR *gam-ri*⸣
7 MAR AN.BAR^{meš} ^{Id}⸢*gu-la*⸣-[××]
ma-⸢*ḫir*⸣ *ina muḫ-ḫi ḫi-*⸢*ru*⸣*-t*[*u*$_2$]
⸢ID$_2$⸣ *ina* IGI ^{Id}U.GUR-PAP
(blank)
Rev. (blank)
^{iti}GU$_4$ UD.⸢26$^?$⸣.KAM MU.29.⸢KAM⸣
^{d}AG-NIG$_2$.⸢DU-URU$_3$ LUGAL⸣ TIN.⸢TIR^{ki}⸣

14 minas of processed iron (in the form of) seven iron spades were received from Gula-×; they are at the disposal of Nergal-nāṣir for the excavation of the canal.
Month II, day 26$^?$, year 29 of Nebuchadnezzar, king of Babylon.

130. NCBT 966

Copy: Plate XXX
Date: 21.XI.-- (Kan–Npl)
Summary: *maḫir* receipt: iron items + accounting note

For Nanāya-ēreš see **No. 125.**

Obv. 1 GUN 30 MA.NA AN.BAR
2 *si*$^?$*-im-mil-e-ti ša*$_2$ ⸢^{udu}SISKUR⸣^{meš}
10 EME^{meš} *ša*$_2$ AN-*e*
1 *na-aš*$_2$*-ḫi-ip-ti*
1-*en qul-mu-u*$_2$
2-*ta* GIDRU-*a-ta* 1^{en} *su-up-pi-in-*⸢*nu*$^?$⸣
6 *na-al-pat-a-ta* 2 *ma-*⸢*ak-ka*⸣-[*su*]
Lo.E. 2 *mat-qa-<ne*$_2$*>-e ša*$_2$ *a-šar-*⸢×⸣ [(×)]
^{Id}*na-na-a*-KAM IG[I$^{!?ir}$ (×)]
^{iti}ZIZ$_2$ UD.21.KA[M (MU.×.KAM)]
Rev. 2 GUR 2 BAN$_2$ LAL-*ṭi ša*$_2$ 10[(×) ^{I}…]
2 GUR 1 (PI) 4 BAN$_2$ *ša*$_2$$^?$ 12$^?$ ^{I}LU$_2$-⸢^{d}⸣[*na-n*]*a-a*
2 GUR 5 BAN$_2$ *ša*$_2$ 11° ^{I}*bi-*[*bi-a*]$^?$
3 (PI) 2 BAN$_2$ *ša*$_2$ 8 ^{I}URU-⸢*lu-mur*⸣

1 talent 30 minas of iron (in the form of) two *grills* (*grates*) for the sacrificial sheep, ten *wedges* of the canopy, one shovel, one *qulmû*-axe, two rods, one (brick moulding) *suppinnu*-tool, six *scrapers*, two *makkasu*-bowls, two mounts for …, *received* from Nanāya-ēreš; Month XI, day 21, [(year ×)].
2 kor, minus 2 *sūtu*, *for* ten(+), […]; 2;1.4.0, *for* 12, Amīl-Nanāya; 2;0.5.0 *for* 11, Bi[*bēa*]; 0;3.2.0, *for* 8, Ālu-lūmur.

2 The use of *simmiltu* as part of the sacrifice apparatus is otherwise unknown.[15] Although the meaning "ladder" is more common, the *simmiltu* in the present context may have simply been a metal grid on which carcasses were roasted (not necessarily in one piece).
3 The translation "*wedge*" for *lišānu* (lit. "tongue) is based on context, and the fact that *lišānu* can be used for blades and tools whose shape is reminiscent of a tongue.
7 For *nalpattu*, see glossary.
11–14 The meaning of these lines and their relation to the iron items above are unclear.

131. NCBT 972

Copy: Plate XXXI
Date: 02.VIII.07 --
Summary: *maḫir* receipt: iron items + accounting

Obv. 2 [(+) MA].NA 3 ⸢GIN$_2$⸣ <AN.BAR>
1 MAR AN.BAR$^!$ *ap-pat*
u kam-mat ^{Id}AG-PAP ⸢IGI^{ir}⸣
Lo.E. 1 UDU.NITA$_2$ *ina*$^!$ UGU$^!$
^{giš}*gan-*⸢*gan*⸣*-na-ta*
Rev. *ne$_2$-ki*[*s*] ^{iti}APIN
UD.2.KAM MU.7.KAM

2 (+) minas 3 shekels <of iron> (in the form of) one iron spade, a tip, and a dowel were received from Nabû-nāṣir; one sheep *was slaughtered on account of* the pot stands.
Month VIII, day 2, year 7.

3 The name ^{Id}AG-PAP was originally read ^{Id}AG-NUMUN-<MU>, i.e., the well-attested smith; see Payne 2007, 318, listed s.v. Nabû-zēru-iddin. The reading ^{Id}AG-PAP, however, requires no emendation and results in a proper name. Unlike Nabû-zēru-iddin, however, Nabû-nāṣir cannot be identified in additional texts and the tablet cannot be dated.
4–6 The context of these lines and their relation to the previous iron items are unclear.

132. NCBT 721

Copy: Plate XXXI
Date: 13.IV.19 Nbk
Summary: *maḫir* receipt: iron tools[16]

Obv. 26 ⸢MA⸣.NA 58 GIN$_2$ AN.BAR *gam-ri*

[15] The reading of *si-im-mil-e-ti* as a form of *simirtu* / *semeru*, a metal ring of some sort, makes little sense.
[16] A previous edition is included in Payne 2007, 74.

20 MAR^{meš} 4 *se-ra-pi*
ša$_2$ *gi-iz-zu*
5-*ta* NIG$_2$.GAL$_2$.LA^{me}
^{Id}*na-na-a*°-SISKUR$_2$
Lo.E. ⸢A⸣ ^{I}IR$_3$-*a* ^{lu_2}SIMUG
IGI^{ir}
Rev. (blank)
^{iti}ŠU UD.13.KAM MU.19.KAM
^{d}AG-NIG$_2$.DU-URU$_3$
LUGAL TIN.TIR^{ki}

26 minas 58 shekels of processed iron (in the form of) twenty spades, four shears for shearing, and five sickles, received from Nanāya-uṣalli, son of Ardāya, the smith.
Month IV, day 13, year 19 of Nebuchadnezzar, king of Babylon.

5 Nanāya-uṣalli is read Nanāya-aḫu-uṣur in Payne 2007, and is assumed to be the brother of Nanāya-uṣalli (Payne 2007, 322). A collation of the other presumed attestation of Nanāya-aḫu-uṣur, VS 20, 4: 3, will probably prove to be ^{Id}*na-na-a*-SISKUR$_2$ rather than ^{Id}*na-na-a*-ŠEŠ-URU$_3$ (as copied); thus all attestations refer to the same individual: Nanāya-uṣalli / Ardāya.

133. NCBT 752

Copy: Plate XXXI
Date: 02.III.18 Nbk
Summary: *maḫir* receipt: iron tools

Obv. ⸢12⸣ MAR AN.BAR^{me}
4 *na-aḫ-šip-<ti>* AN.BAR^{me}
ša$_2$ TA ⸢UNUG⸣^{ki} *na-ša*$_2$-*tu*$_2$$^{!}$
^{Id}AG-*u*$_2$-*ter-ri*
Lo.E. IGI^{ir}
Rev. (blank)
^{iti}⸢SIG$_4$ UD.2⸣.KAM MU.18.KAM
^{d}AG-NIG$_2$.DU-⸢URU$_3$⸣ LUGAL TIN.TIR^{ki}

Twelve iron spades and four iron shovels that were brought from Uruk were received from Nabû-uterri.
Month III, day 2, year 18 of Nebuchadnezzar, king of Babylon.

3 Note that the tools were brought *from* Uruk. The text was probably written in the countryside and was later brought back to Uruk (by Nabû-uterri?) as proof of delivery.

134. YBC 9068

Copy: Plate XXXI
Date: 05.IX.14 Nbk
Summary: *maḫir* receipt: iron tools

Obv. 1 MA.NA ⸢⅓⸣ 5 GIN$_2$ AN.BAR *gam-ru*

1 $^{\text{an.bar}}$*qul-mu-u*$_2$
^{I}*ina-qi*$_2$*-bi-*^{d}EN*-li-im-*⸢*mir*⸣
$^{\text{lu}_2}$SIMUG AN.BAR I[GI]*-ir*⸣
Rev. (blank)
^{iti}GAN UD.5.KAM MU.⸢14⸣.KAM
^{d}AG-NIG$_2$.DU-URU$_3$
Up.E. LUGAL TIN.TIR^{ki}

1 mina 25 shekels of processed iron (in the form of) one iron *qulmû*-axe were received from Ina-qibīt-Bēl-limmir, the blacksmith.
Month IX, day 5, year 14 of Nebuchadnezzar, king of Babylon.

2 Note $^{\text{an.bar}}$*qul-mu-u*$_2$, with AN.BAR as a determinative, for expected *qul-mu-u*$_2$ AN.BAR.

135. YBC 9293

Copy: Plate XXXI
Date: 15.XI.32 Nbk
Summary: *maḫir* receipt: iron items

Obv. 3 *a-ḫa-nu ša*$_2$ ⸢ḪAR AN.BAR^{me}⸣
1 *iz-qa-ti* AN.⸢BAR⸣
1 ^{giš}MAR AN.BAR
ša$_2$ NIG$_2$.GA *ša*$_2$ *ina* IGI
Lo.E. ^{Id}KUR.GAL*-lu-*⸢*u*$_2$*-šal*⸣*-l*[*im*]
6 ^{I}*ina*-SUḪ$_3$-SUR ⸢A ^{I}⸣^{d}*na-na-a-*⸢ŠEŠ⸣-MU
Rev. $^{\text{lu}_2}$⸢A.KIN*-šu*$_2$⸣ IGI^{ir}
^{iti}ZIZ$_2$ UD.15.KAM MU.3⸢2.KAM⸣
^{d}AG-NIG$_2$.DU-URU$_3$ LUGAL TIN.TIR⸢^{ki}⸣

Three iron manacle rings, one iron fetter, one iron spade from the (temple) stores that were at the disposal of Amurru-lū-šalim, were received from Ina-tēšî-ēṭir, son of Nanāya-aḫu-iddin, his messenger.
Month XI, day 15, year 32 of Nebuchadnezzar, king of Babylon.

136. YBC 9428

Copy: Plate XXXII
Date: 13.VI.19 Nbk
Summary: *maḫir* receipt: iron tools

Obv. 3 ½ MA.NA AN.BAR *gam-ru*
2-*ta ṣib-te-e-ti*
^{Id}*na-na-a-u*$_2$*-ṣal-lu*
A ^{I}IR$_3$*-a* $^{\text{lu}_2}$⸢SIMUG⸣
IGI^{ir}
Rev. (blank)
^{iti}KIN UD.13.KAM MU.⸢19⸣.KAM
^{d}AG-NIG$_2$.DU-URU$_3$ LUGAL TIN.TIR^{ki}

3 ½ minas of processed iron (in the form of) two fetters were received from Nanāya-uṣalli, son of Ardāya, the smith.
Month VI, day 13, year 19 of Nebuchadnezzar, king of Babylon.

137. YBC 9423

Copy: Plate XXXII
Date: 04.VIII.27 Nbk
Summary: accounting note: iron tools from *iškaru*

The tablet is unfired. Although no verb is mentioned, the text should be seen as an equivalent of a *maḫir* receipt.

Obv. 7 MA.NA AN.BAR *gam-ru*
5 GIR$_2$ AN.BAR^{me}
ša$_2$ iš-ka-ru
^{Id}EN-NIGIN$_2$^{ir} ^{lu2}SIMUG
Rev. (blank)
^{iti}APIN UD.4.KAM MU.27.KAM
^{d}AG-NIG$_2$.DU-URU$_3$ LUGAL TIN.TIR$^{⸢ki⸣}$

7 minas of processed iron (in the form of) five iron daggers, which are the *iškāru*-obligation of Bēl-upaḫḫir, the smith.
Month VIII, day 4, year 27 of Nebuchadnezzar, king of Babylon.

138. YBC 3989

Copy: Plate XXXII–XXXIII
Date: --.--.17 Nbk
Summary: tabulated account: iron[17]

Obv.	AN.BAR SUM^{nu}	AN.⸢BAR *gam-ri*⸣ <<*ri*>> IGI	*i-di* SUM^{nu} *{eras.}*
	1 GUN 13 MA 10 GIN$_2$ AN.BAR	1 GUN 1 ⸢MA.NA AN.<BAR>⸣ *gam-ri*	5 GIN$_2$ *gir$_2$-u* LA$_2$ KU$_3$.BABBAR
	a-na dul-lu ina IGI	1 *na-aḫ-ši[p-t]i*	^{I}IR$_3$-^{d}AG A ^{I}*id*!-*di*!-*ia$_2$* {eras.}
	^{I}IR$_3$-^{d}AG A ^{I}*ša$_2$*-^{d}AG-*šu-u*	15 *ḫa-lil-a-nu*	GIŠ ^{iti}ŠE UD.27.KAM MU.15.KAM
	^{iti}ŠE UD.28.KAM MU.15.KAM	^{I}IR$_3$-^{d}AG A ^{I}*ša$_2$*-^{d}AG-*šu-u*	4 ⸢GIN$_2$⸣ 4^{tu2} 2^{u2} KU$_3$!.BABBAR! GIŠ
	42 MA.NA	IGI^{ir} ^{iti}BARA$_2$ UD.3.KAM MU.⸢16?⸣.KAM	⸢^{iti}SIG$_4$? UD.7?⸣.KAM MU.15.KAM
	^{iti}ŠE UD.⸢27⸣.KAM	12 MA.NA ⸢40⸣ GIN$_2$ AN.BAR ⸢*gam-ri*⸣	5 <GIN$_2$> ⸢^{Id}AG-ŠEŠ⸣-MU A ^{I}*id-di-ia* GIŠ
		3 MAR AN.BAR$^{⸢meš⸣}$	^{iti}⸢DU$_6$ UD⸣.13.KAM MU.16.KAM
		1 *na-aḫ-šip-ti*	
		9 NIG$_2$.GAL$_2$.LA$^{⸢meš⸣}$	
		šu-ri-e u šik-kat^{meš}	
		ša$_2$ 5 MAR AN.<BAR>^{meš}	3 ½ GIN$_2$ KU$_3$.BABBAR
		^{I}IR$_3$-^{d}AG A ^{I}*ša$_2$*-^{d}AG-*šu-u*	^{I}*ina-qi$_2$-bit*-^{d}EN-ZALAG$_2$ GIŠ
		IGI^{ir} 2 ½ GIN$_2$ KU$_3$.BABBAR	^{iti}ŠE UD.26.KAM
		re-ḫe-et i-di-šu$_2$ GIŠ	⸢MU.15.KAM⸣
Lo.E.		^{iti}ŠU UD.10.KAM MU.⸢17⸣.KAM	2 ⸢½ GIN$_2$⸣ ^{iti}⸢ŠE?⸣
		13 ½ MA.NA 5 GIN$_2$ AN.BAR *gam-ri*	UD.30.KAM MU.16.KAM GIŠ

17 The text is translated and discussed by Payne in Jursa 2010, 690–1.

		4° *ḫa-*⸢*lil-a-ni*⸣	MU.15.KAM
Rev.		28 ½ MA.NA AN.BAR	3 GIN$_2$ KU$_3$.BABBAR *ina i-di-šu*$_2$
		^{I}IR$_3$-^{d}AG A ^{I}*ša*$_2$-^{d}AG-*šu-u*	^{Id}AG-ŠEŠ-MU GIŠ ^{iti}ŠE UD.16.KAM
	28 MA.NA AN.BAR	IGI^{ir} ^{iti}KIN UD.13.KAM MU.16.KAM	× MU.15.KAM
	ina IGI ^{I}IR$_3$-^{d}AG	7 GIN$_2$ KU$_3$.BABBAR ^{I}IR$_3$-^{d}AG	
	A ^{I}*ša*$_2$-^{d}AG-*šu-u*	A ^{I}*ša*$_2$-^{d}AG-*šu-u* GIŠ	
	^{iti}SIG$_4$ UD.23.KAM	^{iti}DU$_6$ UD.9.KAM MU.16.KAM	
	MU.17.KAM	3 GIN$_2$ ^{iti}SIG$_4$ UD.26.KAM	5 GIN$_2$ ^{I}*ina-qi*$_2$*-bit*-^{d}EN-ZALAG$_2$ GIŠ
		MU.⸢17.KAM⸣ ^{I}IR$_3$-^{d}AG	^{iti}ŠE UD.16.KAM MU.15.KAM
		A ^{I}⸢*ša*$_2$-^{d}AG-*šu-u*⸣ GIŠ	2 ½ GIN$_2$ ^{I}*ina-qi*$_2$*-bit*-^{d}EN-ZALAG$_2$ GIŠ
		8 MA.⸢NA ⅓⸣ GIN$_2$ AN.BAR *gam-*⸢*ri*⸣	^{iti}KIN$^{!}$ UD.24.KAM MU.16.KAM
		5 MAR AN.BAR^{meš} IGI^{ir}	2 GIN$_2$ ^{iti}ŠE UD.12.KAM
		[^{it}]^{i}SIG$_4$ UD.26.KAM MU.17.<KAM>	MU 16.KAM
		5 ⸢× × ×⸣	⸢3$^{?}$⸣ GIN$_2$ ^{iti}SIG$_4$ UD.14[(+×)].KAM
		[(×)]	MU.17.KAM
Up.E.		⸢UD⸣ ⸢9⸣.KAM	1 ½ GIN$_2$ ^{i}[^{ti}SI]G$_4$ UD.⸢15⸣[(+×).KAM]
		MU.15.[KAM]	MU.10[+×.KA]M GIŠ

Iron given (to the smiths):	Processed iron received (from the smiths):	Wages given (to the smiths):
1 talent 13 minas 10 shekels of iron are at the disposal of Arad-Nabû, son of Ša-Nabû-šū for work; Month XII, day 28, year 15.	1 talent 1 mina of processed iron (in the form of) one shovel (and) fifteen *ḫālilu*-tools were received from Arad-Nabû, son of Ša-Nabû-šū; Month I, day 3, year 16?.	Arad-Nabû, son of *Iddia*, withdrew 4 ²³⁄₂₄ shekels of silver; Month XII, day 27, year 15. He (also) withdrew 4¼ shekels as *second* (*instalment*) of silver; Month III?, day 07?, year 15.
42 minas (of iron *are also at his disposal*); Month XII, day 27.	12 minas 50 shekels of processed iron (in the form of) three iron spades, one shovel, nine sickles, *šūrû*-tools and pegs for five iron spades, were received from Arad-Nabû, son of Ša-Nabû-šū. He withdrew 2 ½ shekels of silver (as) the remainder of his wages; Month IV, day 10, year 17.	Nabû-aḫu-iddin, son of Iddia, withdrew 5 shekels (of silver); Month VII, day 13, year 16.
	13 ½ minas 5 shekels of processed iron (in the form of) four *ḫālilu*-tools (and) 28 ½ minas of iron were received from Arad-Nabû, son of Ša-Nabû-šū; Month VI, day 13, year 16.	Ina-qibīt-Bēl-limmir withdrew 3 ½ shekels of silver; Month XII, day 26, year 15. (He also withdrew) 2 ½ shekels; Month XII, day 30, year 16. year 15: Nabû-aḫu-iddin withdrew 3 shekels of silver from his wages; Month XII, day 16, year 15.

28 minas of iron are at the disposal of Arad-Nabû, son of Ša-Nabû-šū; Month III, day 23, year 17.	Arad-Nabû, son of Ša-Nabû-šū, withdrew 7 shekels silver; Month VII, day 9, year 16.	Ina-qibīt-Bēl-limmir withdrew 5 shekels; Month XII, day 16, year 15.
	Arad-Nabû, son of Ša-Nabû-šū, withdrew 3 shekels; Month III, day 26, year 17. 8 minas 20 shekels of processed iron (in the form of) 5 iron spades were received (from him); Month III, day 26, year 17. … (3–4 lines damaged)	Ina-qibīt-Bēl-limmir withdrew 2 ½ shekels (of silver); Month VI, day 24, year 16. 2 shekels; Month XII, day 12, year 16. 3 shekels; Month III, day 14(+), year 17. He withdrew 1 ½ shekels; Month III, day 10(+), year 10(+).

ii,28–30 The original text for this section of the summary account is also preserved, PTS 3425: 8 MA.NA ⅓ GIN$_2$ AN.BAR *gam-[ri]* / 5 MAR AN.<BAR>^{meš} / ^{I}IR$_3$-^{d}AG A-*šu*$_2$ *ša*$_2$ / ^{I}*ša*$_2$-^{d}AG-*šu-u*$_2$ ^{lu_2}SIMUG ⌜IGI^{ir}⌝ / 3 GIN$_2$ KU$_3$.BABBAR *ina i-di-šu*$_2$ / GIŠ.

139. YBC 9274

Copy: Plate XXXIII
Date: 17.V.25 Nbk
Summary: withdrawal (*našû*) note: iron tools

Obv. ⌜5⌝ MA.NA AN.BAR *gam-ri* 4 ^{giš}MAR AN.BAR^{meš}
(tiny line) 1 *qul-mu-u*$_2$ 2 NIG$_2$.GAL$_2$.LA^{me}
a-na dul-lu ša$_2$ ^{giš}KIRI$_6$ *ša*$_2$ ^{giš}GEŠTIN
ša$_2$ *ina* E$_2$ ^{I}*ša*$_2$-*ma-a*ʾ-DINGIR
^{Id}INNIN$^{!}$-MU-KAM A ^{Id}AG-PAP^{me}-GI GIŠ
Rev. ^{iti}NE UD.17.KAM MU.25.KAM
^{d}AG-NIG$_2$.DU-URU$_3$ LUGAL TIN.TIR^{ki}

Ištar-šumu-ēreš, son of Nabû-aḫḫē-šullim, withdrew 5 minas of processed iron (in the form of) four iron spades, one *qulmû*-axe, (and) two sickles for the work of the vineyard that is in Bīt-Šamaʾ-il.
Month V, day 17, year 25 of Nebuchadnezzar, king of Babylon.

140. NCBT 417

Copy: Plate XXXIII
Date: 01(+).I.08 Nbn
Summary: *ina pāni* note: spades

Obv. ⌜2 ^{giš}⌝*mar-ri*⌜^{me}⌝
ina IGI ^{lu_2}*u*$_2$-*dan-na*-⌜*a-a*⌝
1 *ina* IGI ^{I}*ta*-⌜*at*⌝-*tan-nu*
4 ^{iti}BARA$_2$ UD.1[(+×).KA]M
Lo.E. MU.⌜8.KAM⌝

Rev. ⸢^{d}AG-NI$_{2}$.TUK⸣
L[UGAL TIN.TIR^{ki}]

Two spades are at the disposal of the Udanneans. One (spade) is at the disposal of Tattannu. Month I, day 1(+), year 8 of Nabonidus, k[ing of Babylon].

141. YBC 9209

Copy: Plate XXXIV
Date: 13$^{?}$.XII.10 Nbk
Summary: *ina pāni* + withdrawal (*našû*) notes: silver

Obv. 30 MA.NA ⸢^{na_4}⸣GUG ⸢ŠAM$_{2}$⸣ [10 MA.NA KU$_{3}$.BABBAR]
ina pa-ni ^{Id}EN-*ka*-⸢*ṣir*⸣ A-*šu*$_{2}$ *ša*$_{2}$ ^{I}GI$^{?}$-⸢^{d}AG$^{?}$⸣ [(×)]
ina lib$_{3}$-*bi* ⸢8$^{!}$⸣ MA.NA KU$_{3}$.BABBAR-*šu*$_{2}$ *ina* ⸢UGU *dul*⸣-[*lu*]
a-na ⸢^{lu_2}⸣*qi*$_{2}$-*i-pi a-na* ŠUK.ḪI.A^{me} [(×)]
ša$_{2}$ ^{lu_2}RIG$_{7}$^{me} *id*-⸢*din-nu* $^{Id?}$⸣[×(×)]
e-⸢*ṭir*⸣ 2 MA.NA KU$_{3}$.BABBAR *re*-[*ḫe*(-*et* ×)]
⸢*a-na* ^{Id}EN-MU *u*$_{3}$ ERIN$_{2}$^{me} *ša*$_{2}$$^{?}$⸣ [× × SUM$^{?na}$]
PAP 10 MA.NA KU$_{3}$.BABBAR ŠAM$_{2}$ 30 M[A.NA]
⸢^{na_4}⸣GUG *ina* <IGI> ^{Id}EN-*ka-ṣir* ⸢*u*$_{3}$⸣
Lo.E. 10 MA.NA KU$_{3}$.BABBAR *ul-tu* ŠA$_{3}$ KU$_{3}$.BABBAR *pit*$_{2}$-*qu* ⸢*ir-bi*⸣
ša$_{2}$$^{!(T.\ a)}$ ^{iti}ŠE ^{Id}MAŠ-⸢LUGAL⸣-PAP ^{lu_2}*qi*$_{2}$-*i-pi* ⸢GIŠ⸣
Rev. 4 MA.NA 10 GIN$_{2}$ ^{I}*ṣil-la-a* A-*šu*$_{2}$
ša$_{2}$ ^{I}*mar-duk-a* ^{lu_2}UMBISAG *ša*$_{2}$ ^{I}*ṣil-la-a*
⸢*a-na ku-mu*⸣ ZU$_{2}$.LUM.MA-*šu*$_{2}$ *ša*$_{2}$ *a-na* E$_{2}$.AN.NA
id-din-⸢*nu it-ta-ši*⸣
<PAP> 24 MA.NA 10 GIN$_{2}$ KU$_{3}$.BABBAR *pit*$_{2}$-*qu ir-bi*
ša$_{2}$ ^{iti}ŠE *i-na* NIG$_{2}$.GA
^{iti}ŠE UD.13$^{?}$.KAM MU.10.KAM
^{d}AG-NIG$_{2}$.DU-URU$_{3}$ LUGAL TIN.TIR^{ki}

30 minas of carnelian, at a price of [10 minas of silver], are at the disposal of Bēl-kāṣir, son of *Mušallim-Nabû*; from that, 8 minas of silver for work for the *qīpu* was paid to … <who> gave (it) for the salaries of the temple serfs. 2 minas of silver, the re[mainder, *was given*] to Bēl-iddin and the workers *of the* […]; a total of 10 minas of silver, the price of 30 mi[nas] of carnelian are at <the disposal of> Bēl-kāṣir.
Additionally, Ninurta-šarru-uṣur, the *qīpu*, withdrew 10 minas of silver from the smelted silver, the income of month XII; 4 minas 10 shekels of silver (paid for) Ṣillāya, son of Marduka. The scribe of Ṣillāya withdrew (the silver) in lieu of his (i.e., Ṣillaya's) dates that he gave to Eanna; <total of> 24 minas 10 shekels of smelted silver, the income of month XII, from the temple stores.
Month XII, day 13$^{?}$, year 10 of Nebuchadnezzar, king of Babylon.

12–15 For the syntax of the passage to work without emendation, we need to assume that a short entry ("… silver (for) Ṣillāya …") was explained in full by a sentence beginning in line 13: "the scribe of …"

16 The total of 24 minas 10 shekels is 10 minas higher than the two added sums; 10 minas (l. 10) +

4 minas 10 shekels (l. 12). The fact that exactly 10 minas are missing, that is one Winkelhaken, suggests that this is the result of a simple scribal error in one of the figures.

142. NCBT 135

Copy: Plate XXXIV
Date: 21.II.16 Nbk
Summary: *ina pāni* note: stones

Obv. [× M]A.⸢NA NA$_4$ *sam*⸣*-mu*
[*a*]-⸢*na dul-lu*⸣ *ina* IGI
[^{I}]⸢^{d}INNIN-NUMUN-DU$_3$⸣ A ^{I}MU-^{d}AMAR.⸢UTU⸣
⸢^{lu_2}KAB.SAR⸣
Rev. (blank)
⸢^{iti}⸣GU$_4$ UD.21.⸢KAM⸣
⸢MU⸣.16.KAM ^{d}AG-NIG$_2$.DU-⸢URU$_3$⸣
[LU]GAL TIN.⸢TIR^{ki}⸣

[× mi]na(s) of red stone is / are at the disposal of Ištar-zēru-ibni, son of Iddin-Marduk, the jeweler, for work.
Month II, day 21, year 16 of Nebuchadnezzar, king of Babylon.

143. YBC 3990

Copy: Plate XXXV
Date: --.XII.12 --
Summary: accounting inventory: multiple items

Obv. PAP 1 ½$^{!}$ GUN ⸢8$^{?}$ ½$^{?}$ MA⸣.NA 7 GIN$_2$ ^{sik_2}ZA.GIN$_3$.KUR.RA
4 GUN 44 MA.NA 50 GIN$_2$ *in-za-ḫu-re-e-ti*
2 ½ ⸢GUN 4⸣ ½ MA.NA 5 GIN$_2$ ^{na_4}*gab-bu-u$_2$ ša$_2$ mi-ṣir*
⸢3 MA.NA⸣ [(×+)] 8 ⸢GIN$_2$⸣ 4^{tu_2} KU$_3$.BABBAR
5 ⸢GUN⸣ 5 MA.NA SIK$_2$.ḪI.A
44 GUR ZU$_2$.LUM.MA 10 GUR ŠE.BAR
14 GUN 1 MA.NA ⅓ ⸢GIN$_2$⸣ ^{giš}ḪAB
⸢22⸣ MA.⸢NA⸣ 17 GIN$_2$ ^{gada}*ṭu-ma-nu e-lat*
^{gada}*ṭu-ma-nu ša$_2$ ina* ŠU^{II} ^{lu_2}*pu-ṣa-a-a* GIŠ^{u_2}
1 ⸢GUN 22 (+×) MA.NA ×⸣ [GIN$_2$$^{?}$ ^{sik_2}ḪE$_2$.me.da$^{?}$] ⸢^{giš}*in-za*⸣*-ḫu-*⸢*re-e*⸣*-tu$_2$*
10 ⸢GUN 4$^{?}$2 MA.NA⸣ [^{na_4}]⸢*gab-bu-u$_2$ ša$_2$ ka*⸣*-šap-pu*
10 MA.NA 50 GIN$_2$ *ḫa-*⸢*at*⸣*-ḫu-re-e-*⸢*ti*⸣
PAP *ša$_2$ ul-tu* ^{iti}BARA$_2$ MU.8.KAM
a-⸢*di qi$_2$*⸣*-it ša$_2$* ^{iti}ŠE MU.12.KAM GIŠ^{u_2}
Rev. (uninscribed)

Total: 1 ½ talents *8* ½ minas 7 shekels of purple wool; 4 talents 44 minas 50 shekels of *inzaḫurētu*-dye; 2 ½ talents 4 ½ minas 5 shekels of alum from Egypt; 3 minas 8[+×]¼ shekels of silver; 5 talents 5 minas of wool; 44 kor of dates; 10 kor of barley; 14 talents 1 mina 20 shekels of madder; 22 minas 17 shekels of *ṭumānu*-linen thread, apart from the *ṭumānu*-linen thread that was withdrawn from the linen weavers; 1 talent 22(+) minas [× *shekels of*

red wool (*dyed with*)] *inzaḫurētu*-dye; 10 talents *42* minas of alum from Kašappu; 10 minas 50 shekels of apple-color dye.
(All of the above is) the total withdrawn from month I, year 8 until the end of month XII, year 12.

144. NBC 4692

Copy: Plate XXXIV
Date: 11.IX.18 Nbk
Summary: accounting inventory: textiles

Obv. 27 ^{tug_2}KUR.RA^{meš}
ša$_2$ TA UNUG^{ki} ^{I}*ša*$_2$*-du-nu*
u ^{Id}AG-*re-eḫ-ti*-URU$_3$ *iš-šu*$_2$*-nu*
ina lib$_3$*-bi* 20 ^{tug_2}⸢KUR.RA^{me}⸣
a-na ^{tug_2}*šir-a-a*[*m* ×]
⸢*ki*⸣*-i* SUR-*ru* [× × ×]
Lo.E. 28 *a-na* ^{I}TIN^{s}[^{u} (×)]
Rev. A ^{I}*ḫaš-di-i*[*a* (×)]
28 *a-na* ^{Id}*in-nin-*⸢MU-URU$_3$⸣
a-na ^{lu_2}*ši-ra-ku a-na muḫ-ḫi*
dul-la ina ŠU^{II} ^{I}*si-lim-*^{d}EN A ^{I}*re-ḫe-e-t*[*i*]
šu-⸢*bul*⸣ 3 *a-na* ^{munus}*za-ke-e-ti*
ša$_2$ *a-na muḫ-ḫi dul-la šap-ra* SUM^{nu}
re-ḫe 7 ^{tug_2}KUR.RA^{me} *ina* E$_2$ NIG$_2$.GA
Up.E. ^{iti}GAN UD.11.KAM MU.18.KAM
16 ^{d}AG-NIG$_2$.DU-URU$_3$ LUGAL TIN.TIR^{ki}

Twenty-seven capes that Šadûnu and Nabû-reḫti-uṣur withdrew from Uruk: of which, when they paid twenty capes for *šir'am*-garments, [they …]; twenty-eight for Balāssu, son of Ḫašdia; twenty-eight for Innin-šumu-uṣur for the temple serfs, on account of the work, delivered via Silim-Bēl, son of Rēḫētu; three were given to the *zakītu*-women who were sent for the work; the balance, seven capes, are in the storehouse.
Month IX, day 11, year 18 of Nebuchadnezzar, king of Babylon.

14 These seven garments must be related to the "27 (l. 1) minus 20 (l. 4)" garments mentioned in ll. 1–5.

145. NCBT 597

Copy: Plate XXXIV
Date: [×].XI.16 --
Summary: *ina pāni* note: garments

Obv. ⸢18$^{?}$ ^{gada}⸣*la-*⸢*ri-pe-e*⸣
⸢13⸣ ^{gada}*bu-u*$_2$*-*⸢*ṣu*⸣
6 ^{gada}⸢*ṭi*⸣*-pa-nu sad-ru* [(...)]
6 ^{gada}*šid-*⸢*da-nu*⸣ [(...)]
ina pa-ni ^{lu_2}⸢×⸣ [ ]
Lo.E. ^{iti}ZIZ$_2$ ⸢UD⸣.[×.KAM]

MU.⸢16.KAM⸣
Rev. (uninscribed)

*Eigh*teen *laripu*-garments, thirteen (pieces of) byssus, six compressed linen cloths of standard quality, (and) six linen curtains are at the disposal of the ....
Month XI, day [×], year 16.

146. NBC 4563

Copy: Plate XXXIV
Date: 31.XII.17 -- (Npl/Nbk)
Summary: *ina pāni* note: textile

The weaver Nanāya-iddin is attested between 9 Npl (Eames Q2) and 15 Nbk (NBC 4909); see Payne 2007, 189.

Obv. ⅓ 7 ⸢GIN$_2$⸣ ^{sik_2}ZA.⸢GIN$_3$⸣ *a-na* ^{tug_2}*lu-bar*
ša$_2$ ^{d}UTU ½ MA.NA ^{gada}*ṭu-man*$^{!}$-⸢*ni*⸣
a-na gu$_2$°-*ḫal-ṣa-ta*$^{!}$
ša$_2$ ^{tug_2}*lu-bu-uš ša*$_2$ ^{d}UTU
ina ⸢IGI⸣ ^{Id}*na-na-*⸢*a*-MU⸣
Lo.E. ^{lu_2}⸢UŠ⸣.BAR
Rev. (blank)
^{iti}ŠE° UD.13.KAM
MU.17.KAM

27 shekels of purple cloth for the *lubāru*-garment of Šamaš and ½ mina of *ṭumānu*-linen thread for the fringe of the clothing of Šamaš are at the disposal of Nanāya-iddin, the weaver.
Month XII, day 31, year 17.

147. NCBT 706

Copy: Plate XXXV
Date: 25.III.40 Nbk
Summary: accounting note: textile

Obv. 2 MA.NA ^{tug_2}*mu-ṣip-pe-e-ti*
a-na u$_2$*-ka-pe-*⸢*e*⸣
ša$_2$ ^{I}*gu-za-nu* A [^{I}]^{d}AG-EN-MU^{me}
a-na SIK$_2$.ḪI.A
ina NIG$_2$.GA
Rev. ^{iti}SIG$_4$ UD.25.KAM
MU.40.KAM
^{d}AG-NIG$_2$.DU-URU$_3$
LUGAL TIN.TIR^{ki}

2 minas of *muṣiptu*-cloth for a pack-saddle of Gūzānu, son of Nabû-bēl-šumāti, are in the temple stores for wool.
Month III, day 25, year 40 of Nebuchadnezzar, king of Babylon.

5 While the text clearly states that the *muṣiptu*-cloth is in the temple stores at the moment, the exact nature of the recorded transaction is unclear. If the *muṣiptu*-cloth were to come from the pack-saddle, then we would expect it to be *ša*$_2$* *u*$_2$*-ka-pe-*⸢*e*⸣ (rather than *a-na u*$_2$*-ka-pe-*⸢*e*⸣).

148. NBC 4750

Copy: Plate XXXV
Date: 14.II.31 Nbk
Summary: inventory list: cultic garments

Obv. 1 ^{tug_2}*lu-bar*
1 ^{gada}*šal-ḫu*
1 ^{sik_2}*iš-ḫa-<na>-be*
1 ^{tug_2}*ḫu-la-nu*
3 ^{tug_2}MAŠ$_2$
2 ^{sik_2}ḪE$_2$.ME.DA
2 ^{sik_2}ZA.GIN$_3$.KUR.RA
1 ^{gada}*šal-ḫu*
11 ^{tug_2}*ḫu-ṣa-ne*$_2$*-e*
ina ŠA$_3$ 1 *ša*$_2$ *ta-bar-ri*
1 ⸢^{tug_2}⸣*me-ze-eḫ*
PAP ⸢^{tug_2}⸣*mi-*⸢*iḫ*⸣*-ṣi*
Lo.E. *ša*$_2$ ^{d}GAŠAN *ša*$_2$ UNUG⸢^{ki}⸣
Rev. ^{iti}⸢GU$_4$⸣ UD.14.KAM
MU.31.KAM
^{d}AG-NIG$_2$.DU-URU$_3$ LUGAL E^{ki}

One *lubāru*-garment, one linen *šalḫu*-cloth, one *išḫanabe*-garment, one *ḫullānu*-coat, three *ṣibtu*-garments, two red wool garments, two purple garments, one linen *šalḫu*-cloth, eleven *ḫuṣannu*-sashes, of which one of red wool, one *mezēḫu*-band, total of the woven cloth of the Lady-of-Uruk.
Month II, day 14, year 31 of Nebuchadnezzar, king of Babylon.

8 It is unclear why the scribe would separate the two linen *šalḫu*-cloths (ll. 2, 8).

149. YBC 9582

Copy: Plate XXXVI
Date: 09.IV.24 Nbk
Summary: *maḫir* receipt: cloth

Obv. ½ GUN 6 MA.NA 10 GIN$_2$
mi-iḫ-ṣu 1 ^{tug_2}*gid*$_2$*-lu-u*$_2$
ša$_2$ KA$_2$ *za-ra-ti*
⸢*ša*$_2$⸣ ^{d}*na-na-a*
[×] ⸢×⸣ *ta-ri-ti*
[*ša*$_2$$^?$ ^{s}]^{ik_2}ḪE$_2$.ME.DA < *u* ^{sik_2}ZA.GIN$_3$>$^?$.KUR.RA
Lo.E. [*ša*$_2$ ^{g}]^{iš}ḪAB ^{Id}EN-*iq-bi*
[A-*šu*$_2$ *ša*$_2$] ^{Id}AG-GI

Rev. [^{lu_2}U]Š.BAR IGI^{ir}
10 [^{it}]^{i}ŠU UD.9.KAM
MU.24.KAM
^{d}AG-NIG$_2$.DU-URU$_3$
Up.E. LUGAL TIN.TIR^{ki}

½ talents 6 minas 10 shekels of woven cloth (for) a (door) curtain for the entrance of the tent of Nanāya […] … *nurse-(garment)* [of] red *<and purple>* wool (dyed with) madder were received from Bēl-iqbi, [son of] Nabû-ušallim, the weaver.
Month IV, day 9, year 24 of Nebuchadnezzar, king of Babylon.

5 *ta-ri-ti*; possibly from *tārītu*, a nursemaid. For the Assyrian king dressed in a similar garment in cultic context, see SAA X, 275: r.4.

150. YBC 9636

Copy: Plate XXXV
Date: 19.XII.09 (Npl/Nbk)
Summary: *maḫir* receipt: cloth

Iqīšāya (l. 6), a weaver, is attested between 13 Npl (GC 2, 62) and 13 Nbk (**No. 172**); see Payne 2007, 174–5.

Obv. 24 ⅚ MA.NA
⌜TUG$_2$⌝ BABBAR-*u*$_2$
te-ḫir-ti
4 *ša*$_2$ *ki-di-ne*$_2$*-e*
Lo.E. ⌜*a*⌝*-na* <<*a-na*>> ⌜ḪAR$^{?}$⌝^{me}
Rev. *a-na* ^{I}⌜BA^{ša_2}⌝*-a* ⌜SUM⌝^{na}
^{I}BA^{ša_2}*-a*
IGI^{ir}
9 ^{iti}ŠE UD.19.KAM
Up.E. MU.9.KAM

24 ⅚ minas of white cloth, the remainder of cotton, (which) was given to Iqīšāya for …, was received from Iqīšāya.
Month XII, day 19, year 9.

5 The context makes the reading ḪAR^{me}, "rings," difficult to accept.

151. YBC 3464

Copy: Plate XXXVI
Date: (×+)9.--.12 (*Nbk*)
Summary: *maḫir* receipt: garments

The restoration of the name Kudurru is based on the small space at the head of line 3. If correct, then he should be identified with Kudurru/Bēl-nāṣir, attested 1–4 Nbk (see Payne 2007, 177).

Obv. 6 ^{tug_2}⌜*ṣib-tu*$_4$ << *tu*$_4$>>⌝ GAL^{me}
34 MA.NA *ḫa-a-*⌜*ṭu*⌝
[^{I}NIG$_2$.D]U ^{lu_2}UŠ.BAR *ma*$^!$*-ḫir*°
[UD.(×)]9.KAM MU.12.KAM
Rev. (uninscribed)

Six large *ṣibtu*-garments (*and*) 34 minas in stock, were received from [*Kudu*]*rru*, the weaver. Month --, day (×+)9, year 12.

2 Note the relatively large amount of material, 34 minas (17 kg.). It is unclear whether this is total weight of the garments or whether this is leftovers from their manufacture; see **No. 91** for a similar case regarding iron tools. The fact that no material is specified may point to the latter.

3 The final *ḫir* seems to be written over an ^{iti}. The name of the month is indeed missing, and the scribe probably forgot to rewrite it at the beginning of line 4.

152. YBC 9457

Copy: Plate XXXVI
Date: 05.II.23 Nbk
Summary: *maḫir* receipt: silver

The tablet is unfired.

Obv. 1 ^{tug_2}KUR.RA *a-na* 1 ½ GIN$_2$ ⌜KU$_3$.BABBAR⌝
1 ⌜GIN$_2$⌝ KU$_3$.BABBAR *ḫa-a-ṭu*
⌜16$^?$⌝ ^{dug}*nam-za-a-ta ša*$_2$ *a-bat-tu*$_4$
⌜*a-na*⌝ ½ GIN$_2$ KU$_3$.BABBAR
⌜PAP 3 GIN$_2$ KU$_3$.BABBAR *ša*$_2$⌝ $^{I⌜d}$AG-*mu-še-ti-iq*-UD.DA⌝
Lo.E. ⌜A⌝ ^{I}*šu-la-a* ⌜*id*⌝-[*di-nu*]
^{Id}EN-TIN^{it} A [^{I}× × (×)]
Rev. IGI^{ir}
(blank)
^{iti}GU$_4$ UD.5.KAM MU.23.[KA]M
^{d}AG-NIG$_2$.DU-URU$_3$ LUGAL TIN.TIR^{ki}

One cape (for) 1 ½ shekels of silver, 1 shekel of stock silver, *sixteen abattu*-fermenting(?) vats for ½ shekel of silver; a total of 3 shekels of silver, which Nabû-mušētiq-uddê, son of Šulāya, ga[ve], was received from Bēl-uballiṭ, son of [...].
Month II, day 5, year 23 of Nebuchadnezzar, king of Babylon.

2 The one shekel of *kaspu ḫâṭû* refers to the physical silver rather than the various amounts of silver mentioned before and after, which refer to the account value of other items.

3 This is the only attestation of *abattu* fermenting vats (*namzītu*) known to us, though note the *abattu* vessel: *u*$_2$*-de-e u* ^{dug}*a-bat-tu*$_4$ (Dar 468). Furthermore, one shekel of silver for sixteen vats is an unreasonably low price for specialized vessels (which would probably be of a decent size). M. Jursa (1995, 123) showed that the *abattu* must have been an organic material, rather than stone, as

most often the term is translated.[18] In other contexts, the *abattu* is said to be burned (*ana kīri*, e.g., YOS 17, 130; YOS 19, 216), removed from a field (e.g., YOS 6, 33), dried (e.g., BIN 1, 32), given to sheep (Nbn 523), and used as building material (NCBT 34).

153. NBC 4652

Copy: Plate XXXVI
Date: 15.II.25 Nbk
Summary: *maḫir* receipt: textile

Obv. 9 MA.NA ⅔ 5 GIN$_2$ ^{tug2}*mi-iḫ-ṣu*
ana dal-ti ša$_2$ ^{tug2}*za-ra-ti*
10 GIN$_2$ ^{sik2}*ta-bar-ri* ^{giš}ŠA$_3$.ḪAB
^{Id}EN-*iq-bi* ^{lu2}UŠ.BAR IGI^{ir}
(blank)
Rev. ^{iti}GU$_4$ UD.15.⸢KAM MU⸣.25.KAM
^{d}AG-NIG$_2$.DU-URU$_3$ LUGAL TIN.TIR^{ki}

9 minas 45 shekels of woven cloth for the door of the tent and 10 shekels of red wool (dyed with) madder were received from Bēl-iqbi, the weaver.
Month II, day 15, year 25 of Nebuchadnezzar, king of Babylon.

3 For the spelling of *ḫurātu* ^{giš}ŠA$_3$.ḪAB, rather then the usual ^{giš}ḪAB, see Thavapalan 2020, 331. The exact nature of this variant is unclear.

154. NBC 4934

Copy: Plate XXXVII
Date: 03(+).VII.10 Nbn
Summary: *maḫir* receipt: textile

Obv. ⸢1 ^{tug2}⸣[ ]
⸢1 ^{tug2}*lu-bar ša$_2$*$^{?}$ ×⸣ [ ]
⸢1 ^{tug2}MAŠ$_2$ *ša$_2$* ^{d}× ×⸣ [ ] ⸢GAL$^{?}$⸣^{me}
ina lib$_3$-[b]i 5 ⸢TUR^{me}⸣ [ ] ⸢× × ×⸣
10 ½ GIN$_2$ ^{sik2}ḪE$_2$.ME.DA *ša$_2$* ⸢*in-za-ḫu-re*⸣*-e-tu$_2$*
1 ^{tug2}NIG$_2$.IB$_2$.⸢LA$_2$ *ša$_2$* ^{d}GAŠAN *ša$_2$* UNUG^{ki}⸣
14 ½ GIN$_2$ *ṭi-im ša$_2$* ⸢^{sik2}ḪE$_2$.ME.DA ^{giš}⸣ḪAB
1 MA.NA 12 ½ GIN$_2$ *gu-ḫal-ṣa-a-tu$_2$*
⸢*ša$_2$*⸣ ^{sik2}ḪE$_2$.ME.DA *u* ⸢^{sik2}ZA⸣.GIN$_3$.KUR.RA
⸢^{I}*ṣil*⸣*-la-a* ^{lu2}UŠ.BAR *ma-ḫi-ir*
Rev. 18 ⅔ MA.NA ^{tug2}⸢*mi*⸣*-iḫ-ṣu* BABBAR-*u$_2$*
1 ^{tug2}MAŠ$_2$ *ša$_2$* ⸢^{d}⸣GAŠAN *ša$_2$* UNUG^{ki} 1 ^{tug2}MAŠ$_2$
ša$_2$ ^{d}*na-na-a* 15 ^{tug2}NIG$_2$.IB$_2$.LA$_2$^{meš} *u*° ⸢*ṭi-im*⸣
14 ½ GIN$_2$ *ṭi-im ša$_2$* ^{sik2}ḪE$_2$.ME.DA ^{giš}ḪAB
1 MA.NA 12 ½ GIN$_2$ *gu-ḫal-ṣa-a-ti*

[18] Note, for example, TCL 9, 69: 32 (SbB 2, 71) and SbB 2, 131: 9 (PTS 2767), both mistakenly translated as "gravel" in Levavi 2018.

ša$_2$ ^{sik_2}ḪE$_2$.ME.DA *u* ^{sik_2}ZA.GIN$_3$.KUR.RA
(blank)
^{I}NUN.ME *u* ^{Id}UTU-DU-A *ma-aḫ-ru*
⸢^{iti}DU$_6$ UD.3(+×).KAM⸣ MU.10.KAM ^{d}AG-⸢NI$_2$.TUK⸣
[LUGAL TIN.TIR]⸢^{ki}⸣

One […]-garment; one *lubāru*-garment of […]; one *ṣibtu*-garment of … […] *large*, of which five are small […] …; 10 ½ shekels of red wool (dyed with) *inzaḫurētu*-dye; one *nēbeḫu*-sash of the Lady-of-Uruk, 14 ½ shekels of thread of red wool (dyed with) madder; 1 mina 12 ½ shekels of fringe of red and purple wool; (all these) were received from Ṣillāya, the weaver. 18 minas 40 shekels of white woven cloth; one *ṣibtu*-garment of the Lady-of-Uruk, one *ṣibtu*-garment of Nanāya, fifteen *nēbeḫu*-sashes and thread; 14 ½ shekels of thread of red wool (dyed with) madder; 1 mina 12 ½ shekels of fringe of red and purple wool; (all these) were received from Apkallu and Šamaš-mukīn-apli.
Month VII, day 3(+), year 10 of Nabonidus [king of Babylon].

155. NCBT 90

Copy: Plate XXXVI
Date: 25.IX.24 Nbk
Summary: *maḫir* receipt: textile

Obv. 1 TUG$_2$ *ša*$_2$-⸢*pu-u*$_2$⸣ *ša*$_2$ *ta-bar-ru*
ḫu-ra-tu$_4$ *a-na ki-di-ne*$_2$*-e*
^{I}DU$_3$-^{d}INNIN A ^{lu_2}TUG$_2$.BABBAR
IGI^{ir}
(blank)
Rev. ^{iti}GAN ⸢UD⸣.25.KAM
MU.24.KAM ^{d}AG-NIG$_2$.DU-URU$_3$
LUGAL TIN.TIR^{ki}

One embroidered cloth of red wool (dyed with) madder for cotton was received from Ibni-Ištar, descendant of Ašlāku.
Month IX, day 25, year 24 of Nebuchadnezzar, king of Babylon.

1 For *šapû*, to embroider, see Quillien 2022, 430–1. Note that in the present case, however, it is also possible to maintain the meaning "thick"; see Beaulieu 2003, 387.

156. NCBT 240

Copy: Plate XXXVII
Date: 30.XI.41 Nbk
Summary: *maḫir* receipt: yarn

Obv. 10 GIN$_2$ ^{gada}*ṭi-im*
^{I}⸢^{d}*na-na*⸣*-a*-MU
^{lu_2}*pu*-⸢*ṣa*⸣*-a-a* IGI⸢^{ir}⸣
Rev. ^{iti}ZIZ$_2$ UD.30.KAM
MU.41.KAM

^{d}AG-NIG$_2$.DU-URU$_3$
LUGAL$^!$ TIN.⸢TIR^{ki}⸣

10 shekels of yarn were received from Nanāya-iddin, the linen weaver.
Month XI, day 30, year 41 of Nebuchadnezzar, king of Babylon.

157. NCBT 1069

Copy: Plate XXXVII
Date: --.XII.09 --
Summary: withdrawal (*našû*) + *ina pāni* list: garments

Obv. 4 ^{tug_2}MAŠ$_2$ *ṣab-tu* ⸢×⸣ [(×)]
1 ^{tug_2}*ḫul-la-nu* [(×)]
1 ^{tug_2}*me-ze-eḫ* [(×)]
3 ^{tug_2}*par-ši-gu*
2 ^{gada}*šal-ḫu ša*$_2$ *te-ne*$_2$*-e*
1 ^{gada}*šal-ḫu ša*$_2$ DINGIR *ina* UGU E$_2$ *pa-pa-ḫi*
u$_2$*-ši-bi*
2 ^{gada}*šal-ḫu ša*$_2$ *pa-ru-uk-ti*
⸢1⸣ ^{gada}*šal-ḫu ša*$_2$ DINGIR *ina* E$_2$.KISAL
ina UGU *u*$_2$*-ši-bi*
3 ⸢^{gada}⸣*šal-ḫu ša*$_2$ *ku-ub-bur*
1 ⸢^{gada}⸣*šal-ḫu* ^{lu_2}*za-zak-ku* GIŠ
⸢PAP⸣ *ša*$_2$ *ina* IGI ^{lu_2}*um-man-ni ša*$_2$ TIN.TIR^{ki} GIŠ^{u}
^{iti}ZIZ$_2$ UD.26.KAM MU.9.⸢KAM⸣
1 ^{tug_2}*ta-bar-ri a-na* [(×)]
Lo.E. ^{uru}*u*$_2$*-dan-n*[*i*]
1 ^{tug_2}⸢MAŠ$_2$⸣ *ina* IGI
^{I}*ša*$_2$-^{d}A[G-*šu-u*]
Rev. 2 ^{tug_2}*par-ši-g*[*u* (×)]
1 ^{tug_2}*mu-ze-*⸢*eḫ*⸣ [(×)]
{eras.} 13 *kib-su-nu* GIŠ^{u}
⸢1 ^{gada}⸣*par-ši-gu ina* IGI
⸢^{I}*si-lim*-^{d}EN⸣ *ša*$_2$ ^{lu_2}ŠA$_3$.TAM *it-ba-*[*lu*$^?$]
1 ^{gada}*šal-ḫu ša*$_2$ *a-na ta-kil-tu*$_2$$^{!(T. šu_2)}$ SUM.NA
1 ⸢^{gada}*šal-ḫu*⸣ *a-na* ⸢*šub*⸣*-ti ša*$_2$ ^{d}EN
1 ^{gada}*šal-ḫu ša*$_2$ *kib-su ina* IGI ^{I}NIG$_2$.DU
^{iti}ŠE MU.⸢9⸣.KAM

Four *ṣibtu*-garments *attached* (*with*) …, one *ḫullānu*-coat, one *mezēḫu*-band, three *paršīgu*-headdresses, two replacement linen *šalḫu*-cloths, one linen *šalḫu*-cloth for a god placed at the cella, two linen *šalḫu*-cloths for a canopy canvas, one linen *šalḫu*-cloth for a god placed at the courtyard-chapel, three linen *šalḫu*-cloths for a thick (garment), one linen *šalḫu*-cloth withdrawn by the *zazakku*; (this is) all that was withdrawn from the craftsmen of Babylon, Month XI, day 26, year 9.
One red wool cloth for Udannu, one *ṣibtu*-garment at the disposal of Ša-Na[bû-šū], two *paršīgu*-headdresses, one *mezēḫu*-band, 13 *kibsu*-fabrics, were withdrawn.

One linen *paršīgu*-headdress at the disposal of Silim-Bēl, which the *šatammu* took away, one linen *šalḫu*-cloth given for blue-purple cloth, one linen *šalḫu*-cloth for the pedestal of Bēl, one linen *šalḫu*-cloth for *kibsu*-fabrics at the disposal of Kudurru.
Month XII, day 9.

21 An alternative reading might be 13 *kib-su* NU UD^{lu}, "13 un-washed *kibsu*-fabrics."

26 Kudurru might be the weaver attested in **No. 151**; see note there. The possibly identical first name, however, is not enough for a positive identification.

158. NBC 8363

Copy: Plate XXXVIII
Date: 15.I.27 Nbk
Summary: withdrawal (*našû*) note: garments

Obv. [×] ⸢^{tug_2}⸣KUR.RA *ša*$_2$ *a-na*
[× GI]N$_2$ KU$_3$.BABBAR *ina* ŠU^{II} ^{I}LU$_2$-^{d}*na-na-a*
[(×) *i*]*n*$^?$*-na-ša*$_2$*-a*ʾ
[*a-n*]*a zi-*⸢*ku*⸣*-tu*
⸢*ša*$_2$ *ta-ḫap*⸣*-šu*$_2$ *ša*$_2$ ⸢^{d}URU$_3$⸣-INIM-*su*
Lo.E. *u* ⸢^{d}UNUG^{ki}-*i*⸣*-ti*
^{I}⸢IR$_3$⸣-^{d}*in-*⸢*nin*⸣
Rev. ⸢^{lu_2}⸣TUG$_2$.BABBAR GIŠ
2 BAN$_2$ ŠIM.LI *ša*$_2$ ⸢*ta-ḫap*⸣*-šu*$_2$
ša$_2$ ^{d}URU$_3$-INIM-⸢*su*⸣
u ^{d}UNUG⸢^{ki}-*i-ti*⸣
⸢^{I}⸣*na-din* ^{lu_2}UŠ.BAR GIŠ
Up.E. [^{it}]^{i}BARA$_2$ UD.15.KAM
[MU].27.KAM
Le.E. ⸢^{d}AG⸣-NIG$_2$.⸢DU⸣-[URU$_3$]
⸢LUGAL TIN⸣.[TIR^{ki}]

Arad-Innin, the washerman, withdrew [×] capes, which were collected from Amīl-Nanāya for × shekels of silver, for cleaning the blanket of Uṣur-amāssu and Urkayītu. Nādinu, the weaver, withdrew 2 *sūtu* of juniper for the blanket of Uṣur-amāssu and Urkayītu.
Month I, day 15, year 27 of Nebuchadnezzar, king of Babylon.

159. NCBT 856

Copy: Plate XXXVIII
Date: 24.III.39 Nbk
Summary: withdrawal (*našû*) note: garments

Obv. 6 GUN 40 MA.NA
^{tug_2}KUR.RA^{meš} ⸢*ša*$_2$ 80⸣ ^{lu_2}ERIN$_2^{me}$
ina pi-ir-ri ša$_2$ ^{iti}ŠU NE *u* KIN
^{Id}*in-nin*-NUMUN-DU$_3$ *u*$^{(over\ a\ DIŠ)}$ ^{I}*ina*-SUḪ$_3$-SUR
GIŠ^{u_2}
Lo.E. ⸢*ina lib*$_3$*-bi*⸣ 8 MA.NA *ina* NIG$_2$.GA

Rev. (blank)
^{iti}SIG$_4$ UD.24.KAM MU.39.KAM
^{d}AG-NIG$_2$.DU-URU$_3$ LUGAL TIN.TIR^{ki}

Innin-zēru-ibni and Ina-tēšî-ēṭir withdrew 6 talents 4 minas of capes for eighty workers from the workforce of months IV, V, and VI; thereof, 8 minas are (still) in the temple stores. Month III, day 24, year 39 of Nebuchadnezzar, king of Babylon.

1–2 The 6 talents 4 minas of capes divided by 80 men come out 5 minas per cape, which is the standard weight at Uruk; see, e.g., PTS 2443, BM 114480. In **No. 174** we find 4 minas 15 shekels per cape, and in **No. 168** we find 4–5 minas per cape.

160. NCBT 826

Copy: Plate XXXVIII
Date: 09.XI.18 Nbk
Summary: accounting note: garment

Obv. 1-*et* ^{tug_2}⸢*šir*⸣-*a-am*
a-na 1 ⸢½⸣ GIN$_2$ KU$_3$.BABBAR
ša$_2$ ^{f}*ba-ni-ti*-^{d}⸢*in-nin*⸣
⸢A⸣-*šu*$_2$ *ša*$_2$ ^{I}⸢NUMUN-*ia*⸣
Rev. (blank)
^{iti}ZIZ$_2$ UD.9.KAM MU.18.KAM
^{d}AG-NIG$_2$.DU-URU$_3$
LUGAL TIN.TIR^{ki}

One *šir'am*-garment for 1 ½ shekels of silver of ^{f}Bānītu-Innin daughter (text: son) of Zēria. Month XI, day 9, year 18 of Nebuchadnezzar, king of Babylon.

161. YBC 4808

Copy: Plate XXXVIII
Date: undated (Nbk)
Summary: withdrawal (*našû*) note: garments

Although it is not explicitly stated in the text, it seems that all individuals were members of the same decury, and that Nabû-aḫu-iddin in l. 14 is the one from l. 6. The latter should be identified as Nabû-aḫu-iddin/Nanāya-ēreš, a decurion during the mid-reign of Nebuchadnezzar; his multiple attestations in epistolographic sources are listed in Levavi 2018, 642–3 (with further discussions throughout the book).

Obv. 1 ^{tug_2}*šir-a-am*
^{Id}UTU-ŠEŠ-MU
1 ^{tug_2}*šir-a-am* ^{Id}EN-SUḪUŠ-*ia*-DU
A ^{I}E$_2$.AN.NA-⸢*li-pi*-URU$_3$⸣
Lo.E. *ša*$_2$ *ina* 10^{ti}
6 *ša*$_2$ ⸢^{Id}AG⸣-ŠEŠ-MU
Rev. A $^{Id!}$*na-na-a*-KAM
4 ½ GIN$_2$ KU$_3$.BABBAR *ku-um*

3 ^{tug_2}*šir-a-am*
^{I}E$_2$.AN.NA-DU$_3$
Up.E. ^{I}ŠEŠ^{me}-*ši*
u ^{I}DUG$_3$.GA-IM-^{d}15
ša$_2$ ina 10^{ti}
Le.E. *ša$_2$* ^{Id}AG-ŠEŠ-MU
GIŠ^{u_2}

One *širʾam*-garment (*for*) Šamaš-aḫu-iddin; one *šir ʾam*-garment (*for*) Bēl-išdīa-ukīn, son of Eanna-līpi-uṣur, who are from the decury of Nabû-aḫu-iddin, son of Nanāya-ēreš; 4 ½ shekels of silver instead of three *širʾam*-garments (*for*) Eanna-ibni, Aḫḫēšu and Ṭāb-šār-Ištar, who are from the decury of Nabû-aḫu-iddin; withdrawn.

162. YBC 9533

Copy: Plate XXXIX
Date: 12.IV.36 Nbk
Summary: withdrawal (*našû*) note: garments and wool

Obv. 1 ^{tug_2}*šir-*⸢*a-am*⸣
⸢*u$_3$*⸣ 2 MA.NA SIK$_2$.ḪI.A
ku-um ^{tug_2}KUR.⸢RA⸣-*šu$_2$*
ša$_2$ MU.36.KAM
^{I}TUKUL-*ti*-^{d}15
Lo.E. ^{lu_2}*mu-kab-bu-u$_2$*
Rev. *it-*⸢*ta-ši*⸣
(blank)
^{iti}ŠU UD.12.KAM
MU.36.KAM
^{d}AG-NIG$_2$.DU-UR[U$_3$]
Up.E. LUGAL ⸢TIN.TIR⸣[^{ki}]

Tukulti-Ištar, the tailor, withdrew one *širʾam*-garment and 2 minas of wool instead of his cape for year 36.
Month IV, day 12, year 36 of Nebuchadnezzar, king of Babylon.

163. NBC 8350

Copy: Plate XXXIX
Date: 11.I.13(+) (*Nbk*)
Summary: *ina pāni* note: linen

Amīl-Nanāya (l. 7) is probably the linen weaver, son of Šullumāya, attested between 18 Nbk (GC 2, 278) and 3$^{?}$ Ner$^{?}$ (PTS 3322); see Payne 2007, 155–6.

Obv. 30 MA.NA ^{gada}*ḫal-ṣ*[*u* (×)]
a-na ^{gada}*gid$_2$-da-lu-*[*u$_2$* (×)]
ša$_2$ pa-ni ^{d}*na-na-*⸢*a ina*⸣ I[GI ^{I}…]
22 MA.NA ^{gada}⸢*ḫal*⸣-[*ṣu* (×)]

5 *a-na* ^{gada}*gid*$_2$*-da-*⸢*lu*⸣*-*[*u*$_2$ (×)]
ša$_2$ ⸢*pa-ni*⸣ ^{d}URU$_3$-INIM-*s*[*u* (×)]
Lo.E. *ina* IGI ⸢^{I}⸣LU$_2$-⸢^{d}*na-na-a*⸣ [*u*]
Rev. ^{I}SUM.NA-*a* A ^{I}⸢*mar*⸣*-d*[*uk*]
(blank)
$^{iti!}$BARA$_2$^{o} UD.11.KAM MU.13.[(+×).KAM]

30 minas of combed linen for the curtain that is before Nanāya are at the disposal of [PN]. 22 minas of combed linen for the curtain that is before Uṣur-amāssu are at the disposal of Amīl-Nanāya [and] Iddināya, son of Marduk.
Month I, day 11, year 13(+).

2 For a discussion of *gidlû*, see Beaulieu 2003, 381–2.

164. NCBT 146

Copy: Plate XXXIX
Date: 26.V.25 Nbk
Summary: *ina pāni* note: linen

Obv. 5 MA.NA 50 GIN$_2$
GADA.ḪI.A *a-na* ⸢*dul-lu*⸣
ina IGI ^{I}*ḫaš-*⸢*di*⸣*-ia*
A ^{Id}⸢*na-na-a-*KAM⸣
Rev. ⸢^{iti}⸣NE$^{!}$ UD.26.KAM
6 MU.25.KAM ⸢^{d}AG-NIG$_2$⸣.DU-URU$_3$
LUGAL TIN.⸢TIR^{ki}⸣

5 minas 50 shekels of linen are at the disposal of Ḫašdia, son of Nanāya-ēreš, for work.
Month V, day 26, year 25 of Nebuchadnezzar, king of Babylon.

165. NCBT 242

Copy: Plate XXXIX
Date: 11.V.25 Nbk
Summary: *ina pāni* note: linen

Obv. 1 ½ MA.NA 8 GIN$_2$
GADA.ḪI.A *a-na*
dul-lu ina IGI
^{I}*ḫaš-di-ia*
5 A ^{Id}*na-na-a-*KAM
Rev. ^{iti}NE UD.11.KAM
MU.25.KAM ^{d}AG-NIG$_2$.DU-URU$_3$
LUGAL TIN.TIR^{ki}

1 mina 38 shekels of linen for work are at the disposal of Ḫašdia, son of Nanāya-ēreš.
Month V, day 11, year 25 of Nebuchadnezzar, king of Babylon.

166. YBC 9470

Copy: Plate XXXIX
Date: 13.VI.24 Nbk
Summary: *ina pāni* note: linen

Obv. 8 MA.NA GADA.ḪI.A *a-*⸢*na*⸣
dul-lu ina pa-ni ^{I}*ḫaš-*⸢*di-ia*$_{2}$⸣
A ^{Id}*na-na-a*-KAM
⸢8⸣ MA.NA *ina pa-ni*
[^{Id}*na*]-*na-a*-MU
Lo.E. [A ^{I}L]U$_{2}$-^{d}*na-na-a*
Rev. ⸢^{lu_2}⸣*pu-ṣa-a-a*
(blank)
^{iti}KIN ⸢UD⸣.13.KAM
MU.24.KAM ^{d}AG-NIG$_{2}$.DU-URU$_{3}$
LUGAL TIN.TIR^{ki}

8 minas of linen for work are at the disposal of Ḫašdia, son of Nanāya-ēreš; 8 minas are at the disposal of Nanāya-iddin, son of Amīl-Nanāya, the linen weaver.
Month VI, day 13, year 24 of Nebuchadnezzar, king of Babylon.

167. YBC 9385

Copy: Plate XL
Date: 01.XII.31+ Nbk
Summary: *maḫir* receipt: linen

Obv. ⅔ MA.NA ^{gada}⸢*ṭu*⸣*-man-ni*
^{Id}*na-na-a*-MU
A ^{I}LU$_{2}$-^{d}*na-na-a* ^{lu_2}*pu-*⸢*ṣa*⸣-[*a-a*]
IGI^{ir}
Rev. (blank)
^{iti}ŠE UD.1.KAM MU.31[(+×).KAM]
^{d}AG-NIG$_{2}$.DU-URU$_{3}$ ⸢LUGAL TIN.TIR^{ki}⸣

40 minas of *ṭumānu*-linen thread were received from Nanāya-iddin, son of Amīl-Nanāya, the linen weaver.
Month XII, day 1, year 31+ of Nebuchadnezzar, king of Babylon.

168. NBC 4920

Copy: Plate XL–XLI
Date: 05.×.05 Cyr
Summary: issue (*nadin*) list: wool

Obv. [SIK$_{2}$.ḪI].⸢A⸣ *a-na* ^{tug_2}KUR.RA$^{⸢meš⸣}$ *ša*$_{2}$ ^{munus}*za-*⸢*ki-tu*$_{2}$ SUM⸣^{nu}
[ITI].⸢×⸣ UD.10.KAM MU.5.KAM *ku-raš* LUGAL E$^{⸢ki⸣}$ LUGAL KUR.KUR

---

5 MA.NA ^{f}*bu-ra-šu*$_{2}$

	4 MA.NA	^{f}*an-di-ia*
	4 MA.NA	^{f}⸢*li*⸣-*i*ʾ-*du-u*ʾ
	2 MA.NA	^{fd}⸢*aš*$_2$⸣-*ka*-ʾ-*i-tu*$_4$-*ṭa-bat*
	2 MA.NA	^{I}*ta*-⸢*ri*⸣-*bi*
	4 MA.NA	^{f}*ana*-E$_2$.AN.NA-*ḫa*-⸢*am-mat*⸣
	4 MA.NA	^{f}*a-ḫat*-AD-*šu*$_2$
	4 MA.NA	^{f}⸢*a-mat*⸣-*a*
	4 MA.NA	^{I}⸢*zab-di*⸣-*ia*
	2 MA.NA	^{fd}*aš*$_2$-⸢*ka*⸣-ʾ-*i-tu*$_4$-*ṭa-bat* ⸢DUMU⸣.SAL-*su*
	4 MA.NA	^{f}⸢*ba*!⸣-*zi-i-tu*$_4$
	⸢1 (+×)⸣ MA.NA	^{I}*za-an-zi-i-ri* ⸢DUMU⸣-*šu*$_2$
	⸢1 (+×)⸣ MA.NA	^{I}IR$_3$?-^{d}*bu-ne-ne* DUMU-*šu*$_2$
	1 MA.NA	^{f}UD-*si*-⸢*aš*$_2$/*pa*⸣-*a*ʾ
	⸢4⸣ MA!.NA	^{f}*a-mat-a*
	2 MA.NA	^{f}*na-ḫiš-ša*$_2$-*i-mur-šu*$_2$
	(blank)	
	⸢PAP?⸣ 51 MA.NA	
	9 *ša*$_2$ *iš-kar*	
Rev.	[× M]A.⸢NA⸣	⸢^{f} [×]-⸢×-×⸣[(× ×)]⸣
	⸢4?⸣ MA.NA	⸢^{f}DUG.GA-*a-tu*$_4$⸣
	4 MA.NA	⸢^{f}×-$^{d?}$*na*?-*na*?-*a*?-×-×⸣
	4 MA.NA	⸢^{f}× × × ×⸣
	2 MA.NA	⸢^{f}× × × ×⸣-*ni*
	4 MA.NA	^{f}*m*[*i*]-*ṣa-t*[*u*$_4$]
	4 MA.NA	^{fd}*aš*$_2$-⸢*ka*-ʾ-*i-tu*$_4$⸣-*ṭa-bat*
	4 MA.NA	^{f}*bi*-[*n*]*i*-⸢*tu*$_4$⸣
	2 MA.NA	^{f}*ša*$_2$-*ḫi*-[*na*]-⸢*tu*$_4$⸣
	4 MA.NA	^{f}*a*$^{!(T. za)}$-*šar-ši*-⸢*i*-AMA⸣
	1 MA.NA	^{f}*ḫi-pa-a*
	4 MA.NA	⸢^{f}⸣[×]-⸢×⸣-⸢*ta*?⸣-*a*
	4 MA.NA	^{f}[*a-ḫat*]-AD-*šu*$_2$
	4 MA.NA	^{fd}⸢*in-nin*⸣-*e-ṭe*$_3$-*rat*
	4 MA.NA	^{f}*ši*-⸢*da*⸣-*a*
	1 MA.NA	^{Id}UR.IDIM-DINGIR-*u*$_2$-*a*
	4 MA.NA	^{f}*ina*-^{d}*na-na-a-ul-tar-ra-aḫ*
	1 MA.NA	^{Id}*na-na-a*-MU
	4 MA.NA	^{f}*mi-ṣa-tu*$_4$
	1 MA.NA	^{f}⸢*li*⸣-*i*ʾ-*du-u*ʾ
	4 MA.NA	^{I}*a-na*-E$_2$-*šu*$_2$
	4 MA.NA	^{f}*ka*?!-*am-na*?!-*a*ʾ
	[×+] 1 MA.NA	^{f}*taš-li-mu*
	[PAP?.P]AP 1 GUN 14 MA.<NA>	
Up.E.	[(× ×)] 15 *ša*$_2$ *iš-kar*	

[Wool] for capes, given to *zakītu*-women; Month ×, day 10, year 5 of Cyrus king of Babylon, king of all the lands:
5 minas (to) ^{f}Burāšu; 4 minas (to) ^{f}Andia; 4 minas (to) ^{f}*Līdū*; 2 minas (to) ^{f}Aškaʾ ītu-ṭābat; 2 minas

(to) Tarību; 4 minas (to) ^{f}Ana-Eanna-ḫammat; 4 minas (to) ^{f}Aḫāt-abīšu; 4 minas (to) ^{f}Amātā; 4 minas (to) Zabdia; 2 minas (to) ^{f}Aška᾿ītu-ṭābat, his daughter; 4 minas (to) ^{f}Bazītu; 1(+) mina(s) (to) Zanzīru, her son; 1(+) mina(s) (to) Arad-Bunene, her son; 1 mina (to) ^{f}UD*sipā*; 4 minas (to) ^{f}Amātā; 2 minas (to) ^{f}*Naḫiš-ša-īmur(u)šu*; total of 51 minas; nine for the *iškāru*-obligation.
[×] minas (to) ^{f}[...]; 4 minas (to) ^{f}Ṭābatu; 4 minas (to) ^{f}×-Nanāya-×; 4 minas (to) ^{f}...; 2 minas (to) ^{f}...-ni; 4 minas (to) ^{f}Mīṣātu; 4 minas (to) ^{f}Aška᾿ītu-ṭābat; 4 minas (to) ^{f}Binītu; 4 minas (to) ^{f}*Šaḫinatu*; 4 minas (to) ^{f}Ašar-šī-*ummu*; 1 mina (to) ^{f}Ḫīpāya; 4 minas (to) ^{f}...-*tāya*; 4 minas (to) ^{f}[Aḫāt]-abīšu; 4 minas (to) ^{f}Innin-ēṭirat; 4 minas (to) ^{f}Šidâ; 1 mina (to) Ur(i)dimmu-ilūa; 4 minas (to) ^{f}Ina-Nanāya-ultarraḫ; 1 mina (to) Nanāya-iddin; 4 minas (to) ^{f}Mīṣātu; 1 mina (to) ^{f}*Līdū*; 4 minas (to) Ana-bītišu; 4 minas (to) *Kamnā*; 1(+) minas (to) ^{f}Tašlīmu; total of 1 talent 14 minas; 15 for the *iškāru*-obligation.

14, 15 If the tally of 51 (l. 19), and if 17 is indeed the figure in l. 17, then both l. 14 and 15 probably list 2 minas each.

20, 43 The figures 9 and 15, referring to *iškāru* obligations, are unclear; the number of individuals listed on the Obv. and Rev. is greater than 9 and 15 respectively. Still, it seems most reasonable that an unknown grouping of the names should correspond to *iškāru* assignments.

169. NBC 4679

Copy: Plate XL
Date: 25.I.-- (Nbk–Nbn)
Summary: issue (*nadin*) note: silver

Apkallu (l. 4) is attested between 26 Nbk (OECT 10, 315) and 10 Nbn (**No. 154**); see Payne 2007, 157–8.

Obv. [× GI]N$_2$ KU$_3$.BABBAR *ba-ab-t*[*u*$_4$]
[×] MA.NA ⌜KU$_3$⌝.BABBAR *a*-⌜*na*⌝
ta-kil-tu$_4$ *a-na*
^{I}NUN.ME *na-din*
⌜^{iti}⌝BARA$_2$ UD.25.KAM
Rev. (uninscribed)

[× she]kels of silver, part of the [×] minas of silver for blue-purple wool, were given to Apkallu.
Month I, day 25.

1 For *bābtu* see commentary to **No. 97**: 5.

170. NCBT 1057

Copy: Plate XL–XLI
Date: undated (Npl–Nbk)
Summary: accounting inventory: wool for silver

For Kudurru (l. 19), a weaver, see **No. 151**.

Obv. 11 GUN 15 ⌜MA.NA SIK$_2$.ḪI⌝.A *ša*$_2$ 2 ½ MA.NA KU$_3$.⌜BABBAR⌝
^{I}*ša*$_2$-*pi-i*-^{d}EN {eras.} ⌜DUMU⌝ ^{Id}AG-ŠEŠ^{meš}-SUM.NA

36 GUN *ša*$_2$ 8 ˹MA˺.NA KU$_3$.BABBAR ^{I}*ku-na-a* A ^{Id}EN-MU
20 GUN 15 MA.˹NA SIK$_2$˺.ḪI.A *ša*$_2$ 4 ½ MA.NA KU$_3$.BABBAR
^{I}˹*e-zu*˺*-pa-šir*$_3$
[×] GUN ^{I}MU-DU ˹9˺ GUN 40 MA.NA ^{I}˹NUMUN˺-DU
1 GUN ^{I}*aḫ-ḫu-tu* 1 GUN ^{Id}EN-KAR^{ir}
1 GUN 20 MA.NA ^{Id}EN-TIN^{it} A ^{I}ŠEŠ^{meš}-*ša*$_2$*-a*
a-na ⅓ GIN$_2$ KU$_3$.BABBAR

[4+] ½ GUN *ša*$_2$ 1 MA.NA KU$_3$.BABBAR
[*ina*] IGI ^{I}*šul-lu-mu*

Lo.E. [×+] 86 {20}
Rev. 4 ½ GUN SIK$_2$.ḪI.A ˹*ša*$_2$˺ 1 MA.NA KU$_3$.BABBAR ˹I˺[...]
18 GUN 8 MA.NA *ša*$_2$ 4$^{!?}$ MA.NA {eras.} KU$_3$.BABBAR
^{Id}AG-KAR^{ir} DUMU ^{I}EN-*šu*$_2$*-nu* IGI
3 MA.NA ˹*re-e*˺*-ḫi ša*$_2$ ½ MA.NA KU$_3$.GI

˹1˺ GUN SIK$_2$.ḪI.A *a-na* 15 GIN$_2$ KU$_3$.BABBAR ^{Id}EN-MU-GAR^{un}
˹3˺6 MA$^{!}$.NA {eras.} *a-na* 9 GIN$_2$ KU$_3$.BABBAR (blank)
˹8˺ MA.NA {eras.} ^{I}NIG$_2$.DU
3[+× GU]N 10 MA.NA ^{lu_2}UŠ.BAR^{meš}
1 ˹GUN˺ *ina* IGI ^{lu_2}*qi*$_2$*-i-pi*
8 MA.NA ˹*ina* IGI˺ ^{I}*mu-še-zib-*^{d}AMAR.UTU 30 MA.NA ^{I}*za-bi-da-a*
1 GUN ˹^{Id}AMAR.UTU˺-LUGAL-*a-ni* 42 MA.NA ˹I˺*e-zu-pa-šir*$_3$$^{?}$

Up.E. PAP 1 ME 16 G[U]N 42$^{?}$ MA.NA {eras.}
ša$_2$ 21 MA.NA ˹⅔?˺ [ ] GIN$_2$ KU$_3$.BABBAR
Le.E. 22 ½ ˹5˺ 4[(×)] 22

11 talents 15 minas of wool for 2 ½ minas of silver, Ša-pî-Bēl, son of Nabû-aḫḫē-iddin; 36 talents for 8 minas of silver, Kūnāya, son of Bēl-iddin; 20 talents 15 minas of wool for 4 ½ minas of silver, Ezu-pašir; [×] talents, Šumu-ukīn; 9 talents 40 minas, Zēru-ukīn; 1 talent, Aḫḫūtu; 1 talent, Bēl-ēṭir; 1 talent 20 minas, Bēl-uballiṭ, son of Aḫḫēšāya, for 20 shekels of silver.
[4] ½ talent for 1 mina of silver, [at the] disposal of Šullumu.
[×] 86; 4 ½ talents of wool for 1 mina of silver, [...]; 18 talents 8 minas for 4 minas of silver, *received from* Nabû-ēṭir, son of Bēlšunu; 3 minas are the balance of ½ mina of gold.
1 talent of wool for 15 shekels of silver, Bēl-šumu-iškun; 36 minas for 9 shekels of silver, ø, 8 minas, Kudurru; 3(+) talents 10 minas, the weavers; 1 talent at the disposal of the *qīpu*; 8 minas at the disposal of Mušēzib-Marduk; 30 minas Zabidāya; 1 talent, Marduk-šarrāni; 42 minas, Ezu-pašir.
Total of 116 talents 42 minas for 21 minas *40*(+) shekels of silver; 22 ½ 5 4(+) 22.

14 4$^{!}$, text: *ša*$_2$. Although it has only three wedges, 3 would have been written as three vertical wedges and not as a *ša*$_2$.

171. YBC 9368

Copy: Plate XLI
Date: 13.I.26 Nbk
Summary: *ina pāni* note + withdrawal (*našû*) note: wool

Obv. [× MA].⸢NA SIK$_2$⸣.ḪI.A
[*a*]-⸢*na*⸣ *dul-lu ina* IGI
[^{I}]⸢*na*⸣-*din* A-*šu*$_2$ *ša*$_2$ ^{Id}U.GUR-PAP
A ^{lu2}UŠ.BAR ^{iti}BARA$_2$
UD.13.KAM MU.⸢26⸣.KAM
^{d}AG-NIG$_2$.DU-URU$_3$
Lo.E. [L]UGAL TIN.TIR^{ki}
Rev. ^{Id}AG-*a-na-*⸢*bil-ti*⸣-*e-re-ḫi*
^{lu2}*qal-la-šu*$_2$ ⸢GIŠ⸣

[× mi]nas of wool are at the disposal of Nādinu, son of Nergal-nāṣir, descendant of Išparu, for work.
Month I, day 13, year 26 of Nebuchadnezzar, king of Babylon.
Nabû-ana-bilti-ēreḫ, his slave, withdrew (the above-mentioned wool).

172. NCBT 710

Copy: Plate XLI
Date: 25.I.13 Nbk
Summary: *ina pāni* note: wool

Obv. ⸢5⸣ GIN$_2$ ^{sik2}*ta-bar-*⸢*ri*⸣
10 GIN$_2$ ^{sik2}*ta-*⸢*kil-ti*⸣
a-na dul-lu ša$_2$ ⸢TUG$_2$ *ša*$_2$$^{!(T.\ a)}$ *za-ra-tu*$_2$⸣
ina IGI ^{I}BA^{ša2}-*a* ^{lu2}⸢UŠ⸣.BAR
Rev. ^{iti}BARA$_2$ UD.25.KAM MU.13.KAM
^{d}AG-NIG$_2$.DU-URU$_3$ LUGAL TIN.TIR^{ki}

5 shekels of red wool and 10 shekels of purple wool are at the disposal of Iqīšāya, the weaver, for the work of the cloth of the tent.
Month I, day 25, year 13 of Nebuchadnezzar, king of Babylon.

173. YBC 9411

Copy: Plate XLII
Date: 24.XIIb.[×] Nbk
Summary: *ina pāni* note: wool

Obv. {three lines erased}
3 MA.NA SIK$_2$.ḪI.A *a-na*
ṣi-pi ša$_2$ *ta-bar-ri*
[*gid*$_2$$^{?}$-*l*]*u*$^{!?(T.\ [a]š_2)}$⸣-*u*$_2$$^{!?(T.\ lu)}$ *ša*$_2$ *za-ra-ti*
Lo.E. [*i*]*na* IGI ^{Id}EN-E ^{lu2}UŠ.BAR
Rev. (blank)

[^{iti}]⸢DIRI.ŠE.KIN.KUD.DA⸣ UD.24.KAM
[MU.×.KAM] ^{d}AG-NIG$_2$.DU-PAP LUGAL ⸢E⸣[^{ki}]

3 minas of wool for the red dyeing of the (*door*) *curtain* of the tent are at the disposal of Bēl-iqbi, the weaver.
Month XIIb, day 24, [year ×] of Nebuchadnezzar, king of Babylon.

1 Some of the erased lines are partialy readable, or reconstructable: {^{1} … MU ^{2} *ša*$_2$ … *ina* IGI ^{3} ^{Id}*na-na-a*-KAM$^{?}$ ^{lu2}*pu-ṣa-a-a*}.

174. NCBT 641

Copy: Plate XLII–XLIII
Date: 19.IV.38 Nbk
Summary: accounting inventory: textiles

Obv. 1 ^{tug2}KUR.RA 4 MA.NA 15 GIN$_2$ ⸢KI⸣.<LA$_2$>
a-na ⸢8$^{?}$⸣ ½ MA.NA SIK$_2$.ḪI.A ^{f}*bu-ʾ-i-tu*$_2$
1 ⸢^{tug2}KUR.RA⸣ 1 ^{tug2}*šir-a-am a-na* 2 ½ GIN$_2$ ⸢*bit*⸣*-qa*
⸢*ša*$_2$ ^{I}KI-E$_2$⸣.AN.NA-*bu-di-ia*$_2$ *ina* NIG$_2$.⸢GA⸣
1 ⸢^{tug2}KUR.RA⸣ *a-na* 1 ½ GIN$_2$ *ina šad*^{da}*-di-šu*$_2$
[(*ša*$_2$)] MU.38.KAM ⸢*ša*$_2$ $^{I⸢d}$EN-DU$_3^{uš}$
2 ⸢^{tug2}⸣KUR.RA^{me} *a-na* 4 GIN$_2$ 4^{tu2}
ša$_2$ ^{Id}AG-DU-IBILA$^{!}$ A ^{I}ŠEŠ-MU-$^{d!}$AMAR.UTU
1 ^{tug2}KUR.RA ⸢*a-na*⸣ 2 ½ GIN$_2$ ⸢KU$_3$⸣.BABBAR
Lo.E. <<*ina*>> *ša*$_2$ ^{Id}AG-ŠEŠ-MU A ^{I}LU$_2$-^{d}AG ⸢*ina* ŠA$_3$⸣ ½ GIN$_2$
Rev. *it-ta-ši*
½ MA.NA 4^{tu2} KU$_3$.BABBAR *ina* KU$_3$.BABBAR ⸢*ša*$_2$⸣ *ina* IGI
{eras.} ^{Id}AG-DU-ŠEŠ *ina* ŠU^{II} ^{I}ZALAG$_2$-*e-a* A ^{I}LU$_2$-⸢^{d}AG⸣
2 ^{tug2}KUR.RA^{meš} *a-na* 4 GIN$_2$ KU$_3$.BABBAR *ša*$_2$ ^{I}*tab-ne*$_2$*-e-a*
A ^{Id}AG-DU$_3^{uš}$ *ina* NIG$_2$.GA
1 ^{tug2}KUR.RA *a-na* 2 GIN$_2$ ⸢*ša*$_2$⸣ ^{I}IR$_3$-^{d}*in-nin*
A ^{Id}AG-MU-DU$_3$ *ina* KU$_3$.BABBAR *ša*$_2$ *ina* IGI-*šu*$_2$
⸢1 ^{tug2}KUR.RA⸣ *a-na* 7 MA.NA 10 GIN$_2$ *ša*$_2$ SIK$_2$.ḪI.A
[-*i*]*n*$^{?}$*-du-u*$_2$ DUMU.SAL-*su ša*$_2$ ^{I}*na-din ina* NIG$_2$.GA
[KU$_3$].⸢BABBAR⸣ *ša*$_2$ *ina* IGI ^{Id}AG-DU-A
[ ] A ^{I}*mar*-⸢*duk*⸣
Up.E. ⸢^{iti}ŠU⸣ UD.20.1.LA$_2$.KAM MU.38.KAM
^{d}AG-NIG$_2$.DU-URU$_3$ LUGAL TIN.TIR⸢^{ki}⸣

One cape weighing 4 minas 15 shekels, for 8 ½ minas of wool (*of/from*) ^{f}Buʾitu; one cape and one *šir ʾam*-garment for 2 ⅝ shekels of Itti-Eanna-būdia from the temple stores; one cape for 1 ½ shekels, from his *box* [(*for/of*)] year 38, of Bēl-īpuš; two capes for 4 ¼ shekels of Nabû-mukīn-apli, son of Aḫu-iddin-Marduk; one cape for 2 ½ shekels of silver of Nabû-aḫu-iddin, son of Amīl-Nabû, *for/from* which he withdrew ½ shekels; 30 ¼ (shekels of) silver from the silver that is at the disposal of Nabû-mukīn-aḫi (*delivered*) via Nūrea, son of Amīl-Nabû; two capes for 4 shekels of silver of Tabnēa, son of Nabû-īpuš are from the temple stores; one cape for 2 shekels of Arad-Innin, son of Nabû-šumu-ukīn, from the silver at his disposal; one cape for 7 minas 10 shekels of wool; [...] the daughter of Nādinu from the temple stores, [...] silver that is at the disposal of Nabû-mukīn-apli [... ...], son of Marduk. Month IV, day 19, year 38 of Nebuchadnezzar, king of Babylon.

5 The unclear *šad*^{da}-*di-šu*$_2$ is read as a form of *šaddu*, box. For textile being stored in *šaddu* boxes, see Nbn 1090: 5, Nbn 1121: 11, 15. The one attestation listed in the CAD (Š/I, 32) for *šad(d)ādu* as a textile, JSOR 11 131, 37: 19, is an Old Akkadian text and cannot be of relevance here.

175. NBC 4707

Copy: Plate XLII
Date: 13.VIII.38$^?$ Nbk
Summary: accounting inventory: silver

Obv. ⸢8⸣ GIN$_2$ KU$_3$.BABBAR *ša*$_2$ ^{I}*šu-la-a* A ^{I}NUMUN-*ia*$_2$
1 GIN$_2$ *ša*$_2$ ^{Id}EN-DU$_3$ A ^{I}*na-din*
a-na SIK$_2$.ḪI.A *ina* NIG$_2$.GA
(blank)
Rev. (blank)
[^{i}]^{ti}APIN UD.13.KAM MU.⸢38$^?$⸣.<KAM>
[^{d}A]G-NIG$_2$.DU-URU$_3$ ⸢LUGAL TIN.TIR^{ki}⸣

8 shekels of silver of Šulāya, son of Zēria, (and) 1 shekel of Bēl-ibni, son of Nādinu, for wool, are in the temple stores.
Month VIII, day 13, year 38$^?$ of Nebuchadnezzar, king of Babylon.

176. NCBT 632

Copy: Plate XLII–XLIII
Date: 13.II.14 (Nbn)
Summary: issue (*nadin*) list + *maḫir* receipt: textiles[19]

Innin-šumu-uṣur is attested between 40 Nbk (**No. 246**) and 15 Nbn (YOS 19, 47); see Payne 2007, 172. For a discussion on the different colors attested in the text, see Thavapalan 2020. Two noticable aspects regarding scribal practice are the irregular shape of the tablet and the shortcut "MA" for "MA. NA."

Obv. PAP 5 GUN 24 ⸢MA⸣.NA SIK$_2$.ḪI.A
15 MA 7 GIN$_2$ ^{sik2}*ta-kil-tu*$_2$
37 MA 8 ½ GIN$_2$ ^{gada}*ṭu-ma-nu*
21 MA 16 GIN$_2$ *in-za-*⸢*ḫu-re*⸣*-tu*$_2$
1 (GUN) 36 ⅔ MA 5 GIN$_2$ ^{sik2}ZA.GIN$_3$ *ša*$_2$ KA ŠEN
2 ½ MA ^{na4}*gab-u*$_2$ *ša*$_2$ ^{kur}*mi-ṣir*
50 ½ ⸢MA⸣ ^{giš}ḪAB
8 ⅔ ⸢MA 6⸣ ½ GIN$_2$ ^{sik2}ḪE$_2$.ME.DA *ša*$_2$ *in-za-ḫu-re-tu*$_2$
20 MA ^{na4}*gab-u*$_2$ *ša*$_2$ *ka-šap-pi*
½ MA 7 GIN$_2$ *tuk-riš*

19 A previous edition is included in Payne 2007, 128–9.

3 MA ^{sik_2}IR$_3$-U$_2$-MA-MEŠ
ša$_2$ *a-di* UD.5.KAM *ša*$_2$ ^{iti}ZIZ$_2$
ša$_2$ MU.12.KAM *a-na dul-lu*
a-na ^{Id}*in-nin*-MU-URU$_3$ *na-ad-nu*
ina ŠA$_3$ 25 MA.NA ⅓ 6 ⅔ GIN$_2$ ^{tug_2}*m*[*i-iḫ*]-*ṣ*[*u*]
ša$_2$ ^{sik_2}ZA.GIN$_3$ *ša*$_2$ KA ŠEN
Lo.E. ⸢9⸣ MA.⸢NA⸣ 2 ½ GIN$_2$ ^{gada}*ṭu*-[*ma-nu*]
Rev. 1⸢2⸣ MA ⸢48$^?$ ⅓⸣ GIN$_2$ KI.MIN [×]
36° MA ⸢9⸣ ⅔ GIN$_2$ KI.MIN ^{sik_2}⸢ḪE$_2$⸣.[ME.DA *ša*$_2$ ×]
3 MA 12 GIN$_2$ 3 4$^{tu_2.me}$ *gir*$_2$-*u*$_2$ ⸢KI⸣.MIN
ša$_2$ ^{sik_2}ḪE$_2$.ME.DA *ša*$_2$ *in-za-ḫu-re-tu*$_4$
1 MA.NA 53 GIN$_2$ *bit-qa* KI.MIN *ša*$_2$ ^{sik_2}ZA.GIN$_3$.⸢KUR⸣.RA
⅓ 8 GIN$_2$ KI.MIN *ša*$_2$ *tuk-riš*
⅔ MA.NA 7 ½ GIN$_2$ KI.MIN *ša*$_2$ ^{sik_2}ḪAŠḪUR
a-di UD.14.KAM *ša*$_2$° ^{iti}GU$_4$ MU.13.KAM
^{Id}*in-nin*-MU-URU$_3$ *ma-ḫi-ir*

Total: 5 talents 24 minas of wool: 15 minas 7 shekels of purple wool, 37 minas 8 ½ shekels of *ṭumānu*-linen thread, 21 minas 16 shekels of *inzaḫurētu*-dye, 1 (talent) 36 minas 45 shekels of "fresh" purple wool, 2 ½ minas of alum from Egypt, 50 ½ minas of madder, 8 minas 46 ½ shekels of red wool (dyed with) *inzaḫurētu*, 20 minas of alum from Kašappu, 37 shekels of red-purple wool, 3 minas of … wool; (all of) which was given to Innin-šumu-uṣur up through Month XI, day 5, year 12, for work.
From this, 25 minas 26 ⅔ shekels of *wo*[*ven cloth*] of "fresh" purple wool, 9$^?$ minas 2 ½ shekels of *ṭumānu*-linen thread, 12 minas 48 ⅓ (+) shekels ditto […], 36 minas 9 ⅔ shekels ditto of red [wool (dyed with) …], 3 minas 12 $^{18}/_{24}$ ditto of red wool (dyed with) *inzaḫurētu*, 1 mina 53 ⅛ shekels ditto of purple wool, 28 shekels ditto of red-purple wool, and 47 ½ shekels ditto of apple-colored wool, have been received from Innin-šumu-uṣur up through Month II, day 14, year 13.

5, 16 "Fresh," *ša pî ruqqi*, lit. from the mouth of the cauldron; see Payne 2007, 137 n. 245. Thavapalan (2020, 193) suggests that this refers to a relatively dark(er) shade of blue-purple.
11 ^{sik_2}IR$_3$-U$_2$-MA-MEŠ is unclear. The context suggests a type of dyed wool.

177. NCBT 758

Copy: Plate XLIII
Date: 03.XIIb.42 Nbk
Summary: *maḫir* receipt + *ina pāni* note: wool

Obv. ⅚ MA.NA 5 GIN$_2$ ^{sik_2}*ta-kil-ti*
(tiny line) *a-di gu-ra-*⸢*bi*⸣
ša$_2$ *a-na* 9 GIN$_2$ KU$_3$.BABBAR ^{I}NUN.ME
DUMU ^{lu_2}UŠ.BAR *ul-tu* TIN.TIR⸢^{ki}⸣
im-ḫu-ru a-na E$_2$.AN.NA
(tiny line) *ma-ḫi-*⸢*ir*⸣
ina lib$_3$-*bi* ⅔ MA.NA 4^{tu_2} *bit-*⸢*qa*⸣
Lo.E. *a-na dul-lu*

ina IGI ^{I}*ṣil-la-a*
Rev. A ^{I}*na-din* $^{\text{lu}_2}$UŠ.BAR
(blank)
^{iti}DIRI.ŠE.KIN.KUD UD.3.KAM
MU.42.KAM
Up.E. ⸢^{d}AG⸣-NIG$_2$.DU-URU$_3$
LUGAL ⸢TIN⸣.TIR⸢^{ki}⸣

55 shekels of purple wool, together with a sack, which Apkallu, descendant of Išparu, received from Babylon for 9 shekels of silver, were received (from him) for Eanna; thereof 40 ⅜ shekels are at the disposal of Ṣillāya, son of Nādinu, the weaver, for work.
Month XIIb, day 3, year 42 of Nebuchadnezzar, king of Babylon.

178. YBC 3512

Copy: Plate XLIV
Date: [… *Nbk*]
Summary: *maḫir* receipt: garments

For Kudurru (l. 11), a weaver, see **No. 151**.

Obv. 1 TUG$_2$ $^{\text{sik}_2}$⸢ḪE$_2$.ME.DA × × ×⸣
GAL-*ti* 2 ⸢$^{\text{tug}_2}$GU$_2$.E$_3$⸣ TUR^{me}
1 $^{\text{tug}_2}$*ṣa-pu-u* 6 $^{\text{tug}_2}$*par-ši-gu*^{me}

---

7 ⸢$^{\text{tug}_2}$UR$_2$ DARA$_2$-*ti* GAL-*ti*^{me}
8 $^{\text{tug}_2}$*ṣib-ti* TUR^{me}
1 $^{\text{tug}_2}$*me-ze-eḫ* GADA$^{!}$ BABBAR-*u*
Rev. [×] $^{\text{tug}_2}$*ne$_2$-bi-ḫu* 3 MA.NA 10 GIN$_2$
⸢SIK$_2$⸣ *ta-*⸢*bar*⸣ *ša$_2$ ḫaš-ḫu-re-tu$_2$ ḫa-a-ṭu*
PAP 1 GUN ⸢21 MA.NA⸣ [× GI]N$_2$
$^{\text{tug}_2}$*mi-iḫ-*[*ṣu* × ×] ⸢× ×⸣ [ ]
^{I}NIG$_2$.DU ⸢*ma*$^{?}$⸣-[*ḫir*$^{?}$ × × ×]
⸢^{iti}⸣[× MU.×.KAM … LUGAL]
Up.E. TIN.[TIR^{ki}]

One large cloth of red wool …, two small *naḫlaptu*-(outer) garments, one *ṣapû*-dyed garment, six *paršīgu*-headdresses.
Seven large *sūnu*-cloth strips (with) *nēbettu*-belts, eight small *ṣibtu*-garments, one white linen *mezēḫu*-band, [×] *nēbeḫu*-sash, 3 minas 10 shekels of red (dyed with) apple-color dye wool are in stock.
Total of 1 talent 21 minas, [×] shekels of woven cloth … received from Kudurru.
[Month ×, day ×, year × of RN, king of] Babylon.

179. NBC 4645

Copy: Plate XLIV
Date: 19.III.04 (Nbk)
Summary: *maḫir* receipt (with heading): silver

Arad-Innin / Kūnāya (ll. 3–4) is attested between 7 Npl (GC 2, 74) and 9 Nbk (GC 1, 12).

Obv. KU$_3$.BABBAR *ša$_2$ a-˹na˺* SIK$_2$.ḪI.A *maḫ-˹ra˺*
^{iti}SIG$_4$ UD.19.KAM MU.˹4˺.KAM
6 MA.NA ^{I}IR$_3$-^{d}INNIN.˹NA˺
A-*šu$_2$ ša$_2$* ^{I}*ku*$^{?!}$*-na-a*
½ MA.NA ^{Id}AG$^{!}$-IBILA-MU
A ^{Id}EN-NIGIN$_2$^{ir}
[×] GIN$_2$ *gi-ru-u* LA$_2$ ^{Id}AG-A-MU
A ^{Id}EN-TIN^{it}
[×] ˹GIN$_2$˺ ^{I}IR$_3$-˹*ia$_2$*˺ ^{lu_2}ŠU.I
[*u$_3$*$^{?}$] ^{I}A-*a*
[× × × ^{I}]˹^{d}˺*na-na-a*-TIN^{it}
Rev. (blank)
˹^{iti}SIG$_4$˺ UD.19.KAM
[(×) M]U.˹4$^{?}$˺.KAM
Up.E. [(RN)]

Silver that was received for wool, Month III, day 19, year 4: 6 minas (from) Arad-Innin, son of Kūnāya; ½ mina (from) Nabû-aplu-iddin, son of Bēl-upaḫḫir; [×] minus ⅛ shekel (from) Nabû-aplu-iddin, son of Bēl-uballiṭ; [×] shekels (from) Ardia, the barber, [*and*] Aplāya [...] Nanāya-uballiṭ.
Month III, day 19, year 4 of [...].

11 It is possible, perhaps probable, that the break contains a relationship between Aplāya and Nanāya-uballiṭ. Since no such individual is known, we have not restored it here.

180. YBC 11471

Copy: Plate XLIV
Date: 11(+).III.× Nbk
Summary: withdrawal (*našû*) note(?) + *maḫir* receipt (?): wool

Obv. ˹12˺ MA.NA ˹SIK$_2$˺.[ḪI.A]
2 GIN$_2$ KU$_3$.BABBAR *ḫa-a-*[*ṭu*]
ku-um i-di ^{gi}[^{š}MA$_2$]
ša$_2$ AN.BAR *ina lib$_3$-bi a-n*[*a*]
i-lu-u$_2$ ^{Id}*na-na-˹a˺*-[×]
A ^{I}*ki-rib-ti it-˹t*[*a-ši* ( )]
8 MA.NA SIK$_2$.ḪI.A *ša$_2$* 2 ^{t}[$^{ug_2?}$]
Lo.E. 2 ˹GIN$_2$˺ KU$_3$.BABBAR *ḫa-a-ṭu* <<*i*-[(*di*>>)]
9 ˹*ku*˺*-um i-di* ^{giš}MA$_2$ ˹×˺ [ ]
Rev. *ša$_2$* AN.BAR *ina lib$_3$-bi a-na* TIN.TI[R^{ki}]

na-šu-u$_2$ ^{I}⸢^{d}*na-na*⸣-[*a*-×]
A ^{Id}AG-SU$^?$ ⸢*ma*$^?$-*ḫi*$^?$-*ir*$^?$⸣ [( )]
(blank)
⸢^{iti}SIG$_4$ UD.11(+×).KAM⸣ M[U.×.KAM]
^{d}AG-⸢NIG$_2$.DU-URU$_3$⸣ LUG[AL TIN.TIR^{ki}]

12 minas of wool […] 2 shekels of silver in stoc[k …] instead of the rent for the [boat, ...] of iron, of which […] was loaded, Nanāya-[…], son of Kiribtu, withdrew.
8 minas of wool for two *ga[rments* (…)], 2 shekels of silver in stock, instead of the rent of the boat […] that carried iron to Babylon; (*all these*) *were received by* Nanāya-[…], son of Nabû-*erība*.
Month III, day 11(+), year [×] of Nebuchadnezzar, king of Babylon.

181. NBC 4765

Copy: Plate XLV
Date: 21.II.31 Nbk
Summary: withdrawal (*našû*) note: wool

Obv. ⸢2 ½⸣ [(×)] GUN SIK$_2$.ḪI.A *ša*$_2$ *muš-šu-re-e*-⸢*ti*⸣
(tiny line) ⅓ ⸢GIN$_2$⸣
⸢*a-na* 30⸣ MA.NA *ša*$_2$ ^{I}DU$_3$-*a* A-*šu*$_2$ *ša*$_2$ ^{I}*tab-ne*$_2$-*e-a* GIŠ^{ú}
[^{I}]⸢$^{d?}$EN$^?$-TIN⸣ ^{lu_2}UŠ.BAR *it-ta-ši*
[× M]A.NA *a-na* 2 ½ GIN$_2$ *ina* KU$_3$.BABBAR-*šu*$_2$
[*ša*$_2$ *i-na*] ⸢NIG$_2$⸣.GA ^{I}*gi-mil-lu* A-*šu*$_2$ *ša*$_2$ ^{I}NUMUN-*ia*$_2$ GIŠ
[×] ⸢MA.NA⸣ *ša*$_2$ 1 GIN$_2$ KU$_3$.BABBAR *ina* ŠE.ZIZ$_2$.A$_4$$^{!(T. bar)}$-*šu*$_2$
[× (×)] ⸢*ša*$_2$⸣ ^{iti}GU$_4$ ^{I}IR$_3$-*ia*$_2$
[× MA].NA *ša*$_2$ 1 GIN$_2$ ^{Id}INNIN$^!$.NA-NUMUN-⸢TIL⸣
Lo.E. A-*šu*$_2$ *ša*$_2$ ^{I}TIN^{su}
Rev. [(×+)] ⸢1 MA⸣.NA *ša*$_2$ 1 GIN$_2$ *a-na* 2 *ma-ši-ḫu*
ša$_2$ ŠE.ZIZ$_2$.A$_4$ ^{Id}AG-*di-i-ni-e-pu-uš* GIŠ
2 MA.NA *ša*$_2$ ½ GIN$_2$ ^{I}*tab-ne*$_2$-*e-a*
{× × × × A}
^{iti}GU$_4$ UD.21.KAM MU.31.KAM
^{d}AG-NIG$_2$.DU-URU$_3$ LUGAL E^{ki}

2 ½ talents of wool from free-range (sheep), ⅓ shekel, for 30 minas that Ibnāya, son of Tabnēa, withdrew, *Bēl*-uballiṭ, the weaver, withdrew; [×] mina for 2 ½ shekels from his silver, [which is in] the temple stores, Gimillu, son of Zēria, withdrew; [×] mina for 1 shekel of silver from his emmer, ... of month II—Ardia; [×] mina for 1 shekel, Innin-zēru-šubši, son of Balāssu; 1[(+×)] mina for 1 shekel for 2 *mašīḫu* of emmer, Nabû-dīni-īpuš withdrew; 2 minas for ½ shekel, Tabnēa; {…}
Month II, day 21, year 31 of Nebuchadnezzar, king of Babylon.

1–3 Given the expected rate of ca. 4 minas of wool for 1 shekel of silver, the conversion intended in these lines is unclear. For 4m / 1š see l. 13, and see Kleber 2010, 603–5 for wool prices in this period.

1 *muš-šu-re-e*-⸢*ti*⸣, free-range (sheep); see *ṣe-e-nu muš-šu-re-ti ul-tu* EDEN ⸢*i*⸣-*na* ⸢ŠU^{II}⸣ ^{lu_2}DUMU DU$_3$-*i*^{meš} *i-bu-ku*-⸢*ma*⸣ (YOS 7, 146: 5–6), and see CAD U, 310, s.v. *uššuru* (adj.) b).

4 A reading [^{I}]⸢*na*⸣-*din*, rather than [^{I}]⸢$^{d?}$EN$^?$-TIN⸣ may be considered.

182. YBC 9494

Copy: Plate XLIV
Date: 29.IV.24 Nbk
Summary: withdrawal (*našû*) note: wool

Obv. 2 MA.NA
^{sik_2}ZA.⸢GIN$_3$⸣.KUR.RA
ši-ir-⸢ṭu⸣
⸢*ša$_2$*⸣ *ku-si-ti*
⸢*a*⸣*-na* ⸢ḪI⸣ IM
Lo.E. [^{I}]^{d}EN-*iq-*⸢*bi*⸣
Rev. ⸢^{lu_2}UŠ⸣.BAR GIŠ
(blank)
[^{it}]^{i}ŠU UD.29.KAM
[M]U.24.KAM
^{d}A[G] -NIG$_2$.DU-URU$_3$
⸢LUGAL TIN⸣.TIR^{ki}

Bēl-iqbi, the weaver, withdrew 2 minas of purple wool strips of the *kusītu*-garment for ....
Month IV, day 29, year 24 of Nebuchadnezzar, king of Babylon.

5 ⸢ḪI⸣ IM; one might consider reading *bir*$^{!(T. ḫi?)}$*-im* for *birmu* "for (making a) multicolored (garment)," but this remains a conjecture.

8 The month may be DU$_6$ rather than ŠU.

183. YBC 9510

Copy: Plate XLV
Date: 04.II.11 Nbk
Summary: withdrawal (*našû*) note: wool

Obv. ⅓ 3 GIN$_2$ ^{sik_2}ZA.GIN$_3$.KUR.RA^{o}
ina ^{sik_2}ZA.GIN$_3$.KUR.RA
ša$_2$ ^{tug_2}*lu-bar ša$_2$* ^{d}GAŠAN *ša$_2$* ⸢UNUG⸣^{ki}
16 GIN$_2$ ^{gada}*ṭu-man-ni*
⸢*a*⸣*-na lu-bu-*⸢*uš*⸣*-ti*
Lo.E. *ša$_2$* ^{iti}GU$_4$ UD.14.KAM
Rev. ^{I}*na-din* ⸢A⸣ ^{lu_2}UŠ.BAR GIŠ
(blank)
^{iti}GU$_4$ UD.⸢4⸣.KAM MU.11.KAM
^{d}AG-NIG$_2$.DU-URU$_3$ LUGAL TIN.TIR^{ki}

Nādinu, descendant of Išparu, withdrew 23 shekels of purple wool from the purple wool of the *lubāru*-garment of Lady-of-Uruk (and) 16 shekels of *ṭumānu*-linen thread for the clothing ceremony of Month II, day 14.
Month II, day 4, year 11 of Nebuchadnezzar, king of Babylon.

184. YBC 9574

Copy: Plate XLV
Date: 20.X.33 Nbk
Summary: *ina pāni* note: hair + withdrawal (*našû*): silver

Obv. 1 GUN *šar-ti a-na*
saq-qa-a-ta ina pa-ni
^{Id}U.GUR-*ina*-SUḪ$_3$-⸢SUR⸣ A ^{I}*za-bi-da-a*
1 GUN *ina* IGI ^{I}DU$_3$-^{d}INNIN A ^{Id}AG-⸢MU-DU$_3$⸣
18 4$^{!?}$<^{tu_2}> GIN$_2$ KU$_3$.BABBAR *ina* KU$_3$.BABBAR-*šu*$_2$
ša$_2$ *ina* NIG$_2$.GA ^{Id}UTU-KAL <GIŠ>
Rev. (blank)
^{iti}AB UD.20.KAM MU.33.KAM
^{d}AG-NIG$_2$.DU-URU$_3$ LUGAL TIN.TIR^{ki}

1 talent of (goat) hair for sacks is at the disposal of Nergal-ina-tēšî-ēṭir, son of Zabidāya; 1 talent is at the disposal of Ibni-Ištar, son of Nabû-šumu-ibni; Šamaš-udammiq <withdrew> 18 ¼? shekels of silver, from his silver that was in the temple stores.
Month X, day 20, year 33 of Nebuchadnezzar, king of Babylon.

185. NCBT 477

Copy: Plate XLV
Date: 07.V.19 Nbk
Summary: withdrawal (*našû*) note: goat hair

Obv. 40 GUN ⸢*šar*⸣-*ti*°
ša$_2$ ^{I}A-*a* A-*šu*$_2$ *ša*$_2$ ^{I}*da*-⸢*di*⸣-*ia*$_2$
⸢TA⸣ UNUG^{ki} *iš-ša*$_2$-*a*ʾ
39 GUN 57 MA.NA
⸢*ki*⸣-*i i-ḫi-ṭu*
Lo.E. *a-na* E$_2$.SAG.GIL
it-ta-din
Rev. (blank)
^{iti}NE UD.7.KAM MU.19.KAM
^{Id}AG-NIG$_2$.DU-URU$_3$ LUGAL TIN.⸢TIR⸣^{ki}

(Of) the 40 talents of (goat) hair that Aplāya, son of Dadia, brought from Uruk, after weighing it, he gave to Esagil (only) 39 talents 57 minas (of goat hair).
Month V, day 7, year 19 of Nebuchadnezzar, king of Babylon.

186. YBC 9547

Copy: Plate XLVI
Date: 29.III.24 Nbk
Summary: *ina pāni* note: alum and dye

Obv. 12 MA.NA ^{na_4}*gab*$^{!}$-⸢*bu-u*$_2$⸣
20 MA.NA$^{!}$ ^{giš}ḪAB° *ša*$_2$ ⸢*a*°-*na*⸣ [× × (×)]-*tu*$_2$ *bit-qa* ⸢KU$_3$.BABBAR⸣

(tiny inserted line) *maḫ-ru*
a-na ṣi$^{!}$*-ip ša*$_2$ ⸢*ṣu-up-pa-a*⸣*-ta*
ina IGI ^{Id}EN-*iq*-⸢*bi*⸣
^{lu2}UŠ.<BAR>
Rev. (blank)
^{iti}SIG$_4$ UD.29.KAM
MU.24.KAM
9 [^{d}A]G-NIG$_2$.DU-URU$_3$
Up.E. LUGAL TIN.TIR^{ki}

12 minas of alum and 20 minas of madder, which were received for [×]+⅛ (shekels) of silver, are at the disposal of Bēl-iqbi, the weaver, for dyeing the strips of combed wool.
Month III, day 29, year 24 of Nebuchadnezzar, king of Babylon.

187. YBC 9431

Copy: Plate XLVI
Date: 29.XI.23 Nbk
Summary: *ina pāni* note: dye

Obv. [× MA.N]A ^{u2}*ḫaš-ḫu-re*-⸢*e-ti*⸣
[×+] ⸢3⸣ ½ GIN$_2$ ^{sik2}ZA.GIN$_3$.⸢KUR⸣.RA
[*a-n*]*a* ^{tug2}*a-di-la-nu ša*$_2$ $^{tug2!(T. LU)}$⸢BAR.DUL$_8$⸣^{me}
⸢*ša*$_2$⸣ ^{d}GAŠAN *ša*$_2$ ⸢UNUG^{ki} *u*$_3$ *ša*$_2$ ^{d}*gu-la*⸣
⸢*u*$_3$⸣ ^{tug2}*par-ši*-⸢*gu*⸣^{me} *ina* IGI
Lo.E. ⸢I⸣*na*-⸢*di*⸣*-nu* A-*šu*$_2$ *ša*$_2$
⸢I⸣^{d}U.GUR-⸢PAP A $^{lu2!}$UŠ.BAR⸣
Rev. (blank)
[^{it}]^{i}ZIZ$_2$ UD.29.KAM MU.23.KAM
[^{d}A]G-NIG$_2$.DU-URU$_3$ LUGAL TIN.TIR^{ki}

[× min]as of apple-color dye and [(×)]3 ½ shekels of purple-dye for the tassels of the *kusītu*-garments of the Lady-of-Uruk and of Gula, and (for) the *paršīgu*-headdresses are at the disposal of Nādinu, son of Nergal-nāṣir, descendant of Išparu.
Month XI, day 29, year 23 of Nebuchadnezzar, king of Babylon.

188. YBC 9540

Copy: Plate XLVI
Date: 19.V.24 Nbk
Summary: *ina pāni* note: dye

Obv. 20 MA.NA ^{giš}ḪAB
a-na dul-lu ina pa-ni
^{Id}EN-*iq-bi* A ^{Id}AG-GI
^{lu2}UŠ.BAR
Rev. (blank)
^{iti}NE UD.20.1.LA$_2$.KAM
MU.24.KAM ^{d}AG-NIG$_2$.DU-URU$_3$

LUGAL TIN.⸢TIR^{ki}⸣

20 minas of madder for work are at the disposal of Bēl-iqbi, son of Nabû-ušallim, the weaver.
Month V, day 19, year 24 of Nebuchadnezzar, king of Babylon.

189. YBC 11613

Copy: Plate XLVI
Date: 06.VI.08 Cyr
Summary: issue (*nadin*) list: wheat

Obv. GIG.BA *ša*$_2$ *a-na* ⸢ŠUK$^?$.ḪI.A <*ša*$_2^?$> *pir-*<*ir*>*-ri*⸣
a-na ^{lu2}UN^{meš} ⸢E$_2$ SUM.NA⸣
^{iti}KIN UD.6.KAM MU.8.KAM ^{I}*kur-a*[*š*]

---

1 GUR 1 PI ^{Id}UTU-MU ^{lu2}⸢NAGAR⸣ $^{<giš>}$I[G]

---

1 GUR 2 (PI) 4 BAN$_2$ ^{I}NUMUN-*tu*$_2$ E$_2$ UDU.NITA$_2$

⸢1 GUR 2 BAN$_2$⸣ ^{I}*gi-mil-lu* ^{lu2}UŠ.BAR ⸢*bir*⸣*-m*[*u*]

---

2 GUR 3 (PI) 2 BAN$_2$ ^{Id}UTU-⸢ŠEŠ⸣-MU ^{lu2}I$_3$.DU[$_8$]
⸢*ina lib*$_3$°*-bi*⸣ 1 PI ^{Id}UTU°-ŠEŠ-MU NU$^{!(T. pap)}$ IGI

[×] ⸢GUR⸣ ^{Id}UTU-TIN^{it} ^{lu2}IR$_3$ E$_2$.GAL

[×] ⸢GUR {2 BAN$_2$}⸣ ^{Id}UTU-BA^{ša2} *ša*$_2$ E$_2$ GU$_4$

(blank)

Rev. (uninscribed)

Wheat that was given as *salaries of the workforce* for the temple personnel; Month VI, day 6, year 8 of Cyrus:
1;1.0.0 (for) Šamaš-iddin, the doors carpenter; 1;2.4.0 (for) Zērūtu, of the sheep shed; 1;0.2.0 (for) Gimillu, the weaver of colored cloth; 2;3.2.0 (for) Šamaš-aḫu-iddin, the porter, of which Šamaš-aḫu-iddin did not (*yet*) receive 1.0.0; × (for) Šamaš-uballiṭ, the master-builder; × (for) Šamaš-iqīša, of the ox stable.

190. YBC 4165

Copy: Plate XLVII
Date: undated (*Nbk*)
Summary: issue (*nadin*) list: grain

Six of the individuals listed in the text may be identified elsewhere. However, it must be stressed that all cases are based on only one additional attestation of a two-tier name, and so none of these additional attestations is solid: Amīl-Nanāya/Nergal-ušallim in YBC 3525 (7 Nbk), Iddin-Nabû/Nergal-ušallim in YOS 17, 97 (16 Nbk), Nergal-iddin/Nergal-ušallim in YBC 3830 (0a Ner), Šamaš-iddin/Nabû-ēṭir in GC 2, 39 (20 Npl), Šamaš-zēru-iqīša/Nabû-iddin in PTS 2808 (16 Nbk), Zēria/Nabû-iddin in YBC 9251 (41? Nbk). Assuming that at least some of these identifications hold, the present text should probably be dated to the reign of Nebuchadnezzar.

Up.E. [ŠE.BAR ša$_2$ ^{ga}]^{rim}a-šur-re-ti šu-pa-⸢li?⸣-[tu$_2$]
Obv. [ša$_2$ ŠU^{II} ^{I}]⸢ḫa⸣-du-ru ^{lu2}SIPA ša$_2$ ^{I}ḫa-⸢te!-ki⸣
[u ša$_2$ ŠU^{II}]⸢^{Id}AG⸣-a-a-lu ^{lu2}⸢SIPA? ša$_2$⸣ ^{I}ḫa-te-ki
[ša$_2$ E$_2$?] ^{lu2}°GAR UMUŠ PAP° ^{lu2}°er-re-<šu$_2$> ⸢maš°-ḫa°-tu°⸣
s[UM.NA]

---

3 GUR ⸢ŠE⸣.ZIZ$_2$.A$_4$ ^{Id}AG-na-din-ŠEŠ ^{lu2}ENGAR ša$_2$ ^{d}⸢u$_2$⸣-ṣur-a-mat-su
4 GUR ^{I}NUMUN-u$_2$-tu ^{lu2}NAGAR
2 GUR ⸢ŠE.BAR⸣ 4 GUR ŠE.ZIZ$_2$.A$_4$ ^{I}ba-la-ṭu A-⸢šu$_2$⸣
ša$_2$ ^{Id}EN-⸢SU⸣ ina E$_2$ ^{d}PA
18 GUR ša$_2$ da-lu ^{I}ta°-ri-bi ina E$_2$ ^{d}AG
18 GUR ^{I}ZALAG$_2$-^{d}UTU ^{lu2}⸢qal⸣-la ša$_2$ ^{Id}EN-ŠEŠ-MU 9 GUR ḪA.LA
5 GUR ^{I}kal-ba-a A ^{I}NUMUN-ia$_2$ 1 KA$_2$ ⸢me⸣-e ŠU^{II}
10 GUR ^{I}kal-ba-a u° ^{I}⸢id°-di-ia⸣ 2^{u2} KA$_2$
10 GUR ^{I}kal-⸢ba-a⸣ šal-šu$_2$ KA$_2$ ša$_2$ da-lu
12 GUR° ^{I}KI-^{d}AMAR.UTU-TIN ⸢A⸣ ^{I}UNUG:$^{ki°}$-a°-a {eras.}
25 GUR ^{Id}AG-GAL$_2$^{ši} ⸢A⸣ ^{I}i-di-u$_2$-a ša$_2$ da-lu
4 GUR° ^{I}KI-^{d}AMAR.UTU-TIN u ^{I}GI-^{d}⸢AMAR.UTU⸣
46 GUR ^{I}NUMUN-ia A ^{Id}AG-⸢MU⸣
1 GUR $^{Id°}$UTU-NUMUN-BA^{ša2} A ^{Id}AG-MU
8 GUR ⸢ŠE.BAR⸣ 1 GUR ŠE.ZIZ$_2$.A$_4$ ^{I}kur-ban-ni-^{d}⸢AMAR.UTU⸣
2 GUR ^{Id}AG-NUMUN-DU$_3$ ^{uru}kal-za-a-a
Rev. 17 GUR ⸢ŠE.BAR⸣ ina ŠE.ZIZ$_2$.A$_4$ ^{I}kal-⸢ba-a⸣
20 GUR ŠE.BAR 1 GUR 2 (PI) 3 BAN$_2$ ŠE.GIG ^{I}LU$_2$-^{d}na-na-⸢a A⸣ ^{Id}⸢U.GUR⸣-GI
10 GUR ^{I}LU$_2$-^{d}na-na-a u ^{Id}INNIN.NA-NUMUN-DU$_3$
5 GUR ^{Id}U.GUR-MU A ^{Id}U.GUR-GI
45 GUR ^{I}nad-na-a A ^{I}A-a 15 GUR° ḪA!.LA
27 GUR ^{I}kal-ba-a A ^{I}NUMUN-ia$_2$ ma-a-a-ri
3 GUR 2 (PI) 3 BAN$_2$ ŠE.BAR 2 (PI) 3 BAN$_2$ ŠE.ZIZ$_2$.A$_4$ ^{I}MU-^{d}AG A ^{Id}U.GUR-GI
3 GUR ^{Id}UTU-MU A ^{Id}AG-SUR
3 (PI) 2 BAN$_2$ ŠE.ZIZ$_2$.A$_4$ ^{Id}AG-mu-še-tiq$_2$-u$_2$-da
3 GUR ^{Id}AG-ŠEŠ^{meš}-šul-lum A ^{Id}⸢AMAR.UTU-NUMUN$^{!? (T.til)}$⸣-DU$_3$
4 GUR ^{Id}EN-NIGIN$_2$^{ir} A ^{Id}UTU-SUR
18 GUR ^{I}ta-ri-bi ša$_2$ da-lu ina E$_2$ ^{d}AG
{eras.} 4 GUR 2 (PI) 3 BAN$_2$ ḪA.LA
2 GUR ŠE.BAR 4 GUR ŠE.ZIZ$_2$.A$_4$ ^{I}ba-la-ṭu
A ^{Id}EN-<e>-ri-bi$^{(sic)}$ 1 GUR ŠE.BAR 2 GUR ŠE.ZIZ$_2$.A$_4$ ḪA.LA

[Barley from the] lower Aššurītu irrigation district, [under the responsibility] of Ḫadūru, the shepherd of *Ḫateki*, [and under the responsibility] of Nabû-ayyālu, the shepherd of *Ḫateki*, [of the household(?)] of the governor (of Uruk) – (this is for) all the sharecroppers – it was measured out (and) del[ivered].

3 kor emmer, Nabû-nādin-aḫi, plowman of Uṣur-Amāssu; 4 kor, Zērūtu, the carpenter; 2

kor barley, 4 kor emmer, Balāṭu, son of Bēl-erība, in the Nabû temple; 18 kor, (from a field irrigated) by bucket, Tarību in the Nabû temple; 18 kor, Nūr-Šamaš, slave of Bēl-aḫu-iddin, 9 kor (is his) share; 5 kor, Kalbāya, son of Zēria, first installment, *mê qātē* (land), 10 kor, Kalbāya and Iddia, second installment; 10 kor, Kalbāya, third installment, (field irrigated) by bucket; 12 kor, Itti-Marduk-balāṭu, son of Urukāya; 25 kor, Nabû-ušabši, son of *i-di-u*$_2$*-a*, (field irrigated) by bucket; 4 kor, Itti-Marduk-balāṭu and Mušallim-Marduk; 46 kor, Zēria, son of Nabû-iddin; 1 kor, Šamaš-zēru-iqīša, son of Nabû-iddin; 8 kor barley, 1 kor emmer, Kurbanni-Marduk; 2 kor, Nabû-zēru-ibni *the Kalzean*; 17 kor barley, in emmer, Kalbāya; 20 kor barley, 1;2.3.0 of wheat, Amīl-Nanāya, son of Nergal-ušallim; 10 kor, Amīl-Nanāya and Innin-zēru-ibni; 5 kor, Nergal-iddin, son of Nergal-ušallim; 45 kor, Nadnāya, son of Aplāya, 15 kor (is *his*) share; 27 kor, Kalbāya, son of Zēria, (field worked) with the *majāru*-plow; 3;2.3.0 barley, 0;2.3.0 emmer, Iddin-Nabû, son of Nergal-ušallim; 3 kor, Šamaš-iddin, son of Nabû-ēṭir; 0;3.2.0 emmer, Nabû-mušētiq-uddê; 3 kor, Nabû-aḫḫē-šullim, son of Marduk-*zēru*-ibni; 4 kor, Bēl-upaḫḫir, son of Šamaš-ēṭir; 18 kor, Tarību, (field irrigated) by bucket, in the Nabû temple, 4;2.3.0 (is *his*) share; 2 kor barley, 4 kor emmer, Balāṭu, son of Bēl-erība; 1 kor barley, 2 kor emmer, (*his*) share.

12 The *mê qātē* refers to the method of irrigation, in contrast to bucket irrigation (*ša dāli*, ll. 10, 14, 16, 33). B. Janković notes that "the term probably signifies the availability of water, rather than a particular irrigation technique. Literally, the 'water of the hand' indicated precisely that water was at hand, i.e. readily" (Janković 2013, 281). The *mê qātē* fields were productive, so it seems, and thus the payments demanded from the plowmen were higher than those from bucket irrigation; see Janković 2013, 277–82. For other attestations of the related *bīt mê* (*ša*) *qātē*, see YOS 21, 208 (Janković 2013, 279), NCBT 630 (Janković 2013, 274), NCBT 677 (Janković 2013, 280), YBC 3543 (Janković 2013, 281), and BE 9, 7 (from the Murašû archive).

36 Despite the problematic spelling, ^{Id}EN-*ri-bi* must be the father of the same Balāṭu listed in lines 6–7.

191. NCBT 434

Copy: Plate XLVIII
Date: 21.X.12 Nbk
Summary: issue (*nadin*) note: silver

For the edition of the text see page 4 in the introduction.

192. NCBT 1100

Copy: Plate XLVIII
Date: undated (Nbk)
Summary: payment (*apil*) note: salaries[20]

Ṭāb-Uruk (l. 1) is attested between 10(+) and 16 Nbk (GC 1, 174, UCP 9/2, 12 respectively); see Payne 2007, 200.

Obv. ^{Id}15-*re-ṣu-u-a ša*$_2$ ^{I}DUG$_3$.GA-UNUG^{ki} ^{lu2}UŠ.BAR
^{I}GISSU-^{d}*na-na-a ša*$_2$ ^{Id}*na-na-a-*⸢ŠEŠ-MU⸣ A ^{Id}EN-*nu-uḫ-šu*$_2$
PAP 2 *ša*$_2$ ^{Id}EN-*u*$_2$*-še-zib* A ^{Id}*na-na-a-*⸢MU⸣

[20] A previous edition is included in Payne 2007, 21.

	ŠUK°.ḪI.A^{me} *ša*$_2$ ^{iti}GAN *a-pil*
Rev.	(^{uninscribed} except for overflow from Obv.)

Ištar-rēṣūʾa for Ṭāb-Uruk, the weaver; Ṣilli-Nanāya for Nanāya-aḫu-iddin, son of Bēl-nuḫšu; total: two for whom Bēl-ušēzib, son of Nanāya-iddin, was paid the salaries of month IX.

193. NCBT 1318

Copy: Plate XLVIII
Date: undated (Nbk)
Summary: summary withdrawal (*našû*) list: salaries

Ḫašdia (ll. 21′, 23′) is attested between 18 Nbk (GC 2, 278) and 8 Nbn (Eames Q22); see Payne 2007, 168. Note also the two relatively rare names Rikis-kalāma-Bēl (47′) and Nabû-maqtu-šatbi (39′, 53′), both attested here and in NCBT 194 (22 Nbk), which probably points to a close chronological horizon.

Obv.	[beginning broken]	
	[ ]	⸢GIŠ⸣
	[ ]-⸢*ta*?⸣	GIŠ
	[ ]⸢×⸣-*u*$_2$-*ṣu*	GIŠ
	[ ]⸢×⸣ DI KA	GIŠ
	[^{I}×]-MU-DU ^{lu_2}BAN	GIŠ
	[^{Id}]⸢×⸣-NUMUN-TIL	GIŠ
	[^{Id}A]G?-NUMUN-GIŠ	GIŠ
	[^{I}*n*]*a-din*	GIŠ
	[^{I}]⸢^{d}INNIN⸣.NA-MU-PAP	
	[ ]	GIŠ
	[^{it}]^{i}AB *ša*$_2$ 7 ^{lu_2}ERIN$_2$^{me} *ša*$_2$ ŠUK LUGAL	
	[ ] ⸢^{I}LU$_2$⸣-^{d}*na-na-a*	GIŠ

	[ ]-⸢DU⸣-IGI	GIŠ
	[^{I}*re-m*]*ut*	GIŠ
	[ ] ⸢×⸣ [× (×)]-⸢^{d}⸣*na-na-a*	GIŠ
	[ ] ⸢DINGIR?⸣-KA-*ia*-URU$_3$	GIŠ
	[ ] ⸢^{I}IR$_3$⸣-^{d}AG ^{lu_2}I$_3$.DU$_8$	GIŠ
	[(×)] *re-ḫe-et* NINDA.ḪI.A *ša*$_2$ ^{iti}GAN ^{Id}15-DU-IGI	GIŠ

	1 ^{Id}*na-na-a*-MU ^{lu_2}SIPA MUŠEN	GIŠ
	1 ^{Id}15-*re-ṣu-u-a* ^{lu_2}SIPA MUŠEN	GIŠ
	1 ^{I}*ḫaš-di-ia* ^{lu_2}*pu-ṣa-a-a*	GIŠ
	1 ^{Id}INNIN.NA-MU-PAP ^{lu_2}UŠ.BAR	GIŠ
	1 ^{I}DU$_3$-^{d}15 A-*šu*$_2$ *ša*$_2$ ^{I}*ḫaš-di-ia*	GIŠ
	1 ^{I}*ina*-GISSU-^{d}*na-na-a* ^{lu_2}BAḪAR$_2$	GIŠ
	1 ^{I}*re-mut* ^{lu_2}NAGAR	GIŠ
	2 *ša*$_2$ ^{iti}AB ^{Id}*na-na-a*-ŠEŠ-MU ^{lu_2}*si-pir*	GIŠ
	2 *ša*$_2$ ^{iti}AB ^{Id}AG-ŠEŠ-MU ^{lu_2}*si-pir*	GIŠ
	1 ^{I}*ina*-GISSU-^{d}U.GUR A ^{Id}AG-BA^{ša_2}	GIŠ
	1 ^{I}*ša*$_2$-^{d}AG-*šu-u*$_2$ *ina* ŠE.BAR *ša*$_2$ *ir-bi*	GIŠ

1 ^{I}IR$_3$-^{d}AG GIŠ
1 ^{I}NUMUN-*ia* A ^{I}ŠEŠ^{meš}-*ša*$_2$-*a* ⸢GIŠ$^{?}$⸣ [(×)]
Lo.E. 1 $^{I⸢d⸣}$*na-na-a*-KAM A ^{Id}*na-na-⸢a*-PAP GIŠ⸣
{1} ^{I}{eras.}
^{I}
^{I}
Rev. ^{I}
^{I}
1 ^{Id}AG-NUMUN-BA^{ša_2} A ^{I}*za-bi-da-a* GIŠ
1 ^{Id}AG-ŠUB-ZI *ša*$_2$ ^{lu_2}GAR KUR
1 ^{I}DUG$_3$.GA-IM-^{d}15 *ša*$_2$ ^{Id}UTU-TIN^{it}
1 ^{Id}AG-*ke-šir*$_3$ A ^{Id}*na-na-a*-PAP-MU
1 ^{I}LU$_2$-^{d}*na-na-a* *ša*$_2$ ^{I}IR$_3$-*a*
1 ^{Id}AG-EN-URU$_3$ *ša*$_2$ ^{Id}AG-ŠEŠ-MU
1 ^{Id}AG-⸢ŠEŠ⸣-PAP *ša*$_2$ ^{Id}*na-na-a*-SISKUR$_2$
1 ^{Id}AG-ŠEŠ-MU A ^{Id}AG-NUMUN-BA^{ša_2}
1 ^{Id}INNIN.NA-MU-PAP A ^{I}*za-bi-da-a*
1 ^{I}DIM-DU$_3$.A.BI-^{d}EN *ša*$_2$ ^{Id}IGI.⸢DU⸣-NUMUN-DU$_3$ GIŠ
1 ^{Id}15-NUMUN-DU$_3$ DUMU-*šu*$_2$ GIŠ
[ ] ^{Id}UTU-MU A ^{Id}AG-ŠEŠ-MU GIŠ
[ ] $^{I⸢}$*lu-mur*⸣-*dum-qi*$_2$-^{d}15 *ša*$_2$ ^{I}*gi-mil-lu* GIŠ
[ ] ⸢^{I}⸣IR$_3$-*ia* {× × ×} A ^{I}LU$_2$-^{d}*na-na-a* GIŠ
[^{I}*i*]*na*-GISSU-^{d}*na-na-a* *ša*$_2$ LUGAL {×} GIŠ
[^{Id}A]G-ŠUB-ZI *ša*$_2$ ^{I}*re-mut* GIŠ
[^{Id}]⸢×⸣-NUMUN-BA^{ša_2} ^{lu_2}I$_3$.DU$_8$ GIŠ
[^{I}*ina*-GIS]SU-^{d}EN ^{lu_2}AŠGAB GIŠ
[ ]-*ia*$_2$ GI MU DI GIŠ
[^{Id}×-M]U-DU A ^{Id}*na-na-a*-KAM GIŠ
[ ]-*a* A ^{Id}AG-ŠEŠ-MU
[ ]-⸢×⸣ A ^{I}IR$_3$-*ia*$_2$ *ša*$_2$ KI ŠUK.ḪI.A LUGAL [*š*]*ap-ru* GIŠ
[ ] { × ×}
[^{lu_2}*za-b*]*il ku-du-ru*
[ ] ⸢*u*⸣ ^{I}*re-mut*
[ ]⸢KAM⸣
[remainder broken]

[…] withdrew [one; …] withdrew [one; …] withdrew [one; …] withdrew [one; ×]-šumu-ukīn, the archer withdrew [one]; ^{d}×-zēru-šubši withdrew [one]; *Nabû*-zēru-līšir withdrew [one]; Nādinu withdrew [one]; Innin-šumu-uṣur […; …] withdrew [one]; month X, seven workmen for royal rations; […] Amīl-Nanāya [(…)] withdrew.

[^{d}×]-ālik-pāni withdrew [one]; [Rīm]ūt withdrew [one; ×]-Nanāya withdrew [one]; *Ilu*-pīya-uṣur withdrew [one]; Arad-Nabû, the porter withdrew [one]; […] the remainder of the bread of month IX, Ištar-ālik-pāni withdrew.

Nanāya-iddin, the bird-herder, withdrew one; Ištar-rēṣū ʾa, the bird-herder, withdrew one; Ḫašdia, the linen weaver, withdrew one; Innin-šumu-uṣur, the weaver, withdrew one; Ibni-Ištar, son of Ḫašdia, withdrew one; Ina-ṣilli-Nanāya, the potter, withdrew one; Rēmūtu, the carpenter, withdrew one; Nanāya-aḫu-iddin, the alphabet scribe, withdrew two for month X;

Nabû-aḫu-iddin, the alphabet scribe, withdrew two for month X; Ina-ṣilli-Nergal, son of Nabû-iqīša, withdrew one; Ša-Nabû-šū withdrew one from the barley income; Arad-Nabû withdrew one; Zēria, son of Aḫḫēšāya, withdrew one; Nanāya-ēreš, son of Nanāya-nāṣir, withdrew one. (five pre-written *Personenkeils* followed by blanks).
Nabû-zēru-iqīša, son of Zabidāya, withdrew one; Nabû-maqtu-šatbi (withdrew) one for the governor (of the Sealand); Ṭāb-šār-Ištar (withdrew) one for Šamaš-uballiṭ; Nabû-kēšir, son of Nanāya-aḫu-iddin, (withdrew) one; Amīl-Nanāya (withdrew) one for Ardāya; Nabû-bēl-uṣur (withdrew) one for Nabû-aḫu-iddin; Nabû-aḫu-uṣur (withdrew) one for Nanāya-uṣalli; Nabû-aḫu-iddin, son of Nabû-zēru-iqīša, (withdrew) one; Innin-šumu-uṣur, son of Zabidāya, (withdrew) one; Rikis-kalāma-Bēl withdrew one for IGI.DU-zēru-ibni; his son, Ištar-zēru-ibni, withdrew one; Šamaš-iddin, son of Nabû-aḫu-iddin, withdrew one; Lūmur-dumqi-Ištar withdrew one for Gimillu; Ardia, son of Amīl-Nanāya, withdrew one; Ina-ṣilli-Nanāya withdrew one for the *king/royal;* Nabû-maqtu-šatbi withdrew one for Rīmūt; ×-zēru-iqīša, the porter, withdrew one; Ina-ṣilli-Bēl, the leatherworker, withdrew one; […] … withdrew one; [×-šu]mu-ukīn, son of Nanāya-ēreš, withdrew one; […], son of Nabû-aḫu-iddin, withdrew one; […], son of Ardia, who was sent with royal rations, withdrew one; […], the basket-carrier, […] and Rēmūtu […] ….

26′, 27′ The signs 2 *ša*$_2$ ^{iti}AB are densely written by the scribe in order to allow for the alignment with the rest of the lines in this section.

29′ The signs *ina* ŠE.BAR *ša*$_2$ *ir-bi* are written in a smaller script.

194. YBC 11652

Copy: Plate XLIX
Date: 08.[×].13 Nbk
Summary: withdrawal (*našû*) list: salaries

Obv. [×] ⸢½ ^{giš}*ma-ši*⸣-[*ḫu* × ×]⸢^{me}⸣
[ ] ⸢ŠUK.ḪI⸣.A *ša*$_2$ ^{i}[^{ti}×]
⸢I⸣[^{l}]^{u_2}ERIN$_2$^{meš} [*a-na* GN]$^{?}$
⸢*il-la-ku*⸣ ^{I}⸢^{d}U.GUR-×⸣
A ^{Id}*na-na-a*-KAM
^{Id}AG-SISKUR$_2$ [A ^{I}]⸢×⸣[× (×)]
⸢*u*⸣ ^{I}*mu-še-zib*-^{d}EN GI[Š]
Lo.E. ⸢15 ŠUK⸣.ḪI.A *ša*$_2$ ⸢^{iti}⸣[×]
Rev. ⸢*ša*$_2$ (1)5$^{?}$ ^{lu_2}⸣*ki-zu*-⸢*u*$_2$⸣[(^{meš})]
ša$_2$ ^{lu_2}*qi*$_2$-⸢*i-pi*⸣ ^{Id}UTU-⸢SU⸣ G[IŠ]
5 ŠUK.ḪI.A *ša*$_2$ ^{iti}ŠU *u* ^{it}[^{i}NE]
ša$_2$ ^{Id}*na-na-a*-MU ^{lu_2}*sa*-[*sin-nu* (?)]
^{I}LU$_2$-^{d}*na-na-a* A ^{I}*za-kir* [GIŠ]$^{?}$
2 ½ ŠUK.ḪI.A *ša*$_2$ ^{iti}GU$_4$
⸢^{I}*šu-la*⸣-*a* A ^{I}IR$_3$-*a* GIŠ
[× ŠUK.ḪI].⸢A⸣ *ša*$_2$ ^{iti}GU$_4$ ^{Id}INNIN.NA-NUMUN-DU$_3$ [GIŠ]$^{?}$
Up.E. [^{iti}× U]D.8.KAM MU.13⸣.KAM
[^{Id}AG-NIG$_2$.DU-U]RU$_3$ LUGAL ⸢TIN.TIR^{ki}⸣
Le.E. ⸢3$^{?}$⸣ ½ {eras.} ŠUK.ḪI.A *ša*$_2$ ^{i}[^{ti}×]
⸢I⸣*ki*-⸢*rib*⸣-*ti* [(GIŠ)]

Nergal-[…], son of Nanāya-ēreš, Nabû-uṣalli, [son of …], and Mušēzib-Bēl withdrew [× ×] ½ *mašī*[*ḫu* …] salaries of mo[nth ×, *for PN*] and the workers who went [to GN].
Šamaš-erība withdrew 15 salaries for month [×] for 15 *kizû*-attendants of the *qīpu*.
Amīl-Nanāya, son of Zākiru, [withdrew] 5 salaries for months IV and [V] for Nanāya-iddin, the *bo*[*w-maker*].
Šulāya, son of Ardāya, withdrew 2 ½ salaries for month II.
Innin-zēru-ibni [withdrew × salaries] for month II.
Month [×], day 8, year 13 of [Nebuchadn]ezzar, king of Babylon.
Kiribtu [withdrew] 3 ½ salaries for month [×].

195. YBC 9328

Copy: Plate XLIX
Date: 06.II.12 Nbk
Summary: accounting note: salaries

Obv. 2 ŠUK.ḪI.A^{meš} $^{\text{I⸢d}}$AG-NUMUN-MU⸣
u ^{I}*mu-še-zib*-^{d}EN DUMU-*šu*$_2$
1 ŠUK.ḪI.A ^{I}MU-URU$_3$ $^{\text{lu}_2}$NAGAR
1 ^{giš}*ma-ši-ḫu* ^{I}*ba-bi-ia*$_2$ $^{\text{lu}_2}$I$_3$.DU$_8$
u$_3$ ^{Id}AG-DU$_3$-ŠEŠ $^{\text{lu}_2}$I$_3$.DU$_8$
Rev. (blank)
^{iti}GU$_4$ UD.6.KAM MU.12.KAM
^{d}PA-NIG$_2$.DU-PAP LU[GAL TIN.TIR^{ki}]

Two salaries (for) Nabû-zēru-iddin and Mušēzib-Bēl, his son; one salary (for) Šumu-uṣur, the carpenter; 1 *mašīḫu* (for) Bābia, the porter, and Nabû-bān-aḫi, the porter.
Month II, day 6, year 12 of Nebuchadnezzar, ki[ng of Babylon].

196. YBC 9330

Copy: Plate XLIX
Date: 01(+).III.21 (Nbk)
Summary: withdrawal (*našû*) list: salaries

Nādinu (l. 2) is attested between 20 Npl (GC 2, 39) and 35 Nbk (PTS 2792); see Payne 2007, 251.

Obv. ŠUK.ḪI.A^{me} *ša*$_2$ ⸢ITI⸣ [× (×)]
1 (PI) 4 BAN$_2$ $^{\text{I⸢}}$*na-din*⸣ $^{\text{lu}_2\text{⸢}}$KU$_3$$^{?}$.DIM$^{?\text{⸣}}$
5 BAN$_2$ ^{Id}AG-⸢NIGIN$_2$$^{?\text{⸣}ir}$ $^{\text{lu}_2}$NA[GAR (×)]
1 PI ^{I}GISSU-^{d}*na-na-a* $^{\text{lu}_2\text{⸢}}$I$_3$.DU$_8$⸣
1(PI) 2 BAN$_2$ ^{I}[^{d}A]G$^{?}$-LU$^{?}$-KAM [^{l}]$^{\text{u}_2}$BAN
ša$_2$ $^{\text{iti⸢}}$×⸣
Lo.E. ^{iti}SIG$_4$ UD.1[(+×)].⸢KAM⸣ [M]U.21.KAM
Rev. (uninscribed)

The salaries of month [×]: 0;1.4.0 (for) Nādinu, the gold[smith]; 5 *sūtu* (for) Nabû-upaḫḫir, the carpenter, 1 *pānu* (for) Ṣilli-Nanāya, the porter, 0;1.2.0 (for) Nabû-×-ēreš, the archer; of month …
Month III, day 1(+), year 21.

197. YBC 11491

Copy: Plate L
Date: 15.VII$^?$.05 (*Camb*)
Summary: accounting note: salaries

The master-builder Amīl-Nanāya may be identified as the one attested in PTS 2126. While the latter text is undated too, it can be roughly dated to the reign of Cambyses based on prosopography.[21]

Obv. 2-*ta* ŠUK.ḪI.A⸢^{me}⸣
⸢*ša*$_2$⸣ ^{iti}KIN *u* ⸢^{iti}⸣[DU$_6$]$^?$
^{I}LU$_2$-^{d}*na-na*-⸢*a*⸣
^{lu2}IR$_3$-E$_2$.G[AL]
Rev. ⸢*in*⸣-*da*-⸢*ḫar*$^?$⸣[(×)]
⸢^{iti}DU$_6$$^?$ UD.15⸣.[KAM]
⸢MU.5.KAM⸣

Amīl-Nanāya, the master-builder, *received* two salaries for month VI and month [*VII*].
Month VII$^?$, day 15, year 5.

5 A perfect form of *maḫāru* is unexpected. Unlike the common stative *maḫir* form, it must mean that Amīl-Nanāya received the salaries, rather than the salaries were received from him. If this were the case, however, we would expect the more common *eṭir* or *apil* form; see, e.g., **Nos. 192, 219, 309**. An alternative reading may be to read ⸢*in*⸣-*da*-⸢*aš*$_2$$^!$⸣-*ḫ*[*u*/*i*], from *mašāḫu*, to measure.

198. NBC 4919

Copy: Plate L
Date: undated
Summary: withdrawal (*našû*) list: salaries

This tablet is written along both axes; the obverse and top half of the reverse are written in portrait format, while the bottom half of the reverse is in landscape. None of the carpenters can be identified with certainty.

Obv. ^{lu2}NAGAR^{meš} *ša*$_2$ ŠUK.ḪI.A *ša*$_2$ ^{iti}GAN
(tiny line) GIŠ^{u2}
^{I}*šu-ma-a* ^{Id}*a*-⸢*nu*⸣-DU$_3$^{uš}
^{Id}AG-NUMUN-GIŠ
^{Id}UTU-MU
^{Id}*a-nu*-NUMUN-DU$_3$
10° 5° {eras.}
⸢25⸣
^{I}NUMUN-*ia*$_2$ *u* ⸢A⸣^{me}-*šu*$_2$ *ša*$_2$ ^{iti}GAN
^{I}*muk-ke*$^!$-*e-a* {eras.}
^{Id}INNIN-DU-A
^{I}NUMUN-*tu*$_2$ *u* ^{I}*ana*-E$_2$-*šu*$_2$ [(×)]

---

[21] E.g., Dannu-aḫḫēšu-ibni: YBC 3784 (1 Bar) and possibly VS 20, 138 (5 Camb); Anu-šarru-uṣur, *qīpu* of Eanna 17 Nbn–4 Camb.

^{Id}*na-na-a*-MU ^{lu2}NAGAR ^{giš}⸢IG⸣[^{meš}]
Lo.E. ^{Id}AG-*mu-še-tiq*$_2$-UD.⸢DA⸣
Rev. (upper half, portrait, badly damaged)
⸢×⸣ ⸢4 (GUR)⸣
⸢3 (GUR)⸣
⸢× 10⸣
⸢20 6$^?$ × ×⸣
(lower half, landscape)
⸢^{I}*e-rib-šu*$_2$⸣
⸢^{Id}AG$^?$-NUMUN-DU$_3$⸣
⸢^{I} *u*$_2^?$-*qu-pi*$^?$⸣
⸢^{I}*šu-la*⸣-*a*
⸢^{Id}*na-na*⸣-*a*-MU$^?$
⸢^{Id}*na-na-a*⸣-ŠEŠ-MU$^?$
⸢^{Id}*na-na*⸣-*a*-ŠEŠ-KAM$^?$
⸢^{I}E$_3$-*ana*⸣-ZALAG$_2$ {eras.}
⸢^{Id}*in-nin*⸣-NUMUN-GAL$_2^{ši}$
^{iti}GAN {eras.} GIŠ

The carpenters who withdrew salaries for month IX: Šumāya, Anu-īpuš, Nabû-zēru-līšir, Šamaš-iddin, Anu-zēru-ibni: 15 (kor), 25 …; Zēria and his sons for month IX; Mukkēa, Ištar-mukīn-apli, Zērūtu and Ana-bītīšu, Nanāya-iddin, the doors carpenter, Nabû-mušētiq-uddê; (partially erased tallies) …
(landscape) Erībšu, *Nabû*-zēru-ibni, *Uqūpu*, Šulāya, Nanāya-*iddin*, Nanāya-aḫu-*iddin*, Nanāya-aḫu-*ēreš*, Lūṣi-ana-nūri, Innin-zēru-šubši: they withdrew (the salaries in) month IX.

23–5 The last sign in all of these names could be read as either MU or KAM.

199. YBC 6859

Copy: Plate XLIX
Date: 18.XI.28 Nbk
Summary: withdrawal (*našû*) list: silver

Obv. 14 GIN$_2$ 4^{tu2} KU$_3$.BABBAR *ku-um* 6 ½ GIN$_2$ KU$_3$.BABBAR ŠAM$_2$
saḫ-le-e ša$_2$ *a-na* ^{Id}U.GUR-PAP
id-di-in 6 ½ GIN$_2$ *gir*$_2$-*u*$_2$ LA$_2$
(tiny line) *ša*$_2$ *a-na* ^{I}*na-din u* ^{lu2}ERIN$_2^{me}$ *ša*$_2$ *a-na muḫ-ḫi ka-lak*$^!$-*ki ša*$_2$ ID$_2$ ^{I}IR$_3^?$-^{d}EN *ib*$^?$-*ku*$^?$
1 GIN$_2$ *ša*$_2$ *a-na tak*$^!$-*ka-su-u*$_2$
a-na ^{lu2}TUG$_2$.BABBAR^{me} SUM^{nu}
4^{tu2} *bit-qa ša*$_2$ *a-na*
Lo.E. ^{lu2}*ši-rak* GIG^{me} *id-di-nu*
Rev. ^{I}*ki-rib-tu*$_2$ A-*šu*$_2$ *ša*$_2$ ^{I}*na-din* GIŠ
11 GIN$_2$ KU$_3$.BABBAR *ina* 15 GIN$_2$ KU$_3$.BABBAR
^{I}*ša*$_2$-^{d}AG-*šu*$_2$-*u*$_2$ ^{lu2}GAR UMUŠ *ina* ^{iti}AB
a-na E$_2$.AN.NA *id-di-in* ^{Id}AG-ŠEŠ^{me}-⸢MU⸣
(tiny line) DUMU-[*šu*$_2$] GIŠ <<AŠ>>
^{iti}ZIZ$_2$ UD.18.KAM MU.28.KAM

^{d}AG-NIG$_2$.DU-URU$_3$ LUGAL E^{ki}
Up.E. {⸢14? ½? GIN$_2$ 4^{tu_2} KU-UM⸣}

14 ¼ shekels of silver, instead of 6 ½ shekels of silver, the price of cress, which he gave to Nergal-nāṣir; 6 11/24 shekels, which (was *given*) for Nādinu and the workers whom Arad-Bēl *took* for the silo on the canal; 1 shekel that was given for *takkasû*-loaves for the washermen; 3/8 (shekels) that were given for the sick temple serfs: (all of these) Kiribtu, son of Nādinu, withdrew.
11 shekels of silver from the 15 shekels (that) Ša-Nabû-šū, the governor (of Uruk), gave to Eanna in month X, Nabû-aḫḫē-iddin, [his] son, withdrew.
Month XI, day 18, year 28 of Nebuchadnezzar, king of Babylon.

4 The verb is difficult; we take it as a preterite of *abāku*, even though this should be *i-bu-ku*.
16 It must be assumed that this erased line was written as the first line of the tablet, only to be erased and rewritten at the top of the obverse.

200. NBC 4557

Copy: Plate L
Date: 17.X.06 (Npl/Nbk)?
Summary: payment (*apil*) + withdrawal (*našû*) note: salaries

Lâbâši/Ṭāb-šār-Bēl (l. 3) may be attested in PTS 2261, 19 Npl, in a similar context.

Obv. 3-*ta* ŠUK.ḪI.A^{me} 3 ITI^{me}
^{iti}APIN ^{iti}GAN *u* ^{iti}AB
^{I}*la-ba-ši* A-*šu*$_2$ *ša*$_2$ ^{I}DUG$_3$.GA-IM$^{!(T. a?)}$-^{d}EN
a-pil
2 GUR *ina* GAL-*tu*$_2$
Lo.E. ^{I}DU$_3$-^{d}⸢15⸣ DUMU
^{lu_2}GALA GIŠ
Rev. 1 PI ITI$^{!}$.GAN ^{iti}AB
^{Id}AMAR.UTU-NUMUN-DU$_3$ ^{lu_2}IR$_3$ E$_2$.⸢GAL GIŠ?⸣
^{iti}AB UD.17.KAM
MU.6.KAM

Lâbâši, son of Ṭāb-šār-Bēl, was paid three salaries for three months: VIII, IX and X. Ibni-Ištar, son of the lamentation priest, withdrew 2 kor (measured) in the large (*sūtu* measure).
Marduk-zēru-ibni, the master-builder, *withdrew* 1 *pānū* (for) months IX and X.
Month X, day 17, year 6.

201. NCBT 95

Copy: Plate LI
Date: 2(+).VIII.30(+) Nbk
Summary: withdrawal (*našû*) note: salaries

Obv. 1 BAN$_2$ 3 SILA$_3$ I$_3$.GIŠ
1 (PI) 1 BAN$_2$ 3 SILA$_3$ *saḫ-le-⸢e⸣*

1 (PI) 1 BAN$_2$ 3 SILA$_3$ MUN.ḪI.A
ŠUK.ḪI.A *ša*$_2$ 50 ERIN$_2{}^{me}$ *ša*$_2$ *ḫal-*⸢*pu*⸣
⸢*ša*$_2$⸣ *dul-lu ina* E$_2$.AN.NA *ip-*⸢*pu-uš*⸣
ša$_2$ ^{iti}APIN
Lo.E. *u*$_3$ 15 *u*$_4$*-mu*
ina ^{iti}⸢GAN⸣
Rev. ^{Id}⸢*in-nin*⸣-NUMUN-DU$_3$ A ^{I}⸢EN-*šu*$_2$*-nu*⸣$^{?}$
^{I}*la-ba-ši*
u ^{lu2}GAL 10me *it-ta-šu*$_2$*-u*
(blank)
^{iti}⸢APIN⸣ UD.2[(+×).KA]M
MU.30[(+×).KAM]
^{d}AG-NIG$_2$.DU-U[RU$_3$ LUGAL TIN.TIR^{k}]^{i}

Innin-zēru-ibni, son of *Bēlšunu*, Lâbâši, and the decurions withdrew 0;0.1.3 of oil, 0;1.1.3 cress and 0;1.1.3 salt (as) the salaries of fifty workers of the substitutes who work in Eanna for month VIII and fifteen days in month IX.
Month VIII, day 2(+), year 30(+) of Nebuchadnez[zar king of Babylon].

4–5 The end of these lines seems to have been added later. For *ṣābu ša ḫalpi*, see Kleber 2008, 111.
9 The reading ^{I}⸢EN-*šu*$_2$*-nu*⸣ is uncertain, and one may also consider ^{I}⸢*na-din*$^{?}$⸣.

202. NCBT 948

Copy: Plate LI
Date: undated (Nbk)
Summary: accounting inventory: (outgoing) silver

Several of the decurions can be identified in the following dateable attestations: Aḫu-lūmur/Nabû-aḫu-ēreš: PTS 2267 (17 Npl), YBC 9407 (17 Nbk); Nanāya-uṣalli/Ṭāb-Uruk: YBC 9407 (17 Nbk), UCP 9/2, 25 (28 Nbk), YBC 4119 (34 Nbk), PTS 2035 (36 Nbk); Nergal-ēṭir/Nabû-erība: PTS 2267 (17 Npl), NCBT 995 (18 Npl); Rēmūtu/Aḫu-ēreš: YBC 9407 (17 Nbk). Although some are attested as early as 17 Nabopolassar, the tablet was probably written around the mid-reign of Nebuchadnezzar.

Twenty-one of the twenty-seven tallied entries are preserved. This allows us to reconstruct the number of broken lines as six. The quantities are written on the left edge together with the *Personenkeils* on the obverse and the first half of the reverse.

(Le.E. ↓)
Up.E. KU$_3$.BABBAR *ša*$_2$ *a-na su-u*ʾ*-ut-*⸢*ti*⸣
a-na ^{lu2}GAL 10^{meš} *ša*$_2$ *a-na* [×]
ša$_2$ ^{uru}E$_2$-^{I}*da-ku-ru il-l*[*i-ku*]

Obv. 10 GIN$_2$ ^{I} ^{d}AG-PAP A-*šu*$_2$ *ša*$_2$ ^{Id}AG-⸢DA$^{?}$⸣
10 GIN$_2$ ^{I} ^{d}EN-SUR A-*šu*$_2$ *ša*$_2$ ^{I}ŠEŠ^{meš}*-lu-*⸢*mur*⸣
10 GIN$_2$ ^{I} ŠEŠ-IGI A-*šu*$_2$ ⸢*ša*$_2$⸣ ^{I}⸢^{d}AG⸣-ŠEŠ-KAM
10 GIN$_2$ ^{I} *re-mut* A-*šu*$_2$ *ša*$_2$ ^{I}ŠEŠ-⸢KAM⸣
10 GIN$_2$ ^{I} ^{d}U.GUR-SUR A-*šu*$_2$ *ša*$_2$ ^{Id}AG-SU
10 GIN$_2$ ^{I} *re-mu-tu* ^{lu2}UŠ.BAR
10 GIN$_2$ ^{I} ^{d}AG-MU-KAM A-*šu*$_2$ *ša*$_2$ ^{I}AŠ.TE-DINGIR

10 GIN$_2$ ^{I} *ki-din*-^{d}ŠU$_2$ A-*šu*$_2$ *ša*$_2$ ^{I}*e-riš*
10 GIN$_2$ ^{I} TIN.TIR^{ki}-*a-a* A-⸢*šu*$_2$ *ša*$_2$⸣ ^{I}*ša*$_2$-^{d}AG-*šu*$_2$-*u*
10 GIN$_2$ ^{I} ^{d}*na*-⸢*na-a*-SISKUR A-*šu*$_2$ *ša*$_2$ ^{I}DUG$_3$.GA-UNUG^{ki}⸣
(lower edge of Obv. is broken: three lines are missing)
Rev. (upper edge of Rev. is broken: three lines are missing)
⸢10 GIN$_2$ ^{I}⸣ [ ]
10 GIN$_2$ ^{I} ⸢^{d}EN⸣-[ ]
10 GIN$_2$ ^{I} SUM.⸢NA-*a* A⸣-*šu*$_2$ *ša*$_2$ ^{I}⸢×⸣-[×]-⸢×⸣
10 GIN$_2$ ^{I} ^{d}AG-NUMUN-DU A-*šu*$_2$ *ša*$_2$ ^{I}LU$_2$-^{d}*na-na-a*
10 GIN$_2$ ^{Id}UTU-DU$_3$ A-⸢*šu*$_2$ *ša*$_2$⸣ ^{I}GI-⸢^{d}⸣AMAR.UTU
10 GIN$_2$ ^{I}KI.NE-*a-a* A-*šu*$_2$ *ša*$_2$ ^{I}URU-*lu-mur*
10 GIN$_2$ ^{I}E$_2$.AN.NA-DU$_3$ A-*šu*$_2$ *ša*$_2$ ^{Id}UTU-MU
10 GIN$_2$ ^{I}KI.NE-*a-a* A-*šu*$_2$ *ša*$_2$ ^{Id}EN-DU$_3$^{u}[^{š}]
10 GIN$_2$ ^{Id}*na-na-a*-KAM A-*šu*$_2$ *ša*$_2$ ^{Id}AMAR.UTU-PAP
10 GIN$_2$ ^{I}*mar-duk* A-*šu*$_2$ *ša*$_2$ ^{Id}UTU-MU
10 GIN$_2$ ^{Id}*na-na-a*-SISKUR$_2$ A-*šu*$_2$ *ša*$_2$ ^{Id}UTU-MU
(blank)
⸢PAP 27⸣ ^{lu_2}GAL 10^{meš}
111 111 111 10 111 111 111 10 111 111 1

Silver for the support (money given) to the decurions, who went to/for […] of/at Bīt-Dakūri:
10 shekels, Nabû-nāṣir, son of Nabû-lēʾi; 10 shekels, Bēl-ēṭir, son of Aḫu-lūmur; 10 shekels, Aḫu-lūmur, son of Nabû-aḫu-ēreš; 10 shekels, Rēmūtu, son of Aḫu-ēreš; 10 shekels, Nergal-ēṭir, son of Nabû-erība; 10 shekels, Rēmūtu the weaver; 10 shekels, Nabû-šumu-ēreš, son of *Kussî-ili*; 10 shekels, Kidin-Marduk, son of Ērišu; 10 shekels, Bābilāya, son of Ša-Nabû-šū; 10 shekels, Nanāya-uṣalli, son of Ṭāb-Uruk, [… … … … … …]; 10 shekels, […]; 10 shekels, Bēl-[...]; 10 shekels, Iddināya, son of ...; 10 shekels, Nabû-zēru-ukīn, son of Amīl-Nanāya; 10 shekels, Šamaš-ibni, son of Mušallim-Marduk; 10 shekels, Kinūnāya, son of Ālu-lūmur; 10 shekels, Eanna-ibni, son of Šamaš-iddin; 10 shekels, Kinūnāya, son of Bēl-īpuš; 10 shekels, Nanāya-ēreš, son of Marduk-nāṣir; 10 shekels, Marduk, son of Šamaš-iddin; 10 shekels, Nanāya-uṣalli, son of Šamaš-iddin; total of twenty-seven decurions.
(tally): 111 111 111 10 111 111 111 10 111 111 1

1 The form *su-uʾ-ut-*⸢*ti*⸣, to the best of our knowledge, is otherwise unattested. The word must be connected to the verb *sêdu* ("to help," CAD S, 206), and is likely influenced by Aramaic סעד, which was integrated to produce a new word based on the Akkadian *purrust*-form, meaning "support (money)." Note also the possibly related *suʾudu*, which the CAD translates as "a payment of gratuity?" (CAD S, 427).[22]

32′ For a succinct explanation of how this series of vertical wedges and Winkelhaken add up to 27, see the commentary for **No. 213**, and see Levavi (2022) for a full discussion and this tally system with further attestations.

[22] The possible connection of *suʾudu* to Arm סעד is rejected by Abraham and Sokoloff 2011, 50, No. 218.

203. NBC 4774

Copy: Plate LI
Date: 09.III.19 --
Summary: accounting inventory: salaries

None of the listed individuals can be properly identified.

Obv. ⸢8 GIN$_2$ KU$_3$.BABBAR *ša*$_2$ ^{I}TIN$^{tu?}$ A-*šu*$_2$ *ša*$_2$ ^{I}*ša*$_2$-$^{d?}$AG$^{?}$⸣-[*šu*$_2$]
⸢1 GIN$_2$ ^{Id}AG-SUR-ZI^{meš}⸣ [(×)]
⸢7 GIN$_2$ ^{II}SUM.NA-*a* A-*šu*$_2$ *ša*$_2$ ^{Id}EN-×⸣
⸢3 GIN$_2$ ^{II}*na-din*-ŠEŠ ^{lu_2}NAGAR⸣
⸢4 GIN$_2$ *re*-⸢*mut* A-*šu*$_2$ *ša*$_2$⸣ ^{I}IR$_3$-^{d}*gu-la*⸣
⸢5$^{?}$ GIN$_2$ KU$_3$.BABBAR$^{?}$ × *u*$_2$$^{?}$ 10 GIN$_2$ ^{I}*re-ḫe-e-tu*$_4$⸣
⸢10 GIN$_2$ ^{Id}EN-MU⸣
⸢6$^{?}$⸣ MA.NA ŠUK.ḪI.A *ša*$_2$ ^{iti}⸢SIG$_4$$^{?}$ × ×⸣ ^{d}×
Rev. ⸢20 GIN$_2$$^{?}$ × × × ŠUK.⸢ḪI.A⸣ × ×⸣ ITI [×]
⸢^{iti}ŠU$^{?}$ ^{I}DU$_3$-^{d}15 × *ina* ⸢DA⸣$^{?}$ ×⸣
9 GUN SIK$_2$.ḪI.A ŠAM$_2$
⸢3 MA.NA KU$_3$.BABBAR *ša*$_2$ $^{<I>d}$AG-KAL A-*šu*$_2$ *ša*$_2$ ^{Id}AG-NUMUN-MU$^{?}$⸣
⸢*e-ṭir* ^{iti}SIG$_4$ UD.9.KAM MU.19.KAM⸣
20 MA.NA SIK$_2$.ḪI.A ŠUK.ḪI.A *ša*$_2$ ^{iti}GAN
⸢^{iti}AB *u* ^{iti}ZIZ$_2$ ^{Id}15-MU-KAM⸣
⸢× RU$^{?}$ TA$^{?}$ ^{iti}SIG$_4$ UD.9.KAM⸣
Up.E. ⸢MU.19$^{?}$.KAM⸣

8 shekels of silver of *Balāṭu*, son of *Ša-Nabû-šū*; 1 shekel, Nabû-ēṭir-napšāti; 7 shekels, Iddināya, son of Bēl-...; 3 shekels, Nādin-aḫi, the carpenter; 4 shekels, Rēmūtu, son of Arad-Gula; *5* shekels *and* 10 shekel, Rēḫētu; 10 shekels, Bēl-iddin; *6* minas, the salaries of month III ..., 20 *shekels* ... salaries ... month [×], month *IV*, Ibni-Ištar, *on the writing board* ...; 9 talents of wool, (at) the price (of) 3 minas of silver, which Nabû-udammiq, son of Nabû-zēru-iddin, was paid, Month III, day 9, year 19; 20 minas of wool, the salaries of month IX, month X, and month XI, Ištar-šumu-ēreš ..., Month III, day 9, year 19.

1 The spelling ^{I}TIN$^{tu?}$ for Balāṭu is difficult and the reading is therefore questionable.
6 The line is transcribed and translated according to the visible traces, although it does not work as one coherent entry. It is possible that the middle of the line is to be read, LA$_2$ 10 KU$_3$.BABBAR. If true, that means that the initial figure must be higher than 10, certainly not 5 as read above.
8–10 Tiny script; these lines seem to have been added later.

204. NCBT 162

Copy: Plate LII
Date: 03.V.31 Nbk
Summary: issue (*nadin*) note: silver

Obv. 2 GIN$_2$ ⸢KU$_3$.BABBAR⸣ *a*-⸢*na*⸣
^{I}*ina*-SUḪ$_3$-SUR A ^{Id}*na-na*-<*a*>-KAM
⸢*u* ^{Id}⸣AMAR.UTU-MU-DU$_3$

⸢A-*šu*$_2$ *ša*$_2$⸣ ^{I}TIN^{su}
⸢*ša*$_2$ *a-na*⸣ ^{lu_2}*ši-rak*
Lo.E. *ḫal-qu-*⸢*tu šap*⸣*-ru*
na-din
Rev. (blank)
^{iti}⸢NE⸣ UD.3.KAM MU.31.KAM
^{d}AG-NIG$_2$.DU-⸢URU$_3$⸣ [LUGAL E^{k}]^{i}

2 shekels of silver were given to Ina-tēšî-ēṭir, son of Nanāya-ēreš, and Marduk-šumu-ibni, son of Balāssu, who were sent for (i.e., 'sent after') the escaped temple serfs.
Month V, day 3, year 31 of Nebuchadnezzar, king of Babylon.

205. GCBC 84

Copy: Plate LII
Date: 15.XI.32 Nbk
Summary: withdrawal (*našû*) note: silver

Obv. 1 ½ GIN$_2$ KU$_3$.BABBAR ŠUK.ḪI.A-*su*
ša$_2$ ^{iti}APIN *u* ^{iti}GAN
$^{I⸢d}$AG⸣-ŠEŠ-MU ^{lu_2}*se-pir*
⸢*it*⸣*-ta-ši*
Rev. (blank)
^{iti}GAN UD.15.KAM MU.32.KAM
^{d}AG-NIG$_2$.DU-URU$_3$ LUGAL TIN.TIR^{ki}

Nabû-aḫu-iddin, the alphabet scribe, withdrew 1 ½ shekel of silver, his salary for months VIII and IX.
Month XI, day 15, year 32 of Nebuchadnezzar, king of Babylon.

206. NCBT 243

Copy: Plate LII
Date: 14.X.17 Nbk
Summary: withdrawal (*našû*) note: silver

Obv. 1 ⸢½ GIN$_2$ KU$_3$⸣.BABBAR
a-na ^{lu_2}ḪUN.GA$_2$^{meš}
ša$_2$ *tam-lu-u*$_2$ *ša*$_2$ E$_2$ NIG$_2$.GA
^{I}SUM.NA-*a* GIŠ
Rev. (blank)
^{iti}AB UD.14.KAM
MU.⸢17⸣.KAM
⸢^{d}AG⸣-NIG$_2$.⸢DU⸣-URU$_3$
Up.E. ⸢LUGAL⸣ [TIN.TI]R^{ki}

Iddināya withdrew 1 ½ shekels of silver for the hired men for (work on) the terrace of the storehouse.
Month X, day 14, year 17 of Nebuchadnezzar, king of Babylon.

207. NCBT 961

Copy: Plate LII
Date: 12.XI.32 Nbk
Summary: withdrawal (*našû*) note: silver

Obv. 3-*ta* 4$^{tu_2.me}$ KU$_3$.BABBAR *ir-bi*
ŠUK.ḪI.A *ša*$_2$ ^{iti}ZIZ$_2$
ša$_2$ ^{I}*ina*-GISSU-^{d}*na*-⸢*na-a*⸣
^{lu_2}*mu-kab-bu*-⸢*u*$_2$⸣
^{I}*ina*-GISSU-^{d}EN-*ab-ni*
Lo.E. *it-ta-ši*
Rev. 1 GIN$_2$ *bit*-⸢*qa*⸣ LA$_2$
a-na ṣi-di-ti-šu$_2$*-nu*
^{Id}AG-AŠ-URU$_3$ *ša*$_2$ ^{Id}IDIM-NUMUN-BA^{ša_2}
u ^{I}NUMUN-*ia ša*$_2$ *it-ti*
^{lu_2}GAL 10me *u* ^{Id}*in-nin*-NUMUN-GAL$_2^{ši}$
⸢A-*šu*$_2$⸣ *ša*$_2$ ^{Id}*na-na-a*-SISKUR
[*a*]-⸢*na* UGU⸣ *dul-lu*
Up.E. [*šap*]-⸢*ru*⸣ [*i*]*t-ta-šu*$_2$*-u*$_2$
⸢^{iti}⸣ZIZ$_2$ UD.12.KAM MU.32.K[AM]
Le.E. ^{d}AG-NIG$_2$.DU-URU$_3$
⸢LUGAL⸣ TIN.TIR^{ki}

Ina-ṣilli-Bēl-abni withdrew ¾ shekels of silver, (from) the income, the salary of month XI of Ina-ṣilli-Nanāya, the tailor.
Nabû-ēdu-uṣur withdrew ⅞ shekels (of silver) for the (travel) provisions of Ea-zēru-iqīša and Zēria, who were sent with the decurions and Innin-zēru-šubši, son of Nanāya-uṣalli, on account of work.
Month XI, day 12, year 32 of Nebuchadnezzar, king of Babylon.

7–14 The relative clause in ll. 9–14 (*ša*$_2$ … [*šap*]-*ru*) is positioned awkwardly, as it would be expected to follow *ṣi-di-ti-šu*$_2$*-nu*.

208. NCBT 471

Copy: Plate LII
Date: 01.XIIb.17(+) Nbk
Summary: withdrawal (*našû*) note: silver + issue (*nadin*) note: barley

Obv. 1 ⸢GIN$_2$ KU$_3$⸣.BABBAR *a-na*
^{lu_2}ḪUN.GA$_2^{meš}$ *ša*$_2$
⸢*a-gur-ru*⸣ *a-na* E$_2$ NIG$_2$.⸢GA⸣
i-zab-bi-⸢*lu*⸣
⸢^{I}⸣^{d}AG-NUMUN-GAL$_2^{ši}$ ⸢GIŠ⸣
Lo.E. 1 BAN$_2$ 3 SILA$_3$ ŠE.BAR *a-na*
Rev. ^{lu_2}⸢ḪUN.GA$_2$⸣ *ša*$_2$ *a-ma*-⸢*ri*⸣
i-ka-as-su-u$_2$ *na-din*
^{iti}DIRI.ŠE.K[IN.K]UD

UD.1.KAM MU.17[(+×).K]AM
⸢^{d}AG⸣-NIG$_2$.⸢DU-URU$_3$⸣
Up.E. ⸢LUGAL⸣ TIN.TIR^{ki}

Nabû-zēru-šubši withdrew 1 shekel of silver for the hired workers who carry the baked bricks to the storehouse; 0;0.1.3 barley were given for the hired worker who stacked the brick pile. Month XIIb, day 1, year 17(+) of Nebuchadnezzar, king of Babylon.

209. NCBT 1176

Copy: Plate LIII
Date: 10.II.18 Nbk
Summary: withdrawal (*našû*) note: silver

Obv. 1 GIN$_2$ *ina* ŠUK-*šu*$_2$ ^{Id}AG-ŠEŠ-MU$^{!}$
A ^{Id}*na-na-a*-KAM GIŠ
½ GIN$_2$ ^{Id}⸢INNIN⸣-*na*-⸢MU⸣-PAP ^{lu_2}AD.KID
ina ŠUK-*šu*$_2$ GIŠ
^{iti}GU$_4$ UD.10.KAM MU.⸢18⸣.KAM
^{d}AG-NIG$_2$.DU-URU$_3$ LUGAL TIN.TIR^{ki}
⸢10$^{?}$⸣ ½ GIN$_2$ *a-na* 5 GUR 1 (PI) 1 BAN$_2$ 3 ⸢SILA$_3$⸣ ŠE.BAR
Lo.E. ⸢*ina* UD^{meš}⸣ *ša*$_2$ ^{Id}AG-EN-MU^{meš}
^{I}*na-ṣir* GIŠ
6 GIN$_2$ *ina* ^{iti}SIG$_4$ ^{Id}AG-⸢PAP$^{?}$-(×)⸣ [GIŠ]
Rev. 12 GIN$_2$ KU$_3$.BABBAR *a-na* ŠE.BAR
ina UD^{me}-*šu*$_2$ *ša*$_2$ ^{iti}SIG$_4$
IGI ^{d}GAŠAN *ša*$_2$ UNUG^{ki}
^{Id}EN-*ka-ṣir* A ^{I}LU$_2$-^{d}IDIM GIŠ
5 GIN$_2$ *re-ḫe-et*
Up.E. *i-di ša*$_2$ ^{lu_2}*qal-li* ⸢*u*⸣
^{lu_2}AD.KID ^{I}IR$_3$-^{d}EN GIŠ
Le.E. 1 GIN$_2$ 4^{tu_2} 8 [(×)] GIŠ
⸢*a*⸣-*na* UGU ŠE.BAR <^{I}>DU-⸢×⸣
GIŠ^{u}

Nabû-aḫu-iddin, son of Nanāya-ēreš, withdrew 1 shekel from his salary; Innin-šumu-uṣur, the reed-worker, withdrew ½ shekel from his salary; Month II, day 10, year 18 of Nebuchadnezzar, king of Babylon.
Nāṣir withdrew 10 ½ shekels, for 5;1.1.3 barley from the days of Nabû-bēl-šumati; Nabû-*nāṣir*(-×) [withdrew] 6 shekels in month III; Bēl-kāṣir, son of Amīl-Ea, withdrew 12 shekels of silver for the barley of his days of month III before the Lady-of-Uruk; Arad-Bēl withdrew 5 shekels, the remainder of the wages of the slave and the reed-worker; Mukīn-× withdrew 1 ¼ (shekels), *the eighth* (*withdrawal*), on account of barley.

18 The figure 8 is unclear. It may refer to the fact that this is the 8th withdrawal listed in the tablet, but this requires counting the 5 shekels listed in ll. 15–17 as two entries: one for the slave and one for the reed-worker. Alternatively, we may read 1 GIN$_2$ 4^{tu_2} 8 [KU$_3$].BABBAR$^{!(T. giš)}$, which would work with the following line, but still leaves the figure 8 unexplained.

210. NCBT 148

Copy: Plate LIII
Date: 01.I.13 Nbk
Summary: accounting note: (outgoing) silver

Obv. 1 GIN$_2$ KU$_3$.BABBAR *a-na* ^{Id}INNIN.NA-NUMUN-⸢DU$_3$⸣
u ^{I}⸢*šu-la*⸣-*a ša*$_2$ *a-na pa-ni*
^{lu_2}2^{u_2} ⸢*il*⸣-*li-ku*
½ GIN$_2$ *a*-⸢*na* ^{lu_2}⸣*um-man-nu*
⸢*ša*$_2$⸣ ^{giš}*šil-ta-ḫu ib-bu*-⸢*ku*⸣
Lo.E. ⸢3 IGI⸣.4.GAL$_2$.LA^{meš} *a-na*
Rev. ^{giš}*ḫi*-⸢*il*?⸣-*li*
(blank)
^{iti}BARA$_2$ UD.1.KAM MU.13.KAM
^{d}AG-NIG$_2$.DU-URU$_3$ LUGAL TIN.TIR$^{⸢ki⸣}$

1 shekel of silver for Innin-zēru-ibni and Šulāya, who went to the deputy (of the Sealand); ½ shekel for the craftsmen who will bring the arrows; ¾ (shekels) for the reed casings. Month I, day 1, year 13 of Nebuchadnezzar, king of Babylon.

3 The *šanû* in the Eanna archive refers to the *šanû* of the Sealand. In 13 Nbk this is Nabû-ēṭir-napšāti. On the Sealand officials in the Eanna archive see Levavi 2021.

211. NBC 4623

Copy: Plate LIII
Date: 06.VIII.32 Nbk
Summary: issue (*nadin*) note: silver

Obv. 2 GIN$_2$ KU$_3$.BABBAR *a-na bu-le-e*
a-na ^{Id}EN-NIGIN$_2$^{ir}
u ^{I}*mu-še-zib*-^{d}EN
^{lu_2}SIMUG^{me} SUM^{nu}
[×] GIN$_2$ 2ta ŠU$^{II.me}$
Lo.E. [*a*]-⸢*na*⸣ 2 ME 20 ^{giš}*šil*-⸢*ta-ḫu*⸣
[*a*]-*na* ^{Id}AG-MU-DU$_3$
Rev. ⸢^{lu_2}⸣AŠGAB *ma-sin*^{sic}-*ni*
na-di-in
(blank)
^{iti}APIN UD.6.KAM
MU.32.KAM
Up.E. ^{d}AG-NIG$_2$.DU-URU$_3$ LUGAL E^{ki}

2 shekels of silver were given to Bēl-upaḫḫir and Mušēzib-Bēl, the smiths, for firewood. [×+] ⅔ shekels (of silver) were given to Nabû-šumu-ibni, the *shoemaker/bow-maker leatherworker*, for 220 arrows.
Month VIII, day 6, year 32 of Nebuchadnezzar, king of Babylon.

8 Two possibilities come to mind regarding the unclear *ma-sin-ni* in ⸢^{lu_2}⸣AŠGAB *ma-sin*^{sic}*-ni*. First, it may stand for *mešēnu*, "sandals," perhaps to be read *ma-eš-ni*. Alternatively, we may read *sa*$^!$*-sin-ni* for *sasinnu*, the bow-maker. In this case, one might suggest reading ⸢^{lu_2}⸣$^{.zadim!}$*sa*$^!$*-sin-ni*.

212. NBC 4779

Copy: Plate LIII
Date: undated (late Nbk–Camb)
Summary: inventory list: silver credits

Erībšu (l. 12) is attested from 40 <Nbk> (PTS 2648) to 0a Camb (BIN 2, 114); see Payne 2007, 166.

Obv. KU$_3$.BABBAR *ra-šu-*⸢*tu*⸣ *ša*$_2$ *ina* IGI ERIN$_2$⸢^{meš}⸣

⅓ 8 GIN$_2$ KU$_3$.BABBAR ^{Id}UTU-MU-⸢DU A ^{I}*šu-ma*$^!$*-a*⸣
10 GIN$_2$ ^{I}⸢*ki*⸣*-na-a* A ^{I}DU$_3$-⸢^{d}INNIN⸣ A ^{I}*pir-u*ʾ
⅓ 9 GIN$_2$ ^{Id}AG-*ik-ṣur* ⸢A ^{Id}U.GUR-MU-DU$_3$⸣
1 MA.NA ^{Id}AG-MU A ^{I}⸢LU$_2$-^{d}*na-na-a*⸣ ^{lu_2}AŠGAB
18 ½ GIN$_2$ ^{I}*ḫaš-*⸢*di*⸣*-ia* A ^{I}*ia-mi-na-a*ʾ
5 GIN$_2$ 4^{tu_2} ⸢*ša*$_2$⸣ AB$_2$.GAL.MI$_2$.AL ^{I}⸢ŠU A ^{I}NUMUN⸣*-ia*
4 ½ GIN$_2$ ^{I}GI-⸢^{d}⸣AMAR.UTU A ^{Id}AMAR.UTU-⸢NUMUN-DU$_3$⸣
u ^{Id}AMAR.UTU-NUMUN-DU$_3$ A ^{I}*e-tel-lu*
4 ½ GIN$_2$ ^{I}*ba-ni-ia* A ^{I}⸢^{d}AG-PAP⸣
1 [G]IN$_2$ ^{I}ŠU A ^{I}⸢IR$_3$⸣*-a*
⸢½ GIN$_2$⸣ ^{I}*e-rib-šu*$_2$ ^{lu_2}UŠ.BAR
⸢2⸣ GIN$_2$ 4^{tu_2} *ša*$_2$ ^{I}SUM-*nu-nu* A ^{I}⸢*šu-la*⸣*-a*

Rev. (uninscribed)

Silver credit that is at the disposal of the workers:
28 shekels of silver (for) Šamaš-šumu-ukīn, son of Šumāya; 10 shekels (for) Kīnāya, son of Ibni-Ištar, descendant of Pirʾu; 29 shekels (for) Nabû-ikṣur, son of Nergal-šumu-ibni;
1 mina (for) Nabû-iddin, son of Amīl-Nanāya, the leatherworker; 18 ½ shekels (for) Ḫašdia, son of Iaminā; 5 ¼ shekels for cows (for) Gimillu, son of Zēria; 4 ½ shekels (for) Mušallim-Marduk, son of Marduk-zēru-ibni, and Marduk-zēru-ibni, son of Etellu; 4 ½ shekels (for) Bānia, son of Nabû-nāṣir; 1 shekel (for) Gimillu, son of Ardāya; ½ shekel (for) Erībšu, the weaver; 2 ¼ shekels of Iddinunu, son of Šulāya.

1 This passage may mean that the credit "was owed" to the workers. The phrasing, however, with *ina pāni* rather than *ina muḫḫi*, is ambiguous.

5 The amount given to the leatherworker stands out as especially high.

6 The name ^{I}*ia-mi-na-a*ʾ, rendered above as Iaminā, must be West Semitic. The reading is clear, and should not be seen as a form of Yamanāya, Greek, which is usually spelled *ia-man-na-a*, or a close variant.

8–9 It is unclear whether Mušallim-Marduk and Marduk-zēru-ibni are father and son.

213. NCBT 529

Copy: Plate LIV
Date: undated (Nbk)
Summary: accounting inventory: silver, gold, wool

Nādinu (l. 12′) is attested between 20 Npl (GC 2, 39) and 35 Nbk (PTS 2792); see Payne 2007, 251. Another possible identification is of Nabû-erība/Bulluṭāya in YOS 17, 41 (12 Nbk).

The previously unknown and unique (ac)counting method, or tallying, used throughout the text, lines 3′–4′, 15′, 21′, 23′, and 25′, as well as in **No 202**: 32, was deciphered based on these two cases and is discussed in Levavi 2022. This led to the identification of similar cases in GC 2, 187, GC 2, 364, UCP 9/1 I, 13, UCP 9/1 II, 10, and NBC 4783 (= Levavi 2022, no. 5). Here, suffice it to give a brief summary of this tally system, which is essentially a base-10 clustering.[23] When tallying the numbers, the scribe added each individual wedge to its former until he reached 10. A Winkelhaken was then written after the nine individual wedges denoting (in the present case) 10, and the scribe then started over, counting wedges until he reached 10 again. Importantly, the individual wedges were grouped in threes, which resulted in something that could be read either as "3(+)3(+)3, 10" …, or as: "1$^{(+)}$1$^{(+)}$1 (+) 1$^{(+)}$1$^{(+)}$1 (+) 1$^{(+)}$1$^{(+)}$1, 10 …" This grouping practice, which is called "chunking,"[24] was used even in cases where the tally was smaller than 10; see lines 15′, 21′, 23′, and 25′. In other cases, each series (of nine verticals chunked in threes followed by a Winkelhaken) could represent one hundred instead of a ten; see GC 2, 364, NBC 4783 (= Levavi 2022, no. 5), UCP 9/1 I, 13, UCP 9/1 II, 10, discussed in Levavi 2022.

The several gold/silver-to-wool conversions listed in the text are noteworthy. The gold-to-wool conversion rate (ll. 4′–5′) is 1(š):36(m). The 4 ⅓ minas of silver received from Mušēzib-Marduk and Nabû-iqīša (l. 6′) cannot stand for the 1 mina 50 shekels of gold (l. 5′) as this is too low a price for the gold. It must be assumed that the 6 ½ minas of silver in the temple stores (l. 8′) are to be added to that. Ultimately, the broken lines at the head of the tablet and the scribal problems in l. 7′ (see comment below) prevent a proper understanding of the relationship between the sums of silver (including the balance) and gold listed in these lines.

Nine silver-to-wool conversions are listed in lines 9′–27′. All but one reflect a similar silver (shekels) to wool (minas) rate of 1:2 ½; the one exception, 7 ½ talents, the price of 3 minas of silver (ll. 15′–16′) is of 1: 2 ⅔. These conversion rates are extremely low, that is, the wool is very expensive.

Obv. [beginning broken]
[××] ⸢× ŠAM$_2$ 13 GIN$_2$ KU$_3$.BABBAR⸣
[^{I}]⸢^{d}⸣*uraš*-MU A ^{I}ŠEŠ^{me}-*e-šu$_2$ e-ṭir*
⸢111⸣ 111 111 10 111 111 111 10
⸢111⸣ 111 111 10 PAP 30 GUN SIK$_2$.ḪI.A
$^{(tiny\ line)}$ [ŠA]M$_2$ 1 MA.NA 50 GIN$_2$ KU$_3$.GI
⸢PAP 4⸣ ⅓ MA.NA KU$_3$.BABBAR ^{I}*mu-še-zib*$^{!}$-^{d}AMAR.UTU
u ^{Id}AG-BA^{ša_2} $_{(over\ another\ line)}$ ⸢*ma*-LIŠ^{sic}⸣-*ru-u*ʾ *re-ḫi* {× (-E)}$^{?}$
6 ½ MA.NA KU$_3$.BABBAR-*šu$_2$ ina* IGI$^{!}$ NIG$_2$.⸢GA⸣
12$^{!}$ GIN$_2$ KU$_3$.BABBAR ŠAM$_2$ 30 MA.NA SIK$_2$.ḪI.A
⸢*ina* IGI⸣ ^{Id}AMAR.UTU-SU A ^{I}⸢SUM⸣.NA-ŠEŠ KU$_3$.BABBAR *ina*$^{!(T.nu)}$ IGI

[23] The rationale somewhat resembles the base 5 clustering tally, which is probably known to most readers: I$_{(=1)}$ II$_{(=2)}$ III$_{(=3)}$ IIII$_{(=4)}$ ~~IIII~~$_{(=5)}$.

[24] See Levavi 2022: 2.

⅓ 4 GIN$_2$ ŠAM$_2$ 1 GUN
{*ina* IGI} ^{I}*na-din* A ^{I}*mar-duk* ^{lu2}KU$_3$.DIM ⌜IGI^{ir}⌝
50 MA.NA SIK$_2$.ḪI.A ŠAM$_2$ ⅓ GIN$_2$ KU$_3$.BABBAR
^{I}⌜*li*$^{?}$⌝-*šir*$_3$ *ša*$_2$ ^{lu2}UMBISAG KUR *e-ṭir*
111 111 1 ½ PAP 7 ½ GUN
Lo.E. [ŠA]M$_2$ 3 ⌜MA⌝.NA KU$_3$.BABBAR
^{Id}AMAR.UTU-MU-PAP A ^{Id}AG-NUMUN-MU
e-ṭir
Rev. 1 GUN ŠAM$_2$ ⅓ 4 GIN$_2$ KU$_3$.BABBAR
^{Id}AG-*eri*$_4$-*ba* A ^{I}*bul-luṭ-a e-ṭir*
111 1 PAP 4 GUN ŠAM$_2$ ⅓ MA.NA 6 GIN$_2$ KU$_3$.BABBAR
^{Id}*uraš-u*$_2$-*še-zib* A ^{I}NIG$_2$.BA ^{lu2}2^{u} *e-ṭir*
111 11 PAP 5 GUN ŠAM$_2$ 2 MA.NA KU$_3$.BABBAR
^{Id}AG-LUGAL-PAP A ^{Id}EN-DU$_3$ *e-ṭir*
111 11 PAP 5 GUN ŠAM$_2$ 2 MA.NA KU$_3$.BABBAR
^{I}*na-din a-na* E$_2$ *e-ṭir*
⅓ GIN$_2$ ŠAM$_2$ 50 MA.NA ^{Id}AG-SUR
^{lu2}*mu-la-la e-ṭir*
2 ⅔ MA.NA 7 GIN$_2$ *ina* ŠA$_3$ IGI^{ir}
3 MA.NA *re-ḫi* [(×)]

[…] price of 13 shekels of silver, paid (to) Uraš-iddin, son of Aḫḫēšu. 111 111 111 10, 111 111 111 10, 111 111 111 10; total of 30 talents of wool, the price of 1 mina 50 shekels of gold. Total of 4 ⅓ minas of silver *received from* Mušēzib-Marduk and Nabû-iqīša. *The balance*, 6 ½ minas of silver, is at the disposal of the temple stores.
12 shekels of silver, the price of 30 minas of wool, are at the disposal of Marduk-erība, son of Nādin-aḫi. The silver is at the disposal of <…>.
24 shekels of silver, the price of 1 talent, received from Nādinu, son of Marduk, the goldsmith.
50 minas of wool, the price of 20 shekels of silver, paid (to) Līšīr, (*man*) *of* the scribe of the (*Sea*)land.
111 111 111 1 ½, total of 7 ½ talents, the price of 3 minas of silver, paid (to) Marduk-šumu-uṣur, son of Nabû-zēru-iddin.
1 talent, the price of 24 shekels of silver, paid (to) Nabû-erība, son of Bulluṭāya.
111, 1; total of 4 talents, (at the) price of 26 shekels of silver, paid to Uraš-ušēzib, son of Qīštu, the deputy (*of the Sealand*).
111, 11; total of 5 talents, the price of 2 minas of silver, paid (to) Nabû-šarru-uṣur, son of Bēl-ibni.
111, 11; total of 5 talents, price of 2 minas of silver, Nādinu paid (to) the temple.
20 shekels, the price of 50 minas, paid (to) Nabû-ēṭir, the feeble-minded.
Thereof 2 minas 47 shekels were received. The balance is 3 minas.

7′ The spelling ⌜*ma*-LIŠ^{sic}⌝-*ru-uʾ* must stand for *maḫrū*. Despite the resemblance of the LIŠ sign to UD, the reading ⌜*ma-aḫ*$_3$$^{!}$⌝-*ru-uʾ* is difficult and unlikely. Alternative readings such as ⌜*ma-aḫ*$^{!}$/*ḫa*$^{!}$⌝-*ru-uʾ* may be slightly preferable, though there is little to no resemblance between the sign LIŠ and *aḫ* or *ḫa* that would explain such a scribal error.

10′ The "suspended" KU$_3$.BABBAR *ina*$^{!(T.nu)}$ IGI is difficult as it is unclear whether the scribe simply forgot to write the name of the said individual, or the entire phrase is redundant. Whatever the answer may be, this peculiarity, as well as the errors in l. 7′ and the erased {*ina* IGI} in l. 12′, perhaps illustrate a lack of concentration by the scribe.

14′ The title of *ṭupšar māti*, "scribe of the land" is known from only one other contemporary source: UCP 9/2, 59: 4–5; see Kleber 2008, 325–6. Based on the use of *mātu* in the Eanna archive as referring to the Sealand, it seems reasonable that the *ṭupšar māti* was the scribe of the (sea)land. As noted by Kleber, the reading of KUR as *ekallu* (i.e., *ṭupšar ekalli*), is also possible, but seems less likely in the context of the Eanna archive.

28′ For *mulālu*, feeble-minded or mentally week, see Jursa 2001.

214. NBC 4780

Copy: Plate LIV
Date: 10(+).X.01(+) [Nbn–Camb]
Summary: withdrawal (*našû*) note: multiple items

The following dateable attestations form the chronological horizon of the text: Nādinu/Bēl-aḫḫē-iqīša (assuming that he is the temple scribe from the Egibi family) is attested between 5 Nbn (PTS 3049) and 5 Camb (YOS 7, 176); Marduk-šumu-iddin/Nabû-aḫḫē-bulliṭ (descendant of Balāṭu?): 1 Am (GC 2, 78) – 3 Camb (AnOr 8, 71); Arad-Innin/Nabû-naʾid: 1 Nbn (YOS 19, 284) – 3 Nbn (GC 1, 333).

Obv. ⅚ MA.NA KU$_3$.BABBAR ^{I}*na-di-nu* A-*šu*$_2$
ša$_2$ ^{Id}EN-PAP^{me}-BA^{ša_2} *a-na* UGU ^{lu_2}LUNGA⸢^{me}⸣
3 ⸢GIN$_2$ *bit-qa*⸣ ^{Id}AMAR.UTU-MU-MU A ^{Id}AG-PAP^{me}-TIN
(blank)
⸢38⸣ MA.NA ⸢15 GIN$_2$ *ḫa*⸣-*at-ḫu-re-e-tu*$_2$
⸢*ša*$_2$ ^{I}×⸣[× × ×] ⸢A ^{I}⸣*ka-re-e-a*
1 ½ MA.NA 7 GIN$_2$ KU$_3$.BABBAR ŠAM$_2$ 11 ⸢MA$^?$.NA$^?$⸣
^{Id}AG-MU-MU *it-ta-ši*
Lo.E. 50 GIN$_2$ *ir-bi ša*$_2$ *ul-tu* [(ø)]
UD.11.KAM *ša*$_2$ ^{iti}GAN *a-na qu-u*[*p*$^?$-*pi*$^?$]
(tiny line) *ša*$_2$ KA$_2$ *i-ru-bu*
Rev. 4 MA.NA ⅓ 6 GIN$_2$ KU$_3$.BABBAR *a*$^!$-⸢*na*⸣ [(ø)]
5 *kiš-ka-na-ne*$_2$-*e ša*$_2$ ⸢^{giš}× ×⸣
⸢*ša*$_2$ *a-na* ^{I}IR$_3$⸣-^{d}*in-nin* A ^{Id}AG-I
⸢*ma-ḫi-ir*⸣
(blank)
^{iti}⸢AB UD.10⸣[(+×).KAM] ⸢MU.1(+×).KAM⸣
[…]-⸢× LUGAL TIN.TIR^{ki}⸣

Nādinu, son of Bēl-aḫḫē-iqīša, (withdrew) 50 shekels of silver on account of the brewers; Marduk-šumu-iddin, son of Nabû-aḫḫē-bulliṭ, (withdrew) 3 ⅛ shekels; [PN], son of Karēa, (withdrew) 38 minas 15 shekels of apple-color dye; Nabû-šumu-iddin withdrew 1 mina 37 shekels of silver, the price of 11 *minas* (…); 50 shekels, the income that has come into the "cashbox of the gate" since Month IX, day 11; 4 minas 26 shekels of silver *for* …; five *kiškanê*-wood, *for*/*of* …, which were received for Arad-Innin, son of Nabû-naʾid.
Month X, day 10(+), year 1(+) of [RN].

215. YBC 11443

Copy: Plate LV
Date: --.IV.04 Camb
Summary: issue (*nadin*) list: salaries (barley)

Obv. ⸢ŠE⸣.BAR *ša*$_2$ *a-na* ŠUK.⸢ḪI⸣.A^{me} ^{I}⸢*la-ba*⸣*-a-ši*$^{!}$
u ^{Id}UTU-ŠEŠ-MU *ul-tu* ^{iti}GU$_4$ *a-di*
^{iti}ŠU MU.4.KAM ^{I}*kam-bu-zi-ia*$_2$ LUGAL TIN.TIR^{ki}
LUGAL KUR.KUR *id-di-nu*

---

5 GUR ^{Id}*na-na-a*-KAM ^{lu2}⸢GAL⸣ E$_2$ *kil-li*
2 GUR ^{I}E$_2$.AN.NA-DU$_3$ 1 ^{lu2}SIPA ⸢MUŠEN⸣^{me}
2 GUR ⸢^{I}E$_2$.AN⸣.NA-DU$_3$ 2^{u2} KA$_2$
3 ⸢GUR⸣ ⸢^{I}⸣^{d}*dan-nu*-ŠEŠ^{me}-*šu*$_2$-DU$_3$ ^{lu2}*mu-ša*$_2$*-kil* MUŠEN^{me}
⸢2$^{?}$ GUR⸣ ^{Id}INNIN-DU A ^{lu2}I$_3$.DU$_8$ *ša*$_2$ *a-ki-tu*$_4$
⸢3$^{?}$⸣ GUR 3 (PI) 4 BAN$_2$ 3 QA ŠUK.ḪI.A *ša*$_2$ ^{lu2}A.BAL^{meš}
[(×)] ^{lu2}*za-bil ku-du-ru* ^{Id}*na-na-a*-ŠEŠ-MU
[× GU]R ⸢^{f}⸣*tab-lu-ṭu u* ^{f}*bu*-⸢*ra*$^{?}$⸣-*šu*$_2$ *a-na qe*$_2$-⸢*me*⸣
[ŠE$^{?}$].BAR *a-na ki-is*-⸢*sat* 3 (PI) 3$^{?}$ ban$_2$$^{?}$⸣ [ ]
[ ] ⸢× × ×⸣ [ ]
(remainder of Obv. broken)

Rev. (beginning of Rev. broken)
⸢1(+) GUR⸣ [ ]
1 GUR ^{I}⸢IR$_3$-^{d}⸣[ ]
1 GUR ^{Id}UTU-ŠEŠ⸢^{meš}⸣-[×]
2 GUR ^{Id}AG-EN-*šu*$_2$*-nu* ^{lu2}EN.N[UN]
1 GUR ^{I}*u*$_2$*-bar ša*$_2$ ŠU^{II} ^{Id}KUR.GAL-LUGAL-⸢*a-ni*⸣
1 GUR ^{I}IR$_3$-^{d}*na-na-a* ^{lu2}EN *ma-aṣ*-⸢*ṣar*⸣*-tu*$_4$
2 (pi) 3 ban$_2$ ^{Id}UR.IDIM-DINGIR-*u*$_2$*-a* ^{lu2}AŠGAB
2 GUR ^{I}E$_2$.AN.NA-DU$_3$ ^{lu2}SIPA MUŠEN^{meš}
1 GUR ^{I}*la-ba-a*-⸢*ši*⸣-^{d}15
1 GUR ^{I}*a-ta-ṣur-u*$_2$*-ba-ku*-^{d}INNIN
1 GUR ^{f}*a-na-tab-ni-šu*$_2$ *ša*$_2$ *ina* ⸢ŠU⸣^{II} ^{f}⸢*tab-lu*⸣-*ṭu*

Barley that Lâbâši and Šamaš-aḫu-iddin distributed for salaries from month II to month IV, year 4 of Cambyses, king of Babylon, king of the world:
5 kor (for) Nanāya-ēreš, the prison overseer; 2 kor (for) Eanna-ibni, first (installment), the bird-herder; 2 kor (for) Eanna-ibni, second installment; 3 kor (for) Dannu-aḫḫēšu-ibni the bird feeder; *2* kor (for) Ištar-ukīn, son of the porter of the Akītu (temple); *3*;3.4.3 (for) the salaries of the water-drawers; [(× for)] basket-carriers (and$^{?}$) Nanāya-aḫu-iddin; [× ko]r (for) ^{f}Tabluṭu and ^{f}Burāšu for flour [... bar]ley for fodder; *0;0.3.3* [...] ... [...]
(*Break*)
1(+) kor (for) [...]; 1 kor (for) Arad-[DN]; 1 kor (for) Šamaš-aḫḫē-[...]; 2 kor (for) Nabû-bēlšunu, the watchman; 1 kor (for) Ubāru, standing for Amurru-šarrāni; 1 kor (for) Arad-Nanāya, the chief of the watch; 0;2.3.0 (for) Ur(i)dimmu-ilūa, the leatherworker; 2 kor (for) Eanna-ibni, the bird-herder; 1 kor (for) Lâbâši-Ištar; 1 kor (for) *Attaṣar-ubâki*-Ištar; 1 kor (for) ^{f}Ana-tabnîšu, via ^{f}Tabluṭu.

10′ The name ^{I}*a-ta-ṣur-u*$_2$*-ba-ku-*^{d}INNIN is otherwise unknown to us. The first element is assumed to be a first person perfect (or preterite I/3?) form of *naṣāru,* the second, a first person present of *bu*”*û* with an accusative suffix. It might be rendered as “I have been careful in my search for you, O Ištar.”

216. YBC 11938

Copy: Plate LIV
Date: 02.II.02 Nbn
Summary: *ina pāni* note: barley

The tablet is lentil-shaped. While this is not a common feature, there are known lentil-shaped tablets from the Eanna archive; e.g., Kleber 2017, no. 95 (PTS 2324) and Kleber 2017, no. 156 (PTS 3004).

Obv. ⸢5 GUR⸣ ŠE.BAR *a-na* NINDA.ḪI.A
ša$_2$ ⸢^{lu_2}⸣NAGAR^{me} *ša*$_2$ TA
UD.1.KAM *ša*$_2$ ^{iti}⸢GU$_4$⸣ *ina* IGI
^{I}LUGAL-UŠ$_2$-TIN^{it}
^{iti}GU$_4$ UD.2.K[AM]
[M]U.2.K[AM]
Lo.E. ^{d}AG-N[I$_2$.TUK]
Rev. LUGAL TIN.[TIR^{ki}]

5 kor of barley for the bread of the carpenters from day 1 of month II is at the disposal of Šarru-mītu-uballiṭ.
Month II, day 2, year 2 of Nabonidus, king of Babylon.

217. NCBT 643

Copy: Plate LV
Date: 10.IX.33 Nbk
Summary: issue (*nadin*) list: barley

Obv. ⸢ŠE⸣.BAR *ir-bi ša*$_2$ ^{iti}GAN *ša*$_2$ *a-na maš-*⸢*šar-ti*⸣
ša$_2$ ^{iti}AB *u*$_3$ ŠUK^{me} *ša*$_2$ ^{lu_2}RIG$_7$^{me}
SUM.NA^{tu_4} ⸢ITI⸣°.GAN UD.10.KAM MU.33.KAM
^{d}AG-NIG$_2$.DU-URU$_3$ LUGAL TIN.TIR^{ki}

---

15 *ma-ši-ḫu*	^{Id}AMAR.UTU-MU-MU
6	^{Id}AG-MU-GIŠ
6	^{Id}AG-DU$_3$-⸢ŠEŠ⸣
5	^{I}GAR-MU
5	^{I}EN-*šu*$_2$*-nu*
5	^{I}IR$_3$-^{d}*in-nin*
5	^{Id}AG-*ke-šir*$_3$
4	^{Id}AG-SUR
⸢PAP⸣ <51>$^{?}$ *ša*$_2$ ^{I}DU$_3$-*ia* A $^{I\circ d}$AG-PAP$^{!(T.\ qa)meš!(T.\ d.30)}$ -DU$_3$	
⸢4⸣	^{Id}*in-nin*-MU-URU$_3$
⸢8⸣	^{I}NUMUN-DU

Rev. 4 ^{Id}AG-ŠEŠ^{meš}-MU
5 *ša*$_2$ ^{I}TIN ^{I}*na-din*
10 *ša*$_2$ ^{I}DU$_3$-*ia* ^{Id}U.GUR-TIN^{iṭ}
4 ^{Id}UTU-KAL
6 *ina* UD^{me} *ša*$_2$ ^{iti}BARA$_2$ ^{I}KAR-^{d}EN
6 ^{I}*gi-mil-lu ša*$_2$ ^{Id}UTU-KAL GIŠ^{u2}
22 *ma-ši-ḫu ša*$_2$ ŠE.BAR 3 *re-ḫe-et*
ŠAM$_2$ AB$_2$.MAḪ$_2$$^{!}$ PAP 28 *ma-ši-ḫu*
ŠUK.ḪI.A *ša*$_2$ 14 ^{lu2}*mu-saḫ-ḫi-re-e*
^{I}*ina*-SUḪ$_3$-SUR ^{lu2}*si-pir*
1 *šal-šu ina* ŠUK.ḪI.A-*šu*$_2$ *ša*$_2$ ^{iti}GAN
^{Id}*na-na-a*-MU ^{lu2}*mu-ša*$_2$*-kil* MUŠEN.ḪI.A
2 ^{Id}EN-NIGIN$_2$^{ir} *u* ^{I}IR$_3$-*a* ^{lu2}NAGAR^{me}
2 *ina* ŠUK.ḪI.A-*šu*$_2$ *ša*$_2$ ^{iti}GAN ^{Id}AG-EN-MU^{me}
ša$_2$ UGU *qu-up-pu*
⸢2⸣ ŠUK-*su ša*$_2$ ^{iti}GAN ^{Id}INNIN-*u*$_2$*-da*
Up.E. ⸢*ša*$_2$⸣ ^{I}*gi-mil-lu ša*$_2$ UGU UDU.⸢NITA$_2$ GIŠ^{u2}⸣

Barley, the income of month IX, which was given for the *maššartu* of month X and the salaries of the temple serfs, Month IX, day 10, year 33 of Nebuchadnezzar, king of Babylon: 15 *mašīḫu*s (for) Marduk-šumu-iddin; 6 (for) Nabû-šumu-līšir; 6 (for) Nabû-bān-aḫi; 5 (for) Šākin-šumi; 5 (for) Bēlšunu; 5 (for) Arad-Innin; 5 (for) Nabû-kēšir; 4 (for) Nabû-ēṭir; total <51> of Bānia, son of Nabû-aḫḫē-ibni.
4 (*mašīḫu*s for) Innin-šumu-uṣur; 8 (for) Zēru-ukīn; 4 (for) Nabû-aḫḫē-iddin; 5 (of) Balāṭu, (son of/and/for)? Nādinu; 10 (of) Bānia, (son of/and/for)? Nergal-uballiṭ; 4 (for) Šamaš-udammiq; 6 from the days of month I (of/for?) Mušēzib-Bēl; 6 (for) Gimillu, which Šamaš-udammiq withdrew; 22 *mašīḫu*s of barley, 3 are the remainder, price of a young cow; total of 28 *mašīḫu*s, the salaries of fourteen agents.
Ina-tēšî-ēṭir, the alphabet scribe, 1 ⅓ (*mašīḫu*) from his salary of month IX (for) Nanāya-iddin, the bird feeder; 2 (*mašīḫu*s) (for) Bēl-upaḫḫir and Ardāya, the carpenters; 2 from his salary of month IX (for) Nabû-bēl-šumāti, the (one) in charge of the cashbox; 2, his salary of month IX (for) Ištar-uddu, which Gimillu, who is in charge of the sheep, withdrew.

13 The missing amount, calculated as 51, must be a scribal error.
The reading $^{I\circ d}$AG-PAP$^{!(T.\ qa)meš!(T.\ d.30)}$-DU$_3$ may alternatively be read $^{I\circ d}$AG-PAP$^{<<me>>meš}$-DU$_3$, which would result in the same name, but fewer emendations.

218. NBC 4567

Copy: Plate LVI
Date: 07.V.12 --
Summary: *maḫir* receipt: barley

Obv. 1 (PI) 4 BAN$_2$ ŠE.BAR ŠUK.ḪI.A *ša*$_2$ ^{iti}NE
^{I}*šu-la-a* ^{lu2}GALA
⸢IGI$^{\circ ir}$⸣ {eras.} ^{iti}NE UD.7.KAM
Lo.E. MU.12.KAM
Rev. (uninscribed)

0;1.4.0 barley, salary for month V, *was received from* Šulāya, the lamentation priest.
Month V, day 7, year 12.

1–3 It is unclear why the lamentation (*kalû*) priest would deliver salaries to the temple. A more reasonable scenario would be the priest withdrawing, *ittaši* (GIŠ), the barley. The signs, however, even though traces of previous erased signs are visible, clearly read IGI^{ir}. It may therefore be argued that this text presents the "northern," active, usage of *maḫir*, i.e., Šulāya indeed received the barley; see Jursa 2005, 46. Additionally, and not less problematic, is the fact that the priest receives *kurummatu* rather than prebendary income.

219. NBC 4710

Copy: Plate LVI
Date: 03.VI.21 --
Summary: payment (*apil*) note: barley

Obv. 1 GUR 3 (PI) 4 BAN$_2$ 3 SILA$_3$ ŠE.B[AR]
ŠUK.ḪI.A *ša*$_2$ 7$^!$ ITI^{me} ^{iti}⸢BARA$_2$⸣
^{iti}GU$_4$ ^{iti}SIG$_4$ ^{iti}⸢ŠU⸣
^{iti}NE ^{iti}KIN *u* ⸢^{iti}DU$_6$⸣
^{I}*na-din* ^{lu_2}⸢ŠITIM⸣
Lo.E. *a-pil*
Rev. ^{iti}KIN UD.3.KAM
MU.21.KAM

Nādinu, the builder, was paid 1;3.4.3 barley, salary for seven months: I–VII.
Month VI, day 3, year 21.

1–2 Dividing the salary of 1;3.4.3 (315 liters) barley by the seven months of work comes to 45 liters (0;1.1.3) per month. This is exactly half of the standard 90 liters per month used in Uruk during the reign of Nebuchadnezzar onwards (see Jursa 2010, 672).

220. YBC 9491

Copy: Plate LVI
Date: 04.XII.13 Nbk
Summary: payment (*eṭir*) note: barley

Obv. 4 BAN$_2$ ½ SILA$_3$ ŠE.BAR
NINDA.ḪI.A-*šu*$_2$ *ša*$_2$ *ul-tu*
UD.3.KAM *a-di*
4 UD.16.KAM
Lo.E. ⸢^{lu_2}⸣NAGAR *e-*⸢*ṭir*⸣
Rev. (blank)
^{iti}ŠE UD.4.KAM
MU.13.KAM
⸢^{d}AG-NIG$_2$⸣.DU-URU$_3$
Up.E. LUGAL TIN.TIR^{ki}

The carpenter was paid 0;0.4.½ barley, his bread from days 3–16.
Month XII, day 4, year 13 of Nebuchadnezzar, king of Babylon.

221. NCBT 680

Copy: Plate LVI
Date: 05.IX.0a [AM–Nbn]
Summary: personnel list + accounting note

Amīl-Nanāya (l. 10) is attested between 18 Nbk (GC 2, 278) and 3$^?$ Ner$^?$ (PTS 3322); see Payne 2007, 155. Bēl-aḫḫē-iddin / Bēlšunu (l. 5) may be identified in PTS 2157 (43 Nbk). Nanāya-aḫu-iddin/Arrab l. 8), if he is the oil-presser attested in **No. 272**: 3, then the latter would be his last known attestation, 31 Nbk, while his earliest would be in 14 Nbk (NBDMich. 32).

Obv.	^{I}NIG$_2$.DU A-šu$_2$ ša$_2$ ^{Id}A[G$^?$-…	]
	^{Id}na-na-a-SISKUR$_2$ [A-šu$_2$ ša$_2$ ^{I}	]
	^{Id}AG-ŠEŠ-MU A-šu$_2$ ⸢ša$_2$ ^{I}⸣LU$_2$-^{d}A[G$^?$]	⸢ša$_2$ ^{I}⸣[ ]
	^{I}LU$_2$-^{d}na-⸢na-a A-šu$_2$ ša$_2$⸣ ^{Id}UTU-MU	ša$_2$ ^{I}⸢SUM$^?$⸣.[NA$^?$-(×)]
	^{Id}EN-ŠEŠ^{me}-MU A-šu$_2$ ša$_2$ ^{I}EN-šu$_2$-nu	ša$_2$ ^{I}⸢ŠEŠ⸣$^?$-[×]-⸢×-×⸣
	^{Id}ŠU$_2$-NUMUN-DU$_3$ ^{lu2}IR$_3$-E$_2$.GAL	ša$_2$ ^{I}IR$_3$-^{d}⸢INNIN.NA ša$_2$ ^{Id}ag$^?$-NUMUN-×⸣
	^{Id}na-na-a-SISKUR$_2$ A-šu$_2$ ša$_2$ ^{Id}na-na-a-KAM	ša$_2$ ^{Id}na-na-a-⸢ŠEŠ-× A ^{I}×-×⸣
	^{Id}na-na-a-ŠEŠ-MU A-šu$_2$ ša$_2$ ^{I}ar$_2$-rab	ša$_2$ ^{I}si-lim-^{d}EN A ^{I}⸢SUM.NA-a⸣
Lo.E.	⸢^{I}⸣IR$_3$-a A-šu$_2$ ša$_2$ ^{Id}na-na-a-KAM ^{lu2}MA$_2$.LAḪ$_4$	
	^{Id}UTU-PAP ^{lu2}pu-ṣa-a-a ⸢ša$_2$⸣ ^{I}LU$_2$-^{d}na-na-a ^{lu2}pu-ṣa-⸢a⸣-[a]	
Rev.	PAP 10 ^{lu2}SIPA^{me} ša$_2$ a-na ^{kur}i-zal-la šap-ra	
	⸢3⸣ MA.NA ⅓ GIN$_2$ KU$_3$.BABBAR a-na ŠUK.ḪI.A^{me}-šu$_2$-nu iḫ-te-eṭ	
	⸢a⸣-na a$^!$-me-lu ⅓ GIN$_2$ KU$_3$.BABBAR 2 MA.NA a-na 2 ANŠE^{me} ina IGI-šu$_2$-<nu>	
	⸢PAP⸣ 5 MA.NA ⅓ ⸢GIN$_2$⸣ KU$_3$.BABBAR <<IT>> {eras.}	
	(blank)	
	^{iti}⸢GAN⸣ UD.5.KAM [	]
Up.E.	MU.SAG.⸢NAM.LUGAL⸣ […, LUGAL TIN.TIR^{ki}]	
Rev.*	(written sideways)	
	1	[(×)]
	1	[(×)]
	1	[(×)]
	1	[(×)]
	{eras.}	
	PAP 20	1
	^{Id}EN-PAP	ina ⸢IGI$^?$-šu$_2$$^?$⸣[(×)]

Kudurru, son of *N*[*abû*-…]; Nanāya-uṣalli, [son of …]; Nabû-aḫu-iddin, son of Amīl-*N*[*abû*] for […]; Amīl-Nanāya, son of Šamaš-iddin, for *Iddin*-[DN]; Bēl-aḫḫē-iddin, son of Bēlšunu, for *Aḫu*-…; Marduk-zēru-ibni, the master-builder of Arad-Innin for Nabû-zēru-×; Nanāya-uṣalli, son of Nanāya-ēreš, for Nanāya-aḫu-…, *son of* …; Nanāya-aḫu-iddin, son of Arrab, for Silim-Bēl, son of Iddināya; Ardāya, son of Nanāya-ēreš, the boatman; Šamaš-nāṣir, the linen weaver; for Amīl-Nanāya, the linen weaver; total of ten shepherds who were sent to Izalla.
He weighed 3 minas 20 shekels of silver for their salaries at 20 shekels of silver per man, 2

minas for two donkeys are at his disposal; total of 5 minas 20 shekels silver.
Month IX, day 5, year 0a [..., king of Babylon].

(*written sideways:) ...; total of 20 ... Bēl-nāṣir, *at his disposal.*

3ff. From the aligning of ll. 6–8 it is clear that the right side of ll. 3–5 drops. The break at the upper right corner prevents us from tracing the lining at the head of the tablet.

12 The subject of *iḫṭēṭ* is the head of this group of men—perhaps Bēl-nāṣir mentioned on the reverse, or else Kudurru, the first man on the list.

14 The last sign, *it*, seems superflous. It may have been intended to be the beginning of a perfect from of *našû*.

222. NBC 4732

Copy: Plate LVII
Date: 04.X.38 Nbk
Summary: withdrawal (*našû*) note: barley

Obv. 5 GUR 2 PI 3 SILA$_3$ ⸢ŠE⸣.BAR
a-na ŠUK *ša*$_2$ MUNUS^{me} *ša*$_2$ *ina* E$_2$
^{Id}EN-⸢ŠEŠ⸣^{me}-SU *ṣab-*⸢*ta*⸣
^{I}*nu-ḫa-a* ⸢*it-ta*⸣*-ši*
[(×+)] 1 GUR 1 (PI) 4 BAN$_2$ *a-na*
Lo.E. [SI]K$_2^{!}$.ḪI.A *ša*$_2$ KA$_2$
Rev. [^{Id}A]G-*re-ṣu-u*$_2$*-a*
GIŠ
(blank)
⸢^{iti}⸣AB UD.4.KAM MU.38.KAM
^{d}AG-NIG$_2$.DU-URU$_3$ LUGAL TIN.TIR^{ki}
(textile/basket$^?$ impressions on both sides of the tablet)

Nuḫāya withdrew 5;2.0.3 barley for the rations of the women held in the house of Bēl-aḫḫē-erība. Nabû-rēṣū'a withdrew 1(+);1.4.0 kor for the wool of the gate.
Month X, day 4, year 38 of Nebuchadnezzar, king of Babylon.

2 Given the seemingly temporary situation of the held women, *kurummatu* is translated here as "rations" rather than "salaries" (as the general practice throughout this volume).

223. NCBT 139

Copy: Plate LVII
Date: 21.VII.<×> Nbk
Summary: withdrawal (*našû*) note: barley

Obv. 5 BAN$_2$ ŠE.BAR *ina* ŠUK.ḪI.A-*šu*$_2$
^{I}MU-DU ^{lu2}AD.KID GIŠ
⸢5 BAN$_2$⸣ ^{I}*ina*-GISSU-^{d}⸢*na*⸣*-na-a*
⸢*ša*$_2$⸣ *a-na ṣa-rap*
Lo.E. [(×)] *a-gur-ru* ⸢*šap*⸣*-ri*

6 GIŠ
Rev. (blank)
^{iti}DU$_6$ UD.21.KAM <MU.×.KAM>
^{d}AG-NIG$_2$.DU-URU$_3$
LUGAL TIN.TIR^{ki}

Šumu-ukīn, the reed-worker, withdrew 5 *sūtu* of barley from his salary. Ina-ṣilli-Nanāya, who was sent to fire bricks, withdrew 5 *sūtu* (of barley).
Month VII, day 21, <year ×> of Nebuchadnezzar, king of Babylon.

224. NCBT 197

Copy: Plate LVII
Date: 23.II.15 Nbk
Summary: withdrawal (*našû*) note: barley[25]

Obv. 90 ^{giš}*ma-ši-ḫu ša*$_2$ 1 PI ⌜AM$_3$⌝
ŠE.BAR *ir-bi ša*$_2$ ^{Id}*na-na-a*-MU <A$^?$>
^{Id}AG-GI ^{I}GI-^{d}AMAR.UTU
A ^{Id}AG-MU-⌜PAP⌝ *ina* UD^{meš}
5 *ša*$_2$ ^{Id}UTU-NUMUN-BA^{ša_2} GIŠ
Rev. (blank)
^{iti}GU$_4$ UD.23.KAM MU.15.KAM
^{d}AG-NIG$_2$.DU-URU$_3$ LUGAL TIN.TIR⌜^{ki}⌝

Mušallim-Marduk, son of Nabû-šumu-nāṣir, withdrew 90 *mašīḫu*s, each measuring 1 *pānu*, of barley, the income of Nanāya-iddin <son of$^?$> Nabû-ušallim, from the days of Šamaš-zēru-iqīša.
Month II, day 23, year 15 of Nebuchadnezzar, king of Babylon.

1 The *mašīḫu* used here, containing 36 *qû*, is smaller than the standard *mašīḫu* of Eanna that contained 45 *qû*; see Beaulieu 1989; Janković 2013, 11–2.

2 The reading of the last sign in ^{Id}*na-na-a*-KAM$^?$ (Nanāya-ēreš) is uncertain, and the name may also be read ^{Id}*na-na-a*-MU$^?$ (Nanāya-iddin).

2–3 There is neither *u* nor A(-*šu*$_2$ *ša*$_2$) between Nanāya-iddin and Nabû-ušallim, yet this is most probably one individual (rather than two); most probably Nanāya-iddin/Nabû-ušallim the weaver, for whom see Payne 2007, 189.

225. NCBT 82

Copy: Plate LVII
Date: 03.X.21 Nbk
Summary: withdrawal (*našû*) note: barley

Obv. 1 ^{giš}*ma-ši-*⌜*ḫu*⌝ *ša*$_2$ ŠE.BAR *ina* ŠUK.ḪI.A$^!$-*šu*$_2$
ša$_2$ ^{iti}AB ^{Id}*na-na-a*-⌜SISKUR⌝ GIŠ
^{I}*ina*-GISSU-^{d}*na-na-a*

[25] A previous edition is included in Payne 2007, 146.

^{lu_2}I$_3$.DU$_8$ *ša*$_2$ E$_2$ *te-en-ne*$_2$*-e* GIŠ
Rev. (blank)
^{iti}AB UD.3.KAM MU.21.KAM
^{d}AG-NIG$_2$.DU-URU$_3$ LUGAL TIN.TIR^{ki}

Nanāya-uṣalli withdrew 1 *mašīḫu* of barley from his salary for month X; Ina-ṣilli-Nanāya, the porter of the *annex*, withdrew (1 *mašīḫu*).
Month X, day 3, year 21 of Nebuchadnezzar, king of Babylon.

4 E$_2$ *te-en-ne*$_2$*-e* is taken as a form of *bīt tēnê*. The meaning "annex," CAD T, 345, s.v. *tānû* 3, is uncertain.

226. NCBT 950

Copy: Plate LVIII
Date: 29.I.32 Nbk
Summary: withdrawal (*našû*) note: barley

Obv. 10 ^{giš}⸢*ma*⸣*-ši-ḫu ša*$_2$ ŠE.BAR *ir-bi*
re-⸢*ḫe-et*⸣ ŠUK.ḪI.A*-šu*$_2$*-nu ša*$_2$ *a-di*
UD.⸢15.KAM⸣ *ša*$_2$ ^{iti}GU$_4$ ^{Id}*na-na-a-*⸢SISKUR$_2$⸣
ša$_2$ 10^{ti} *ša*$_2$ ^{Id}*na-na-a-*KAM
^{I}⸢*lu-mur-dum-qi*$_2$⸣-^{d}15 ^{I}I-^{d}15
^{Id}*in-nin-*NUMUN-BA^{ša_2} ^{Id}*na-na-a-*⸢ŠEŠ-MU⸣
^{I}°LU$_2$-^{d}*na-na-*⸢*a*⸣ *u* ^{Id}AG-⸢KAD$_2$⸣
Lo.E. ⸢*ša*$_2$⸣ *a-na* IGI ^{lu_2}ŠA$_3$.TAM
9 ⸢*u*$_3$⸣ ^{lu_2}UMBISAG E$_2$ *šap-ru*
Rev. *it-ta-šu*$_2$*-u*$_2$
1 *re-ḫe-et* ŠUK.ḪI.A*-šu*$_2$
ša$_2$ ^{iti}BARA$_2$ ^{I}*lu-mur-dum-qi*$_2$-^{d}15
^{lu_2}GAL ^{giš}*sik-kat*^{me} *it-*⸢*ta-ši*⸣
1 *šal-šu*$_2$ *re-ḫe-et* ŠUK.ḪI.A*-šu*$_2$*-*⸢*nu*⸣
⸢*ša*$_2$⸣ ^{iti}BARA$_2$ ^{I}*ša*$_2$-^{d}INNIN*-u*$_2$*-da*
^{lu_2}U.ZADIM GI^{me} *u* ^{I}ŠEŠ*-it-tab-*⸢*ši*⸣
it-ta-šu$_2$*-u*$_2$
Up.E. ^{iti}BARA$_2$ UD.29.KAM MU.32.⸢KAM⸣
^{d}AG-NIG$_2$.DU-⸢URU$_3$ LUGAL⸣ TIN.TIR⸢^{ki}⸣

Nanāya-uṣalli of the decury of Nanāya-ēreš, Lūmur-dumqi-Ištar, Na'id-Ištar, Innin-zēru-iqīša, Nanāya-aḫu-iddin, Amīl-Nanāya, and Nabû-kāṣir, who were sent before the *šatammu* and the temple scribe, withdrew 10 *mašīḫus* of barley, (from) the income, the remainder of their salaries up to day 15 of month II.
Lūmur-dumqi-Ištar, the *rab sikkati*, withdrew 1 (*mašīḫu*), the remainder of his salary of month I.
Ša-Ištar-uddu the bow and reed (arrow) maker, and Aḫu-ittabši withdrew ⅓ (*mašīḫu*), the remainder of their salaries of month I.
Month I, day 29, year 32 of Nebuchadnezzar, king of Babylon.

227. NBC 4773

Copy: Plate LVIII
Date: 20.VI.14 Nbk
Summary: withdrawal (*našû*) note: *irbu*

Obv. [ŠE.BAR]$^?$ ⸢ir-bi⸣ ša$_2$ ^{iti}KIN UD.20.K[AM] MU.⸢14.KAM⸣
⸢^{d}AG⸣-NIG$_2$.DU-URU$_3$ LUGAL TIN.TIR⸢^{ki}⸣

---

4 ^{giš}ma-ši-ḫu ina UD^{me} ša$_2$ ^{I}ṣil-la-a
⸢^{iti}DU$_6$⸣ IGI ^{d}GAŠAN ša$_2$ SAG ^{Id}AG-ke-šir$_3$ GIŠ
5 ina UD^{meš}-šu$_2$ ša$_2$ ^{iti}DU$_6$ ^{Id}U.GUR-PAP GIŠ
2 ina UD^{me} ša$_2$ ^{I}ša$_2$-^{d}AG-šu-u$_2$ ⸢^{iti}⸣DU$_6$
IGI ^{d}GAŠAN ša$_2$ UNUG^{ki} ^{I}bul-luṭ A ^{Id}gu-la-NUMUN-DU$_3$ ⸢GIŠ⸣
2 ina UD^{me} ša$_2$ ^{Id}UTU-NUMUN-BA$^{\text{ša2}}$ ša$_2$ ⸢^{iti}⸣APIN
^{I}A-a A ^{I}DU$_3$-a $^{\text{lu2}}$A.KIN ša$_2$ ^{I}IR$_3$-⸢^{d}AG⸣ GIŠ
Lo.E. ⸢5⸣ SILA$_3$ ša$_2$ 4 mu-ra-ši-ia u 1 ⸢SILA$_3$⸣
at-tu-šu$_2$ ^{I}si-lim-^{d}EN $^{\text{lu2}}$I$_3$-DU$_8$ ⸢GIŠ⸣
Rev. 3 BAN$_2$ ša$_2$ 11 ERIN$_2^{\text{meš}}$ ^{I}a-qar-a GIŠ
4 BAN$_2$ ša$_2$ ERIN$_2^{\text{meš}}$ ša$_2$ E$_2$ GUR$_7^{\text{meš}}$
^{Id}na-na-a-MU GIŠ
1 BAN$_2$ 1 SILA$_3$ ^{I}ta-ri-bi ^{Id}INNIN.NA-NUMUN-DU$_3$
^{Id}na-na-a-ŠEŠ-MU u ^{Id}30-na-din-MU GIŠ⸢$^{\text{u2}}$⸣
4 SILA$_3$ ^{I}ri-kis-DU$_3$.A.BI-^{d}EN u$_3$
2 ERIN$_2^{\text{meš}}$-šu$_2$ GIŠ$^{\text{u2}}$
[×] ⸢$^{\text{lu2}}$pu⸣-ṣa-a-a u$_3$ 2 ERIN$_2^{\text{meš}}$-⸢šu$_2^?$⸣
[(×)] ⸢ša$_2$⸣ it-ti-šu$_2$ GIŠ$^{\text{u2}}$

[*Barley*] income of Month VI, day 20, year 14 of Nebuchadnezzar, king of Babylon: Nabû-kēšir withdrew 4 *mašīḫus* from the days of Ṣillāya (of) month VII before Bēltu-ša-rēš; Nergal-nāṣir withdrew 5 (*mašīḫus*) from his days of month VII; Bulluṭ, son of Gula-zēru-ibni, withdrew 2 (*mašīḫus*) from the days of Ša-Nabû-šū (of) month VII before the Lady-of-Uruk; Aplāya, son of Ibnāya, the messenger of Arad-Nabû, withdrew 2 from the days of Šamaš-zēru-iqīša of month VIII; Silim-Bēl, the porter, withdrew 5 *qû* for four wildcats and 1 *qû* for himself; Aqara withdrew 3 *sūtu* for eleven workers; Nanāya-iddin withdrew 4 *sūtu* for the workers of the depots; Tarību, Innin-zēru-ibni, Nanāya-aḫu-iddin, and Sîn-nādin-šumi withdrew 0;0.1.1; Rikis-kalāma-Bēl and two of his workers withdrew 4 *qû*; [...] the linen weaver and two of his workers withdrew [...] who are with him.

10 Kleber (2018) argues that the ration-receiving *murašûs* in temple archives were large wildcats used by fowlers during bird hunts; she suggests identifying it as a caracal. Regardless of the specific identification, there is no justification for the CAD's (M/II, 218–9) separation of *murašû* A (wildcat) and *murašû* B (meaning uncertain).

228. NCBT 495

Copy: Plate LVIII
Date: 15?.XI.12 Nbk
Summary: withdrawal (*našû*) note: silver

Obv. 2 GIN$_2$ KU$_3$.BABBAR ^{Id}*na-na-a*-ŠEŠ-MU
^{lu2}UŠ.BAR *i-na* ŠUK.ḪI.A-*šu*$_2$
ša$_2$ ^{iti}AB
it-ta-ši
Rev. (blank)
^{iti}ZIZ$_2$ ⸢UD.15?⸣.KAM
MU.12.[KAM]
^{Id}AG-NIG$_2$.⸢DU⸣-PAP

Nanāya-aḫu-iddin, the weaver, withdrew 2 shekels of silver from his salary of month X. Month XI, day 15, year 12 of Nebuchadnezzar.

229. YBC 3513

Copy: Plate LIX
Date: 14.IX.18 Nbk
Summary: withdrawal (*našû*) list: dates and barley

Obv. 5 BAN$_2$ ZU$_2$.LUM.MA ^{I}⸢×⸣ [ ]
ša$_2$ *a-na* UGU PA ḪI? [ ]
2 BAN$_2$ ŠE.BAR ^{I}*i-sin-na-*[*a-a*]
3 BAN$_2$ 2 SILA$_3$ ZU$_2$.LUM.MA NINDA.ḪI.⸢A-*šu*$_2$⸣-[*nu* ^{I}… *u*]
ERIN$_2$^{me} *ša*$_2$ UGU ⸢NIG$_2$⸣.BUR$_3$.BUR$_3$-⸢*tu*$_4$? GIŠ^{u_2}⸣
⸢1 BAN$_2$⸣ 2 SILA$_3$ *ša*$_2$ ⸢2⸣ UD-*mu*! 2 ^{lu2}*ši-rak* ⸢GIG⸣^{me} GIŠ^{u}
4 SILA$_3$ ^{I}ŠEŠ-*lu-mur ṣab-tu* GIŠ
1 BAN$_2$ ŠE.BAR ^{I}MU-DU ⸢^{lu2}AD.KID⸣ GIŠ
Lo.E. ⸢1 BAN$_2$⸣ 2 SILA$_3$ *ša*$_2$ 2 ⸢UD⸣ ^{Id}AG-⸢ŠEŠ⸣^{meš}-MU
u ^{Id}AG-NUMUN-DU ^{lu2}UŠ.BAR^{me} GIŠ^{u}
Rev. 1 BAN$_2$ 2 SILA$_3$ *ana* ŠUK.ḪI.A *ša*$_2$ *iṣ*-⸢*ṣur*⸣ ^{Id}*na-na-a*-MU GIŠ
1 BAN$_2$ 2 SILA$_3$ ZU$_2$.LUM.MA NINDA.ḪI.A-*šu*$_2$-*nu ša*$_2$ 2 *u*$_4$-*mu*
^{I}KI-E$_2$.AN.NA-*bu-di-ia*$_2$ *u* ^{I}DIM-DU$_3$.A-^{d}EN! GIŠ^{u}
(blank)
⸢^{iti}⸣GAN UD.14.KAM MU.18.KAM ^{d}AG-NIG$_2$.DU-U[RU$_3$]
LUGAL TIN.TIR^{ki}

[PN withdrew] 5 *sūtu* of dates … on account of […]. Isinnāya [withdrew] 2 *sūtu* of barley. [PN and] the men in charge of the *drilling* withdrew 0;3.2.0 dates, th[eir] bread. Two sick temple serfs withdrew 0;1.2.0 for two days. Aḫu-lūmur, the prisoner, withdrew 4 *qû*. Šumu-ukīn, the reed-worker, withdrew 1 *sūtu* of barley. Nabû-aḫḫē-iddin and Nabû-zēru-ukīn, the weavers, withdrew 0;1.2.0 for two days. Nanāya-iddin withdrew 0;1.2.0 as salary for the birds. Itti-Eanna-būdia and Rikis-kalāma-Bēl withdrew 0;1.2.0 dates, their bread, for two days.
Month IX, day14, year 18 of Nebuchadnezzar, king of Babylon.

5 The phrase *ša muḫḫi pālišti* is unknown, and the word is word *pāliš(t)u* itself is generally attested in earlier periods; see CAD P, 68, s.v. *pallišu*. The reading, nonetheless, is relatively secure and we know of no better alternative understanding.

230. NCBT 1165

Copy: Plate LIX
Date: undated (ca. Nbk 30)
Summary: accounting inventory: barley

Regarding Nādinu (l. 12), of the three weavers named Nādinu listed in Payne 2007 (pp. 182–4), Nādinu/Nadnāya//Išparu (attested 30–36$^?$ Nbk) and Nādinu/Nergal-nāṣir//Išparu (attested 21–36 Nbk) should be considered. An individual named Šamaš-udammiq is attested in several texts around the same time in the context of salaries and ration withdrawals; e.g., **Nos. 217**, **304**, and see also YBC 9545 (27 Nbk) in which Šamaš-udammiq receives barley from the *upnu* of the temple scribe.

Obv. ⸢60^{šu}⸣ 4 GUR ⸢3° (PI)⸣ 2 BAN$_2$ ŠE°.BAR° *u* ZU$_2$.LUM.⸢MA⸣
ŠE.ZIZ$_2$.A$_4$ *u*$_3$ ŠE.GIŠ.I$_3$ *u*$_2$*-pu-un*
ša$_2$ 9 *lim* 7.ME GUR ŠE.⸢BAR⸣ *ša*$_2$ ⸢*ul*⸣*-tu*
^{iti}BARA$_2$ *a-di lib*$_3$*-bi* ^{iti}ŠE MU.29.KAM
⸢*a*⸣*-di* 2 *lim*$^!$ GUR ŠE.BAR *ša*$_2$ ^{lu2}ENGAR$^{!me}$
[*ina*] ⸢*lib*$_3$⸣*-bi* 3 [GU]R 1 (PI) 1 BAN$_2$ 3 SILA$_3$ *re-ḫe-et*
[Z]U$_2$.LUM.MA *ša*$_2$ ^{Id}AG-MU-DU *ina* ^{uru}E$_2$*-gi-la-nu*
[^{Id}]⸢×⸣-NUMUN-DU *u* ^{I}*še-el-li-bi*
[ ] × × [ ] ⸢× ×⸣ *ina* ŠE.BAR
Lo.E. [ ] ⸢ME$^?$ *ša*$_2$⸣ [^{I}]⸢^{d}AG-MU⸣-DU
[ ] ⸢×⸣ [ ] ⸢× ŠU$^?$ U$_2$⸣
Rev. [ ] ⸢*ša*$_2$ ^{I}*na*⸣*-din* ^{lu2}UŠ.BAR GIŠ$^{⸢u⸣}$
[(×+)] ⸢2 GUR⸣ 2 (PI) 3 BAN$_2$ *ina* ŠE.BAR *ša*$_2$ ^{Id}EN.LIL$_2$-MU-DU$_3$
[(×)] *ša*$_2$ ^{Id}U.GUR*-re-ṣu-u*$_2$*-a* GIŠ^{u2}
11 GUR 3 (PI) 4 BAN$_2$ 3 SILA$_3$ ŠE.BAR *u* ZU$_2$.LUM.MA *ša*$_2$ ^{Id}UTU-KAL GIŠ^{u}
37 GUR 2 (PI) 1 BAN$_2$ *ša*$_2$ ^{lu2}UMBISAG-E$_2$
ina ŠE.BAR *ša*$_2$ *muḫ-ḫi-šu*$_2$ *a-na* E$_2$.AN.NA *iḫ-ḫi-si*
PAP 72 GUR 1 (PI) 2 BAN$_2$ *it-*⸢*ta-ši*⸣
7 (GUR) 3 PI *ina* ŠE.BAR *ša*$_2$ ⸢^{lu2}⸣[× (×)]
MU.30.KAM *it-ta-ši*

64;3.2.0 barley and dates, emmer and sesame, the *upnu* allotment for the 9,700 kor of barley that is from month I until the middle of month XII of year 29, including the 2,000 kor of barley of the plowmen; thereof, 3;1.1.3, the remainder of the dates of Nabû-šumu-ukīn, are in Bīt-Gilāni; … ^{d}×-zēru-ukīn and Šellibi […] … from the barley … of/which Nabû-šumu-ukīn … […] … that Nādinu, the weaver, withdrew.
2(+);2.3.0 from the barley of Enlil-šumu-ibni that Nergal-rēṣū'a withdrew.
11;3.4.3 barley and dates that Šamaš-udammiq withdrew.
37;2.1.0 of the temple scribe, from the barley that returned to Eanna at his expense; he withdrew a total of 72;1.2.0.
7;3.0.0 from the barley that the [… (official)] withdrew [for] year 30.

2 The *upnu*, literally "handful/fist," is 1/150, or 0.66%; see Jursa and Levavi 2021. In the present context, 9700 (kor) divided by 64;3.2.0 (kor) gives us 150.001. The same 1/150 ratio is found in other first millennium Babylonian sources; e.g., 12 *akalu* is the *upnu* of 1 *kurru* (RA 16 125 ii: 8, a 9th century *kudurru*); 8 ⅔ (*mašīḫus*) is the *upnu* of 1301 (*mašīḫus*) (GC 2, 291: 1–5, 22 Nbk). On the significance of the *upnu* within Eanna's administration and further discussion regarding its wider context, see Jursa and Levavi 2021.

7 For Bīt-Gilāni, see OECT 12, AB 233; YOS 7, 196; YOS 17, 42.

231. NBC 4613

Copy: Plate LVIII
Date: 22.III.32 Nbk
Summary: accounting inventory: barley

Obv. 5 GUR ŠE.BAR *ina maš-šar-ti-šu*$_2$
ša$_2$ ^{iti}ŠU ^{iti}NE *u* ^{iti}KIN
^{I}*bul-luṭ* A ^{I}⌜^{d}⌝*gu-la*-NUMUN-DU$_3$
5 GUR 2 (PI) 3 BAN$_2$ ^{Id}AG-MU-GIŠ
PAP 10 GUR 2 (PI) 3 BAN$_2$ ŠE.BAR
⌜*ša*$_2$ ^{Id}AG-*si*⌝-*lim* A$^{!}$ ^{I}⌜^{d}⌝UTU-NUMUN-DU$_3$
Lo.E. ⌜*a*⌝-*na* ⌜SIK$_2$.ḪI.A⌝ *ina* NIG$_2$.GA
Rev. (blank)
^{iti}SIG$_4$ UD.22.KAM MU.32.KAM
^{d}AG-NIG$_2$.DU-URU$_3$ LUGAL TIN.⌜TIR⌝^{ki}

5 kor of barley from his *maššartu* of months IV, V, and VI, (to) Bulluṭ, son of Gula-zēru-ibni, (and) 5;2.3.0 (to) Nabû-šumu-līšir; a total of 10;2.3.0 barley of Nabû-silim, son of Šamaš-zēru-ibni for (i.e., "in lieu of") wool, are in the temple stores.
Month III, day 22, year 32 of Nebuchadnezzar, king of Babylon.

1–7 Although unexpected, it seems that *maššartu* payments that were meant to be in wool were to be given in barley; the opposite transaction would be expected in the Eanna. Regardless, the barley is said to still be stored in the temple for the time being. An alternative reading would be: *5 kor of barley, his maššartu of months IV, V, and VI, (for) Bulluṭ, son of Gula-zēru-ibni, (and) 5;2.3.0 (for) Nabû-šumu-līšir; a total of 10;2.3.0 barley (originally paid) by Nabû-silim, son of Šamaš-zēru-ibni for wool, (which is still) in the temple stores*. Although this would resolve the above-mentioned issue, the main problem with this reading would be the reference to the wool that is still in the temple. If this wool was indeed unrelated to the *maššartu* payments, there would be no reason to specify it in the present record.

232. YBC 6863

Copy: Plate LIX
Date: 23.IX.24 Nbk
Summary: promissory note: barley

The text is not directly related to craftsmen per se, and was included in the volume based on prosopography; e.g., the witness Nādinu/Nergal-nāṣir//Išparu, a weaver attested 21–36 Nbk (see Payne 2007, 183), and the scribe Ibni-Ištar/Nabû-zēru-ukīn//Ašlāku, a washerman attested 3 Nbk–

4 Nbn (see Payne 2007, 169–71).

Obv. ⸢8⸣ ^{giš}*ma-ši-ḫu ša*$_2$ ŠE.BAR *ku-*⸢*um*⸣
8 ^{giš}*ma-ši-ḫu ša*$_2$ ŠE.ZIZ$_2$.A$_4$
NIG$_2$.GA ^{d}INNIN UNUG^{ki} *u* ^{d}*na-na-a*
ina UGU ^{I}TIN^{su} A-*šu*$_2$ *ša*$_2$ ^{I}*šu-ma-a*
A ^{I}*na-ba-a-a ina* ^{iti}GU$_4$
ina ^{giš}*ma-ši-ḫu ša*$_2$ E$_2$.AN.⸢NA⸣
⸢*ina* E$_2$⸣.AN.NA *i-nam-din*
Rev. ⸢^{lu_2}⸣*mu-kin-nu* ^{I}⸢^{d}⸣U.GUR-PAP
A-*šu*$_2$ *ša*$_2$ ^{I}*a-qar-a* A ^{Id}EN-A-URU$_3$
^{I}*na-din* A-*šu*$_2$ *ša*$_2$ ^{Id}U.GUR-PAP A ^{lu_2}UŠ.BAR
^{I}KAR-^{d}EN A-*šu*$_2$ *ša*$_2$ ^{I}A-*a* A ^{I}*ar*$_2$*-rab-tu*$_2$
^{I}MU-DU A-*šu*$_2$ *ša*$_2$ ^{Id}AG-NUMUN-DU$_3$
⸢*u*⸣ ^{lu_2}UMBISAG ^{I}DU$_3$-^{d}15 A-*šu*$_2$ *ša*$_2$
^{Id}AG-NUMUN-DU$^{!}$ A ^{lu_2}TUG$_2$$^{!}$.BABBAR
UNUG^{ki} ^{iti}GAN UD.23.KAM
Up.E. MU.24.KAM ^{d}AG-NIG$_2$.DU-URU$_3$
LUGAL TIN.TIR⸢^{ki}⸣

8 *mašīḫus* of barley, instead of 8 *mašīḫus* of emmer, the property of Ištar-of-Uruk and Nanāya, are owed by Balāssu, son of Šumāya, descendant of Nabāya. He will give it in month II in Eanna, in the *mašīḫu* of Eanna.
Witnesses: Nergal-nāṣir, son of Aqara, descendant of Bēl-aplu-uṣur; Nādinu, son of Nergal-nāṣir, descendant of Išparu; Mušēzib-Bēl, son of Aplāya, descendant of Arrabtu; Šumu-ukīn, son of Nabû-zēru-ibni, and the scribe Ibni-Ištar, son of Nabû-zēru-ukīn, descendant of Ašlāku.
Uruk, Month IX, day 23, year 24 of Nebuchadnezzar, king of Babylon.

233. YBC 8838

Copy: Plate LIX
Date: 26.II.08(+) Nbk
Summary: withdrawal (*našû*) note: barley

Obv. ⸢5 BAN$_2$⸣ ŠE.BAR NINDA.ḪI.A *ša*$_2$ TA°
UD.25.KAM *a-*⸢*di*⸣ UD.30.KAM
ša$_2$ 2 ^{lu_2}*mu-ša*$_2$*-kil* UDU.NITA$_2$^{me}
^{I}*i-sin-na-a-a* GIŠ
3 BAN$_2$ ŠUK *ša*$_2$ *mu-ra-ši-*⸢*i*⸣
Lo.E. *ša*$_2$ 2 UD ^{I}*ar*$_2$*-rab* GIŠ
Rev. 1 BAN$_2$ 3 ^{lu_2}*ši-rak* GIG ⸢× ^{lu_2}⸣-×
GIŠ^{u_2}
1 BAN$_2$ 3 ^{lu_2}UŠ.BAR^{meš} GIŠ^{u_2}
(blank)
[^{iti}G]U$_4$$^{?}$ UD.26.KAM
Up.E. [MU.(×+)]8.KAM ^{d}AG-NIG$_2$.DU-URU$_3$
LUGAL TIN.TIR^{ki}

Isinnāya withdrew 5 *sūtu* of barley for bread, for days 25–30, for two sheep feeders. Arrab withdrew 3 *sūtu*, the rations of the wildcats, for two days. (The) … withdrew 1 *sūtu* (for) three sick temple serfs. Three weavers withdrew 1 *sūtu*.
Month II, day 26, year 8(+) of Nebuchadnezzar, king of Babylon.

5 For *murašû*, wildcats, see note to **No. 227**: 10.

234. NBC 4637

Copy: Plate LX
Date: 04.VI.30 Nbk
Summary: withdrawal (*našû*) note: barley

Obv. ⸢6⸣ *ma-ši-ḫu ša*$_2$ ŠE.BAR *ina* UD^{me}
ša$_2$ ^{iti}DU$_6$ *ša*$_2$ ^{I}*na-din* A ^{I}*nad-na-a*
^{I}NUN.ME GIŠ
a-di 1 *ša*$_2$ ^{Id}UTU-MU-DU
^{lu2}*man-di-di* ⸢*iš-šu*⸣-[*u*$_2$]
Rev. (blank)
^{iti}KIN UD.4.KAM MU.30.KAM
^{d}AG-NIG$_2$.DU-URU$_3$ LUGAL TIN.TIR$^{⸢ki⸣}$

Apkallu withdrew 6 *mašīḫus* of barley for the days of month VII of Nādinu, son of Nadnāya, including one that Šamaš-šumu-ukīn, the measuring official, withdrew.
Month VI, day 4, year 30 of Nebuchadnezzar, king of Babylon.

235. YBC 9557

Copy: Plate LX
Date: ×.IX.26 Nbk
Summary: delivery (*šūbulu*) note: silver + withdrawal (*našû*): beer

Obv. 15 GIN$_2$ KU$_3$.BABBAR *a-na* AN.BAR
ina ŠU^{II} $^{I⸢}$*gi*⸣*-mil-lu* A ^{I}IR$_3$-*a*
šu-bu-ul
2 GIN$_2$ *a-na* KAŠ.⸢SAG⸣ *ša*$_2$ *a-na*
^{lu2}*um-man-nu* SUM^{nu}
⸢^{I}⸣*re-mut ša*$_2$ E$_2$ GUR$_7$^{meš} GIŠ
Rev. (blank)
$^{iti⸢}$GAN$^{?}$ UD.×.KAM MU⸣.26.<KAM>
^{d}AG-NIG$_2$.DU-⸢URU$_3$ LUGAL⸣ TIN.TIR^{ki}

15 shekels of silver for iron were delivered by Gimillu, son of Ardāya. Rēmūtu of the depots withdrew 2 shekels for high quality beer that was given to the craftsmen.
Month IX, day ×, year 26 of Nebuchadnezzar, king of Babylon.

236. NCBT 1115

Copy: Plate LX
Date: 15.IV.10 N[bn]
Summary: *maḫir* receipt: beer

Madān-ēreš (l. 4) is attested in multiple texts from the reign of Nabonidus in the context of beer distribution.[26]

Obv. 5 BAN$_2$ KAŠ.ḪI.A
a-na ^{lu_2}TUG$_2$.BABBAR^{meš}
ina UGU ^{tug_2}BAR.⸢DUL$_8$⸣
^{I}DI.KUD-KAM
5 IGI^{ir}
Rev. (blank)
^{iti}ŠU UD.⸢15⸣.[KAM]
MU.10.KAM ^{d}A[G-I]
LUGAL TIN.TIR$^{⸢ki⸣}$

5 *sūtu* of beer for the washermen on account of the *kusītu*-garments were received from Madān-ēreš.
Month IV, day 15, year 10 of Nab[onidus], king of Babylon.

237. NCBT 1127

Copy: Plate LX; photograph of reverse on Plate LXXXIX
Date: 26.VIII.38 (Nbk)
Summary: *maḫir* receipt: beer

For Gimillu (l. 5) in the context of beer for various purposes, see **Nos. 235, 238–240, 242, 244** and multiple texts starting from 23 Nbk (NCBT 816) onwards.

Obv. 1 *dan-nu a-na* E$_2$ ⸢KAŠ$^?$⸣
1 *dan-nu a-na*
^{lu_2}UŠ.BAR^{me}
4 3 BAN$_2$ *a-na* ⸢E$_2$⸣ UDU.NITA$_2^{!(T.\ babbar)}$
Lo.E. ⸢I⸣ŠU IGI$^{!⸢ir⸣}$
Rev. (seal impression; Ehrenberg, AUWE 18, 97)
^{iti}APIN UD.26.KAM
MU.38.KAM

One *dannu*-vat (of beer) for the *brewery*, one *dannu*-vat for the weavers and 3 *sūtu* for the sheep shed were received from Gimillu.
Month VIII, day 26, year 38.

[26] See, e.g., Knopf 1939 XXV B SC-27 (2 Nbn), YOS 19, 173 (4 Nbn), YOS 6, 8 (4 Nbn), YOS 19, 174 (4 Nbn), Knopf 1939 XXI A SC-24 (4 Nbn), Sack CD, 3 (5 Nbn), YOS 19, 175 (5 Nbn), YOS 6, 245 (9 Nbn), *Iraq* 59, 24 (10+ Nbn), YOS 6, 19 (10 Nbn), YOS 19, 176 (10 Nbn), YOS 19, 177 (10 Nbn), YOS 19, 178 (10 Nbn), YOS 19, 179 (10 Nbn), YOS 19, 180 (10 Nbn), YOS 19, 181 (10 Nbn), YOS 19, 182 (10 Nbn), YOS 19, 183 (Nbn), YOS 19, 184 (10 Nbn), YOS 19, 185 (10 Nbn), YOS 19, 186 (11 Nbn), YOS 19, 187 (11 Nbn).

238. NCBT 251

Copy: Plate LX
Date: 17.XIIb.36 Nbk
Summary: *maḫir* receipt: beer

Obv. 3 BAN$_2$ KAŠ *a-⸢na⸣ par-⸢su⸣*
ina UGU *šu-⸢kut⸣-ti*
ša$_2$ ^{d}URU$_3$-INIM-*su*
⸢*u* ^{d}⸣UNUG^{ki}-⸢*a*⸣-*a-i-tu*$_2$
Lo.E. ^{I}*gi-⸢mil⸣-lu*
6 IGI^{ir}
Rev. (blank)
^{iti}DIRI.ŠE.KIN.KUD
UD.17.KAM MU.36.⸢KAM⸣
9 ^{d}AG-⸢NIG$_2$⸣.DU-URU$_3$
Up.E. LUGAL TIN.TIR^{ki}

3 *sūtu* of beer to be apportioned on account of the (work on / ritual of the) jewelry of Uṣur-amāssu and Urkayītu were received from Gimillu.
Month XIIb, day 17, year 36 of Nebuchadnezzar, king of Babylon.

1–4 Our translation slightly differs from that of Beaulieu, "3 *sâtus* of beer for the selection concerning (the ritual involving) the jewelry of Uṣur-amāssu and Urkayītu" (Beaulieu 2003, 265). The ritual reconstructed in Beaulieu's translation is uncertain, and as he notes, this would be the only attestation of this jewelry related ritual. Cf. the parallel phrasing in **No. 240** in which the beer is given for the smelting of bronze.

239. NCBT 258

Copy: Plate LXI; photograph of reverse on Plate LXXXIX
Date: 06.III.38 Nbk
Summary: *maḫir* receipt: beer

Obv. 5 BAN$_2$ KAŠ.ḪI.A
a-na ^{lu_2}KAB.SAR^{me}
u ^{lu_2}KU$_3$.DIM^{me}
4 ^{I}*gi-mil-lu*
Lo.E. *ma-ḫi-ir*
Rev. ^{iti}SIG$_4$ UD.6.KAM
MU.38.KAM
^{d}AG-NIG$_2$.DU-URU$_3$
[LUG]AL TIN.TIR^{ki}
(seal impression; Ehrenberg, AUWE 18, 14)

5 *sūtu* of beer for the jewelers and the goldsmiths were received from Gimillu.
Month III, day 6, year 38 of Nebuchadnezzar, king of Babylon.
(Seal)

240. NCBT 913

Copy: Plate LXI; photograph of reverse on Plate LXXXIX
Date: 15.XI.-- (*late Nbk*)
Summary: *maḫir* receipt: beer

For Gimillu (l. 5), see comment in **No. 237**.

Obv. ⸢3 BAN$_2$⸣ KAŠ.ḪI.A *a-na*
par-si ša$_2$ ina muḫ-ḫi
pi-it-qu a-na
4 ^{lu_2}SIMUG$^!$ ZABAR^{meš}
Lo.E. ^{I}ŠU IGI^{ir}
Rev. ^{iti}ZIZ$_2$ UD.15.KAM
(seal impression; Ehrenberg, AUWE 18, 17)

3 *sūtu* of beer, to be apportioned to the bronzesmiths on account of smelting, were received from Gimillu.
Month IX, day 15.
(Seal)

241. NCBT 97

Copy: Plate LXI
Date: 26.III.16 Nbk
Summary: withdrawal (*našû*) and issue (*nadin*) note: silver

Obv. 1 GIN$_2$ *mi-šil bit-⸢qa* KU$_3$.BABBAR⸣ *ša$_2$* KAŠ.SAG
ša$_2$ a-na ^{lu_2}⸢UMBISAG⸣^{meš} ⸢*id*⸣*-din* ^{I}NUMUN-*tu$_2$* ⸢GIŠ⸣
⸢½⸣ GIN$_2$ *ḫal-⸢lu⸣-ru* LA$_2$-*ṭi*
^{I}*a-⸢qar⸣-a* GIŠ
5 ⸢4⸣*-tu$_2$ bit-qa a-na* KAŠ.SAG
a-na ^{lu_2}*um-man-nu na-⸢din⸣*
Rev. (blank)
^{iti}⸢SIG$_4$⸣ [UD].⸢26$^?$⸣.KAM MU.16.⸢KAM⸣
^{d}AG-⸢NIG$_2$⸣.D[U-UR]U$_3$ LUGAL$^!$ TIN.TIR^{ki}

Zērūtu withdrew 1 1/16 shekels of silver for high-quality beer that he gave to the scribes. Aqara withdrew 4/10 shekel. 3/8 (shekels) were given to the craftsmen for high-quality beer.
Month III, day 26$^?$, year 16 of Nebuchadnezzar, king of Babylon.

1 1 *šiqlu mišil bitqa* could be understood as, 1+ a half of 1/8, i.e., 1 1/16. Alternatively, it may be read, 1+½ + 1/8, i.e., 1 5/8. The former seems to be a better reading given the syllabic *mi-šil*; c.f. 2 ½ GIN$_2$ ⸢*bit*⸣*-qa* (**No. 174**: 3) for expressing the fraction in 2 5/8.

242. NCBT 663

Copy: Plate LXII
Date: 17.I.35 Nbk
Summary: accounting inventory: barley and dates

Obv. ⸢7 GUR⸣ ŠE.BAR 32 GUR 2 (PI) 3 BAN$_2$ ⸢ZU$_2$.LUM⸣.MA
PAP 39 GUR 2 (PI) 3 BAN$_2$ ŠE.BAR
u$_3$ ZU$_2$.LUM.MA *ša*$_2$ *ina* ^{giš}BAN$_2$
ša$_2$ ^{I}TIN^{su} A ^{I}*ina*-SUḪ$_3$-SUR ^{Id}AMAR.UTU-MU-GIŠ
A ^{I}TIN^{su} *u*$_2$*-še-la-a*ʾ *e-la-tu*$_4$
5 GUR 2 (PI) 5 BAN$_2$ ŠE.BAR *ša*$_2$ *a-na*
^{lu_2}NU.GIŠ.KIRI$_6^{meš}$ *ša*$_2$ ^{giš}GEŠTIN *id-di-nu*
^{iti}BARA$_2$ UD.7.KAM MU.35.KAM
^{d}AG-NIG$_2$.DU-URU$_3$ LUGAL TIN.TIR^{ki}

---

ina lib$_3$*-bi* 6 GUR ŠE.BAR
23 GUR ZU$_2$.LUM.MA ^{Id}15-MU-KAM
A ^{Id}AG-MU-DU *u* ^{I}*ki-na-a*
^{lu_2}*man-di-di a-na* NIG$_2$.GA *in-da-aš*$_2$*-ḫu*
1 GUR ZU$_2$.LUM.MA *a-na*
^{I}*gab-ri-ia*$_2$ ^{lu_2}NU.GIŠ.KIRI$_6$ *ša*$_2$ ^{giš}GEŠTIN
⸢5⸣ GUR *a-na* KAŠ.ḪI.A
Lo.E. ⸢*a*⸣-*na* ^{I}*gi-mil-lu* A ^{I}⸢IR$_3$-*a*⸣
{three lines erased}
Rev. 1 GUR *a-na i-di* ^{giš}MA$_2$
2 (PI) 3 BAN$_2$ *a-na* NINDA.ḪI.A *ša*$_2$ ^{lu_2}MA$_2$.LAḪ$_4^{me}$
u ^{lu_2}*ša*$_2$*-di-di*^{me}
1 (PI) 2 BAN$_2$ 3 SILA$_3$ 1^{en} ^{lu_2}ḪUN.GA$_2$
1 GUR *ina ma-la-ti-šu*$_2$
^{Id}AG-MU-DU ^{lu_2}⸢SITIM⸣

7 kor of barley and 32;2.3.0 dates; a total of 39;2.3.0 barley and dates that Marduk-šumu-līšir, son of Balāssu, brought as part of the *sūtu*-obligation of Balāssu, son of Ina-tēšî-ēṭir. (This is) apart from 5;2.5.0 barley that were given to the vintners; Month I, day 7, year 35 of Nebuchadnezzar, king of Babylon.
Thereof, Ištar-šumu-ēreš, son of Nabû-šumu-ukīn, and Kīnāya, the measuring official(s), measured 6 kor of barley and 23 kor of dates for the temple stores; 1 kor of dates for Gabria, the vintner; 5 kor for beer for Gimillu, son of Ardāya; 1 kor for the rent of a boat; 0;2.3.0 for the bread of the boatmen and boat-towers; 0;1.2.3 for one hired worker; 1 kor from his *malītu*-offering(s) (for) Nabû-šumu-ukīn, the builder.

23 An alternative reading would be ^{Id}AG-MU-DU ^{lu_2}⸢BAN GIŠ⸣, Nabû-šumu-ukīn, the archer, withdrew; cf. NBDMich 68 (18 Nbk) in which we find a certain bowman (^{lu_2}BAN) named Nabû-šumu-ukīn.

243. NBC 4653

Copy: Plate LXI
Date: --.VI.32 Nbk
Summary: *ina pāni* note: multiple entries (*imittu*)

Obv. 2 GUR 2 (PI) 3 BAN$_2$ ⸢ZU$_2$.LUM⸣.MA SAG.DU ZAG
ša$_2$ ^{Id}EN-MU A ^{I}*mun-na-bi-ti*
ina IGI ^{Id}EN-TIN^{it} A ^{Id}EN-ŠEŠ^{me}-SU
⸢2⸣ GUR *ša*$_2$ ^{Id}EN-MU A-*šu*$_2$ *ša*$_2$ ^{I}*mun-na-bi-ti*
5 [(×)] *ša*$_2$*-nu-u*$_2$ KA$_2$ *ina pa-ni*
[^{I}]⸢^{d}⸣UTU-SIG$_5^{iq}$ A ^{Id}EN-ŠEŠ^{me}-BA^{ša_2}
[× GU]R ⸢2 (PI) 3 BAN$_2$⸣ *ša*$_2$ ^{I}*tab-ne*$_2$*-e-a*
[A ^{I}(×)]A-⸢*a ina* IGI⸣ ^{Id}AG-SU
Lo.E. [× × ^{I}]^{d}*in-*⸢*nin*⸣-NUMUN-DU$_3$
Rev. [× × ^{d}]⸢*na-na-a ina* IGI ^{Id}INNIN$^{?}$⸣-SU
11 [(×+) 4 B]AN$_2$ ⸢*ša*$_2$ ^{Id}INNIN$^{?}$-NUMUN-DU$_3$ A ^{I}*ta*⸣*-rib*
[(×+)] ⸢4 BAN$_2$⸣ ^{Id}INNIN-NUMUN-⸢DU$_3^{?}$ A ^{Id}EN⸣-GI
⸢1⸣ (PI) 1 BAN$_2$ 3 SILA$_3$ ^{Id}INNIN.NA-NUMUN-⸢TIL$^{?}$⸣ A ^{I}NUN.ME
1 (PI) 4 BAN$_2$ *ša*$_2$ ^{I}LU$_2$-^{d}*na-na-a* ^{lu_2}*pu-ṣa-a-a*
15 *ina* IGI ^{Id}AG-ŠEŠ^{me}-MU A ^{lu_2}I$_3$.DU$_8$
(blank)
Up.E. ^{iti}KIN MU.32.KAM
^{d}AG-NIG$_2$.DU-URU$_3$ LUGAL TIN.TIR⸢^{ki}⸣

2;2.3.0 dates, the principal of the impost of Bēl-iddin, son of Munnabittu, are at the disposal of Bēl-uballiṭ, son of Bēl-aḫḫē-erība; 2 kor of Bēl-iddin, son of Munnabittu, the second installment, are at the disposal of Šamaš-udammiq, son of Bēl-aḫḫē-iqīša; [×];2.3.0 of Tabnēa, [son of] Aplāya are at the disposal of Nabû-erība [...] Innin-zēru-ibni [...]-Nanāya are at the disposal of *Ištar*-erība; [×;×].4.0 of *Ištar*-zēru-ibni, son of Tarību; [×;×].4.0 of Ištar-zēru-*ibni*, son of Bēl-ušallim; 0;1.1.3 of Innin-zēru-*šubši*, son of Apkallu; 0;1.4.0 of Amīl-Nanāya, the linen weaver, are at the disposal of Nabû-aḫḫē-iddin, descendant of Atû. Month VI, day --, year 32 of Nebuchadnezzar, king of Babylon.

244. NCBT 170

Copy: Plate LXII
Date: 28.IV.42 Nbk
Summary: issue (*nadin*) list: dates and barley

Up.E. ^{iti}ŠU UD.28.KAM MU.42.KAM
⸢^{d}AG-NIG$_2$⸣.DU-URU$_3$ LUGAL TIN.TIR^{ki}
Obv. ŠE.BAR *u* ZU$_2$.LUM.MA *ša*$_2$ *a-*⸢*na*⸣ ŠUK.ḪI.A
ša$_2$ ^{iti}NE *a-na* ^{lu_2}⸢RIG$_7$⸣^{me}
5 *ša*$_2$ *a-na* KUR *tam-ti*$_3$ *šap-ru* SUM^{n}[^{u}]

---

1 (PI) 4 BAN$_2$	3 (PI) 2 BAN$_2$	^{Id}*na-na-a*-ŠEŠ-MU A ⸢^{I}*la*⸣*-ba-ši*
1 (PI) 4 BAN$_2$	3 (PI) 2 BAN$_2$	^{Id}AG-*mu-še-*<<*ti*>>*-tiq*$_2$-<UD>.DA ⸢A ^{I}⸣^{d}EN-⸢NIGIN^{ir}⸣
1 (PI) 4 BAN$_2$	3 (PI) 2 BAN$_2$	^{I}*gi-mil-lu* ⸢A⸣ ^{I}IR$_3$-^{d}*gu-la*

1 (PI) 4 BAN$_2$ 3 (PI) 2 BAN$_2$ ^{I}LU$_2$-^{d}*na-na-a* A ^{Id}INNIN-*a-lik*-IGI
1 (PI) 4 BAN$_2$ 3 (PI) 2 BAN$_2$ ^{I}*gi-mil-lu* A ^{I}⸢*nad*$^{?}$-*na*$^{?}$-*a*$^{?}$⸣
1 (PI) 4 BAN$_2$ 3 (PI) 2 BAN$_2$ ^{I}*gu-za-nu* A ^{Id}⸢*na-na*⸣-[*a*-×]
Rev. (blank)
2 (PI) 3 BAN$_2$ *ina* KAŠ.ḪI.A *ša*$_2$ UD.15.KAM *ša*$_2$ ^{iti}ŠU
id-di-nu ^{I}*gi-mil-lu* A ^{I}IR$_3$-*a*
it-ta-ši
1 GUR ŠUK-⸢*su ša*$_2$⸣ ^{iti}KIN ^{Id}UTU-MU
A ^{Id}UTU-TIN^{it}

Month IV, day 28, year 42 of Nebuchadnezzar, king of Babylon. Barley and dates that were given as the salaries of month V to the temple serfs who were sent to the Sealand: 0;1.4.0 (barley) and 0;3.2.0 (dates were given to each): Nanāya-aḫu-iddin, son of Lâbâši; Nabû-mušētiq-uddê, son of Bēl-upaḫḫir; Gimillu, son of Arad-Gula; Amīl-Nanāya, son of Ištar-ālik-pāni; Gimillu, son of *Nadnāya*; Gūzānu, son of Nanāya-×. Gimillu, son of Ardāya withdrew 0;2.3.0 (as partial payment) for the beer that he gave on Month IV, day 15. Šamaš-iddin, son of Šamaš-uballiṭ, (withdrew) 1 kor (for) his salary for month VI.

245. NCBT 631

Copy: Plate LXIII
Date: 16.X.32$^{?}$ Nbk
Summary: issue (*nadin+našû*) note: salaries in dates

Strictly speaking, in accordance with the typology used in this volume, the present text contains a *nādin* clause (as part of its heading, l. 2), an *ina pāni* clause (l. 15′), and a *našû* clause (l. 16′). Nonetheless, the main function of the text is that of an issue (*nadin*) list. The withdrawal (*našû*) clause is secondary, and even more so is the *ina pāni* note.

Obv. [ZU$_2$].⸢LUM.MA *ša*$_2$⸣ *a-na* ŠUK.ḪI.A^{meš} *ša*$_2$ ⸢^{iti}⸣[A]B ZIZ$_2$ ⸢ŠE⸣
[*a*]-⸢*na*⸣ ^{lu_2}*um-man-ni*^{me} SUM.NA ^{iti}AB ⸢UD.16⸣.KAM
[MU.(×+)]22.KAM ^{d}AG-NIG$_2$.DU-URU$_3$ LUGAL TIN.TIR^{ki}
1 2 ^{Id}AG-ŠEŠ^{meš}-GI A ^{Id}EN-*u*$_2$-*še-zib*
1 2 ^{Id}AG-NUMUN-BA^{ša_2} A ^{I}DU$_3$-*a*
1 2 ^{Id}INNIN.NA-MU-PAP A ^{I}A-*a*
1 2 ^{Id}*a-nu*-MU-DU$_3$ A ^{Id}DI.KUD-KAM
1 2 ^{Id}INNIN.NA-NUMUN-TIL A ^{I}*re*-⸢*mut*⸣
1 2 ^{I}*gi-mil-lu* A ^{Id}AG-⸢NUMUN-BA$^{!ša_2}$⸣
1 2 ^{I}KI-SIG-^{d}AG A ^{I}*šu-la-a*
PAP 7 ^{lu_2}⸢NAGAR⸣^{meš}
2 ^{I}⸢GAR⸣-MU A ^{Id}AG-PAP
⸢2$^{?}$⸣ ^{I}LU$_2$-^{d}*na-na-a* A ^{I}*tab-ne*$_2$-*e-a*
2 ^{I}KAR-^{d}EN A ^{I}⸢*ta*⸣-*qiš*-^{d}ME.ME
2 ^{Id}*na-na-a*-URU$_3$ A ^{I}N[UMU]N-TIN.⸢TIR⸣^{ki}
2 ^{I}IR$_3$-^{d}INNIN.NA A ^{I}*ba-laṭ-su*
2 ^{I}*ba-la-ṭu* A ^{I}*tab-ne*$_2$-*e-a*
2 ^{I}⸢BA⸣^{ša_2}-^{d}INNIN.NA A ^{I}*min*$_3$-⸢*su*-DINGIR⸣
½ 1 ^{I}[^{d}×]-⸢NUMUN⸣-DU$_3$ A ^{I}⸢^{d}⸣[× ×]

⸢PAP 8 ^{lu_2}KAB.SAR^{meš}⸣
(lower edge broken)
Rev. [ ]⸢× ×⸣
[ ]-*da-a*
[^{Id}INNIN-MU-DU$_3$ A ^{I}]⸢^{d}AG⸣-MU-DU
⸢1⸣ ^{Id}EN-DU$_3$ A ^{Id}⸢*na*⸣-*din*
1 2 ^{I}DUG$_3$.GA-*ia* A ^{I}EN-NUMUN
NU ^{I}A-*a* A ^{I}⸢*da*⸣-*di-ia*
PAP 8 ^{lu_2}KU$_3$.DIM^{me}
1 3 ^{Id}AG-⸢MU-DU$^{?}$⸣ ^{lu_2}ŠITIM
½ 2 ^{I}*ba-bi-ia*$_2$ A ^{Id}AMAR.UTU-KAM
½ 2 ^{Id}INNIN.NA-NUMUN-TIL A ^{I}⸢^{d}EN-DU$_3$⸣
½ 2 ^{Id}AMAR.⸢UTU⸣-MU-URU$_3$
PAP 3 ^{lu_2}SIMUG ZABAR
½ 1 ^{I}⸢*šu*⸣-*ma-a* ^{lu_2}BUR.GUL
ša$_2$ ^{Id}⸢AG⸣-PAP-MU A-*šu*$_2$ *ša*$_2$ ^{I}IR$_3$-*a* A ^{Id}⸢EN⸣-[×]
ina IGI ^{I}*ša*$_2$-^{d}*na-na-a-taš-met*
⸢^{Id}AG-DU$_3$⸣-ŠEŠ A ^{I}A-*a* ŠUK.ḪI.<A>-*su* *ša*$_2$ ^{iti}ZIZ$_2$ GIŠ

Dates that were given as the salaries of months X, XI and XII [for] the craftsmen; Month X, day 16, year *32* of Nebuchadnezzar king of Babylon:
1 (and/for) 2, Nabû-aḫḫē-šullim, son of Bēl-ušēzib; 1 (and/for) 2, Nabû-zēru-iqīša, son of Ibnāya; 1 (and/for) 2, Innin-šumu-uṣur, son of Aplāya; 1 (and/for) 2, Anu-šumu-ibni, son of Madān-ēreš; 1 (and/for) 2, Innin-zēru-šubši, son of Rēmūtu; 1 (and/for) 2, Gimillu, son of Nabû-zēru-iqīša; 1 (and/for) 2, Itti-enši-Nabû, son of Šulāya; total of seven carpenters.
2, Šākin-šumi, son of Nabû-nāṣir; 2, Amīl-Nanāya, son of Tabnēa; 2, Mušēzib-Bēl, son of Taqīš-Gula; 2, Nanāya-nāṣir, son of Zēr-Babili; 2, Arad-Innin, son of Balāssu; 2, Balāṭu, son of Tabnēa; 2, Iqīša-Innin, son of Minsu-ilī; ½ (and/for) 1, [×]-zēru-ibni, son of …; total of eight jewelers.
(*several lines broken*)
[…] …;[…]-dāya; […, Ištar-šumu-ibni, son of] Nabû-šumu-ukīn; 1, Bēl-ibni, son of Nādinu; 1 (and/for) 2, Ṭābia, son of Bēl-zēri; *none*, Aplāya, son of Dadia; a total of eight goldsmiths.
1 (and/for) 3, Nabû-šumu-*ukīn*, the builder; ½ (and/for) 2, Bābia, son of Marduk-ēreš; ½ (and/for) 2, Innin-zēru-šubši, son of Bēl-ibni; ½ (and/for) 2, Marduk-šumu-uṣur; total of three bronzesmiths.
½ (and/for) 1, Šumāya, the seal cutter of Nabû-aḫu-iddin, son of Ardāya, descendant of Bēl-×, at the disposal of Ša-Nanāya-tašmēt.
Nabû-bān-aḫi, son of Aplāya, withdrew his salary of month XI.

246. NCBT 667

Copy: Plate LXII
Date: 28.III.40 Nbk
Summary: *maḫir* receipt: dates

Obv. 3 (PI) 4 BAN$_2$ 3 SILA$_3$ ZU$_2$.⸢LUM⸣.MA *ina* ŠUK.ḪI.A *ša*$_2$ ^{iti}⸢SIG$_4$⸣
ša$_2$ ^{Id}*in-nin*-MU-URU$_3$ ^{lu_2}UŠ.BAR
a-na muḫ-ḫi ^{Id}UTU-MU-DU A ^{I}*šu-la-a* IGI^{ir}

1 GUR 3 (PI) *ša*$_2$° *zi-ku-tu ša*$_2$ *lu-bu-*⸢*uš-ti*⸣
^{I}*šu-ma-a* A ^{I}DU$_3$-⸢^{d}15⸣ [GIŠ]
(blank)
Rev. (blank)
^{iti}SIG$_4$ UD.28.KAM MU.40.KAM
^{d}AG-NIG$_2$.DU-⸢URU$_3$⸣ LUGAL TIN.TIR^{ki}

0;3.4.3 dates from the salary of month IV of Innin-šumu-uṣur, the weaver, were received on the account of Šamaš-šumu-ukīn, son of Šulāya.
1;3.0.0 for the cleaning of the clothing Šumāya, son of Ibni-Ištar [has withdrawn].
Month III, day 28, year 40 of Nebuchadnezzar, king of Babylon.

247. YBC 9141

Copy: Plate LXIV
Date: 11.IV$^{?}$.20 Nbk
Summary: withdrawal (*našû*) account: dates

Obv. ZU$_2$.L[UM.M]A ⸢*ša*$_2$⸣ *ina* ⸢ŠUK⸣.ḪI.A-*šu*$_2$-*nu ša*$_2$ ^{iti}BARA$_2$
ša$_2$ *a-n*[*a* ^{l}]^{u_2}GAL 10^{meš} *ša*$_2$ *dul-lu*
ina [(×) ^{ur}]^{u}*ia-a-da-qu* SUM.NA

⸢40⸣ [^{gi}]^{š}*ma-šiḫ* ^{I}*re-mut* A ^{Id}U.GUR-MU GIŠ
⸢40⸣ [^{gi}]^{š}*ma-šiḫ* ^{Id}AG-DU$_3$-ŠEŠ A ^{I}ŠEŠ-*lu-mur* GIŠ
PAP 80 ^{giš}*ma-šiḫ* GIŠ^{u_2}
Rev. (blank)
^{iti}⸢ŠU$^{?}$⸣ UD.11.KAM MU.20.KAM
^{d}AG-NIG$_2$.DU-URU$_3$ LUGAL TIN.TIR^{ki}

Dates that were given from their salaries of month I to the decurions who worked in Iādaqu: Rēmūtu, son of Nergal-iddin, withdrew 40 *mašīḫus*; Nabû-bān-aḫi, son of Aḫu-lumur, withdrew 40 *mašīḫus*; they withdrew a total of 80 *mašīḫus*.
Month IV$^{?}$, day 11, year 20 of Nebuchadnezzar, king of Babylon.

7 ^{iti}⸢ŠU⸣ might alternatively be read ^{iti}⸢ZIZ$_2$⸣ (XI).

248. YBC 9315

Copy: Plate LXIV
Date: 18.IX.38$^{?}$ Nbk
Summary: withdrawal (*našû*) note: dates

Obv. 20 GUR ZU$_2$.LUM.MA {eras.}
ina ZU$_2$.LUM.MA *ša*$_2$ ^{Id}AG-ŠEŠ^{me}-GI
⸢A-*šu*$_2$⸣ *ša*$_2$ ^{Id}AG-KAL ^{Id}INNIN-ŠEŠ-⸢MU⸣
⸢A-*šu*$_2$⸣ *ša*$_2$ ^{I}A-*a* ^{lu_2}KU$_3$.DIM
⸢^{lu_2}A⸣.KIN-*ri ša*$_2$ ^{Id}EN-*ka-šid-*⸢*a-a-bi*⸣
^{lu_2}[SA]G LUGAL *ša*$_2$ *muḫ-ḫi*
r[*e*$^{?}$-*ḫ*]*e*$^{?}$-⸢*e*⸣-*ti it-ta-ši*

Rev. ⸢^{iti}GAN⸣ UD.18.KAM MU.⸢38$^{?}$⸣.KAM
⸢^{d}AG⸣-NIG$_2$.DU-URU$_3$ ⸢LUGAL TIN$^{!(T.\ ḫi)}$.TIR^{ki}⸣
(blank)
(7+ large horizontal wedges on Rev.)

Ištar-aḫu-iddin, son of Aplāya, the goldsmith (and) messenger of Bēl-kāšid-ayyabi, the courtier, overseer of the remainders (of the sacrificial meal), withdrew 20 kor of dates from the dates of Nabû-aḫḫē-šullim, son of Nabû-udammiq.
Month IX, day 18, year 38$^{?}$ of Nebuchadnezzar, king of Babylon.

249. NCBT 81

Copy: Plate LXIV
Date: --.III.40 Nbk
Summary: accounting note: flour

Obv. TA UD.18.KAM *ša*$_2$ ^{iti}SIG$_4$
a$^{!}$*-di-i* UD.24^{sic}.KAM
ša$_2$ ^{iti}SIG$_4$ *ša*$_2$ *u*$_4$*-mu*
⸢3 SILA$_3$⸣ ZID$_2$.DA *a-na*$^{!}$
^{I}⸢^{d}AG⸣-NUMUN-BA^{ša_2} ^{lu_2}NAGAR
Rev. ⸢^{I}⸣^{d}⸢AMAR⸣.UTU-MU-MU
⸢*in-di*⸣*-lik*
ITI$^{!}$.SIG$_4^{!}$ *ša*$_2$ MU.40.KAM
^{Id}AG-NIG$_2$.DU-URU$_3$ LUGAL E^{ki}
PAP 4 BAN$_2$ ZID$_2$.DA

From the 18th day of month III to the 24th, Marduk-šumu-iddin *advised for* 3 *qû* of flour (*to be given*) daily to Nabû-zēru-iqīša, the carpenter.
Month III, year 40 of Nebuchadnezzar, king of Babylon.
A total of 4 *sūtu* of flour.

2 The date should reflect eight, not seven, days: total of 4 *sūtu* (= 24 *qû*) = 3 *qû* (daily) × 8 (days).
7 The reading *in-di-lik* is relatively certain. A form of *malāku* in the present context, however, is unexpected and difficult. An alternative reading, *in-di-ṭu*$^{!}$ (for **in-da-ṭu*, *maṭû*) would perhaps fit the context slightly better, but would be epigraphically and grammatically problematic.

250. NCBT 1023

Copy: Plate LXIV
Date: 19.IX.34 Nbk
Summary: *ina pāni* note: barley

Obv. [×] GUR ŠE.BAR *ir-bi*
a-na ZID$_2$.DA
ina pa-ni ^{I}*ša*$_2$*-du-nu*
^{lu_2}GAL ⸢E$_2$⸣ *ki-li*
Rev. (blank)
^{iti}GAN UD.20.1.LA$_2$.KAM

MU.34.KAM
^{d}AG-NIG$_{2}$.DU-URU$_{3}$
[LU]GAL TIN.TIR^{ki}

[×] kor of barley from the income are at the disposal of Šadûnu, the prison overseer for (the grinding of) flour.
Month IX, day 19, year 34 of Nebuchadnezzar, king of Babylon.

251. NCBT 812

Copy: Plate LXIV
Date: 22.XII.41 Nbk
Summary: *maḫir* receipt: (barley)$^{?}$

Obv. 1 GUR *ša*$_{2}$ ^{I}*ra-šil*
^{lu2}GAL-DU$_{3}$
ša$_{2}$ *a-na qe*$_{2}$*-me*
a-na ^{lu2}AŠGAB^{meš}
id-din-nu
Lo.E. ^{I}⸢^{d}INNIN⸣-*re-ṣu-*⸢*u*$_{2}$*-a*⸣
Rev. *ma-*⸢*ḫi*⸣*-ir*
^{iti}ŠE$^{!}$ UD.22.KAM
MU.41.KAM
^{d}AG-NIG$_{2}$.DU-URU$_{3}$
Up.E. LUGAL TIN.TIR^{ki}

1 kor (of barley$^{?}$) of Rāšil, the date gardener, which he gave for the flour for the leatherworkers, was received from Ištar-rēṣū'a.
Month XII, day 22, year 41 of Nebuchadnezzar, king of Babylon.

1 The *rab banê* Rāšil may be identified as the son of Marduka, attested in PTS 2824 (36 Nbk). Two possible earlier attestations (both with no title) are YOS 17, 21 (13 Nbk) and YBC 3767 (11 Nbk, desc. of Kidin-Marduk).

252. NCBT 166

Copy: Plate LXV
Date: 11.II.22 Nbk
Summary: issue (*nadin*) note: silver

Obv. 4 ½ GIN$_{2}$ KU$_{3}$.BABBAR ŠAM$_{2}$ 3 GUR ŠE.BAR
ša$_{2}$ *a-na* GI^{meš} *a-na*
^{I}SUM-*nu-nu* A ^{Id}EN-BA^{ša2} SUM^{nu}
9 ME ^{gi}*ku-zu-ul-lu*
um-ma IGI^{ir}
1 GIN$_{2}$ KU$_{3}$.BABBAR *a-na* GI^{meš}
ina IGI-*šu*$_{2}$
Lo.E. ⸢7⸣ GIN$_{2}$ 2ta ŠU$^{II.meš}$
Rev. *a-na* 1 *lim* 3 ME

ku-zu-ul-lu
ša$_2$ GI^{meš} SUM^{in}
(blank)
^{iti}GU$_4$ UD.11.KAM
MU.22.KAM
Up.E. ^{d}AG-NIG$_2$.DU-URU$_3$
LUGAL TIN.TIR^{ki}

(Record concerning) 4 ½ shekels of silver, the price of 3 kor of barley, which was given to Iddinunu, son of Bēl-iqīša, for reeds. (Regarding) 900 reed bundles it is said: they were received from him. 1 shekel of silver for the reeds is at his disposal. He was (in total) given 7 ⅔ (shekels of silver) for 1,300 bundles of reeds.
Month II, day 11, year 22 of Nebuchadnezzar, king of Babylon.

253. NCBT 92

Copy: Plate LXV
Date: 11.X.16 Nbk
Summary: delivery (*šūbulu*) note: silver

Obv. ⸢1 ½ GIN$_2$⸣ KU$_3$.BABBAR ⸢*a-na* GI⸣^{meš}
⸢3 GIN$_2$ *a-na a-bat-ti*⸣ *ina* IGI $^{I⸢}$IR$_3$⸣-$^{d⸢}$*na-na*⸣-*a*
⸢*ina* ŠU^{II}⸣ $^{I⸢d}$AG⸣-AŠ-URU$_3$
a-⸢*na*⸣ $^{I⸢d}$AG⸣-EN-*i*$_3^{?!(T.du_2)}$-*li*$_2^{?!}$
⸢*šu-bul*⸣
Rev. (blank)
^{iti}AB UD.11.K[AM]
MU$^{!}$.⸢16⸣.KAM ⸢^{d}AG⸣-NIG$_2$-D[U-UR]U$_3$
LUGAL TIN.⸢TIR^{ki}⸣

1 ½ shekels of silver for reeds (and) 3 shekels (of silver) for *abattu*-wood, (which are) at the disposal of Arad-Nanāya, were delivered by Nabû-ēdu-uṣur to Nabû-bēl-ili.
Month X, day 11, year 16 of Nebuchadnezzar, king of Babylon.

4 For *abattu* as organic material rather than stones, see Jursa 1995, 123 and commentary to **No. 152**: 3. For a shipment of *abattu*-wood for Nabû-bēl-ili, see also **No. 254**, written five days earlier. A week after the present text, Nabû-bēl-ili receives a shipment of bricks; YOS 17, 232.

254. NCBT 473

Copy: Plate LXV
Date: 06.X16 Nbk
Summary: delivery (*šūbulu*) note: silver + issue (*nadin*) note: reed

For a similar shipment of *abattu*, see **No. 253**.

Obv. 5 GIN$_2$ KU$_3$.BABBAR *a-na*
a-bat-tu$_4$ SUM^{in}
ina ŠU^{II} ^{I}*la-qi*$_2$*-i-pi*

a-na ^{Id}AG-EN-*i*$_3$-*li*$_2$$^{!}$
šu-bul
Lo.E. ⸢2⸣ ½ GIN$_2$ *a-na* GI^{me}
⸢*a*⸣-*na* ^{gi}*sal-le-e*
Rev. *na-din*
(blank)
^{iti}AB UD.6.KAM
MU.16.KAM ⸢^{d}AG⸣-NIG$_2$.DU-URU$_3$
LUGAL TIN.TIR^{ki}

5 shekels of silver were given for the *abattu*-wood; (it) was delivered by Lāqīpu to Nabû-bēl-ilī. 2 ½ shekels were given for reeds for *sellu*-baskets.
Month X, day 6, year 16 of Nebuchadnezzar, king of Babylon.

255. NCBT 901

Copy: Plate LXV
Date: undated (mid Nbk)
Summary: accounting note: reed items

Obv. *ina* 2 GIN$_2$ KU$_3$.BABBAR
ša$_2$ ^{Id}AG-SUR *a-na* ^{I}MU-DU ^{iti}⸢GAN⸣
a-na GI^{meš} *id-di-nu*
5 *gu-zu-ul-lu*
a-na ⸢E$_2$⸣ ŠU^{II}
Lo.E. 6 *nu-us-uḫ-ḫe-e*
20 *sel-li a-na* E$_2$
Rev. ^{lu_2}ŠA$_3$.TAM
2 *nu-us-uḫ-ḫe-e*
5 *sel-li a-na* E$_2$ ^{lu_2}*qip-pu*
2 *bu-ra-ne*$_2$-*e*
a-na E$_2$ ^{lu_2}ŠA$_3$.TAM

From the 2 shekels of silver that Nabû-ēṭir gave to Šumu-ukīn (in) month IX for reeds: five reed bundles for the *bīt qātē*, six *nusḫu*-baskets, twenty *sellu*-baskets for the *bīt šatammi*, two *nusḫu*-baskets and five *sellu*-baskets for the *bīt qīpi*, two reed mats for the *bīt šatammi*.

2 For Šumu-ukīn, the reed worker, see **No. 229** (18 Nbk) and **No. 260** (17 Nbk).

5 For the *bīt qātē* (lit. hand house), albeit at a slightly later period (in the context of the Rēš temple), see Baker 2013.

7–8 To the best of our knowledge this is the only attestation of the *bīt šatammi*.

10 The spelling of ^{lu_2}*qip-pu* for *qīpu* (rather than *qi-i-pu*) is unexpected. The determinative ^{lu_2} and the doubling of the <*p*> after the vowel, indicating /ī/, leaves no doubt that the form is *qīpu*.[27] The only other attestation of the *bīt qīpi* known to us is in the unpublished YBC 4187 in the context of the building of Nebuchadnezzar's palace in Babylon.

[27] Furthermore, the determinative ^{lu_2} clearly distinguishes this attestation from the Ḫarri-kibbi canal (RGTC 8: 351), as well as from the E$_2$ *kib-bi* (or *qip-pi*) in BE 9, 15: 5, 9.

256. YBC 7372

Copy: Plate LXVI
Date: undated
Summary: accounting inventory: reeds

None of the listed men can be properly identified and the tablet cannot be dated.

Obv. 75 *qa-ne$_2$-e* ^{I}*ki-in-ne$_2$-e*
21 ^{I}*šul-lu-mu*
⌜32⌝ ^{I}IR$_3$-*ia* A ^{Id}AG-ŠEŠ-MU
[×] ^{I}LUGAL-*kit-ti-i-ra-am*
⌜22(+) ^{I}*am*⌝-*mi-ia*
⌜6$^{?}$ × × ×⌝*mu-ṣu-u$_2$*
⌜*ša$_2$* ^{I}*a*$^{?}$-*mi-ia*⌝
Lo.E. ⌜12 ^{Id}AMAR$^{?}$.UTU$^{?}$-MU-GAR^{un}⌝
Rev. ⌜12$^{?}$ ^{Id}DU$_3$-*tu$_4$*$^{?}$-KAM⌝
⌜21$^{?}$⌝ ^{I}ŠEŠ$^{!}$-*im-me-e*
13 ^{I}*a-a-bi*
6 ^{Id}AG-DU$_3$
18 ⌜^{Id}AG⌝-TIN^{su}-E
18 ^{Id}*za-ba$_4$-ba$_4$*-DU-A

Seventy-five reeds, Kinnê; twenty-one, Šullumu; thirty-two, Ardia, son of Nabû-aḫu-iddin; [×], Šarru-kitti-irâm, twenty-two(+) *A(m)mia, six, …-muṣu for A(m)mia*; twelve *Marduk-šumu-iškun*; *twelve* Bānītu-ēreš; *twenty-one*, Aḫu-imme; thirteen, Ayyabi; six Nabû-ibni; eighteen Nabû-balāssu-iqbi; eighteen Zababa-mukīn-apli.

6–7 Although the traces seem to suggest that …-*muṣu* received reeds for (*ša$_2$*) *A*(*m*)*mia*, the fact that *A*(*m*)*mia* is already listed (l. 5), …-*muṣu* might actually be his son.

257. NCBT 891

Copy: Plate LXVI
Date: 26.VIII.22 Nbk
Summary: *ina pāni* note: reed mats

Obv. 3 ^{gi}*bu-ra-ne$_2$-e*
ina IGI ^{Id}AG-*na-din*-MU
4 *ina* IGI ^{Id}AG-NUMUN-BA^{ša_2}
PAP 7 ⌜^{gi}⌝*bu-ra-ne$_2$-e*
a-na 1 G[IN$_2$] ⌜*šal*⌝-*šu$_2$* 1 GIN$_2$ KU$_3$.BABBAR
na-šu-nu^{sic} [KU$_3$].BABBAR-*šu$_2$-nu*
ina NIG$_2$.G[A]
Rev. (blank)
^{iti}APIN UD.26.KAM
MU.22.KAM ^{d}AG-NIG$_2$.DU-⌜URU$_3$⌝
LUGAL TIN.TIR^{ki}

Three reed mats at the disposal of Nabû-nādin-šumi, four at the disposal of Nabû-zēru-iqīša: a total of seven reed mats were taken for 1 ⅓ shekels of silver. Their [sil]ver is in the temple stores.
Month VIII, day 26, year 22 of Nebuchadnezzar, king of Babylon.

258. NCBT 747

Copy: Plate LXVI
Date: 03.V.12 Nbk
Summary: *ina pāni* note: silver and reed

Obv. 5 ⸢GIN$_2$⸣ KU$_3$.BABBAR *a-na* ^{giš}⸢UR$_3$⸣
u$_3$ GI^{meš} *ina* IGI
^{I}I-^{d}⸢AMAR.UTU⸣
A ^{Id}AG-NUMUN-⸢GAL$_2$^{ši}⸣
^{lu_2}ŠITIM$^{!}$
Rev. (blank)
^{iti}NE UD.3.KAM
⸢MU.12⸣.KAM ^{d}AG-NIG$_2$.⸢DU-URU$_3$⸣
LUGAL TIN.TIR^{ki}

5 shekels of silver for beams and reeds are at the disposal of Na'id-Marduk, son of Nabû-zēru-šubši, the builder.
Month V, day 3, year 12 of Nebuchadnezzar, king of Babylon.

259. YBC 8783

Copy: Plate LXVI
Date: 09.V.17 Nbk
Summary: issue (*nadin*) note: barley

Obv. 3 BAN$_2$ 3 SILA$_3$ ŠE.BAR
a-⸢*na*⸣ *i-di*
^{lu_2}*at-kal-uš-še-e*
ša$_2$ GI^{meš} *iš-šu*$^{!}$-⸢*nu*⸣
SUM^{at}
Rev. ^{iti}NE UD.9.KAM
MU.17.KAM ^{d}AG-NIG$_2$.DU-URU$_3$
LUGAL TIN.TIR^{ki}

0;0.3.3 barley was given for the wages of the carrier(s) who brought the reeds.
Month V, day 9, year 17 of Nebuchadnezzar, king of Babylon.

260. NCBT 140

Copy: Plate LXVI
Date: 03.III.17 Nbk
Summary: *maḫir* receipt: reed mats

Obv. 96 ^{gi}*bu-ru-u*$_2$
^{I}MU-DU ^{I}IR$_3$-^{d}⸢INNIN$^{!}$.NA⸣

	u ^{Id}AG-*u*$_2$-*ṣur-šu*$_2$
4	^{lu2}AD.KID^{meš}
Lo.E.	⸢*iš*⸣-*ka*-⸢*ru*⸣
Rev.	*ša*$_2$ ^{iti}⸢GU$_4$ *maḫ-ru*⸣
	(blank)
	^{iti}SIG$_4$ UD.3.⸢KAM⸣
	MU.17.⸢KAM⸣ ^{d}AG-NIG$_2$.DU-⸢URU$_3$⸣
	LUGAL TIN.TIR^{ki}

Ninety-six reed mats, the *iškāru*-obligation of month II, were received from Šumu-ukīn, Arad-Innin and Nabû-uṣuršu, the reed-workers.
Month III, day 3, year 17 of Nebuchadnezzar, king of Babylon.

261. NCBT 808

Copy: Plate LXVII
Date: 15.VII.31 Nbk
Summary: *ina pāni* note: goats and hides

As phrased, the leather dyer is said to receive live goats, rather than carcasses or hides. While this is unexpected, note a similar practice recorded in **No. 281**: 18.

Obv.	⸢50$^{?}$⸣ MAŠ$_2$.GAL
	a-na ^{kuš}*du-še-e*
	u$_3$ ^{kuš}*ṣal-lu*
	ina IGI ^{I}NUMUN-*tu*$_2$
5	[^{I}]^{u2}*ṣa-rip* ⸢^{kuš}*du*⸣-[*še*]-⸢*e*⸣
Rev.	(blank)
	^{iti}DU$_6$ UD.15.KAM
	MU.31.KAM
	^{d}AG-NIG$_2$.DU-URU$_3$
Up.E.	[LU]GAL TIN.⸢TIR⸣^{ki}

Fifty billy-goat (*hides*) for (making) *dušû*(-colored)-leather and tanned hides are at the disposal of Zērūtu, the leather dyer.
Month VII, day 15, year 31 of Nebuchadnezzar, king of Babylon.

262. NCBT 838

Copy: Plate LXVII
Date: 08.IV.08 Nbk
Summary: *ina pāni* note: leather

Obv.	30 ^{kuš}⸢*du*⸣-[*šu-u*$_2$ *a-na*]
	dul-⸢*lu ša*$_2^{?}$⸣ [× (×) *ina* IGI]
	^{Id}AG-NUMUN-B[A-*ša*$_2$ A ^{Id}UTU$^{?}$]-⸢SU ^{lu2}AŠGAB$^{!}$⸣
	11 ^{kuš}*du-šu*$^{!(T.\ ba)}$-⸢*u*$_2$⸣ [× (×)]
5	*ša*$_2$ ^{kuš}*za-ra*-⸢*ti ina pa-ni*⸣
	^{I}E$_2$.AN.NA-*li-pi*-PAP ^{lu2}AŠGAB

Rev. (blank)

^{iti}ŠU UD.8.KAM MU.8.KAM

^{d}AG-NIG$_2$.DU-PAP LUGAL E^{ki}

Thirty (pieces of) *du*[*šû*(-colored)]-leather [for] the work of [... are at the disposal of] Nabû-zēru-iqīša, [son of *Šamaš*]-erība, the leatherworker.
Eleven (pieces of) *dušû*(-colored)-leather [...] for tents are at the disposal of Eanna-līpu-uṣur, the leatherworker.
Month IV, day 8, year 8 of Nebuchadnezzar, king of Babylon.

3 The reconstruction of Šamaš-erība's name is based on Nabû-zēru-iqīša/Šamaš-erība, a leatherworker attested in PTS 2461 (3 Ner) and PTS 3327 (0a Nbn). While the large gap between these two attestations and the present tablet is not inconceivable, it must be taken into account.

263. NCBT 444

Copy: Plate LXVII
Date: 14(+).X.-- --
Summary: inventory note: hides and sinews

Obv. 8 MA.NA 15 GIN$_2$

^{kuš}*ṣal-la*

50 GIN$_2$ ⸢*gi*⸣-*du*

^{iti}DU$_6$ UD.28.KAM

Rev. 4 MA.NA ⸢^{kuš}*ṣal-la*⸣

6 ^{iti}APIN U[D.×.KAM]

6 ½° MA.NA ⸢5⸣ [(+×) GIN$_2$] <^{kuš}*ṣal-la*>

1 MA.NA *gi*-[*du*]

^{iti}AB UD.⸢14⸣[(+×).KAM]

8 minas 15 shekels of tanned hides, 50 shekels of sinew: Month VII, day 28;
4 minas of tanned hides: Month VIII, day [×];
6 minas 35 [shekels of tanned hides], 1 mina sin[ew]: Month X, day 14(+).

1–5 Unlike the *gidu*, the *ṣallu* hides are typically not measured by weight.

264. NCBT 431

Copy: Plate LXVII
Date: 13.*IX*.20(+) Nbk
Summary: issue (*nadin*) note: hides

Obv. ⸢1⸣ GIN$_2$ KU$_3$.BABBAR *a-na* 2 KUŠ^{meš}

ša$_2$ ^{lu_2}SIMUG SUM^{nu}

(blank)

Rev. (blank)

^{iti}GAN$^{!?}$ UD.13.KAM MU.20[(+×).KAM]

^{d}AG-NIG$_2$.DU-URU$_3$ LUGAL TIN.⸢TIR^{ki}⸣

1 shekel of silver was given for two hides for the smiths.
Month *IX*, day 13, year 20(+) of Nebuchadnezzar, king of Babylon.

1–2 Note that there is no individual specified as receiving the hides.
3 Month name may alternatively be read AB$^{!}$.

265. NCBT 1033

Copy: Plate LXVII
Date: [×].VIII.06 [Nbn/Cyr]
Summary: *maḫir* receipt: hides

The leatherworker Innin-zēru-iddin/Zērūtu is attested during the reign of Nabonidus (e.g., YOS 6, 205; YOS 19, 280) until 7 Cyr (AnOr 8, 5).

Obv. 3 ^{kuš}*ṣal-lu*
^{Id}*in-nin*-NUMUN-MU
A ^{I}NUMUN-*tu*$_2$ IGI^{ir}
Rev. (blank)
⸢^{iti}⸣APIN ⸢UD⸣.[×.KAM]
MU.6.K[AM …]
LUGAL [TIN.TIR^{ki}]

Three tanned hides were received from Innin-zēru-iddin, son of Zērūtu.
Month VIII, day [×], year 6 of […], king of [Babylon].

266. NCBT 127

Copy: Plate LXVIII
Date: 21.I.35 Nbk
Summary: *maḫir* receipt: hides

Obv. [60]-*šu* ^{kuš}*ḫa-li-ṣa-nu*
ša$_2$ ^{iti}ŠE *u* ^{iti}BARA$_2$
ina ^{kuš}*ši-ḫa-ṭu*
ša$_2$ ŠUK.ḪI.A *ša*$_2$ ^{lu_2}ŠA$_3$.TAM
⸢*ša*$_2$⸣ *ina* IGI-*šu*$_2$
Lo.E. ⸢I⸣IR$_3$-^{d}*na-na-a*
Rev. A ^{I}DUG$_3$.GA-IM-⸢d⸣15
⸢IGI⸣^{ir}
^{iti}BARA$_2$ UD.21.KAM
MU.35.KAM
⸢^{d}AG⸣-NIG$_2$.DU-URU$_3$
Up.E. [L]UGAL TIN.TIR^{ki}

Sixty flayed skins for months XII and I, from the *šiḫṭu* hides of the salaries of the *šatammu* that are at his disposal, were received from Arad-Nanāya, son of Ṭāb-šār-Ištar.
Month I, day 21, year 35 of Nebuchadnezzar, king of Babylon.

267. NCBT 152

Copy: Plate LXVIII
Date: 28.I.43 Nbk
Summary: *maḫir* receipt: hides

Obv. 11 ^{kuš}*du-šu-u*$_2$
^{Id}AG-DU-A
A-*šu*$_2$ *ša*$_2$ ^{I}NUMUN-*u*$_2$-*tu*$_2$
ma-ḫi-ir
Rev. (blank)
^{iti}BARA$_2$ UD.28.KAM
MU.43.KAM
^{d}AG-NIG$_2$.DU-URU$_3$
Up.E. LUGAL TIN.TIR^{ki}

Eleven (pieces of) *dušû*(-colored)-leather were received from Nabû-mukīn-apli, son of Zērūtu.
Month I, day 28, year 43 of Nebuchadnezzar, king of Babylon.

268. NCBT 727

Copy: Plate LXVIII
Date: 29.XII.22 Nbk
Summary: *maḫir* receipt: hides

For the edition of the text see page 3 in the introduction.

269. NCBT 709

Copy: Plate LXVIII
Date: 21.VII.42 Nbk
Summary: *maḫir* receipt: various tools

Obv. ⸢×⸣ ^{kuš}*til-lu rak-su*
2 MAR AN.BAR$^{⸢\text{meš}⸣}$
3 *qul-ma-a-ta*
3 NIG$_2$.GAL$_2$.LA^{meš}
^{I}*e-rib-šu*$_2$ A ^{I}*re-ḫe-e-tu*$_2$
⸢*ša*$_2$⸣ *a-na* UGU *bu-le-e*
Lo.E. *iš-šu-u*$_2$
Rev. *ma-ḫi-ir*
(blank)
^{iti}DU$_6$ UD.21.KAM
⸢MU⸣.42.⸢KAM ^{d}AG⸣-NIG$_2$.DU-URU$_3$
LUGAL TIN.TIR^{ki}

× bundled quivers, two iron spades, three *qulmû*-axes and three sickles were received from Erībšu, son of Rēḫētu, who withdrew (them) for (cutting) firewood.
Month VII, day 21, year 42 of Nebuchadnezzar, king of Babylon.

270. NCBT 122

Copy: Plate LXVIII
Date: 21.IX.21 Nbk
Summary: withdrawal (*našû*) note: hides

For the edition of the text see page 4 in the introduction.

271. NCBT 843

Copy: Plate LXIX
Date: 19.IX.38 Nbk
Summary: withdrawal (*našû*) note: iron tools

Obv. 2 ^{kuš}*til-lu* ⸢*rak-su*⸣-*tu*
2 ⸢*az*⸣-*ma-ra-ne*$_2$-*e* AN.BAR
⸢*it*⸣-*ti* ^{I}KAR-^{d}EN
A ^{I}A-*a* ⸢*ša*$_2$⸣ *a-na* UGU ⸢ŠE.BAR⸣
[*a-n*]*a*⸢^{uru}⸣*sa-na-aṣ-ru*
[*ša*]*p-ru na-šu-u*$_2$
Lo.E. ⸢^{I}⸣IR$_3$-^{d}AG A ^{I}*re-ḫe-e-tu*$_2$
Rev. ⸢^{lu_2}⸣A.KIN-*šu*$_2$ *it-ta-ši*
(blank)
^{iti}GAN UD.20.1.LA$_2$.KAM MU.38.KAM
^{d}AG-NIG$_2$.DU-URU$_3$
LUGAL TIN.TIR^{ki}

Two bundled quivers and two iron lances have been taken with Mušēzib-Bēl, son of Aplāya, who was sent to Sanaṣru for barley; Arad-Nabû, son of Rēḫētu, his (i.e., Mušēzib-Bēl's) messenger, withdrew (them).
Month IX, day 19, year 38 of Nebuchadnezzar, king of Babylon.

5 The town of Sanaṣru is otherwise unknown. Note the once attested deity Bēl-sanaṣru in YOS 6, 145: 1, who seems to be connected with Gula. Beaulieu (2003, 274) mentions a possible identification with IGI.DU, though he seems to ultimately reject it.

272. YBC 9539

Copy: Plate LXIX
Date: 01.VIII.31 Nbk
Summary: delivery (*šūbulu*) note: silver + issue (*nadin*) note: oil

Obv. [× ×] ⸢KU$_3$.BABBAR⸣ *ina* KU$_3$.BABBAR *ša*$_2$ *a-na*
[× ×] ⸢×⸣ [×]-*ti a-na* TIN.TIR^{ki}
[*ina*] ⸢ŠU⸣^{II} ^{Id}*na-na-a*-ŠEŠ-MU
⸢A-*šu*$_2$ *ša*$_2$⸣ ^{I}*ar*$_2$-*rab šu*-⸢*bul*⸣
⸢1 BAN$_2$$^{?}$⸣ I$_3$.GIŠ *ša*$_2$ *nu-u*$_2$-*ru*
ša$_2$ ⸢^{iti}APIN⸣ *a-na*
Lo.E. ^{Id}AG-MU-⸢DU⸣ ^{lu_2}⸢ŠITIM⸣
na{eras.}-*din* {eras.}

Rev. (blank)
^{iti}APIN UD.1.KAM MU.31.KAM
^{d}AG-NIG$_2$.DU-URU$_3$ LUGAL TIN.TIR^{ki}

[×] silver, from the silver that is for […] …, was delivered to Babylon by Nanāya-aḫu-iddin, son of Arrab. *1 sūtu* of oil for the lamp of month VIII was given to Nabû-šumu-ukīn, the builder. Month VIII, day 1, year 31 of Nebuchadnezzar, king of Babylon.

273. NCBT 797

Copy: Plate LXIX
Date: 23.XI.0a Nbk
Summary: accounting inventory: oil

Obv. ½ SILA$_3$ ⸢I$_3$⸣.[GIŠ$^?$] ⸢×⸣-*a-a*
½ SILA$_3$ ^{Id}⸢AMAR⸣.[UTU]-⸢SU⸣ ^{lu2}SIMUG
½ SILA$_3$ ^{Id}EN-*ni-ip-šar-ri*
⸢½⸣ SILA$_3$ ^{I}*kal-[b]a-a*
⸢½⸣ SILA$_3$ ^{I}⸢*mar-duk*⸣-*a* ^{lu2}SIMUG
½ SILA$_3$ ^{I}⸢DU$_3$-^{d}⸣15 A-*šu$_2$ ša$_2$* ^{Id}EN-DU$_3$
Lo.E. ½ SILA$_3$ ^{I}*re-mut* A ^{Id}EN-PAP-MU
Rev. 1 SILA$_3$ ^{I}*šu-la-a* A ^{I}*i-sin-na-a-a*
½ SILA$_3$ ^{I}*ta-qi$_2$-ša$_2$-^{d}gu-la*
^{iti}ZIZ$_2$ UD.23.KAM PAP 5 SILA$_3$
MU.SAG.NAM.LUGAL.LA
⸢^{d}AG⸣-NIG$_2$.DU-URU$_3$ ⸢LUGAL⸣ E^{ki}

½ *qû* of o[*il*]…-*āya*, ½ *qû*, Marduk-erība the smith; ½ *qû* Bēl-nipšari; ½ *qû* Kalbāya; ½ *qû* Marduka, the smith; ½ *qû* Ibni-Ištar, son of Bēl-ibni; ½ *qû* Rēmūtu, son of of Bēl-aḫu-iddin; 1 *qû* Šulāya, son of of Isinnāya; ½ *qû* Taqīš-Gula; Month XI, day 23, total of 5 *qû*.
Year 0a of Nebuchadnezzar, king of Babylon.

274. NCBT 762

Copy: Plate LXIX
Date: 28.VI.42 Nbk
Summary: withdrawal (*našû*) note: oil

Obv. ⸢8⸣ NINDA.ḪI.A I$_3$.⸢GIŠ⸣
ša$_2$ nu-u$_2$-ru
ša$_2$ E$_2$-^{d}URU$_3$-INIM-*su*
ša$_2$ UD.29.KAM
ša$_2$ ^{iti}KIN
Lo.E. ⸢*u$_3$* UD⸣.13.KAM
Rev. *ša$_2$* ^{iti}DU$_6$
^{Id}AG-*mu-še-tiq$_2$*-UD.DA
A-*šu$_2$ ša$_2$* ^{I}A-*a it-ta-ši*
^{iti}KIN UD.28.KAM
MU.42.KAM

^{d}AG-NIG$_2$.DU-⸢URU$_3$⸣
Up.E. LUGAL TIN.TIR^{k}[^{i}]

Nabû-mušētiq-uddê, son of Aplāya, withdrew 8 *aklu* of oil for the lamps of the Uṣur-amāssu temple for Month VI, day 29, and Month VII, day 13.
Month VI, day 28, year 42 of Nebuchadnezzar, king of Babylon.

8 Nabû-mušētiq-uddê was the *šangû* of the *bīt ḫilṣi*; see note to **No. 57**: 5.

275. NBC 4532

Copy: Plate LXX
Date: 21.I.19 -- (Npl–Nbk)
Summary: *ina pāni* note: wax

The only known datable attestation of Kidinnu / Šadûnu (ll. 5–6) is PTS 3460, 17 Npl; see Payne 2007, 244.

Obv. 1 MA.NA DUḪ.LAL$_3$
a-na ra°-ka-su
ša$_2$ ḫi-mir-ti ša$_2$
gan-gan ša$_2$ me°-<*e*> ŠU^{II}
Rev. *ina* IGI ^{I}*ki-din-nu*
6 A ^{I}*ša$_2$-du-nu*
(blank)
^{iti}BARA$_2$ UD.21.KAM
Up.E. MU.19.KAM

1 mina of wax for binding the *crack* of the pot stand for the hand(-washing) water (basin), is at the disposal of Kidinnu, son of Šadûnu.
Month I, day 21, year 19.

3 *ḫimirtu* must derive from *ḫemēru* whose range of meanings, "to pucker, contract" (CAD Ḫ, 169, s.v. *ḫemēru*), "austrocknen" (AHw, 315, s.v. *ḫamāru*), and the context of this text support the translation offered here.

276. NCBT 895

Copy: Plate LXX
Date: undated
Summary: inventory note (unclear)

Obv. ⸢7$^{?}$⸣ GUN 37 MA.NA AN.BAR
⸢1$^{?}$⸣ GUN *a-ḫu-us-su*
48 MA.NA ⸢^{na_4}*gab-bu-u$_2$*⸣
10 MA.NA ⸢DUḪ.LAL$_3$⸣
5 [(×)] *ša$_2$* ^{I}I-^{d}AMAR.UTU
[(×)] DUMU *bar-sip^{ki}*
⸢*ul*⸣ *pa-ri-is*
Rev. (uninscribed)

7 talents 37 minas of iron, 1 talent of *aḫussu*-soda, 48 minas of alum, 10 minas of wax, of Na'id-Marduk, the Borsippean; *it is not* (*yet*) *separated*.

7 The exact nuance expressed by *parāsu* in the present context is not immediately clear. The first apparent option seems to be relating to allocations or apportions of the above listed goods. This, however, would be odd in the present context, as it makes little sense to produce a record of something that did not happen. The answer probably lies in the middle. These products were indeed allocated for the Borsippeans, but were not put out/prepared for them yet.

277. NCBT 564

Copy: Plate LXX
Date: 01.I$^?$.36 Nbk
Summary: withdrawal (*našû*) note: honey

Obv. ⸢4 NINDA⸣.ḪI.A LAL$_3$
ša$_2$ 4 UD.EŠ$_3$.EŠ$_3$^{me} *ša*$_2$ ⸢^{iti}KIN⸣
ša$_2$ *mut-ta-qu* ^{I}DUG$_3$.GA-⸢IM-E$_2$-DINGIR⸣
6 NINDA.ḪI.A ⸢*ša*$_2$⸣ 2 UD.EŠ$_3$.⸢EŠ$_3$⸣^{me}
ša$_2$ NINDA *qu-lu-pu* ^{Id}[×]-⸢GI⸣ GIŠ
⸢8⸣ NINDA.⸢ḪI.A⸣ *ša*$_2$ 4 UD.EŠ$_3$.[EŠ$_3$^{me}]
Lo.E. ⸢*ša*$_2$⸣ [× ×] ⸢×⸣ ^{I}*iq-ba-*[*a*]
[*it*]-⸢*ta-ši*⸣
Rev. (blank)
[^{it}]^{i}⸢BARA$_2$$^?$ UD.1.KAM⸣ MU.36.KAM
[^{d}AG-NIG$_2$.DU]-⸢URU$_3$ LUGAL⸣ TIN.TIR^{ki}

Ṭāb-šār-bīt-ili (withdrew) 4 *aklu* of honey for four festival days in month VI for *muttāqu*-sweetcakes.
[DN]-ušallim withdrew 6 *aklu* for two festival days for *qullupu*-sweetcakes.
Iqbā[*ya*] withdrew 8 *aklu* for four festival days for [...].
Month I, day 1, year 36 of [Nebuchadn]ezzar, king of Babylon.

3, 5 For *muttāqu* and *qullupu* sweetcakes for the festival, see, e.g., **No. 304**: 29′, 31′; TCL 13, 233.

278. NCBT 817

Copy: Plate LXX
Date: 20.XII.41 Nbk
Summary: withdrawal (*našû*) note: sesame

Obv. 1 (PI) 1 BAN$_2$ 3 SILA$_3$ ⸢ŠE.GIŠ.I$_3$⸣
a-⸢*na*⸣ *gi-*⸢*ne*$_2$*-e*⸣
^{Id}AG-DU$_3$-ŠEŠ
4 A ^{I}IR$_3$-^{d}AG
Lo.E. *it-ta-ši*
Rev. ^{iti}ŠE UD.20.KAM
MU.41.KAM
^{d}AG-NIG$_2$.DU-URU$_3$

LUGAL TIN.TIR$^{⸢ki⸣}$

Nabû-bān-aḫi, son of Arad-Nabû, withdrew 0;1.1.3 sesame for the *ginû*-offerings.
Month XII, day 20, year 41 of Nebuchadnezzar, king of Babylon.

279. NCBT 1105

Copy: Plate LXXI
Date: 20.VII.-- --
Summary: *ina pāni* note: wood + (unrelated)$^?$ tallies

The tablet rotates on its vertical axis. *Kabtia* (l. 3), if the reconstruction is correct, cannot be identified.

Obv. ⸢60^{šu}⸣ 7 ^{giš}*da*$^!$*-ap-*⸢*pi*⸣
ša$_2$ *šur-i-ni*
ina IGI ^{I}*kab-<ti>-ia*$^{!?}$
4 *u*$_3$ ^{lu2}NAGAR$^{!meš}$
Lo.E. ^{iti}DU$_6$ UD.20.KAM

Rev. 1 ME 50 1 ME 20

Sixty-seven crossbeams of cypress are at the disposal of *Kabtia* and the carpenters.
Month VII, day 20.
(*unrelated* tallies)$^?$: 150, 120.

6 It is unclear how, if at all, the numbers on the reverse relate to the obverse. The unusual rotation axis may argue against such a connection.

280. YBC 9536

Copy: Plate LXXI
Date: 30.XII.32 Nbk
Summary: *maḫir* receipt: silver + *ina pāni* note

Obv. 3 ½ GUN MUN.ḪI.A
a-na ½ GIN$_2$ KU$_3$.BABBAR
ina il-ki ša$_2$ UGU ^{lu2}UNUG^{ki}*-a-a*
^{lu2}*ki-niš-ti* ^{Id}AMAR.UTU-⸢NUMUN-DU$_3$⸣
⸢A⸣-*šu*$_2$ *ša*$_2$ ^{Id}AG-MU
ma-ḫi-ir
Lo.E. *a-na gi-ne*$_2$*-e*
Rev. *ina* IGI ^{Id}AG-GI
A-*šu*$_2$ *ša*$_2$ $^{I⸢d}$EN-MU⸣ ^{lu2}MU {(⸢×-TU$_4$⸣)}
(blank)
^{iti}ŠE UD.⸢30.KAM⸣
MU.32.KAM
^{d}AG-NIG$_2$.DU-URU$_3$
Up.E. LUGAL TIN.TIR^{ki}

3 ½ talents of salt for ½ shekel of silver from the *ilku*-obligation owed by the Urukean priests were received from Marduk-zēru-ibni, son of Nabû-iddin; it is at the disposal of Nabû-ušallim, son of Bēl-iddin, the *baker*, for the *ginû*-offerings.
Month XII, day 30, year 32 of Nebuchadnezzar, king of Babylon.

9 The signs at the end of the line, ^{lu_2}MU {(⸢×-TU$_4$⸣)}, may not have been erased but simply damaged.

281. YBC 16253

Copy:	Plate LXXI
Date:	undated (mid Nbk–mid Nbn)
Summary:	accounting inventory: livestock

Although prosopography does not help with the dating of the text, the chronological horizon can be established based on format and terminology. The following notes are all based on Pirngruber 2021. Around the mid-reign of Nebuchadnezzar, livestock inventories in the Eanna archive changed from a landscape to a portrait format. The earliest portrait format tablet is NCBT 199 (edited in Pirngruber 2021, 92), dated to 23 Nbk, and it is relatively safe to say that our present text postdates it. Another important development first attested in NCBT 199 is the transition in lamb terminology from BAR.GAL and BAR.MI$_2$ to the syllabic *ka-lum* and *par-rat*.[28] This transition is less clear-cut than the tablet format noted above and there is a gradual change continuing into the reign of Nabonidus. Importantly, the spelling BAR.MI$_2$ is last attested in PTS 2640 (edited in Pirngruber 2021, 96), dated to 10 Nbn. From that point onward, only the syllabic *par-rat* is attested.

Obv.	{× × × ×}	
	38	*ka-lum*
	60^{šu}	*par-rat*
	⸢PAP⸣	(blank)
	16	⸢MAŠ$_2$.GAL⸣ [(×)]
	53	⸢UZ$_3$^{me}⸣
	12	⸢MAŠ$_2$.TUR⸣
	24	⸢SAL.AŠ$_2$⸣.[GAR$_3$]
	PAP	[(× ×)]
Lo.E.	⸢× ×⸣ [× ×]	
Rev.	^{Id}UTU-⸢×⸣ [× ×]	
	3 ⸢*ša$_2$* <^{I}>^{d}AG-AD$^{?}$-URU$_3$$^{?}$⸣	
	5 BAR.GAL *gaz-za*	
	a-na u$_2$-ru-⸢*u$_2$*⸣	
	9 BAR$^{!}$.GAL *ina* ⸢ŠA$_3$$^{?}$ 3 ×⸣	
	3 *ka-lum ina lib$_3$-bi* × ×	
	2 MAŠ$_2$.GAL	
	^{lu_2}*ṣa-rip* ^{kuš}DUḪ.ŠI.A	

Thirty-eight male lambs, sixty female lambs, total (blank); sixteen billy-goats, fifty-three

28 Note the exceptional spelling ^{udu}*ka-lu-me* in NCBT 2313: 2 (edited in Pirngruber 2021, 92), written in 18 Npl. This shows an early use of *kalūmu* in the Eanna archive, though it is significant that the spelling *ka-lu-me* differs from the later standardized *ka-lum*.

goats, twelve kids, twenty-four female kids, total [(×)]. … […] Šamaš-… […]; three of Nabû-*abu-uṣur*; five shorn young male sheep for the stable; nine young male sheep, three of which …; three male lambs, of which …; two billy-goats (for) the leather dyer.

1 It is not entirely clear whether the first line is erased or eroded.

10 The head of the line may read ⸢*ina* IGI ^{I}⸣[…], but the traces are too faint to affirm the reading.

18 For the leather dyer apparently receiving live animals, see also **No. 261**.

282. YBC 6926

Copy: Plate LXXII
Date: undated (late Nbk–Camb)
Summary: accounting inventory: animals (and by-products)

Innin-šumu-uṣur / Ṭāb-Uruk (l. 13) is attested between 40 Nbk (NCBT 667 = **No. 246**) and 15 Nbn (YOS 19, 74); see Payne 2007, 172–3 (and p. 200 for his father Ṭāb-Uruk). Datable attestations of additional individuals listed are: Aḫu-ilia / Abu-ilāhī: YOS 6, 209 (15 Nbn); Gimillu / Arad-Innin: GC 1, 323$^{?}$ (10 Nbn), BM 113273 (15 Nbn), *Iraq* 59, 25 (1 Ner), TCL 13, 164 (4 Camb); Ibnāya / Nabû-aḫḫē-šullim: YOS 6, 142 (11 Nbn), GC 2, 102 (1 Cyr), BM 113485 (2 Cyr), BM 114449 (3 Cyr); Mušēzib-Bēl / Mušallim-Marduk: Nbk 124$^{?}$ (21 Nbk); Nanāya-aḫu-iddin / Nergal-ina-tēšî-ēṭir: YBC 3830 (0a Ner), PTS 2344$^{?}$ (1 Ner, edited in Janković 2013, 49–50), YOS 7, 132 (2 Camb); Šulāya / Šamaš-zēru-ibni: BIN 1, 174 (14 Nbn), BM 113385 (16 Nbn), SBTU 5, 299 (6 Xer). Taken together, prosopography points to a late Nbk–Camb date for the present text.

Obv. [× UDU].BAR.GAL *ša*$_2$ ⸢^{I}*ib*⸣-*na-a* A ^{Id}AG-PAP^{me}-G[I]
⸢14$^{?}$⸣ UDU.BAR.GAL *ša*$_2$ ^{I}*ba-as-si-ia* A ^{I}*u*$_2$-*zu-ub-bat*-⸢DINGIR⸣
20 UDU.BAR.GAL *ša*$_2$ ^{I}KAR-^{d}EN A ^{I}GI-^{d}AMAR.UTU
5 UDU.BAR.GAL *ša*$_2$ ^{Id}*na-na-a*-ŠEŠ-MU A ^{Id}U.GUR-*ina*-SUḪ$_3$-SUR
5 ⸢UDU⸣.BAR.GAL *ša*$_2$ ^{I}*ga-du-u*$_2$ A ^{Id}AG-GI
8 UDU.BAR.GAL *ša*$_2$ ^{I}ŠEŠ-*li-ia* A ^{I}⸢AD⸣-*i-la-ḫi-i*$^{?}$
PAP 1 ME 3 *ina* ŠA$_3$ 79 $^{\text{lu}_2}$SIPA SA$_2$.DUG$_4$
24 *a-na u*$_2$-*re-e*
2 BAN$_2$ 3 SILA$_3$ I$_3$.NUN$^{!}$.NA ^{I}*šu-la-a* A ^{Id}UTU-NUMUN-DU$_3$
6 KUR.GI$^{\text{mušen.me}}$ ^{I}(blank) $^{\text{lu}_2}$MUŠEN.DU$_3$
9 GIN$_2$ *tuk-riš u* $^{\text{sik}_2}$ZA.GIN$_3$.KUR.RA *u* $^{\text{sik}_2}$ḪE$_2$.MA.DA ^{giš}ḪAB
1 $^{\text{tug}_2}$*mu-ṣip-ti* ŠU^{II} *ša*$_2$ E$_2$ *ḫi-il-ṣu*
^{Id}*in-nin*-MU-URU$_3$ A-*šu*$_2$ *ša*$_2$ ^{I}DUG$_3$.GA-UNUG$^{!\text{ki}}$
4 UZ.TUR$^{\text{mušen.me}}$ *ir-bi ša*$_2$ ^{Id}EN-ŠEŠ^{me}-SU
75 ⸢U$_8$⸣ 12 *ka-lum* 31 *par-rat*
1 ⸢MAŠ$_2$⸣.GAL 4 ⸢UZ$_3$⸣^{me} 1 MAŠ$_2$.TUR
PAP 1 ME 24 *ṣe-e-nu ina* IGI ^{I}DU$_3$-^{d}INNIN
1 AB$_2$.GAL {eras.} 1 AB$_2$ 3^{ti} 1 AB$_2$ 2^{ti}
PAP 3 *ir*$^{!}$-*bi ina* IGI ^{I}ŠU A ^{I}IR$_3$-^{d}⸢*in-nin*⸣
13 <UDU>.BAR.GAL *a-na u*$_2$-*ru-u*$_2$
{eras.}
Lo.E. 1 MAŠ$_2$.GUB
Rev. {erased tallies}

[×] young male sheep of Ibnāya, son of Nabû-aḫḫē-šullim; *fourteen* young male sheep of Basia, son of Uzīb-Baytil; twenty young male sheep of Mušēzib-Bēl, son of Mušallim-Marduk; five young male sheep of Nanāya-aḫu-iddin, son of Nergal-ina-tēšî-ēṭir; five young male sheep of Gadû, son of Nabû-ušallim; eight young male sheep of Aḫu-ilia, son of Abu-ilāhī; total of 103, seventy-nine of which (are for / with) the offering shepherd (and) twenty-four are for the stables.
0;0.2.3 ghee (of) Šulāya, son of Šamaš-zēru-ibni; six geese (of) $^{mr.}$ø, the bird-catcher; 9 shekels of red-purple wool, purple wool, and red wool, *ḫūratu*-dye, one *muṣiptu*-cloth, *property* of the *bīt ḫilṣi*, (*of*) Innin-šumu-uṣur, son of Ṭāb-Uruk; four ducks, the income of Bēl-aḫḫē-erība; seventy-five ewes; twelve male lambs, thirty-one female lambs; one billy-goat; four goats; one kid; total of 124 sheep and goats at the disposal of Ibni-Ištar.
One cow; one three-year-old cow; one two-year-old cow; total of three, the income at the disposal of Gimillu, son of Arad-Innin.
Thirteen young male sheep for the stables; { } one young goat.
{erased tallies}

2 The renderring Uzīb-Baytil for ^{I}*u$_2$-zu-ub-bat*-⸢DINGIR⸣ follows the corrigenda to Thissen's 2017 review of Nielsen 2015.[29]

283. NCBT 479

Copy: Plate LXXIII
Date: 17.XII.14 (Nbn / Dar)
Summary: *maḫir* receipt: ducks + allocation of sheep

For Šamaš-iddin (l. 2), a bird-catcher, see **No. 122**.

Obv. 10 ⸢UZ⸣.TUR^{mušen}
^{Id}UTU-MU IGI^{ir}
(blank)
^{iti}ŠE UD.17.KAM
MU.14.KAM
Rev. 2 UDU.NITA$_2$ UD.17.KAM *ša$_2$* ^{iti}ŠE
6 *a-na* ^{lu_2}*um-man*

Ten ducks were received from Šamaš-iddin; Month XII, day 17, year 14.
Two sheep, 17th of Month XII, (were given) for / to the craftsmen.

284. NCBT 760

Copy: Plate LXXIII
Date: 17.XII.21 Nbk
Summary: *maḫir* receipt: sheep

Obv. 10 UDU.NITA$_2$^{meš} *ša$_2$ a-na*
^{d}UTU *šap-ru-ụ$_2$*
2 UDU.NITA$_2$^{me} *ša$_2$ a-na*

29 See Thissen 2021.

^{lu_2}*um-man-ni* SUM^{u_2}

Lo.E. ^{I}TUKUL-*ti*-^{d}AMAR.UTU

⌜A⌝ ^{I}NIG$_2$.DU

Rev. [^{lu_2}S]IPA-⌜*i*⌝ IGI^{ir}

(blank)

^{iti}ŠE UD.17.KAM

MU.21.KAM ^{d}AG-NIG$_2$.DU-URU$_3$

LUGAL TIN.TIR^{ki}

Ten sheep that were sent for (the temple of) Šamaš and two sheep that were given for the craftsmen were received from Tukulti-Marduk, son of Kudurru, the shepherd.
Month XII, day 17, year 21 of Nebuchadnezzar, king of Babylon.

285. NBC 4602

Copy: Plate LXXIII
Date: undated (Nbn–Cyr)
Summary: accounting inventory: sheep and iron

Ibni-Ištar/Šumu-ukīn (l. 9′) is attested between 2 Ner (NBC 4883, edited in Sack 1979, 112–3) and 7 Cyr (YBC 11553).

Obv. (beginning broken)

⌜24$^{?}$ U$_8$ *ša*$_2$$^{?}$⌝ [ ]

17 ⌜U$_8$⌝ ^{I}AD$^{?}$-*qi*$_2$-*i*-⌜*ni*$^{?}$⌝ […]

24 ⌜U$_8$⌝ ^{I}BA^{ša_2} [(×)]

14 U$_8$ ^{Id}UTU-MU-DU A [^{I}…]

13 U$_8$ ^{Id}AG-*na-din*-MU […]

2 *pu-ḫal* 16 U$_8$ 1 UZ$_3$

ša$_2$ ^{Id}AG-I

4 U$_8$ *ša*$_2$ ^{Id}AG-ŠEŠ^{me}-MU A ^{Id}AG-*il*$^{!?}$-*ta*$^{?}$-⌜*ma*$^{?}$-$^{??}$⌝

10 U$_8$ ^{I}DU$_3$-^{d}INNIN A ^{I}MU-DU

23 U$_8$ 3 UZ$_3$ ^{Id}EN-ŠEŠ^{me}-SU$^{!(T.\ zu)}$

A$^{!}$ ^{I}*i-di-i*$^{?}$-DINGIR

2 MA.NA 10 GIN$_2$ AN.BAR *gam-ru* 1 *qul-mu-u*$_2$ *ik-ri*$^{!(T.\ ḫu)}$ AN.BAR

^{I}DU$_3$-^{d}INNIN IGI^{ir}

Rev. (blank)

60$^{šu?}$ *a-na* ⅚ MA.NA *ina* IGI ^{lu_2}GAL *bu-li*$_3$

(several free lines with traces of tallies)

20

(blank)

5

1

4$^{?}$ 6$^{?}$/7$^{?}$ ⌜×⌝

ina/1

^{iti}G[AN$^{?}$]

[remainder broken]

[…] Twenty-four ewes of / from [PN]; seventeen ewes (of / from) *Abu-qīni*; twenty-four ewes (of / from) Iqīšāya; fourteen ewes (of / from) Šamaš-šumu-ukīn, son of [PN]; thirteen ewes (of / from) Nabû-nādin-šumi; two rams, sixteen ewes, and a goat of / from Nabû-na'id; four ewes for / from Nabû-aḫḫē-iddin, son of Nabû-iltama'; ten ewes (of / from) Ibni-Ištar, son of Šumu-ukīn; twenty-three ewes, three goats (of / from) Bēl-aḫḫē-erība, son of Idī-il; 2 minas 10 shekels in processed iron (in the form of) one iron *qulmû*-axe (*and*) an iron *ikru*?, were received from Ibni-Ištar; 60 (shekels)? for ⅚ mina are at the disposal of the herd supervisor.
(unclear tallies)
Month *I*[*X*].

12′ *ik-ri*$^{!(T.\,hu)}$; the nature of this tool is unclear. The reading *ri*$^{!(T.\,hu)}$ is based on 2 *qul-mu-u*$_2$ *ik-ru* AN.BAR in PTS 2200: 5.

286. NCBT 702

Copy: Plate LXXIV
Date: undated (*Camb*)
Summary: accounting inventory: varia

Two possible identifications are: Šamšamānu / Arad-Nabû in BM 113407 (0a Camb), and Marduk-šāpik-zēri / Balāṭu in NCBT 1012 (4 Camb) and BM 113429 (7 Camb).

Obv. 15 ^{udu}*ka-lum ša*$_2$ ^{I}*ša*$_2$*-am-ša*$_2$*-ma-n*[*u*]
A ^{I}IR$_3$-^{d}AG *ina* ŠA$_3$ 3 *a-na u*$_2$*-ru*$^{!(T.\,nu)}$*-u*$_2$
12 *ina pa-ni* ^{I}*gu-za-nu* $^{lu_2\circ}$SIPA SA$_2$.DUG$_4$
^{iti}BARA$_2$ UD.23.KAM
1 *pag-ra ša*$_2$ UDU.NITA$_2$ *a-na* 1 (PI) 1 BAN$_2$ 3 SILA$_3$ ZU$_2$.LUM.MA
ina ŠUK.ḪI.A-*šu*$_2$ ^{Id}UTU-NUMUN-GAL$_2$^{ši} A ^{I}DU$_3$*-ia*$_2$
^{iti}BARA$_2$ UD.26.KAM
16 GIN$_2$ KU$_3$.⸢BABBAR⸣ *ša*$_2$ 16 GUR° ŠE.BAR *la-bi-ri*
ša$_2$ *a-na maš-*⸢*šar*⸣*-ti a-na* ^{lu_2}LUNGA^{me} *u* ^{lu_2}MUḪALDIM^{me}
SUM.NA ^{Id}AMAR.UTU-DUB-NUMUN A ^{I}*ba-la-ṭu*
^{iti}BARA$_2$ UD.27.KAM UD.28.KAM
18 ½ GIN$_2$ ^{gada}*ṭi-mu* ^{Id}AG-SIPA-*u*$_2$*-a* ^{lu_2}*p*[*u-ṣa*]-⸢*a*⸣*-a* IGI^{ir}
4 BAN$_2$ 4 SILA$_3$ ŠE.GIŠ.⸢I$_3$⸣ ^{Id}⸢60-DU$_3$⸣ ^{lu_2}I$_3$.⸢SUR⸣ [(ø) GI]Š?
2 BAN$_2$ ⸢1⸣ SILA$_3$ ŠE.GIŠ.I$_3$ *ša*$_2$ ^{Id}ENŠADA -⸢× ×⸣ [ ]
^{iti}GU$_4$ U[D.×.KAM]
⸢7 *ka*⸣*-lum ša*$_2$ ^{I}⸢DU⸣-[ ]
[ ] ⸢× ×⸣ [ ]
(remainder of Obv. broken)
Rev. (beginning of Rev. broken)
(blank)
{*ina* / 1}
{11(+) / IG[I]}
{⸢7?⸣}
{ }
{⸢3?⸣}

Fifteen male lambs of Šamšamānu, son of Arad-Nabû; three of which are for the stable (and) twelve are at the disposal of Gūzānu the offering shepherd; Month I, day 23.
One sheep carcass, for 0;1.1.3 dates, from his salary, (for) Šamaš-zēru-šubši, son of Bānia; day 26 of month I.
16 shekels of silver for 16 kor of the old barley, which was given to the brewers and the bakers for the(ir) *maššartu*, (for) Marduk-šāpik-zēri, son of Balāṭu; days 27 and 28 of month I.
18 ½ shekels of thread linen received from Nabû-rēʾûa the linen weaver.
Anu-ibni, the (ø)? oil-presser, withdrew 0;4.4.0 sesame.
0;2.1.0 sesame of Nusku-… […]; da[y [×] of month II. Seven male lambs of / which Mukīn-[…] … […]
{erased(?) tally}

287. NBC 4693

Copy: Plate LXXV
Date: 04.V.27 Nbk
Summary: witnessed accounting note: silver

Obv. *ina* ⸢⅔? MA⸣.NA 8 GIN$_2$ KU$_3$.BABBAR *ša*$_2$ UD.4.KAM
ša$_2$ ⸢^{iti}⸣NE MU.27.KAM
^{d}AG-NIG$_2$.DU-URU$_3$ LUGAL TIN.TIR^{ki}
ina ŠU^{II} ^{Id}AMAR.UTU-EN-*šu*$_2$-*nu* ^{lu2}ŠA$_3$.TAM
⸢*ina lib*$_3$⸣-*bi* 4 GIN$_2$ *šal-šu*$_2$ 1 GIN$_2$ KU$_3$.BABBAR
a-na ⸢1-*en*? UDU⸣.NITA$_2$ *ša*$_2$ *a-na*
Lo.E. ⸢^{lu2}⸣ŠA$_3$.TAM *na-din*
Rev. *ina* GUB-*zu* *ša*$_2$ ^{Id}AMAR.UTU-SUR
A-*šu*$_2$ *ša*$_2$ ^{Id}AG-NUMUN-SI.SA$_2$
u ^{Id}KUR.GAL-*šu*$^{!(T.\ ba)}$-*zib-an-ni*
^{lu2}*ma-la-ḫu*-⸢*e*⸣
^{iti}NE UD.⸢4⸣.[KA]M
MU.27.KAM ^{d}AG-NIG$_2$.DU-URU$_3$
Up.E. LUGAL TIN.TIR^{ki}

Of the 48 shekels of silver for Month V, day 4, year 27 of Nebuchadnezzar, king of Babylon, under the responsibility of Marduk-bēlšunu, the *šatammu*: thereof 4 ⅓ shekels of silver were given for one sheep that is for the *šatammu*. (Written) in the presence of Marduk-ēṭir, son of Nabû-zēru-līšir, and Amurru-šūzibanni, the boatman.
Month V, day 4, year 27 of Nebuchadnezzar, king of Babylon.

11 Note the spelling ^{lu2}*ma-la-ḫu*-⸢*e*⸣. It may be speculated that the scribe had the plural form in mind, possibly referring to both witnesses.

288. NCBT 780

Copy: Plate LXXIV
Date: undated
Summary: personnel list

None of the listed individuals can be identified elsewhere.

Obv. ⸢$^{Id?}$15$^{?}$-GI ^{lu2}KU$_3$$^{?}$⸣.[DIM$^{?}$]
^{Id}AG-MU ^{lu2}⸢NAGAR *qu*⸣-*t*[*a-nu*]
^{Id}U.GUR-MU ^{lu2}SIMUG
^{Id}*in-nin*-MU-URU$_3$ ^{lu2}ŠITIM
^{Id}*na-na-a*-MU ^{lu2}ŠITIM
3 ^{lu2}EN.NUN E$_2$-NIG$_2$.GA^{meš}
PAP 8
(blank)
Rev. ^{lu2}°GAL *šir*$_3$-*ku* 2
5 ⸢ERIN^{meš} *ša*$_2$⸣ ^{lu2}GAL *šir*$_3$-*ku*
PAP 7 ^{lu2}GAL ⸢*šir*$_3$⸣-*ku*

Ištar-ušallim, the *goldsmith*; Nabû-iddin, the *fine woodwork* carpenter; Nergal-iddin, the smith; Innin-šumu-uṣur, the builder; Nanāya-iddin, the builder; three watchmen of the storehouses; total of eight (men). Overseer of serfs - two; five workers of the overseer of serfs; total: seven overseers of serfs.

2 *Nagār qutāni*: see glossary.
8–10 The seven overseers in the final line must be the two overseers (l. 8) + five workers (l. 9). It is unclear why the five workers (*ṣābu*) are counted as overseers (*rab širku*) in l. 10.

289. NCBT 671

Copy: Plate LXXIV
Date: undated
Summary: note regarding a shearing commitment

None of the listed individuals can be identified elsewhere.

Obv. 10 {eras.} ^{lu2}⸢*mu-saḫ-ḫ*[*ir-ri*]
15 {eras.} ^{lu2}ḪUN.GA$_2$^{me}
5 {^{lu2}} ^{lu2}*za-bil ku-du-ru*
PAP 30 {eras.} ERIN$_2$^{me} {eras.}
a-[*n*]*a* ⸢*gaz*⸣-*za ina* IGI
^{I}*e*°-*rib-šu*$_2$ *u* ^{Id}AG-*a-a*-⸢*lu*⸣
11 ^{lu2}*za-bil ku-du-ru*
ina IGI ^{Id}U.GUR-MU-DU$_3$
pu-ut ri-iq-ti ša$_2$ *gaz-za*
u$_3$ E$_2$-*ta*⸣-*nu na-ši*
Rev. (uninscribed)

Ten agents, fifteen hired workers, five basket-carriers; total of thirty men for the shearing are at the disposal of Erībšu and Nabû-ayyalu. Eleven basket-carriers are at the disposal of Nergal-šumu-ibni. He is responsible in case of *idleness* in the shearing as well as (the work) within the temple.

9 *ri-iq-ti* is taken as an unexpected form of either *rīqu* (adj., no noun) or *rīqūtu*, in the sense of "interruption (i.e., idleness) in the work."

290. NCBT 488

Copy: Plate LXXV
Date: 12.IX.06 (Npl)
Summary: note regarding serfs + *ina pāni* note: iron

Kudurru's (i.e., Nebuchadnezzar's) term as the *šatammu* was 0a–9 Npl.

Obv. ^{I}*ina*-GISSU-^{d}*na-na-a*
^{lu_2}*šir*$_3$*-ku ša*$_2$ ^{I}NIG$_2$.DU ^{lu_2}ŠA$_3$.TAM
ina E$_2$.AN.NA
^{I}*ša*$_2$-^{d}AG-*šu*$_2$*-u*$_2$ ^{lu_2}*šir*$_3$*-ku ša*$_2$ ⸢^{d}AG⸣
ina IGI ^{I}MU-^{d}AG A-*šu*$_2$ *ša*$_2$ ^{I}*ap-la-a*
Lo.E. ^{iti}GAN UD.12.KAM MU.6.KAM
Rev. 6 5/6 MA.NA AN.BAR *ina* IGI
^{Id}AG-NUMUN-MU ^{lu_2}SIMUG {eras.}

Ina-ṣilli-Nanāya, the temple serf of Kudurru, the *šatammu*, is in Eanna.
Ša-Nabû-šū, the temple serf of Nabû, is at the disposal of Iddin-Nabû, son of Aplāya.
Month IX, day 12, year 6.
6 5/6 minas of iron are at the disposal of Nabû-zēru-iddin, the smith.

1–3 The fact that Ina-ṣilli-Nanāya is referred to as the temple serf of Kudurru, i.e., the *šatammu* (and future king Nebuchadnezzar) is noteworthy. Cases in which serfs are designated as *širku ša* PN usually occur when the slave was dedicated to the temple during his master's lifetime. This, however, is not likely to be the case here. First, Nebuchadnezzar could not have been older than 10–15 at this point, which would make the future (suspended) dedication of Ina-ṣilli-Nanāya an extremely early and unlikely action by his master.[30] Furthermore, the text clearly states that Ina-ṣilli-Nanāya is in the temple, rather than in Kudurru's place. The phrasing of the text seems to suggest that Ina-ṣilli-Nanāya's serfhood was vis-à-vis Kudurru in his capacity as the *šatammu*. This is the only case in which a serf is said to be of the *šatammu*, and it is certainly possible that Kudurru's royal affiliation was behind this practice. According to NBC 4514, written about a year after our text (Month III, day 14, year 7 of Nabopolassar), a certain Nādinu, son of Iddinaya, owes the temple silver as the "purchase price" of two sons of his, one of whom bears the name Ina-ṣilli-Nanāya. Notably, the tablet is witnessed by the palace scribe, a high-ranking royal official, Amurru-udammiq (*qīpu* of Eanna), Anu-aḫu-iddin (*šakin ṭēmi* of Uruk), and Kudurru, the *šatammu*, himself. This might be the same Ina-ṣilli-Nanāya, whose father might

30 One could also speculate that the age of the slave might have played a part, as it was potentially a way for a master to dispose of an aging slave. This, however, cannot be substantiated due to the nature of the available sources, which would not, or at least do not, address such a rationale by dedicators.

have tried to ransom him (against credit) from the temple.

291. NCBT 1006

Copy: Plate LXXV
Date: undated
Summary: personnel list

None of the listed individuals can be identified elsewhere.

Obv. ^{I}⸢LU$_2$⸣-^{d}*na*-⸢*na*⸣-*a* (blank)
^{I}⸢LU$_2$⸣-^{d}AG *ša*$_2$ ^{I}*e-zu-u-pa-šir*$_2$
^{Id}AG-SUḪUŠ-*ia*$_2$-DU *ša*$_2$ ^{Id}U.GUR-MU
⸢^{I}⸣^{d}15-*re-ṣu-u*$_2$-*a* *ša*$_2$ ^{I}*šu-ma-a*
^{I}ŠEŠ-*it-tab-ši* *ša*$_2$ ^{I}KI.NE-*nu-na-a-a*
PAP 5 ^{I}LU$_2$-^{d}*na-na-a*
Rev. ^{Id}⸢*na*⸣-*na-a*-KAM ^{lu2}MA$_2$.LAḪ$_4$
^{I}*bul*-⸢*luṭ*⸣-*a* (blank)
^{I}LU$_2$-^{d}*na-na-a-rib/kal-bi*
PAP 3 ^{Id}*na-na-a*-KAM
PAP 8 ERIN$_2$^{meš} ^{lu2}*qi*$_2$-*pi*
a-na TIN.TIR^{ki} *il-tap-par*
Up.E. ŠUK.ḪI.A *ša*$_2$ ^{iti}SIG$_4$
⸢*in-da*$^{?}$⸣-*an-ṭa*

Amīl-Nanāya, Amīl-Nabû for Ezu-pašir, Nabû-išdīa-ukīn for Nergal-iddin, Ištar-rēṣūʾa for Šumāya, Aḫu-ittabši for Kinūnāya; total of five (men headed by) Amīl-Nanāya. Nanāya-ēreš, the boatman, Bulluṭāya, Amīl-Nanāya-*ribi*; total of three (men headed by) Nanāya-ēreš: (thus,) the *qīpu* sent a total of eight people to Babylon. The(ir) salaries for month III *are missing*.

9 The name Amīl-Nanāya-ribi is unclear and must stand for something else. Both Amīl-Nanāya and Nanāya-ribi are possible, but not the three components together. An alternative reading for the penultimate sign is of course *kal*, thus *kalbi* (as in Ša-pî-kalbi or Kalbi-DN), yet this does not solve the problem. The confusion regarding the element ur in ^{I}UR-DN names, to be read either as Amīl-DN or Kalbi-DN[31] provokes thoughts of some complicated scribal games between LU$_2$ = *amīlu* = UR = *kalbu*. This, however, seems to be a mere coincidence, and does not help with the reading of the name. Finally, the final element might be a way to distinguish the present Amīl-Nanāya from his namesake in lines 1, 6.

12. 14$^{?}$ The use of perfect forms in main clauses is noteworthy. While certainly not unattested, it is uncharacteristic for administrative texts.[32]

14 The form *in-da-an-ṭa* is challenging. Not only is the (voiceless) *ṭṭ* > *nṭ* shift in *an-ṭa* unexpected, the "original" double *ṭṭ*, in what would be taken as a perfect form, is unclear. Theoretically, *in-da-an-ṭa* could be read as a Gt present form, in the sense of *"(the salaries) are missing respectively (for each individual)." Neither dictionary, however, lists the Gt as a productive form of *maṭû*.

[31] See the appendix in Sandowicz 2018.

[32] Note especially the relatively common use of *našû* in the perfect form; e.g., **No. 162**: 7, **No. 230**: 18, 20.

292. NCBT 1024

Copy: Plate LXXV
Date: undated
Summary: personnel list

None of the listed individuals can be identified elsewhere. The tablet is a near, though not a complete, duplicate of **No. 293**. The main difference is Nanāya-taklāk for Amīl-Nanāya (l. 10), who is not listed in **No. 293**, and Amīl-Nabû / Aḫḫēa (**No. 293**: 4), who is not listed in the present text.

Obv. ^{I}KI.NE-*a-a* A ^{I}SUM.NA-*a*
^{Id}AG-*tak-lak ša*$_2$$^{!}$ ^{Id}AG-<*za-k*>*ir*$^{(T.\ ḫa)}$-MU
^{I}LU$_2$-^{d}*na-na-a* A ^{Id}U.GUR-*u*$_2$-*še-zib*
^{Id}AG-*na-din*-MU A ^{I}*šul-lum-a*
^{Id}AG-MU A ^{Id}EN-*ana*-KUR-*šu*$_2$
^{Id}EN-AD-PAP *ša*$_2$ $^{I⸢d⸣}$KUR.GAL-KAL
Rev. ^{Id}EN-PAP ^{lu2}*ma-la-ḫu*
^{Id}*na-na-a*-KAM A ^{I}*i-ba-a*
^{Id}AG-NUMUN-MU A ^{Id}AG-*u*$_2$-*še-zib*
^{Id}*na-na-a-tak-lak ša*$_2$ ^{I}LU$_2$-^{d}*na-na-a*
PAP 10 *ša*$_2$ ^{I}KI.NE-*a-a*

Kinūnāya, son of Iddināya; Nabû-taklāk, for Nabû-zākir-šumi; Amīl-Nanāya, son of Nergal-ušēzib; Nabû-nādin-šumi, son of Šullumāya; Nabû-iddin, son of Bēl-ana-mātišu; Bēl-abu-uṣur, for Amurru-udammiq; Bēl-nāṣir, the boatman; Nanāya-ēreš, son of Ibāya; Nabû-zēru-iddin, son of Nabû-ušēzib; Nanāya-taklāk, for Amīl-Nanāya; total of ten (men) of Kinūnāya.

2 Note that the (near) duplicate **No. 293**, line 2 has ^{I}*ana*-^{d}15-*tak-lak*, rather than ^{Id}AG-*tak-lak*. The two must be the same individual. Furthermore, from **No. 293**: 2 we also see that the second name must be Nabû-zākir-šumi. And so, despite the possible reading ^{Id}AG-*ḫa-mu* for Nabû-ḫanû (c.f. ^{Id}AG-*ḫa-mu-u*, read Nabû-ḫanû in BM 96535: 4 (= Zadok 2005/2006, No. 187), it seems best to emend the present text text to ^{Id}AG-<*za-k*>*ir*$^{(T.\ ḫa)}$-mu; i.e., assuming that the *ḫa* sign is in fact the end of the expected *kir* sign. This might be a possible case of the scribe's eye "jumps over," *aberratio oculi*, when copying from a (third) original.

8 Nanāya-ēreš / Ibāya is identified as a bronzesmith in **No. 293**.

293. NCBT 1189

Copy: Plate LXXVIII
Date: undated
Summary: personnel list

None of the listed individuals can be identified elsewhere. The tablet is a near, though not a complete, duplicate of **No. 292**. The main difference is Amīl-Nabû/Aḫḫēa (l. 4), who is not listed in **No. 292**, and Nanāya-taklāk for Amīl-Nanāya (**No. 292**: 10), who is not listed in the present text. See above for more on the relationship between these tablets.

Obv. ^{I}KI.NE-*a*-<*a*> A ^{I}SUM.NA-*a*
^{I}*ana*-$^{d⸢}$15$^{⸣}$-*tak-lak ša*$_2$ ^{Id}AG-*za-kir*-MU

^{I}LU$_2$-^{d}*na-na-a* A $^{Id°}$U.GUR°-*u*$_2$-*še-zib*
^{I}LU$_2$-^{d}AG A ^{I}ŠEŠ^{meš}-*e-a* ^{lu_2}AŠGAB$^{!}$
^{Id}AG-*na-din*-MU A ^{I}*šul-lum-a*
^{Id}AG-MU A ^{Id}EN-*ana*-KUR-*šu*$_2$
Rev. ^{Id}AG-AD-URU$_3$ *ša*$_2$ ^{Id}KUR.GAL-KAL
^{Id}EN-PAP ^{lu_2}*ma-la-ḫu*
^{Id}*na-na-a*-KAM A ^{I}*i-ba-a* ^{lu_2}SIMUG ZABAR
^{Id}AG-NUMUN-MU A ^{Id}AG-*u*$_2$-*še-zib* KI.<MIN>$^{?}$
PAP 10 *ša*$_2$ ^{I}KI.NE-*a-a*

Kinūnāya, son of Iddināya; Ana-Ištar-taklāk, for Nabû-zākir-šumi; Amīl-Nanāya, son of Nergal-ušēzib; Amīl-Nabû, son of Aḫḫēa, the leatherworker; Nabû-nādin-šumi, son of Šullumāya; Nabû-iddin, son of Bēl-ana-mātišu; Nabû-abu-uṣur, for Amurru-udammiq; Bēl-nāṣir, the boatman; Nanāya-ēreš, son of Ibāya, the bronzesmith; Nabû-zēru-iddin, son of Nabû-ušēzib, *ditto*; total of ten (men) of Kinūnāya.

294. YBC 11085

Copy: Plate LXXVIII
Date: [×.×].07 [Nbn]
Summary: personnel list

For Innin-šumu-uṣur/Ṭāb-Uruk see **No. 282**. For Nabû-šarru-uṣur's term as the commissioner of Eanna, 1–13 Nbn, see Kleber 2008, 36.

Obv. [beginning broken]
[ ] ⸢*bar*⸣
[^{I}]⸢^{d}AG⸣-LUGAL-URU$_3$
[^{lu_2}EN *pi-qit*]-*ti* ⸢E$_2$⸣.AN.NA
[^{iti}× UD.(×+)]⸢2.KAM MU.7.KAM⸣
[^{Id}AG-I] LUGAL ⸢TIN.TIR^{ki}⸣
[^{Id}*in*]-⸢*nin*-MU-URU$_3$$^{?}$ A ^{I}DUG$_3$.GA⸣-UNUG^{ki}
[^{Id}*in*]-*nin*$^{?}$-[ ] ⸢A⸣ ^{Id}*na-na-a*-MU
[ ]⸢*šu*$_2$$^{?}$⸣[(A) ^{Id}*n*]*a-na-a*-MU
[ ] ⸢×⸣ [ ] ⸢^{lu_2}*ṣa-pe-e*⸣
^{Id}⸢UTU⸣-M[U$^{?}$ $^{lu_2?}$*pu-ṣa*]-⸢*a-a*⸣$^{?}$
^{Id}UT[U-× (×) ^{lu_2}]⸢*pu-ṣa*⸣-[*a-a*]
[(×)]1 ^{I}DU$_3$-^{d}⸢15⸣ [ ] ⸢×⸣
[(×)]1 ^{lu_2}SIMUG ⸢ZABAR⸣ [ ]
[(×)]1 ^{lu_2}NAGAR ^{giš}⸢IG^{me}⸣ [ ]
[(×)] ^{lu_2}AŠGAB^{m}[^{e}]
[(×)] ^{lu_2}AD.KID [ ]
Rev. [(×)] ^{lu_2}⸢IR$_3$-E$_2$.GAL⸣ [ ]
[(×)] ^{I}ŠEŠ-*lu-mur u* ^{lu_2}⸢ERIN$_2$⸣[^{me}]
[(×)] ^{Id}U.GUR-MU-DU$_3$ *u* ^{lu_2}E[RIN$_2$^{me}]
[(×)] ^{lu_2}BUR.GUL^{me} *u*$_3$ [ ]
[(×)] ^{lu_2}BAḪAR$_2$^{me} [(×)]
[(PAP ×) ^{l}]^{u_2}ERIN$_2$^{me}

[...] ... [...] Nabû-šarru-uṣur, [the commissio]ner of Eanna, [... month ×, day (×+)]2, year 7 [of Nabonidus], king of Babylon:
Innin-šumu-uṣur, son of Ṭāb-Uruk; [In]nin-[...], son of Nanāya-iddin; [... (son of)] Nanāya-iddin; [...], the dyer; Šamaš-*id*[*din*, the laund]erer; Šamaš-[×, the] launde[rer]; [(×+)]1, Ibni-Ištar [...]; [(×+)]1, the bronzesmith; [(×+)]1, the doors carpenter [(...)]; [(×)], the leatherworkers; [(×)], the reed-worker(s) [(...)]; [(×)], the master-builder(s) [(...)]; [(×)], Aḫu-lūmur and (his$^?$) workers; [(×)], Nergal-šumu-ibni and (his$^?$) workers; [(×)], the seal cutters; [(×)], the potters [(...)]; [*total of* ×] workers.

295. YBC 6846

Copy: Plate LXXVIII
Date: undated (Nbn)
Summary: personnel list

Erībšu (l. 9) is attested between 0a AM (AUWE 5, 4) and 14 Nbn (BIN 1, 174); see Payne 2007, 303. Ištar-aḫu-iddin (l. 6) is probably to be identified as the one attested in **No. 296**: 47 ([Nbn]).

Obv. ⸢I⸣^{d}UTU-DU$_3$-ŠEŠ
^{I}SUM.NA-*a*
2 ^{lu_2}ERIN$_2^{me}$
4 E$_2$ GU$_4$ *ša*$_2$ LUGAL
3 ^{lu_2}*gaz*$^{!(T.\ gu_2)}$-*zi-zi*^{me}
I⸢d⸣15°-ŠEŠ-MU
^{I}*ša*$_2$-^{d}INNIN-*u*$_2$-*da*
1 ^{lu_2}SIMUG ZABAR
1 *ša*$_2$ <*ina*> ŠU^{II} ^{I}KU$_4$-*šu*$_2$
^{I}*nim-ša*$_2$-⸢{eras.}*tu*$_4$⸣
Rev. 1 *ša*$_2$ ⸢*ina* ŠU^{II}⸣ ^{I}UR-*a*
^{Id}AG-SUR

Šamaš-bān-aḫi, Iddināya, two workmen, four (men of) the royal ox stables, three *shearers*, Ištar-aḫu-iddin, Ša-Ištar-uddu, one bronzesmith, one under the responsibility of Erībšu, *Nimšātu*, one under the responsibility of Kalbāya, Nabû-ēṭir.

296. YBC 9027

Copy: Plates LXXVI–LXXVII
Date: 19.V.[× Nbn]
Summary: personnel list

Several of the listed individuals are well attested in the Eanna archive. The following are but a few examples: Bēl-ēṭir (l. 37), 3 Nbn (see Payne 2007, 160); Bēl-iqbi (l. 21), 14–25 Nbk (see Payne 2007, 162); Bēl-upaḫḫir (l. 46) 14–32 Nbk (see Payne 2007, 302); Dannu-aḫḫēšu-ibni (l. 30), 8 Nbn (see Payne 2007, 164); Dannu-aḫḫēšu-ibni (l. 20), 16 Nbn–5 Cyr (see Payne 2007, 163); Eanna-šumu-ibni (l. 36), 3 Nbn (see Payne 2007, 165); Ēdūa (l. 46), 3 Nbn–5 Camb (see Payne 2007, 303); Erībšu (l. 18), 2 Nbn–0a Camb (see Payne 2007, 166–7).

Obv. [UD.(×+)]⸢19⸣.KAM *ša*$_2$ ^{iti}NE

[ ]⸢×⸣

[^{I}*gi*]-⸢*mil-lu*⸣ [(×)] ⸢A⸣ ^{Id}AG-NUMUN-BA^{ša_2}
^{Id}*a-nu-um*-MU-DU$_3$ A ^{I}DI.KUD-APIN^{eš}
^{I}KI-SIK-^{d}AG A ^{I}*šu-la-a*
^{Id}UTU-ŠEŠ-MU A ^{Id}AG-ŠEŠ^{me}-GI
^{Id}UTU-MU-MU A ^{Id}UTU-NUMUN-⸢BA⸣-*ša*$_2$
^{I}*ni-din*$^{!}$*-ti* A ^{Id}AG-*mu*-⸢*še-tiq*$_2$⸣-UD.⸢DA⸣ *ina na-aš*$_2$*-par-ti*
PAP 5^{sic} ${}^{lu_2.giš}$NAGAR *qu-ta-nu*

---

^{Id}*in-nin-na*-MU-URU$_3$ A ^{I}DUG$_3$.GA-UNUG^{ki}
^{I}*ina*-SUḪ$_3$-SUR *u*° ^{Id}*a-nu*-LUGAL-URU$_3$ ⸢DUMU⸣^{me} *ša*$_2$ ^{I}*re-mut*
^{I}IR$_3$-^{d}EN *u* ^{Id}UTU-SUR DUMU^{me} *ša*$_2$ ^{I}*si-lim*-^{d}EN
^{I}*kal-ba-a* A ^{Id}AG-*si-lim ina na-aš*$_2$*-par-ti*
^{I}*ki-i*-^{d}UTU *ina* UD.UNUG⸢^{ki}⸣
^{Id}15-ŠEŠ-MU *ina pa-ni* ^{I}⸢*ki-din*$^{?}$⸣
^{I}LU$_2$-^{d}*na-na-a* ^{lu_2}⸢GIG⸣
PAP 9 ^{lu_2}UŠ.BAR *bir-mu*

---

^{I}*e-rib-šu*$_2$ A ^{Id}*na-na-a*-MU *u* ^{Id}UTU-NUMUN-DU$_3$ DUMU-*šu*$_2$
^{I}IR$_3$-^{d}*in-nin-na* A ^{f}*a-na*-E$_2$-*šu*$_2$ ^{munus}*za-ki-tu*$_2$
^{Id}*dan-nu*-ŠEŠ^{me}-*šu*$_2$-DU$_3$ A ^{f}*a-na-ta-ba-ni-šu*$_2$ KI.MIN
^{I}*gi-mil-lu* A ^{Id}EN-*iq-bi ina* TIN.TIR^{ki}
^{I}*u*$_2$*-bar* A ^{I}LU$_2$-^{d}*na-na-a ina* UD.UNUG^{ki}
⸢^{I}⸣^{d}15-LUGAL-URU$_3$ *ša*$_2$ ^{lu_2}GAR KUR *ina na-aš*$_2$*-par-ti*
PAP 7 (blank)

---

^{Id}UTU-MU-DU A° ^{I}*ḫaš-di-ia*
^{Id}*na-na-a*-MU ⸢DUMU$^{!}$⸣-*šu*$_2$ ^{I}DU$_3$-^{d}15 ŠEŠ-⸢*šu*$_2$⸣
^{I}*re-e-mu-tu* ⸢*ša*$_2$⸣ ^{Id}MAŠ-LUGAL-URU$_3$
⸢^{I}⸣*ni-din-ti* ŠEŠ-*šu*$_2$
Lo.E. ⸢^{I}⸣^{d}AG-*di-i-ni*-DU$_3$^{uš} *ša*$_2$ ^{I}BAD$_3$-*la*-⸢*a*⸣
[^{Id}]*dan-nu*-ŠEŠ^{me}-*šu*$_2$-DU$_3$ A ^{Id}AG-AŠ-URU$_3$
ina TIN.TIR^{ki}
Rev. ⸢^{I}⸣MU-MU ŠEŠ-*šu*$_2$ *ina* UD.UNUG^{ki}
^{I}*ṣa-ṣi-ru* {^{lu_2}} KI.MIN
[PAP] ⸢9⸣ ^{lu_2}*pu-ṣa-a-a*

---

^{I}⸢^{d}⸣UTU-MU A ^{Id}*na-na-a*-MU
^{I}E$_2$.AN.NA-MU-DU$_3$° A ^{I}*šu-la-a*
^{Id}EN-SUR A ^{I}IR$_3$-^{d}AG
^{I}IR$_3$-^{d}*in-nin* ŠEŠ-*šu*$_2$
^{Id}*na-na-a*-MU *ina* TIN.TIR^{ki}
^{Id}AG-SUR-ZI^{me} *ina na-aš*$_2$*-par-ti*
^{Id}15-*re-ṣu-u*$_2$*-a ina* UD.UNUG^{ki}
^{Id}UTU-*ka-ṣir u* ^{Id}UTU-ŠEŠ-MU$^{!}$ DUMU^{meš}
(tiny inserted line) *ša*$_2$ ^{I}MU-URU$_3$

^{Id}UTU-MU *u* ^{Id}⸢*a-nu*⸣-LUGAL-URU$_3$ ⸢DUMU⸣^{me} *ša*$_2$ ^{I}*še-el-li-bi*
PAP 9 ^{lu_2}*pu-ṣa-a-a ša*$_2$ ŠU^{II} ^{Id}UTU-MU

---

^{I}DU$_3$-^{d}15 A ^{Id}EN-NIGIN$_2$^{ir} ^{I}*e-du-u*$_2$*-a* ^{lu_2}*qal-la-šu*$_2$
^{Id}15-ŠEŠ-MU A ^{Id}AG-GAL$_2$^{ši}
^{Id}EN-KAR-^{d}UTU A ^{Id}15-NUMUN-DU$_3$
^{I}IR$_3$-^{d}AG *u* ^{I}*u*$_2$*-bar* <*ša*$_2$> *a-na bu-le-e šap-ru*
PAP 5 ^{lu_2}SIMUG ⸢AN⸣.BAR

---

^{Id}UTU-DU$_3$ ^{Id}UTU-DINGIR-[*u*$_2$]-⸢*a*⸣ ^{Id}INNIN-*u*$_2$*-kin*
^{I}*ba-ku-u*$_2$*-a* ^{Id}AG-TIN$^{⸢su⸣}$-E
^{I}*nad-na-a* A ^{I}*gi-mil-lu*
^{I}DU$_3$-^{d}15 {A ^{I}} *ina* UD.UNUG^{ki}
^{I}*id-di-ia it-ti* ^{I}*kal-ba-a* ^{lu_2}GAL ⸢*ka-a-ri*⸣
^{I}IR$_3$$^{!}$-^{d}ME.ME *u* ^{Id}⸢*dan*⸣*-nu*-ŠEŠ^{me}-*šu*$_2$-DU$_3$ *ina na-aš*$_2$*-par-ti*
PAP 10 ^{lu_2}AŠGAB^{meš}

---

^{I}KI-^{d}EN-*ab-ni* ^{I}IR$_3$-⸢*ia*$_2$⸣ DUMU-*šu*$_2$
^{I}*na-din ina* TIN.TIR^{ki} ^{I}*ana*-^{d}15-*tak-lak*
⸢*ina* UD.UNUG^{ki}⸣ ^{Id}*dan-nu*-⸢ŠEŠ^{me}⸣-*šu*$_2$-DU$_3$ A ^{munus}*za-ki-tu*$_2$
[PAP ×] ^{lu_2}*mu-šal-lim-ma-nu*
[^{I}]*ḫaš-da-a* ^{Id}*na-na-a*-[×] ⸢×⸣
Up.E. [ ]⸢^{Id}AG⸣-*ba-ni a*$^{!}$*-na bu*-⸢*le-e*⸣
[ ]-⸢×⸣ *ina* UD.UNUG^{ki}
[PAP × ^{lu_2}]SIMUG AN.BAR *ša*$_2$ ŠU^{II} ^{I}*ḫaš-d*[*a-a*]
Le.E.$_{I}$ [^{I}]⸢^{d}*in*⸣*-nin*-NUMUN-GAL$_2$^{ši} ^{I}E$_2$.AN.NA-⸢*lip*⸣-URU$_3$
[^{I}I]R$_3$-*ia*$_2$ ^{I}DU$_3$-*ia*$_2$ ^{I}*gi-mil-lu* ^{I}*u*$_2$*-qu-pu*$^{!}$
[^{I}]^{d}*na-na-a*-ŠEŠ-MU A ^{Id}AG-SUR *ina* UD.UNUG$^{⸢ki⸣}$
^{I}MU-URU$_3$ *u* ^{I}*gu-za*-⸢*nu*⸣ *ina* TIN.TIR^{ki}
^{I}⸢NUMUN-*ia*$_2$⸣-[*a*] A ^{Id}*in-nin*-MU-URU$_3$ ^{lu_2}GIG
^{Id}UTU-NUMUN-DU$_3$ A ^{Id}AG-DU-IBILA$^{?}$

Le.E.$_{II}$ ^{Id}UTU-NUMUN-DU$_3$ A ^{I}KI-^{d}UTU-TIN
^{I}*zu-um-bu* ŠEŠ-*šu*$_2$
^{Id}*dan-nu*-ŠEŠ^{me}-*šu*$_2$-<DU$_3$> ^{lu_2}GIG
^{I}SUM.NA-*a* A ^{munus}*za-ki-tu*$_2$

[ ] 19th(+) day of month V [ ] ...:
Gimillu, son of Nabû-zēru-iqīša; Anu-šumu-ibni, son of Madān-ēreš; Itti-enši-Nabû, son of Šulāya; Šamaš-aḫu-iddin, son of Nabû-aḫḫē-šullim; Šamaš-šumu-iddin, son of Šamaš-zēru-iqīša; Nidintu, son of Nabû-mušētiq-uddê, a proxy; total of five*sic* *fine woodwork* carpenters. Innin-šumu-uṣur, son of Ṭāb-Uruk; Ina-tēšî-ēṭir and Anu-šarru-uṣur, sons of Rēmūtu; Arad-Bēl and Šamaš-ēṭir, sons of Silim-Bēl; Kalbāya, son of Nabû-silim, a proxy; Kî-Šamaš, in Larsa; Ištar-aḫu-iddin, (standing) for Kidinnu; Amīl-Nanāya, sick; total of nine weavers of colored cloth.
Erībšu, son of Nanāya-iddin, and Šamaš-zēru-ibni, his son; Arad-Innin, son of ^{f}Ana-bītišu, a *zakītu*-woman; Dannu-aḫḫēšu-ibni, son of ^{f}Ana-tab(a)nîšu, ditto; Gimillu, son of Bēl-iqbi,

in Babylon; Ubāru, son of Amīl-Nanāya, in Larsa; Ištar-šarru-uṣur, (man) of the governor (of the Sealand), a proxy; total of seven (blank).

Šamaš-šumu-ukīn, son of Ḫašdia; Nanāya-iddin, his son; Ibni-Ištar, his brother; Rēmūtu, (man) of Ninurta-šarru-uṣur; Nidintu, his brother; Nabû-dīni-īpuš, (man) of Dūrlāya; Dannu-aḫḫēšu-ibni, son of Nabû-ēdu-uṣur, in Babylon; Šumu-iddin, his brother, in Larsa; Ṣāṣiru, ditto; [total of] nine linen weavers.

Šamaš-iddin, son of Nanāya-iddin; Eanna-šumu-ibni, son of Šulāya; Bēl-ēṭir, son of Arad-Nabû; Arad-Innin, his brother; Nanāya-iddin, in Babylon; Nabû-ēṭir-napšāti, a proxy; Ištar-rēṣūa, in Larsa; Šamaš-kāṣir and Šamaš-aḫu-iddin, sons of Šumu-uṣur; Šamaš-iddin and Anu-šarru-uṣur, sons of Šellibi; total of nine linen weavers under the responsibility of Šamaš-iddin.

Ibni-Ištar, son of Bēl-upaḫḫir; Ēdūa, his slave; Ištar-aḫu-iddin, son of Nabû-ušabši; Bēl-eṭēri-Šamaš, son of Ištar-zēru-ibni; Arad-Nabû and Ubāru, who were sent for firewood; total of five blacksmiths.

Šamaš-ibni; Šamaš-ilua; Ištar-ukīn; Bākûa; Nabû-balāssu-iqbi; Nadnāya, son of Gimillu; Ibni-Ištar, in Larsa; Iddia, with Kalbāya, the harbor overseer; Arad-Gula and Dannu-aḫḫēšu-ibni, proxy / ies; total of ten leatherworkers.

Itti-Bēl-abni; Ardia, his son; Nādinu, in Babylon; Ana-Ištar-taklāk, in Larsa; Dannu-aḫḫēšu-ibni, son of a *zakītu*-woman; [total of ×] *mušallimānus*.

[...] Ḫašdāya; Nanāya-...; [...]; Nabû-bāni, for firewood [...] ..., in Larsa; [total of ×] blacksmiths under the responsibility of Ḫašdāya.

Innin-zēru-šubši; Eanna-līpu-uṣur; Ardia; Bānia; Gimillu; Uqūpu; Nanāya-aḫu-iddin, son of Nabû-ēṭir, in Larsa; Šumu-uṣur and Guzānu, in Babylon; Zēria, son of Innin-šumu-uṣur, sick; Šamaš-zēru-ibni, son of Nabû-mukīn-*apli*.

Šamaš-zēru-ibni, son of Itti-Šamaš-balāṭu; Zumbu, his brother; Dannu-aḫḫēšu-ibni, sick; Iddināya, son of a *zakītu*-woman.

9 *Nagār qutāni*: see glossary.

14 Note the reading ^{I}*ki-i-*^{d}UTU, rather than *qi*$_2$-*bi-*^{d}UTU, as read in Payne 2013, 190 (rendered again Qibi-Šamaš in p. 142).

18–24 These seven men are not identified by their profession, but they are known to be weavers; see Payne 2007 for prosopography.

20 We propose to normalize the second name as Ana-tabnîšu, taking the noun *tabnû*, as an otherwise unattested variant of *tabnītu*.

61 The CAD (M/II, 256) translates *mušallimānu*, presumably based on context, as 1. (a craftsman), 2. (uncertain meaning), while the AHw's (p. 680) "Überbringer" relies on the derivation from *šalāmu*. In the present case, the context indeed points to a craftsman (alongside the blacksmiths, leatherworkers, etc.), but derivation from *šlm* gives too wide a semantic range.

297. YBC 9268

Copy: Plate LXXIX
Date: 11.VIII.22 Nbk
Summary: personnel list

Obv. ^{I}⸢*ta-ri-*[*bi* A ^{I}]
^{Id}AG-ŠEŠ-MU ⸢A $^{\mathrm{Id?}}$ ×⸣[ ]
^{I}SUM.NA-ŠEŠ A ^{Id}AG-ḪI.⸢LI$^{!?}$⸣-[DINGIR$^{\mathrm{meš?}}$]

^{I}*mu-še-zib*-^{d}EN A ^{Id}U.GUR-SUR
^{I}*ba-la-ṭu* A ^{I}LU$_2$-^{d}*na-na-a*
^{Id}*na-na-a*-ŠEŠ-MU A ^{I}EN-*šu*$_2$-*nu*
^{Id}*na-na-a*-ŠEŠ-MU A ^{Id}AG-MU
^{Id}AG-MU-DU A ^{Id}AMAR.UTU-MU-DU$_3$
^{Id}EN-*at-ta*-DA *ša*$_2$ ^{Id}AMAR.UTU-DUB-NUMUN
^{I}*re-mut* A ^{I}*šu-ma-a*
^{Id}AG-SUR-ZI^{meš} A ^{I}*ḫaš-di-ia*$_2$
PAP 11 *ina* IGI ^{I}*ta-rib*

---

^{I}I-^{d}INNIN A ^{Id}AG-NUMUN-MU
^{Id}AG-SUR A ^{Id}*na-na-a*-KAM
^{Id}AG-ŠEŠ-MU A ^{Id}AG-NUMUN-BA^{ša_2}
^{Id}INNIN-MU-KAM A ^{Id}AG-ŠEŠ-MU
[^{I}]⸢KI-E$_2$.AN.NA⸣-*bu-di-ia*$_2$ ^{lu_2}SIPA *iṣ-ṣur*
Lo.E. ⸢^{I}⸣*ina*-GISSU-^{d}*na-na-a* A ^{Id}U.⸢GUR-×⸣
Rev. ^{I}⸢^{d}INNIN-*re-ṣu*⸣-*u*$_2$-*a* *ša*$_2$ ^{I}IGI-⸢*dum-qi*$_2$⸣-[^{d}×]
^{Id}⸢*na-na*⸣-*a*-MU ^{lu_2}AŠGAB
^{I}SUM.NA-*a* *ša*$_2$ ^{Id}EN-ŠEŠ^{meš}-SU [(×)]
^{I}⸢*šu-la*⸣-*a* A ^{Id}AG-ŠEŠ^{meš}-GI
PAP 10 ^{lu_2}ERIN$_2^{me}$ *ina* IGI ^{I}I-⸢^{d}INNIN⸣
^{Id}AG-*ana*${}^{!}$-*ka-a-šu*$_2$-*at-kal* *ša*$_2$ ^{I}*tab-ne*$_2$-*e-a*
^{Id}INNIN-NUMUN-DU$_3$ A ^{I}ŠEŠ^{meš}-*ša*$_2$-*a*
^{I}IR$_3$-^{d}INNIN.NA A ^{I}⸢KI⸣.NE-*na-a-a*
^{I}IR$_3$-^{d}ME.ME A ^{I}LU$_2$-^{d}*na-na-a*
^{I}LU$_2$-^{d}*na-na-a* A ^{Id}AG-NUMUN-DU$_3$
^{I}*la-ba-ši u* ^{Id}AG-ŠEŠ-MU 1^{en} ^{lu_2}ENGAR
^{Id}AG-*si-lim* A ^{I}*ki-na-a*
^{I}IGI-*dum-qi*$_2$-^{d}INNIN A ^{I}DUG$_3$.GA-IM-E$_2$.AN.NA
^{Id}EN-*iq-bi* A ^{Id}AG-GI
(tiny line) ^{Id}*na-na-a*-KAM A ^{Id}⸢*na-na-a*-ŠEŠ^{meš}-MU⸣
PAP 10 ^{lu_2}ERIN$_2^{me}$ *ina* IGI ${}^{I⸢d⸣}$[AG-*ana-ka-a-šu*$_2$-*at-k*]*al*⸢×
⸢PAP⸣ 31${}^{!}$ ^{lu_2}ER[IN$_2^{meš}$]
[(+ one line broken?)]
Le.E. ^{iti}APIN UD.11.KAM MU.22.KAM
^{d}AG-NIG$_2$.⸢DU⸣-KAM LUGAL TIN.TIR^{ki}

Tarību, [son of ...]; Nabû-aḫu-iddin, son of ...; Nādin-aḫi, son of Nabû-*ku*[*zub-ilī*]; Mušēzib-Bēl, son of Nergal-ēṭir; Balāṭu, son of Amīl-Nanāya; Nanāya-aḫu-iddin, son of Bēlšunu; Nanāya-aḫu-iddin, son of Nabû-iddin; Nabû-šumu-ukīn, son of Marduk-šumu-ibni; Bēl-atta-talê, for Marduk-šāpik-zēri; Rēmūtu, son of Šumāya; Nabû-ēṭir-napšāti, son of Ḫašdia; total of eleven (men) are at the disposal of Tarību.

Na'id-Ištar, son of Nabû-zēru-iddin; Nabû-ēṭir, son of Nanāya-ēreš; Nabû-aḫu-iddin, son of Nabû-zēru-iqīša; Ištar-šumu-ēreš, son of Nabû-aḫu-iddin; Itti-Eanna-būdia, the bird-herder; Ina-ṣilli-Nanāya, son of Nergal-...; Ištar-rēṣū'a, for Lūmur-dumqi-[DN]; Nanāya-iddin, the leatherworker; Iddināya, for Bēl-aḫḫē-erība; Šulāya, son of Nabû-aḫḫē-šullim; total of ten men at the disposal of Na'id-Ištar.

Nabû-ana-kâšu-atkal, for Tabnēa; Ištar-zēru-ibni, son of Aḫḫēšāya; Arad-Innin, son of Kinūnāya; Arad-Gula, son of Amīl-Nanāya; Amīl-Nanāya, son of Nabû-zēru-ibni; Lâbâši and Nabû-aḫu-iddin, one plowman (of the two)?; Nabû-silim, son of Kīnāya; Lūmur-dumqi-Ištar, son of Ṭāb-šār-Eanna; Bēl-iqbi, son of Nabû-ušallim; Nanāya-ēreš, son of Nanāya-aḫḫē-iddin; total of ten men at the disposal of [Nabû-ana-kâšu-atkal].
(Grand) total: thirty-one me[n (...)].
Month VIII, day 11, year 22 of Nebuchadnezzar, king of Babylon.

9 The name ^{Id}EN-*at-ta*-DA is attested CT 56, 439: 6 (19 Nbk) from Sippar; read Bēl-attaDA(?) in Joannès 1994. The name should probably be read Bēl-atta-talê, "Bēl you are able," alternatively "you are (my)? strength."

23–24 While there is no ruling between these two lines, there is a small gap separating the two lists.

29 It seems that only one of the two, Lâbâši and Nabû-aḫu-iddin, is counted in this decury.

298. NBC 4864

Copy: Plate LXXIX
Date: undated (late Nbk–Cyr)
Summary: personnel list

The following datable attestations form the chronological horizon for the tablet: Amīl-Nanāya, 24 Nbk[33] (UCP 9/2, 21); Ērišu, Nbn (YOS 19, 115), see Payne 2007, 304; Innin-zēru-šubši, 43 Nbk (PTS 2629), see Payne 2007, 309; Kalbāya, Nbn–5 Cyr (YOS 19, 115, NBC 4598), see Payne 2007, 176; Nanāya-iddin, 39 Nbk–5 Cyr (GC 1, 145, NBC 4598), see Payne 2007, 187; Šamaš-iddin, 0a–6 Nbn (PTS 2038, YOS 6, 74).

Obv. ^{I}IR$_{3}$-^{d}*in-nin* A-*šu*$_{2}$
ša$_{2}$ ^{I}*a*$^{!}$-*na*-^{d}INNIN-*tak-lak*
^{Id}*in-nin*-NUMUN-GAL$_{2}^{\check{s}i}$
u ^{I}*e-riš* ^{lu_2}⸢SIMUG⸣ AN.BAR
^{Id}UTU-MU *u* ^{Id}⸢*na-na*⸣-*a*-MU
^{lu_2}*pu-ṣa-a-a*
^{I}*gi-mil-lu* ^{lu_2}AŠGAB
^{I}LU$_{2}$-^{d}*na-na-a* *u* ^{I}SUM.NA-ŠEŠ
ša$_{2}$ ŠUK.ḪI.A LUGAL
^{I}*kal-ba-a* *u* ^{Id}UTU-DU$_{3}$ <^{lu_2}>UŠ.BAR^{m}[$^{e(\check{s})}$]
PAP 10 ^{lu_2}ERIN^{me}
{eras.}
{eras.}
Rev. (uninscribed)

Arad-Innin, son of Ana-Ištar-taklāk; Innin-zēru-šubši and Ērišu, the blacksmith(s); Šamaš-iddin and Nanāya-iddin, the linen weaver(s); Gimillu, the leatherworker; Amīl-Nanāya and Nādin-aḫi, (who are in charge) of the royal rations; Kalbāya and Šamaš-ibni, the weavers; a total of ten workmen.

33 He is likely to be identified in GC 1, 151. Although the text is undated, the mention of Tyre points to a 30 Nbk onwards date for the tablet. For the "late Tyre dossier" in the Eanna archive see Van der Brugge and Kleber 2016.

299. YBC 15720

Copy: Plate LXXX
Date: undated (*early Nbk*)
Summary: tabulated accounting inventory

The identification of Nabû-aḫu-iddin, the bronzesmith (l. 19′), as the one mentioned attested in YOS 17, 325: 8 (8 Nbk), and possibly Nabû-zēru-iddin, the [*smith*] (l. 13′, multiple attestations Npl–Nbk), point to an early Nebuchadnezzar date of the tablet.

Obv. (beginning broken)

PAP 10 [(+×)]			[ ]
PAP 12			[ ]
PAP 9		2	⸢*ša*$_2$ ^{I}*ša*$_2$-*du*⸣-[*nu* (A ^{I}...)]
PAP 6		{+1}	*ša*$_2$ ^{I}DUG$_3$.GA A ^{I}⸢×⸣[ ]
PAP 11			*ša*$_2$ ^{I}*e-zu-u*$_2$-*pa-š*[*ir*$_3$] [(A ^{I}...)]
⸢PAP 8⸣			*ša*$_2$ ^{I}SUM.NA-*a* ⸢A⸣ [ ]
[PAP ×]			*ša*$_2$ ^{Id}EN-SUR ⸢A⸣ [ ]
⸢PAP 10⸣ [(+×)]		⸢1?⸣	*ša*$_2$ ^{I}ŠEŠ^{me}-*ša*$_2$-*a* ⸢A?⸣[ ]
PAP ⸢8⸣		⸢1⸣	*ša*$_2$ ^{I}E$_2$.AN.NA-*l*[*i-pi*-URU$_3$ (...)]
PAP ⸢9?⸣		⸢4?	*ša*$_2$⸣ ^{Id}U.GUR-MU ⸢A⸣ [ ]
PAP [ ]		2	⸢*ša*$_2$⸣ ^{I}DUG$_3$.GA-UNUG^{k}[^{i}]
PAP [ ]			⸢*ša*$_2$⸣ [^{I}]⸢^{d}EN/AG-×-× A⸣ [ ]
[PAP ×]		13	⸢*ša*$_2$⸣ [^{I}]⸢^{d}AG⸣-NUMUN-MU ^{I}[^{lu_2}SIMUG?]
⸢PAP 9?⸣		2 GIŠ	*ša*$_2$ ^{I}⸢*na*⸣-[*din*?] ⸢A ^{I}SUM?-*a*? ×⸣ [(...)]
PAP 11 [(+×)]			*ša*$_2$ ^{I}⸢^{d}AG⸣-[×-M]U? A ^{I}⸢*nad-na*⸣-[*a*]
PAP ⸢9?⸣		1	*ša*$_2$ ^{Id}AG-⸢GAL$_2$⸣^{ši} ^{lu_2}ŠITIM [ ]
PAP ⸢6⸣		1	*ša*$_2$ ^{Id}*u*[*ra*]*š*-MU A ^{Id}*na-na-a*-KAM
PAP 8		4	*ša*$_2$ ^{I}IR$_3$-⸢*ia*$_2$⸣ A ^{I}*nad-na-a*

	PAP 17			*ša*$_2$ ^{Id}AG-š[E]š-MU $^{\text{lu}_2}$SIMUG ZABAR
20′	PAP 13			*ša*$_2$ ^{I}SUM.NA-[Š]EŠ$^{?}$ $^{\text{lu}_2}$NAGAR^{me}
	⸢PAP⸣ 8			⸢*ša*$_2$ ^{I}*ša*$_2$-^{d}AG-*šu*$_2$-*u*⸣ $^{\text{lu}_2}$NAGAR^{me}
	⸢PAP 11⸣		⸢4⸣	*ša*$_2$ ^{I}⸢×⸣[ ] $^{\text{lu}_2}$⸢UŠ.BAR^{me}⸣
	[PAP] ⸢8$^{?}$⸣			*ša*$_2$ ^{I}⸢^{d}⸣[EN/AG-...]
24′	[PAP ×]			⸢*ša*$_2$ ^{Id}⸣[EN/AG-...]
Lo.E.	[PAP] ⸢10⸣[(+×)]		⸢1	*ša*$_2$ ^{I}⸣[ ]
Rev.	⸢PAP 6$^{?}$ ½⸣		2 GIŠ	^{I}⸢DUG$_3$$^{?}$⸣.G[A$^{?}$]
	⸢PAP⸣ 10		8 GIŠ	^{Id}*n*[*a-na-a*-×]
	⸢PAP⸣ 11			^{I}LU$_2$-^{d}*n*[*a-na-a*]
	⸢PAP⸣ 3 ½			^{Id}UTU-⸢*u*$_2$$^{?}$⸣-[ ]
30′	⸢PAP⸣ 13		4 GIŠ	*ša*$_2$ ^{Id}UTU-⸢×⸣ [$^{\text{lu}_2}$×]⸢^{me}⸣
	⸢PAP⸣ 13		2 GIŠ	*ša*$_2$ ^{Id}INNIN.N[A-× $^{\text{lu}_2}$×]^{me}
	⸢PAP 12⸣		1	*ša*$_2$ ^{I}*ta*-[ ]^{me}
	⸢PAP 11⸣		1	*ša*$_2$ ^{Id}AG-⸢*u*$_2$$^{?}$⸣[ ] ⸢×⸣
	PAP 8		⸢1$^{?}$⸣	*ša*$_2$ ^{Id}AG-⸢×⸣[ ]
35′	PAP 8		1	*ša*$_2$ ^{I}*ki*-⸢*din*$^{?}$⸣ [ ]
	⸢PAP 7$^{?}$⸣		3	*ša*$_2$ ^{I}⸢^{d}U⸣.[GUR-×]
	PAP ⸢13$^{?}$⸣		1	*ša*$_2$ ^{Id}AG-[ ]
	PAP 9		2 GIŠ	*ša*$_2$ ^{I}⸢*ina*⸣-GIS[SU$^{?}$-^{d}×]
	PAP 6		[×	*ša*$_2$] ⸢^{I}⸣[ ]
40′	PAP 12		11 [	*ša*$_2$ ^{I}]
	⸢PAP⸣ 8		1[(×)	*ša*$_2$ ^{I}]

PAP 14		10[(×) *ša*$_2$ ^{I}]
PAP 8		[(×) *ša*$_2$ ^{I}]
PAP ⸢9⸣		[(×)] ⸢*ša*$_2$ ^{I}⸣[ ]
PAP 9		1 GIŠ *ša*$_2$ ^{I}⸢×⸣[ ]
PAP 10		4 *ša*$_2$ ^{I}*ša*$_2$-[ ]
PAP 7$^?$		1 *ša*$_2$ ^{I}⸢*na*$^?$⸣[ ]
PAP 7		2 *ša*$_2$ ^{I}⸢×⸣[ ]
PAP 8		2 ⸢GIŠ⸣ *ša*$_2$ ^{I}[ ]
[PAP] ⸢8$^?$⸣		2 GIŠ *ša*$_2$ ^{I}⸢*na*$^?$⸣[ ]
[PAP ×]		⸢1⸣ *ša*$_2$ ⸢^{I}×⸣ [ ]

(remainder broken)

total: 10[(+)]		[ ]
total: 12		[ ]
total: 9		2 of Šadû[nu, (son of)]
total: 6		of Ṭābia, son of [ ]
total: 11		of Ezu-pašir, [(son of)]
total: 8		of Nadnāya, son of [ ]
[total: ×]		of Bēl-ēṭir, son of [ ]
total: 10[(+)]		*1* of Aḫḫēšāya, son of [ ]
total: 8		1 of Eanna-l[īpu-uṣur (son of)]
total: *9*		*4* of Nergal-iddin, son of [ ]
total: [×]		2 of Ṭāb-Uruk [(son of)]
total: [×]		of *Bēl*/*Nabû*-..., son of [ ]

[total: ×]		13	of Nabû-zēru-iddin, the [*smith*]
total: *9*		2 *GIŠ*	of N*ā*[*din*], son of *Nadnāya* [( )]
total: 11[(+)]			of Nabû-[×-*id*]*din*, son of Nadnāya
total: *9*		1	of Nabû-ušabši, the builder
total: 6		1	of Uraš-iddin, son of Nanāya-ēreš
total: 8		4	of Ardia, son of Nadnāya
total: 17			of Nabû-aḫu-iddin, the bronzesmith
total: 13			of Nādin-*aḫi*, carpenters
total: 8			of Ša-Nabû-šū, carpenters
total: 11		4	of …, weavers
[total]: *8*			of [ ]
[total: ×]			of [ ]
[total]: 10[(+)]		1	of [ ]
total: *6½*		2 *GIŠ*	Ṭa[b-…]
total: 10		8 *GIŠ*	N[anāya-×]
total: 11			Amīl-N[anāya]
total: 3½			Šamaš-*u*[ ]
total: 13		4 *GIŠ*	of Šamaš-…, […]s
total: 13		2 *GIŠ*	of Innin-[…, …]s
total: 12		1	of Ta[…, …]s
total: 11		1	of Nabû-*u*[ ]
total: 8		*1*	of Nabû-…
total: 8		1	of Kidin[ ]

total: *7*		3	of Ne[rgal-×]
total: *13*		1	of Nabû-[ ]
total: 9		2 *GIŠ*	of Ina-ṣil[li-DN]
total: 6		[	of …]
total: 12		11	[of …]
total: 8		1[(+)	of …]
total: 14		10[(+)	of …]
total: 8		[(×)	of …]
total: 9		[(×)]	of […]
total: 9		1 *GIŠ*	of … [ ]
total: 10		4	of Ša[ ]
total: *7*		1	of *Na*[…]
total: 7		2	of … [ ]
total: 8		2 *GIŠ*	of […]
[total]: *8*		2 *GIŠ*	of *Na*[…]
[total: ×]		1	of … […]

14′ Also ll. 26′, 27′, 30′, 31′, 38′, 45′, 49′, 50′: The form and meaning of GIŠ is unclear. It may stand for a form of *našû* and thus indicate an amount that was already withdrawn by the listed individual. In this case, however, the difference between these and the multiple entries with secondary figures but with no GIŠ is unclear.

300. NCBT 1031

Copy: Plate LXXIX; photograph of reverse on Plate LXXXIX
Date: 24.V.21 (Nbk)
Summary: *ina pāni* note(?): unclear

Taqīš-Gula may cautiously be identified as the *kabšarru* Taqīš-Gula//Kiribtu//Nūr-Sîn, attested 18 Npl–9 Nbk; see Payne 2007, 276. According to the Neo-Babylonian chronicle ABC 5: 8–10, Nabopolassar died in the eighth day of Abu. It is thus unlikely that year 21 refers to Nabopolassar's reign, as it would have been two and a half weeks past his death.

Obv. ⸢1$^?$ *mas*$^?$-*sa*$^?$⸣-*ni*
^{I}*ta-qiš*-^{d}ME.<ME>
a-na bat-qa ša$_2$ *ir*-⸢*tu*$_2$⸣
^{iti}NE UD.24.⸢KAM⸣
Lo.E. MU.21.KAM
Rev. (a sketch of a rosette/flower)

1 ... (*at the disposal of*) Taqīš-Gula, for the repair of the breast (ornament).
Month V, day 24, year 21.

1 The word ⸢*mas*$^?$-*sa*$^?$⸣-*ni*, if the reading is correct, is unclear; a variant of *maššânu*, "tongs," is unlikely. Also problematic would be to read the final -*ni* as part of an *ina pāni* clause. First, the preceding traces do not seem to fit. Additionally, this clause would have been placed after the *ana batqa* clause.

301. NBC 4606

Copy: Plate LXXXI
Date: 11.I.[×] Nbk
Summary: inventory list: chariot equipment

The text closely resembles Pinches 1928, 132–4 in both content and format.[34] Pinches's text seems to be better preserved and requires collation, especially given the schematic facsimile, which makes it much more difficult to reinterpret the several problematic parts in the edition.

Obv. [*u*$_2$-*de-e ša*$_2$ ^{giš}GIGIR]
[ ] ⸢× ×⸣ [ ] ⸢× ITI$^?$⸣.B[ARA$_2$$^?$ *ša*$_2$$^?$]
[*si-in*]-⸢*qu*⸣-*ma* ⸢*ina*$^?$⸣ [ŠU$^{II?}$] ^{lu_2}SIPA AN[ŠE.KUR.RA^{meš} IGI$^{?u?}$]

2$^?$-⸢*ta*⸣ *iš-pat* KU$_3$.G[I *a*]-⸢*a*⸣-*ri* ⸢KU$_3$⸣.G[I]
[(1+)] 2 GIR$_2$ AN.BAR KU$_3$.BA[BBAR$^?$ × ×] ⸢SIK$_2$$^?$ ×⸣ [ ]
4 *me-ṭu*^{meš} S[A]G.DU ⸢×⸣[ ]
2-*ta* ^{giš}BAN^{me} ⸢KU$_3$.BABBAR⸣ SAG.DU [ ]
2 *ka-la-pu* S[A]G.DU *u* ⸢×⸣[ ]
2 NIG$_2$.GUL$^{?!(T. ugu)}$ <AN>.BAR [×]⸢×⸣^{meš} K[U$_2$.GI/BABBAR]
2 *qu-ul*-⸢*le*⸣-*e* K[U$_3$.GI/BABBAR]
2 *ḫu-na-qa*-⸢*nu*⸣ *u a-a-r*[*i-šu*$_2$-*nu ša*$_2$ KU$_3$.GI/BABBAR]
6 *ḫi-in-ša*$_2$-*nu* [S]AG.DU *u* ⸢×⸣ [ ]
1 *ad-du* [(×) S]AG.DU [ ]
56 *a-a-ri* [K]U$_3$.GI TUR^{me} ⸢*ša*$_2$⸣ [UGU *pu-ug*]-⸢*da-a-tu*$_2$⸣
10 *a-a-r*[*i*] KU$_3$.GI GAL^{m}[^{e} *ša*$_2$ UGU *p*]*u-ug-da-a-tu*$_2$
2 ⸢$^{giš?}$⸣[× ×] ⸢×⸣ KU$_3$.GI ⸢2-*ta a*/*ša*$_2$$^?$ *ṣab*$^?$⸣ *tu*$_4$ KU$_3$.GI
1-*et*$^!$ *a*$^!$-*a*-[*r*]*i-it-tu*$_4$ KU$_3$.BABBAR
6 ME 12 *ši-ḫu* KU$_3$.GI *ša*$_2$ UGU

---

[34] Regarding format, Pinches's tablet contains a similar, though not identical (see below) heading. Additionally, unlike the present tablet, most lines in the main text in Pinches's tablet seem to have been indented midway, giving the appearance of two columns. This, however, dose not seem to be related to actual content, and might have more to do with the fact that Pinches's facsimile was mechanically produced (rather than an actual hand-copy). The tablet requires collation.

pu-ug-da-a-ta ina lib$_3$*-bi* 3 *ina* <^{giš}>*šad*$^!$*-du ša*$_2$ *bat-qa*
2-*ta* NIG$_2$^{o}.⸢GAL$_2$⸣.LA^{me} AN.BAR
2-*ta ku-us-bir-tu*$_3$$^{!me}$ KU$_3$.BABBAR *ša*$_2$ *ḫu-na-qa-nu* KU$_3$.BABBAR
2 *sa*$^{?!(T.\ e_2)}$*-ḫa-ri* KU$_3$.BABBAR *sik-kat*$_2$*-šu*$_2$*-nu* KU$_3$.BABBAR
1 GIR$_2$ AN.BAR *ir-bi*
Lo.E. 1 *ša*$_2$*-a-ri(-)i-šiṭ-ṭu* KU$_3$.BABBAR
1 *iš-tuḫ-ḫu* SAG.DU
10 *il-du* KU$_3$.GI
Rev. 16 *a-a-ri* KU$_3$.GI GAL^{me}
ša$_2$ ⸢UGU$^!$⸣ *na-at-tul-lum-*⸢*me*⸣
ina lib$_3$*-bi* 1 *ina* ^{giš}*šad-du ša*$_2$ *bat-qa*
40 *nu-*⸢*ur*$_2$⸣*-mu* KU$_3$.GI
50 *la-*⸢*ru ša*$_2$$^?$⸣ *nu-ur*$_2$*-mu-u*$_2$ LA$_2$*-u*$_2$
(blank)
⸢PAP$^?$ ⸢*u*$_2$$^?$*-de*$^?$⸣ *ša*$_2$ ^{giš}GIGIR *ša*$_2$ ⸢*si*$^?$⸣-[*in-q*]*u-*⸢*ma*$^{!?}$⸣
^{I}⸢UR⸣-[*a*]$^?$ A ^{Id}EN-ŠEŠ-⸢GAL$_2$⸣^{ši}
^{lu_2}SI[PA A]NŠE.KUR.RA^{me} ⸢IGI^{u_2}⸣
ina lib$_3$-[*bi* (×)] 3 UD SAL ⸢KU$_3$⸣.[GI / BABBAR]
(blank)
^{iti}BARA$_2$ U[D.(×+)]⸢11.KAM M[U.×.KAM]
^{d}AG-NIG$_2$.D[U-URU$_3$] ⸢LUGAL⸣ T[IN.TIR^{ki}]

[*Equipment of the chariot* …] … […] … […] … *month I* [… that was] examined and [*received from*] the hor]se-herders: two quivers of gol[d … r]osettes of gol[d (×); (×+)] two iron daggers, *sil*[*ver* …] *wool* … […]; four *mēṭu*-maces *of/for the head* […]; two silver bows *of/for the head;* two *kalapu*-axes *of/for the head and* […]; two *iron* mattocks … of si[lver / g[old …]; two *qullu*-rings of si[lver / g[old …]; two (horse) collars and [*their*] rosettes [of silver / gold]; six *ḫinšus of/for the head and* […]; one throwing-stick *of/for the head* [(…)]; fifty-six small rosettes of gold for [the bri]dles; ten large rosettes of gold [for the b]ridles; two … of gold; two … of gold; one silver cowrie; 612 *šīḫu*-ornaments of gold for the bridles, three of which are in the repair box; two iron sickles; two silver *cover / bases* of silver (horse) collars; two silver *saḫḫarru*-bowls (*with*) their silver *pin racks;* one iron dagger, (*from the*) income; one *šāri*$^?$ *išiṭṭi*$^?$ of silver; one whip *of/ for the head;* ten golden *bases;* sixteen large gold rosettes for the harness, one of which is in the repair box; forty gold pomegranates; fifty *branches* of pomegranates are *missing;* total of equipment of the chariot that was examined and received from *Kalbāya,* son$^?$ of$^?$ Bēl-aḫu-šubši, the horse-herder. Of which, [(×+)]three … *si*[*lver / g*[*old*].
Month I, day 11, [year ×] of Nebucha[dnezzar], king of Ba[bylon].

1′–3′ Cf. the heading in Pinches 1928, 132–4:

u$_2$*-de-e ša*$_2$ ^{giš}GIGIR *ša*$_2$ ^{d}UD *ša*$_2$ *ina* ŠU^{II} ^{lu_2}SIPA ANŠE <KUR>.R[A]
si-in-qu-ma a-na ^{Id}+EN-ŠEŠ^{meš}-MU A-*šu*$_2$ *ša*$_2$ ^{Id}+AG-⸢×⸣[(×)]
na-ad-nu UD.KIB.NUN^{ki} ^{iti}GU$_4$ UD.14.KAM MU.13.KAM
^{Id}+AG-A-PAP LUGAL TIN.TIR^{ki}

The traces on our tablet cannot be perfectly reconciled with the phrasing on the Sippar tablet. Furthermore, the two tablets were written in different places (Uruk and Sippar) and under two different kings (Nebuchadnezzar and Nabopolassar). The form of *sanāqu* and the reference to the *rē'i-sisê,* however, show that the two tablets must have been written in a very similar context.

6′ Also ll. 7′, 8′, 12′, 13′, 25′: The exact meaning of SAG.DU, presumably for *qaqqadu*, is unclear, but we assume that parts of the horses' headgear are meant.

9′ The GUL$^{?!(T.\ ugu)}$ <bar>.BAR sequence might also be read UD$^{!(T.\ u)}$.KA.BAR, i.e., ZABAR, bronze. Then, however, the NIG$_2$/*ša*$_2$ sign would stand for the object/tool, which in turn means that another sign was probably omitted between the signs NIG$_2$ and ZABAR$^!$.

11′, 21′ For *ḫunāqu*, see glossary.

18′ The *šīḫu*-ornament is unknown. It might be related to the fruit-shaped *šiḫittu*, on which see Beaulieu 2003, 388.

21′ *ḫu-na-qa-nu*; see comment to l. 11′ above.

22′ For *kusibirītu* as a base, or possibly a cover, see Jursa 2006–2008, 225.

23′ The *sikkatu*, usually a peg or a pin, if indeed related to the bowls, were probably used to hang or fasten the bowls.

24′ For *šāri*$^?$ *išiṭṭi*$^?$, see glossary.

28′ The *natt/ddulu* was a part of the harness, not the entire device (CAD N/II, 120).

33′–34′ The plural form ^{lu_2}SI[PA A]NŠE.KUR.RA^{me} (l. 34′) conflicts with the single horse-herder named in l. 33′. Either *Kalbāya* was not the son of Bēl-aḫu-šubši – rather these are two separate herders – or *Kalbāya* represented a group of horse-herders.

35′ The signs UD SAL ⸢KU$_3$⸣ might be read UD.MUNUS.⸢ḪUB$_2^!$⸣ for *algamēšu* stone, though it is unclear how that would fit in the context. Following the *maḫir* clause, the *ina libbi* probably refers to the entire list. The function and the content of such a clause in this position is unclear.

302. YBC 9273

Copy: Plate LXXXI
Date: 12.VI.[×] Nbk
Summary: account settlement: silver[35]

Obv. ⅓ GIN$_2$ KU$_3$.BABBAR *ša*$_2$ *a-na* KI.L[AM]
ša$_2$ GADA.ḪI.A *ina* ŠU^{II} ^{I}*ina*-SUḪ$_3$-[SUR]
A-*šu*$_2$ *ša*$_2$ ^{I}*tab-ne*$_2$*-e-a* A ^{I}ZALAG$_2$-⸢^{d}30⸣
u$_3$ ^{Id}*na-na-a*-MU
^{lu_2}*pu-ṣa-a-a a-na* EDIN
$^{(tiny\ line)}$ *šu-bu-lu*
2 GUN 20 MA.NA
Lo.E. ⸢GADA⸣.ḪI.A *a-na* 18 GIN$_2$ 2$^{⸢ta⸣}$
R.E. ŠU$^{II.me}$ KU$_3$⸣.BABBAR
Rev. ⸢*maḫ*⸣*-ru* 3ta 4$^{tu_2.me}$
a-na i-di ANŠE *u*$_3$ *pi-*⸢*ir-su*⸣
½ GIN$_2$ KU$_3$.BABBAR *a-na* NIG$_2$.GA
bit-qa pa-ri-⸢*du*$^{?*}$⸣
PAP ⅓ GIN$_2$ KU$_3$.BABBAR ⸢×⸣ [(×)]
NIG$_2$.KA$_9$ *it-ti-š*[*u*$_2$*-nu ep*$_2$*-šu*]
^{iti}KIN UD.12[(+×).KAM MU.×.KAM]
Up.E. ^{d}AG-NIG$_2$.DU-URU$_3$
⸢LUGAL TIN⸣.TIR$^{⸢ki⸣}$

35 A previous edition is included in Payne 2007, 109–10.

20 shekels of silver were sent overland with Ina-tēšî-ēṭir, son of Tabnēa, descendant of Nūr-Sîn, and Nanāya-iddin, the linen weaver, for the pur[chase] of linen.
2 talents 20 minas of linen were received (from them, at a cost of) 18 ⅔ shekels of silver; ¾ (shekels of silver) were for the hire of a donkey and (its) weaned foal; ½ shekel of silver were (returned) to the temple store; ⅛ (shekel) for / in *pa-ri-du*$^?$. A total of 20 shekels silver [...]. The account with t[hem is settled].
Month VI, day 12, [year ×] of Nebuchadnezzar, king of Babylon.

13 The reading of the last sign as *du* is uncertain; cf. the reading *pa-ri-*[*is*], translated as "*withheld*" in Payne 2007, 109. The meaning of *pa-ri-*⸢*du*$^?$⸣ is unclear. The CAD (p. 185, *s.v. parīdu*) states "a qualification of silver," while Jursa (2010, 147, note 844) sees it as a commodity. See also Abraham and Sokoloff 2011, 44, no. 165, who rightly reject Von Soden's interpretation as related to Aramaic פרידא, but cannot offer an ulternative interpretation.

13 The listed silver amounts to 20 $^1/_{24}$ shekels.

303. NBC 4859

Copy: Plate LXXXII
Date: undated (Nbn)
Summary: accounting inventory: multiple items

The chronological horizon of the tablet can be established based on the following: Bēl-iddin (l. 23′) is attested between 13 Nbn (PTS 2282) and 1 Nbk IV (YOS 17, 301); see Payne 2007, 161; Nanāya-aḫu-iddin (l. 41′) is attested between 12 Nbk and 14 Nbn (BIN 1, 174); see Payne 2007, 185; Nabû-rēmu-šukun (ll. 26′, 29′) is probably to be identified in TCL 12, 116 (16 Nbn) and PTS 2301 (OrAn 25, 36–7 No. 5) (17 Nbn).

Obv. [upper and left edges broken (much of the Obv. is damaged)]
[ ]⸢× ×⸣
[MA].⸢NA⸣ KU$_3$.BABBAR *id-di-nu*
[*ša*$_2$]⸢× × ×⸣ [ ]⸢*a-di*⸣ 1 MA.NA KU$_3$.BABBAR
[ ]⸢TIN.TIR^{ki}⸣ [ ] *id-di-nu* [ ]⸢×⸣
[ ]⸢× ×⸣ [ ]⸢A⸣ [ ]
[(×+)] 1 GUR ŠE.BAR *ina* ⸢ŠUK⸣.[ḪI.A]
[GU]R$^?$ ^{Id}U.GUR-*na-ṣir* ^{I}⸢×⸣ [ ]
[ ]⸢× *ša*$_2$ *it-ti*⸣ ^{I}*la-a-b*[*a-ši* ( )]
[ ]⸢*ša*$_2$ *a-na*⸣ UGU *ṣe*-⸢*e*⸣-[*nu*]
[(×+)] ⸢1 GUR ŠE⸣.BAR *ina* ŠUK.ḪI.A^{me}-*šu*$_2$-[(*nu*)]
[ ]⸢× *kal*$^?$⸣ -*ia u* 2ta ⸢LI$^{?!}$⸣[ ]
[G]UR ŠE.BAR *ina* ŠUK.ḪI.A^{me}-*šu*$_2$-*nu* [ ]
[ ]⸢DU$^?$ ERIN$_2$$^?$⸣^{meš}-*šu*$_2$ *ša*$_2$ *ina* UGU ^{lu2}ER[IN$_2$]
[ ] TIN.TIR⸢^{ki}⸣ *id-di-nu*
[ ]⸢×⸣ [*a*$^?$]-⸢*na*⸣ *ṣi-di-ti-šu*$_2$-*nu i-di* ⸢ANŠE⸣^{meš}
[ ]⸢MA$_2$⸣ [^{meš}] *ša*$_2$ SIK$_2$.ḪI.A *ina lib*$_3$-*bi u*$_2$-*še-lu-nu*
⸢× GUN⸣ SIK$_2$.⸢ḪI⸣.[A] ⸢*ša*$_2$⸣ *a-na i-di* ^{kuš}*maš-ki-ru*
[*ša*$_2$] ⸢SIK$_2$.ḪI.A⸣ *ul-tu* ^{uru}A.GA.DE$_3$^{ki} *ina lib*$_3$-*bi u*$_2$-*še-lu-nu*
⸢*ina lib*$_3$-*bi* ½ GUN SIK$_2$⸣.ḪI.A GI$_6$^{meš} *ki-i* KA 10 MA.NA SIK$_2$.ḪI.A
[*a*]-*na* ⸢1 GIN$_2$⸣ KU$_3$.BABBAR *na-ad-na*
[(×+)] ⸢4⸣ MA.NA ⅓ 1 GIN$_2$ 3ta *re-bat* KU$_3$.BABBAR ⸢⅓ GUN⸣ SIK$_2$.ḪI.A

⸢*ma-ḫi-ir*⸣ *re-*[*e*$^?$]*-ḫu* 51 GIN$_2$ 3ta *re-bat* KU$_3$.BABBAR *ina* IGI-*šu*$_2$
[(×+)] 1 MA.NA 13 GIN$_2$ ^{gada}*ṭu-ma-nu* ^{Id}EN-MU ^{lu_2}UŠ.BAR
⸢2⸣ ME ŠEŠ.MUŠEN ^{I}*la-qi*$_2$*-pi ma-ḫi-ir*
3 GUN { }SIK$_2$.ḪI.A *ša*$_2$ 40 GUR 4 PI ⸢ŠE.BAR⸣
[(×)] 11 GIN$_2$ KU$_3$.BABBAR ^{Id}AG-ARḪUŠ-*šu-*⸢*kun*⸣
Lo.E. [×] GUN 10 MA.NA *ša*$_2$ 21 GUR ŠE.BAR
^{Id}UTU-*eri*$_4$*-ba*
⸢6⸣ GUN *ša*$_2$ ^{Id}AG-ARḪUŠ-*šu-kun* ^{lu_2}A.[KIN$^?$]
Rev. *ša*$_2$ ^{Id}U.GUR-DU$_3$^{uš} GIŠ^{u_2} *ina* IGI ^{I}[^{u_2}×]
6 GUN SIK$_2$.ḪI.A 3 GUN SIK$_2$.UZ$_3$ *ša*$_2$ 3 ME GUR ŠE.BAR
a-di 1 GUN SIK$_2$.ḪI.A *ša*$_2$ ^{I}*ši-ib-ḫi-ia iš-šu-u*$_2$
^{I}*ša*$_2$*-am-ša*$_2$*-ma-nu* $^{lu_2!}$A.KIN *ša*$_2$ ^{Id}AG-EN-*šu*$_2$*-nu*
3 GUN 25 ½ MA.NA *ša*$_2$ 54 GUR 2 (PI) 3 BAN$_2$ ŠE.BAR 6 GIN$_2$ KU$_3$.BABBAR
[(×)] ^{I}*ba-la-ṭu* A-*šu*$_2$ *ša*$_2$ ^{I}GI-^{d}AMAR.UTU
⸢41° ⅓ MA.NA° *ša*$_2$ 12 GUR 2 PI 1 BAN$_2$$^{?°}$ ŠE.BAR *ina maš-šar-ti-šu*$_2$ ^{I}KA$_5$.A
⸢½⸣ GUN 45 MA.NA 50 GIN$_2$ *ša*$_2$ 31 GUR 3 (PI) 4 BAN$_2$ ŠE.BAR
^{Id}30-KAM *ina lib*$_3$*-bi* 10 GUR ^{I}*še-el-li-bi*
½ GUN 1 ½ MA.NA *ša*$_2$ 9 GUR 2 (PI) 3 BAN$_2$ ^{I}*na-din*
13 MA.NA *ša*$_2$ 3 GUR 4 (PI) 3 BAN$_2$ ^{Id}*na-na-a-*ŠEŠ-MU
22 ½ MA.NA *ša*$_2$ 6 GUR 3 (PI) 4 BAN$_2$ 3 SILA$_3$ ^{I}IR$_3$-^{d}EN
⸢8⸣ GUN *ša*$_2$ 1 ME 44° GUR° ŠE° .BAR ^{Id}UTU-DU-IBILA
1 ⅚ MA.NA 5 GIN$_2$ *ša*$_2$ 3 GUR 2 (PI) 4 BAN$_2$ ^{I}*im-bi-ia*
1 [(+×)] GUN 50 MA.NA *ša*$_2$ 33 GUR ŠE.BAR *a-di* 11 ⸢GUR 2(PI)⸣ [× BAN$_2$] ⸢ŠE.BAR⸣
[(×)] ⸢*ša*$_2$⸣ ^{Id}UTU-DU-IBILA ^{I}KAR-^{d}AMAR.UTU
[(×+)] ⸢2⸣ MA.NA *ša*$_2$ 11 GUR$^{!}$4 PI *ina* ŠA$_3$ 3 GUR *ša*$_2$ ⸢×⸣ [ ]
[ ] ⸢$^{I?!}$*na*$^{?!}$⸣*-din-*A A ^{Id}AMAR.UTU-MU-MU
[× G]U[N] ⸢36⸣ ⅚ MA.NA *ša*$_2$ 31 G[UR] ⸢4$^?$ (PI)⸣ 4 BAN$_2$ ^{Id}*in-nin-*MU-URU$_3$
[(×+)] 2 MA.NA ⸢⅓⸣ GIN$_2$ *ša*$_2$ 4 GUR ⸢3(+$^?$) (PI) 1(+) BAN$_2$⸣ [^{Id}×-M]U-MU
20 MA.NA *ša*$_2$ 9 GUR 3$^{!?}$ (PI) 1$^{!?}$ BAN$_2$ ⸢^{I}⸣^{d}AG-TIN^{su}-E ^{lu_2}*tar-den-ne-e*
⸢58$^?$⸣ MA.NA *ša*$_2$ ⸢19$^?$ GUR⸣ 2 (PI) 2 BAN$_2$ ^{Id}*a-nu-ik-ṣur*
⸢51$^?$⸣ MA.NA *ša*$_2$ ⸢10$^?$⸣ GIN$_2$ 4^{tu_2} ^{I}SUM.NA-*a*
[(×+)] 1 MA.NA *ša*$_2$ 1 ½ GIN$_2$ ^{Id}DI.KUD-LUGAL-URU$_3$
[× ×] ⸢× × × × × ×⸣
[^{Id}]⸢AG$^?$⸣-ŠEŠ-MU
[the rest is broken]

[(beginning broken) … mi]na(s) of silver (that) … gave […] … including 1 mina of silver [that …] Babylon ... gave […] … […] … […] 1(+) kor of barley from the salaries […] kor, Nergal-nāṣir, … […] which was [*sent/intrusted*] with Lâbâši [...] on account of the sheep and goats […] 1(+) kor of barley from their/his salaries […] … *and* 2 … [… ×] kor of barley from their salaries […] … his workers, who are in charge of the *workers* […] [in/to/from$^?$] Babylon, gave […] for their (travel) provisions, rent of donkeys […] boat[s] in which they brought the wool.
× talents of wool for the rent of the rafts with [which] they brought the wool from Akkad; from this, ½ talent of black wool was given at the rate of 10 minas of wool for 1 shekel of silver; 4(+) minas 21 ¾ shekels of silver (for) ⅓ talent of wool, was received; the balance, 51 ¾ shekels of silver, is at his disposal; 1(+) mina 13 shekels of *ṭumānu*-linen thread, Bēl-iddin, the weaver; two-hundred *marratu*-birds were received from Lāqīpi.

3 talents wool for 40;4.0.0 barley; 11(+) shekels silver, Nabû-rēmu-šukun; × talents 10 minas for 21 kor of barley, Šamaš-erība; 6 talents, which Nabû-rēmu-šukun, the *mes*[*senger*] of Nergal-īpuš withdrew, are at the disposal of the ....
6 talents of wool, 3 talents of (goat) hair for 300 kor of barley, including 1 talent of wool that *Šibḫia* withdrew, (is at the disposal of?) Šamšamānu, the messenger of Nabû-bēlšunu.
3 talents 25 ½ minas (of wool) for 54;2.3.0 barley (and) 6 shekels of silver, Balāṭu, son of Mušallim-Marduk; 41 ⅓ minas for 12;2.1.0 barley from the *maššartu* of Šellibi; ½? talent 45 minas 50 shekels for 31;3.4.0 barley, Sîn-ēreš, thereof 10 kor, Šellibi; ½ talent 1 ½ minas for 9;2.3.0, Nādinu; 13 minas for 3;4.3.0, Nanāya-aḫu-iddin; 22 ½ minas for 6;3.4.3, Arad-Bēl; 8 talents for 144 kor of barley, Šamaš-mukīn-apli; 1 ⅚ minas 5 shekels for 3;2.4.0, Imbia; 1(+) talent 50 minas for 33 kor of barley including 11;2.×.0 barley of Šamaš-mukīn-apli (and) Mušēzib-Marduk; 2(+) minas for 11;4.0.0, thereof 3 kor [...] *Nādin-apli*, son of Marduk-šumu-iddin; × talents 36 ⅚ minas for 31;4?.4.0, Innin-šumu-uṣur; 2(+) minas 20 shekels for 4;3?.1.0, [DN]-šumu-iddin; 20 minas for *9;3.1.0*, Nabû-balāssu-iqbi, the *younger*; 58 minas for 19?;2.2.0, Anu-ikṣur; *51* minas for 10 ¼ shekels, Iddināya; 1(+) mina for 1 ½ shekels, Madān-šarru-uṣur ... ... [... ...*Na*]*bû*-aḫu-iddin [remainder broken].

19′ Ten minas of wool for one shekel of silver is a very low price for wool, which probably explains why this specific price is mentioned. It would also be reasonable to assume that the low price has to do with the fact that this is "black wool," a rare term in administrative context.[36] Throughout the long sixth century, wool prices averaged 3.57 minas of wool per 1 shekel, with the lowest rate being 6.67 minas of wool per 1 shekel of silver (CT 55, 754); see table 96 in Jursa 2010, 616–7. Given that all other undamaged conversion rates listed in the tablet are for barley (with another exception of goat hair in l. 31′), we cannot evaluate this low wool price internally.

44′ The conversion of 1 ⅚ minas 5 shekels (of wool) for 3;2.4.0 (barley) reflects an extremely high wool price: 1 kor (berley): ⅗ mina (wool). Other complete rates in the text are 1 kor barley: 3.333–6.577 mina wool.

51′ The expected meanings of ^{lu2}*tar-den-ne-e* (young, secondary, crown prince) are difficult in the present context. As an official, the *tard/tennu* is unknown from first millennium sources. Even less likely, in this context, is the military official *tartannu*.

304. NBC 4891

Copy: Plate LXXXIII
Date: undated (Cyr–Camb 9?)
Summary: accounting inventory: multiple items

The following selected prosopography forms the chronological horizon of the tablet: Ardia/Šākin-šumi (l. 17): Sack CD, 55 (5 Nbn), AnOr 8, 50 (5 Cyr); Innin-šumu-uṣur/Gimillu (l. 16): YOS 7, 144 (3 Camb); Ištar-ālik-pāni/Ibnāya (l. 7), YBC 4164 (6 Camb); Nanāya-iddin/Innin-aḫḫē-iddin (l. 14) YOS 7, 198 (6 Camb), see Payne 2007, 271. This Nbn–Camb timeframe can be narrowed further by the mention of the work on the wall of Babylon (l. 2). The "Babylon wall dossier" in the Eanna archive is know from 9 Cyr (AnOr 8, 60) until 1 Nbk IV (YBC 4173); see Kleber 2008, 187–8.

Obv. 2 ½ MA.NA KU$_3$.BABBAR *i-na* ŠUK.⸢ḪI.A^{me}⸣ *ša*$_2$ ^{lu2}ERIN$_2$^{me}
ša$_2$ BAD$_3$ TIN.TIR^{ki} *ina* ⸢ŠU^{II} ^{Id}*na-na-a*-MU⸣ A ^{Id}EN-BA^{ša2}

[36] Cf. the possible gloss GE$_6$ (YBC 9030: iii), writeen on the left edge; see Payne 2008 for an edition and Quillien 2022, 222–3.

a-na ^{lu2}qi$_2$-i-pi šu-bu-ul
1 (PI) 4 BAN$_2$ ŠE.BAR a-na ki-is-sa-tu$_4$ ša$_2$ TU.KUR$_4$^{mušen} $^{I⸢d}$dan⸣-nu-PAP^{me}-⸢šu$_2$-DU$_3$⸣
3 GUR ŠE.BAR ki-is-sa-tu$_4$ ša$_2$ 15 UZ.TUR^{mušen}
ša$_2$ li-i-šu$_2$ i-na pa-ra-su ša$_2$ ^{iti}GAN $^{Id⸢}$dan-nu-PAP⸣^{me}-šu$_2$-DU$_3$
16 ^{udu}ka-lum A MU.AN.NA ša$_2$ ^{Id}INNIN-DU-IGI A$^{!(T. ša_2)}$ ^{I}DU$_3$-⸢a⸣
7 ^{udu}ka-lum A MU.AN.NA ša$_2$ ^{I}ša$_2$-⸢am⸣-ša$_2$-⸢ma-nu A⸣ ^{I}[IR$_3$$^{?}$-^{d}A]G
a-na u$_2$-ru-u$_2$
(blank)
^{iti}APIN UD.6.KAM UD.7.⸢KAM⸣ UD.⸢8⸣.KAM MU.3.KAM
2 ½ GUN ṣu-ba-a-ta $^{Id⸢}$na⸣-na-a-MU IGI^{ir}
2 GUR ZU$_2$.LUM.MA ma-ak-ka-si ⸢ina maš⸣-šar-ti-šu$_2$
^{I}ni-din-ti ⸢A $^{I⸣}$DU$_3$-^{d}15
2 GUR ina ŠUK-šu$_2$ ^{Id}na-na-a-⸢MU$^{?}$⸣ A ^{Id}INNIN.NA-⸢PAP⸣^{me}-MU ^{I}[^{lu2}KA]B.SAR
1 GUR KI.MIN ^{Id}UR.IDIM-DINGIR-⸢u$_2$⸣-a ^{lu2}AŠGAB
{eras.} 2 (PI) 3 BAN$_2$ i-na maš-šar-ti-šu$_2$ ^{Id}in-⸢nin⸣-MU-URU$_3$ A ^{I}ŠU ⸢{^{I}ŠU$^{?}$}⸣
2 (PI) 3 BAN$_2$ KI.MIN ^{I}IR$_3$-ia A ^{I}GAR-MU
[PA]P 6 GUR ZU$_2$.LUM.MA eš-ru-u$_2$ ša$_2$ $^{Id⸢}$30⸣-KAM A ^{Id}AG-MU-SI.⸢SA$_2$⸣
[^{it}]^{i}APIN UD.9.KAM {eras.} <<2>>
[×] UDU^{me} ⸢i^{o}⸣-na^{o} ṣib-tu$_4$ ša$_2$ ^{Id}UTU-NUM[UN-D]U$_3$ A ^{I}tab-ne$_2$-⸢e⸣-a
[×] UDU^{me} KI.MIN ša$_2$ $^{Id⸢}$UTU⸣-NUMUN-GAL$_2$^{ši} A ^{Id}IGI.DU-⸢ŠU-GIŠ-BI⸣-ZA-ŠU$_2$$^{?}$
[×] UDU^{me} KI.MIN ša$_2$ ^{I}ki-rib-tu A $^{I⸢d}$AG⸣-NUMUN-GAL$_2$^{ši}
[×] ⸢× × ×⸣ UDU^{me} ša$_2$ ^{lu2}GAL MAŠ$_2$^{me} ša$_2$ ^{Id}na-na-a-[×]
[ ] ⸢× × i$^{?}$-di$^{?}$⸣ [× (×)] ⸢a-na⸣ [ ]
(remainder of Obv. is broken)
Rev. (beginning of Rev. is broken)
[ ] ⸢×⸣ [ ]
[ ]-e ša$_2$ KA$_2$ i-ru-b[u]
[ ] ⸢×⸣ i-na ŠUK^{me} ša$_2$ ka-a$^{!}$-du $^{I⸢d}$× × ×⸣
[ŠE].⸢GIŠ⸣.I$_3$ ^{Id}in-nin-MU-URU$_3$ ^{lu2}I$_3$.SUR SA$_2$.⸢DUG$_4$⸣
[ ] ⸢ša$_2$ 8⸣ UD.EŠ$_3$.EŠ$_3$^{me} ša$_2$ qu-ul-lu-pu ša$_2$ TA
[UD.×.K]AM ša$_2$ ^{iti}KIN$^{!}$ a-di qi$_2$-it ^{iti}GAN ^{I}MU-^{d}EN ina ŠA$_3$ ⸢1$^{?}$ (PI) 2 BAN$_2$ ^{I}na$^{?}$-din$^{?}$⸣
[(×+)]1 (PI) 5 BAN$_2$ i-na ŠE.GIŠ.I$_3$ ša$_2$ mut-ta-qu ša$_2$ ^{iti}GAN ^{I}na$^{?}$-din
1 BAN$_2$ ša$_2$ ma-ka-a-ta ^{I}ni-din-ti
1 BAN$_2$ ša$_2$ ri-kis li-li-su ZABAR ša$_2$ ^{iti}DU$_6$ ^{Id}AG-[M]U$^{?}$-URU$_3$
^{iti}APIN UD.11.KAM
3 ⅓ MA.NA AN.BAR 1 na-aš$_2$$^{?!(T. ah)}$-ḫi$^{?}$-ip-tu$_4$ ša$_2$ ^{I}re-mut-dingir ^{lu2}ša$_2$ muḫ-ḫi$^{?}$ q[u$^{?}$-up-pi$^{?}$]
a-na dul-lu ina IGI ^{I}SUM.NA-<a> ^{lu2}SIMUG AN.BAR
1 GU$_4$ 3^{u2} KU$_3$ ina re-ḫi ša$_2$ ^{I}ta-lim A ^{I}DU$_3$-^{d}INNIN
a-na u$_2$-ru-⸢u$_2$⸣
(blank)
(remainder was written after clay started to dry)
6 GUR 1 BAN$_2$ ŠE.GIŠ.I$_3$ i-na ŠU^{II} ^{I}gu-⸢za⸣-nu ^{lu2}A.KIN ša$_2$ ^{lu2}ŠA$_3$.TAM ⸢TA⸣ ED[IN × × × ×] ⸢×⸣
4 GUR 2 BAN$_2$ 5 SILA$_3$ ŠE.GIŠ.I$_3$ ina ŠU^{II} $^{I⸢}$TU × $^{I?}$IR$_3$$^{?}$-^{d}EN$^{?}$ × LUGAL$^{?}$ KUR GIŠ⸣
1 ⸢MA.NA⸣ 16 ½ GIN$_2$ KU$_3$.BABBAR i-na i-di ša$_2$ 30 ^{lu2}ḪUN.GA$_2$^{me}
ša$_2$ E$_2$ ka-a-du EN.NUN-tu$_4$ i-nam-⸢ṣar⸣-ru ša$_2$ ul-tu
UD.1.KAM ša$_2$ ^{iti}GAN ina ŠU^{II} ^{Id}UTU-KAL A ^{I}ina-SUḪ$_3$-SUR
a-na ^{Id}15-DU-IGI šu-bu-ul

15 ^{udu}*ka-lum ša*$_2$ ^{Id}*na-na-a*-MU A ^{I}AD-DU
3 {×} ^{I}*ni-din-ti u* ^{I}DU$_3$-*ia*$_2$ A^{me} *ša*$_2$ ^{I}ZALAG$_2$-⸢*e-a*⸣
PAP ⸢18⸣ *a-na u*$_2$-*ru-u*$_2$

---

2 ½ minas of silver were delivered via Nanāya-iddin, son of Bēl-iqīša, to the *qīpu* for the salaries of the workers at the wall of Babylon; 0;1.4.0 barley, fodder of the doves (to) Dannu-aḫḫēšu-ibni; 3 kor of barley, fodder for fifteen ducks (fattened) with dough, for the allocation of month IX, (to) Dannu-aḫḫēšu-ibni; sixteen one-year-old male lambs of Ištar-ālik-pāni, son of Ibnāya, (and) seven one-year-old male lambs of Šamšamānu, son [*Arad*-Na]bû, (were delivered) to the stable; month VIII, days 6, 7, (and) 8, year 3. 2 ½ talents of cloth were received from Nanāya-iddin; 2 kor of quality dates (to) Nidintu, son of Ibni-Ištar, for his *maššartu*; 2 kor (to) Nanāya-iddin, son of Innin-aḫḫē-iddin, the jeweler, for his salary. 1 kor (to) Ur(i)dimmu-ilūa, the leatherworker, *ditto*; 0;2.3.0 (to) Innin-šumu-uṣur, son of Gimillu, for his *maššartu*; 0;2.3.0 (to) Ardia, son of Šākin-šumi, *ditto*; altogether 6 kor of dates, the tithes of Sîn-ēreš, son of Nabû-šumu-līšir, month 8, day 9. [×] sheep, the *ṣibtu*-tax of Šamaš-zē[ru-ib]ni, son of Tabnēa; [×] sheep, *ditto* of Šamaš-zēru-šubši, son of IGI.DU-… [×] sheep, *ditto* of Kiribtu, son of Nabû-zēru-šubši. [×] … sheep of the *ṣibtu*-tax overseer, which Nanāya-[× …] … *rent* … to/for […].
$^{Rev.}$ […] … […] of the gate, entered […] … for the salaries of the guard-posts, PN … […] oil, (to) Innin-šumu-uṣur the oil-presser of the regular offerings; […] for eight festival days, for the *qullupu*-sweetcakes from [day ×] of month VI until the end of month IX, (to) Iddin-Bēl, of which 0;1.2.0 (are for) *Nādinu*; [×];1.5.0 in sesame for the *muttāqu*-cakes of month IX (to) Nādinu; 1 *sūtu* for the *makūtu*-cake (to) Nidintu; 1 *sūtu* for the ritual arrangement of the bronze kettledrum of month VII (to) Nabû-šumu-uṣur; month VIII, day 11. 3 ⅓ minas of iron (for) one shovel for Rēmūt-ili, who is in charge of the c[*ashbox*], for the works, are at the disposal of Iddināya the blacksmith; one three-year-old *pure* ox from the balance of Talīmu, son of Ibni-Ištar, (entered) the stable.
6;0.1.0 sesame [(delivered)] via Guzānu, messenger of the *šatammu*, from the step[pe …]; 4;0.2.5 sesame Arad-Bēl … withdrew via …; 1 mina 16 ½ shekels of silver, the salaries of thirty hired men, who are keeping the watch in the guard-post from the first day of month IX, were delivered via Šamaš-udammiq, son of Ina-tēšî-ēṭir, to Ištar-ālik-pāni; fifteen male lambs of Nanāya-iddin, son of Abu-ukīn; three (lambs of) Nidintu and Bānia, sons of Nūrea; altogether eighteen (were delivered) to the stable.

33′ For *rikis lilissi* and the interpretation as "ritual arrangement of the kettle drum," see Gabbay 2014, 155.

35′ Given the two spelling variants for *našḫiptu* and the possible š:ḫ metathesis (see commentary to **No. 101**: 3), the spelling *na-aš*$_2^{?!(\text{T. }aḫ)}$-*ḫi*$^?$-*ip-tu*$_4$ may be taken as another variant: **naḫḫiptu*.

305. YBC 3529

Copy: Plate LXXXIV
Date: undated (Nbn–Cyr)
Summary: *ina pāni* list: various items

The following attestations form the chronological horizon of the tablet: Erībšu (l. 13), (possibly) YOS 19, 160 (1 Nbn); Silim-ili (l. 22), e.g., BM 114524 (16 Nbn), PTS 2089 (1 Cyr), and BM 114528 (5 Camb); Šamaš-ibni/Gimillu (l. 21), YOS 6, 237 (15 Nbn).

Obv. 2 ^{giš}IG^{me} *ša*$_2$ ^{giš}UR$_3$ *ša*$_2$ E$_2$ ^{I}*ṣil-la-a*
[A]-⸢*šu*$_2$⸣ *ša*$_2$ ^{I}LU$_2$-^{d}*na-na-a ina* E$_2$ ^{Id}*in-nin*-NUMUN-DU$_3$
[A]-*šu*$_2$ *ša*$_2$ ^{I}IR$_3$-⸢*ia*$_2$⸣
[× ^{giš}]⸢IG⸣^{me} ⸢*zu-uḫ-ḫu*⸣ *ina* IGI ^{Id}*in-nin*-ŠEŠ-MU
[A-*šu*$_2$ *ša*$_2$] ⸢I⸣^{d}EN-DA
[× ^{giš}I]G^{me} ^{I}IR$_3$-*ia*$_2^{!(T.\ za)}$ A ^{Id}U.GUR-MU-DU$_3$
[ ]⸢*ti*?⸣ *ina* IGI ^{Id}INNIN-DU-IGI
[^{it}]^{i}NE UD.11.KAM
[ ] ⸢AN⸣.BAR *ina* IGI ^{I}*la-ba-ši*
[$^{I?}$]⸢NIG$_2$?⸣.DU? ⸢^{iti}⸣NE UD.14.KAM
Lo.E. [× *az*?-*ma*?] ⸢*ru*⸣-*u*$_2$ *ina* IGI ^{I}*u*$_2$-*bar*
[ ] ⸢*ša*$_2$? *u*$_2$ ^{Id}AG?⸣-:IR$_3$ ^{iti}NE UD.17.KAM
Rev. [ ] ⸢*e*?⸣-*ru* [*ina*] ⸢IGI⸣ ^{I}KU$_4$-*šu*$_2$ ^{lu2}IR$_3$-⸢E$_2$⸣.<GAL>
[ ] ⸢*saq*⸣-*qa-a-ti ina* IGI ^{Id}*in-nin-kib-su*-AD-URU$_3$
[(×+)] ⸢1⸣ *qul-mu-u*$_2$ AN.BAR 1 *ma-ti-qu*
5 ½ MA.NA AN.BAR KI.LA$_2$.BI *ina pa-ni*
^{Id}EN-SUR *u* ^{Id}*dan-nu*-ŠEŠ^{me}-*šu*$_2$-DU$_3$
ša$_2$ UD$^{!}$.UNUG^{ki} ^{iti}NE UD.25.KAM
1 *ṣib-te-e-ti ina* IGI ^{I}EN-*šu*$_2$-*nu*
A ^{I}*na-din*
2 ^{kuš}DUḪ.ŠI.A *ina* IGI $^{I⸢d}$UTU-DU$_3$⸣ A ^{I}ŠU
Up.E. 4 ḪAR AN.BAR^{me} *ina* IGI ^{I}*si*-⸢*lim*-DINGIR⸣
<<*ša*$_2$ *muḫ-ḫi*>> ^{lu2}*ša*$_2$ *muḫ-ḫi qu-up-pu*
4 NIGIN? KA$_2^{me}$
Le.E. 2 [ ]

Two beams for doors from the house of Ṣillāya, son of Amīl-Nanāya, are in the house of Innin-zēru-ibni, son of Ardia; [×] door reed mats at the disposal Innin-aḫu-iddin, [son of] Bēl-lēʾi; [× do]ors, Ardia, son of Nergal-šumu-ibni; [...] at the disposal of Ištar-ālik-pāni [... mon]th V, day 11. [...] of iron at the disposal of Lâbâši; [...] *Kudurru;* month V, day 14. [× *lan*]*ces* at the disposal of Ubāru; [...], *Arad-Nabû,* month V, day 17. [...] *copper,* at the disposal of Erībšu, the master-builder; [...] sacks are at the disposal of Innin-kibsu-abi-uṣur; one(+) iron *qulmû*-axe, one *mount,* weighing 5 ½ minas of iron, are at the disposal of Bēl-ēṭir and Dannu-aḫḫēšu-ibni of Larsa; month V, day 25.
One (pair of) fetters at the disposal of Bēlšunu, son of Nādinu; two (pieces of) *dušû*(-colored)-leather are at the disposal of Šamaš-ibni, son of Gimillu; four iron rings are at the disposal of Silim-ili, the (one) in charge of the cashbox; four ... *installments;* 2 [...].

1 The text reads "doors of beams," but "beams of doors" must be meant.

12 The name ⸢^{Id}AG?⸣-IR$_3$ is difficult. If the reading of the IR$_3$ sign is correct, then the scribe may have had Arad-Nabû in mind but reversed the order of the elements. Although this is a highly unusual scribal error, it might be compared with the probable switch of beams and doors in line 1.

15 The spelling *ma-ti-qu* is cautiously taken as a faulty singular form of *matqanu*. The alternative reading *ba-ti-qu* may be suggested in light of the AHw entry for *bātiqu,* meaning 3 "ein Gerät aus Eisen" (AHw, 115). However, the only reference is to a presumed Pl. form, *ba-ti-qa-nu* (Nbn 784: 9), which in all likelihood is simply another attestation of *matqanu* (as indeed read in CAD M/I, 413, s.v. *matqanu* b).

23 Silim-ili was the *ša rēš šarri ša muḫḫi quppi šarri*, 15 Nbn–6 Camb; Kleber 2008, 37. Therefore, although difficult, one may suggest reading *ša*$_2$ SAG$^{!}$ LUGAL$^{!}$ *ša*$_2$ *muḫ-ḫi qu-up-pu*.

306. GCBC 705

Copy: Plate LXXXIV
Date: undated (ca. *late Nbk*)
Summary: *ina pāni* note: (not specified)

Gimillu may cautiously be identified as the carpenter attested as working with writing boards in GC 1, 399 (40 Nbk) and GC 2, 189 (43 (Nbk).

Obv. ⸢1 ½ MA.NA ^{giš}DA⸣
⸢*ina* IGI ^{I}*gi-mil-lu*⸣
Rev. (uninscribed)

1 ½ minas (in/for$^{?}$ the) writing boards are at the disposal of Gimillu.

307. NCBT 1154

Copy: Plate LXXXV
Date: undated (late Nbk–Nbn)
Summary: *maḫir* receipt: multiple complex entries

The following attestations form the chronological horizon of the tablet: Ištar-zēru-ibni/Šulāya (l. 5), YOS 6, 90 (7 Nbn); Kalbāya/Amīl-Nanāya (l. 6), GC 1, 168 (32 Nbk); Nabû-aḫḫē-bulliṭ/Nanāya-ibni (l. 10), FLP 1543 (31 Nbk), PTS 2949 (39 Nbk); Nabû-zēru-iqīša/Nanāya-ibni (l. 1), YBC 7380 (21 Nbk), YBC 9222 (35 Nbk), PTS 3082 (37 Nbk), PTS 2346 (1 Ner); Nūrea/Iqīšāya (l. 9), PTS 2344 (1 Ner); Šumu-uṣur/In[nin-zē]ru-ibni (l. 13), GC 1, 168 (32 Nbk).

Obv. $^{I⸢d}$AG⸣-NUMUN-BA$^{⸢ša_2}$ A⸣ ^{Id}*na-na-⸢a*-DU$_3$⸣
⸢^{Id}AG⸣-ŠEŠ^{me}-⸢URU$_3^{?}$⸣
$^{I⸢}$*ar*$_2$⸣-*rab* ⸢ŠEŠ⸣-*šu*$_2$
$^{I⸢}$SUM.NA-*a*⸣ A ^{I}*šu-la-a*
5 $^{Id⸢}$15⸣-NUMUN-DU$_3$ ŠEŠ-*šu*$_2$
^{I}*kal-ba-a* A ^{I}LU$_2$-^{d}*na-na-a*
^{I}*la-ba-ši* ŠEŠ-*šu*$_2$
$^{I⸢}$KU$_4$⸣-*šu*$_2$ A ^{I}BA^{ša_2}-⸢*a*⸣
^{I}ZALAG$_2$-*e-a* ŠEŠ-<*šu*$_2$>
10 ^{Id}AG-PAP^{me}-TIN A $^{Id⸢}$*na-na*⸣-*a*-DU$_3$
^{I}ZALAG$_2$-*e-a* ⸢ŠEŠ-*šu*$_2$⸣
[^{I}]LU$_2$-^{d}*na-na-a* ⸢ŠEŠ⸣-[*šu*$_2$]
Lo.E. [^{I}(×)]-MU-URU$_3$ A ^{Id}*i*[*n-nin*-NU]MUN-DU$_3$

---

14 [× *ma*]-⸢*ši*⸣-*ḫu* ⸢TA⸣
Rev. $^{uru?}$*ma*-⸢*aḫ*⸣$^{?}$-*ra-ga-a*$^{?}$ ⸢GIŠ⸣
13 GIN$_2$ ^{I}*ana*-E$_2$-*šu*$_2$
MU.39.KAM *u* MU.40.KAM
4 ⸢^{tug_2}⸣KUR.RA^{me} *u*$_3$ 6 GIN$_2$ KU$_3$.BABBAR

^{Id}AG-MU-DU$_3$ ^{lu_2}AŠGAB
⸢1 ^{tug_2}⸣KUR.RA 4 GIN$_2$ KU$_3$.BABBAR ^{Id}EN-PAP^{me}-[×]
(Le.E. ↓) 3 ^{tug_2}KUR.RA 4 ^{tug_2}⸢*šir-a-am*⸣
$^{(a)}$ 1 (PI) 4 BAN$_2$ ŠE.GIŠ.⸢I$_3$⸣ $^{(c)}$ 5 GIN$_2$ KU$_3$.BABBAR ^{I}ŠU A ^{I}⸢^{d}*na-na*⸣-[*a*-×]
$^{(b)}$ ⸢*ša*$_2$$^?$ *ta-lam*⸣ I$_3$.GIŠ
1 ⸢MA$^?$⸣ *ina* ŠU^{II} ^{f}*ni-šu-nu*
1 ^{tug_2}⸢KUR⸣.RA 1 ^{tug_2}⸢*šir*⸣-*a*-⸢*am*⸣
ina ŠU^{II} ^{f}*za-bu-ub-tu*$_4$
ša$_2$ *ina ḫa-la-tu*
⸢PAP⸣ KU$_3$.BABBAR *ša*$_2$ ^{I}*u*$_2$-*paq* GIŠ⸢^{u_2}⸣

Nabû-zēru-iqīša, son of Nanāya-ibni; Nabû-aḫḫē-uṣur; Arrab, his brother; Iddināya, son of Šulāya; Ištar-zēru-ibni, his brother; Kalbāya, son of Amīl-Nanāya; Lâbâši, his brother; Erībšu, son of Iqīšāya; Nūrea, <his> brother; Nabû-aḫḫē-bulliṭ, son of Nanāya-ibni; Nūrea, his brother; Amīl-Nanāya, his brother; Šumu-uṣur, son of In[nin-zē]ru-ibni: (they$^?$) withdrew [x *ma*]*šīḫu* from (the town of) *Ma-aḫ-ra-ga-a*.
13 shekels, Ana-bītišu, year 39 and 40; four capes and 6 shekels of silver, Nabû-šumu-ibni, the leatherworker; one cape, 4 shekels of silver, Bēl-aḫḫē-[…]; three capes, four *šir'am*-garments, 0;1.4.0 sesame for$^?$ one *talammu* container of oil, (*and*) 5 shekels of silver, Gimillu, son of Nanāya-[…]; one *ma*<*šīḫu*>$^?$ via ^{f}*Nišunu*, one cape, one *šir'am*-garment via ^{f}*Zabubtu*, who/that are in (*the town of*) *Ḫalatu*; total of the silver that Upāqu withdrew.

15 $^{uru?}$*ma*-⸢*aḫ*$^?$⸣-*ra-ga-a*$^?$: no such town is known from other sources. A town by the name of *maḫ-ra-a-a'* is attested in PSBA 38, pl. 1: 19 (see RGTC 8: 217, s.v. Maḫrā), which would still require a significant correction to one of the readings. The final *-ga-a* may alternatively be read as *-ta*, though this does not help with the identification of this place name.

22_{a+b+c} Both of the lines following l. 21 start on the left edge, and were clearly meant by the scribe as one entry. Moreover, if the reading ⸢*ša*$_2$$^?$⸣ before *ta-lam* is right, then it would make more sense that this phrase follows 1 (PI) 4 BAN$_2$ ŠE.GIŠ.⸢I$_3$⸣ above it, only then one should read 5 GIN$_2$ KU$_3$.BABBAR ^{I}ŠU A ^{I}⸢^{d}*na-na*⸣-[*a*-×]. Thus, we read as follows: $^{(a)}$ 1 (PI) 4 BAN$_2$ ŠE.GIŠ.⸢I$_3$⸣ $^{(b)}$ ⸢*ša*$_2$$^?$⸣ *ta-lam* I$_3$.GIŠ $^{(c)}$ 5 GIN$_2$ KU$_3$.BABBAR ^{I}ŠU A ^{I}⸢^{d}*na-na*⸣-[*a*-×]. Although this kind of reorganization is certainly a conjecture, it is clear from the use of the left edge that the arrangement of these lines was "improvised" by the scribe, and so an irregular layout is less problematic.

23 The ⸢MA$^?$⸣ may be an abbreviation for *mašīḫu*.

25 The name ^{f}*Zabubtu* is, to the best of our knowledge, unknown elsewhere. It is unclear whether this is the feminine form of the name Zumbu, "fly."

308. NBC 4597

Copy: Plates LXXXV–LXXXVI
Date: undated (late Nbk–Camb)
Summary: accounting inventory: varia

The following attestations form the chronological horizon of the tablet: Anu-zēru-ibni (l. 2′), YOS 7, 137 (3 Camb), see Payne 2007, 156; Bēl-iddin (l. 23′), 13 Nbn (PTS 2282) until 1 Nbk IV (YOS 17, 301), see Payne 2007, 161; Dannu-aḫḫēšu-ibni (l. 6′), 13 Nbn (UCP 9/2, 35) until 6 Camb (Sack CD, 45), see Payne 2007, 163; Iddināya/Innin-šumu-uṣur (l. 12′), 2 Camb (BM 114601) until 6 Camb (GC 2, 104); Innin-šumu-uṣur (l. 4′), 40 Nbk (**No. 246**) until 15 Nbn (YOS 17, 74), see Payne 2007, 172; Innin-zēru-

šubši (ll. 8′, 31′), 0a Ner (YOS 19, 115) until 4 Cyr (YOS 7, 32), see Payne 2007, 173–4; Nabû-kēšir/Iqīšāya (l 17′), YOS 7, 87 (Cyr); Nanāya-aḫu-iddin (*rab bīt kīli*, l. 33′), YOS 7, 97 (0a Camb); Nidintu (l. 34′), 8 Cyr (YOS 7, 95) until 8 Camb (PTS 2188), see Payne 2007, 325;

Obv. [ ] ˹× × ×˺ [ ]
[ ] ˹^{Id}*a-nu*-NUMUN˺-DU$_3$ ^{lu2}*pu-ṣa-a-a* ˹IGI^{ir}˺
[ ] ˹^{I}BA˺^{ša2} ^{lu2}UŠ.BAR *bir-mu*
[ ] ˹^{Id}*in-nin*-MU-˹URU$_3$ IGI^{ir}˺
[ ]-*ḫu-tu a-na ṣu*-˹*up-pa-a-tu*$_2$˺
[^{Id}*dan-nu*-ŠEŠ^{m}]^{eš}-*šu*$_2$-DU$_3$ ^{lu2}*pu*-[*ṣa*]-*a-a*
[ ] ˹× KU$^?$˺ NU *a-na* ˹*dul-lu*˺
[^{Id}*in-n*]*in*-NUMUN-GAL$_2^{ši}$ ^{lu2}˹UŠ.BAR$^!$ *bir*˺-*mu*
[ ] ˹× × ×˺ [GI]N$_2$ KU$_3$.BABBAR *ina* IGI ^{I}IR$_3$-^{d}EN
[ ] ˹× × × ×˺ [ ] ˹GIN$_2$˺ KU$_3$.BABBAR *ina* IGI ^{Id}AG-˹*it-tan*˺-*nu*
[ ] ˹2(+×) GIN$_2$ KU$_3$.BABBAR *ina* IGI˺ [^{Id}×]-˹ŠEŠ˺-MU A ^{I}IR$_3$-^{d}*na-na-a*
[$^{I?}$]˹DU$_3^?$-^{d}INNIN$^?$˺.NA ^{I}˹SUM.NA˺-*a* A ^{Id}*in-nin*-MU-URU$_3$ IGI^{ir}
[ ] ˹*ma-ak-ṣa-ru*˺ *ša*$_2$ ˹*ti-ib*˺-*nu* ^{I}*gu-za-nu ma-ḫi-ir*
[^{iti}S]IG$_4$ UD.15.KAM UD.16.KAM
(blank)
[× (×)] UDU.BAR.SAL *ir-bi ša*$_2$ ^{I}NUMUN-*ia* A ^{I}*ta-li-mu*
˹1(+×)˺ *par-rat ir-bi ša*$_2$ ^{II}*si-lim*-DINGIR PAP 22 *par-rat a-na qa-bu-ut*$^!$-*tu*$_4$
(tiny line) *ina* IGI ^{Id}AG-*ke*-˹*šir*$_3$˺ A ^{I}BA^{ša2}-*a*
˹1(+×)˺ GUN 5 ⅚ MA.NA SIK$_2$.ḪI.A *ša*$_2^!$ 20 GUR ŠE.BAR
[*ina*$^?$] ˹ŠUK.ḪI.A˺^{me}-*šu*$_2$-*nu* ^{lu2}*mu-saḫ-ḫi-re-e ša*$_2$ ^{Id}AG-ŠEŠ-MU
[× MA.NA] ˹SIK$_2$˺.ḪI.A *ša*$_2$ 6 GUR ŠE.BAR 5 ^{lu2}ḪUN.GA$_2$ *ša*$_2$ ^{giš}MA$_2$ ˹^{tug2}BAR.DUL$_8$˺
[*a-na* TIN].˹TIR˺^{ki} *i-šad-da*-˹*du*˺
[ ] ˹NA$^?$˺ U$_2$ MU *a-na* E$_2$.KI[SAL]
Rev. [ ] ˹^{I}˺*ina*-GISSU-^{d}*na-na-a*
[ ] *a-na su-u*$_2$-*nu ša*$_2$ A^{me} ŠU^{II}
ša$_2$ E$_2$ ^{d}URU$_3$-˹INIM-*su*˺ *ku-um* ^{tug2}UR$_2$ *a-ri-du* <<NA>>
2 GUN 5 ½ MA.NA SIK$_2$.ḪI.A *a-na dul-lu*
ina IGI ^{Id}EN-MU ^{lu2}UŠ.BAR
6 *pag*$^!$-*ru ša*$_2$ TU.KUR$_4^{mušen}$ ^{Id}*dan-nu*-PAP^{me}-*šu*$_2$-DU$_3$ IGI^{ir}
^{iti}SIG$_4$ UD.17.KAM
7 MA.NA *mi-iḫ-ṣi* BABBAR-*u*$_2$ 3 *ṣu-up-pa-a-tu*$_4$
^{Id}*in-nin*-NUMUN-GAL$_2^{ši}$ ^{lu2}UŠ.BAR *bir-mu* IGI^{ir}
6 MA.NA ⅓ GIN$_2$ AN.BAR 6 [*a*]-*ḫa-a-nu ša*$_2$ ḪAR^{meš}
šu-ub-bu-ru-tu ^{Id}*na-na-a*-ŠEŠ-MU
^{lu2}GAL E$_2$ *ki-li ma-ḫi-ir a-na dul-lu ina* IGI ^{I}*ni-din-tu*$_2$
˹5˺ ME 38 GUR 3 (PI) 2 BAN$_2$ ŠE.BAR *ina* ^{giš}BAN$_2$ *ša*$_2$ ^{I}DA-^{d}AMAR.UTU *u* ^{Id}AG-KAL
˹*ša*$_2$˺ MU.5.KAM *ina* ŠU^{II} ^{Id}*na-na-a*-ŠEŠ-MU *u* ^{I}TIN *a-na* NIG$_2$.GA
[(×+)] 3 ⅓ MA.NA SIK$_2$.ḪI.A *ša*$_2$ 7 GUR ŠE.BAR *ina* ŠUK.ḪI.A^{me}
[ ] ˹^{lu2}˺E$_2$RIN^{meš}-*šu*$_2$ ^{I}*ina*-GISSU-^{d}*na-na-a*
[ ] *ma-ak-ṣa-ru ša*$_2$ *ti-ib-nu* ^{Id}KUR.GAL-LUGAL-˹*a-ni* IGI^{ir}˺
[*m*]*a-ak-ṣa-ru* ^{I}IR$_3$-*ia* A ^{I}*kal-ba*-[*a*]
[ITI].˹SIG$_4$˺ UD.18.˹KAM˺ [ ]
[remainder broken]

[…]… […] received from Anu-zēru-ibni, the linen weaver; […] Iqīšā(*ya*), the weaver of colored cloth, […] received from Innin-šumu-uṣur; […] … for strip(s) of combed wool [… Dannu-aḫḫ]ēšu-ibni, the linen weaver, […] … for (the) work [(of) …, … Inn]in-zēru-šubši, the weaver of colored cloth, [… shek]el(s) of silver is at the disposal of Arad-Bēl; […] … shekel(s) of silver is at the disposal of Nabû-ittannu; […(×+)]2 shekels are at the disposal of [×]-aḫu-iddin, son of Arad-Nanāya; […] *Ibni*-Innin received from Iddināya, son of Innin-šumu-uṣur; × bundles of straw were received from Guzānu—[month I]II, days 15 and 16. [×] female lambs, the income of Zēria, son of Talīmu; one(+) female lamb(s), the income of Silim-ili, a total of twenty-two lambs for the fold are at the disposal of Nabû-kēšir, son of Iqīšāya; 1 talent, 5 ⅚ minas of wool for 20 kor of barley [for/*from*] the salaries for the agents of Nabû-aḫu-iddin; [× minas of] wool for 6 kor of barley (for) five hired men who tow the boat of *kusītu*-garments [to Baby]lon; […] … for the [court]yard-chapel [... …] Ina-ṣilli-Nanāya [...] for the *sūnu*-cloth strip (i.e., towel) for the hand(-washing) water (basin) of the Uṣur-amāssu temple, instead of the removed *sūnu*-cloth strip; 2 talents 5 ½ minas of wool are at the disposal of Bēl-iddin, the weaver, for work; six carcasses of doves were received from Dannu-aḫḫēšu-ibni – month III, day 17.
7 minas of white woven cloth (in the form of) three strips of combed wool were received from Innin-zēru-šubši, the weaver of colored cloth; 6 minas 20 shekels of iron (in the form of) broken manacles rings were received from Nanāya-aḫu-iddin, the prison overseer, (they are) at the disposal of Nidintu for work; 538;3.2.0 barley from the *sūtu*-obligation of Ileʾʾi-Marduk and Nabû-udammiq of year 5, [(were received)] via Nanāya-aḫu-iddin and Balāṭu for the temple stores; [×+]3 ½ minas of wool for 7 kor of barley from the salaries […] of the workmen of Ina-ṣilli-Nanāya; [×] bundles of straw were received from Amurru-šarrāni; [×] bundles (from) Ardia, son of Kalbāya [...] month III, day 17 [...] [rest is broken]

3 The rendering of Iqīšāya for BA^{ša_2} is problematic, since the name is normally written BA^{ša_2}-*a*. The spelling BA^{ša_2} is usually used for the second element, which would be preceded by a DN.

309. NBC 4627

Copy: Plate LXXXVI
Date: 26.[×].13 [Npl]
Summary: payment (*eṭir*) note: silver

The straightforward laconic phrasing of the tablet seems to be hiding a quite remarkable episode: a father selling his son, the reed-worker, to the Eanna temple. To the best of our knowledge, keeping in mind that the sold reed-worker is not a slave, this kind of a sale is otherwise undocumented in contemporary records. Having said that, our text is not the only record dealing with this case. The present text must be related to YOS 3, 158 (= SbB 2, 20), a letter by IGI.DU-zēru-ibni to Nabû-nādin-šumi (temple scribe, ca. 10–15 Npl and later *šatammu*, 15 Npl–3 Nbk) regarding a somewhat unclear business involving Rēḫētu, his kinsmen (*qīnu*), and silver. In YOS 3, 158, the relations between IGI.DU-zēru-ibni, Rēḫētu, and the silver are not laid out. Since the selling of Rēḫētu is not hinted at, and it is a very unlikely course of events, the SbB 2 (i.e., Levavi's) translation inserts an interruptive "(from)," in one of IGI.DU-zēru-ibni's key statements: "*The Lady-of-Uruk knows that I did not receive (from) Rēḫētu a surplus of silver, rather less.*"[37] The present text makes it clear, however, that the silver was actually the (purchase) price of Rēḫētu. Thus, the SbB 2 translation should be amended to: *The Lady-of-Uruk*

37 ^{d}GAŠAN *ša*$_2$ UNUG^{ki} *lu ti-i-de ki-i* KU$_3$.BABBAR *a-tar* ^{I}*re-ḫe-e-ti am-ḫu-ru al-la ki-i* [*ma*]-*ṭu-u*$_2$ (YOS 3, 158: 10–14).

knows that I did not receive (for) Rēḫētu a surplus of silver, rather less."

Although YOS 3, 158 is not dated, its addressee, Nabû-nādin-šumi, establishes a timeframe of 10 Npl – 3 Nbk. The only 13th regnal year within this timeframe is 13 Npl, which should be established for both texts.[38] As for IGI.DU-zēru-ibni, the writer of the letter, he is probably to be identified as the chief priest (*šangû*) of Udannu (Levavi 2018, 149, 252), later listed in the *Hofkalender* of Nebuchadnezzar (*terminus post quem* 7 Nbk; ^{Id}IGI.DU-NUMUN-*i-bi*$_2$-*in* ^{lu2}E$_2$.BAR ^{uru}*u*$_2$-*da-an-nim*, col. vii*: 9′). The fact he is not identified as such in the present text might point to an earlier phase of his career, prior to his appointment.

Obv. ⌜10 MA.NA⌝ NIG$_2$.GA ^{d}*iš-tar u* ^{d}*na-na-a*
⌜ŠAM$_2$⌝ ^{I}*re-ḫe-e-ti* ^{lu2}AD.KID
^{Id}AG-NUMUN-MU DUMU-*šu*$_2$
^{Id}IGI.DU-NUMUN-DU$_3$ A-*šu*$_2$ *ša*$_2$ ^{I}*ša*$_2$-^{d}AG-*šu*$_2$-*u*
e-ṭir
(blank)
Rev. (blank)
⌜^{iti}⌝[× UD].⌜26.KAM MU.13.KAM⌝
[^{d}AG-A-URU$_3$ LUGAL] ⌜TIN.TIR^{ki}⌝

IGI.DU-zēru-ibni, son of Ša-Nabû-šū, was paid 10 minas (of silver from) the temple store of Ištar and Nanāya, the (purchase?) price of Rēḫētu, the reed-worker, (and) Nabû-zēru-iddin, his son.
Month [×], day 26, year 13 of [Nabopolassar, king of] Babylon.

310. NCBT 1016

Copy: Plate LXXXVI
Date: 12.I.23 Nbk
Summary: withdrawal and delivery note

Obv. 10 [(+)] GIN$_2$ KU$_3$.BABBAR *a-na* ZU$_2$.LUM.⌜MA *ina* ŠU^{II}⌝[^{I}×-×(×)]
(tiny line) ⌜A ^{I}ŠEŠ$^{?}$-*u*$_2$-<*tu*> *u* ^{I}*ina*-SUḪ$_3$-SUR A [^{I}*ta*]*b-ne*$_2^{!}$-*e-a*
5 GIN$_2$ KU$_3$.BABBAR *ina i-di-šu*$_2$ ^{giš}MA$_2$-*šu*$_2$ ^{Id}EN-KAR
A-*šu*$_2$ *ša*$_2$ ^{I}*ša*$_2$-^{d}AG-*šu-u*$_2$ ^{lu2}MA$_2$.LAḪ$_4$ GIŠ
4 GIN$_2$ *i-di* ^{giš}MA$_2$-*šu*$_2$ ^{Id}AG-EN-*šu*$_2$-*nu* A ^{Id}EN-⌜×⌝-[×]
2 GIN$_2$ *u*$_2$-*de-e* ^{lu2}BAḪAR$_2$ *u* GI[^{meš}]$^{?}$
⌜*ina* ŠU^{II}⌝ ^{I}NUMUN-*ia*$_2$ A ^{I}ŠEŠ^{meš}-*ša*$_2$-*a šu-bul*
Lo.E. 6 ½ GIN$_2$ *gir*$_2$-*u a-na* 3 *ne*$_2$-*sip ša*$_2$ ⌜I$_3$.GIŠ⌝
Rev. [*ina* š]U^{II} ^{I}⌜*ina*-SUḪ$_3$⌝-SUR A ^{I}*tab-ne*$_2$-*e-a* ⌜*šu-bul*⌝
⌜6$^{?}$ GIN$_2$⌝ *a-na i-di* ^{giš}MA$_2$ *ina* ⌜ŠU^{II}⌝
[^{I}]^{d}AG-ŠEŠ^{meš}-MU A ^{lu2}⌜UŠ⌝.BAR *u* ^{I}NUMUN-⌜*tu*$_2^{?}$⌝
(tiny line) A-*šu*$_2$ *ša*$_2$ ^{Id}*gu-la*-NUMUN-DU$_3$ *šu-bul*
2 GIN$_2$ *a-na ti-ib-ni ina* ŠU^{II} ^{Id}INNIN$^{!}$.NA-NUMUN-⌜MU$^{?}$⌝
A-*šu*$_2$ *ša*$_2$ ^{I}TIN^{su} *šu-bul*
^{iti}BARA$_2$ UD.12.KAM MU.23.KAM

[38] Note that YOS 3, 158 is dated to 16 Npl–3 Nbk in Levavi 2018, 252, based on the assumption that Nabû-nādin-šumi was already the šatammu at the time of the letter (rather than still temple scribe).

⸢^{d}AG⸣-NIG$_2$.DU-URU$_3$ LUGAL TIN.TIR^{ki}

10(+) shekels of silver for dates via [...], son of *Aḫḫūtu*, and Ina-tēšî-ēṭir, son of Tabnēa(.) Bēl-ēṭir, son of Ša-Nabû-šū, the boatman, withdrew 5 shekels of silver for the rent of his boat. Nabû-bēlšunu, son of Bēl-×, (withdrew) 4 shekels for the rent of his boat. 2 shekels (for) potter wares and reeds were delivered by Zēria, son of Aḫḫēšāya.
6 $^{13}/_{24}$ shekels for three *nēsepu*-containers of oil were delivered via Ina-tēšî-ēṭir, son of Tabnēa.
6 shekels for the rent of a boat were delivered via Nabû-aḫḫē-iddin, descendant of Išparu, and Zērūtu, son of Gula-zēru-ibni.
2 shekels for straw were delivered via Innin-zēru-*iddin*, son of Balāssu.
Month I, day 12, year 23 of Nebuchadnezzar, king of Babylon.

1–2 The first entry seems to be missing a verb. Alternatively, these lines are part of the following entry ending with *našû* in l. 4.

5 In YBC 9239 we find a boatman by the name of Nabû-bēlšunu / Nabû-šumu-ukīn. This reading might be possible for the present case, as the father's name is written on the curving edge of the tablet.

13 The last sign of the name Innin-zēru-*iddin* is unclear, MU or KAM, and the name may be read Innin-zēru-*ēreš*.

311. YBC 9223

Copy: Plate LXXXVII
Date: *18*.IX.*39* Nbk
Summary: record of interrogation

Obv. ^{Id}EN-*na-din*-A A-*šu*$_2$ *ša*$_2$ ^{I}NUMUN-TIN.⸢TIR^{ki}⸣
A ^{I}DA-^{d}AMAR.UTU
^{I}EN-*šu*$_2$-*nu* A-*šu*$_2$ *ša*$_2$ ^{Id}AG-PAP^{meš}-MU
A ^{I}*e-gi-bi*
^{I}*gi-mil-lu* A<-*šu*$_2$ *ša*$_2$> ^{I}⸢NUMUN⸣-*ia*$_2$ A ^{I}*ši-gu-u*$_2$-*a*$^{!(\mathrm{T.}\ ša_2)}$
⸢^{I}⸣^{d}AG-DU$_3$-ŠEŠ A-*šu*$_2$ ⸢*ša*$_2$⸣ ^{I}MU-^{d}AMAR.UTU A ^{I}ZALAG$_2$-⸢^{d}⸣30
⸢^{I}⸣*gi-mil-lu* A-*šu*$_2$ *ša*$_2$ ^{Id}EN-ŠEŠ-MU
⸢^{Id}EN⸣-DU$_3$ A-*šu*$_2$ *ša*$_2$ ^{I}*na-din* A ^{I}*ba-bu*$^{!}$-*tu*$_2$
Lo.E. ⸢*an-nu-tu*⸣ $^{\mathrm{lu_2}}$*mu-kin-ne*$_2$-*e* <*ša*$_2$>
ina ⸢IGI⸣-*šu*$_2$-*nu* ^{Id}AG-DU$_3$-ŠEŠ A-*šu*$_2$ *ša*$_2$
Rev. ^{I}IDIM-⸢*ia*⸣ A ^{I}⸢*ba-la-ṭu*⸣
^{I}ŠU-^{d}UTU A-*šu*$_2$ *ša*$_2$ ^{I}K[I]-⸢^{d}⸣UTU-TIN
$^{\mathrm{lu_2}}$KU$_4$ E$_2$ *ša*$_2$ ^{d}URU$_3^{!}$-INIM-*su*
^{giš}*šad-du ša*$_2$ *bat-qa ša*$_2$ E$_2$ *pa-pa-ḫa*
ša$_2$ ^{d}URU$_3$-INIM-*su pe-tu-u*$_2$
⸢*a*⸣-*na* IGI ^{Id}AMAR.UTU-MU-MU A<-*šu*$_2$ *ša*$_2$> ^{Id}AG-TIN⸢^{su}⸣-E
[A ^{I}]ŠU-^{d}*na-na-a* $^{\mathrm{lu_2}}$EN *pi-qit*-⸢*ti*⸣
[*u*] ⸢$^{\mathrm{lu_2}}$⸣*qi*$_2$-*i-pu iš-šu-nim-ma* ^{Id}⸢AMAR⸣.[UTU]-⸢MU-MU⸣
⸢*iq*⸣-*ba-aš*$_2$-*šu*$_2$-*nu-tu um-ma mi-nam-ma* ⸢*pe-ti*⸣
⸢*a-na*⸣ ^{Id}AMAR.UTU-MU-MU *iq-bu-u*$_2$
Up.E. ⸢*um-ma*⸣ *qi*$_2$-*bu ina* IGI-*ni-ni pi*-⸢*ti*⸣
⸢^{iti}⸣GAN UD.⸢18$^{?}$⸣.KAM ⸢MU.39$^{?}$⸣.[KAM]
Le.E. ^{d}AG-NIG$_2$.DU-⸢URU$_3$⸣

⸢LUGAL⸣ TIN.TIR^{ki}

Bēl-nādin-apli, son of Zēr-Bābili, descendant of Ilèi-Marduk; Bēlšunu, son of Nabû-aḫḫē-iddin, descendant of Egibi; Gimillu, son of Zēria, descendant of Šigûa; Nabû-bān-aḫi, son of Iddin-Marduk, descendant of Nūr-Sîn; Gimillu, son of Bēl-aḫu-iddin; Bēl-ibni, son of Nādinu, descendant of Babūtu—these are the witnesses in whose presence Nabû-bān-aḫi, son of Kabtia, descendant of Balāṭu, Gimil-Šamaš, son of Itti-Šamaš-balāṭu, the 'temple enterers' of Uṣur-amāssu, (and) the opened repair box of the cella of Uṣur-amāssu were brought before Marduk-šumu-iddin, son of Nabû-balāssu-iqbi, [descendant of] Gimil-Nanāya, the commissioner, and the *qīpu*. Marduk-šumu-iddin asked them: "Why is it opened?" They said to Marduk-šumu-iddin: "There was an order before us (stating): 'Open (it).'"
Month IX, day *18*, year *39* of Nebuchadnezzar, king of Babylon.

312. YBC 9155

Copy: Plate LXXXVII
Date: 12.VI.42 Nbk
Summary: record of a testimony

Obv. $^{I⸢d}$AG-ŠEŠ$^{⸣meš}$-MU A-*šu$_2$ ša$_2$* ^{I}*nad-⸢na⸣-a* A ^{lu_2}UŠ.BAR
^{I}[ ] ⸢A⸣-*šu$_2$ ša$_2$* ^{I}*ta-qiš-^{d}gu-la* A ^{I}*ḫa-mi-⸢ša$_2$$^{?}$⸣*(-×)
⸢^{I}⸣[A]-⸢*šu$_2$*⸣ *ša$_2$* ^{Id}AG-ŠEŠ^{meš}-TIN^{it}
[^{Id}AG-SUR-ZI^{meš} A]-*šu$_2$ ša$_2$* ^{Id}EN-BA^{ša_2} A $^{I\circ d}$EN-A-URU$_3$
[^{I}×-×-$^{d?}$ME$^{?}$].⸢ME$^{?}$⸣ A-*šu$_2$ ša$_2$* ^{I}*ša$_2$*-KA-^{d}EN A ^{I}LU$_2$-^{d}IDIM
[^{I}]-NUMUN-GAL$_2$^{ši} A-*šu$_2$ ša$_2$* ^{I}⸢TIN^{su}⸣
[^{I}] ⸢×⸣ A-*šu$_2$ ša$_2$* ^{Id}AG-TIN^{su}-E ⸢A ^{I}⸣[ ]-⸢A⸣
[*u*] ⸢^{Id}AMAR.UTU⸣-MU-GIŠ A-*šu$_2$ ša$_2$* ^{I}TIN^{su} ⸢A ^{I}⸣[ ]
an-nu-tu ^{lu_2}*mu-*[*kin-ne-e* (×)]
Lo.E. *ša$_2$ ina* IGI-*šu$_2$-nu* ^{I}DUG$_3$.GA-⸢×⸣[(×) A-*šu$_2$ ša$_2$* ... (A ...)]
^{lu_2}EN.NUN-*ti ša$_2$ ina* ⸢E$_2$⸣.[AN.NA$^{?}$]
Rev. *a-na* ^{Id}AMAR.UTU-MU-MU ⸢A-*šu$_2$ ša$_2$* ^{Id}⸣[AG-TIN^{su}-E]
A ^{I}ŠU-^{d}*na-na-a u* ^{lu_2}EN^{meš} *piq-⸢ne$_2$-e⸣-*[*ti*]
ša$_2$ E$_2$.AN.NA *iq-bu-u$_2$ um-ma*
UD.11.KAM UD.12.KAM *ša$_2$* ^{iti}⸢KIN⸣ *man-zal-ti*
^{lu_2}MUḪALDIM-*u$_2$-tu ina muḫ-ḫi* ^{I}EN-*šu$_2$-nu* A-*šu$_2$ ša$_2$*
^{Id}AG-ŠEŠ^{meš}-MU A ^{I}*e-gi$_3$-bi al-la*
ina° *muḫ-ḫi ra-bi-i ša$_2$ še-e-ri* 3 BAN$_2$
u ina muḫ-ḫi tar-din-nu ša$_2$ še-e-ri 1 BAN$_2$
tak-ka-su-u$_2$ a-na ^{d}GAŠAN *ša$_2$* UNUG^{ki}
⸢*ul*⸣ *iq-ru-ub* ^{iti}KIN UD.12.KAM
Up.E. MU.42.KAM ^{d}AG-NIG$_2$.DU-URU$_3$
LUGAL TIN.TIR^{ki}

Nabû-aḫḫē-iddin, son of Nadnāya, descendant of Išparu, [...], son of Taqīš-Gula, descendant of *Ḫamiša*, [...], son of Nabû-aḫḫē-bulliṭ, [Nabû-ēṭir-napšāti] , son of Bēl-iqīša, descendant of Bēl-aplu-uṣur, [×-*Gul*]*a*$^{?}$, son of Ša-pî-Bēl, descendant of Amīl-Ea, [DN]-zēru-šubši, son of Balāssu, [...], son of Nabû-balāssu-iqbi, descendant of [...]-*a*, and Marduk-šumu-līšir, son of Balāssu, descendant of [...]; these are the wi[tnesses] in whose presence Ṭāb-..., [son of ...] the watch, who

was (in duty) in E[anna$^?$], said to Marduk-šumu-iddin, son of [Nabû-balāssu-iqbi], descendant of Gimil-Nanāya, and the commissioners of Eanna as follows: on the 11th–12th days of month VI, except for the 3 *sūtu* for the main (meal of) the morning and the 1 *sūtu* for the second (meal of) the morning the *takkasû*-loaf of the Lady-of-Uruk, (which is) the baker's temple service incumbent on Bēlšunu, son of Nabû-aḫḫē-iddin, descendant of Egibi, was not offered.
Month VI, day 12, year 42 of Nebuchadnezzar, king of Babylon.

2 ^{I}*ḫa-mi-ša*$_2$; alternatively, ^{I}*ḫa-mi-ṣ*[*a*] or ^{I}*ḫa-gi*[*g*-(×)], all unclear.

12 for the name of Marduk-šumu-iddin's father, see **No. 311**: 16–17. Later, 1 Ner–2 Nbn, he will serve as the governor of Uruk (*šākin ṭēmi*).

313. YBC 7391

Copy: Plate LXXXVII
Date: [×.×.×] Nbn
Summary: summons guarantee

Obv. [*pu-ut* GI]R$_3$ ⸢*ša*$_2$⸣ ^{I}*ka-re-e-a* A-*šu*$_2$ *ša*$_2$ ^{Id}AG-ŠEŠ$^{⸢meš}$-MU⸣
[*ša*$_2$ ^{I}]MU-DU *a-ki-i sar-tu*$_4$ *iṣ-ba-tu-šu*$_2$
u ⸢*a-ki-i*⸣ *mu-ur-ṣi*-⸢*šu*$_2$$^!$⸣ *a-di-i* ḪAR^{meš} AN.BAR *ul-tu* E$_2$ *kil-lu*
a-na ^{Id}EN-GI A-*šu*$_2$ *ša*$_2$ ^{Id}UTU-MU A ^{I}MU^{meš}
a-na bul-lu-ṭu id-din-nu-šu$_2$ ^{Id}EN-GI
⸢A⸣-*šu*$_2$ *ša*$_2$ ^{Id}UTU-MU A ^{I}MU^{meš} *ina* ŠU^{II} ^{I}MU-DU
A-*šu*$_2$ *ša*$_2$ ^{Id}EN-NUMUN A ^{I}*ba-si-ia ša*$_2$ *muḫ-ḫi*
^{giš}BAN$_2$ *ša*$_2$ ^{d}GAŠAN *ša*$_2$ UNUG^{ki} *na-ši u*$_4$*-mu*
ša$_2$ ^{I}MU-DU *re-eš* ^{II}*ka-re-e-a*
⸢*i-na-šu-u*$_2$⸣ ^{Id}EN-GI *ib-ba-kam*-⸢*ma*⸣
Lo.E. ⸢*a-na*⸣ ^{I}MU-DU *i-nam-din-su ki-i*
la i-tab-kam-ma la ⸢*it*⸣*-tan-nu-šu*$_2$
Rev. *ḫi*-⸢*ṭu ša*$_2$⸣ DINGIR *u* LUGAL ⸢*i*⸣*-šad-dad*
(blank)
^{lu2}*mu*-⸢*kin*⸣*-nu* ^{I}*ba*$^!$*-la-ṭu* A-*šu*$_2$ *ša*$_2$ ^{I}IR$_3$-^{d}AG
A ^{lu2}I$_3$.SUR-GI.NA ^{Id}UTU-DU-A A-*šu*$_2$ *ša*$_2$
⸢^{Id}*na*⸣*-na-a*-KAM A ^{I}*ki-din*-^{d}AMAR.UTU ^{I}*na-di-nu*
⸢A-*šu*$_2$ *ša*$_2$ ^{Id}AG-*mu*⸣*-še-tiq*$_2$-UD.DA A ^{I}*bu-u*$_2$*-ṣu*
[^{I}]⸢A-*a*⸣ A-*šu*$_2$ *ša*$_2$ ^{I}KI.NE-*na-a-a u* ^{lu2}UMBISAG
[ ]-⸢^{d}15⸣ A-*šu*$_2$ *ša*$_2$ ^{I}*ša*$_2$-KA-^{d}EN [(×)]
[ ] ^{iti}[×]
Up.E. [ ] ⸢^{d}AG-I⸣
[LUGAL TIN].⸢TIR⸣^{ki}

Šumu-ukīn, son of Bēl-zēri, descendant of Basia, the rent-farmer of the Lady-of-Uruk, arrested (Karēa) because of a crime, and (later), due to his sickness, he transferred (him) in shackles from the prison to Bēl-ušallim, son of Šamaš-iddin, descendant of Šumāti, so that he might heal him. Bēl-ušallim guarantees vis-à-vis Šumu-ukīn for the presence of Karēa, son of Nabû-aḫḫē-iddin.
The day Šumu-ukīn demands the presence of Karēa, Bēl-ušallim shall bring him forth and hand him over to Šumu-ukīn. If he does not bring him forth and hands him over, he shall

bear the guilt of (an offence against) god and king.
Witnesses: Balāṭu, son of Arad-Nabû, descendant of Ṣāḫit-ginê; Šamaš-mukīn-apli, son of Nanāya-ēreš, descendant of Kidin-Marduk; Nādinu, son of Nabû-mušētiq-uddê, descendant of Bûṣu; Aplāya, son of Kinūnāya, and the scribe [...]-Ištar, son of Ša-pî-Bēl, descendant of ... [×.×.×] Nabonidus, [king of Bab]ylon.

1–8 The translation above diverges substantially from the original Akkadian structure for the sake of clarity. A closer, though cumbersome, translation would be: "*Bēl-ušallim, son of Šamaš-iddin, descendant of Šumāti, guarantees, vis-à-vis Šumu-ukīn, son of Bēl-zēri, descendant of Basia, the rent-farmer of the Lady-of-Uruk, for the presence of Karēa, son of Nabû-aḫḫē-iddin, whom Šumu-ukīn arrested because of a crime, and (later) due to his sickness, transferred in fetters from prison to Bēl-ušallim, son of Šamaš-iddin, descendant of Šumāti, so that he might heal him.*"

13 The translation of *ḫīṭu* as "the guilt of (an offence against)," rather than the more common "penalty," is based on Magdalene, Wunsch, and Wells 2019, who present an in-depth discussion of the term and its context.

314. YBC 9179

Copy: Plate LXXXVIII
Date: 10.VIII.35 Nbk
Summary: summons guarantee

Obv. ⸢^{I}IR$_{3}$⸣-^{d}AG A-*šu*$_{2}$ *ša*$_{2}$ ^{I}*i-di-i*ʾ-DINGIR
u ^{I}IR$_{3}$-^{d}AG A-*šu*$_{2}$ *ša*$_{2}$ ^{I}EN-*šu*$_{2}$-*nu*
pu-ut ^{I}⸢^{d}U.GUR⸣-TIN^{it} *u* ^{I}*e-rib-šu*$_{2}$ <<×>>
A^{meš} ⸢*ša*$_{2}$ ^{I}*i-sin*⸣-*na-a-a* ^{lu2}NA.GADA
ša$_{2}$ ^{d}⸢GAŠAN *ša*$_{2}$ UNUG^{ki}⸣ *ina* ŠU^{II} ^{Id}30-MU
⸢^{lu2}*qi*$_{2}$-*i*⸣-*p*[*i ša*$_{2}$ E$_{2}$.A]N.NA *na-šu-u*$_{2}$
[*ina*] ⸢^{iti}⸣SI[G$_{4}$$^{?}$ *ib-ba-ku*]$^{?}$-*šu*$_{2}$-*nu-im*-⸢*ma*⸣
[*ina* U]NUG⸢^{ki} *a-na*⸣ ^{Id}30-⸢MU⸣
Lo.E. ⸢^{lu2}*qi*$_{2}$⸣-*i-pi ša*$_{2}$ ⸢E$_{2}$.AN.NA⸣ [(×)]
⸢*i*⸣-*nam-din-šu*$_{2}$-⸢*nu*⸣ [*ki-i*]
Rev. *la i-tab-ku-n*[*u*(-*im-ma*) *la i*]*t-tan*$^{!}$-⸢*nu*$^{!}$⸣
ina re-e-ḫi ša$_{2}$ UGU ^{I}⸢*i-sin-na-a-a*⸣
AD-*šu*$_{2}$$^{!}$-*nu a-na* ^{d}⸢GAŠAN⸣ *ša*$_{2}$ UNUG^{ki} [*i-nam*]-*di-nu*
u ^{Id}30-MU ^{Id}U.GUR-TIN^{it} *u* [^{I}]⸢KU$_{4}$$^{?}$⸣-*šu*$_{2}$
a-ki-i re-ḫe-et re-e-ḫe ša$_{2}$ UGU
AD-*šu*$_{2}$-*nu u*$_{2}$-*ba-a*ʾ 1^{en} *pu-ut*
(tiny line) *ša*$_{2}$ 2^{i} *na-šu-u*$_{2}$
^{lu2}*mu-kin-nu* ^{I}MU-DU A-*šu*$_{2}$ *ša*$_{2}$ ^{I}*re-mut*
^{I}*na-din* A-*šu*$_{2}$ *ša*$_{2}$ ^{Id}U.GUR-PAP A ^{lu2}UŠ.BAR
^{I}⸢^{d}AG-SUR-ZI⸣^{me} A-*šu*$_{2}$ *ša*$_{2}$ ^{I}⸢^{d}EN-BA⸣^{š}[^{a2}]
Up.E. [A] ^{Id}⸢EN⸣-A-PAP ⸢^{Id}INNIN$^{?}$⸣-MU-KAM A-*šu*$_{2}$ *ša*$_{2}$ ^{Id}AG-PA[P^{me}]-GI
[A] ^{I}⸢AM-^{d}*a-nu*$_{3}$⸣ ^{lu2}UMBISAG ^{Id}AG-DU$_{3}$-Š[EŠ]
[A]-*šu*$_{2}$ *ša*$_{2}$ ^{I}DU$_{3}$-*a* A ^{I}*e*$_{2}$-*kur-za-kir* ^{uru}⸢×⸣[×]
⸢^{iti}APIN$^{?}$⸣ UD.10.KAM MU.35.KAM
Le.E. [^{d}]AG-NIG$_{2}$.DU-URU$_{3}$
[L]UGAL TIN.TIR^{ki}

Arad-Nabû, son of Idī-il, and Arad-Nabû, son of Bēlšunu, guarantee vis-à-vis Sîn-iddin, the *qīpu* of Eanna, for Nergal-uballiṭ and Erībšu, sons of Isinnāya, the herder of the Lady-of-Uruk. In month *III,* they will bring them forth and give them to Sîn-iddin, the *qīpu* of Eanna, in Uruk.
[If] they do not bring them forth and give them, they will pay from the balance due from Isinnāya, their father, to the Lady-of-Uruk. *Furthermore,* Sîn-iddin will hold Nergal-uballiṭ and Erībšu accountable for the rest of the balance due from their father. Each one guarantees for the other.
Witnesses: Šumu-ukīn, son of Rēmūtu; Nādinu, son of Nergal-nāṣir, descendant of Išparu; Nabû-ēṭir-napšāti, son of Bēl-iqīša, [descendant of Bē]l-aplu-uṣur; *Ištar*-šumu-ēreš, son of Nabû-aḫḫē-šullim, [descendant of] Rīm-Anu, (and) the scribe Nabû-bān-aḫi, son of Ibnāya, descendant of Ekur-zākir. (Town of) [...]. Month VIII, day 10, year 35 of Nebuchadnezzar, king of Babylon.

7 ⌜^{iti}⌝SI[G$_4$, possibly ⌜^{iti}⌝Š[E. The restored form *ib-ba-ku*?]-*šu*$_2$-*nu-im*-⌜*ma*⌝ is clearly problematic. The last four signs after the break, however, are clear, and a form of *abāku* must be sought; cf. *la i-tab-ku-n*[*u*] in l. 11.

315. YBC 3715

Copy: Plate LXXXVIII
Date: 06.X.40 Nbk
Summary: work contract: laundry[39]

Note that in most of the NA signs the scribe drops one of the *Winkelhakens* and the vertical wedge is preceded by only two strokes.

Obv. *ul-tu* UD.1.KAM *ša*$_2$ ^{iti}AB MU.40.KAM
^{d}AG-NIG$_2$.DU-URU$_3$ LUGAL TIN.TIR^{ki}
^{Id}*na-na-a*-MU A-*šu*$_2$ *ša*$_2$ ^{I}LU$_2$-^{d}*na-na-a*
^{Id}*in-nin*-MU-URU$_3$ A-*šu*$_2$ ^{I}LU$_2$-^{d}*na-na-a*
A-*šu*$_2$ *ša*$_2$ ^{I}*šul-lum-a* $^{Id!}$*na-na-a*-MU
A ^{fd}*na-na-a-re-ṣu-ni* ^{munus}*za-ka-t*[*u*$_4$]
u ^{Id}UTU-MU A$^{!(T.\ ša_2)}$ ^{I}*bu-ša*$_2$*-a* PAP 5 ^{lu_2}*pu-ṣa*-⌜*a*⌝-*a*
⌜*ina*⌝ MU.AN.NA 5 ^{gada}*gi-da-la-ne*$_2$*-e* *ša*$_2$ ⌜KA$_2$⌝ E$_2$ *pa-pa-ḫu*
⌜*ša*$_2$⌝ ^{d}GAŠAN ⌜*ša*$_2$⌝ UNUG^{ki} ^{d}*na-na-a*
[^{d}*u*$_2$]-*ṣur*-INIM-*su* ^{d}*gu-la u* ^{d}IGI.⌜DU⌝
Lo.E. [× × ×] ⌜×⌝ *ša*$_2$ ⌜*gu-ḫal*⌝-*ṣa-a-ta u* ⌜*ki*⌝-*ša*$_2$*-du*
[× ×] ⌜*ub*?-*bar*?⌝^{meš} *ša*$_2$ KAL MU.AN.NA
Rev. *ip-pu*-⌜*šu*⌝-*ma a-na* E$_2$.AN.NA *i-nam-di-nu*
mam-ma ul-tu muḫ-ḫi dul-li-šu$_2$*-nu*
a-na dul-lu ša$_2$*-nam-ma ul ib-bak-šu-nu-tu*
ŠUK.ḪI.A-*su-nu a-ḫi* ŠE.BAR *u a-ḫi* ZU$_2$.LUM.MA
ul-tu E$_2$.AN.NA *i-nam-šu-u*$_2$
^{lu_2}*mu-kin-nu* ^{Id}UTU-KAL A-*šu*$_2$ *ša*$_2$ ^{I}BA^{ša_2}-*a* A ^{lu_2}SIPA$^{!}$ ⌜GU$_4$⌝
^{Id}EN-*na-din*-A A-*šu*$_2$ *ša*$_2$ ^{I}NUMUN-TIN.TIR^{ki} A ^{I}DA-^{d}AMAR.UTU
^{Id}AMAR.UTU-SU A-*šu*$_2$ *ša*$_2$ ^{I}DU$_3$-*a* A ^{I}*e-gi*$_3$*-bi*
^{I}*mar-duk* A-*šu*$_2$ *ša*$_2$ ^{Id}AMAR.UTU-PAP A ^{I}ŠU-^{d}*na-na-a*

[39] A previous edition is included in Payne 2007, 101–2.

Up.E. [lú]UMBISAG [Id]AG-DU-A A-*šu*$_2$ *ša*$_2$ [I]NUMUN-*ia*
UNUG[ki] [iti]AB UD.6.KAM MU.40.KAM
[d]AG-NIG$_2$.DU-⸢URU$_3$⸣ LUGAL TIN.TIR[ki]

Beginning on day 1 of month X, year 40 of Nebuchadnezzar, king of Babylon, Nanāya-iddin, son of Amīl-Nanāya, Innin-šumu-uṣur, his son, Amīl-Nanāya, son of Šullumāya, Nanāya-iddin, son of [f]Nanāya-rēṣûni, a *zakītu*-woman, and Šamaš-iddin, son of Bušāya—a total of five linen weavers—will annually make five curtains for the gate(s) of the cella(s) of the Lady-of-Uruk, Nanāya, Uṣur-amāssu, Gula and [d]IGI.DU … of the cords and necklace …s of the entire year, and they will deliver (them) to Eanna.
No one shall remove them from their work for other work. They shall withdraw their salaries half in barley and half in dates from Eanna.
Witnesses: Šamaš-udammiq, son of Iqīšāya, descendant of Rē'i-alpi; Bēl-nādin-apli, son of Zēr-Bābili, descendant of Ile''i-Marduk; Marduk-erība, son of Ibnāya, descendant of Egibi; Marduk, son of Marduk-nāṣir, descendant of Gimil-Nanāya, (and) the scribe Nabû-mukīn-apli, son of Zēria.
Uruk, Month X, day 6, year 40 of Nebuchadnezzar, king of Babylon.

INDICES

Personal Names

The names in this index are listed in an alphabetical order. Each name is taken as a unit, disregarding hyphens and glottal ʾ signs. Damaged or incomplete name elements, marked with either × or …, are placed at the end of the alphabetical sequence.

Prosopographical work incorporated in this index is limited. Multiple attestations are listed together only if they were identified as a single individual in Payne 2007, or if there are clear indications within the present corpus. This means that namesakes who are listed separately below are not necessarily different individuals.[1] Given the focus of this volume on craftsmen, priority is given to individuals whose title/profession is known. The order of listing, in general, is identifiable protagonists, protagonists with only first name, fathers of protagonists.

Professional and personal attributes are stated only if they are attested in the text. A minor exception is references to Payne 2007, in which case professional attributes are given in parentheses. The sigla *, +, and ^ mark multiple attributes of a single individual that are attested in different texts.[2] Royal names in date formulas are not listed.

Orthographic variants are presented following the normalized form.[3] Individual spellings are given only in uncertain or exceptional cases. Line numbers in square brackets refer to a fully restored name.

Regarding normalization, conventions and consistency were generally preferred over historical accuracy. The following examples illustrate the main potential diversities and ambiguities.

- DN-A-MU is rendered DN-aplu-iddin (rather than DN-apla-iddina)
- DN-LUGAL-URU$_3$ is rendered DN-šarru-uṣur (rather than DN-šar(ra)-uṣur)
- *-ia* endings are rendered -ia; thus, NUMUN-*ia* is read Zēria (rather than Zēriya)
- *-Ca-a* endings are rendered -āya (rather then -â); thus, *kal-ba-a* is read Kalbāya (rather than Kalbâ)
- *-CV-ʾ* endings are rendered -CV̄; thus - *ia-mi-na-aʾ* is read Iaminā[4]
- Accusative is rendered *-u* in the Sg. and *-ē* in the Pl.
- E$_2$.AN.NA is rendered Eanna (rather than Ayakku); ^{d}MAŠ is rendered Ninurta (rather than Inušt); ^{d}EN.LIL$_2$ is rendered Enlil (rather than Illil)
- Noun names and nominalized participles are rendered with a nominal ending; thus, Nādinu (not Nādin) and Rēmūtu (not Rēmūt), regardless of spelling
- Unless specifically noted by orthography, final verbal elements in three-part names are read in

---

1 This is perhaps especially problematic in a few cases of several female namesakes listed on a single tablet. Our poor understanding and knowledge regarding female prosopography prevents us from identifying or distinguishing these women from each other.

2 Note, for example, the entry *nappāḫu**, f. of Ibni-Ištar+ 137:4*; 211:2*; 296:46+. Here, the individual is identified as a first *nappāḫu* in the first two attestations, and as the father of Ibni-Ištar in the third. An exception to this is ancestors of multiple descendants.

3 The use of the determinative ^{meš} vs. ^{me} is not considered a variant.

4 Note the exception of the family name *pir-uʾ*, which is conventionally rendered Pirʾu.

the imperative; thus, DN-N-bulliṭ/šullim (rather than DN-N-uballiṭ/ušallim). Two-part names, however, are rendered DN-uballiṭ/ušallim

– MU-MU names, with or without a DN, are read as "noun-verb" (rather than "participle-noun"); thus, (DN-)MU-MU = (DN-)šumu-iddin[5]

The following abbreviations are used: anc. = ancestor; br. = brother; desc. = descendant; f. = father; mo. = mother

Abu-ilāḫī (⌜AD⌝-*i-la-ḫi-i*ʾ)
1. f. of Aḫu-ilia 282:6

Abu-qīni (AD$^?$-*qi*$_2$-*i*-⌜*ni*$^?$⌝)
1. 285:2′

Abu-ukīn (AD-DU)
1. f. of Nanāya-iddin 304:45′

Abu-ul-īde (AD-NU.ZU)
1. *sepīru*(?) 106:4

ᶠAḫat-abīšu (*a-ḫat*-AD-*šu*$_2$)
1. 168:9
2. 168:33$^?$ ([*a-ḫat*]-AD-*šu*$_2$)

Aḫḫēa (ŠEŠ^{meš}-*e-a*)
1. f. of Amīl-Nabû 293:4
2. f. of Nabû-šumu-ibni 105:3

Aḫḫēšāya (ŠEŠ^{me}-*ša*$_2$-*a*)
1. son of […] 299:8′
2. 105:7
3. f. of Bēl-uballiṭ 170:8
4. f. of Ištar-zēru-ibni 297:25
5. f. of Zēria 193:31′; 310:7

Aḫḫēši (ŠEŠ^{me}-*e-šu*$_2$, ŠEŠ^{me}-*ši*)
1. 105:1
2. 161:11
3. f. of Uraš-iddin 213:2′

Aḫḫūtu (*aḫ-ḫu-tu*)
1. 170:7
2. f. of […] 310:2$^?$ (ŠEŠ$^?$-*u*$_2$-<*tu*>)

Aḫu-… (⌜ŠEŠ$^?$⌝-[×]-⌜×-×⌝)
1. 221:5

Aḫu-ēreš (ŠEŠ-KAM)
1. f. of Rēmūtu 202:7

Aḫu-iddin-Marduk (ŠEŠ-MU-^{d}AMAR.UTU)
1. 19:4
2. f. of Nabû-mukīn-apli 174:8

Aḫu-imme (ŠEŠ$^!$-*im-me-e*)
1. 256:10

Ahu-ittabši (ŠEŠ-*it-tab-ši*)
1. 226:16
2. 291:5

Aḫu-ilia (ŠEŠ-*li-ia*)
1. son of Abu-ilaḫī 282:6

Aḫu-lūmur (ŠEŠ$^{(meš)}$-*lu-mur*, ŠEŠ-IGI)
1. son of Nabû-aḫu-ēreš, *rab ešerti* 202:6
2. 229:7
3. 294:18′
4. f. of Bēl-ēṭir 202:5

Ālu-lūmur (URU-*lu-mur*)
1. 130:14
2. f. of Kinūnāya 202:25

ᶠAmātā (*a-mat-a*)
1. 168:10
2. 168:17

Amīl-Ea (LU$_2$-^{d}IDIM)
1. f. of Bēl-kāṣir 209:14
2. anc. of [×-*Gul*]*a*$^?$/Ša-pî-Bēl 312:5

Amīl-Nabû (LU$_2$-^{d}AG)
1. son of Aḫḫēa, *aškāpu* 293:4
2. 291:2
3. f. of Nabû-aḫu-iddin and Nūrea 174:10, 13
4. f. of Nabû-aḫu-iddin 221:3$^?$ (LU$_2$-^{d}A[G$^?$])

Amīl-Nanāya (LU$_2$-^{d}*na-na-a*)
1. *arad ekalli* 197:3
2. *išpar birmi* 296:16
3. *kabšarru*, son of Tabnēa (br. of Balāṭu?) 245:13 (see Payne 2007, 263, with no further attestations)
4. *pūṣāya*, son of Šullumāya$^+$ and f. of Nanāya-iddin* (grandfather of Innin-šumu-uṣur) 158:2; 163:7; 166:6*; 167:3*; 221:10; 243:14; 315:3*, 4$^+$ (see Payne 2007, 155–6)
5. *rēʾû*, son of Šamaš-iddin 221:4
6. *ša kurummat šarri* 298:8
7. son of Ištar-ālik-pāni 244:9
8. son of Nabû-zēru-ibni 297:28

[5] Names in the "participle-noun" pattern require syllabic spelling; e.g., ^{d}AG-*na-din*-MU (Nabû-nādin-šumi).

6. f. of Innin-šumu-uṣur 245:6
7. f. of Ištar-aḫu-iddin 248:2
8. f. of Mušēzib-Bēl, desc. of Arrabtu 232:11
9. f. of Mušēzib-Bēl 271:4
10. f. of Nabû-bān-aḫi 245:16′
11. f. of Nabû-mušētiq-uddê 57:6; 274:9
12. f. of Nadnāya 190:26
13. f. of Tabnēa 243:8

Aqara (*a-qar-a*)
1. 227:12
2. 241:4
3. f. of Nergal-nāṣir, desc. of Bēl-aplu-uṣur 232:9

Arad-Bēl (IR$_3$-^{d}EN)
1. *išpar birmi*, son of Silim-Bēl and br. of Šamaš-ēṭir 296:12 (see Payne 2007, 158)
2. 199:4
3. 209:17
4. 303:41′
5. 304:40′
6. 308:9′

Arad-Bunene (IR$_3^{?}$-^{d}*bu-ne-ne*)
1. son of ^{f}Bazītu, br. of Zanzīru 168:15

Arad-Gula (IR$_3$-^{d}ME.ME, IR$_3$-^{d}*gu-la*)
1. *aškāpu* 296:56
2. son of Amīl-Nanāya 297:27
3. 64:3
4. f. of Gimillu 244:8
5. f. of Rēmūtu 203:5

Arad-Innin (IR$_3$-^{d}*in-nin*, IR$_3$-^{d}INNIN.NA)
1. *ašlāku* 158:7 (see Payne 2007, 158, with no further attestations)
2. *atkuppu* 260:2
3. *kabšarru*, son of Balāssu 245:16 (see Payne 2007, 263–4)
4. *nappāḫu* 62:5 (see Payne 2007, 295)
5. *pūṣāya*, son of Arad-Nabû and br. of Bēl-ēṭir 296:38 (see Payne 2007, 159, with no further attestations)
6. son of Ana-Ištar-taklāk 298:1
7. son of ^{f}Ana-bītišu (*zakītu*-woman) 296:19
8. son of Kinūnāya 297:26
9. son of Kūnāya 179:3
10. son of Mušallim-Marduk 55:3
11. son of Nabû-naʾid 214:13
12. son of Nabû-šumu-ukīn 174:16
13. 55:10
14. 217:10
15. 221:6
16. f. of Gimillu 282:19

Arad-Nabû (IR$_3$-^{d}AG)
1. *atû* 193:17′
2. *nappāḫ parzilli* 296:49 (see Payne 2007, 295–6)
3. son of Bēlšunu 314:2
4. son of Iddia 138:iii 3
5. son of Idī-il 314:1
6. son of Rēḫētu 271:7
7. son of Ša-Nabû-šū 104:3, 5; 138:i 4, 22, ii 5, 13, 20, 22, 26 (see Payne 2007, 296)
8. 193:30′
9. 227:9
10. 305:12
11. f. of Balāṭu, desc. of Ṣāḫit-ginê 313:14
12. f. of Bēl-ēṭir and Arad-Innin 296:37
13. f. of Nabû-bān-aḫi 278:4
14. f. of Šamšamānu 286:2; 304:8

Arad-Nanāya (IR$_3$-^{d}*na-na-a*)
1. *aškāpu*, f. of Eanna-līpi-uṣur and ^{f}Baba-eṭerat, husband of ^{f}Ana-Nanāya-šī 105:9
2. *bēl maṣṣarti* 215:6′
3. son of Ṭāb-šār-Ištar 266:6
4. 253:2
5. f. of [×]-aḫu-iddin 308:11′

Arad-[DN] (⸢IR$_3$-^{d}⸣[...])
1. 215:2′

Ardāya (IR$_3$-*a*)
1. *nagāru* 217:28
2. *reʾû*, son of Nanāya-ēreš 221:9
3. 193:42′
4. f. of Gimillu[6] 212:11; 235:2; 242:17; 244:13
5. f. of Nabû-aḫu-iddin, desc. of Bēl-× 245:14′
6. f. of Nanāya-uṣalli[7] 132:6; 136:4

6 Given the context of the different attestations, it is likely that Ardāya, the father(s) of Gimillu, Nanāya-uṣalli, and Šulāya, is the same individual and this was a family of smiths.

7 See note 6.

7. f. of Šulāya[8] 103:7; 194:15

Ardia (IR$_3$-*ia*)
1. *gallābu* 179:9
2. *mušallimānu*, son of Itti-Bēl-abni 296:58
3. son of Amīl-Nanāya 193:51′
4. son of Kalbāya 308:40′
5. son of Nabû-aḫu-iddin 256:3
6. son of Nadnāya 299:18′
7. son of Nergal-šumu-ibni 305:6
8. son of Šākin-šumi 304:17
9. 181:8
10. 296:67
11. f. of [...] 193:59′
12. f. of Innin-zēru-ibni 305:3

Arrab (*ar$_2$-rab*)
1. 233:6
2. br. of Nabû-aḫḫē-uṣur 307:3
3. f. of Nanāya-aḫu-iddin 221:8
4. f. of Nanāya-aḫu-iddin 272:4

Arrabtu (*ar$_2$-rab-tu$_2$*)
1. anc. of Mušēzib-Bēl / Aplāya 232:11

ᶠAšar-*šī-ummu* (*a*$^{!}$(T:ZA)-*šar-ši-*⌜*i*-AMA⌝)
1. 168:30

ᶠAškaʾitu-ṭābat (^{d}⌜*aš$_2$-ka-ʾ-i-tu$_4$-ṭa-bat*)
1. 168:6
2. 168:27
3. daughter of Zabdia 168:12

Ašlāku (^{lu_2}TUG$_2$.BABBAR)
1. anc. of the *ṭupšarru* Ibni-Ištar / Nabû-zēru-ukīn 155:3; 232:14

Attaṣar-ubâki-Ištar (*a-ta-ṣur-u$_2$-ba-ku*-^{d}INNIN)
1. 215:10′

Atû (^{lu_2}I$_3$.DU$_8$)
1. anc. of Nabû-aḫḫē-iddin 243:15

Ayyabi (*a-a-bi*)
1. 256:11

ᶠBaba-eṭerat (^{d}*ba-ba$_6$-e-ṭe-*⌜*rat*⌝)
1. daughter of Arad-Nanāya 105:11

Bābia (*ba-bi-ia$_2$*, *ba-bi-ia*)
1. *atû* 195:4
2. *nappāḫu**, *nappāḫ siparri*+, son of Marduk-ēreš 70:6*; 245:9′+ (see Payne 2007, 297)

Bābilāya (TIN.TIR^{ki}-*a-a*)
1. son of Ša-Nabû-šū, *rab ešerti* 202:12

Babūtu (*ba-bu*$^{!}$*-tu$_2$*)
1. anc. of (the *kutimmu*) Bēl-ibni/ Nādinu 311:8

Bākûa (*ba-ku-u$_2$-a*)
1. *aškāpu* 296:52

Balāssu (TIN^{su}, *ba-laṭ-su*)
1. *nappāḫ siparri* 61:4 (see Payne 2007, 297, with no further attestations)
2. son of Ḫašdia 144:7
3. son of Ina-tēšî-ēṭir and f. of Marduk-šumu-līšir 242:4, 5
4. son of Nanāya-īpuš 107:2
5. son of Šumāya, desc. of Nabāya 45:3; 232:4
6. 30:4
7. f. of Arad-Innin 245:16
8. f. of Innin-zēru-iddin 310:14
9. f. of Innin-zēru-šubši 71:12
10. f. of Innin-zēru-šubši 181:10
11. f. of [DN]-zēru-šubši 312:6[9]
12. f. of Marduk-šumu-ibni 113:3
13. f. of Marduk-šumu-ibni 204:4
14. f. of Marduk-šumu-līšir, desc. of [...] 312:8

Balāṭu (*ba-la-ṭu*, TIN$^{tu?}$)
1. *kabšarru*, son of Tabnēa (br. of Amīl-Nanāya?) 245:17 (see Payne 2007, 264–5)
2. son of Amīl-Nanāya 297:5
3. son of Arad-Nabû, desc. of Ṣāḫit-ginê 313:14
4. son of Bēl-erība 190:8, 35
5. son of Ina-tēšî-ēṭir 26:3 (see Payne 2007, 234)
6. son of Mušallim-Marduk 303:35′
7. son of Ša-Nabû-šū 203:1
8. son of Šumāya 115:2
9. 217:17
10. 308:36′
11. f. of Marduk-šāpik-zēri 286:10
12. anc. of Nabû-bān-aḫi / Kabtia 311:11

8 See note 6.

9 Possibly f. of [Innin]-zēru-šubši; see **Nos. 71**:12 and **181**:10.

Bānia (DU$_3$-*ia*, DU$_3$-*ia*$_2$, *ba-ni-ia*)
1. son of Bēl-rēmanni 117:5
2. son of Nabû-aḫḫē-ibni 217:13
3. son of Nabû-balāssu-iqbi 71:13
4. son of Nabû-nāṣir 212:10
5. son of Nūrea, br. of Nidintu 304:46′
6. 217:18
7. 296:67
8. f. of Šamaš-zēru-šubši 286:6

Bānītu-ēreš (^{d}DU$_3$-*tu*$_4$$^{?}$-KAM)
1. 256:9

^{f}Bānītu-Esagil (DU$_3$-*tu*$_2$-<E$_2$>.SAG.IL$_2$)
1. 37:4

Basia (*ba-si-ia, ba-as-si-ia*)
1. son of Uzīb-Baytil 282:2
2. anc. of the *ša muḫḫi sūti* Šumu-ukīn/Bēl-zēri 313:6

^{f}Bazītu (⸢*ba*$^{!}$⸣-*zi-i-tu*$_4$)
1. mo. of Zanzīru and Arad-Bunene 168:13

Bēl/Nabû-... (⸢^{d}EN/AG-×-×⸣)
1. son of [...] 299:12′

Bēl-abu-uṣur (^{d}EN-AD-PAP)
1. 292:6

Bēl-aḫḫē-erība (^{d}EN-PAP^{me}-SU, ^{d}EN-ŠEŠ^{me}-SU)
1. son of Idī-il 285:10′
2. son of Marduka 47:4
3. 30:5
4. 222:3
5. 282:14
6. 297:21
7. f. of Bēl-uballiṭ 243:3

Bēl-aḫḫē-iddin (^{d}EN-ŠEŠ^{me}-MU)
1. *rē*ʾ*û*, son of Bēlšunu 221:5
2. son of Nabû-zēru-ibni 47:3

Bēl-aḫḫē-iqīša (^{d}EN-PAP^{me}-BA^{ša_2}, ^{d}EN-ŠEŠ^{me}-BA^{ša_2})
1. f. of Nādinu 214:2
2. f. of Šamaš-udammiq 243:6

Bēl-aḫḫē-[...] (^{d}EN-PAP^{me}-[×])
1. 307:20

Bēl-aḫu-iddin (^{d}EN-ŠEŠ-MU)
1. f. of Rēmūtu* and Itti-Marduk-balāṭu* 5:5*; 11:3; 31:10* (see Payne 2007, 234–5)
2. 190:11
3. f. of Gimillu 311:7
4. f. of Rēmūtu 273:7[10]

Bēl-aḫu-šubši (^{d}EN-ŠEŠ-⸢GAL$_2$⸣-*ši*)
1. f. of(?) Kalbāya 301:33′

Bēl-ana-mātišu (^{d}EN-*ana*-KUR-*šu*$_2$)
1. son of Nabû-ušallim 105:5
2. f. of Nabû-iddin 292:5; 293:6

Bēl-aplu-uṣur (^{d}EN-A-URU$_3$, ^{d}EN-A-PAP)
1. anc. of Nabû-ēṭir-napšāti/Bēl-iqīša and Nergal-nāṣir/Aqara 25:5; 232:9; 312:4; 314:21

Bēl-atta-talê (^{d}EN-*at-ta*-DA)
1. 297:9

Bēl-īpuš (^{d}EN-DU$_3$^{uš})
1. 126:2
2. 174:6
3. f. of Kinūnāya 202:27

Bēl-erība (^{d}EN-⸢SU⸣, ^{d}EN-<*e*>-*ri-bi*$^{(sic)}$)
1. f. of Balāṭu 190:9, 36

Bēl-eṭēri-Šamaš (^{d}EN-KAR-^{d}UTU)
1. *nappāḫ parzilli*, son of Ištar-zēru-ibni 296:48 (see Payne 2007, 299, with no further attestations)

Bēl-ēṭir (^{d}EN-SUR, ^{d}EN-KAR, ^{d}EN-KAR^{ir})
1. *ašlāku*, son of Arad-Nabû and br. of Arad-Innin 296:37 (see Payne 2007, 160)
2. *malāḫu*, son of Ša-Nabû-šū 310:3
3. *rab ešerti*, son of Aḫu-lūmur 202:5
4. son of [...] 299:7′
5. Larsean 305:17
6. 170:7

Bēl-ibni (^{d}EN-DU$_3$, ^{d}EN-*ib-ni*)
1. *kutimmu**, son of Nādinu^{+}, desc. of Babūtu 1:6*; 3:5*; 4:8*; 9:[1]*; 36:4*; 53:5*; 175:2^{+}; 245:4′$^{+}$; 311:8^{+} (see Payne 2007, 235–7)
2. *nappāḫ siparri**, son of Nabû-zēru-ibni and f. of Innin-zēru-šubši^{+}, br. of Marduka, and Šulāya 54:4; 60:3*; 70:5;+ 245:10′+ (see Payne 2007, 300–1)
3. f. of Ibni-Ištar 273:6
4. f. of Nabû-šarru-uṣur 213:242′
5. f. of Nanāya-aḫu-iddin 116:9

[10] Quite possibly to be identified as the goldsmith from **No. 11**:3 (father in **Nos. 5**:5 and **31**:10).

Bēl-iddin (^{d}EN-MU)
1. *išparu* 303:23′; 308:27′ (see Payne 2007, 161–2)
2. son of Munnabittu 243:2, 4
3. 141:7
4. 203:7
5. f. of Kūnāya 170:3
6. f. of Nabû-ušallim 280:9

Bēl-iqbi (^{d}EN-*iq-bi*, ^{d}EN-E)
1. *išparu**, son of Nabû-ušallim+ and f. of Gimillu^ 149:7*+; 153:4*; 173:4*; 182:6*; 186:5*; 188:3*+; 270:3*; 296:21^; 297:32+ (see Payne 2007, 162)
2. son of Iqīšāya 116:6
3. f. of Gimillu 296:21
4. 128:8

Bēl-iqīša (^{d}EN-BA^{ša_2})
1. f. of Iddinunu 252:3
2. f. of Nabû-ēṭir-napšāti, desc. of Bēl-aplu-uṣur 25:6; 312:4; 314:20
3. f. of Nanāya-iddin 304:2

Bēl-išdīa-ukīn (^{d}EN-SUḪUŠ-*ia*-DU)
1. son of Eanna-līpi-uṣur 161:3

Bēl-kāṣir (^{d}EN-*ka-ṣir*)
1. son of Amīl-Ea 209:14
2. son of Mušallim-Nabû 141:2, 9

Bēl-kāšid-ayyabi (^{d}EN-*ka-šid-*⌜*a-a-bi*⌝)
1. *ša rēš šarri ša muḫḫi rehēti* 248:5

Bēl-lēʾi (^{d}EN-DA)
1. f. of Innin-aḫu-iddin 305:5

Bēl-nādin-apli (^{d}EN-*na-din*-A)
1. son of Zēr-Bābili, desc. of Ileʾʾi-Marduk 311:1; 315:19

Bēl-nāṣir (^{d}EN-PAP)
1. *malāḫu* 292:7; 293:8
2. 221:22
3. f. of Innin$^{?}$-zēru-[×] 18:10

Bēl-nipšari (^{d}EN-*ni-ip-šar-ri*)
1. 273:3

Bēl-nuḫšu (^{d}EN-*nu-uḫ-šu*$_2$)
1. f. of Nanāya-aḫu-iddin 192:2

Bēl-rēmanni (^{d}EN-*re-man-ni*)
1. f. of Bānia 117:5

Bēl-šumu-iškun (^{d}EN-MU-GAR^{un})
1. 170:17

Bēlšunu (EN-*šu*$_2$-*nu*)
1. *bēl piqitti*(?), [son of(?)] Ša-Nabû-šū 56:3
2. son of Nabû-aḫḫē-iddin, desc. of Egibi 311:3; 312:16
3. son of Nādinu 305:19
4. 55:2
5. 217:9
6. f. of Arad-Nabû 314:2
7. f. of Bēl-aḫḫē-iddin 221:5
8. f. of Innin-zēru-ibni 201:9?
9. f. of Nabû-ēṭir 170:15
10. f. of Nanāya-aḫu-iddin 297:6

Bēl-tuklātūʾa (^{d}EN-*tu-kul-*⌜*la*$^{!}$⌝-*tu-u*$_2$-*a*)
1. 121:3

Bēl-uballiṭ (^{d}EN-TIN^{iṭ})
1. *išparu* 181:4 (⌜$^{d?}$EN$^{?}$-TIN⌝, possibly ⌜*na*⌝-*din*, Nādinu)
2. son of Aḫḫēšāya 170:8
3. son of Bēl-aḫḫē-erība 243:3
4. son of [...] 152:7
5. f. of Nabû-aplu-iddin 179:8

Bēl-upaḫḫir (^{d}EN-NIGIN^{ir}, ^{d}EN-NIGIN$_2$^{ir})
1. *nagāru* 217:28
2. *nappāḫu*, son of Nādinu 110:3
3. *nappāḫu**, f. of Ibni-Ištar^{+} 137:4*; 211:2*; 296:46^{+} (see Payne 2007, 302)
4. son of Šamaš-ēṭir 190:32
5. f. of Nabû-aplu-iddin 179:6
6. f. of Nabû-mušētiq-uddê 244:7

Bēl-ušallim (^{d}EN-GI)
1. son of Šamaš-iddin, desc. of Šumāti 313:4, 5, 10
2. f. of Ištar-zēru-ibni 243:12

Bēl-ušēzib (^{d}EN-*u*$_2$-*še-zib*)
1. son of Nanāya-iddin 192:3
2. f. of Nabû-aḫḫē-šullim 245:4

Bēl-zēri (^{d}EN-NUMUN)
1. 107:11
2. f. of Šumu-ukīn, desc. of Basia 313:7
3. f. of Ṭābia 245:5′

Bēl-[...]
1. *rab ešerti* 202:21 (⌜^{d}EN⌝-[...])
2. f. of Iddināya 203:3 (^{d}EN-×)
3. f. of Nabû-bēlšunu 310:5 (^{d}EN-⌜×⌝-[×])
4. anc. of Nabû-aḫu-iddin/Ardāya 245:14′ (^{d}⌜EN⌝-[×])

Bibēa (*bi-bi-e-a*)
1. 126:7
2. 130:13$^{?}$ (*bi-*[*bi-a*$^{?}$])

^{f}Binītu (*bi-[n]i-⌜tu$_4$⌝*)
1. 168:28

^{f}Bu'itu (*bu-'-i-tu$_2$*)
1. 174:2

Bulluṭ (*bul-luṭ*)
1. son of Gula-zēru-ibni 227:7; 231:3

Bulluṭāya (*bul-luṭ-a*)
1. 291:8
2. f. of Nabû-erība 213:20′

^{f}Burāšu (*bu-ra-šu$_2$*)
1. 168:3
2. 215:12

Bûṣu (*bu-u$_2$-ṣu*)
1. anc. of Nādinu / Nabû-mušētiq-uddê 313:17

Bušāya (*bu-ša$_2$-a*)
1. f. of Šamaš-iddin 315:7

Dadia (*da-di-ia*)
1. f. of Aplāya 185:2; 245:6′

Dannu-aḫḫēšu-ibni (^{d}*dan-nu*-ŠEŠ^{me}-*šu$_2$*-DU$_3$, ^{d}*dan-nu*-PAP^{me}-*šu$_2$*-DU$_3$)
1. *aškāpu* 296:56
2. *mušākil iṣṣūri* 215:8
3. *mušallimānu*, son of a *zakītu*-woman 296:60 (see Payne 2007, 163)
4. *pūṣāya*, son of Nabû-ēdu-uṣur and br. of Šumu-iddin 296:30 (see Payne 2007, 164)
5. *pūṣāya* 308:6′ (see Payne 2007, 163)
6. son of ^{f}Ana-tabnîšu (*zakītu*) 296:20 (see Payne 2007, 163)
7. Larsean 305:17
8. 296:74
9. 304:4, 6
10. 308:28′

Dūrlāya (BAD$_3$-*la-⌜a⌝*)
1. 296:29

Eanna-ibni (E$_2$.AN.NA-DU$_3$)
1. *rab ešerti*, son of Šamaš-iddin 202:26
2. *rē'i iṣṣūri* 215:6, 8′
3. 161:10
4. 215:7

Eanna-līpi-uṣur (E$_2$.AN.NA-*li-pi*-PAP, E$_2$.AN.NA-*li-pi*-URU$_3$, E$_2$.AN.NA-*lip*-URU$_3$, E$_2^{!}$.AN.NA$^{!}$-*li-pu*-PAP)
1. *aškāpu* 262:6
2. son of Arad-Nanāya 105:10
3. 296:66
4. 299:9′
5. f. of Bēl-išdīa-ukīn 161:4

Eanna-šumu-ibni (E$_2$.AN.NA-MU-DU$_3$)
1. *pūṣāya*, son of Šulāya 296:36 (see Payne 2007, 165)

Ea-zēru-iqīša (^{d}IDIM-NUMUN-BA^{ša_2})
1. 207:9

Ēdūa (*e-du-u$_2$-a*)
1. *nappāḫ parzilli*, *qallu* (of Ibni-Ištar / Bēl-upaḫḫir) 296:46 (see Payne 2007, 303)

Egibi (*e-gi-bi*, *e-gi$_3$-bi*)
1. anc. of Bēlšunu / Nabû-aḫḫē-iddin and Marduk-erība / Ibnāya 311:4; 312:17; 315:20

Ekur-zākir (*e$_2$-kur-za-kir*)
1. anc. of the *ṭupšarru* Nabû-bān-aḫi / Ibnāya 314:23

Enlil-šumu-ibni (EN.LIL$_2$-MU-DU$_3$)
1. 230:13

Erībšu (KU$_4$-*šu$_2$*, *e-rib-šu$_2$*)
1. *arad ekalli* 305:13
2. *išparu**, son of Nanāya-iddin⁺ and f. of Šamaš-zēru-ibni 212:12*; 296:18⁺ (see Payne 2007, 166–7)
3. *nagāru*(?) 198:19
4. son of Iqīšāya and br. of Nūrea 307:8
5. son of Isinnāya and br. of Nergal-uballiṭ 314:3, 14
6. son of Rēḫētu 269:5
7. 289:6
8. 295:9 (*nappāḫ parzilli*, see Payne 2007, 303)
9. f. of Šamaš-erība 122:9

Ērišu (*e-riš*)
1. *nappāḫu* 298:4 (see Payne 2007, 304)
2. f. of Kidin-Marduk 202:11

Etellu (*e-tel-lu*)
1. f. of Marduk-zēru-ibni 212:9

Ēṭeru (*e-ṭir*)
1. f. of Iddināya 120:3

Ezu-pašir (*e-zu-pa-šir$_3$*, *e-zu-u$_2$-pa-š[ir$_3$]*, *e-zu-u-pa-šir$_2$*)
1. 170:5
2. 170:23
3. 291:2
4. 299:5′

Gabria (*gab-ri-ia*$_2$)
1. *nukaribbu ša karānu* 242:15
Gadû (*ga-du-u*$_2$)
1. son of Nabû-ušallim 282:5
Gimillu (ŠU, *gi-mil-lu*)
1. *aškāpu* 298:7
2. *išpar birmi**, son of Bēl-iqbi+ 189:6*; + 296:21+ (see Payne 2007, 197)
3. *nagāru**, *nagār qutāni*+, son of Nabû-zēru-iqīša 245:9*; 296:3+
4. *ša muḫḫi immeri* 217:32
5. son of Ardāya* 212:11*; 235:2*, 237:5, 238:5, 239:4, 240:5 242:17*, 244:13*
6. son of Arad-Gula 244:8
7. son of Arad-Innin 282:19
8. son of Bēl-aḫu-iddin 311:7
9. son of Nadnāya 244:10
10. son of Nanāya-[…] 307:22
11. son of Zēria 181:6
12. son of Zēria 212:7
13. son of Zēria, desc. of Šigūa 311:5
14. 10:2
15. 193:50′
16. 217:21
17. 296:67
18. f. of Innin-šumu-uṣur 304:16
19. f. of Nadnāya 296:53
20. f. of Šamaš-ibni 305:21
Gimil-Nanāya (ŠU-ᵈ*na-na-a*)
1. anc. of Marduk/Marduk-nāṣir and the *bēl piqitti* Marduk-šumu-iddin/Nabû-balāssu-iqbi 311:17; 312:13; 315:21
Gimil-Šamaš (ŠU-ᵈUTU)
1. *ērib bīti* of Uṣur-amāssu, son of Itti-Šamaš-balāṭu 311:12
Gula-x (ᵈ⌜*gu-la*⌝-[××])
1. 129:2
Gula-zēru-ibni (ᵈ*gu-la*-NUMUN-DU$_3$)
1. f. of Bulluṭ 227:7; 231:3
2. f. of Zērūtu 310:12
Guzānu (*gu-za-nu*)
1. *mār šipri* (of the *šatammu*) 304:39′
2. *rēʾi sattukki* 286:3
3. son of Nabû-bēl-šumāti 147:3
4. son of Nanāya-× 244:11
5. 296:69
6. 308:13′

Ḫadūru (⌜*ḫa*⌝-*du-ru*)
1. *rēʾû* 190:2
Ḫamiša (*ḫa-mi*-⌜*ša*$_2$?⌝)
1. anc. of […]/Taqīš-Gula 312:2
Ḫašdāya (*ḫaš-da-a*)
1. *nappāḫ parzilli* 296:62, 65 (see Payne 2007, 304–5)
Ḫašdia (*ḫaš-di-ia*, *ḫaš-di-ia*$_2$)
1. *pūṣāya**, son of Nanāya-ēreš+, f. of Šamaš-šumu-ukīn^ and Ibni-Ištar^ (grandfather of Nanāya-iddin) 164:3+; 165:4+; 166:2+; 193:21′*, 23′^; 296:25^ (see Payne 2007, 168)
2. *ikkaru* 88:7
3. son of Iaminā 212:6
4. f. of Balāssu 144:8
5. f. of Nabû-ēṭir-napšāti 297:11
Ḫateki (*ḫa-te-ki*)
1. 190:2, 3
ᶠḪīpāya (*ḫi-pa-a*)
1. 168:31

Iaminā (*ia-mi-na-aʾ*)
1. f. of Ḫašdia 212:6
Ibāya (*i-ba-a*)
1. f. of Nanāya-ēreš 292:8; 293:9
Ibnāya (DU$_3$-*a*)
1. son of Nabû-aḫḫē-šullim 282:1
2. son of Tabnēa 181:3
3. f. of Aplāya 227:9
4. f. of Ištar-ālik-pāni 304:7
5. f. of Marduk-erība, desc. of Egibi 315:20
6. f. of Nabû-bān-aḫi, desc. of Ekur-zākir* 71:15 (⌜DU$_3$⌝-*ia*[!sic]); 314:23*
7. f. of Nabû-zēru-iqīša 245:5
Ibni-Innin (⌜DU$_3$?-ᵈINNIN?⌝.NA)
1. 308:12′
Ibni-Ištar (DU$_3$-ᵈINNIN, DU$_3$-ᵈ15)
1. *aškāpu* 296:54
2. *pūṣāya*, son of Ḫašdia and br. of Šamaš-šumu-ukīn 296:26 (see Payne 2007, 168)
3. *ṭupšarru**, son of Nabû-zēru-ukīn*,

desc. of Ašlāku 155:3; 232:13* (see Payne 2007, 169–71)
4. son of Bēl-ibni 273:6
5. *nappāḫ parzilli**, son of Bēl-upaḫḫir* 285:13′; 296:46* (see Payne 2007, 305)
6. son of Ḫašdia 193:23′
7. son of a *kalû*(?) (a junior *kalû*?) 200:6
8. son of Nabû-šumu-ibni 184:4
9. son of Šumu-ukīn 285:9′
10. 203:10
11. 282:17
12. 294:12′
13. f. of Kīnāya, desc. of Pirʾu 212:3
14. f. of Nidintu 304:13
15. f. of Šumāya 246:5
16. f. of Talīmu 304:37′

Iddia (*id-di-ia*)
1. *aškāpu* 296:55
2. 190:13
3. f. of Arad-Nabû (and Nabû-aḫu-iddin?) 138:iii 3$^{?}$ (*id*$^{!}$-*di*$^{!}$-*ia*$_{2}$)
4. f. of Nabû-aḫu-iddin (and Arad-Nabû?) 138:iii 7

Iddin-[DN] (⸢SUM$^{?}$⸣.[NA$^{?}$-...])
1. 221:4

Iddināya (SUM.NA-*a*)
1. *nappāḫ parzillu**, son of Ēṭeru^{+} 120:2^{+}; 304:36′* (see Payne 2007, 321, s.v. Nadnāya; the identification of both cases as one smith is uncertain)
2. *rab ešerti*, son of ... 202:22
3. son of a *zakītu*-woman 296:75
4. son of Bēl-… 203:3
5. son of Innin-šumu-uṣur 308:12′
6. son of Marduk 163:8 (see Payne 2007, 185, s.v. Nadnāya, with no further attestations)
7. son of Nēšu 55:7
8. son of Šulāya and br. of Ištar-zēru-ibni 307:4
9. son of Zabidāya 107:3
10. son of […] 299:6′
11. 107:10
12. 206:4
13. 295:2
14. 297:21
15. 303:52′
16. f. of Kinūnāya 292:1; 293:1
17. f. of Nā[din] 299:14′? (SUM$^{?}$.A$^{?}$)
18. f. of Silim-Bēl 221:8

Iddin-Bēl (MU-^{d}EN)
1. 304:30′

Iddin-Ištar (MU-^{d}INNIN$^{!}$)
1. f. of Nergal-ēṭir 28:4

Iddin-Marduk (MU-^{d}AMAR.UTU)
1. f. of Ištar-zēru-ibni 142:3
2. f. of Nabû-bān-aḫi, desc. of Nūr-Sîn 311:6

Iddin-Nabû (MU-^{d}AG)
1. son of Aplāya 290:5
2. son of Nergal-ušallim 190:28

Iddinunu (SUM-*nu-nu*)
1. son of Bēl-iqīša 252:3
2. son of Šulāya 212:13

Idī-il (*i-di-i*$^{?}$-DINGIR)
1. f. of Arad-Nabû (and probably of Bēl-aḫḫē-erība) 314:1
2. f. of Bēl-aḫḫē-erība (and probably of Arad-Nabû) 285:11′

i-di-u$_{2}$*-a*
1. f. of Nabû-ušabši 190:16

IGI.DU-zēru-ibni (^{d}IGI.DU-NUMUN-DU$_{3}$)
1. son of Ša-Nabû-šū 309:4
2. f. of Ištar-zēru-ibni 193:47′

IGI.DU-… (^{d}IGI.DU-⸢ŠU-GIŠ-BI⸣-ZA-ŠU$_{2}^{?}$)
1. f. of Šamaš-zēru-šubši 304:21

Ileʾʾi-Marduk (DA-^{d}AMAR.UTU)
1. 308:35′
2. anc. of Bēl-nādin-apli / Zēr-Bābili 311:2; 315:19

Ilu-pīya-uṣur (DINGIR$^{?}$⸣-KA-*ia*-URU$_{3}$)
1. 193:16′

Imbāya (*im-ba-a*)
1. f. of Uk(k)umu 32:5

Imbia (*im-bi-ia*)
1. 303:43′

^{f}Ina-Nanāya-ultarraḫ (*ina-*^{d}*na-na-a-ul-tar-ra-aḫ*)
1. 168:37

Ina-qibīt-Bēl-limmir (*ina-qi*$_{2}$*-bit-*^{d}EN-ZALAG$_{2}$, *ina-qi*$_{2}$*-bi-*^{d}EN-*li-im-mir*)
1. *nappāḫ parzilli** 134:3*; 138:iii 12, 25, 27 (see Payne 2007, 308)

Ina-ṣil[li-DN] (*ina*-GIS[SU$^{?}$-^{d}×])
1. 299:38′

Ina-ṣilli-Bēl ([*ina*-GIS]SU-^{d}EN)
1. *aškāpu* 193:55′
Ina-ṣilli-Bēl-abni (*ina*-GISSU-^{d}EN-*ab-ni*)
1. 207:5
Ina-ṣilli-Nanāya (*ina*-GISSU-^{d}*na-na-a*)
1. *atû* 225:3
2. *mukabbû* 207:3
3. *paḫāru* 193:24′
4. *širku* of the *šatammu* Kudurru 290:1
5. son of Nergal-... 297:18
6. 193:52′
7. 223:3
8. 308:23′
9. 308:38′
Ina-ṣilli-Nergal (*ina*-GISSU-^{d}U.GUR)
1. son of Nabû-iqīša 193:28′
Ina-tēšî-ēṭir (*ina*-SUḪ$_{3}$-SUR)
1. *išpar birmi*, son of Rēmūtu and br. of Anu-šarru-uṣur 296:11 (see Payne 2007, 171)
2. *mār šipri* (of Amurru-lū-šalim), son of Nanāya-aḫu-iddin 135:6
3. *sepīru* 217:25
4. son of Nanāya-ēreš 204:2
5. son of Šumu-uṣur 67:5 (see Payne 2007, 308)
6. son of Tabnēa, desc. of Nūr-Sîn* 302:2*; 310:2, 9
7. f. of Balāssu 242:4 (see Payne 2007, 238)
8. f. of Balāṭu 26:4
9. f. of Šamaš-udammiq 304:43′
Innin-[...]
1. son of Nanāya-iddin 294:7′ ([^{d}*in*]-*nin*$^{?}$-[...])
2. 299:31′ (^{d}INNIN.N[A-×])
Innin-aḫḫē-iddin (^{d}INNIN.NA-PAP^{me}-MU, ^{d}*in-nin*-ŠEŠ-MU)
1. son of Bēl-lēʾi 305:4
2. f. of Nanāya-iddin 304:14
^{f}Innin-ēṭirat (*in-nin-e-ṭe*$_{3}$*-rat*)
1. 168:34
Innin-kibsu-abi-uṣur (^{d}*in-nin-kib-su*-AD-URU$_{3}$)
1. 305:14
Innin-šumu-uṣur (^{d}INNIN.NA-MU-PAP, ^{d}INNIN.NA-MU-URU$_{3}$, ^{d}*in-nin*-MU-URU$_{3}$)
1. *atkuppu* 209:3
2. *išparu* 193:22′
3. *išparu**, *išpar birmi*+, son of Ṭāb-Uruk^ 176:14, 26; 246:2*; 282:13^; 294:6′^; 296:10+^; 308:4′ (see Payne 2007, 172–3)
4. *itinnu* 288:4
5. *nagāru*, son of Aplāya 245:6
6. *pūṣāya*, son of Nanāya-iddin 315:4 (see Payne 2007, 172, with no further attestations)
7. *ṣāḫit sattukku* 304:28′
8. son of Gimillu 304:16
9. son of Šārid 120:4
10. son of Zabidāya 193:46′
11. 144:9
12. 193:9′
13. 217:14
14. 303:48′
15. f. of Iddināya 308:12′
16. f. of Zēria 296:70
Innin-zēru-ibni (^{d}INNIN.NA-NUMUN-DU$_{3}$, ^{d}*in-nin*-NUMUN-DU$_{3}$)
1. son of Ardia 305:2
2. son of Bēlšunu 201:9
3. 190:24
4. 194:16
5. 210:1
6. 227:15
7. 243:9 (unclear affiliation)
8. f. of Šumu-uṣur 307:13
Innin-zēru-iddin (^{d}*in-nin*-NUMUN-MU)
1. son of Balāssu 310:13$^{?}$ (^{d}INNIN$^{!}$.NA-NUMUN-⌜MU$^{?}$⌝, possibly Innin-zēru-ēreš)
2. son of Zērūtu 265:2
Innin-zēru-iqīša (^{d}*in-nin*-NUMUN-BA^{ša_2})
1. 226:6
Innin-zēru-šubši (INNIN.NA-NUMUN-TIL, ^{d}*in-nin*-NUMUN-GAL$_{2}^{ši}$)
1. *išpar birmi** 296:66; 308:8′, 31′* (see Payne 2007, 173–4)
2. *nagāru*, son of Rēmūtu 245:8
3. *nappāḫu**, *nappāḫ siparri*+, son of Bēl-ibni 70:5*; 245:10′+ (see Payne 2007, 309–10)
4. son of Apkallu 243:13
5. son of Balāssu 71:11
6. son of Balāssu 181:9

7. son of Nanāya-uṣalli 207:11
8. 298:3 (*nappāḫ parzilli*, see Payne 2007, 309)

Innin?-zēru-[×] (^{I}INNIN$^{!?}$.NA-NUMUN-[×])
1. son of Bēl-nāṣir 18:9

Iqbā[ya] (*iq-ba-[a]*)
1. 277:7

Iqīša-Innin (BA^{ša_2}-^{d}INNIN.NA)
1. *kabšarru*, son of Minsu-ilī 245:18 (see Payne 2007, 268, with no further attestations)

Iqīšāya (BA^{ša_2}-*a*)
1. *išparu** 150:6, 7; 172:4* (see Payne 2007, 174–5)
2. *išpar birmi* 308:3′? (BA^{ša_2})
3. 285:3′? (^{I}BA^{ša_2} [(×)])
4. f. of Bēl-iqbi 116:7
5. f. of Erībšu and Nūrea 307:8
6. f. of Nabû-kēšir 308:17′
7. f. of Šamaš-udammiq, desc. of Rē'i-alpi 315:18

Isinnāya (*i-sin-na-a-a*)
1. *nāqidu ša Bēlet Uruk*, f. of Nergal-uballiṭ and Erībšu, 314:4, 12
2. 229:3
3. 233:4
4. f. of Šulāya 273:8

Išparu (^{lu_2}UŠ.BAR)
1. anc. of Apkallu, Nabû-aḫḫē-iddin, Nabû-aḫḫē-iddin / Nadnāya, Nādinu, and the *išparu* Nādinu / Nergal-nāṣir 171:4; 177:4; 183:7; 187:7; 232:10; 310:11; 312:1; 314:19

Ištar-aḫu-iddin (^{d}INNIN-ŠEŠ-MU, ^{d}15-ŠEŠ-MU)
1. *išpar birmi* 296:15 (see Payne 2007, 175, with no further attestations)
2. *kutimmu*, *mār šipri*, son of Aplāya 248:3 (see Payne 2007, 239–40)
3. *nappāḫ parzilli**, son of Nabû-ušabši+ 295:6; 296:47*+ (see Payne 2007, 310–1, with no further attestations)

Ištar-ālik-pāni (^{d}INNIN-DU-IGI, ^{d}15-DU-IGI, ^{d}INNIN-*a-lik*-IGI)
1. son of Ibnāya 304:7
2. 193:18′
3. 304:44′
4. 305:7
5. f. of Amīl-Nanāya 244:9

Ištar-erība (^{d}INNIN?-SU)
1. 243:10

Ištar-mukīn-apli (^{d}INNIN-DU-A)
1. *nagāru* 198:11
2. son of Zērūtu 109:2

Ištar-nādin-apli (^{d}INNIN-*na*°-⸢*din*-IBILA⸣)
1. son of Nabû-aḫu-[×] 23:2

Ištar-rēṣū'a (^{d}INNIN-*re-ṣu-u_2*-a, ^{d}15-*re-ṣu-u-a*, ^{d}15-*re-ṣu-u_2-a*)
1. *pūṣāya** 192:1; 296:41* (see Payne 2007, 175–6)
2. *rē'i iṣṣūri* 193:20
3. 251:6
4. 291:4
5. 297:19

Ištar-šarru-uṣur (^{d}15-LUGAL-URU$_3$)
1. *ša šakin māti* 296:23 (see Payne 2007, 176, with no further attestations)

Ištar-šumu-ēreš (^{d}INNIN-MU-KAM, ^{d}15-MU-KAM)
1. *mandidu*, son of Nabû-šumu-ukīn 242:11
2. son of Nabû-aḫḫē-šullim, desc. of Rīm-Anu* 139:5, 314:21*
3. son of Nabû-aḫu-iddin 297:16
4. 203:15

Ištar-šumu-ibni (^{d}INNIN-MU-DU$_3$, ^{d}15-MU-DU$_3$)
1. *kutimmu*, son of Nabû-šumu-ukīn* 1:6; 3:4; 4:8; 9:2; 36:3; 52:3; 53:5; 245:[3′]* (see Payne 2007, 240–1)

Ištar-uddu (^{d}INNIN-*u_2-da*)
1. 217:31

Ištar-ukīn (^{d}INNIN-DU, ^{d}INNIN-*u_2-kin*)
1. *aškāpu* 296:51
2. son of the *atû ša akītu* 215:9

Ištar-ušallim ($^{d?}$15?-GI)
1. *kutimmu*(?) 288:1

Ištar-zēru-ibni (^{d}INNIN-NUMUN-DU$_3$, 15-NUMUN-DU$_3$)
1. *kabšarru*, son of Iddin-Marduk 142:3 (see Payne 2007, 269)
2. son of Aḫḫēšāya 297:25
3. son of Bēl-ušallim 243:12
4. son of IGI.DU-zēru-ibni 193:48′
5. son of Šulāya and br. of Iddināya 307:5
6. son of Tarību 243:11
7. f. of Bēl-eṭēri-Šamaš 296:48

Itti-Bēl-abni (KI-^{d}EN-*ab-ni*)
1. f. of Ardia 296:58

Itti-Eanna-būdia (KI-E$_{2}$.AN.NA-*bu-di-ia*$_{2}$, KI-E$_{2}$.AN.NA-*bu-di-ia*)
1. ^{lu2}*ma/ba-la-a* 112:2
2. *rē*ʾ*i iṣṣūri* 297:17
3. 55:11
4. 126:4
5. 174:4
6. 229:13

Itti-enši-Nabû (KI-SIK-^{d}AG)
1. *nagāru*, son of Šulāya 245:10
2. *nagār qutāni*, son of Šulāya 296:5

Itti-Marduk-balāṭu (KI-^{d}AMAR.UTU-TIN, KI-^{d}ŠU$_{2}$-TIN)
1. son of Bēl-aḫu-iddin* and br. of Rēmūtu* 5:5*; 17:6; 20:5; 31:9* (*kutimmu*, see Payne 2007, 242)
2. son of Urukāya 190:15, 17

Itti-Šamaš-balāṭu (KI-^{d}UTU-TIN)
1. f. of Gimil-Šamaš 311:12
2. f. of Šamaš-zēru-ibni and Zumbu 296:72

Kabtia (IDIM-*ia*, *kab*-<*ti*>-*ia*$^{!?}$)
1. 279:3(?) (*kab*-<*ti*>-*ia*$^{!?}$)
2. f. of Nabû-bān-aḫi, desc. of Balāṭu 311:11

Kalbāya (*kal-ba-a*, UR-*a*)
1. *išparu**, *išpar birmi*$^{+}$, son of Nabû-silim^{+} 296:13^{+}; 298:10* (see Payne 2007, 176–7)
2. *rab kāri* 296:55
3. *rē*ʾ*i sîsē*, son of(?) Bēl-aḫu-šubši 301:33′
4. son of Amīl-Nanāya and br. of Lâbâši 307:6
5. son of Zēria 190:12, 13, 14, 22, 27
6. 273:4
7. 295:11
8. f. of Ardia 308:40′

Kalbi-ilāni (UR-DINGIR^{meš})
1. f. of Nādinu 32:4

Kamnā (*ka*$^{?!}$-*am-na*$^{?!}$-*a*ʾ)
1. 168:42

Karēa (*ka-re-e-a*)
1. son of Nabû-aḫḫē-iddin 313:1, 9
2. f. of [...] 214:5

Kidin-Marduk (*ki-din*-^{d}AMAR.UTU, *ki-din*-^{d}ŠU$_{2}$)
1. *rab ešerti*, son of Ērišu 202:11
2. anc. son Šamaš-mukīn-apli / Nanāya-ēreš 313:16

Kidinnu (*ki-din-nu*, *ki-din*)
1. *išpar birmi* 296:15 (see Payne 2007, 177, with no further attestations)
2. son of Šadûnu 275:5 (*kutimmu*, see Payne 2007, 244)

Kidin[(-...)] (*ki*-⸢*din*$^{?}$⸣[(...)])
1. 299:35′

Kīnāya (*ki-na-a*)
1. *mandidu* 242:12
2. son of Ibni-Ištar, desc. of Pirʾu 212:3
3. f. of Nabû-silim 297:30

Kinnê (*ki-in-ne*$_{2}$-*e*)
1. 256:1

Kinūnāya (KI.NE-*a-a*, KI.NE-*na-a-a*, KI.NE-*nu-na-a-a*)
1. *rab ešerti*, son of Ālu-lūmur 202:25
2. *rab ešerti*, son of Bēl-īpuš 202:27
3. son of Iddināya 292:1, 11; 293:1
4. f. of Aplāya 313:18
5. f. of Arad-Innin 297:26
6. 291:5

Kiribtu (*ki-rib-tu*, *ki-rib-tu*$_{2}$, *ki-rib-ti*)
1. son of Nabû-zēru-šubši 304:22
2. son of Nādinu 199:9
3. 194:20
4. f. of Nanāya-[...] 180:6

Kî-Šamaš (*ki-i*-^{d}UTU)
1. *išpar birmi* 296:14 (see Payne 2007, 190, s.v. Qibi-Šamaš, with no further attestations)

Kudurru (NIG$_{2}$.DU)
1. *išparu* 151:3 ([⸢NIG$_{2}$.D]U)[11]
2. *rē*ʾ*û*, son of N[abû-...] 221:1
3. *šatammu* (Nbk) 290:2
4. 157:26
5. 170:19, 178:11 (see Payne 2007, 177)[12]
6. 305:10
7. f. of Tukulti-Marduk 284:6

[11] If the reading is correct, then this Kudurru is most likely the same weaver attested in **No. 170**: 19 (for which, see Payne 2007, 177).

[12] See note 6.

Kūnāya (*ku-na-a*)
1. son of Bēl-iddin 170:3
2. f. of Arad-Innin 179:4

^{f}Kupīti (*ku-pi-ti*)
1. 37:3

Kurbanni-Marduk (*kur-ban-ni*-^{d}AMAR.UTU)
1. 190:20

Kussî-ili (AŠ.TE-DINGIR)
1. f. of Nabû-šumu-ēreš 202:10

Lâbâši (*la-ba-ši, la-a-ba-ši*)
1. *ikkaru*(?) 297:29
2. son of Amīl-Nanāya and br. of Kalbāya 307:7
3. son of Ṭāb-šār-Bēl 200:3
4. 201:10
5. 303:8′
6. 305:9
7. f. of Nanāya-aḫu-iddin 244:6

Lâbâši-Ištar (*la-ba-a-ši*-^{d}15)
1. 215:9′

Lāqīpi (*la-qi*$_2$*-i-pi, la-qi*$_2$*-pi*)
1. 254:3
2. 303:24′

Libluṭ (*lib-luṭ*)
1. *nappāḫu**, *nappāḫ siparri*$^{+}$, son of Nanāya-iddin^{+} 58:3^{+}; 59:4*; 69:4^{+}; 70:4^{+} (see Payne 2007, 312)

^{f}Līdū (*li-i*ʾ*-du-u*ʾ)
1. 168:5
2. 168:40

Līšīr (⸢*li*?⸣*-šir*$_3$)
1. *ṭupšar māti* 213:14′

Lūmur-dumqi-[DN] (IGI-⸢*dum-qi*$_2$⸣-[^{d}×])
1. 297:19

Lūmur-dumqi-Ištar (^{I}IGI-*dum-qi*$_2$-^{d}INNIN, *lu-mur-dum-qi*$_2$-^{d}15)
1. *rab sikkatu* 226:12
2. son of Ṭāb-šār-Eanna 297:31
3. 193:50′
4. 226:5[13]

Lūṣi-ana-nūri (E$_3$-*ana*-ZALAG$_2$)
1. *nagāru*(?) 198:26

m / ba-bi-a?*-p / bu*
1. f. of Rēmūtu 75:7

Madān-ēreš (DI.KUD-KAM, DI.KUD-APIN^{eš})
1. 236:4
2. f. of Anu-šumu-ibni 245:7; 296:4

Madān-šarru-uṣur (DI.KUD-LUGAL-URU$_3$)
1. 303:53′

Marduk (*mar-duk*)
1. *rab ešerti*, son of Šamaš-iddin 202:29
2. son of Marduk-nāṣir, desc. of Gimil-Nanāya 315:21
3. f. of Iddināya 163:8
4. f. of Nādinu 7:4
5. f. of Nādinu 213:12′
6. f. of [...] 174:21

Marduka (*mar-duk-a*)
1. *nappāḫu* 273:5[14]
2. *nappāḫ siparri**, son of Nabû-zēru-ibni, br. of Bēl-ibni^{+}, and Šulāya^{+} 48:3*; 54:4, 13^{+}; 77:6 (see Payne 2007, 314)
3. f. of Bēl-aḫḫē-erība 47:5
4. f. of Ṣillāya 141:13

Marduk-bēlšunu (^{d}AMAR.UTU-EN-*šu*$_2$*-nu*)
1. *šatammu* 287:4

Marduk-ēreš (AMAR.UTU-KAM)
1. f. of Bābia 70:[6]; 245:9′

Marduk-erība (AMAR.UTU-SU)
1. *nappāḫu* 273:2
2. son of Ibnāya, desc. of Egibi 315:20
3. son of Nādin-aḫi 213:10′

Marduk-ēṭir (^{d}AMAR.UTU-SUR)
1. son of Nabû-zēru-līšir 287:8

Marduk-nāṣir (^{d}AMAR.UTU-PAP)
1. f. of Marduk, desc. of Gimil-Nanāya 315:21
2. f. of Nanāya-ēreš 202:28

Marduk-šākin-šumi (^{d}AMAR.UTU-GAR-M[U])
1. 31:2

Marduk-šāpik-zēri (^{d}AMAR.UTU-DUB-NUMUN)
1. son of Balāṭu 286:10
2. 297:9

Marduk-šarrāni (^{d}AMAR.UTU-LUGAL-*a-ni*)
1. 170:23

Marduk-šumu-ibni (^{d}AMAR.UTU-MU-DU$_3$)
1. son of Balāssu 113:2

[13] Although not identified as such, it is reasonable to assume that he is the same individual named as rab *sikkatu* later in the text: 226:12.

[14] Most like he is the son of Nabû-zēru-ibni; see below.

2. son of Balāssu 204:3
3. f. of Nabû-šumu-ukīn 297:8

Marduk-šumu-iddin (AMAR.UTU-MU-MU)
1. *bēl piqitti**, son of Nabû-balāssu-iqbi, desc. of Gimil-Nanāya 311:16*, 18, 20; 312:12
2. son of Nabû-aḫḫē-bulliṭ 214:3
3. 217:5
4. 249:5
5. f. of Nādin-apli 303:47′

Marduk-šumu-iškun (^{d}AMAR$^{?}$.UTU$^{?}$-MU-GAR^{un})
1. 256:8

Marduk-šumu-līšir (^{d}AMAR.UTU-MU-GIŠ)
1. son of Balāssu, desc. of [...]* 242:4; 312:8* (see Payne 2007, 269–70)

Marduk-šumu-uṣur (^{d}AMAR.UTU-MU-URU$_3$, ^{d}AMAR.UTU-MU-PAP, ^{d}ŠU$_2$-MU-PAP)
1. *nappāḫu**, *nappāḫ siparri*$^{+}$, son of Mušēzib-Marduk* 70:7*; 245:11′$^{+}$ (see Payne 2007, 313)
2. son of Nabû-zēru-iddin 213:17′

Marduk-šumu-× (^{d}AMAR.UTU-MU-⸢×⸣)
1. 107:7

Marduk-ušallim (^{d}AMAR.UTU-GI)
1. f. of Nādinu 191:3

Marduk-zēru-ibni (^{d}AMAR.UTU-NUMUN-DU$_3$, ^{d}ŠU$_2$-NUMUN-DU$_3$)
1. *arad ekalli* 200:9
2. *arad ekalli, rēʾû* 221:6
3. son of Etellu (possibly father of Mušallim-Marduk) 212:9
4. son of Nabû-iddin 280:4
5. f. of Mušallim-Marduk 212:8
6. f. of Nabû-aḫḫē-bulliṭ 47:2
7. f. of Nabû-aḫḫē-šullim 190:31

Minsu-ilī (*min*$_3$-*su*-DINGIR)
1. f. of Iqīša-Innin 245:18

^{f}Mīṣātu (*mi-ṣa-tu*$_4$)
1. 168:26
2. 168:39

Mukīn-Marduk (DU-^{d}AMAR.UTU)
1. son of Murānu 106:3

Mukīn-×
1. 209:19 (DU-⸢×⸣)
2. 286:16 (⸢DU⸣-[...])

Mukkēa (*muk-ke*$^{!}$*-e-a*)
1. *nagāru* 198:10

Munnabittu (*mun-na-bi-ti*)
1. f. of Bēl-iddin 243:2, 4

Murānu (*mu-ra-nu*)
1. f. of Mukīn-Marduk 106:3

Mušallim-Marduk (GI-^{d}AMAR.UTU)
1. son of Marduk-zēru-ibni 212:8
2. son of Nabû-šumu-nāṣir 224:3
3. 190:17
4. f. of Arad-Innin 55:4
5. f. of Balāṭu 303:35′
6. f. of Mušēzib-Bēl 282:3
7. f. of Šamaš-ibni 202:24

Mušallim-Nabû (GI$^{?}$-⸢^{d}AG$^{?}$⸣)
1. f. of Bēl-kāṣir 141:2

Mušēzib-Bēl (KAR-^{d}EN, *mu-še-zib*-^{d}EN)
1. *kabšarru*, son of Taqīš-Gula 245:14 (see Payne 2007, 270)
2. *nappāḫu**, *nappāḫ parzilli*$^{+}$, son of Nabû-zēru-iddin^ 95:3^; 96:3*^; 97:3^; 98:6^{+}; 99:3^; 100:6^; 101:5+; 102:3^; 195:2^; 211:3* (see Payne 2007, 314–5)
3. son of Aplāya 271:3
4. son of Aplāya, desc. of Arrabtu 232:11
5. son of Mušallim-Marduk 282:3
6. son of Nergal-ēṭir 297:4
7. 194:7
8. 217:20

Mušēzib-Marduk (KAR-^{d}AMAR.UTU, *mu-še-zib*-^{d}AMAR.UTU)
1. 170:22
2. 213:6′
3. 303:45′
4. f. of Marduk-šumu-uṣur 70:8 (<KAR>-^{d}ŠU$_2$)

Nabāya (*na-ba-a-a*)
1. anc. of Balāssu / Šumāya 45:4; 232:5

Nabû-abu-uṣur (^{d}AG-AD-URU$_3$)
1. 281:12(?)
2. 293:7

Nabû-aḫḫē-bulliṭ (AG-PAP^{me}-TIN, ^{d}AG-ŠEŠ^{meš}-TIN^{iṭ})
1. son of Marduk-zēru-ibni 47:1
2. son of Nanāya-ibni, br. of Nūrea and Amīl-Nanāya 307:10
3. 19:3
4. f. of Marduk-šumu-iddin 214:3
5. f. of [...] 312:3

Nabû-aḫḫē-ibni (^{d}AG-PAP$^{\text{!(T. qa)meš!(T. d.30)}}$-DU$_3$)
1. f. of Bānia 217:13

Nabû-aḫḫē-iddin (^{d}AG-ŠEŠ^{meš}-MU, ^{d}AG-PAP^{meš}-MU)
1. *išparu* 229:9
2. son of Nabû-iltama᾽ 285:8′
3. son of Nadnāya, desc. of Išparu 312:1
4. son of Ša-Nabû-šū 199:12
5. desc. of Atû 243:15
6. desc. of Išparu 310:11
7. 28:2
8. 217:16
9. f. of Bēlšunu, desc. of Egibi 311:3; 312:17
10. f. of Karēa 313:1
11. f. of Ša-pî-Bēl 170:2

Nabû-aḫḫē-šullim (AG-ŠEŠ^{meš}-GI, ^{d}AG-ŠEŠ^{meš}-*šul-lum*, ^{d}AG-PAP^{me}-GI)
1. *nagāru*, son of Bēl-ušēzib 245:4
1. son of Marduk-zēru-ibni 190:31
2. son of Nabû-udammiq 248:2
3. f. of Ibnāya 282:1
4. f. of Ištar-šumu-ēreš, desc. of Rīm-Anu* 139:5, 314:21*
5. f. of Šamaš-aḫu-iddin 296:6
6. f. of Šulāya 297:22

Nabû-aḫḫē-uṣur (^{d}AG-ŠEŠ^{me}-⌜URU$_3$?⌝)
1. br. of Arrab 307:2

Nabû-aḫu-ēreš (^{d}AG-ŠEŠ-KAM)
1. son of Nūrea 18:6
2. f. of Aḫu-lūmur 202:6

Nabû-aḫu-iddin (^{d}AG-ŠEŠ-MU, ^{d}AG-PAP-MU)
1. *ikkaru*(?) 297:29
2. *nagāru* 79:3
3. *nappāḫ siparri* 299:19′ (see Payne 2007, 316)
4. *nappāḫu* 100:9
5. *rē᾽û*, son of Amīl-N[abû] 221:3
6. *sepīru* 193:27′; 205:3
7. son of Amīl-Nabû 174:10
8. son of Ardāya, desc. of Bēl-× 245:14′
9. son of Iddia 138:iii 7, 20 (see Payne 2007, 315–6, with no further attestations)
10. son of Ištar-šumu-ēreš 297:16
11. son of Nabû-zēru-iqīša 193:45′
12. son of Nabû-zēru-iqīša 297:15
13. son of Nanāya-ēreš 161:6, 14
14. son of Nanāya-ēreš 209:1
15. son of ... 297:2
16. 193:43′
17. 303:55′ ([^{d}]⌜AG?⌝-ŠEŠ-MU)
18. 308:19′
19. f. of [...] 193:58′
20. f. of Ardia 256:3
21. f. of Šamaš-iddin 193:49′

Nabû-aḫu-uṣur (^{d}AG-ŠEŠ-PAP)
1. 193:44′

Nabû-aḫu-[×] (^{d}AG-ŠEŠ-[×])
1. f. of Ištar-nādin-apli 23:3

Nabû-ana-bilti-ēreḫ (^{d}AG-*a-na-bil-ti-e-re-ḫi*)
1. *qallu* (of Nādinu / Nergal-nāṣir / / Išparu) 171:8 (see Payne 2007, 179, s.v. Nabû-ana-×-rēḫi)

Nabû-ana-kâšu-atkal (^{d}AG-*ana-ka-a-šu$_2$-at-kal*)
1. 297:24, 34

Nabû-aplu-iddin (^{d}AG-IBILA-MU, ^{d}AG-A-MU)
1. son of Bēl-uballiṭ 179:7
2. son of Bēl-upaḫḫir 179:5

Nabû-ayyālu (^{d}AG-*a-a-lu*)
1. *rē᾽û* 190:3
2. 289:6

Nabû-balāssu-iqbi (^{d}AG-TIN^{su}-E)
1. *aškāpu* 296:52
2. *tardennu* 303:50′
3. 256:13
4. f. of Bānia 71:13
5. f. of Marduk-šumu-iddin, desc. of Gimil-Nanāya 311:16
6. f. of [...], desc. of [...]-a 312:7

Nabû-bān-aḫi (^{d}AG-DU$_3$-ŠEŠ)
1. 217:7
2. *atû* 195:5
3. *nappāḫ parzilli* 296:63 (see Payne 2007, 316, with no further attestations)
4. *ṭupšarru*, son of Ibnāya, desc. of Ekur-zākir* 71:14; 314:22*
5. son of Aplāya 245:16′
6. son of Arad-Nabû 278:3
7. son of Iddin-Marduk, desc. of Nūr-Sîn 311:6
8. son of Kabtia, desc. of Balāṭu 311:10

Nabû-bēl-ili (^{d}AG-EN-*i$_3$-li$_2$*)
1. 253:4; 254:4

5. 198:14
6. f. of Nādinu, desc. of Bûṣu 313:17
7. f. of Nidintu 296:8

Nabû-nādin-aḫi (^{d}AG-*na-din*-ŠEŠ)
1. *ikkaru* 190:6

Nabû-nādin-šumi (^{d}AG-*na-din*-MU)
1. son of Šullumāya 292:4; 293:5
2. 257:2
3. 285:5′

Nabû-na'id (^{d}AG-I)
1. 285:7′
2. f. of Arad-Innin 214:13

Nabû-nāṣir (^{d}AG-PAP)
1. son of Nabû-lē'i 202:4
2. 27:7, 14; 30:3; 38:6 (*kutimmu*, see Payne 2007, 248–9)
3. 131:3 (listed s.v. Nabû-zēru-iddin in Payne 2007, 318)
4. f. of Bānia 212:10
5. f. of Šākin-šumi 245:12

Nabû-*nāṣir*(-×) (^{d}AG-⌜PAP?-(×)⌝)
1. 209:10

Nabû-reḫti-uṣur (^{d}AG-*re-eḫ-ti*-URU$_3$)
1. 144:3

Nabû-rēmu-šukun (^{d}AG-ARḪUŠ-*šu-kun*)
1. *mār šipri* (of Nergal-īpuš) 303: 26′, 29′

Nabû-rēṣū'a ([^{d}A]G-*re-ṣu-u$_2$-a*)
1. 222:7

Nabû-rē'ûa (^{d}AG-SIPA-*u$_2$-a*)
1. *pūṣāya* 286:12 (see Payne 2007, 181)

Nabû-silim (AG-*si-lim*)
1. son of Kīnāya 297:30
2. son of(?) Šamaš-zēru-ibni 231:6
3. f. of Kalbāya 296:13

Nabû-šarru-uṣur (^{d}AG-LUGAL-URU$_3$, ^{d}AG-LUGAL-PAP)
1. [*bēl piqit*]*ti Eanna* 294:2′
2. son of Bēl-ibni 213:24′

Nabû-šumu-ēreš (^{d}AG-MU-KAM)
1. *malāḫu* 117:12
2. son of Kussî-ili, *rab ešerti* 202:10
3. son of Zību 119:2

Nabû-šumu-ibni (^{d}AG-MU-DU$_3$)
1. *aškāp mešēni*(?) 211:7
2. *aškāpu* 307:19
3. son of Aḫḫēa 105:3
4. f. of Ibni-Ištar 184:4
5. 107:1

Nabû-šumu-iddin (^{d}AG-MU-MU)
1. 107:6
2. 214:7

Nabû-šumu-līšir (^{d}AG-MU-GIŠ, ^{d}AG-MU-SI.SA$_2$)
1. desc. of Šangû-Zāriqu 25:3
2. 217:6
3. 231:4
4. f. of Sîn-ēreš 304:18

Nabû-šumu-nāṣir (^{d}AG-MU-PAP)
1. f. of Mušallim-Marduk 224:4

Nabû-šumu-ukīn (^{d}AG-MU-DU)
1. *itinnu* 242:23; 245:8′; 272:7
2. *kutimmu**, son of Nergal-uballiṭ$^{+}$ 6:6*; 8:4*; 29:17*; 39:8*; 45:6*; 7:5^{+} (see Payne 2007, 249–50)
3. son of Marduk-šumu-ibni 297:8
4. son of Nanāya-ēreš 97:7
5. 230:10
6. 230:7
7. f. of [Ištar-šumu-ibni] 245:3′
8. f. of Arad-Innin 174:17
9. f. of Ištar-šumu-ēreš 242:12

Nabû-šumu-uṣur (^{d}AG-[M]U?-URU$_3$)
1. 304:33′

Nabû-taklāk (^{d}AG-*tak-lak*)
1. 292:2[15]

Nabû-udammiq (^{d}AG-KAL)
1. son of Nabû-zēru-iddin 203:12
2. 308:35′
3. f. of Nabû-aḫḫē-šullim 248:3

Nabû-upaḫḫir (^{d}AG-⌜NIGIN$_2$?⌝^{ir})
1. *nagāru* 196:3

Nabû-uṣalli (^{d}AG-SISKUR$_2$)
1. son of [...] 194:6

Nabû-uṣuršu (^{d}AG-*u$_2$-ṣur-šu$_2$*)
1. *atkuppu* 260:3

Nabû-ušabši (^{d}AG-GAL$_2$^{ši})
1. *itinnu* 299:16′
2. son of *i-di-u$_2$-a* 190:16
3. f. of Ištar-aḫu-iddin 296:47

Nabû-ušallim (^{d}AG-GI)
1. *nuḫatimmu*, son of Bēl-iddin 280:8
2. *ša rēš* [*šarri*](?) 125:4
3. f. of Bēl-ana-mātišu 105:5

15 Possibly a mistake for Ana-Ištar-taklāk; see commentary to the text.

4. f. of Bēl-iqbi* and Nanāya-iddin^{+} 149:8*; 188:3*; 224:3(?)$^{+}$; 297:32 (see Payne 2007, 181, in which the texts from the present volume are not listed)
5. f. of Gadû 282:5

Nabû-ušēzib (^{d}AG-*u*$_2$-*še-zib*)
1. f. of Nabû-zēru-iddin 292:9; 293:10

Nabû-uterri (^{d}AG-*u*$_2$-*ter-ri*)
1. 133:4

Nabû-*u*[...] (^{d}AG-⸢*u*$_2^{?}$⸣[...])
1. 299:33′

Nabû-zākir-šumi (^{d}AG-*za-kir*-MU)
1. 292:2 (^{d}AG-<*za-k*>*ir*$^{(T, ḫa)}$-MU); 293:2

Nabû-zēru-ibni (^{d}AG-NUMUN-DU$_3$, ^{d}AG-NUMUN-*ib-ni*)
1. *ikkaru* 105:2
2. *nagāru*(?) 198:20(?)
3. *nappāḫu*, *nappāḫ siparri*, f. of Bēl-ibni, Marduka, and Šulāya 13:5, 7; 31:6; 48:3; 54:4, 14; 60:4; 77:7 (see Payne 2007, 317)[16]
4. Kalzean (^{uru}*kal-za-a-a*) 190:21
5. f. of Amīl-Nanāya 297:28
6. f. of Bēl-aḫḫē-iddin 47:3
7. f. of Šumu-ukīn 232:12

Nabû-zēru-iddin (^{d}AG-NUMUN-MU)
1. *nappāḫu**, *nappāḫ parzillu*$^{+}$, f. of Mušēzib-Bēl^ 72:3; 73:3*; 74:3; 75:4; 76:3, 6; 77:3^{+}; 78:3; 79:2; 80:4; 81:2; 83:2; 84:6; 85:4; 86:3^{+}; 87:4; 88:5*; 89:3*; 90:8^{+}; 91:4; 92:3^{+}; 93:4; 94:3*; 95:4^; 96:4^; 97:3^; 99:4^; 100:7^; 102:4^; 290:8*; 195:1; 299:13′* (see Payne 2007, 317–21)
2. son of Nabû-ušēzib 292:9
3. son of Nabû-ušēzib, *nappāḫ siparri*(?) 293:10
4. son of Rēḫētu 309:3
5. f. of Marduk-šumu-uṣur 213:17′
6. f. of Nabû-udammiq 203:12
7. f. of Na'id-Ištar 297:13

Nabû-zēru-iqīša (^{d}AG-NUMUN-BA^{ša_2})
1. *aškāpu*, [son of(?) Šamaš]-erība 262:3
2. *nagāru*, son of Ibnāya 245:5
3. *nagāru* 249:6
4. *ša kurummat šarri* 63:4
5. son of Nanāya-ibni 307:1
6. son of Zabidāya 193:38′
7. 257:3
8. f. of Gimillu 245:9; 296:3
9. f. of Nabû-aḫu-iddin 193:45′
10. f. of Nabû-aḫu-iddin 297:15

Nabû-zēru-līšir (^{d}AG-NUMUN-GIŠ, ^{d}AG-NUMUN-SI.SA$_2$)
1. *nagāru* 198:4
2. 193:7′
3. f. of Marduk-ēṭir 287:9

Nabû-zēru-šubši (^{d}AG-NUMUN-GAL$_2^{ši}$)
1. 208:5
2. f. of Kiribtu 304:22
3. f. of Na'id-Marduk 258:4

Nabû-zēru-ukīn (^{d}AG-NUMUN-DU)
1. *išparu* 229:10
2. *rab ešerti*, son of Amīl-Nanāya 202:23
3. f. of Ibni-Ištar, desc. of Ašlāku 232:14 (see Payne 2007, 182, not listing the present text)

Nabû-zēru-× (^{d}AG$^{?}$-NUMUN-×)
1. 221:6

Nabû-×-ēreš ([^{d}A]G$^{?}$-LU$^{?}$-KAM)
1. *qaštu* 196:5

Nabû-[×-*id*]*din* (⸢^{d}AG⸣-[×-M]U$^{?}$)
1. son of Nadnāya 299:15′

Nabû-...
1. 299:34′ (^{d}AG-⸢×⸣[...])
2. 299:37′ (^{d}AG-[...])
3. f. of Kudurru 221:1 (^{d}A[G$^{?}$-...])

Nādinu (*na-din*, *na-di-nu*)
1. *išparu**, son of Nergal-nāṣir, desc. of Išparu 158:12*; 171:3; 187:6; 232:10; 314:19 (see Payne 2007, 183–4)
2. *išparu* 230:12[17]
3. *itinnu* 219:5
4. *kutimmu*, son of Marduk*6:5; 7:4*; 8:4; 29:16; 39:7; 45:5; 196:2; 213:12′* (see Payne 2007, 251)
5. *mušallimānu* 296:59

[16] For the sake of clarity, given the multiple attributes of this blacksmith, we refrained from marking the different attestations with *$^{+}$^.

[17] It cannot be determined whether he is the son of Nergal-nāṣir or Nadnāya.

6. son of Bēl-aḫḫē-iqīša 214:1
7. son of Iddināya 299:14′(?) (⌜*na*⌝-[*din*$^{?}$])
8. son of Kalbi-ilāni 32:3
9. son of Marduk-ušallim 191:2
10. son of Nabû-mušētiq-uddê, desc. of Bûṣu 313:16
11. son of Nadnāya 234:2 (*išparu*; see Payne 2007, 183)
12. desc. of Išparu 183:7 (*išparu*; see Payne 2007, 182–3)
13. 193:8′
14. 199:4
15. 213:26′
16. 217:17
17. 303:39′
18. 304:30′
19. 304:31′
20. f. of Bēl-ibni, desc. of Babūtu 311:8
21. f. of Bēl-ibni 175:2
22. f. of Bēl-ibni 245:4′
23. f. of Bēlšunu 305:20
24. f. of Bēl-upaḫḫir 110:3
25. f. of Kiribtu 199:9
26. f. of Ṣillāya 177:10
27. f. of [^{f}…] 174:19

Nādin-aḫi (*na-din*-ŠEŠ, SUM.NA-ŠEŠ)
1. *nagāru* 203:4
2. *nagāru* 299:20′
3. *ša kurummat šarri* 298:8
4. son of Nabû-ku[zub-ilī] 297:3
5. f. of Marduk-erība 213:10′

Nādin-apli (*na*$^{?!}$⌝-*din*-A)
1. son of Marduk-šumu-iddin 303:47′

Nadnāya (*nad-na-a*)
1. son of Ammēni-il 103:6
2. son of Aplāya 190:26
3. son of Gimillu, *aškāpu* 296:53
4. f. of Ardia 299:18′
5. f. of Gimillu 244:10 (⌜*nad*$^{?}$-*na*$^{?}$-*a*$^{?}$⌝)
6. f. of Nabû-[×-id]din 299:15′
7. f. of Nabû-aḫḫē-iddin, desc. of Išparu 312:1
8. f. of Nādinu 234:2

^{f}Naḫiš-ša-īmur(u)šu (*na-ḫiš-ša*$_{2}$*-i-mur-šu*$_{2}$)
1. 168:18

Naʾid-Ištar (I-^{d}INNIN, I-^{d}15)
1. son of Nabû-zēru-iddin 297:13, 23
2. 46:2 (see Payne 2007, 321–2, with no further attestations)
3. 226:5

Naʾid-Marduk (I-^{d}AMAR.UTU)
1. son of Nabû-zēru-šubši, *itinnu* 258:3
2. Borsippean (DUMU *bar-sip*^{ki}) 276:5

Nanāya-aḫḫē-iddin (^{d}*na-na-a*-ŠEŠ^{meš}-MU)
1. f. of Nanāya-ēreš 297:33

Nanāya-aḫu-*ēreš* (^{d}*na-na-a*-ŠEŠ-KAM$^{?}$)
1. *nagāru*(?) 198:25

Nanāya-aḫu-iddin (^{d}*na-na-a*-ŠEŠ-MU, ^{d}*na-na-a*-PAP-MU)
1. *išparu* 228:1 (see Payne 2007, 185–6)
2. *nagāru*(?) 198:24
3. *rab bīt kīli* 308:33′
4. *rēʾû*, son of Arrab 221:8
5. sepīru 193:26′
6. son of Arrab 272:3[18]
7. son of Bēl-ibni 116:8
8. son of Bēl-nuḫšu 192:2
9. son of Bēlšunu 297:6
10. son of Lâbâši 244:6
11. son of Nabû-ēṭir 296:68
12. son of Nabû-iddin 297:7
13. son of Nergal-ina-tēšî-ēṭir 282:4
14. 122:6
15. 215:11
16. 226:6
17. 227:16
18. 303:40′ (*išpar birmi*, see Payne 2007, 185–6)
19. 308:36′
20. f. of Ina-tēšî-ēṭir 135:6
21. f. of Nabû-kēšir 193:41′

Nanāya-aḫu-… (^{Id}*na-na-a*-⌜ŠEŠ-×)
1. son of … 221:7

Nanāya-īpuš (^{d}*na-na-a*-DU$_{3}$$^{!uš}$)
1. f. of Balāssu 107:2

Nanāya-ēreš (^{d}*na-na-a*-KAM)
1. *malāḫu* 291:7, 10
2. *nappāḫu* 111:2(?) (^{d}*n*[*a-na-a*-KAM$^{?}$])
3. *nappāḫ siparri**, son of Ibāya 292:8; 293:9*
4. *rab bīt kīli* 215:5
5. *rab ešerti* son of Marduk-nāṣir 202:28

18 Note the herder by that name is attested in **No. 221**:8.

6. son of Nanāya-aḫḫē-iddin 297:33
7. son of Nanāya-nāṣir 193:32′
8. son of Ša-Nabû-šū 108:3
9. 105:4
10. 125:3; 128:5; 130:9 (*nappāḫ parzilli*, see Payne 2007, 322–3)
11. 226:4
12. f. of Ardāya 221:9
13. f. of Hašdia 164:4; 165:5; 166:3 (see Payne 2007, 186; the present texts are not listed)
14. f. of Ina-tēšî-ēṭir 204:2
15. f. of Nabû-aḫu-iddin 161:7
16. f. of Nabû-aḫu-iddin 209:2
17. f. of Nabû-ēṭir 297:14
18. f. of Nabû-šumu-ukīn 97:8
19. f. of Nanāya-uṣalli 221:7
20. f. of Nergal-[...] 194:5
21. f. of Šamaš-mukīn-apli, desc. of Kidin-Marduk 313:16
22. f. of Uraš-iddin 299:17′
23. f. of [DN-šu]mu-ukīn 193:57′

Nanāya-ibni (*na-na-a*-DU$_{3}$)
1. f. of Nabû-aḫḫē-bulliṭ, Nūrea, and Amīl-Nanāya 307:10
2. f. of Nabû-zēru-iqīša 307:1

Nanāya-iddin (^{d}*na-na-a*-MU)
1. *aškāpu* 297:20
2. *išparu* 146:5 (see Payne 2007, 189)
3. *itinnu* 288:5
4. *kabšarru*, son of Innin-aḫḫē-iddin 304:14 (see Payne 2007, 271)
5. *mušākil iṣṣūri* 217:27
6. *nagār dalti* 198:13
7. *nagāru*(?) 198:23
8. *pūṣāya**, son of Amīl-Nanāya, f. of Innin-šumu-uṣur* 166:5; 167:2; 315:3* (see Payne 2007, 188)
9. *pūṣāya*, son of ᶠNanāya-rēṣûni 315:5 (see Payne 2007, 188)
10. *pūṣāya*, son of Šamaš-šumu-ibni / Ḫašdia 296:26 (see Payne 2007, 189)
11. *pūṣāya* 156:2
12. *pūṣāya* 296:39; 298:5; 302:4 (see Payne 2007, 187–8)
13. *rē'i iṣṣūri* 193:19
14. *sa*[*sinnu*] 194:12
15. son of Abu-ukīn 304:45′
16. son of Bēl-iqīša 304:2
17. <son of> Nabû-ušallim 224:2[19]
18. 168:38
19. 227:14
20. 229:11
21. 304:11
22. f. of [...] 294:8′
23. f. of [In]nin-[...] 294:7′
24. f. of Bēl-ušēzib 192:3
25. f. of Erībšu (grandfather of Šamaš-zēru-ibni) 296:18
26. f. of Libluṭ 58:4; 69:4; 70:4*(*nappāḫ siparri*, see Payne 2007, 323–4)
27. f. of Šamaš-iddin 296:35

Nanāya-nāṣir (^{d}*na-na-a*-URU$_{3}$, ^{d}*na-na-a*-PAP)
1. *kabšarru*, son of Zēr-Babili 245:15 (see Payne 2007, 271, s.v. Nanāya-uṣur, with no further attestations)
2. f. of Nanāya-ēreš 193:32′

ᶠNanāya-rēṣûni (^{d}*na-na-a-re-ṣu-ni*)
1. *zakītu* mo. of Nanāya-iddin 315:6

Nanāya-*šar-di-nu* (^{d}*na-na-a-*⌈*šar*?⌉*-di-nu*)
1. 107:6

Nanāya-taklāk (^{d}*na-na-a-tak-lak*)
1. 292:10

Nanāya-uballiṭ ($^{d⌉}$*na-na-a*-TIN^{it})
1. 179:11 (probably father of Aplāya)

Nanāya-uṣalli (^{d}*na-na-a*-SISKUR$_{2}$, ^{d}*na-na-a*-SISKUR, ^{d}*na-na-a-u*$_{2}$*-ṣal-lu*)
1. *nappāḫu*, son of Ardāya 132:5; 136:3 (see Payne 2007, 322, s.v. Nanāya-aḫu-uṣur, and p. 324)[20]
2. *rab ešerti*, son of Šamaš-iddin 202:30
3. *rab ešerti*, son of Ṭāb-Uruk 202:13
4. *rē'û*, son of [...] 221:2
5. *rē'û*, son of Nanāya-ēreš 221:7
6. 193:44′

[19] Note the probable identification with the weaver attested in **No. 146**:5; see Payne 2007, 189.

[20] It was understood elsewhere that Nanāya-uṣalli and Nanāya-aḫu-uṣur are two brothers (Payne 2007, 322), though it is reasonable to assume that a collation of VS 20, 4 will show the reading to be ^{Id}*na-na-a*-SISKUR$_{2}$ rather than ^{Id}*na-na-a*-ŠEŠ-URU$_{3}$; all attestations refer thus to the same individual.

7. 225:2
8. 226:3
9. f. of Innin-zēru-šubši 207:12

Nanāya-[…]
1. *nappāḫ parzilli* 296:62 (^{d}*na-na-a*-[×] ⸢×⸣) (see Payne 2007, 324, with no further attestations)
2. son of Kiribtu 180:5 (^{d}*na-na-*⸢*a*⸣-[…])
3. son of Nabû-erība 180:11 (⸢^{d}*na-na*⸣-[*a*-…])
4. 299:27′ ^{d}*n*[*a-na-a*-…]
5. 304:23 (^{d}*na-na-a*-[...])
6. f. of Gimillu 307:22 (⸢^{d}*na-na*⸣-[*a*-…])
7. f. of Gūzānu 244:11 ^{d}⸢*na-na*⸣-[*a*-…]

Nāṣir (*na-ṣir*)
1. 209:9

Na[…]
1. 299:47′ (⸢*na*?⸣[…])
2. 299:50′ (⸢*na*?⸣[…])

Nergal-īpuš (^{d}U.GUR-DU$_{3}$^{uš})
1. 303:30′

Nergal-ēṭir (^{d}U.GUR-SUR)
1. *rab ešerti*, son of Nabû-erība 202:8
2. son of Iddin-Ištar 28:4
3. 105:6
4. f. of Mušēzib-Bēl 297:4

Nergal-iddin (^{d}U.GUR-MU)
1. *nappāḫu* 288:3 (see Payne 2007, 325, with no further attestations)
2. son of Nergal-ušallim 190:25
3. son of […] 299:10′
4. 291:3
5. f. of Rēmūtu 121:2

Nergal-ina-tēšî-ēṭir (^{d}U.GUR-*ina*-SUḪ$_{3}$-SUR)
1. son of Zabidāya 184:3
2. f. of Nanāya-aḫu-iddin 282:4

Nergal-nāṣir (^{d}U.GUR-PAP, ^{d}U.GUR-*na-ṣir*)
1. son of Aqara, desc. of Bēl-aplu-uṣur 232:8
2. 129:4
3. 199:2
4. 227:5
5. 303:7′
6. f. of Nādinu, desc. of Išparu 171:3; 187:7; 232:10; 314:19

Nergal-rēṣū’a (^{d}U.GUR-*re-ṣu-u*$_{2}$-*a*)
1. 230:14

Nergal-šumu-ibni (^{d}U.GUR-MU-DU$_{3}$)
1. 289:8
2. 294:19′
3. f. of Ardia 305:6
4. f. of Nabû-ikṣur 212:4

Nergal-uballiṭ (^{d}U.GUR-TIN^{iṭ})
1. son of Isinnāya, br. of Erībšu 314:3, 14
2. son of Šumāya 68:3 (see Payne 2007, 325, with no further attestations)
3. 217:18
4. f. of Nabû-šumu-ukīn 7:5

Nergal-ušallim[21] (^{d}U.GUR-GI)
1. f. of Amīl-Nanāya 190:23
2. f. of Iddin-Nabû 190:28
3. f. of Nergal-iddin 190:25

Nergal-ušēzib (^{d}U.GUR-*u*$_{2}$-*še-zib*)
1. f. of Amīl-Nanāya 292:3; 293:3

Nergal-[…]
1. son of Nanāya-ēreš 194:4 (⸢^{d}U.GUR-×⸣)
2. 299:36′ (⸢^{d}U⸣.[GUR-…])
3. f. of Ina-ṣilli-Nanāya 297:18 (^{d}U.⸢GUR-×⸣)

Nēšu (*ne*$_{2}$-*e-šu*$_{2}$)
1. f. of Iddināya 55:8

Nidintu (*ni-din-ti*, *ni-din-tu*$_{2}$)
1. *nagār qutāni*, son of Nabû-mušētiq-uddê 296:8
2. *pūṣāya*, br. of Rēmūtu 296:28 (see Payne 2007, 190)
3. son of Ibni-Ištar 304:13
4. son of Nūrea, br. of Bānia 304:46′
5. 304:32′
6. 308:34′ (*nappāḫ parzilli*, see Payne 2007, 325)

Nimšātu (nim-ša$_{2}$-tu$_{4}$)
1. 295:10

Ninurta-šarru-uṣur (^{d}MAŠ-LUGAL-PAP, ^{d}MAŠ-LUGAL-URU$_{3}$)
1. *qīpu* 141:11
2. 296:27

^{f}Nišunu (*ni-šu-nu*)
1. 307:23

[21] All three attestations come from one tablet (190), listed within a span of five lines. Note, however, that they are not consecutive, and thus we cannot automatically assign them all to the same individual.

Nuḫāya (*nu-ḫa-a*)
1. 222:4
Nuḫtimmu (*nu-uḫ-tim*!*-mu*)
1. f. of Šalam 105:12
Nūrea (ZALAG$_2$-*e-a*)
1. son of Amīl-Nabû 174:13
2. son of Iqīšāya, br. of Erībšu 307:9
3. son of Nanāya-ibni, br. of Nabû-aḫḫē-bulliṭ and Amīl-Nanāya 307:11
4. f. of Nabû-aḫu-ēreš 18:6
5. f. of Nidintu and Bānia 304:46′
Nūr-Sîn (ZALAG$_2$-^{d}30)
1. anc. of Ina-tēšî-ēṭir / Tabnēa and Nabû-bān-aḫi / Iddin-Marduk 302:3; 311:6
Nūr-Šamaš (ZALAG$_2$-^{d}UTU)
1. *qallu* (of Bēl-aḫu-iddin) 190:11
Nusku-... (^{d}ENŠADA-⌜× ×⌝)
1. 286:14
Pir'u (*pir-u'*)
1. anc. of Kīnāya / Ibni-Ištar 212:3

Qīštu (NIG$_2$.BA)
1. f. of Uraš-ušēzib 213:22′

Rāšil (*ra-šil*)
1. rab banê 251:1
Rēḫētu (*re-ḫe-e-ti, re-ḫe-e-tu$_2$, re-ḫe-e-tu$_4$*)
1. *atkuppu*, f. of Nabû-zēru-iddin 309:2
1. 203:6
2. f. of Arad-Nabû, 271:7
3. f. of Erībšu 269:5
4. f. of Silim-Bēl 144:11
Rē'i-alpi (^{lu_2}SIPA GU$_4$)
1. anc. of Šamaš-udammiq / Iqīšāya 315:18
Rēmūtu (*re-mut, re-mu-tu*)
1. *išparu, rab ešerti* 202:9 (see Payne 2007, 191)
2. *kutimmu**, son of Bēl-aḫu-iddin⁺, br. of Itti-Marduk-balāṭu⁺ 5:4⁺, 8, 10; 17:5; 27:7, 14; 31:9⁺; 35:4* (see Payne 2007, 252–3)
3. *nagāru* 193:25′
4. *pūṣāya*, br. of Nidintu 296:27 (see Payne 2007, 192)
5. *rab ešerti*, son of Aḫu-ēreš 202:7
6. ^{lu_2}[×], son of *m / ba-bi-a*?*-p / bu* 75:7
7. son of Arad-Gula 203:5
8. son of Bēl-aḫu-iddin[22] 273:7
9. son of Nergal-iddin 121:2
10. son of Šumāya 297:10
11. 193:14′
12. 193:53′
13. 193:62′
14. 235:6
15. f. of Ina-tēšî-ēṭir and Anu-šarru-uṣur 296:11
16. f. of Innin-zēru-šubši 245:8
17. f. of Šumu-ukīn 314:18

Rēmūt-ili (*re-mut*-DINGIR)
1. *ša muḫḫi quppi* 304:35′
Rikis-kalāma-Bēl (*ri-kis*-DU$_3$.A.BI-^{d}EN, DIM-DU$_3$.A.BI-^{d}EN, DIM-DU$_3$.A-^{d}EN)
1. *pūṣāya* 227:17
2. 193:47′
3. 229:12
Rīm-Anu (⌜AM-^{d}*a-nu$_3$*⌝)
1. anc. of Ištar-šumu-ēreš / Nabû-aḫḫē-šullim 314:22

Silim-Bēl (*si-lim*-^{d}EN)
1. *atû* 227:11
2. son of Iddināya 221:8
3. son of Rēḫētu 144:11
4. 157:23
5. f. of Arad-Bēl and Šamaš-ēṭir 296:12
Silim-ili (*si-lim*-DINGIR)
1. *ša muḫḫi quppi* 305:22
2. 308:16′
Sîn-ēreš (^{d}30-KAM)
1. son of Nabû-šumu-līšir 304:18
2. 303:38′
Sîn-iddin (^{d}30-MU)
1. *qīpu* 314:5, 8, 14
Sîn-karābu-šime → Bīt-Sîn-karābu-šime (GN)
Sîn-nādin-šumi (^{d}30-*na-din*-MU)
1. 227:16

[22] This individual fits in name and timeframe to the *kutimmu* (son of Bēl-aḫu-iddin and brother of Itti-Marduk-balāṭu), but there is no clear indication that he is indeed a goldsmith.

Ṣāḫit-ginê (^{lu2}I$_{3}$.SUR-GI.NA)
1. anc. of Balāṭu / Arad-Nabû 313:15

Ṣāṣiru (*ṣa-ṣi-ru*)
1. *pūṣāya* 296:33 (see Payne 2007, 192)

Ṣillāya (*ṣil-la-a*)
1. *išparu* 154:10 (see Payne 2007, 192)
2. *išparu*, son of Nādinu 177:9 (see Payne 2007, 193)
3. *ṭupšarru*, son of Marduka 141:12, 13
4. son of Amīl-Nanāya 71:4
5. son of Amīl-Nanāya 305:1
6. 227:3

Ṣilli-Nanāya (GISSU-^{d}*na-na-a*)
1. *atû* 196:4
2. 192:2

Šadûnu (*ša*$_{2}$*-du-nu*, *ša*$_{2}$*-du-ni*)
1. *kutimmu** 2:2; 10:8, 11; 11:8; 16:3$^{?}$; 27:3; 31:12*; 33:1, 12; 128:7 (see Payne 2007, 253–4)
2. *rab bīt kīli* 250:3
3. 144:2
4. 299:3′
5. f. of Kidinnu 275:6

^{f}Šaḫinatu (*ša*$_{2}$*-ḫi-*[*na*]*-*⸢*tu*$_{4}$⸣)
1. 168:29

Ša-Ištar-uddu (*ša*$_{2}$-^{d}INNIN-*u*$_{2}$*-da*, *ša*$_{2}$-^{d}INNIN-*u*$_{2}$*-da*)
1. *sasinnu* 226:15
2. 295:7

Šākin-šumi (GAR-MU)
1. *kabšarru*, son of Nabû-nāṣir 245:12 (see Payne 2007, 275, with no further attestations)
2. 217:8
3. f. of Ardia 304:17

Šalam (*ša*$_{2}$*-lam*)
1. son of Nuḫtimmu 105:11

Šamaʾ-il → Bīt-Šamaʾ-il (GN)

Šamaš-aḫḫē-[…] (^{d}UTU-ŠEŠ$^{⸢meš⸣}$-[…])
1. 215:3′

Šamaš-aḫu-iddin (^{d}UTU-ŠEŠ-MU)
1. *atû* 189:7, 8
2. *nagār qutāni*, son of Nabû-aḫḫē-šullim 296:6
3. *pūṣāya*, son of Šumu-uṣur and br. of Šamaš-kāṣir 296:42 (see Payne 2007, 194)
4. 161:2

Šamaš-bān-aḫi (^{d}UTU-DU$_{3}$-ŠEŠ)
1. 295:1

Šamaš-erība (^{d}UTU-SU, ^{d}UTU-*eri*$_{4}$*-ba*)
1. son of Erībšu 122:9
2. 194:10
3. 303:28′
4. [f. of](?) Nabû-zēru-iqīša 262:3 ([^{d}UTU$^{?}$]-⸢SU⸣)
5. f. of Zērūtu 106:2
6. f. of Zērūtu 268:2

Šamaš-ēṭir (^{d}UTU-SUR)
1. *išpar birmi*, son of Silim-Bēl, br. of Arad-Bēl 296:12
2. f. of Bēl-upaḫḫir 190:32

Šamaš-ibni (^{d}UTU-DU$_{3}$)
1. *aškāpu* 296:51
2. *išparu* 298:10 (see Payne 2007, 195)
3. son of Gimillu 305:21
4. *rab ešerti*, son of Mušallim-Marduk 202:24

Šamaš-iddin (^{d}UTU-MU)
1. *ašlāku*, son of Šellibi, br. of Anu-šarru-uṣur 296:44 (see Payne 2007, 196, with no further attestations)
2. *nagār dalti* 189:4
3. *nagāru* 198:5
4. *pūṣāya*, son of Bušāya 315:7 (see Payne 2007, 195–6)
5. *pūṣāya*, son of Nanāya-iddin 296:35, 45 (see Payne 2007, 196, with no further attestations)
6. *pūṣāya* 294:10′[23]
7. *pūṣāya* 298:5 (see Payne 2007, 195)
8. *ušandû* 122:8
9. son of Nabû-aḫu-iddin 193:49′
10. son of Nabû-ēṭir 190:29
11. son of Šamaš-uballiṭ 244:15
12. 283:2
13. f. of Amīl-Nanāya 221:4
14. f. of Bēl-ušallim, desc. of Šumāti 313:4, 6
15. f. of Eanna-ibni 202:26

[23] This linen weaver is, most probably, either the son of Bušāya or the father of Eanna-ibni; for these linen weavers, see Payne 2007, 195.

16. f. of Marduk 202:29
17. f. of Nanāya-uṣalli 202:30
Šamaš-ilua (dUTU-DINGIR-[u2]-⌜a⌝)
1. *aškāpu* 296:51
Šamaš-īpuš (dUTU-DU3uš)
1. 107:4
2. Šamaš-iqīša (dUTU-BAša2)
1. *ša bīt alpi* 189:10
Šamaš-kāṣir (dUTU-*ka-ṣir*)
1. *pūṣāya*, son of Šumu-uṣur, br. of Šamaš-aḫu-iddin 296:42 (see Payne 2007, 197, with no further attestations)
Šamaš-mukīn-apli (dUTU-DU-A, dUTU-DU-IBILA)
1. son of Nanāya-ēreš, desc. of Kidin-Marduk 313:15
2. 154:17 (see Payne 2007, 197, with no further attestations)
3. 303:42′
4. 303:45′
Šamaš-nāṣir (dUTU-PAP)
1. *pūṣāya, rē'û* 221:10 (see Payne 2007, 197, with no further attestations)
Šamaš-šarru-bulliṭ (dUTU-LUGAL-*bul-liṭ*)
1. *ša qīpi* 118:3
Šamaš-šumu-iddin (dUTU-MU-MU)
1. *nagār qutāni*, son of Šamaš-zēru-iqīša 296:7
Šamaš-šumu-ukīn (dUTU-MU-DU)
1. *mandidu* 234:4
2. *pūṣāya*, son of Ḫašdia and f. of Nanāya-iddin, br. of Ibni-Ištar 296:25 (see Payne 2007, 197–8)
3. son of […] 285:4′
4. son of Šulāya 246:3
5. son of Šumāya 212:2
Šamaš-uballiṭ (dUTU-TINiṭ)
1. *arad ekalli* 189:9
2. 193:40′
3. f. of Šamaš-iddin 244:16
Šamaš-udammiq (dUTU-KAL, dUTU-SIG5iq)
1. son of Bēl-aḫḫē-iqīša 243:6
2. son of Ina-tēšî-ēṭir 304:43′
3. son of Iqīšāya, desc. of Rē'i-alpi 315:18
4. 184:6
5. 217:19
6. 217:21
7. 230:15
Šamaš-*u*[…] (dUTU-⌜u2?⌝-[…])
1. 299:29′
Šamaš-zēru-ibni (dUTU-NUMUN-DU3)
1. son of Erībšu / Nanāya-iddin 296:18 (see Payne 2007, 198, with no further attestations)
2. son of Itti-Šamaš-balāṭu, br. of Zumbu 296:72
3. son of Nabû-mukīn-apli 296:71 (see Payne 2007, 198)
4. son of Tabnēa 304:20
5. f. of(?) Nabû-silim 231:6
6. f. of Šulāya 282:9
Šamaš-zēru-iqīša (dUTU-NUMUN-BAša2)
1. son of Nabû-iddin 190:19
2. 224:5
3. 227:8
4. f. of Šamaš-šumu-iddin 296:7
Šamaš-zēru-šubši (dUTU-NUMUN-GAL2ši)
1. son of Bānia 286:6
2. son of IGI.DU-… 304:21
Šamaš-[×]
1. *pūṣāya* 294:11′ (dUT[U-…])
2. 281:11 (dUTU-⌜×⌝)
3. 299:30′ (dUTU-⌜×⌝)
fŠamḫat (*šam-ḫat*)
1. 37:4
Šamšamānu (*ša2-am-ša2-ma-nu*)
1. *mār šipri* (of Nabû-bēlšunu) 303:33′
2. son of Arad-Nabû 286:1; 304:8
Ša-Nabû-šū (*ša2*-dAG-*šu-u*, *ša2*-dAG-*šu2-u2*)
1. *nagāru* 299:21′
2. *šakin ṭēmi*, f. of Nabû-aḫḫē-iddin 199:11
3. *širku* of Nabû 290:4
4. 157:18 (*ša2*-dA[G-*šu-u*])
5. 193:29′
6. 227:6
7. f. of Arad-Nabû 104:4; 138:i 4, 23, ii 5, 13, 20, 23, 27
8. f. of Bābilāya 202:12
9. f. of Balāṭu 203:1
10. f. of Bēl-ēṭir 310:4
11. [f. of](?) Bēlšunu 56:4
12. f. of IGI.DU-zēru-ibni 309:4
13. f. of Nanāya-ēreš 108:4

Ša-Nanāya-tašmēt (*ša*$_2$-^{d}*na-na-a-taš-met*)
1. 107:1, 4, 5, 8, 12; 245:15′[24]

Šangû-Zāriqu (^{lu_2}E$_2$.BAR-^{d}*za-ri-qu*)
1. anc. of Nabû-šumu-līšir 25:4

Ša-pî-Bēl (*ša*$_2$-KA-^{d}EN, *ša*$_2$-*pi-i*-^{d}EN)
1. son of Nabû-aḫḫē-iddin 170:2
2. f. of [×-Gul]a?, desc. of Amīl-Ea 312:5
3. f. of ... 313:19

Šārid (*ša*$_2$-*rid*)
1. f. of Innin-šumu-uṣur 120:5

Šarru-kitti-irâm (LUGAL-*kit-ti-i-ra-am*)
1. 256:4

Šarru-mītu-uballiṭ (LUGAL-UŠ$_2$-TIN^{it})
1. 216:4

Ša[...] (*ša*$_2$-[...])
1. 299:46′

Šellibi (KA$_5$.A, *še-el-li-bi*)
1. 230:8
2. 303:36′, 38′
3. f. of Šamaš-iddin and Anu-šarru-uṣur 296:44

Šibḫia (*ši-ib-ḫi-ia*)
1. 303:32′

^{f}Šidâ (*ši-da-a*)
1. 168:35

Šigûa (*ši-gu-u*$_2$-*a*)
1. anc. of Gimillu / Zēria 311:5

Širiktu (*ši-rik-ti*)
1. 103:1

Šulāya (*šu-la-a*)
1. *kalû* 218:2
2. *nagāru*(?) 198:22
3. son of Ardāya 103:7
4. son of Ardāya 194:15
5. son of Isinnāya 273:8
6. son of Nabû-aḫḫē-šullim 297:22
7. son of Nabû-zēru-ibni, br. of Bēl-ibni, and Marduka 54:5, 14 (see Payne 2007, 327)
8. son of Šamaš-zēru-ibni 282:9
9. son of Zēria 175:1
10. 210:2
11. f. of Eanna-šumu-ibni 296:36
12. f. of Iddināya and Ištar-zēru-ibni 307:4
13. f. of Iddinunu 212:13
14. f. of Itti-enši-Nabû 296:5
15. f. of Itti-enši-Nabû 245:10
16. f. of Nabû-mušētiq-uddê 152:6
17. f. of Šamaš-šumu-ukīn 246:3

Šullumāya (*šul-lum-a*)
1. f. of Nabû-nādin-šumi 292:4; 293:5
2. f. of Amīl-Nanāya 315:5

Šullumu (*šul-lu-mu*)
1. 170:11
2. 256:2

Šumāti (MU^{meš})
1. anc. of Bēl-ušallim / Šamaš-iddin 313:4, 6

Šumāya (*šu-ma-a*)
1. *nagāru* 198:3
2. *parkullu* 245:13′
3. son of Ibni-Ištar 246:5 (*ašlāku*, see Payne 2007, 198–9)
4. 291:4
5. f. of Balāssu, desc. of Nabāya 45:4; 232:4
6. f. of Balāṭu 115:3
7. f. of Nergal-uballiṭ 68:4
8. f. of Rēmūtu 297:10
9. f. of Šamaš-šumu-ukīn 212:2

Šumu-iddin (MU-MU)
1. *pūṣāya*, son of Nabû-ēdu-uṣur, br. of Dannu-aḫḫēšu-ibni 296:32 (see Payne 2007, 199)

Šumu-ukīn (MU-DU)
1. *atkuppu** 223:2*, 229:8*, 260:2, 255:2
2. *ša muḫḫi sūti*, son of Bēl-zēri, desc. of Basia 313:2, 6, 9, 11
3. son of Nabû-zēru-ibni 232:12
4. son of Rēmūtu 314:18
5. 170:6
6. f. of Ibni-Ištar 285:9′

Šumu-uṣur (MU-URU$_3$)
1. *nagāru* 195:3
2. son of In[nin-zē]ru-ibni 307:13
3. 296:69 (*išpar birmi*, see Payne 2007, 184, s.v. Nādin-aḫi)
4. f. of Ina-tēšî-ēṭir 67:6

[24] Although not specifically stated, the context and prosopography point to Ša-Nanāya-tašmēt being a blacksmith (on both texts).

5. f. of Šamaš-kāṣir and Šamaš-aḫu-iddin 296:43

^{f}Tabluṭu (*tab-lu-ṭu*)
1. 215:12, 11′

Tabnēa (*tab-ne$_2$-e-a*)
1. son of Aplāya 243:7
2. son of Nabû-īpuš 174:14
3. 107:5
4. 181:13
5. 297:24
6. f. of Amīl-Nanāya 245:13
7. f. of Balāṭu 245:17
8. f. of Ibnāya 181:3
9. f. of Ina-tēšî-ēṭir, desc. of Nūr-Sîn* 302:2*; 310:2, 9
10. f. of Šamaš-zē[ru-ib]ni 304:20

Taklāta (*tak-la-a-ta*)
1. 114:2

Talīmu (*ta-lim*, *ta-li-mu*)
1. son of Ibni-Ištar 304:37′
2. f. of Zēria 308:15′

Taqīš-Gula (*ta-qiš-*^{d}ME.ME, *ta-qiš-*^{d}*gu-la*, *ta-qiš$_2$-*^{d}*gu-la*, *ta-qi$_2$-ša$_2$-*^{d}*gu-la*)
1. 78:4 (*kabšarru*, see Payne 2007, 276)
2. 273:9
3. 300:2
4. f. of […], desc. of Ḫamiša 312:2
5. f. of Mušēzib-Bēl 245:14

Tarību (*ta-ri-bi*, *ta-rib*)
1. son of [...] 297:1, 12
2. 127:2
3. 168:7
4. 190:10, 33
5. 227:15
6. f. of Ištar-zēru-ibni 243:11

^{f}Tašlīmu (*taš-li-mu*)
1. 168:43

Tattannu (*ta-at-tan-nu*)
1. 140:3

Ta[…] (*ta-*[…])
1. 299:32′

Tukulti-Ištar (TUKUL-*ti-*^{d}15)
1. *mukabbû* 162:5

Tukulti-Marduk (TUKUL-*ti-*^{d}AMAR.UTU)
1. *rē'û*, son of Kudurru 284:5

Ṭāb (DUG$_3$.GA)
1. 299:4′

Ṭāb-...
1. *ašlāku*, son of […] 312:10 DUG$_3$.GA-⌜×⌝[(×)]
2. 299:26′ (⌜DUG$_3$?⌝-G[A?-...])

^{f}Ṭābatu (DUG.GA-*a-tu$_4$*)
1. 168:22

Ṭābia (DUG$_3$.GA-*ia*)
1. *kutimmu*, son of Bēl-zēri 245:5′ (see Payne 2007, 257, with no further attestations)

Ṭāb-šār-Bēl (DUG$_3$.GA-IM(T: A')-^{d}EN)
1. f. of Lâbâši 200:3

Ṭāb-šār-bīt-ili (DUG$_3$.GA-IM-E$_2$-DINGIR)
1. 277:3

Ṭāb-šār-Eanna (DUG$_3$.GA-IM-E$_2$.AN.NA)
1. f. of Lūmur-dumqi-Ištar 297:31

Ṭāb-šār-Ištar (DUG$_3$.GA-IM-^{d}INNIN, DUG$_3$.GA-IM-^{d}15)
1. 64:6
2. 161:12
3. 193:40′
4. f. of Arad-Nanāya 266:7

Ṭāb-Uruk (DUG$_3$.GA-UNUG^{ki})
1. *išparu**, f. of Innin-šumu-uṣur⁺ 192:1*; 282:13⁺; 294:6′⁺; 296:10⁺ (see Payne 2007, 200)
2. *širku* 105:13
3. 105:8
4. 299:11′
5. f. of Nanāya-uṣalli 202:13

Ubāru (*u$_2$-bar*)
1. *nappāḫ parzilli* 296:49 (see Payne 2007, 329)
2. son of Amīl-Nanāya 296:22 (see Payne 2007, 200)
3. 215:5′
4. 305:11

^{f}UDsipā (UD-*si-*⌜*aš$_2$*/*pa*⌝*-a'*)
1. 168:16

Uk(k)umu (*u$_2$-ku-mu*)
1. son of Imbāya 32:5
2. 12:3

Upāqu (*u$_2$-paq*)
1. 307:27

Uqūpu (*u*$_2$-*qu-pu*, *u*$_2$$^?$-*qu-pi*$^?$)
1. *nagāru*(?) 198:21
2. 296:67

Uraš-iddin (^{d}*uraš*-MU)
1. son of Aḫḫēšu 213:2′
2. son of Nanāya-ēreš 299:17′

Uraš-ušēzib (^{d}*uraš*-*u*$_2$-*še-zib*)
1. *šanû*, son of Qīštu 213:22′

Ur(i)dimmu-ilūa (^{d}UR.IDIM-DINGIR-*u*$_2$-*a*)
1. *aškāpu* 215:7′; 304:15
2. 168:36

Urukāya (UNUG:$^{ki°}$-*a*°-*a*)
1. f. of Itti-Marduk-balāṭu 190:15

Uzīb-Baytil (*u*$_2$-*zu-ub-bat*-DINGIR)
1. f. of Basia 282:2

Zababa-mukīn-apli (^{d}*za-ba*$_4$-*ba*$_4$-DU-A)
1. 256:14

Zabdia (*zab-di-ia*)
1. f. of ^{f}Aška'ītu-ṭābat 168:11

Zabidāya (*za-bi-da-a*)
1. 170:22
2. f. of Iddināya 107:3
3. f. of Innin-šumu-uṣur 193:46′
4. f. of Nabû-zēru-iqīša 193:38′
5. f. of Nergal-ina-tēšî-ēṭir 184:3

^{f}Zabubtu (*za-bu-ub-tu*$_4$)
1. 307:25

Zākiru (*za-kir*)
1. f. of Amīl-Nanāya 194:13

Zanzīru (*za-an-zi-i-ri*)
1. son of ^{f}Bazītu, br. of Arad-Bunene 168:14

Zēr-Babili (NUMUN-TIN.TIR^{ki})
1. f. of Bēl-nādin-apli, desc. of Ile''i-Marduk 311:1; 315:19
1. f. of Nanāya-nāṣir 245:15

Zēria (NUMUN-*ia*, NUMUN-*ia*$_2$)
1. *nagāru* 198:9
2. son of Aḫḫēšāya 193:31′; 310:7
3. son of Innin-šumu-uṣur 296:70
4. son of Nabû-iddin 190:18
5. son of Talīmu 308:15′
6. 30:1
7. 30:2
8. 207:10
9. f. of Anu-šumu-ibni 71:6
10. f. of Gimillu 181:6
11. f. of Gimillu 212:7
12. f. of Gimillu, desc. of Šigūa 311:5
13. f. of Kalbāya 190:12, 27
14. f. of Nabû-mukīn-apli 315:22
15. f. of Šulāya 175:1

Zērūtu (NUMUN-*u*$_2$-*tu*, NUMUN-*u*$_2$-*tu*$_2$, NUMUN-*tu*$_2$)
1. *nagāru* 190:7
2. *nagāru* 198:12
3. *ṣārip dušî*, son of Šamaš-erība* 261:4; 268:2*
4. *ša bīt immeri* 189:5
5. son of Gula-zēru-ibni 310:11
6. son of Šamaš-erība 106:2
7. 241:2
8. f. of Innin-zēru-iddin 265:3
9. f. of Ištar-mukīn-apli 109:3
10. f. of Nabû-mukīn-apli 267:3

Zēru-ukīn (NUMUN-DU)
1. 170:6
2. 217:15

Zību (*zi-i-bu*)
1. f. of Nabû-šumu-ēreš 119:3

Zumbu (*zu-um-bu*)
1. son of Itti-Šamaš-balāṭu, br. of Šamaš-zēru-ibni 296:73

[…]-A ([…]-⸢A⸣)
1. anc. of […] / Nabû-balāssu-iqbi 312:7

^{d}[×]-aḫu-iddin ([^{d}×]-⸢ŠEŠ⸣-MU)
1. son of Arad-Nanāya 308:11′

^{d}[×]-ālik-pāni ([^{d}×]-⸢DU⸣-IGI)
1. 193:13′

…-*āya* (⸢×⸣-*a-a*)
1. 273:1

[…]-dāya ([…]-*da-a*)
1. *kutimmu* 245:2′

[×-*Gul*]*a*$^?$ ([…-$^{d?}$ME$^?$].⸢ME$^?$⸣)
1. son of Ša-pî-Bēl, desc. of Amīl-Ea 312:5

[…]-Ištar ([…]-⸢^{d}15⸣)
1. *ṭupšarru*, son of Ša-pî-Bēl, desc. of […] 313:19

…-*muṣu* (⸢× × ×⸣*mu-ṣu-u*$_2$)
1. 256:6, Possibly son of *A*(*m*)*mia*

[…]-Nanāya
1. 193:15′ ([…]-⸢^{d}⸣*na-na-a*)
2. 243:10 ([…-^{d}]⸢*na-na-a*⸣)

Akkadian Words

Listed below are all the words attested in the corpus, with some minor exceptions. First, the most common independent prepositions, *ana, ina*, and *ša*, are not listed, unless when used in prepositional phrases, such as *ina/ana/ša muḫḫi, ina pāni/qāt* etc. Less frequent prepositions, such as *adi, kī*, and *ultu*, are listed separately. Additionally, the words *māru* and *aplu* are not listed when they are parts of a filiation formula, but are listed when they stand as independent nouns or in phrases (e.g., *mār šipri* or *mār bane*). Similarly, the word *šarru* in date formulas is not listed.

Lemmas are presented according to Late Babylonian conventions, and more specifically, forms that are attested in the corpus. Some deviations from the dictionaries (AHw, CAD) should thus be taken into consideration. Each normalized form is followed by its orthographic variants. Half-brackets and other transliteration conventions are generally omitted. A few exceptions were kept in cases of uncertain attestations. Uncertain readings are marked with [?], while line numbers in square brackets refer to a fully restored word. Cases in which more than one syllabic variation is attested (as minor as it may be) are simply marked as "syl." Like homonyms, some polysemes are listed separately for the sake of simplicity. Thus, for example, *qaqqadu* I, is "principle (amount)" while *qaqqadu* II is "head, top." Lemmas whose meaning can be slightly modified by their logographic spelling, such as PAP/PAP.PAP for *napḫaru*, or KAŠ/KAŠ.SAG for *šikaru*, may be listed separately as (a) and (b).

Epigraphic and grammatical difficulties are not discussed below and no attempt has been made to classify different verbal forms. Some lexical commentary, however, may be added. In line with the overall interest of the volume, the focus of this glossary is material culture, hence the lexical commentary is reserved for selected nouns only. Additionally, it is added in cases of multiple attestations, while comments to single attestations are presented in the edition. Importantly, the translations below derive from the corpus, and there is no attempt at capturing the full semantic range or alternative functions.

abāku (syl.) 199:4; 210:5; 313:10, 12; 314:7, 11; 315:15
"to bring (in/forth), to take"

abattu (syl.) 152:3′; 253:2; 254:2
"*abattu*-wood"; for the problem with 152:3′, see there.

abnu (NA_4) 21:12′; 142:1
"stone"

abu (AD) 314:13, 16
"father"

addu (syl.) 51:13; 301:13′
"throwing-stick"

adi (syl.) 10:2; 25:3; 27:13; 29:15; 33:3, 7, 9; 51:23; 143:14; 176:13, 25; 177:2; 215:2; 220:3; 226:2; 230:5; 233:2; 234:4; 249:2; 303:3′, 28′, 44′; 304:30′; 313:3
1. "including"; 2. "until"

adi libbi (syl.) 230:4
"until the middle (of month ...)"

adīlu (syl.) 187:3
"tassels"

agâ (syl.) 48:8
"these"

agru (^{lu_2}ḪUN.GA_2) 206:2; 208:2, 7; 242:21; 289:2; 304:41′; 308:20′
"hired men/worker(s)"

agû (AGA) 7:2
"crown"

agurru I (syl.) 21:7′, 16′; 38:3
"*agurru*-ornaments"

agurru II (syl.) 208:3; 223:5
"(baked) bricks"

aḫameš (syl.) 21:5′
"together"

aḫānu I (syl.) 135:1; 308:32′
"manacles (rings)"

aḫānu II (syl.) 38:2
"winged"

aḫu I (ŠEŠ) 54:5; 296:26, 28, 32, 38, 73; 307:3, 5, 7, 9, 11, 12
"brother"
aḫu II (syl.) 315:16
"half"
aḫussu (syl.) 276:2
"*aḫussu*-soda"
aki (syl.) 313:2, 3; 314:15
"because of"
akkullu(attu) (NIG$_2$.GUL, syl.) 55:6; 56:2; 128:2, 6, 8; 301:9′
"mattock"; the spelling *ak-kul-lat* (with slight variants in **No. 128**) may be a form of *akkullu*, a hammer/hoe-like tool (CAD A/I, 276), hence, "mattock." The main difficulty is that **Nos. 55, 56** speak of silver, which would not be used for the repair of such agricultural tools. In **No. 128**, on the other hand, we are dealing with iron tools. It is possible that the first two cases deal with ceremonial counterparts of the original object. Whether or not the orthographical differences are significant in this respect is unclear. A cultic version to an agricultural tool is attested for the *marru* spade: *šu-ba-tu$_4$ ša$_2$ mar-ri* "a pedestal for the *marru* spade (symbol)" (Nbn 753:32); 2⌜0⌝ KU$_3$.BABBAR ŠAM$_2$ *mar-ri ša$_2$* KU$_3$.BABBAR "20 shekels of silver is the price of the silver *marru* spade" (Nbn 529: 1).
aklu I (NINDA) 242:19; 274:1; 277:1, 4, 5, 6
"a type of measurement"
aklu II (NINDA) 193:18′; 216:1; 220:2; 229:4, 12; 233:1
"bread"
alāku (syl.) 194:4; 202:3; 210:3
"to go"
alla (syl.) 312:17
"except for ..."
alpu (GU$_4$, see also *bīt a.*) 304:37′
"ox"
amaru (syl.) 208:7
"brick pile"
amēlu (syl.) 221:13
"man"
ana muḫḫi (*a.* UGU, syl.) 16:4; 105:13; 114:3; 117:6; 144:10, 13; 199:4; 207:13; 209:19; 214:2; 229:2; 246:3; 269:6; 271:4; 303:9′
"on account of; for (the purpose of)"
ana pāni (*a.* IGI, syl.) 54:3; 210:2; 226:8; 311:16
"(weighed) against; (went/brought) to/before (PN)"
annutû (syl.) 311:9; 312:9
"these"
apālu (syl.) 192:4; 200:4; 219:6
"to pay"
appatu (syl.) 93:3; 128:3; 131:2
"tip"; as a part of an iron tool.
arad ekalli (^{lu_2}IR$_3$ E$_2$.GAL) 189:9; 197:4; 200:9; 221:6; 294:17′; 305:13
"master-builder"
arādu (syl.) 6:3; 15:3?; 41:6; 308:25′
"to remove; to send down (river)"
arḫu (ITI) 200:1; 219:2
"month"
arṣabu (*ar$_2$-ṣa-a-bat-tu$_4$*) 60:2
"*arṣabu*-tool"
arzallu (*ar$_2$-zal-lu$_4$*) 38:3
"*arzallu*-jewel"; a gold ornament.
ašābu (syl.) 157:7, 10
"to dwell"
ašgik/gû (^{na_4}(UGU.)AŠ.GI$_3$.GI$_3$) 32:2; 51:11
"*ašgikû*-stone"; the reading of ^{na_4}UGU.AŠ.GI$_3$.GI$_3$ (**No. 51**: 11) as *ašgikû* is uncertain; see *ašgikû* 1b), CAD A$_2$, 427.
aškāpu (^{lu_2}AŠGAB) 105:9; 193:55′; 211:8; 212:5; 215:7′; 251:4; 262:3, 6; 293:4; 294:15′; 296:57; 297:20′ 298:7; 304:15
"leatherworker"
ašlāku (^{lu_2}TUG$_2$.BABBAR) 158:8; 199:6; 236:2
"washerman"
ašlu (syl.) 108:1
"rope"
ašnugallu (^{na_4}GIŠ.NU$_{11}$.GAL) 51:8
"alabaster"
aššatu (DAM) 105:10
"wife"
atkalluššu (syl.) 259:3
"carrier"; see Jursa and Weszeli 1996.
atkuppu (^{lu_2}AD.KID) 209:3, 17; 223:2; 229:8; 260:4; 294:16′; 309:2
"reed-worker"
attu (syl.) 227:11
"for (one)self"

atû (^{lu_2}I$_3$.DU$_8$) 189:7; 193:54′; 195:4, 5; 196:4; 215:9; 225:4; 227:11
"porter"

ayar(i)tu (syl.) 51:6; 301:17′
"cowrie (shaped ornament)"

ayaru (syl.) 11:7; 24:4; 34:8, 12; 40:7, 9; 41:1; 42:7; 43:5; 44:1, [6], 9; 51:6, 28; 301:4′, 11′, 14′, 15′, 27′
"rosette (shaped ornament)"; often mentioned alongside ornamental squares (*tenšu*)

azmarû (syl.) 271:2; 305:11?
"lance"

babbanû (syl.) 33:2?
"top quality"

bābtu (KA$_2$-*ti*(-*i*), syl.) 22:11; 27:16; 31:3; 97:5; 105:2, 4; 169:1
"part (of a whole)"; see commentary to **No. 97**: 5.

bābu I (KA$_2$) 8:5; 11:7; 16:1; 149:3; 214:10; 222:6; 304:26′; 315:8
"gate; door; entrance; opening (of an ornament)"

bābu II (KA$_2$) 190:12, 13, 14; 215:7; 243:5; 305:24
"installment"

bāʾiru (^{lu_2}ŠU.KU$_6$) 45:2; 54:7
"fisherman"

balāṭu (syl.) 313:5
"to heal"

batqu (syl., see also *šaddu ša b.*) 1:2, 3; 3:2; 4:7; 5:10; 6:2 7:3; 8:2; 10:10; 14:6; 20:2; 26:2; 27:14?; 34:15; 36:2; 40:6; 45:1; 49:3, 5; 52:1; 55:6; 56:2; 61:2; 62:2; 300:3
"repair"

bēl maṣṣarti (^{lu_2}EN *ma-aṣ-ṣar-tu*$_4$, see also *maṣṣartu* II) 215:6′
"chief of the watch"

bēl piqitti/-nēti (^{lu_2}EN + syl.) 56:3; 294:3′?; 311:17; 312:13
"commissioner"

birti (syl.) 39:6
"between"

bītānu (E$_2$-*ta-nu*) 289:10
"temple"

bitqa (syl.) 1:1; 18:2; 29:10; 49:2, 4; 174:3; 176:22; 177:7; 186:2; 189:7; 207:7; 214:3; 241:1, 5; 302:13
"⅛"

bīt alpi (E$_2$ GU$_4$) 189:10; 295:4
"ox stable"

bīt ḫilṣi (E$_2$ + syl.) 57:4; 69:3; 282:12
"*bīt ḫilṣi*"; an oil press workshop; for the *bīt ḫilṣi*, especially in the context of preparing medicinal ointment, see Joannès 2006.

bīt immeri (E$_2$ UDU.NITA$_2$) 189:5; 237:4
"sheep shed"

bīt išpari (E$_2$ ^{lu_2}UŠ.BAR) 62:4
"weavers' workshop"

bīt kādu (E$_2$ *ka-a-du*) 304:43′
"guard-post"

bīt karê (E$_2$ GUR$_7$, syl.) 65:4; 227:13; 235:6
"depot"

bīt kīli (E$_2$ + syl., see also *rab bīt kīli*) 313:3
"prison"

bīt kisalli (E$_2$ KISAL, see also *kisallu*) 157:9; 308:22′
"courtyard-chapel"

bīt makkūri (E$_2$ NIG$_2$.GA, see also *makkūru*) 144:14; 206:3; 208:3; 288:6
"storehouse"

bīt nuḫatimmi (E$_2$ ^{lu_2}MUḪALDIM, see also *nuḫatimmu* and *nuḫatimmūtu*) 65:5
"bakery"

bīt papāḫu (E$_2$ + syl.) 75:3; 157:6; 311:14; 315:8
"cella"

bīt qātē (E$_2$ ŠU^{II}) 255:5
"*bīt qātē*"

bīt qīpi (E$_2$ ^{lu_2}*qip-pu*) 255:10
"*bīt qīpi*"

bīt sirāšî (E$_2$ ^{lu_2}LUNGA, see also *sīrāšû*) 98:5
"brewers' workshop"; the difference between the *bīt sirāši* and the *bīt šikari* (see below) is not clear; the former relates to the personnel while the latter refers to the product.

bīt šatammi (E$_2$ ^{lu_2}ŠA$_3$.TAM) 255:7–8, 12
"*bīt šatammi*"

bīt šikari (E$_2$ KAŠ?) 237:1
"brewery"; the difference between the *bīt šikari* and the *bīt sirāši* (see above) is not clear; the former relates to the product while the latter refers to the personnel.

bīt talli (E$_2$ ^{giš}*tal*$^{!(T. ḫu)}$-⸢*la*⸣) 11:2
"pole *base*"
bīt tenê (E$_2$ *te-en-ne*$_2$*-e*) 225:4
"*annex*"
bīt ummâni (E$_2$ ^{lu_2}*um-man-nu*) 40:6
"craftsmen's workshop"
bītu I (E$_2$) 222:2; 305:1, 2
"house"
bītu II (E$_2$) 189:2; 213:26′
"temple"
bullu (*bu-le-e*) 211:1; 269:6; 296:49, 63
"firewood"; dried wood and reed.
burāšu (ŠIM.LI) 158:9
"juniper"
būrtu (AB$_2$.MAḪ$_2$) 217:23
"young cow"
burû (syl.) 255:11; 257:1, 4; 260:1
"reed mat"
būṣu (^{gada}*bu-u*$_2$*-ṣu*) 145:2
"byssus"
buʾʾû (*u*$_2$*-ba-a*ʾ) 314:16
"to hold (one) accountable"

daltu (^{giš}IG, see also *nagār d.*) 5:9; 76:2; 153:2; 305:1, 4, 6
"door"
dālû (^{lu_2}A.BAL, see also *ša d.*) 215:10
"water-drawer"
dannu (*dan-nu*) 237:1, 2
"*dannu*-vat"
dapas/ltu (^{tug_2}*da*$^?$*-ap-al-ti*) 123:2
"*dapastu*-cover"; see Quillien 2022, 449–50.
dappu (^{giš}*da*$^!$*-ap-*⸢*pi*⸣) 279:1
"crossbeam"
dišpu (LAL$_3$) 277:1
"honey"
dudittu ([*du-di*]*-it-ti*) 21:5′
"fibula"
dullu (syl.) 6:4; 9:7; 29:16; 59:2; 64:2; 95:2; 96:2; 100:2; 113:4; 126:3; 138:i 3; 139:3; 141:3; 142:2; 144:11, 13; 164:2; 165:3; 166:2; 171:2; 172:3; 176:13; 177:8; 188:2; 201:5; 207:13; 247:2; 262:2; 304:36′; 308:7′, 26′, 34′; 315:14, 15
"work"
dūru (BAD$_3$ TIN.TIR^{ki}) 304:2
"(city) wall"
dušû (^{kuš}DUḪ.ŠI.A, ^{kuš}*du-šu-u*$_2$, see also *ṣārip d.*) 261:2; 262:1, 4; 267:1; 305:21
"*dušû*(-colored)-leather"; for the *dušû* color, see Thavapalan 2020, 244–64.

elat (syl.) 2:1$^?$; 31:1; 143:8; 242:5
"apart from"
eleppu (^{giš}MA$_2$) 180:[3], 9; 242:18; 303:16′; 308:20′; 310:3, 5, 10
"boat"
ellu (KU$_3$) 304:37′
"*pure* (ox)"
elû (syl.) 180:5; 242:5; 303:16′, 18′
"to load; bring (upstream)"
enzu (UZ$_3$) 281:6; 282:16; 285:6′, 10′
"goat"
epēšu (syl.) 104:6; 201:5; 302:[15]; 315:13
"to work; to make (a manufactured product); to settle (an account)"
erēbu (syl.) 27:15; 214:10; 304:26′
"to enter; come in"
ērib bīti (^{lu_2}KU$_4$ E$_2$) 311:13
"temple enterer"
errēšu ($^{lu_2 \circ}$*er-re-*<*šu*$_2$>) 190:4
"sharecropper"
erû (URUDU, syl.) 61:2; 64:1; 305:13$^?$
"copper"
esû (*e-su-u*$_2$) 77:2
"*esû*"; an *esû* iron tool is otherwise unattested.
eṣēdu (*e-ṣe-du*) 97:6
"harvest"
ešertu (10^{ti}, see also *rab ešerti*) 161:5, 13; 226:4
"decury"
ešrû (*eš-ru-u*$_2$) 304:18
"tithe"
eššešu (UD.EŠ$_3$.EŠ$_3$^{me}) 277:2, 4, 6; 304:29′
"festival (days)"
eššu (*eš-šu*$_2$) 65:7
"new"
eṭēru (syl.) 10:13$^?$; 16:5; 19:5; 20:5; 104:8; 141:6; 144:6; 203:13; 213:2′, 14′, 18′, 20′, 22′, 24′, 26′, 28′; 220:5; 309:5
"to pay"

gabû (syl.) 143:3, 11; 176:6, 9; 186:1; 276:3
"alum"

gadû (MAŠ$_2$.TUR) 281:7; 282:16
"kid"
gallābu (^{lu_2}ŠU.I) 179:9
"barber"
gamru (syl.) 68:1; 69:1; 70:1; 78:1; 81:1; 90:1; 97:1; 98:1; 99:2; 100:1, 5; 101:2; 102:2; 103:3; 104:7; 117:1, 8; 129:1; 132:1; 134:1; 136:1; 137:1; 138:ii 1, 2, 7, 16, 18; 139:1; 285:12′
"processed (source material into an object)"
gangannu (syl.) 131:5; 275:4
"pot stand"
gappu (*ga-ap-pi*) 11:5
"quill"
gāzizu (^{lu_2}*gaz*$^{!(T.\ gu_2)}$-*zi-zi*^{me}) 295:5
"shearer"
gazzu (*gaz-za*) 281:13
"shorn"
gidlu (syl.) 149:2; 163:2, 5; 173:3$^?$; 315:8
"curtain"
gīdu (*gi-du*) 263:3, 8
"sinew"
ginû (*gi-ne$_2$-e*) 278:2; 280:7
"*ginû*-offering"
girû (syl.) 4:6; 8:1; 9:4; 17:1; 18:3; 23:1; 29:7; 31:8$^?$; 138:iii 3; 176:20; 179:7; 199:3; 310:8
"$^1/_{24}$ (of a shekel)"
gizzu (syl.) 98:3; 118:2; 132:3; 289:5, 9
"shearing"
guḫalṣu (syl.) 5:3; 21:6′, 8′; 146:3; 154:8, 15; 315:11
1. "wire (of gold)"; 2. "fringes; cords (of wool)"
$^{giš?!}$***gur-ra*** 128:4
unclear; possibly: ^{giš}<*it*>-*qur-ra*, a "spoon"
gurābu (*gu-ra-bi*) 177:2
"sack"
guzullu (*gu-zu-ul-lu*) 255:4
"reed bundle"

ḫabṣu (*ḫab-ṣu-tu*) 24:1
"lustrous"
ḫalāqu (syl.) 50:4
"missing"
ḫālilu (syl.) 103:5; 122:2; 138:ii 3, 18
"*ḫālilu*-tool"; iron tool used alongside shovels (*našḫiptu*) in excavations and maintenance work.
ḫalīṣu (^{kuš}*ḫa-li-ṣa-nu*) 266:1
"flayed skin"
ḫallūru (syl.) 29:10, 14; 34:13; 241:3
"$^1/_{10}$ (of a shekel)"
ḫalpu (*ḫal-pu*) 201:4
"substitute (worker)"
ḫalqu (*ḫal-qu-tu*) 204:6
"escaped (man)"
ḫalṣu (^{gada}*ḫal-ṣu*) 163:1, 4
"combed linen"
ḫandūḫu (syl.) 50:3, 8, 12, 16
"lock part"; see Beaulieu 2003, 12, and several texts cited throughout the study.
ḫargullu (ḪAR.ḪAR, syl.) 50:2, 7, 11, 15
"lock"; see Beaulieu 2003, 12.
ḫarḫarru (syl.) 37:1; 38:4
"chain (of rings)"
ḫašḫūru (^{sik_2}ḪAŠḪUR) 176:24
"apple-colored (wool)"; refers to the color of wool, to be distinguished from *ḫaš*/*tḫurētu*, which was the apple-colored dye; see Thavapalan 2020, 266.
ḫaš/tḫurētu (syl.) 143:12; 178:8; 187:1; 214:4
"apple-color dye"; as noted by Thavapalan (2020, 268), the determinative ^{u_2} in **No. 187**: 1 shows that this was a plant-based dye, used also for the making of other red and red-purple dyes. Though related, the *ḫaš*/*tḫurētu* dye should be distinguished from *ḫašḫūru*, which refers to wool color; see above.
ḫašû (*ḫa-še-e*) 34:2; 40:2, 5; 42:2, 4; 43:2
"*ḫašû*-ornament"
ḫaṭṭu (syl.) (GIDRU-*a-ta*, *ḫa-ṭa-a-ta*) 80:2; 130:6
"rod"; in both cases, of iron.
ḫâṭu I (syl.) 15:2; 33:9; 54:3; 67:2; 91:3; 151:2; 152:2; 178:8
"stock"; weighed material (in hand).
ḫâṭu II (syl.) 13:1, 2; 18:1; 180:2, 8
"instalment"
ḫepû (*ḫi-pa-a-ta*) 71:10
"void (lit. broken, regarding a promissory note)"
ḫiāṭu (syl.) 8:6; 13:10; 185:5; 221:12
"to weigh"
ḫillu (^{gi}*ḫi*-⸢*il*$^?$⸣-*li*) 210:7
"(reed) casing"

ḫimētu (I$_3$.NUN.NA) 282:9
"ghee"

ḫimirtu (*ḫi-mir-ti*) 275:3
"*crack*?"; see edition.

ḫinšu ($^{(na_4)}$*ḫi-in-ša$_2$-nu*) 51:8; 301:12′
Unclear cultic object; attested twice in the Pl form, *ḫi-in-ša$_2$-nu*, listed among ornaments and cultic objects. In **No. 51** we find it may be made out of alabaster, lapis lazuli, *pappardilu*-stone, and *ašgikû*-stone. Another attestation can be found in a similar context, 5 *ḫi-in-šu* (Pinches 1928, 132–4: 15), with no further information regarding material, shape, or function.

ḫirûtu (syl.) 122:3; 129:3
"excavation"

ḫīṭu (*ḫi-ṭu*) 313:13
"guilt of (an offence against …)"

ḫubšu (*ḫu-⸢bu*?⸣*-ša$_2$-nu*) 10:7
"*ḫubšu*-object"; unclear, see edition for commentary.

ḫullānu (syl.) 148:4; 157:2
"*ḫullānu*-coat"; see Quillien 2022, 523.

ḫummušu (syl.) 4:4; 7:1; 18:5, 7; 20:1; 29:5, 13
"⅕"

ḫunāqu (syl.) 51:20; 301:11′, 21′
"(horse) collar"; in **No. 51** it is made of leather and silver. In **No. 301** it is listed among items related to cultic chariots. Its combination of context, materials, and etymology (*ḫnq*) thus point to a choker (a collar), which was part of the harness.

ḫurāṣu (KU$_3$.GI, see also *ḫ. sādu*, and *ḫ. sāmu*, and *nalṭar*) 1:1, 2; 2:1, 3, 5; 3:1; 4:1, 2, 4, 6; 5:6; 6:1; 7:1, 2; 8:1, 6; 9:4, 6; 10:4, 5, 9, 10; 11:1, 4; 13:1, 3, 6, 10; 14:1, 2; 15:1, 2, 4; 16:1; 17:1–4; 18:1, 3, 5, 7; 19:1; 20:1; 21:4′, 7′, 8′, 12′, 14′–21′, 7″–9″, 11″, 12″, 13″–18″; 22:11, 12; 23:1; 24:1, 6; 25:1; 26:1; 271, 8, 9, 13; 28:1, 3; 29:1, 3, 4, 5, 7, 8, 14; 30:1; 31:11; 33:5; 34:1, 2, 8, 9, 12, 13; 35:1; 36:1; 37:1; 38:1, 3, 4, 5; 39:1, 6; 40:1, 5, 7, 9; 41:[1]?; 42:1, 2, 5, [7], [8]; 43:1, 5, 6; 44:1, 9; 51:12, 13, 14, 25; 170:16; 213:5′; 301:4′, 15′, 16′, 18′, 26′, 27′, 30′
"gold"

ḫurāṣu* (*ša*) *sādu (KU$_3$.GI *ša$_2$ sa-a-du*) 24:4–5
"*sādu*-gold"

ḫurāṣu sāmu (KU$_3$.GI SA$_5$, see also *ḫurāṣu sāmu*) 5:1; 10:6; 12:1; 33:1, 3, 8
"red gold"

ḫurātu (^{giš}(ŠA$_3$.)ḪAB, *ḫu-ur-ra-ti**) 123:3?*; 143:7; 149:7; 153:3; 154:7, 14; 155:2; 176:7; 186:2; 188:1; 282:11
"madder"; see Thavapalan 2020, 331–8.

ḫuṣannu (^{túg_2}*ḫu-ṣa-ne$_2$-e*) 148:9
"*ḫuṣannu*-sashes"; see Quillien 2022, 523.

ḫušû (*ḫu-še-e*) 67:4, 7
"scrap (bronze)"

idu (syl.) 104:8; 138:ii 15, iii 1, 19; 180:3, 9; 209:16; 242:18; 259:2; 302:11; 303:15′, 17′; 304:41′; 310:3, 5, 10
1. "wage"; 2. "rent"

ikkaru (^{lu_2}ENGAR) 88:7; 105:2; 190:6; 230:5; 297:29
"plowman"

***ikru*?** (*ik-ru*$^{!(T. ḫu)}$) 285:12′
"an (iron) tool"

ilku (*il-ki*) 280:3
"*ilku*-obligation"

ilu (DINGIR) 157:6, 9; 313:13
"god"

imēru (ANŠE) 221:13; 302:11; 303:15′
"donkey"

immertu (U$_8$) 282:15; 285:1′–6′, 8′, 9′, 10′
"ewe"

immeru (UDU(.NITA$_2$)) 131:4; 270:1; 283:5; 284:1, 3; 286:5; 287:6; 304:20, 21, 22, 23
"sheep"

imittu (ZAG) 243:1
"impost"

ina libbi (*ina* ŠA$_3$/*lib$_3$-bi*) 21:9; 27:2, 6, 12; 33:4; 34:12; 48:6; 126:5; 141:3; 144:4; 148:10; 154:4; 174:10; 176:15; 177:7; 180:4, 10; 189:8; 213:29′; 230:6; 242:10; 281:15, 16; 282:7; 286:2; 287:5; 301:19′, 29′, 35′; 303:16′, 18′, 19′, 38′, 46′; 304:30′
"thereof/from this"

ina muḫḫi (*ina* UGU/*muḫ-ḫi*) 42:6; 71:4, 9; 106:3, 4; 129:3; 131:4; 141:3; 157:6, 10; 232:4; 236:3; 238:2; 240:2; 286:3; 312:16, 18, 19
1. "in regards to/vis-à-vis/for"; 2. owed by

ina pāni (*ina* IGI/*pa-ni*) 1:6; 2:2; 3:4; 4:7; 5:4, 10; 6:5; 7:4; 9:[8]; 10:8, 11; 11:3; 12:3; 13:4, 7;

14:7; 15:6; 18:7; 21:9′; 27:17; 31:9, 12; 32:5; 34:5, 11, 14; 35:4; 36:3; 37:3; 39:2; 46:2; 47:1, 3, 4; 48:2; 50:4; 58:3; 59:2; 60:3; 61:4; 62:5; 63:4; 64:2, 5; 72:3; 73:2; 74:[3]; 75:7; 76:6; 77:6; 78:4; 88:7; 94:2; 95:3; 96:2; 97:7; 100:8; 105:1, 5, 6, 7, 8; 107:1, 3–9, 11, 12; 108:3; 109:2; 110:2; 111:2; 112:2; 113:2; 114:2; 115:2; 116:5; 117:5, 11; 118:3; 119:2; 120:2, 3; 121:2, 3; 122:5, 8, 9; 124:3; 125:4; 126:4, 6; 127:3; 128:7, 8; 129:4; 135:4; 138:i 3, 22; 140:2, 3; 141:1, 9; 142:2; 145:5; 146:5; 157:13, 17, 22, 26; 159:6; 163:3, 7; 164:3; 165:3; 166:2, 4; 170:11, 21, 22; 171:2; 172:4; 173:4; 174:12, 17, 20; 177:9; 184:2, 4; 186:5; 187:5; 188:2; 212:1; 213:8′, 10′; 216:3; 221:13, 22; 243:3, 5, 8, 10, 15; 245:15′; 250:3; 252:7; 253:2; 257:2, 3; 258:2; 261:4; 262:5; 266:5; 275:5; 279:3; 282:17, 19; 285:14′; 289:5, 8; 290:5, 7; 297:12, 23, 24; 303:22′, 30′; 304:36′; 305:4, 7, 9, 11, 13, 14, 16, 19, 21, 22; 306:2; 308:9′, 10′, 11′, 17′, 27′, 34′; 311:10, 21; 312:10
"at the disposal of"

ina qāt (*ina* ŠU^{II}, see also *qātu*) 18:6; 19:2; 25:3; 45:3; 103:1, 5; 105:11; 143:9; 144:11; 158:2; 174:13; 215:11′; 235:2; 253:3; 254:3; 272:3; 287:4; 295:9, 11; 301:3′; 302:2; 304:2, 39′, 40′, 43′; 307:23, 25; 308:36′; 310:1, 7, 9, 10, 13; 313:6; 314:5
1. "via/by/from"; 2. "under the responsibility of"

ina ušuzzu (*ina* GUB-*zu*) 287:8
"in the presence of"

inbu (*in-bi*) 14:1
"fruit (shaped jewels)"

inzaḫurētu (syl.) 143:2, 10; 154:5; 176:4, 8, 21
"*inzaḫurētu*-dye"; see Thavapalan 2020, 330–1, 336.

irbu (syl., see also *irbu ša šarri*) 23:2; 25:2; 29:3; 109:1; 141:10, 17; 193:29′; 207:1; 214:8; 217:1; 224:2; 226:1; 227:1; 250:1; 282:14, 19; 301:24′; 308:15′, 16′
"income"; note that *irbu ša* x refer to "income from x" (rather than "to/for x").

irbu ša šarri (*i. ša*$_2$ LUGAL) 1:1; 29:1
"income from the king"

irtu (GABA) 2:1, 3; 21:16′, 17′; 35:2, 3; 38:2; 39:6; 300:3
"breast (ornament)"

^{sik_2}IR$_3$-U$_2$-MA-MEŠ 176:11
unclear; a type of dyed wool(?) listed alongside dye related materials.

iṣṣūru (*iṣ-*⌜*ṣur*⌝, see also *mušākil iṣṣūri* and *rēʾi iṣṣūri*) 229:11
"bird"

išdu (*il-du*) 301:26′
"base"

išḫanabe (^{sik_2}*iš-ḫa-*<*na*>*-be*) 148:3
"*išḫanabe*-garment"

iškāru (syl.) 99:3; 137:3; 168:20, 45; 260:5
"*iškāru*-obligation"

iškūru (DUḪ.LAL$_3$) 275:1; 276:4
"wax"

išpar birmi (^{lu_2}UŠ.BAR *bir-mu*) 189:6; 296:17; 308:3′, 8′, 31′
"weaver of colored cloth"

išparu (^{lu_2}UŠ.BAR, see also *bīt i.* and *i. birmi*) 146:6; 149:9; 151:3; 153:4; 154:10; 158:12; 170:20; 171:4; 172:4; 173:4; 177:4, 10; 182:6; 186:6; 188:4; 192:1; 193:22′; 202:9; 212:12; 228:2; 229:10; 230:12; 233:9; 237:3; 246:2; 298:10; 299:22′; 303:23′; 310:11; 312:1
"weaver"

išpatu (*iš-pat*) 301:4′
"quiver"

ištuḫḫu (*iš-tuḫ-ḫu*) 301:25′
"whip"

itinnu (^{lu_2}ŠITIM) 219:5; 242:23; 245:8′; 258:5; 272:7; 288:4, 5; 299:16′
"builder"

itti (*it-ti*) 21:14″; 27:15; 104:5; 207:10; 271:3; 296:55; 302:15
"with"

izqātu (*iz-qa-ti*) 135:2
"fetter"

kabšarru (^{lu_2}KAB.SAR) 14:7; 142:4; 239:2; 245:20; 304:14
"jeweler"

kādu (*ka-a*$^{!}$*-du*, see also *bīt k.*) 304:27′
"guard-post"

kakkabtu (MUL) 21:10′; 34:1; 39:3; 40:1, 5; 42:1, 3; 43:1; 85:3
"star"

kakku (*kak*$^{?}$*-ku*$^{?}$) 123:6$^{?}$
"weapon"

kalakku (*ka-lak*$^{!}$*-ki*) 199:4
"silo"
kalapu (*ka-la-pu*) 301:8′
"*kalapu*-axe"
kallu (syl.) 33:6; 49:8; 51:17
"*kallu*-bowl"
kalu (KAL) 315:12
"all"
kalû (^{lu_2}GALA) 200:7; 218:2
"lamentation priest"
kalūmu ($^{(udu)}$*ka-lum*) 281:2, 16; 282:15; 286:1, 16; 304:7, 8, 45′
"male lamb"; both *kalūmu* and *parru* designate male lambs in Neo-Babylonian records. Here, we translate *kalūmu* as a male lamb while *parru* is rendered young male sheep; see Kozuh 2014, 61–3.
kammu (*kam-mat*) 87:3; 93:2; 128:3; 131:3
"dowel"
kanāšu (*i-ka-as-su-u*$_2$) 208:8
"to stack"
kanāzu (syl., in the stat. only) 27:12; 48:10
"to (be) store(d)"
kappu (^{giš}*kap-pu*) 112:1
"*kappu*-bowl"
karānu (^{giš}GEŠTIN); see also *kirû ša karāni* and *nukaribbu ša karāni*
kaspu (KU$_3$.BABBAR, see also *k. peṣū*) 5:9; 12:6, 7; 16:4$^{?}$; 18:2, 4, 8; 25:8; 28:1; 30:1, 2; 45:1; 46:1; 47:1; 48:2, 6; 49:1, 2, 4, 5, 7; 50:1, 2, 3, 6, 7, 8, 14, 15, 16; 51:3, 5–7, 12, 13, 15, 17, 19, 21, 23–28; 52:1, 2; 53:1; 54:1, 3, 6, 7, 10, 11; 55:1, 5; 56:1; 103:1; 106:1; 138:ii 14, 22, iii 2, 5, 12, 19; 141:[1], 3, 7, 8, 10, 16; 143:4; 152:1, 2, 4, 5; 158:2; 160:2; 161:8; 169:1, 2; 170:1, 3, 4, 9, 10, 13, 14, 17, 18, 25; 174:9, 12, 14, 17, 20; 175:1; 177:3; 179:1; 180:2, 8; 181:5, 7; 184:5; 186:2; 191:1; 199:1, 10; 202:1; 203:1, 6, 12; 204:1; 205:1; 206:1; 207:1; 208:1; 209:11; 210:1; 211:1; 212:1, 2; 213:1′, 6′, 8′, 9′, 10′, 13′, 16′, 19′, 21′, 23′; 214:1, 6, 11; 221:12, 13, 14; 228:1; 235:1; 241:1; 252:1, 6; 253:1; 254:1; 255:1; 257:5, 6; 258:1; 264:1; 272:1; 280:2; 286:8; 287:1, 5; 301:5′, 7′, 17′, 21′, 22′, 24′; 302:1, 8, 11, 13; 303:2′, 3′, 20′, 21′, 22′, 26′, 34′; 304:1, 41′; 307:18, 20, 22, 27; 308:9′, 10′, 11′; 310:1, 3
"silver"
kaspu peṣû (KU$_3$.BABBAR BABBAR-*u*$_2$) 48:1
"white silver"
kasūsu (*ka-su-su*)$^{?}$ 21:15′, 11″
"falcon (figurine)"
kī (*ki-i*, see also *kī pî*) 313:11; 314:[10]
"if"
KI.MIN 176:18, 19, 20, 22, 23, 24; 293:10$^{?}$; 296:20, 33; 304:15, 17, 21, 22
"ditto"
kī pî (*ki-i* KA) 303:19′
"at a rate of"
kibsu (syl.) 157:21, 26
"*kibsu*-fabric"
kibtu (ŠE.GIG, GIG.BA) 189:1; 190:23
"wheat"
kidinnu (*ki-di-ne*$_2$*-e*) 150:4; 155:2
"cotton"; see Quillien 2022, 162–3.
kigallu (KI.GAL) 20:2
"pedestal"
kiništu (^{lu_2}*ki-niš-ti*) 280:4
"priests"
kirītu (*ki-rit-ti*) 54:6
"*kirītu*-ornament"
kirru (*ki-ir-ri*) 65:7; 69:2
"*kirru*-vessel"
kirû ša karāni (^{giš}KIRI$_6$ *ša*$_2$ ^{giš}GEŠTIN, see also *karānu* and *nukaribbu ša karāni*) 139:3
"vineyard"
kisallu (KISAL, see also *bīt kisalli*) 49:6
"courtyard"
kissatu (syl.) 215:13; 304:4, 5
"fodder"
kišādu (GU$_2$) 21:13′; 24:2; 39:2, 4; 315:11
"necklace"
kiškanê (*kiš-ka-na-ne*$_2$*-e*) 214:12
"*kiškanê*-wood"
kišukku (syl.) 54:1, 12
"grate"
kittu (*kit-ti*) 33:7
"*kittu*-bowl"
kitû (GADA.ḪI.A) 164:2; 165:2; 166:1; 178:6; 302:2, 8
"linen"
kizû (^{lu_2}*ki-zu-u*$_2$) 194:9
"*kizû*-attendant"
kubburru (*ku-ub-bur*) 157:11
"thick"

kulūlu (*ku-lu-lu*) 14:2, 5; 21:4′
"crown"

kūm ana kūm (syl.) 20:4
"one for the other"

kumāru (*ku-ma-ra-a-ta*) 8:2; 21:4′
"frame(d ornaments)"

kūmu (syl., see also *kūm ana kūm*) 65:8; 161:8; 162:3; 180:3, 9; 199:1; 232:1; 270:2; 308:25′
"instead"

kunāšu (ŠE.ZIZ$_2$.A$_4$) 181:7, 12; 190:6, 8, 20, 22, 28, 30, 35, 36; 230:2; 232:2
"emmer"

kunukku (^{na_4}KIŠIB) 2:3, 4; 5:3; 24:2; 32:1
"cylinder seal (shaped beads)"

kupru (*ku-pur*) 117:6
"bitumen"

kurkû (KUR.GI^{mušen}) 282:10
"goose"

^{tug_2}KUR.RA 144:1, 4, 14; 152:1; 152:1; 159:2; 162:3; 168:1; 174:1, 3, 5, 7, 9, 14, 16, 18; 307:18, 20, 21, 24
"cape"; see Quillien 2022, 505–17. The Akkadian reading for ^{tug_2}KUR.RA is unknown. It was a rectangle piece of woolen garment, of about 2 m × 3.5 m weighing about 2.5 kg., in Uruk. The item itself was multifunctional, given often to soldiers and workers on the road. One would be able to wear it during the day, but also use it for cover at night as a blanket. Imagining a poncho like garment, the ^{tug_2}KUR.RA is translated as a "cape," which one is able to wrap around the body for various uses.

kurṣu (*kur-ṣu*) 39:4
"link (of a necklace)"

kurummatu (ŠUK, see also *kurummat šarri*) 55:9; 141:4; 189:1$^?$; 192:4; 194:2, 8, 11, 14, [16], 19; 195:1, 3; 196:1; 197:1; 198:1; 200:1; 201:4; 203:8, 9, 14; 205:1; 207:2; 209:1, 4; 215:1, 10; 217:3, 24, 26, 29, 31; 218:1; 219:2; 221:12; 222:2; 223:1; 225:1; 226:2, 11, 14; 228:2; 229:11; 233:5; 244:3, 15; 245:1, 16′; 246:1; 247:1; 266:4; 270:2; 286:6; 291:13; 303:6′, 10′, 12′; 304:1, 14, 27′; 308:19′, 37′; 315:16
"salary; in two cases, *kurummatu* is translated as "rations" rather than "salaries": **No. 222**:2 (rations of the women, see note there) and **No. 233**:5 (rations of the wildcats), and see also *kurummat šarri* below.

kurummat šarri (ŠUK.ḪI.A LUGAL, see also *kurummatu*) 63:5; 193:11′, 59′; 298:9
"royal rations"

kus*(*i*)*birītu (syl.) 33:6; 54:11; 301:22′
"*cover / base*"; for *kusibirītu* as a base, or possibly a cover, see Jursa, *RlA 11*: 225.

kusītu (^{tug_2}BAR.DUL$_8$) 34:3, 10; 40:2, 11; 42:4, 6, 10; 43:3, 7; 44:4; 182:4; 187:3; 236:3; 308:20′
"*kusītu*-garment"; see Quillien 2022, 524.

kutimmu (^{lu_2}KU$_3$.DIM) 1:7; 3:5; 4:9; 6:7; 8:4; 9:2; 14:8; 29:17; 31:12$^?$; 34:5, 11, 14; 35:4; 36:[4]; 39:8; 45:7; 52:4; 53:6; 196:2; 213:12′; 239:3; 245:7′; 248:4; 288:1$^?$
"goldsmith"

kuzullu (^{gi}*ku-zu-ul-lu*) 252:4, 10
"reed bundles"

lā (syl.) 21:11′, 14′; 24:3; 189:8; 313:12; 314:11
negation

labānu (*la-ba-nu*) 51:5
"frankincense"

labbu(?) (⸢*lab-ba-nu*⸣) 70:2
"lion"

labīru (*la-bi-ri*) 286:8
"old"

lānu (*la-a-nu*) 33:5; 54:1
"body"

laripu (^{gada}*la-ri-pe-e*) 145:1
"*laripu*-garment"

larû(?) (*la-ru*) 301:31′
"branche"

lēʾu (^{giš}DA) 191:2; 203:10$^?$; 306:1
"writing board"

lillidu (MAŠ$_2$.GUB) 282:22
"young goat"

lišānu (EME) 130:3
"*wedge* (lit. "tongue)"

līšu (*li-i-šu$_2$*) 304:6
"dough"

littu (GIŠ.ŠU$_2$.A) 13:8
"stool"

lītu (AB$_2$.GAL.MI$_2$.AL) 212:7; 282:18
"cow"

lubār mēṭi (^tug2^*lu-bar* ^giš^KU.AN, see also *lubāru* and *mēṭu*) 4:3
"*lubār mēṭi*-headdress"; see Quillien 2022, 525.
lubāru (^tug2^*lu-bar*, see also *lubār mēṭi*) 146:1; 148:1; 154:2; 183:3
"*lubāru*-garment"; see Quillien 2022, 524.
lubuštu (syl.) 146:4; 183:5; 246:4
"clothing"

maddaru (*ma-ad-dar*) 90:7
"*pickaxe*"; see edition.
ma-ag-ga-nu[?] (uncl.) 72:2
unclear; an iron object, see edition.
maḫāru (IGI, syl., see also *nadan u maḫar*) 10:1; 12:7; 16:3; 17:7; 18:2, 4, 6, 10; 27:3; 33:12; 38:6; 39:9; 53:6; 65:5; 66:2; 67:8; 68:4; 69:6; 70:9; 75:4; 76:3; 77:5; 78:3; 79:2; 80:4; 81:3; 82:2, 5; 83:2; 85:4; 86:4; 87:5, 8; 88:6; 89:4; 90:9; 91:5; 92:5; 93:4; 97:4; 98:7; 99:5; 100:7; 101:7; 102:5; 104:7; 124:5; 125:3; 126:3; 127:2; 128:5; 129:3; 130:9; 131:3; 132:7; 133:5; 134:4; 135:7; 136:5; 138:ii 1, 6, 14, 21, 29; 149:9; 150:8; 151:3; 152:8; 153:4; 154:10, 17′; 155:4; 156:3; 167:4; 170:15[?]; 176:26; 177:5, 6; 178:11; 179:1; 180:12; 186:3; 189:8; 197:5[?]; 213:7′[?], 12′, 29′; 214:14; 218:3; 236:5; 237:5; 238:6; 239:5; 240:5; 216:3; 251:7; 252:5; 260:6; 265:3; 266:8; 267:4; 268:4; 269:8; 280:6; 283:2; 284:7; 285:13′; 286:12; 301:34′; 302:10; 303:22′, 24′; 304:11; 308:2′, 4′, 12′, 13′, 28′, 31′, 34′, 39′
"to receive"
māḫiru (KI.LAM) 302:1
"purchase"
māḫiṣu (*ma-ḫi-ṣu*) 58:2; 76:6
"*mallet*"; the great semantic range of the root **mḫṣ* makes it difficult to pinpoint the meaning of *ma-ḫi-ṣu* in context. The simplest solution must be some kind of a tool; i.e. *māḫiṣu* = striker = mallet. The mallet in **No. 58**, however, would be relatively heavy (ca. 2.3 kg.), while at the same time made out of soft bronze, rather than of iron as in **No. 76**). The efficiency of a heavy bronze mallet may be questionable. Alternatively, one may also suggest the object to have been the anvil used for the smith's daily work.
makaddu (*ma*[?!]*-kad-da-nu*) 89:2
"*spatula*(?)"; see edition.
makkasu I (*ma-*⸢*ak-ka*⸣*-*[*su*]) 130:7
"*makkasu*-bowl"
makkasu II (*ma-ak-ka-si*) 304:12
"quality (dates)"
makkūru (NIG$_2$.GA, see also *bīt makkūri* and *makkūr* DN) 49:9; 135:4; 141:17; 147:5; 159:6; 174:4, 15, 19; 175:3; 181:6; 184:6; 213:8′; 231:7; 242:13; 257:7; 302:12; 308:36′; 309:1
"temple store(s)"
***makkūr* DN** (NIG$_2$.GA DN) 71:3; 232:3
"property of DN"
makṣāru (*ma-ak-ṣa-ru*) 308:13′, 39′, 40′
"bundles (of straw)"
makūtu (*ma-ka-a-ta*) 304:32′
"*makūtu*-cake"
^lu2^***ma/ba-la-a*** 112:3
unclear; see edition.
malāḫu (^lu2^MA$_2$.LAḪ$_4$, ^lu2^*ma-la-ḫu*) 117:12; 221:9; 242:19; 287:11; 291:7; 292:7; 293:8; 310:4
"boatman"
malītu (*ma-la-ti*) 242:22
"*malītu*-offering"
mamma (*mam-ma*) 315:14
"(any)one"
mandidu (^lu2^*man-di-di*) 234:5; 242:13
"measuring official"
mandītu (syl.) 21:8′, 11′, 15″; 27:1[?]
"mounting"
manû (syl.) 13:8[?]
"to count/weigh"
manzaltu (*man-zal-ti*) 312:15
"temple service"
manzāzu (*man-za-za*) 51:26
"stand"
maqqāru (*ma-aq-qar*) 100:3, 8
"*maqqāru*-chisel"
mār šipri (^lu2^A.KIN) 135:7; 227:9; 248:5; 271:8; 303:29′; 304:39′
"messenger"
marratu (ŠEŠ.MUŠEN) 303:24′
"*marratu*-bird"
marru (MAR) 51:29; 75:2, 6; 78:2; 82:2; 84:3; 86:2; 87:2; 88:3; 92:2; 93:2; 105:1; 107:1, 2, 4–7, 9,

11; 110:1; 113:1; 117:2, 9; 119:1; 122:7; 127:1, 3; 129:2; 131:2; 132:2; 133:1; 135:3; 138:ii 8, 12, 29; 139:1; 140:1; 269:2
"spade"

marṣu (GIG) 199:8; 229:6; 233:7; 296:70, 74
"sick"

māru (DUMU) 105:11; 199:13
"child / son (of)"

⸢mas$^?$-sa$^{?}$⸣-ni (300:1)
unclear

maṣṣartu I (^{lu_2}EN.NUN) 215:4′; 288:6
"watchman"

maṣṣartu II (EN.NUN-*tu*$_4$, see also *bēl maṣṣarti*) 304:42′; 312:11
"watch (duties)"

mašāḫu (⸢*maš*°-*ḫa*°-*tu*°⸣) 190:4
"to (be) measure(d)"

mašīḫu (syl.) 181:11; 194:1; 195:4; 217:5, 22, 23; 224:1; 225:1; 226:1; 227:3; 232:1, 2, 6; 234:1; 247:4, 5, 6; 307:14, 23$^?$
"*mašīḫu* (measure)"

maškiru (^{kuš}*maš-ki-ru*) 303:17′
"raft"

mašku (KUŠ^{meš}, KUŠ.ḪI.A) 51:18, 20, 22; 264:1; 270:1
"hide; leather"

maššânu (^{giš}*ma-aš*$_2$*-ša*$_2$*-nu*) 123:7
"tongs"

maššartu (*maš-šar-ti*) 217:1; 231:1; 286:9; 303:36′; 304:12, 16
"*maššartu*"; for the *maššartu* in temple administration see Waerzeggers 2010, 61–3.

matqanu (syl.) 130:8; 305:15$^?$
"mount"

maṭû (LA$_2$, syl.) 4:6; 9:5; 13:11; 14:4; 18:2, 5, 7; 20:1; 28:3; 29:6; 30:5; 47:6; 48:9; 130:11; 138:iii 3; 179:7; 199:3; 207:7; 241:3; 291:14; 301:31′
"to be(come) missing / low / little; be(come) less (= minus)"

mayāru (*ma-a-a-ri*) 190:27
"*majāru*-plow"

mê qātê I (A^{me} ŠU^{II}, *me-e* ŠU^{II}) 65:2, 9; 275:4; 308:24′
"hand(-washing) water / hand(-washing) water (basin)"

mê qātē (*me-e* ŠU^{II}) 190:12
"*mê qātē* (land)"; see edition.

mešēnu$^?$ (*ma-sin*^{sic}*-ni*) 211:8
"*shoemaker / bow-making leatherworker*"; see edition.

mēṭu (*me-ṭa-nu*, see *lubār mēṭi*) 51:14; 301:6′
"*mēṭu*-mace"

mezēḫu (^{tug_2}*me-ze-eḫ*) 148:11; 157:3, 20; 178:6
"*mezēḫu*-band"; see Quillien 2022, 527.

miḫṣu (*mi-iḫ-ṣu*) 148:12; 149:2; 153:1; 154:11; 176:15; 178:10; 308:30′
"woven cloth"; see Quillien 2022, 527.

mīnamma (*mi-nam-ma*) 311:19
"why"

mišlu (*mi-šil*) 241:1
"half"

mitḫāru (syl.) 21:11′, 14′; 24:3
"of equal / similar quality"; in *lā mitḫāru* as "various."

mukabbû (^{lu_2}*mu-kab-bu-u*$_2$) 162:6; 207:4
"tailor"

mukinnu (syl.) 71:11; 232:8; 311:9; 312:9; 313:14; 314:18; 315:18
"witness"

mulālu (^{lu_2}*mu-la-la*) 213:28′
"feeble-minded"

murašû (syl.) 227:10; 233:5
"wildcat"; on which see Kleber 2018.

murṣu (*mu-ur-ṣi*) 313:3
"sickness"

musaḫḫiru (syl.) 217:24; 289:1; 308:19′
"agent"

muṣ/za/ibbu 90:2 (*mu-ṣab-bi-it*); 128:2, 6, 7 (*mu-ṣib-bi-ta-nu*)
an unclear iron object; neither the meaning of the iron object is clear, nor if both spellings represent the same word. The context suggests an iron tool. Reading *muzībtu*, "drainage," make little sense, especially given that this was an iron item. "A part of a loom," *muṣabbitu*, might fit, but it is known only from lexical texts. The CAD lists one attestation of *mu-ṣa-bi-ta-nu* in BM 60745: 10 (82-9-18, 719): "an implement," CAD M/II, 340, s.v. *muṣabbitu* 2.

muṣiptu (syl.) 147:1; 282:12
"*muṣiptu*-cloth"

mušaḫḫinu (syl.) 57:1; 62:3; 67:1
"cooking pot"; for the *mušaḫḫinu* cooking pot see Levavi 2022.
mušākil immeri (^{lu_2}*mu-ša$_2$-kil* UDU.NITA$_2$^{me}) 233:3
"sheep feeder"
mušākil iṣṣūri (^{lu_2}*mu-ša$_2$-kil* MUŠEN^{me} / .ḪI.A, see also *iṣṣūru*) 215:8; 217:27
"bird feeder"
mušallimānu (^{lu_2}*mu-šal-lim-ma-nu*) 296:61
"*mušallimānu*"; unclear profession: see edition.
mušēlu (*mu-še-lu-u$_2$*) 98:4
"door latch"; see edition.
mušēzibu (*mu-še-zib-e-ti*) 7:2
"*cover-(plates)*"; see edition.
muššuru (*muš-šu-re-e-ti*) 181:1
"free-range (sheep)"; see edition.
muttāqu (*mut-ta-qu*) 277:3; 304:31′
"*muttāqu*-sweetcake"

nadānu (SUM, syl., see also *nadan u maḫar*) 16:2$^?$; 25:7; 26:5; 29:17; 31:3; 48:8; 52:4; 35:3, 6, 9; 67:6; 70:3; 71:7; 79:3; 104:4; 107:10; 138:i 1, iii 1; 141:5, 15; 144:13; 150:6; 152:6; 157:24; 168:1; 169:4; 176:14; 185:7; 189:2; 191:3; 199:3, 6, 8, 12; 204:7; 208:8; 211:4, 9; 215:4; 217:3; 232:7; 235:5; 241:2, 6; 242:7; 244:5, 13; 245:2; 247:3; 251:5; 252:3, 11; 254:2, 8; 255:3; 259:5; 264:2; 272:8; 284:4; 286:10; 287:7; 303:2′, 4′, 14′, 20′; 313:5, 11, 12; 314:10, 11; 315:13
"give"
nadan u maḫar (*na-dan u ma-ḫar*, see also *maḫāru* and *nadānu*) 104:2
"trade"
nagāru (^{lu_2}NAGAR, see also *n. dalti* and *n. qutāni*) 79:3; 190:7; 193:25′; 195:3; 196:3; 198:1; 203:4; 216:2; 217:28; 220:5; 245:11; 249:5; 279:4; 299:20′, 21′
"carpenter"
nagār dalti (^{lu_2}NAGAR ^{giš}IG^{meš}) 189:4; 198:13; 294:14′
"doors carpenter"
nagār qutāni ($^{lu_2\text{-}(giš)}$NAGAR *qu-ta-nu*) 288:2; 296:9
"*fine woodwork* carpenter"; *qutānu* as a "thin piece of lamber" (CAD Q, 321, s.v. *qutānu* B), hence the suggested understanding of these carpenters as specialists of small-scale delicate wood-work.
naḫāsu (syl.) 49:10; 230:17
"to return"
naḫlaptu (^{tug_2}GU$_2$.E$_3$) 178:2
"*naḫlaptu*-(outer) garment"; see Quillien 2022, 528.
****naḫšiptu*** → *našḫiptu*
nakāsu (syl.) 131:6$^?$
"to (be) slaughter(ed)"
nakmaru (*nak-ma-ru*) 34:7; 40:4, 12; 44:5, 7, 10
"*nakmaru*-basket"
nalpattu (syl.) 90:5; 130:7
"*scraper*"; The translations "small bowl, ladle" (CAD N$_1$, 202) or "Schale, Tiegel" (AHw, 724) are based on the lexical equations such as ^{giš}DILI$_2$.TUR and LU-UD DUG (see references there). While these cannot be simply dismissed, there are some indications that this is not the meaning of *nalpattu* in the context of both the present cases. The very derivation from *lapātu* suggests something to do with contact/touch, rather than a container. Note also in this respect the Amarna attestations with clear reference to handles of ebony (EA 14 ii: 61, iii: 6–7) and claws (*ṣupru*) of gold (ibid. ii: 53). A ladle, and to a lesser extent a bowl, can certainly have a handle, but a claw seems to fit far less. These Amarna *nalpattu* tools seem to be a kind of a pointer, or at least a stick-shaped object, some with ivory handles and some with pointy tips. The ebony-handled *nalpattu*s are said to be of the barber, for which, again, neither a bowl nor a ladle seem to be a good fit. In this context, one may think of hair crochets as possible use of the *nalpattu*. In first millennium sources we find the *nalpattu* used by various craftsmen: smiths (Nbk 92: 6, BIN 1, 173: 5, GC 1, 54: 2), carpenters (BM 56018: 5, BM 57184: 5),[25] and potters (BAM 1, 3 i: 32, Neo-Assyrian).

[25] Bertin's hand-copies of both tablets are available in the British Museum online collection; accessed: 07.10.2020.

We suggest that in all of these cases it is possible to understand the *nalpattu* as an elongated tool meant for decorating and shaping iron or wooden objects.

nalṭar ((KU$_3$.GI) *na-al-tar*) 10:1, 3
"*nalṭar*-gold"; for the *nalṭar* (rather than *naltar*) gold, see Kleber 2016a.

namṣartu (*na-*⌜*aṣ-ṣa*⌝*-*[*ar-tu*]) 84:4$^?$
"*storage jar*"; see edition.

namzītu (^{dug}*nam-za-a-ta*) 152:3$^?$
"fermenting vat"; see edition.

napḫaru (a) (PAP, see also *napḫaru* (b)) 4:6; 10:4; 15:4; 185; 21:18′; 24:6; 29:4; 33:8; 40:9; 41:3; 42:3, 9; 44:[3], 8; 47:6; 49:4; 100:4; 141:8, <16>; 143:1, 13; 148:12; 152:5; 157:13; 168:19; 170:24; 176:1; 178:9; 190:4; 192:3; 202:31; 213:4′, 6′, 15′, 21′, 23′, 25′; 221:11, 14, 21; 230:18; 231:5; 242:2; 247:6; 257:4; 273:10; 281:4, 9; 282:7, 17, 19; 288:7, 10; 291:6, 10, 11; 292:11; 293:11; 296:9, 17, 24, [34], 45, 50, 57, [61], [65]; 297:12, 23, 34, 35; 298:11; 299:1′–51′; 302:13; 304:47′; 307:27; 308:16′; 315:7
"total (of)"

napḫaru (b) (PAP.PAP, see also *napḫaru* (a)) 10:9; 33:3, 11; 168:44$^?$
"grand total"; *napḫaru* (a) and (b) are listed separately only to highlight the specific attestations of *napḫaru* (b).

nappāḫu (^{lu_2}SIMUG, see also *nappāḫ parzilli* and *nappāḫ siparri*) 13:5; 31:6; 55:5; 59:4; 62:6; 70:9; 73:3; 88:5; 89:3; 94:3; 100:8; 110:3; 132:9; 136:4; 137:4; 211:4; 217:13, 23; 264:2; 273:2, 5; 288:3; 289:4; 290:8
"smith"

nappāḫ parzilli (^{lu_2}SIMUG AN.BAR, see also *nappāḫu* and *nappāḫ siparri*) 77:4; 86:4; 90:9; 92:4; 96:5; 98:6–7; 101:6; 111:3; 124:4; 134:4; 296:50, 65; 298:4; 304:36′
"blacksmith"

nappāḫ siparri (^{lu_2}SIMUG ZABAR, see also *nappāḫu* and *nappāḫ parzilli*) 48:4; 58:5; 60:5; 61:4; 69:5; 240:4; 245:12′; 293:9; 294:13′; 295:8; 299:19′
"bronzesmith"

naptanu (*nap-ta-nu*) 63:2
"*naptanu*-meal"

nāqidu (^{lu_2}NA.GADA) 314:4
"herder"

narkabtu ($^{(d/giš)}$GIGIR) 1:4; 301:[1′], 32′
"chariot"

nāru (ID$_2$) 122:3; 129:4; 199:4
"canal"

naṣāru (syl.) 304:42′
"to (keep) watch"

naṣbaru (syl.) 76:2; 128:3
"(door) mounting"

našāḫu (syl.) 242:13
"to measure"

našḫiptu / ****naḫšiptu*** (syl.) 75:3; 101:3*; 103:4; 110:2; 117:4, 9; 122:1; 123:1; 130:4; 133:2*; 138:ii 2*, 9*; 304:35′
"shovel"; The spelling *na-aḫ-šip-ti*, attested four times in the corpus (marked * above) must be a variant for *našḫiptu*. To the best of our knowledge, a *š:ḫ* metathesis is not too frequent, though it may be found for example in cases like *lašḫu* (*laḫšu*); see examples in CAD L, 108, s.v. *lašḫu*. Note also *ḫašḫūru* vs. *šaḫšūru*; GAG § 36c.

našpartu (syl.) 296:8, 13, 23, 40, 56
"proxy"

našû (GIŠ, syl., see also *pūtu n.* and *rēšu n.*) 10:3; 25:11; 54:5, 15; 55:2, 4, 11; 56:4; 103:2; 133:3; 138:ii 15, 22, 27, ii i4, 5, 13, 17, 20, 25, 27, 34; 139:5; 141:11, 15; 143:9, 14; 144:3; 157:12, 13, 21; 158:3, 8, 12; 159:5; 161:15; 162:7; 171:9; 174:11; 180:6, 11; 181:3, 4, 6, 12; 182:6; 183:7; 185:3; 193:*passim*; 194:7, 10, [13], 15, [16], [20]; 198:2, 28; 199:9, 13; 200:7, 9; 201:11; 205:4; 206:4; 207:6, 14; 208:5; 209:2, 4, 14, 17, 18, 20; 214:7; 217:21, 32; 222:4, 8; 223:2, 6; 224:5; 225:2, 4; 226:10, 13, 17; 227:4, 5, 7, 9, 11, 12, 14, 16, 18, 20; 228:4; 229:5–8, 10, 11, 13; 230:12, 14, 15, 18, 20; 233:4, 6, 8, 9; 234:3, 5; 235:6; 241:2, 4; 244:14; 245:16′; 247:4–6; 248:7; 257:6; 259:4; 269:7; 270:3; 271:6, 8; 274:9; 277:5, 8; 278:5; 286:13$^?$; 299:14′$^?$, 26′$^?$, 27′$^?$, 30′$^?$, 31′$^?$, 38′$^?$, 45′$^?$, 49′$^?$, 50′$^?$; 303:28′; 304:40′; 307:15, 27; 310:4; 311:18; 315:17
"to withdraw; to (be) take(n) / carry(/ ied)"

natkapu? ([*n*]*a-at-kap*) 90:6
"awl"; see edition.
natt/ddulu (*na-at-tul-lum-me*) 301:28′
"(part of the) harness"
nāṭilu (*na-ṭi-il-ti*) 52:2
"ladle"; see edition.
nēbeḫu (^{tug2}NIG$_2$.IB$_2$.LA$_2$, ^{tug2}*ne*$_2$*-bi-ḫu*) 154:6, 13; 178:7
"*nēbeḫu*-sash"; see Quillien 2022, 528.
nēbettu (DARA$_2$) 178:4; see Quillien 2022, 528.
"*nēbettu*-belt"
nēsepu (*ne*$_2$*-sip*) 57:2; 310:8
"*nēsepu*-container"
niggallu (NIG$_2$.GAL$_2$.LA) 51:16; 97:2; 114:1; 117:11; 121:1; 132:4; 138:ii 10; 139:2; 269:4; 301:20′
"sickle"
nignakku (NIG$_2$.NA, *nig*$_2$*-nak*) 33:1, 9; 49:5, 9; 51:5
"censer"
nikkassu (NIG$_2$.KA$_9$) 104:1; 302:14
"account"
niqû (^{udu}SIZKUR) 130:2
"sacrificial sheep"
nišū ($^{(lu2)}$UN^{meš}) 25:2; 29:3; 189:2
"people; personnel"
nuḫatimmu (^{lu2}MUḪALDIM, see also *bīt nuḫatimmi* and *nuḫatimmūtu*) 280:9?; 286:9
"baker"
nuḫatimmūtu (^{lu2}MUḪALDIM-*u-tu*, see also *nuḫatimmu* and *bīt nuḫatimmi*) 312:16
"the baker's temple service"
nukaribbu ša karāni (^{lu2}NU.GIŠ.KIRI$_6$ *ša*$_2$ ^{giš}GEŠTIN, see also *karānu* and *kirû ša karāni*) 242:7, 15
"vintner"
nurmû ($^{(na4)}$*nu-ur*$_2$*-mu-u*$_2$) 1:4; 21:7″, 12″; 39:4; 301:30′, 31′
"pomer"
nūru (*nu-u*$_2$*-ru*) 272:5; 274:2
"lamp"
nusḫu (*nu-us-uḫ-ḫe-e*) 255:6, 9
"(reed) *nusḫu*-basket"

pagru (syl.) 286:5; 308:28′
"carcass"
paḫāru (^{lu2}BAḪAR$_2$) 193:24′; 294:21′; 310:6
"potter"
pālištu (NIG$_2$.BUR$_3$.BUR$_3$-*tu*$_4$?) 229:5
"drilling"; see edition.
pa-na-nu 51:22
unclear leather item
pānu I (IGI, see also *pānu* II, *ana p.*, *ina p.*, and *ša p.*) 209:13; 227:4, 7
"in front"
pānu II (IGI, syl., see also *pānu* I, *ana p.*, *ina p.*, and *ša p.*) 17:2, 3
"face"
pappardilu (^{na4}BABBAR.DIL) 39:5; 51:10
"pappardilu-stone"
parāsu (syl.) 238:1; 240:2; 276:7; 304:6
"to (be) apportion(ed)/ allocate(d)
parīdu(?) (*pa-ri-*⌜*du*?⌝) 302:13
unclear; see edition.
parkullu (^{lu2}BUR.GUL) 246:13′; 294:20′
"seal cutter"
parratu (UDU.BAR.SAL, *par-rat*) 281:3; 282:15; 308:15′, 16′
"female lamb"
parru ((UDU.)BAR.GAL) 281:13, 15; 282:1–6, 20
"young male sheep"; both *parru* and *kalūmu* designate male lambs in Neo-Babylonian records. Here, we translate *parru* as young male sheep while *kalūmu* is rendered as a male lamb; see Kozuh 2014, 61–3.
paršīgu ($^{tug2/gada}$syl.) 157:4, 19, 22; 178:3; 187:5
"*paršīgu*-headdress"; see Quillien 2022, 529.
paruktu (*pa-ru-uk-ti*) 157:8
"canopy canvas"; see Quillien 2022, 529.
parzillu (AN.BAR, see also *nappāḫ parzilli*) 8:5; 15:5; 51:12–14, 16; 54:3, 9, 13; 72:1; 73:1; 74:1, 2; 75:1, 2, 7; 76:1, 5; 77:1, 2; 78:1, 2; 79:1; 80:1, 2; 81:1; 82:1, 2; 83:1; 84:1; 85:1–3; 86:1, 2; 87:1–3, 6; 88:1–4; 89:1, 2; 90:1–7; 91:1; 92:1, 2; 93:1–3; 95:2; 96:1; 97:1, 2; 98:1; 99:1, 2; 100:1, 3, 5, 8; 101:1; 102:2; 103:3; 104:1, 7; 105:1; 106:1; 107:1, 2, 4; 108:2; 109:1; 110:1, 2; 111:1; 112:1; 113:1; 114:1; 115:1; 116:1–3; 117:1, 2, 8, 9; 118:1; 119:1; 120:1; 121:1; 112:1, 2, 7; 123:1; 124:1; 125:1; 126:1; 127:1, 3; 128:1; 129:1, 2; 130:1; 131:2; 132:1; 133:1, 2; 134:1, 2; 135:1–3; 136:1; 137:1, 2; 138:passim; 139:1; 180:4, 10; 235:1; 269:2; 271:2; 276:1; 285:12′; 290:7; 301:5′, 20′, 23′; 305:9, 15, 16, 22; 313:3
"iron"

paspasu (UZ.TUR^{mušen}) 282:14; 283:1; 304:5
"duck"

pāšu (*pa-a-šu*$_2$) 79:1; 83:1
"*pāšu*-axe"

patru (GIR$_2$) 51:12; 99:2; 100:1; 137:2; 301:5′, 23′
"dagger"

peṣû (BABBAR-*u*$_2$, see also *kaspu peṣû*) 100:2; 150:2; 154:11; 178:6; 308:30′
"white; cleaning"

petû (syl.) 311:15, 19, 21
"to open"

pidānu (*pi-da-nu*) 13:4, 7
"assaying"

pingu (*pi-in-ga*) 50:1, 6, 10, 14
"knob"; see Beaulieu 2003, 12, and several texts cited throughout the study.

pirru (*pi-ir-ri*) 159:3; 189:1$^?$
"workforce"

pirsu (*pi-ir-su*) 302:11
"weaned (foal)"

pišannu (^{giš}*pi-ša*$_2$*-an-ni*) 37:5
"*pišannu*-box"; see edition.

pitqu (syl.) 16:2, 5; 141:10, 16; 240:3
"smelting"

pû (KA); see *kī pî* and *ša pî ruqqi*

pugudātu (syl.) 301:14′, 15′, 19′
"bridle"

puḫālu (*pu-ḫal*) 285:6′
"ram"

pūṣāya (^{lu_2}*pu-ṣa-a-a*) 143:9; 156:3; 166:7; 167:3; 193:21′; 221:10; 227:19; 243:14; 286:12; 294:10′, 11′; 296:34, 45; 298:6; 302:5; 308:2′, 6′; 315:7
"linen weaver"; see Zawadzki 2006, 61, 66, Quillien 2022, 282–284.

pūtu našû (syl.) 289:9–10; 313:1–8; 314:3–6, 15–16
"to guarantee/be responsible for"

qabû (syl.) 311:19, 20; 312:14
"to say"

qabuttu (*qa-bu-ut*$^!$*-tu*$_4$) 308:16′
"fold"

qabūtu (*qa-bu-ut-tu*$_2$) 63:1
"*qabūtu*-bowl"

qallu (syl.) 171:9; 190:11; 209:16; 296:46
"slave"

qanû (GI^{meš}, syl.) 226:16; 252:2, 6, 11; 253:1; 254:6; 255:3; 256:1; 258:2; 259:4; 310:6
"reed"

qaqqadu I (SAG.DU) 243:1
"principle (amount)"

qaqqadu II (SAG.DU) 301:6′, 7′, 8′, 12′, 13′, 25′
"head, top"

qaqqaru (*qaq-qar-a-nu*) 49:3
"*plate*" (lit. ground); see edition

qaštu I (^{giš}BAN, see also *qaštu* II) 51:24; 301:7′
"bow"

qaštu II (^{lu_2}BAN, see also *qaštu* I) 193:5′; 196:5
"archer"

qātāte (ŠU$^{II.me}$) 6:1; 25:1; 211:5; 252:8; 302:8–9
as fractions in ⅔

qātu (ŠU^{II}, see also *bīt qātē*, *ina qāt*, *mê qātê* I/II, *qātāte*) 39:2, 6; 215:5′; 282:12; 296:45, 65
"hand; authority; property"

qēmu (ZID$_2$.DA, *qe*$_2$-⸢*me*⸣) 215:12; 249:4, 10; 250:2; 251:3
"flour"

qerēbu (syl.) 312:21
"to (be) offer(ed)"

qību (*qi*$_2$*-bu*) 311:21
"order"

qīpu (^{lu_2}*qi*$_2$*-i-pi*) 103:8; 107:10; 118:4; 141:4, 11; 170:21; 194:10; 291:11; 304:3; 311:18; 314:6, 9
"*qīpu* (official)"

qiššû (UKUŠ$_2$) 38:4
"melon (shaped-beads)"

qītu (*qi*$_2$*-it*) 143:14; 304:30′
"end"

qullû (*qu-li-i*) 57:3
"cooking/roasting"

qullu (*qu-ul-le-e*) 301:10′
"*qullu*-ring"

qullupu (syl.) 277:5; 304:29′
"*qullupu*-sweetcake"

qulmû (syl.) 101:4; 108:2; 117:6, 10; 120:1; 130:5; 134:2; 139:2; 269:3; 285:12′; 305:15
"*qulmû*-axe"

quppu (*qu-u*[*p*$^?$*-pi*$^?$]) 214:9
"cashbox"

quppû (*qup-pu-u*$_2$) 90:4
"knife"; see edition.

rab banê (lu2GAL-DU$_3$) 251:2
"date gardener"
rab bīt kīli (lu2GAL E$_2$ *kil-li*, see also *bīt kīli*) 215:5; 250:4; 308:34′
"prison overseer"
rab būli (lu2GAL *bu-li$_3$*) 285:14′
"herd supervisor"
rab ešerti (lu2GAL 10me, see also *ešertu*) 201:11; 202:2, 31′; 207:11; 247:2
"decurion"
rab kāri (lu2GAL *ka-a-ri*) 296:55
"harbor overseer"
rab sikkati (lu2GAL giš*sik-kat*me) 226:13
"*rab sikkati*"; military official.
rab ṣibti (lu2GAL MAŠ$_2$me, see also *ṣibtu*) 304:23
"*ṣibtu*-tax overseer"
rab širki (lu2GAL *šir$_3$-ku*, see also *širku*) 288:8, 9, 10
"overseer of serfs"
rabû (GAL) 38:5; 51:28; 123:7; 151:1; 154:3; 178:2, 4; 200:5; 301:15′, 27′; 312:18
"large"
rakāsu (*ra-ka-su*) 275:2
"binding"
raksu (syl.) 42:10; 94:2; 269:1; 271:1
"bundled; attached"
rapšu (syl.) 91:2; 107:1, 2
"hoe"; the *rapšu* was used alongside *šūrû*-tools and *marru*-spades in excavations. As suggested by etymology, *rapāšu* "to be(come) wide," the *rapšu* was probably between a shovel and a spade, with a wide end able to cut through and remove soil.
rašûtu (*ra-šu-tu*) 106:2; 212:1
"credit"
rebât (syl.) 18:1; 303:21′, 22′
"¼"
rēḫtu (syl.) 71:2; 76:5; 106:1; 138:ii 15; 141:6; 193:18′; 209:15; 217:22; 226:2, 11, 14; 230:6; 314:15
"remainder / rest"
rēḫu (syl.) 9:6; 27:4; 33:12; 144:14; 170:16; 213:7′, 30′; 303:22′; 304:37′; 314:12, 15
"balance"
rēʾû (lu2SIPA, see also *r. iṣṣūri*, *r. sattukki*, and *r. sîsē*) 190:2, 3; 221:11; 284:7
"shepherd"
rēʾi iṣṣūri (lu2SIPA MUŠEN / *iṣ-ṣur*, see also *iṣṣūru* and *rēʾû*) 193:19′, 20′; 215:6, 8′; 297:17
"bird-herder"
rēʾi sattukki (lu2SIPA SA$_2$.DUG$_4$, see also *rēʾû*) 282:7; 286:3
"offering shepherd"
rēʾi sîsē (lu2SIPA AN[ŠE.KUR.RA], see also *rēʾû*) 301:3′, 33′
"horse-herder"
rēšu našû (*re-eš … i-na-šu-u$_2$*) 313:9–10
"to guarantee"
rikis lilissi (*ri-kis li-li-su*) 304:33′
"ritual arrangement of the kettledrum"
rīq(t)u (*ri-iq-ti*) 289:9
"*idleness*"
ri-sa?-a-⸢ta?⸣ 123:5
unclear
ruqqu (ŠEN, see also *ša pî ruqqi*) 33:2; 61:2; 68:2
"cauldron"

sadru (*sad-ru*) 145:3
"standard quality"
saggilmud (na4*sag-gil-mud*) 21:13′; 37:2
"*saggilmud*-stone"; on this mineral, which was interchangeable with *ḫašmānu*, see Thavapalan 2020, 272, 281–3.
SAG SIG KUR ⸢*tu$_4$*⸣ 31:5
unclear; see edition.
saḫḫarru (*sa*?!(T. e2)-*ḫa-ri*) 301:23′
"*saḫḫarru*-bowl"
saḫlû (*saḫ-le-e*) 25:10; 199:2; 201:2
"cress"
sāmtu (na4GUG) 141:1, 9
"carnelian"
sāmu (*sam-mu*, see also *ḫurāṣu sāmu*) 142:1
"red"
sanāqu (*si-in-qu-ma*) 301:3′, 32′
"to (be) examine(d)"
sanḫu (*sa-an-ḫa*, **sa-ma-ḫal*(sic)) 21:7′?*; 38:1?*, 5
"hook"; see note for **No. 38**: 1.
saqqu (syl.) 184:2; 305:14
"sack"
sartu (*sar-tu$_4$*) 313:2
"crime"
sasinnu (lu2(U).ZADIM, syl.) 194:12; 226:16
"bow-maker"

sellu (*sel-li*) 254:7; 255:7, 10
"*sellu*-basket"

semeru (ḪAR) 102:2; 135:1; 150:5$^?$; 305:22; 308:32′; 313:3
"ring; shackles"

sepīru (syl.) 106:4; 193:26′, 27′; 205:3; 217:25
"alphabet scribe"

serpu (*se-ra-pi*) 85:2; 98:2; 118:1; 132:2
"shears"

sigirru$^?$ (*si-gi-ir-ru*) 51:24, 26
"*refined*"; see edition

sikinūnu (TU.KUR$_4$^{mušen}) 304:4; 308:28′
"dove"

sikkatu (syl.) 76:3; 87:8; 88:2; 128:4; 138:ii 11; 301:23′
"peg; pin"

simmiltu (*si*$^?$*-im-mil-e-ti*) 130:2
"*grills* (*grates*)"; see edition.

sinništu (MUNUS) 222:2
"woman"

siparru (ZABAR) 13:9; 31:1, 4; 33:2, 3, 7, 9; 54:2, 12; 57:1; 58:1; 59:1; 61:1; 62:2; 63:1; 65:1, 7; 66:1; 67:1, 4, 7; 68:1, 2; 69:1, 2; 70:1; 71:1, 9; 123:5; 304:33′
"bronze"

sīrāšû ($^{\text{lu}_2}$LUNGA, see also *bīt sirāšî*) 214:2; 286:9
"brewer"

sukullu (AB$_2$.GU$_4$.ḪI.A) 80:3
"cattle (herd)"

suluppu (ZU$_2$.LUM.MA) 141:14; 143:6; 229:1, 4, 12; 230:1, 7, 15; 242:1, 3, 11, 14; 243:1; 244:3; 245:1; 246:1; 247:1; 248:1, 2; 286:5; 304:12, 18; 310:1
"dates"

sūnu ($^{\text{tug}_2}$UR$_2$, *su-u$_2$-nu*) 178:4; 308:24′, 25′
"*sūnu*-cloth strip"; see Quillien 2022, 530.

suppinnu (*su-up-pi-in-*⌜*nu*$^?$⌝) 130:6
"(brick moulding) *suppinnu*-tool"

sūtu I (^{giš}BAN$_2$, syl.) 35:1; 39:1, 6
"*sūtu*-attachments"

sūtu II (BAN$_2$) 66:1
"*sūtu*-bowl"

sūtu III (^{giš}BAN$_2$) 242:3; 308:35′
"*sūtu*-obligation"

su**ʾʾ**uttu (*su-u*ʾ*-ut-ti*) 202:1
"support"; see edition.

ṣabātu (syl.) 21:5′; 49:7; 222:3; 313:5
"to (be) fasten(ed); to be held / arrested"

ṣabītu (MAŠ.DA$_3$) 17:2, 3
"gazelle"

ṣabtu (*ṣab-tu*) 229:7
"prisoner"

ṣābu (ERIN$_2$) 141:7; 159:2; 193:11′; 194:3; 199:4; 201:4; 212:1; 227:12, 13, 18, 19; 229:5; 228:9; 289:4; 291:11; 294:18′, 19′, 22′; 295:3; 297:23, 34, 35; 298:11; 303:13′; 304:1; 308:38′
"men; workers"

ṣāḫitu ($^{\text{lu}_2}$I$_3$.SUR, see also *ṣāḫit sattukki*) 286:13
"oil-presser"

ṣāḫit sattukki ($^{\text{lu}_2}$I$_3$.SUR SA$_2$.DUG$_4$, see also *ṣāḫitu*) 304:28′
"oil-presser of the regular offerings"

ṣallu (syl.) 261:3; 263:2, 5; 265:1; 268:1
"tanned hide"

ṣalmu (GI$_6$) 303:19′
"black"

ṣapitu (*ṣa-pi-ti*) 97:6
"*ṣapitu*-reed"

ṣapû I ($^{\text{lu}_2}$*ṣa-pe-e*) 294:9′
"dyer"

ṣapû II ($^{\text{tug}_2}$*ṣa-pu-u*) 178:3
"*ṣapû*-dyed garment"; see Quillien 2022, 531.

ṣarāpu (*ṣa-rap*) 223:4
"to fire bricks"

ṣārip dušî (*ṣa-rip* DUḪ.ŠI.A, syl.) 261:5; 268:3; 281:18
"leather dyer"

ṣeḫru (TUR) 38:5; 51:27; 154:4; 178:2, 5
"small"

ṣēnu (*ṣe-e-nu*) 282:17; 303:9′
"sheep and goats"

ṣēru (EDIN) 302:5; 304:39′
"steppe; (over)land"

ṣibtētu (syl.) 90:3$^?$; 115:1; 125:2; 136:2; 305:19
"fetter(s)"

ṣibtu I ($^{\text{tug}_2}$MAŠ$_2$, syl.) 148:5; 151:1; 154:3, 12; 157:1, 17; 178:5
"*ṣibtu*-garment"; see Quillien 2022, 531.

ṣibtu II (*ṣib-tu$_4$*, see also *rab ṣibti*) (syl.) 304:20
"*ṣibtu*-tax"

ṣidītu (syl.) 25:11; 207:8; 303:15′
"(travel) provisions"

ṣīpu (syl.) 173:2; 186:4
"dyeing"
ṣubātu (TUG$_2$) 150:2; 155:1; 172:3; 178:1; 304:11
"cloth"
ṣuppātu (syl.) 186:4; 308:5′, 30′
"combed wool"

ša dāli (syl.) 190:10, 14, 16, 33
"(irrigation) by bucket"
ša muḫḫi (*ša$_2$* UGU/*muḫ-ḫi*, see also *ša muḫḫi* ×) 34:3, 10; 40:2, 11; 43:3, 7; 229:5; 230:17; 280:3; 314:12, 15
"of/belonging to (in regard to person/object/obligation)"
ša muḫḫi immeri (*ša$_2$* UGU UDU.NITA$_2$) 217:32
"(one) in charge of the sheep"
ša muḫḫi quppi ($^{(lu_2)}$*ša$_2$* UGU/*muḫ-ḫi qu-up-pu*) 217:30; 304:35′; 305:23
"(one) in charge of the cashbox"
ša muḫḫi reḫēti (*ša$_2$ muḫ-ḫi r*[*e*$^?$-*ḫ*]*e*$^?$-⌜*e*⌝-*ti*) syl. 248:6–7
"overseer of the remainders (of the sacrificial meal)"
ša muḫḫi sūti (*ša$_2$* UGU ^{giš}BAN$_2$) 313:7–8
"rent-farmer"
ša pāni (*ša$_2$* IGI/*pa-ni*) 54:2, 8; 163:3, 6
"(object) that is before (DN)"
ša pî ruqqi (*ša$_2$* KA ŠEN, see also *ruqqu*) 176:5, 16
"fresh"
ša rēš šarri (^{lu_2}SAG LUGAL) 125:5$^?$; 248:6
"courtier"
šadādu (syl.) 308:21′; 313:13
"to tow; to bear (guilt)"
šadânu (^{na_4}KUR) 13:9; 54:8
"hematite"
šaddu (syl., see also *šaddu ša batqa*) 174:5$^?$
"box"
šaddu ša batqa (^{giš}*šad-du ša$_2$ bat-qa*, see also *šaddu*) 4:5; 5:2; 24:8; 29:9, 11; 301:19′, 29′; 311:14
"repair box"
šādidu (^{lu_2}*ša$_2$-di-di*^{me}) 242:20
"boat-tower"
šaḫātu$^?$ (*šu-uḫ-ḫu-tu*) 27:6$^?$
"to clean(?)"
šaḫilu (*ša$_2$*$^{!(T.\ 4)}$-*ḫi-il*$^?$) 128:4$^?$
"bucket"
šakānu (syl.) 9:3; 29:1, 4; 46:1
"to put/place"
šakin māti (^{lu_2}GAR KUR) 193:39′; 296:23
"governor (of the Sealand)"
šākin ṭēmi (^{lu_2}GAR UMUŠ) 190:4; 199:11
"governor (of Uruk)"
ša$_2$-lam 21:19′, 20′, 14″
unclear; see edition.
šalḫu (^{gada}*šal-ḫu*) 21:13″; 148:2, 8; 157:5, 6, 8, 9, 11, 12, 24, 25, 26
"linen *šalḫu*-cloth"; see Quillien 2022, 530 (s.v. *salḫu*)
šalšu I (*šal-šu*) 13:13; 34:13; 39:1; 217:26; 226:14; 257:5; 287:5
"⅓" (one-third)
šalšu II (*šal-šu$_2$*) 190:14
"third" (3rd)
šamnu (I$_3$.GIŠ) 25:9; 51:29; 57:3; 114:3; 201:1; 272:5; 273:1; 274:1; 307:22b; 310:8
"oil"
šamšamu (ŠE.GIŠ.I$_3$) 230:2; 278:1; 286:13, 14; 304:28′, 31,′ 39′, 40′; 307:22a
"sesame"
šamšatu (AŠ.ME) 10:5; 24:1
"sun-disk"
šamû (AN-*e*) 130:3
"canopy"
šanû I (*ša$_2$-nu-u$_2$*) 243:5; 315:15
"second"
šanû II (^{lu_2}2) 27:11$^?$; 210:3; 213:22′
"deputy"
šapāru (syl.) 25:[9]; 114:4; 117:7; 144:13; 193:59′; 204:6; 207:14; 221:11; 223:5; 226:9; 244:5; 271:6; 284:2; 291:12; 296:49
"to send"
šappu (*šap-pe-e*) 15:1; 48:2, 7
"*šappu*-bowl"
šapû (*ša$_2$-pe-e*) 35:3; 155:1
"to embroider"
šāri$^?$ ***išiṭṭi***$^?$ (*ša$_2$-a-ri*(-)*i-še-eṭ-ṭu*, *ša$_2$-a-ri*(-)*i-šiṭ-ṭu*) 51:7; 301:24′
"unclear"; a silver ornament? Though the meaning of the phrase is unclear and its rendering is speculative, the reading of the signs in both cases is certain. Moreover, the phrase is attested in at least one additional text, *ša$_2$-a-ri i-šiṭ-ṭi* (Pinches 1928, 132–4:

11). The rendering and parsing *šāri išiṭṭi* is not trivial. The reading of the first word is based on the clear persistence in all three cases of stressing the length of the first syllable: *ša$_2$-a-*. All three scribes then follow with … *-ri(-)i-*…, which, if taken as one word, would result in the awkward form **šārīšiṭṭi* / *u*. The spelling of the final part, … *še-eṭ-ṭu*, in **No. 51** confirms the reading … *šiṭ-ṭu* in both **No. 301** and in Pinches 1928, 132–4: 11 (read … *šid-di* by pinches), rather than the potential reading … *riṭ-ṭu*.

šarru (LUGAL, see also *irbu ša šarri*, *kurummat šarri*, and *ša rēš šarri*) 102:3; 193:52′; 295:4; 313:13
"king; royal"

šartu (SIK$_2$.UZ$_3$, *šar-ti*) 184:1; 185:1; 303:31′
"(goat) hair"

šatammu (^{lu_2}ŠA$_3$.TAM, see also *bīt šatammi*) 48:7; 157:23; 226:8; 266:4; 287:4, 7; 290:2; 304:39′
"*šatammu* (official)"

šattu (MU.AN.NA) 304:7, 8; 315:8, 12
"year"

šēpu ([GI]R$_3$) 313:1
"self / presence (lit. leg)"; in the phrase *pūt šepē našû*, "to guarantee."

šepūṭu[?] (*še-pu-ṭu*) 11:6
unclear ornament; see edition.

šēru (*še-e-ri*) 312:18, 19
"morning"

šibirru/šibru[?] (*ši-bir*) 5:10
"staff(?)"; see edition.

šiddu (^{gada}*šid-da-nu*) 145:4
"linen curtain"

šiḫ(a)ṭu ($^{(kuš)}$*ši-ḫa-ṭu*) 266:3
"*šiḫṭu* hide"

šīḫu (*ši-ḫu*) 301:18′
"*šīḫu*-ornament"

šikaru (a) (KAŠ, see also *bīt šikarri*) 236:1; 238:1; 239:1; 240:1; 242:16; 244:12
"beer"

šikaru (b) (KAŠ.SAG) 235:4; 241:1, 5
"high-quality beer"

šiltāḫu (^{giš}*šil-ta-ḫu*) 210:5; 211:6
"arrow"

šīmu (ŠAM$_2$) 28:1, 4; 141:1, 8; 199:1; 203:11; 213:1′, 5′, 9′, 11′, 13′, 16′, 19′, 21′, 23′, 27′; 214:6; 217:23; 252:1; 309:1
"price"

šindu / šimtu (⸢*ši-in*$^{?!}$⸣*-du*) 80:3
"branding iron"

šīpātu (SIK$_2$.ḪI.A) 12:6; 143:5; 147:4; 162:2; 168:[1]; 170:1, 4, 13, 17; 171:1; 173:1; 174:2, 18; 175:3; 176:1; 178:8; 179:1; 180:1, 7; 181:1; 203:11, 14; 213:4′, 9′, 13′; 222:6; 231:7; 303:16′–19′, 21′, 25′, 31′, 32′; 308:18′, 20′, 26′, 37′
"wool"

šir'am (syl.) 144:5; 160:1; 161:1, 3, 9; 162:1; 174:3; 307:21, 24
"*šir'am*-garment"; a military garmet; see Quillien 2022 498–502.

širku (^{lu_2}RIG$_7$, ^{lu_2}*šir$_3$-ku*, see also *rab širki*) 105:13; 141:5; 144:10; 199:8; 204:5; 217:2; 229:6; 233:7; 244:4; 290:2, 4
"temple serf"

širṭu (*ši-ir-ṭu*) 182:3
"(wool) strip"

šubburu (syl.) 34:6; 308:33′
"broken"

šubtu (^{giš}KI.TUŠ, *šub-ti*) 3:2; 157:25
"pedestal"

šubullu (syl.) 45:8; 55:8; 103:8; 144:12; 235:3; 253:5; 254:5; 272:4; 302:6; 304:3, 44′; 310:7, 9, 12, 14
"deliver"

šukuttu (*šu-kut-ti*) 1:2; 10:10; 13:6; 21:18′; 24:6; 26:2; 36:2; 238:2
"jewelry"

šulmānu (*šul-ma-nu*) 32:3
"*šulmānu*-offering"

šupālu (*šu-pa-li-*[*tu$_2$*]) 190:1
"lower"

šuqultu (KI.LA$_2$, *šu-qul-tu$_2$*) 8:5; 13:11; 15:5; 34:14; 54:3, 9, 13; 71:2; 174:1[?]; 305:16
"weight; weighing"

šurmīnu (*šur-i-ni*) 279:2
"cypress"

šūrû (syl.) 84:2; 87:7; 88:1; 91:1; 128:3[?]; 138:ii 11
"*šūrû*-tool"; an agricultural iron tool,[26]

[26] Note BM 30436 and BM 41452, in which a bronze *šūrû* is attested. In the latter, the two mentioned *šūrû*s weigh 9 and 4 minas, which far exceeds the normal range of the iron *šūrû*s in the temple archives.

or part of a tool, which was regularly distributed alongside pegs (*sikkatu*), always in a ratio of two pegs per *šūrû*. Though mostly attested as part of a spade (*marru*), the *šūrû* could have been be of a hoe (*rapšu*) as well (e.g., **No. 91**), suggesting that it cannot simply refer to the metal head of the tool. It may be speculated that the *šūrû* was an additional spike that could be attached to different agricultural tools to help breaking through the ground or pushing it aside.

šussullu (syl.) 45:2; 54:7
"(fishermen) chest"

tabālu (*it-ba-*[*lu*$^?$]) 157:23$^?$
"take away"

tabarru (^{sik_2}ḪE$_2$.ME.DA, *ta-bar-ri*) 148:6, 10; 149:6; 153:3; 154:5, 7, 9, 14, 16; 155:1; 157:15; 172:1; 173:2; 176:8, 19, 21; 178:1, 8; 282:11
"red wool"; see Thavapalan 2020, 294–308.

taḫapšu (*ta-ḫap-šu*$_2$) 158:5, 9
"blanket"; see Quillien 2022, 532.

takkasû (*tak-ka-su-u*$_2$) 312:20
"*takkasû*-loaf"

takiltu (^{sik_2}ZA.GIN$_3$(.KUR.RA), syl.) 143:1; 146:1; 148:7; 149:6$^?$; 154:9, 16; 157:24; 169:3; 172:2; 176:2, 5, 16, 22; 177:1; 182:2; 183:1, 2; 187:2; 282:11
"purple"

talammu (*ta-lam*) 307:22b
"*talammu* container"

tamirtu (GARIM) 122:4; 190:1
"irrigation district"

tamlû I (*tam-lu-u*$_2$) 206:3
"terrace"

tamlû II (syl.) 11:7; 16:1$^?$
"inlaid (rosettes)";

tardennu (syl.) 303:50′; 312:19
"second (meal)"; "*younger* (man)"; see note to ^{lu_2}*tar-den-ne-e* in **No. 303**.

tariktu (*ta-ri-ka-a-ta*) 33:4
"*tariktu-ornament*"; see edition.

tārītu (*ta-ri-ti*) 149:5
"*nurse-*(*garment*)"; see edition.

tarkisu (*taš-kis*) 21:19′
"*tarkisu*-ornament"

târu (syl.) 29:7
"to (be) return(ed)"

tēḫirtu (*te-ḫir-ti*) 33:10; 49:8; 150:3
"remainder"

tenšu (syl.) 34:9, 13; 40:8, 10; 41:2; 42:8; 43:6; 44:2, 6, 9
"square (shaped ornament)"; often mentioned alongside ornamental rosettes (*ayaru*)

tēnû (*te-ne*$_2$*-e*) 157:5
"replacement"

tibnu (syl.) 105:14; 308:13′, 39′; 310:13
"straw"

tillu (syl.) 94:1; 269:1; 271:1
"quiver"

tuḫullu$^?$ (*tu-ḫul*$^?$*-la-nu*) 51:15
unclear; made of silver.

tukpītu (^{na_4}*tuk-pi-tu*$_4$) 21:12′
"kidney shape beads"

tukriš (*tuk-riš*) 176:10, 23; 282:11
"red-purple"; For the reading *tuk-riš* rather than ^{sik_2}SAG (for *argamannu*), see Thavapalan 2020, 226–7, van Soldt 1990, 345, n. 165.

tupkītu / *tukpītu* (*tup-kāt*) 17:4
"kidney-shaped bead"

ṭabtu (MUN.ḪI.A) 25:10; 201:3; 280:1
"salt"

ṭīmu (syl.) 154:7, 13, 14; 156:1; 286:12
"thread/yarn"

ṭīpu (^{gada}*ṭi-pa-nu*) 145:3
"compressed (linen) cloth"

ṭumānu (syl.) 143:8, 9; 146:2; 167:1; 176:3, 17; 183:4; 303:23′
"*ṭumānu*-linen thread"

ṭuppu ($^{na_4.im}$DUB) 21:11′, 14′, 15″
"inscribed stones"

ṭupšarru (^{lu_2}UMBISAG, see also *ṭupšar bīti* and *ṭupšar māti*) 71:14; 141:13; 232:13; 241:2; 313:18; 314:22; 315:22
"scribe"

ṭupšar bīti (^{lu_2}UMBISAG E$_2$, see also *ṭupšarru*) 226:9; 230:16
"temple scribe"

ṭupšar māti (^{lu_2}UMBISAG KUR, see also *ṭupšarru*) 213:14′
"scribe of the (*Sea*)land"; see edition.

udû (syl.) 123:4$^?$; 301:32′; 310:6
"equipment; ware"
u'iltu (*u*$_2$-*il*$_3$-*ti*$_3$) 71:8
"promissory note"
ukāpu (*u*$_2$-*ka-pe-e*) 147:2
"pack-saddle"
ul (syl.) 276:7; 312:21; 315:15
"not"
UL.GA^{meš} 21:6′, 17″
unclear
ultu (TA, *ul-tu*, see also *ultu libbi* and *ultu muḫḫi*) 4:5; 5:1; 6:2; 25:2; 29:8, 11, 14; 54:3; 133:3; 143:13; 144:2; 177:4; 185:3; 215:2; 216:2; 220:2; 230:3; 233:1; 313:3; 315:1, 17
"from"
ultu libbi (*ul-tu* ŠA$_3$, see also *ultu*) 141:10
"from"
ultu muḫḫi (*ul-tu* UGU / TA *muḫ-ḫi*, see also *ultu*) 41:4; 44:3; 315:14
"from"
umma (syl.) 252:5; 311:19, 21; 312:14
introducing direct speech
ummânu (^{lu_2}*um-man-nu*, see also *bīt ummâni*) 26:4; 157:13; 210:4; 235:5; 241:6; 245:2; 283:6; 284:4
"craftsman"
ūmu (UD^{meš}, *u*$_4$-*mu*) 201:7; 209:8, 12; 217:20; 224:4; 227:3, 5, 6, 8; 229:6, 9, 12; 233:6; 234:1; 249:3; 313:8
"day"
unīqu (⸢SAL.AŠ$_2$⸣.[GAR$_3$]) 281:8
"female kid"
upnu (*u*$_2$-*pu-un*) 230:2
"*upnu* allotment"; see edition.
uqnû (^{na_4}ZA.GIN$_3$) 21:13′, 15″; 51:9
"lapis lazuli"
urāku (syl.) 78:2, 4
"*urāku*-chisel"
urīṣu (MAŠ$_2$.GAL) 261:1; 281:5, 17; 282:16
"billy-goat"
urmaḫḫu (UR.MAḪ) 1:5, 4:2
"lion (ornament)"
urū (^{giš}UR$_3$) 258:1; 305:1
"beam"
urû (syl.) 126:6; 281:14; 282:8, 20; 286:2; 304:9, 38′, 47′
"stable"
ušandû (^{lu_2}MUŠEN.DU$_3$) 122:8; 282:10
"bird-catcher"
utūnu (UDUN) 9:3, 5; 29:1, 4, 6; 46:2
"kiln"
uṭṭatu (ŠE.BAR) 143:6; 190:8, 20, 22, 23, 28, 35, 36; 193:29′; 208:6; 209:7, 11, 19; 215:1, 13; 216:1; 217:1, 22; 218:1; 219:1; 220:1; 222:1; 223:1; 224:2; 225:1; 226:1; 229:3, 8; 2301, 3, 5, 9, 13, 15, 17, 19; 231:1, 5; 232:1; 233:1; 234:1; 242:1, 2, 6, 10; 244:3; 250:1; 252:1; 259:1; 271:4; 286:8; 303:6′, 10′, 12′, 25′, 27′, 30′, 34′, 36′, 37′, 42′, 44′; 304:4, 5; 308:18′, 20′, 35′, 37′
"barley"

zabālu (*i-zab-bi-lu*) 208:4
"to carry"
zābil kudurri (^{lu_2}*za-bil ku-du-ru*) 193:61′; 215:11; 289:3, 7
"basket carrier"
zakītu (syl.) 144:12; 168:1; 296:19, 60, 75; 315:6
"*zakītu*-woman"
zāratu (^{tug_2}*za-ra-ti*) 149:3; 153:2; 172:3; 173:3; 262:5
"tent"
zazakku (^{lu_2}*za-zak-ku*) 157:12
"*zazakku* (official)"
ze-ri-in-nu-ut-ti 123:3, 4
unclear; see edition.
zēr qišê (NUMUN UKUŠ$_2$) 38:4
"melon seeds (shaped-beads)"
zikûtu (syl.) 158:4; 246:4
"cleaning"
zīmu (*zi-i-mu*) 21:9′
"appearance"
zittu (ḪA.LA) 190:11, 26, 34, 36
"share"
zuḫḫu (*zu-uḫ-ḫu*) 305:4
"reed mat (for doors)"
zumbu (*zu-um-bu*) 123:6
"fly"

Month Names

I Nisannu (BARA$_2$) 48:4; 143:13; 217:20; 219:2; 226:12, 15; 230:4; 247:1; 266:2; 286:4, 7, 11; 301:2′?

II Ayyāru (GU$_4$) 71:6; 176:25; 181:8; 183:6; 194:14, 16; 215:2; 216:3; 219:3; 226:3; 232:5; 260:6; 286:15

III Simānu (SIG$_4$) 29:15, 16; 179:2; 203:8, 13; 209:10, 12; 219:3; 246:1; 249:1, 3; 291:13; 308:14′, 29′; 314:7

IV Dûzu (ŠU) 25:2; 27:10; 194:11; 203:10; 215:3; 219:3; 231:2; 244:1, 12

V Abu (NE) 31:7; 159:3; 194:[11]; 218:1; 219:4; 231:2; 244:4; 287:2; 296:1

VI Ulūlu (KIN) 159:3; 197:2; 219:4; 227:1; 231:2; 244:15; 274:5; 277:2; 304:30′

VII Tašrītu (DU$_6$) 197:2; 219:4; 227:4, 5, 6; 234:2; 263:4; 274:7; 304:33′

VIII Araḫsamnu (APIN) 25:3; 200:2; 201:6; 205:2; 227:8; 263:6; 272:6; 304:10, 34′

IX Kislīmu (GAN) 192:4; 193:18′; 198:1, 9, 28; 200:2, 9; 201:8; 203:14; 205:2; 214:9; 217:1, 3, 26, 29, 31; 255:2; 304:6, 30′, 31′, 43′

X Ṭebētu (AB) 193:11′, 26′, 27′; 199:11; 200:2, 10; 203:15; 217:2; 225:2; 228:3; 245:1, 2; 263:9; 270:3

XI Šabāṭu (ZIZ$_2$) 176:12; 203:15; 207:2; 245:1, 16′

XII Addaru (ŠE) 29:2; 141:11, 17; 143:14; 230:4; 245:1; 266:2

Temples

Akītu (*a-ki-tu*$_4$) 215:9

Ea temple (E$_2$ ^{d}IDIM) 63:3

Eanna (E$_2$.AN.NA) 65:6; 107:7, 9, 11; 141:14; 177:5; 199:12; 201:5; 230:17; 232:6, 7; 290:3; 294:3′; 312:11, 14; 314:6, 9; 315:13, 17

Esagil (E$_2$.SAG.IL$_2$, E$_2$.SAG.GIL) 25:8; 26:5; 185:6

Gula temple (E$_2$ ^{d}*gu-la*) 65:3, 8

IGI.DU temple (E$_2$ ^{d}IGI.DU) 6:2–3

Nabû temple (E$_2$ ^{d}PA, E$_2$ ^{d}AG) 190:9, 10, 32

Uṣur-amāssu temple (E$_2$ ^{d}URU$_3$-INIM-*su*) 5:2; 29:9; 61:3; 274:3; 308:25′

Divine Names

Adapa (^{d}*a-da-pi*) 50:17

Bēl (^{d}EN) 157:25

Bēlet-balāṭi (^{d}GAŠAN-TIN) 54:2, 12

Bēlet / Bēltu (ša) Uruk (^{d}GAŠAN *ša*$_2$ UNUG^{ki}, ^{d}GAŠAN UNUG^{ki}) 1:3; 3:3; 24:7; 34:4; 39:3; 40:3; 42:[5, 6]; 43:4; 50:5; 71:3; 148:13; 154:6, 12; 183:3; 187:4; 209:13; 227:7; 232:3; 312:20; 313:8; 314:5, 13; 315:9

Bēltu-ša-rēš (^{d}GAŠAN *ša*$_2$ SAG) 1:5; 4:3; 50:13; 227:4

Gula (^{d}*gu-la*) 29:[12]; 49:6; 187:4; 315:10

IGI.DU (^{d}IGI.DU) 29:12; 315:10

Ištar (^{d}15, ^{d}*iš-tar*) 5:4, 9; 54:8; 309:1

Kurunnītu (^{d}KAŠ.DIN.NAM, ^{d}KAŠ.⸢NAM⸣:DIN) 35:2; 38:2

Nanāya (^{d}*na-na-a*) 10:11; 14:3, 5; 17:5; 34:11; 39:2, 5, 7; 40:11; 41:5; 42:10; 43:8; 44:4; 50:9; 71:3; 149:4; 154:13; 163:3; 232:3; 309:1; 315:9

Nabû (^{d}AG) 290:4

Šamaš (^{d}UTU) 70:3; 146:2, 4; 284:2

Urkayītu (^{d}UNUG^{ki}-*a-ti*, ⸢^{d}⸣UNUG^{ki}-*a-a-i-tu*$_2$, ^{d}UNUG^{ki}-*i-ti*, ^{d}*aš*$_2$*-ka-i*$^{?}$*-ti*,) 5:7; 20:3; 158:6, 11; 238:4

Uṣur-amāssu (^{d}URU$_3$-INIM-*su*, [^{d}*u*$_2$]-*ṣur*-INIM-*su*) 8:3; 27:2; 53:3?; 158:5, 10; 163:6; 190:6; 238:3; 311:13, 15; 315:10

Geographical Names and Toponyms

Akkad (^{uru}A.GA.DE$_3$^{ki}) 303:18′

Āl-Bēltiya (<^{lu_2}>$^{?}$URU-<^{d}>GAŠAN-*ia*$_2$-*a-a*) 105:12

Aššurītu ([^{ga}]^{rim}*a-šur-re-ti*) 190:1

Babylon (TIN.TIR^{ki}) 157:13; 177:4; 180:10; 272:2; 291:12; 296:21, 31, 39, 59, 69; 303:4′, 14′; 304:2; 308:21′

Birṣu (*bi-ir-ṣ*[*i*]) 8:5

Bīt-Dakūri (^{uru}E$_2$-^{I}*da-ku-ru*) 202:3

Bīt-Gilāni (^{uru}E$_2$-*gi-la-nu*) 230:7

Bīt-Sîn-karābu-šime (^{garim}E$_2$ ^{d}30-*ka-rab*-ŠE.GA) 122:4

Bīt-Šamaʾ-il (E$_2$ ^{I}*ša*$_2$*-ma-a*ʾ-DINGIR) 139:4

Borsippa ((DUMU) *bar-sip*^{ki}) 276:6

Egypt ($^{(kur)}$*mi-ṣir*) 143:3; 176:6

Ḫalatu (*ḫa-la-tu*) 307:26

Iādaqu ([^{ur}]^{u}*ia-a-da-qu*) 247:3

Itu ([uru]*i-ti*) 117:7
Izalla ([kur]*i-zal-la*) 221:11
Kalzu ([uru]*kal-za-a-a*) 190:21
Kašappu (*ka-šap-pu*, *ka-šap-pi*) 143:11; 176:9
Larsa (ud.unug[ki]) 296: 14, 22, 32, 41, 54, 60, 64, 68; 305:18
Ma-aḫ-ra-ga 307:15
Māt tâmti (KUR *tam-ti*$_3$) 244:5
Sanaṣru ([uru]*sa-na-aṣ-ru*) 271:5
Sealand → Māt tâmti
Udannu ([uru]*u*$_2$*-dan-ni*, [lu2]*u*$_2$*-dan-na-a-a*) 140:2; 157:16
Uruk (UNUG[ki], [lu2]UNUG[ki]-*a-a*) 71:15; 133:3; 144:2; 185:3; 232:15; 280:3; 314:8; 315:23

Texts

AnOr 8, 5 192
AnOr 8, 50 226
AnOr 8, 60 226
AnOr 8, 71 161
ARRIM 7, 47 54
AUWE 5, 4 210
AUWE 5, 81 54
AUWE 5, 94 94
BAM 1, 3 i: 32 282
BE 9, 7 143
BE 9, 15 187
BIN 1, 32 120
BIN 1, 127 64
BIN 1, 132 52
BIN 1, 173 282
BIN 1, 174 200, 210, 224
BIN 2, 114 158
BM 30436 289
BM 41452 289
BM 56018 282
BM 57184 282
BM 60745 281
BM 74586 48
BM 96535 208
BM 108858 55
BM 113273 200
BM 113385 200
BM 113407 203
BM 113429 203
BM 113485 200
BM 114449 200
BM 114461 70
BM 114480 124
BM 114524 228
BM 114528 228
BM 114601 231
Camb 18 72
CT 55, 754 226
CT 56, 439 215
Dar 468 119
Eames Q2 116
Eames Q22 144
FLP 1543 230
FLP 1545 63
GC 1, 12 136
GC 1, 51 102
GC 1, 54 282
GC 1, 145 215
GC 1, 151 215
GC 1, 168 230
GC 1, 174 143
GC 1, 323 200
GC 1, 333 161
GC 1, 399 230
GC 2, 39 142, 147, 159
GC 2, 45 40
GC 2, 51 47
GC 2, 54 42
GC 2, 62 118
GC 2, 74 136
GC 2, 78 161
GC 2, 102 200
GC 2, 104 231
GC 2, 187 159
GC 2, 189 230
GC 2, 261 59
GC 2, 273 102
GC 2, 278 166
GC 2, 291 173
GC 2, 304 88
GC 2, 307 101
GC 2, 364 159
GC 2, 389 5
Iraq 59, 24 176
Iraq 59, 25 200
Knopf 1939 XXI A SC-24 176
Knopf 1939 XXV B SC-27 176

UCP 9/1 I, 10 52
UCP 9/1 I, 13 159
UCP 9/1 II, 10 159
UCP 9/1 II, 59 52
UCP 9/2, 12 143
UCP 9/2, 21 215
UCP 9/2, 25 151
UCP 9/2, 35 231
UCP 9/2, 59 161
YBC 3455 45
YBC 3525 141
YBC 3543 143
YBC 3767 185
YBC 3784 148
YBC 3808 63
YBC 3830 141, 200
YBC 4119 151
YBC 4164 226
YBC 4173 226
YBC 4187 187
YBC 7380 230
YBC 9030 226
YBC 9222 230
YBC 9239 235
YBC 9251 142
YBC 9407 96, 102, 151
YBC 9545 172
YBC 11273 78
YBC 11390 41
YBC 11553 202
YBC 11649 45
YBC 11898 71
YOS 3, 158 233, 234
YOS 6, 3 35
YOS 6, 8 176
YOS 6, 19 176
YOS 6, 33 120
YOS 6, 74 215
YOS 6, 90 230
YOS 6, 121 37
YOS 6, 142 200
YOS 6, 145 194
YOS 6, 205 192
YOS 6, 209 200
YOS 6, 218 72
YOS 6, 237 228
YOS 6, 245 176
YOS 7, 23 103
YOS 7, 32 232
YOS 7, 42 83
YOS 7, 69 102
YOS 7, 87 232
YOS 7, 95 232
YOS 7, 97 232
YOS 7, 132 200
YOS 7, 137 231
YOS 7, 144 226
YOS 7, 146 137
YOS 7, 176 161
YOS 7, 196 173
YOS 7, 198 226
YOS 17, 21 185
YOS 17, 41 159
YOS 17, 42 173
YOS 17, 74 231
YOS 17, 97 141
YOS 17, 130 120
YOS 17, 176 71
YOS 17, 220 70
YOS 17, 232 186
YOS 17, 233 94
YOS 17, 245 45
YOS 17, 301 224, 231
YOS 17, 310 105
YOS 17, 316 88
YOS 17, 325 216
YOS 17, 333 72
YOS 17, 334 95
YOS 17, 362 78, 98
YOS 17, 390 51
YOS 19, 47 133
YOS 19, 74 200
YOS 19, 115 215, 232
YOS 19, 160 228
YOS 19, 173 176
YOS 19, 174 176
YOS 19, 175 176
YOS 19, 176 176
YOS 19, 177 176
YOS 19, 178 176
YOS 19, 179 176
YOS 19, 180 176
YOS 19, 181 176
YOS 19, 182 176

BIBLIOGRAPHY

Abraham, Kathleen, and Sokoloff, Michael. 2011. "Aramaic Loanwords in Akkadian — a Reassessment of the Proposals." *AfO* 52: 22–76.

Baker, Heather D. 2013. "Beneath the stairs in the Rēš temple of Hellenistic Uruk. A study in cultic topography and spatial organization." *ZA* 6: 18–42.

Beaulieu, Paul-Alain. 1989. "The capacity of the *mašīḫu* Measure in Neo-Babylonian Eanna." *N.A.B.U.* 1989/65.

Beaulieu, Paul-Alain. 2003. *The Pantheon of Uruk during the Neo-Babylonian Period*. Leiden: Styx, Brill.

Beaulieu, Paul-Alain. Forthcoming. "Tiaras and crowns of Neo-Babylonian deities." In *Material Culture of Babylonia* 1. OLA, edited by Laura Cousin, Louise Quillien and Manon Ramez. Leuven: Peeters.

Ehrenberg, Erica. 1999. *Uruk. Late Babylonian Seal Impressions on Eanna-Tablets*. AUWE 18. Mainz: Philipp von Zabern.

Gabbay, Uri. 2014. *Pacifying the Hearts of the Gods: Sumerian Emesal Prayers of the First Millennium BC*. Heidelberger Emesal-Studien 1. Wiesbaden: Harrassowitz.

Gordin, Shai. 2020. "On the Nature of gištallu in Mesopotamian cultic architecture." *Akkadica* 141: 71–84.

Janković, Bojana. 2013. *Aspects of Urukean Agriculture in the First Millennium BC*. PhD diss., University of Vienna.

Joannès, Francis. 1994. "Une visite du gouverneur d'Arpad." *N.A.B.U.* 1994/20.

Joannès, Francis. 2006. "Traitement des malades et bît hilṣi en Babylonie récente." In *Médecine et médecins au Proche-Orient ancient*. BAR 1528, edited by Laura Battini and Pierre Villard, pp. 73–90. Oxford: Hedges.

Jursa, Michael. 1995. *Die Landwirtschaft in Sippar in neubabylonischer Zeit*. AfO Beih. 25. Vienna: Institut für Orientalistik Universität Wien.

Jursa, Michael. 2001. "Geistesschwache in Sippar." *N.A.B.U.* 2001/67.

Jursa, Michael. 2004a "Accounting in Neo-Babylonian institutional archives: Structure, usage, implications." In *Creating Economic Order*, edited by Michael Hudson and Cornelia Wunsch, pp. 145–98. Bethesda: CDL Press.

Jursa, Michael. 2004b. "Parfüm(rezepte). A. In Mesopotamien." *RLA* 10 5/6: 335–6.

Jursa, Michael. 2005. *Neo-Babylonian Legal and Administrative Documents: Typology, Contents and Archives*. GMTR 1. Münster: Ugarit-Verlag.

Jursa, Michael. 2006–2008. "Die Räucherstoffe." *RLA* 11: 225–9.

Jursa, Michael, with contributions by Joannes Hackl, Bojana Janković, Kristin Kleber, Elizabeth E. Payne, Caronline Waerzeggers, and Michaela Weszeli. 2010. *Aspects of the Economic History of Babylonia in the First Millennium BC. Economic Geography, Economic Mentalities, Agriculture, the Use of Money and the Problem of Economic Growth*. AOAT 377. Münster: Ugarit-Verlag.

Jursa, Michael and Gordin, Shai. 2018. "The Ousting of the Nūr-Sîns." *HeBAI* 7: 42–64.

Jursa, Michael and Levavi, Yuval. 2021. "For a Fistful of Barley: more on the Remuneration of Scribes and State Taxation in the Neo-Babylonian Eanna Temple." *RA* 115: 135–42.

Jursa, Michael and Weszeli, Michaela. 1996. "*atkalluššu, der 'Träger.'" *N.A.B.U.* 1996/26.

Kleber, Kristin. 2005. "Von Bierproduzenten und Gefängnisaufsehern: Dezentrale Güterverteilung und Buchhaltung in Eanna." In *Approaching the Babylonian Economy. Proceedings of the Symposium on the Economic History of Babylonia in the First Millennium Held in Vienna, July 2004*. AOAT 330, edited by Heather D. Baker and Michael Jursa, pp. 289–321. Münster: Ugarit Verlag.

Kleber, Kristin. 2008. *Tempel und Palast. Die Beziehungen zwischen dem König und dem Eanna-Tempel im spätbabylonischen Uruk*. Veröffentlichungen zur Wirtschaftsgeschichte im 1. Jahrtausend v. Chr. 3. AOAT 358. Münster: Ugarit Verlag.

Kleber, Kristin. 2010. "Eanna's trade in wool." In *Aspects of the Economic History of Babylonia in the First Millennium BC. Economic Geography, Economic Mentalities, Agriculture, the Use of Money and the Problem of Economic Growth*. AOAT 377, pp. 595–615. Münster: Ugarit-Verlag.

Kleber, Kristin. 2014. "Zu Waffen und Ausrüstung babylonischer Soldaten in der zweiten Hälfte des 1. Jt. v. Chr." In *Krieg und Frieden im Alten Vorderasien*. AOAT 401, edited by Hans Neumann et al., pp. 429–48. Münster: Ugarit Verlag.

Kleber, Kristin. 2016a. "Arabian gold in Babylonia." *KASKAL* 13: 121–34.

Kleber, Kristin. 2016b. "Sekēru – 'to purify,' not 'to gild.'" *N.A.B.U.* 2016/59.

Kleber, Kristin. 2017. *Spätbabylonische Text zum lokalen und regionalen Handel sowie zum Fernhandel aus dem Eanna-Archiv*. Babylonische Archive 7. Dresden: Islet-Verlag.

Kleber, Kristin. 2018. "Katzen als Jagdhelfer in Mesopotamien." In *Grenzüberschreitungen. Studien zur Kulturgeschichte des Alten Orients. Festschrift für Hans Neumann zum 65. Geburtstag am 9. Mai 2018*. Dubsar 5, edited by Kristin Kleber, Georg Neumann, and Susanne Paulus, pp. 327–48. Münster: Zaphon.

Kleber, Kristin. 2020. "As skilful as Croesus. Evidence for the parting of gold and silver by cementation from Second and First Millennium Mesopotamia and Egypt." In *White Gold: Studies in Early Electrum Coinage*, edited by Peter van Alfen and Ute Wartenberg, pp. 17–34. Jerusalem: American Numismatic Society.

Knopf, Carl Sumner. 1939. "Some Ancient Records from Babylonia." In *So Live the Works of Men. Seventieth Anniversary Volume Honoring Edgar Lee Hewett*, edited by Donald B. Brand and Fred E. Harvey, pp. 231–232 (plates XIX–XXVII). Albuquerque: University of New Mexico.

Kozuh, Michael. 2014. *The Sacrificial Economy. Assessors, Contractors, and Thieves in the Management of Sacrificial Sheep at the Eanna Temple of Uruk (ca. 625–520 B.C.)*. Winona Lake: Eisenbrauns.

Levavi, Yuval. 2014. "*ginnu*-silver from the time of Nebuchadnezzar (and Nabû-aḫḫē-iddin's term as temple administrator)." *N.A.B.U.* 2014/102.

Levavi, Yuval. 2018. *Administrative Epistolography in the Formative Phase of the Neo-Babylonian Empire*. Dubsar 3, SbB 2. Münster: Zaphon.

Levavi, Yuval. 2020. "The Sacred Bureaucracy of Neo-Babylonian Temples." In *Contextualizing Jewish Temples, Brill's Reference Library of Judaism*, edited by Shalom Holtz and Tova Ganzel, pp. 6–22. Leiden/Boston: Brill.

Levavi, Yuval. 2021. "The Interaction between Eanna and the Sealand in the Neo-Babylonian period." In *New Perspectives on Aramaic Epigraphy in Mesopotamia, Qumran, Egypt and Idumea*, edited by Aaren M. Maeir, et al, pp. 17–33. Tübingen: Mohr Siebeck.

Levavi, Yuval. 2022. "Tallying in the Eanna: A Unique Temple Notation Practice." *Iraq* 84, 1–16. Doi:10.1017/irq.2022.8

Levavi, Yuval. Forthcoming. "Basic Prestige: The mušaḫḫinu in Private Babylonian Households." In *Material Culture of Babylonia* 1. OLA, edited by Laura Cousin, Louise Quillien and Manon Ramez, Leuven: Peeters.

Magdalene, Rachel, Wunsch, Cornelia, and Wells, Bruce. 2019. *Fault, Responsibility, and Administrative Law in Late Babylonian Legal Texts*, University Park, PA: Eisenbrauns.

Nielsen, John. 2015. *Personal Names in Early Neo-Babylonian Legal and Administrative Tablets, 747–626 B.C.E.* NISABA 29. Winona Lake, IN: Eisenbrauns.

Payne, Elizabeth E. 2007. *The Craftsmen of the Neo-Babylonian Period: A Study of the Textile and Metal Workers of the Eanna Temple*. PhD diss., Yale University.

Payne, Elizabeth E. 2008. "A Rough Draft of a Neo-Babylonian Accounting Document." In *From the Banks of the Euphrates: Studies in Honor of Alice Louise Slotsky*, edited by Martha Ross, pp. 181–92. Winona Lake, IN: Eisenbrauns.

Payne, Elizabeth E. 2013. "Two tablets from the Yale Babylonian Collection mentioning the guzguzugarment." *N.A.B.U.* 2013/15.

Pearce, Laurie. 1996. "Iron "Stars" in the Neo-Babylonian Period." *N.A.B.U.* 1996/25.

Pinches, Theophilus G. 1928. "The Influence of the Mythology and Heathen Practices of the Canaanites Upon the Hebrews." *JTVI* 60: 122–47.

Pirngruber, Reinhard. 2021. "A Diplomatics Approach to the Eanna Archive: the Livestock Dossier." *AfO* 54: 88–108.

Popova, Olga V., and Quillien, Louise. 2021. "Fabrication and Ritual Use of the *pišannu*-Jewellery Box in Babylonian Temples During the First Millennium BC." In *Material Culture and Food in (Greater) Mesopotamia from the Iron Age to the Parthian Period. 67th Rencontre Assyiologique Internationale – Turin*, Mesopotamia 56: 151–61.

Quillien, Louise. 2022. *Histoire des textiles en Babylonie, 626–484 av. J.-C.* Culture and History of the Ancient Near East 126. Leiden/Boston: Brill.

Sack, Ronald. 1979. "Some Notes on Bookkeeping in Eanna." In *Studies in Honor of Tom B. Jones*. AOAT 203, edited by Marvin A. Powell and Ronald Sack, pp. 111–18. Butzon & Bercker Kevelaer: Ugarit.

Sandowicz, Malgorzata. 2018. "Before Xerxes: The Role of the Governor of Babylonia in the Administration of Justice Under the First Achaemenids." In *Xerxes and Babylonia: The Cuneiform Evidence*, edited by Caroline Waerzeggers and Maarja Seire, pp. 35–62. Leuven/Paris/Bristol: Peeters.

Thavapalan, Shiyanthi. 2020. *The Meaning of Color in Ancient Mesopotamia*. Leiden/Boston: Brill.

Thissen, Cornell. 2017. Review of *Personal Names in Early Neo-Babylonian Legal and Administrative Tablets* by John Nielsen. *BiOr* 74: 129–40.

Thissen, Cornell. 2021. Notes on Thissen 2017, www.academia.edu/34492411/Review_NIELSEN_J_P_2015_in_BiOr_2017_74_1_2_p_129_140; last accessed 12.10.2021.

van der Brugge, Caroline, and Kleber, Kristin. 2016. "The Empire of Trade and the Empires of Force: Tyre in the Neo-Assyrian and Neo-Babylonian Periods." In *Dynamics of Production and Economic Interaction in the Near East in the First Half of the First Millennium BCE*, edited by Juan Carlos Moreno Garcia, pp. 187–222. Oxford: Oxbow.

van Soldt, Wilfred. 1990. "Fabrics and Dyes at Ugarit." *UF* 22: 321–57.

Waerzeggers, Caroline. 2010. *The Ezida Temple of Borsippa: Priesthood, Cult, Archives.* Achaemenid History 15. Leiden: NINO.

Zadok, Ran. 2003. "The representation of foreigners in Neo- and Late-Babylonian legal documents (eighth through second centuries B.C.E.)." In *Judah and the Judeans in the Neo-Babylonian Period*, edited by Oded Lipschits and Joseph Blenkinsopp, pp. 471–589. Winona Lake, IN: Eisenbrauns.

Zadok, Ran. 2005/2006. "The Text Group of Nabû-ēṭer." *AfO* 51: 147–97.

Zaia, Shana. 2021. "Everything Must Go: Consequences of State Construction and of Control in the Levant for the Eanna (591–590 BCE)." *AoF* 48/1: 159–87.

Zawadzki, Stefan. 2006. *Garments of the Gods. Studies on the Textile Industry and the Pantheon of Sippar according to the Texts from the Ebabbar Archive.* Orbis Biblicus et Orientalis 218. Fribourg/Göttingen: Academic Press/Vandenhoeck & Ruprecht.

PLATES

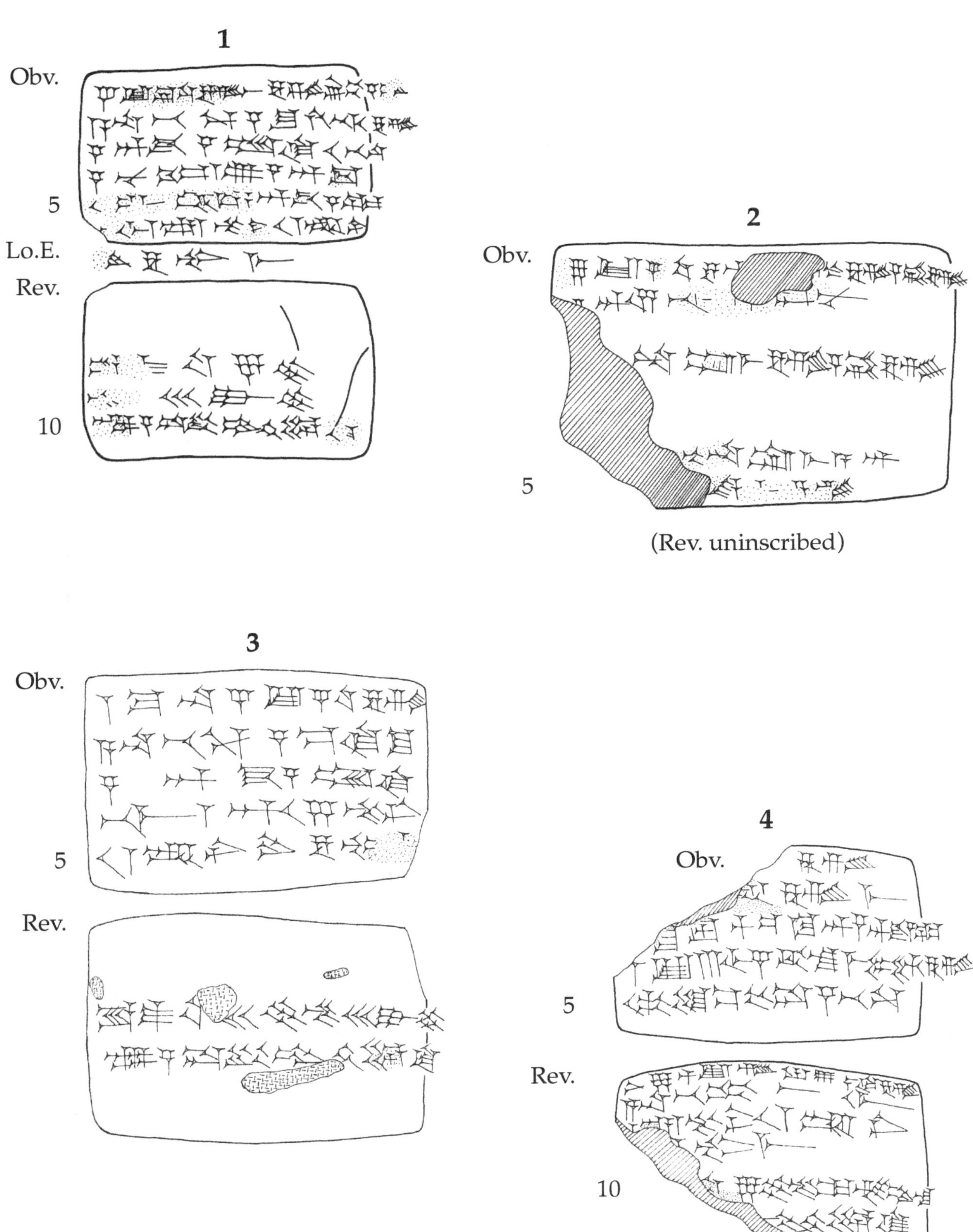
1
Obv.
Lo.E.
Rev.
2
Obv.
(Rev. uninscribed)
3
Obv.
Rev.
4
Obv.
Rev.

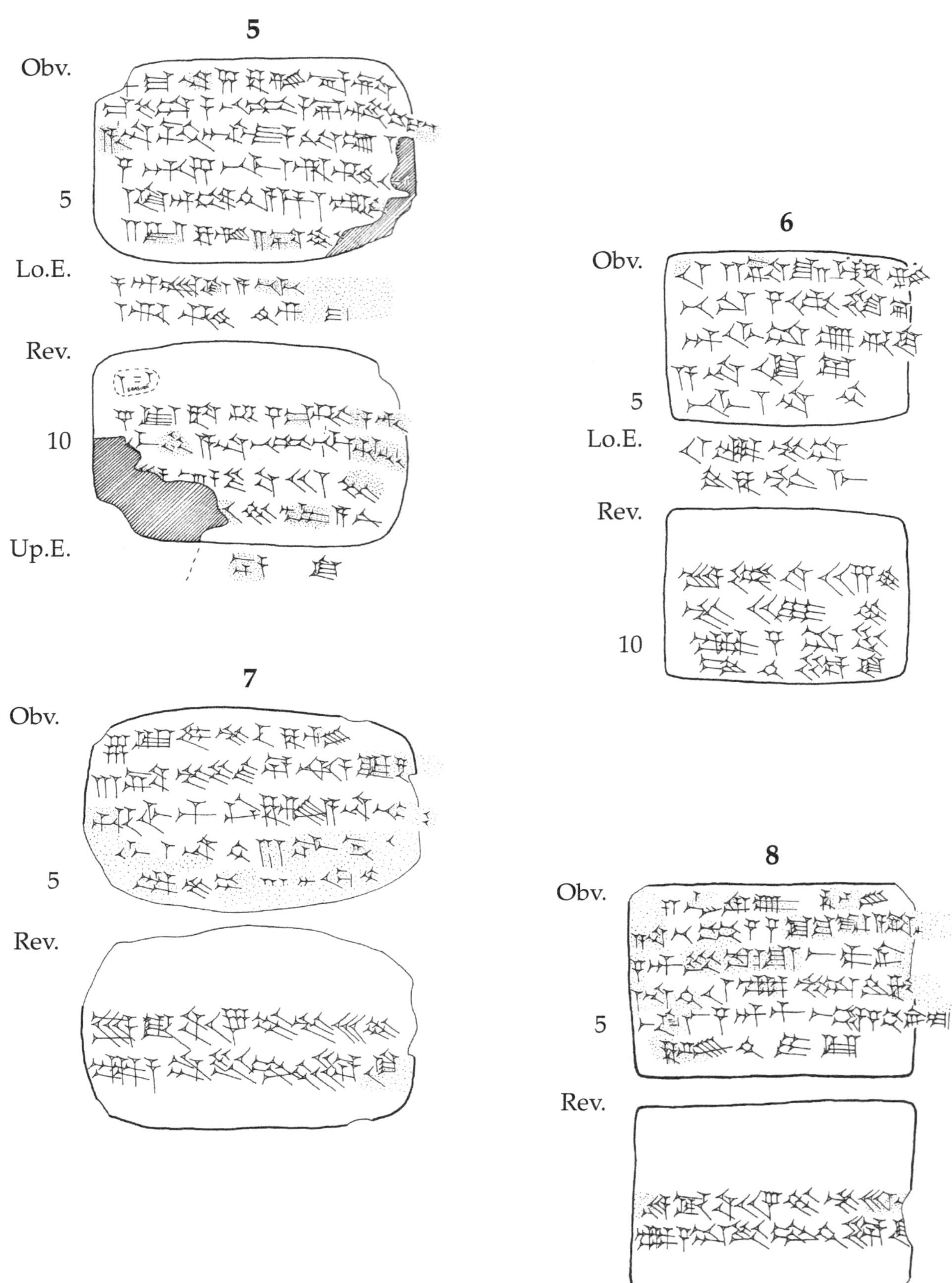
5
Obv.
Lo.E.
Rev.
Up.E.
6
Obv.
Lo.E.
Rev.
7
Obv.
Rev.
8
Obv.
Rev.

9

Obv.

Lo.E.

Rev.

10

Obv.

Lo.E.

Rev.

11

Obv.

Lo.E.

Rev.

12

Obv.

ERASURE

Rev.

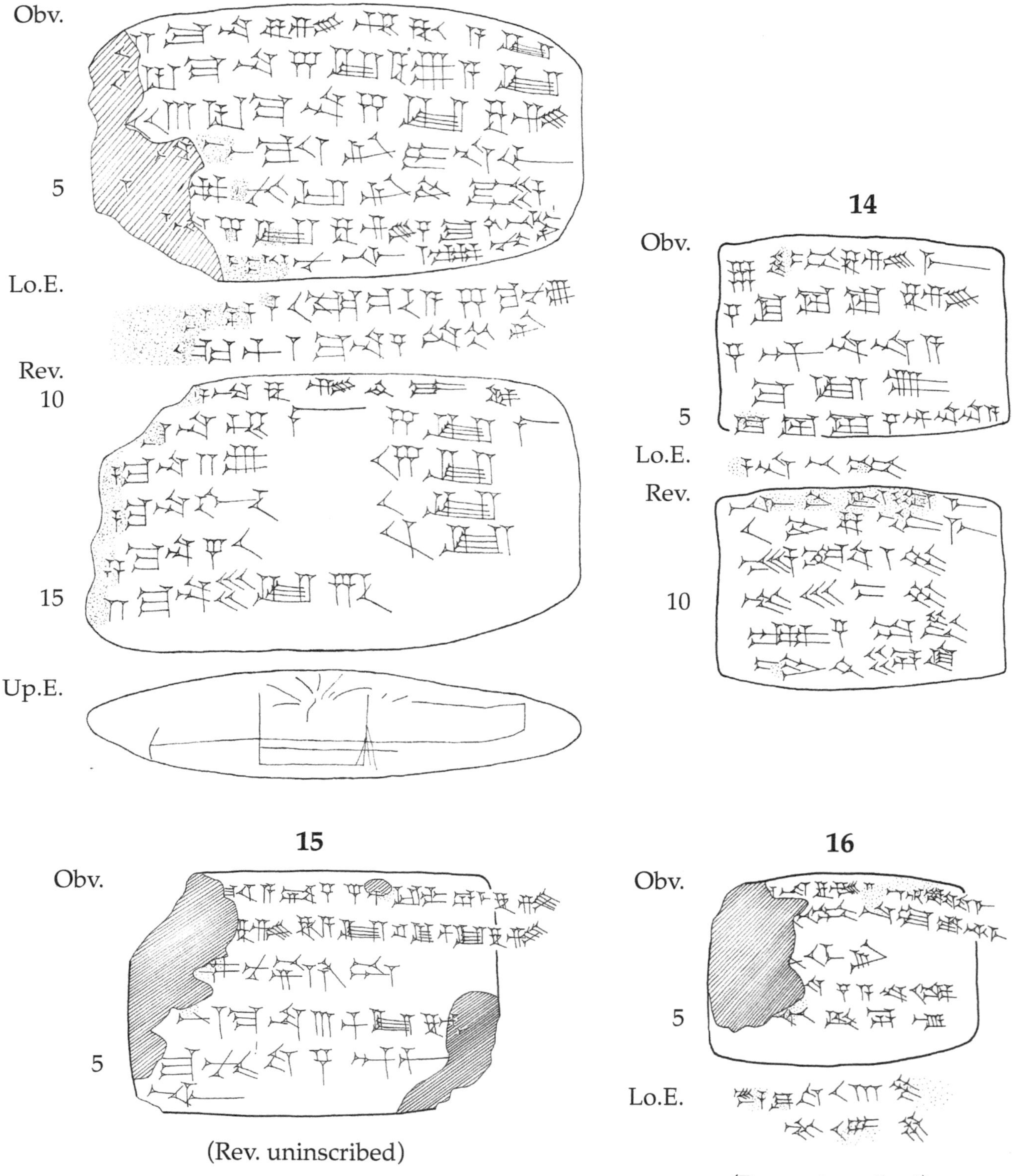
13
Obv.
Lo.E.
Rev.
Up.E.
14
Obv.
Lo.E.
Rev.
15
Obv.
(Rev. uninscribed)
16
Obv.
Lo.E.
(Rev. uninscribed)

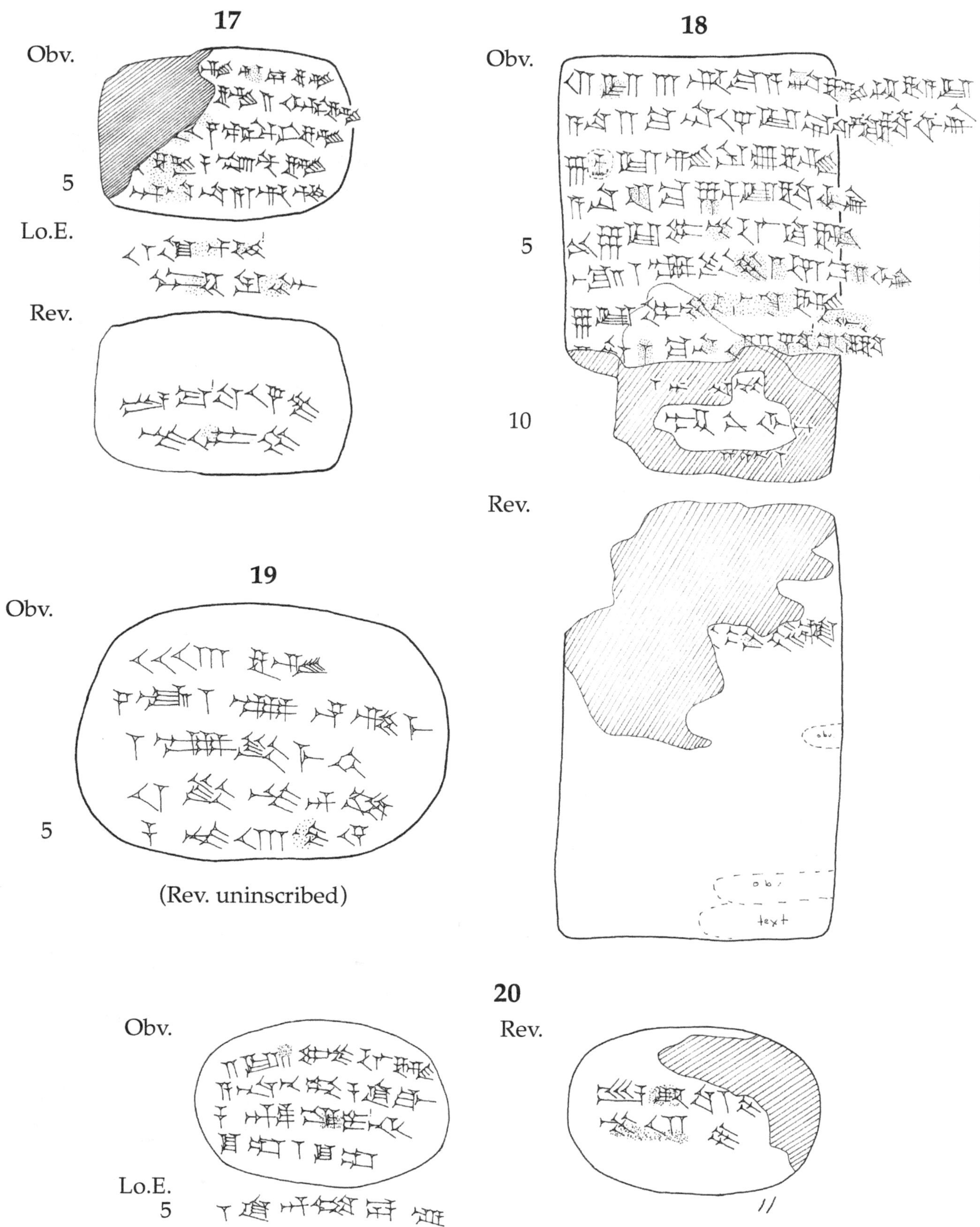
17
Obv.
Lo.E.
Rev.
18
Obv.
Rev.
19
Obv.
(Rev. uninscribed)
20
Obv.
Lo.E.
Rev.

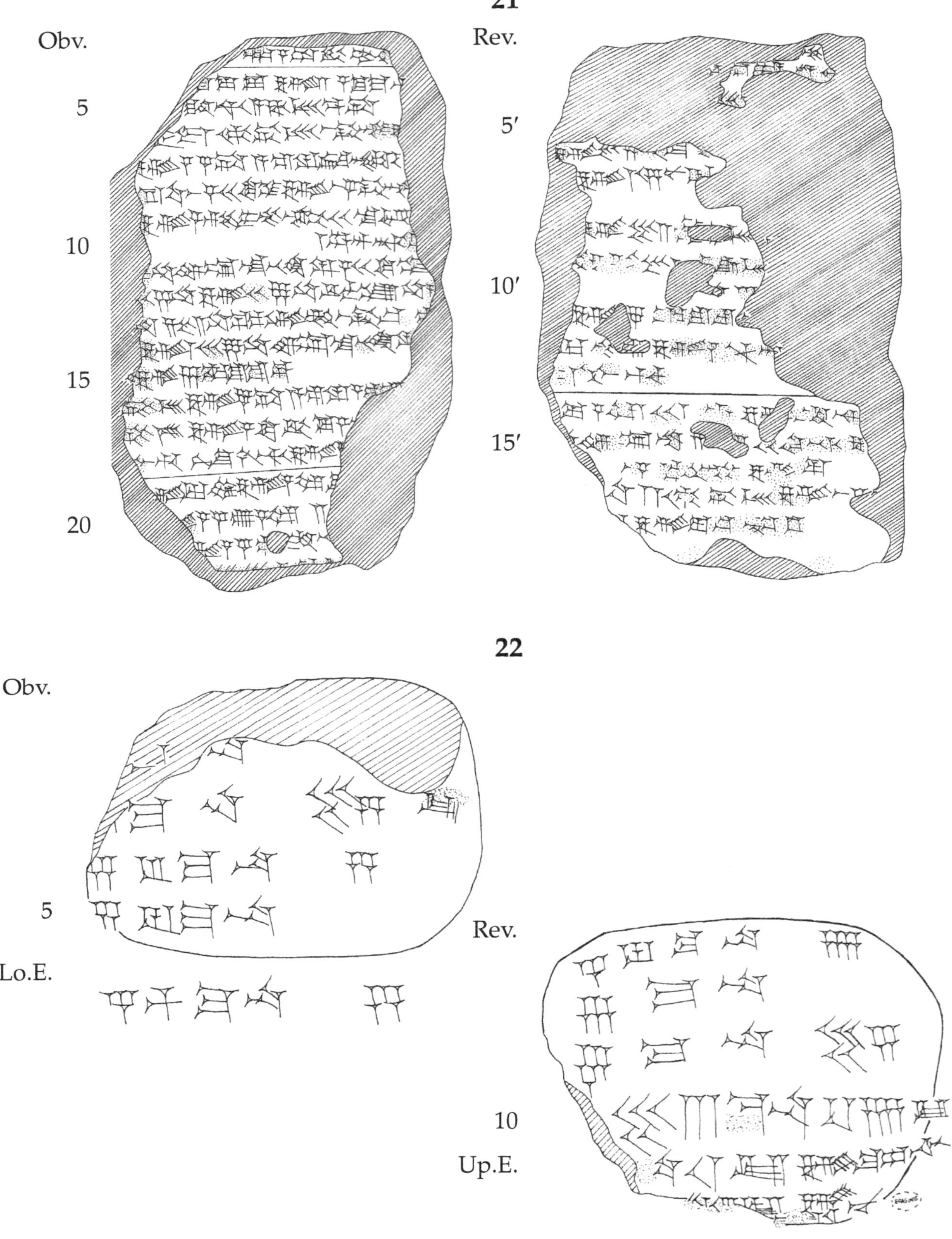
21
Obv.
Rev.
22
Obv.
Lo.E.
Rev.
Up.E.

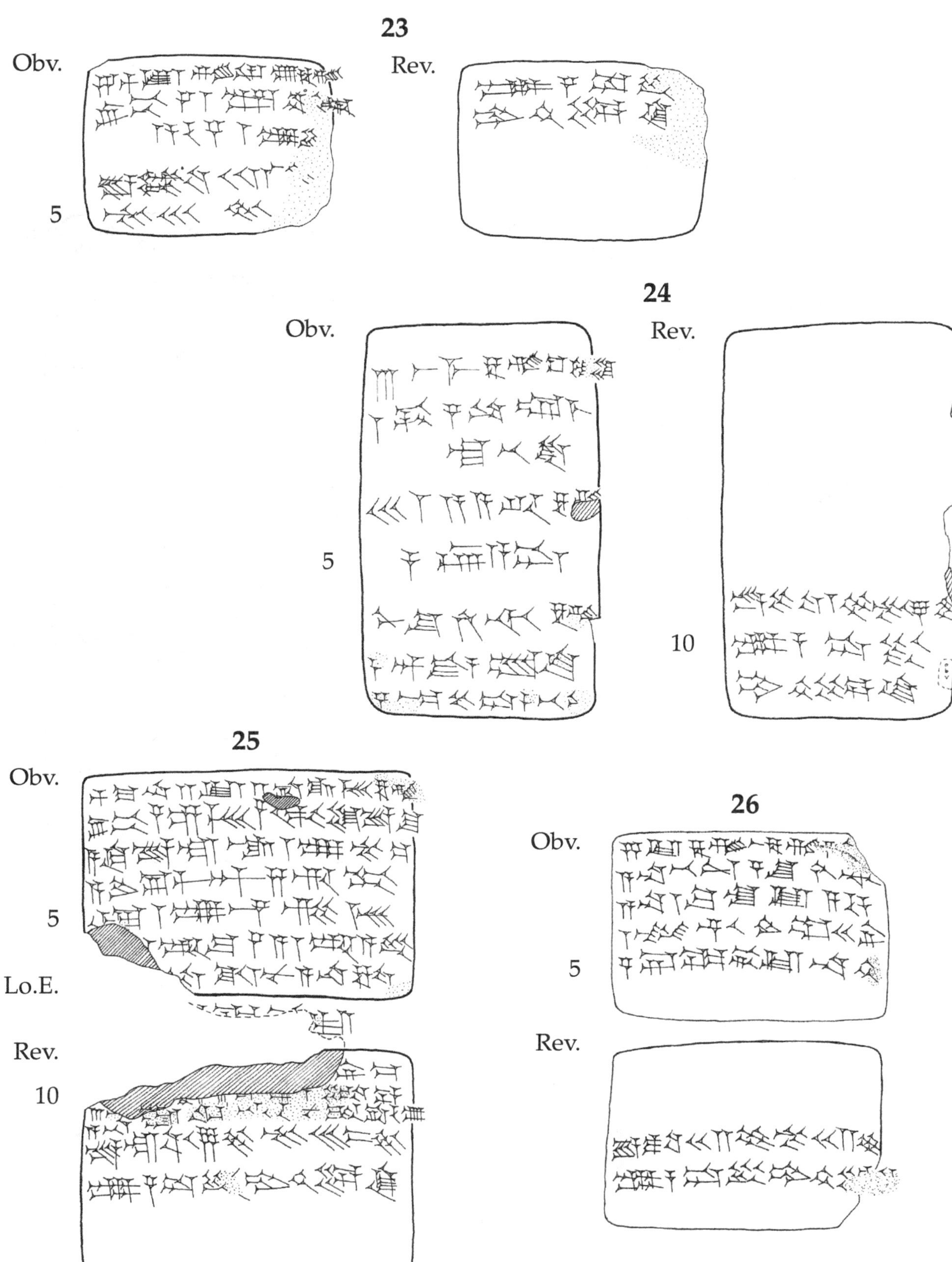
23
Obv.
Rev.
24
Obv.
Rev.
25
Obv.
Lo.E.
Rev.
26
Obv.
Rev.

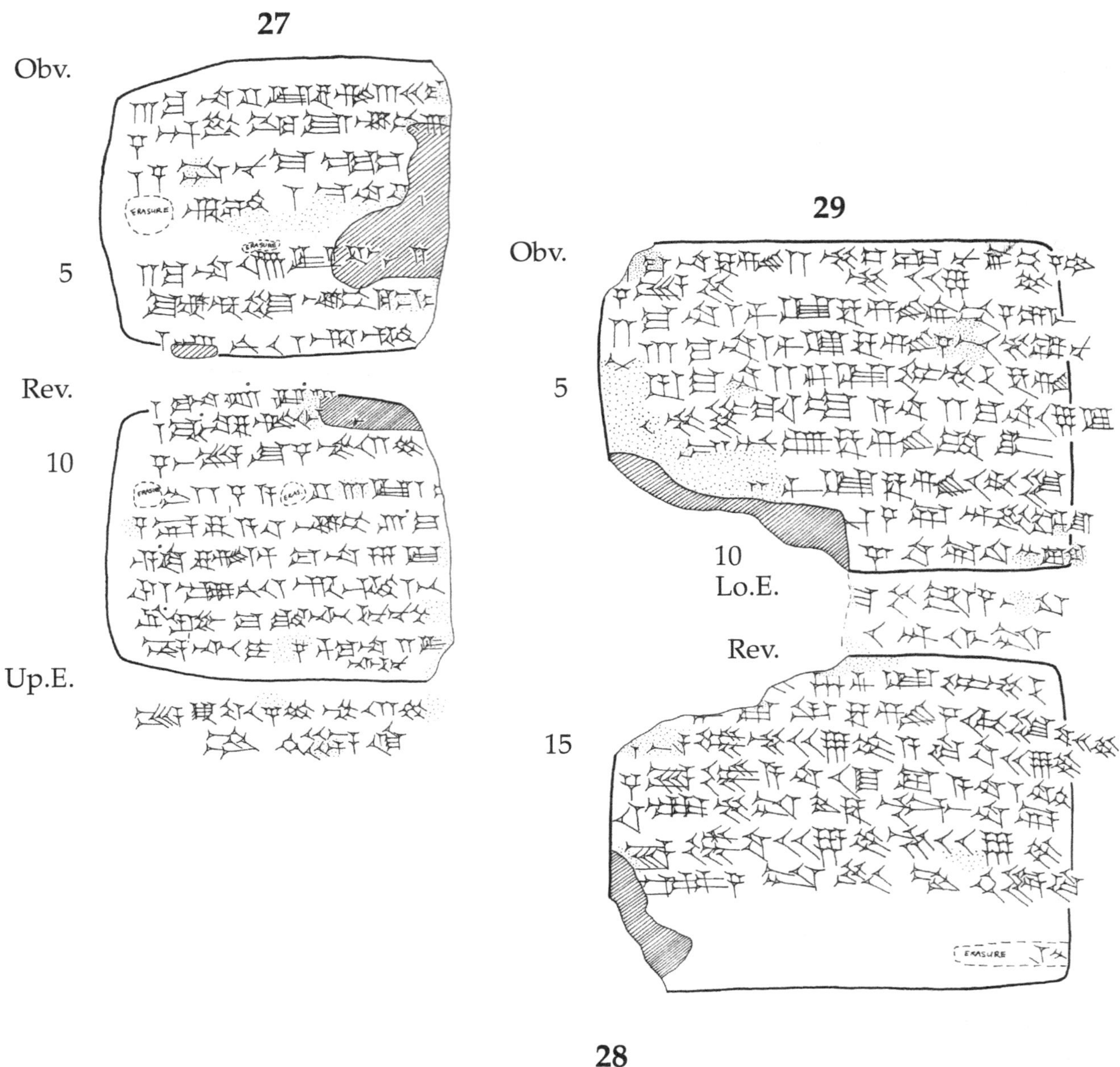

28

Obv.

(Rev. uninscribed)

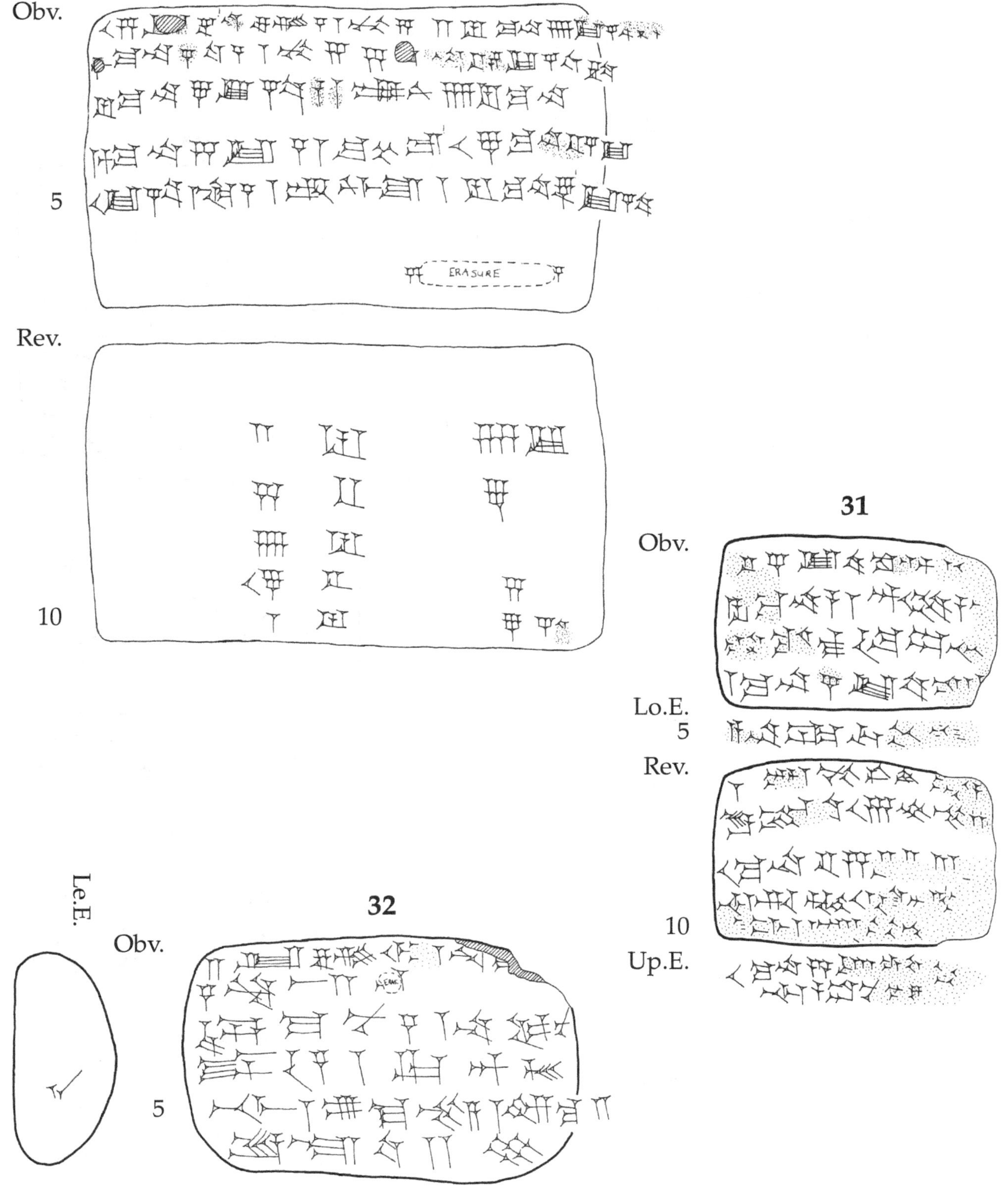
30
Obv.
ERASURE
Rev.
31
Obv.
Lo.E.
Rev.
Up.E.
32
Le.E.
Obv.
(Rev. uninscribed)

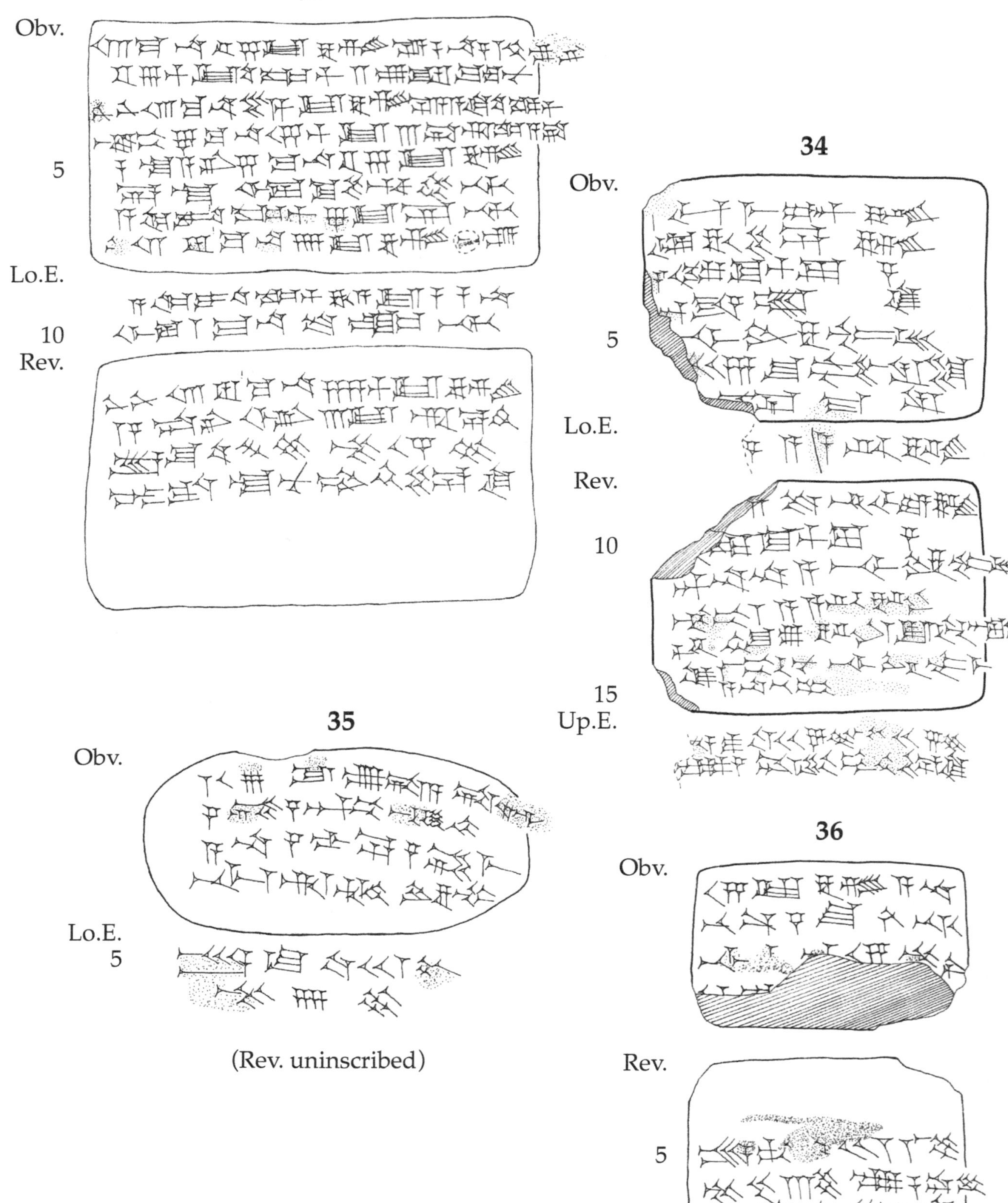
33
Obv.
Lo.E.
Rev.
34
Obv.
Lo.E.
Rev.
Up.E.
35
Obv.
Lo.E.
(Rev. uninscribed)
36
Obv.
Rev.

37

Obv.

Rev.

38

Obv.

Rev.

39

Obv.

Lo.E.

Rev.

40

Obv.

Lo.E.

Rev.

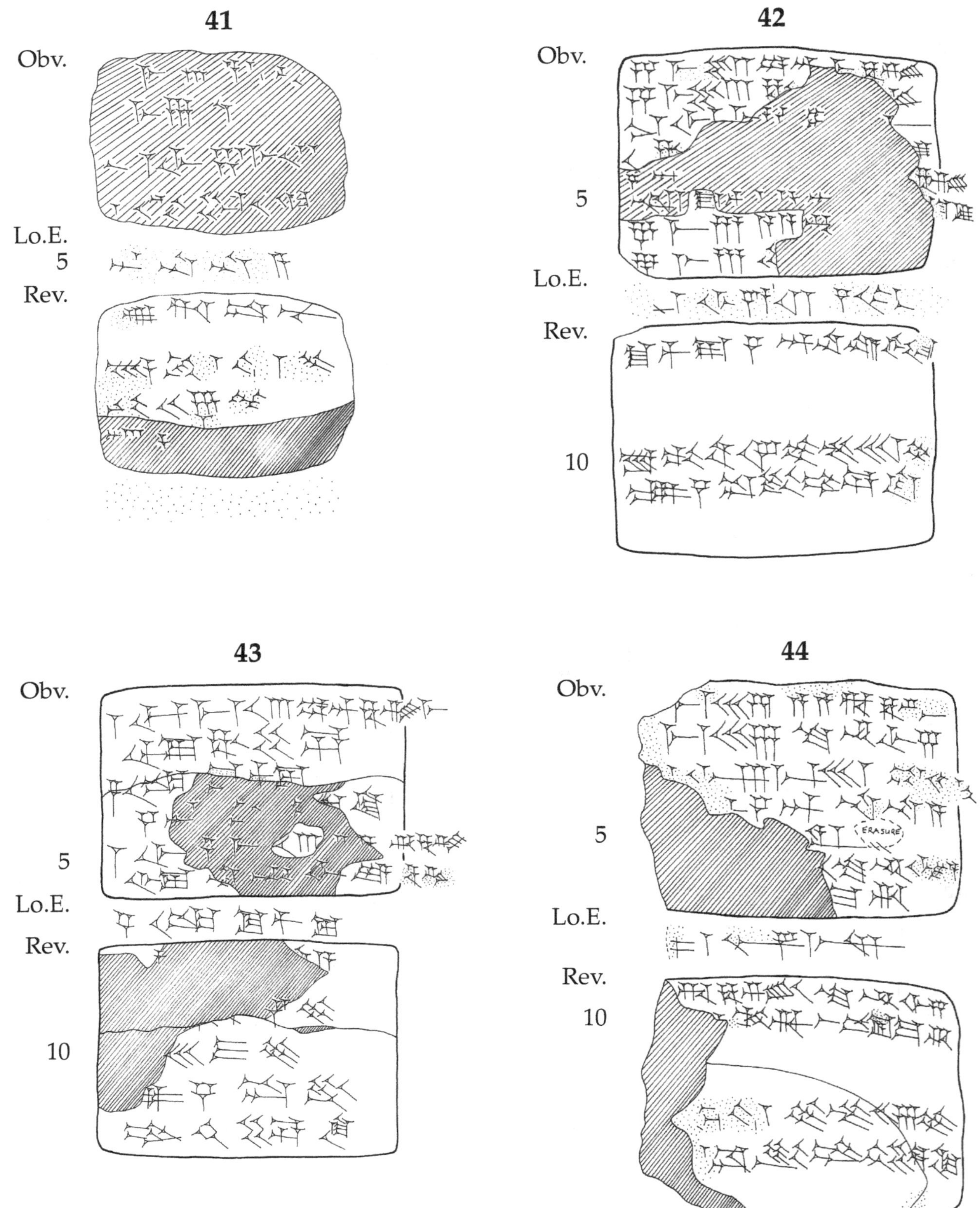
41
Obv.
Lo.E.
5
Rev.
42
Obv.
5
Lo.E.
Rev.
10
43
Obv.
5
Lo.E.
Rev.
10
44
Obv.
5
ERASURE
Lo.E.
Rev.
10

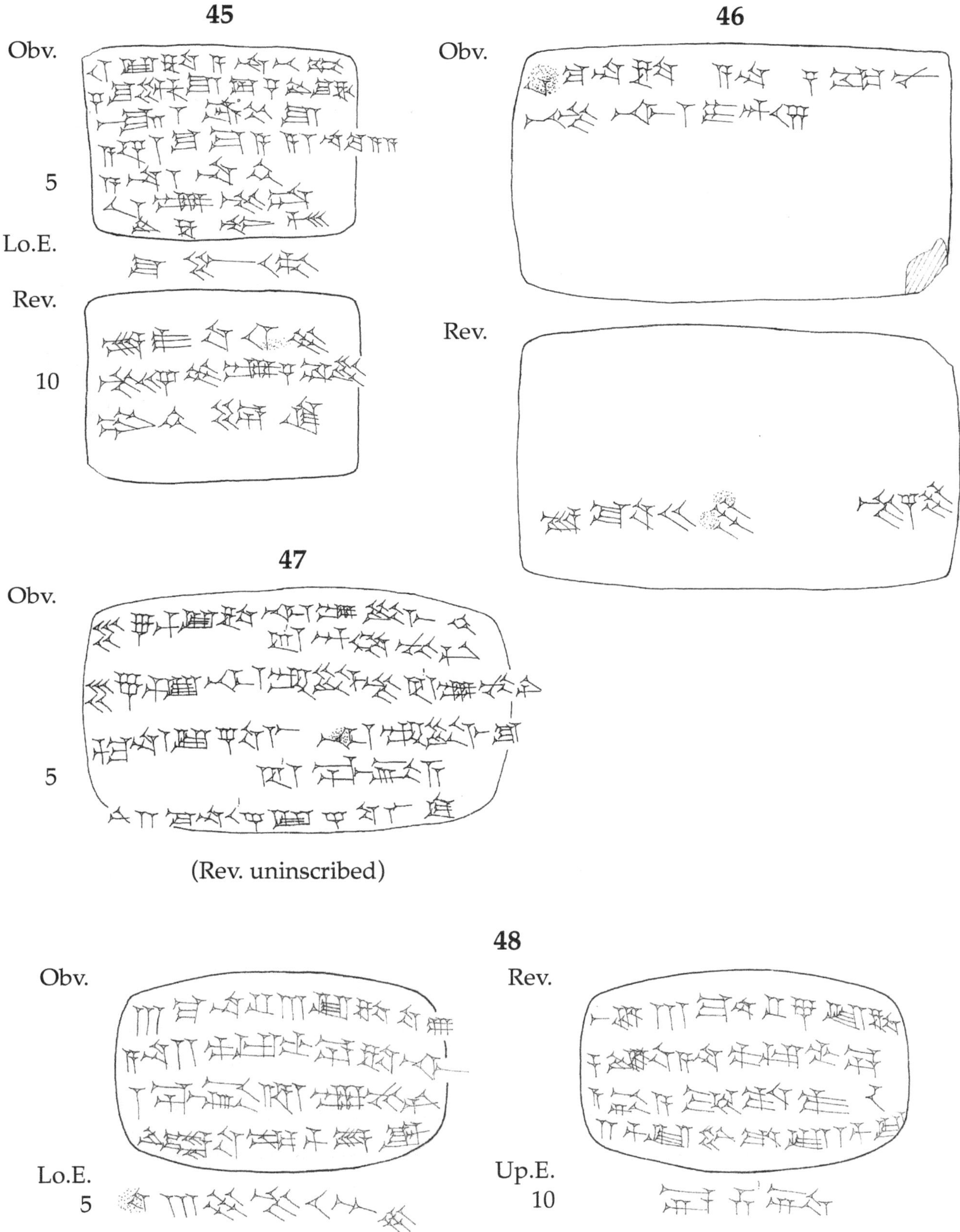
45
Obv.
Lo.E.
Rev.
46
Obv.
Rev.
47
Obv.
(Rev. uninscribed)
48
Obv.
Rev.
Lo.E.
Up.E.

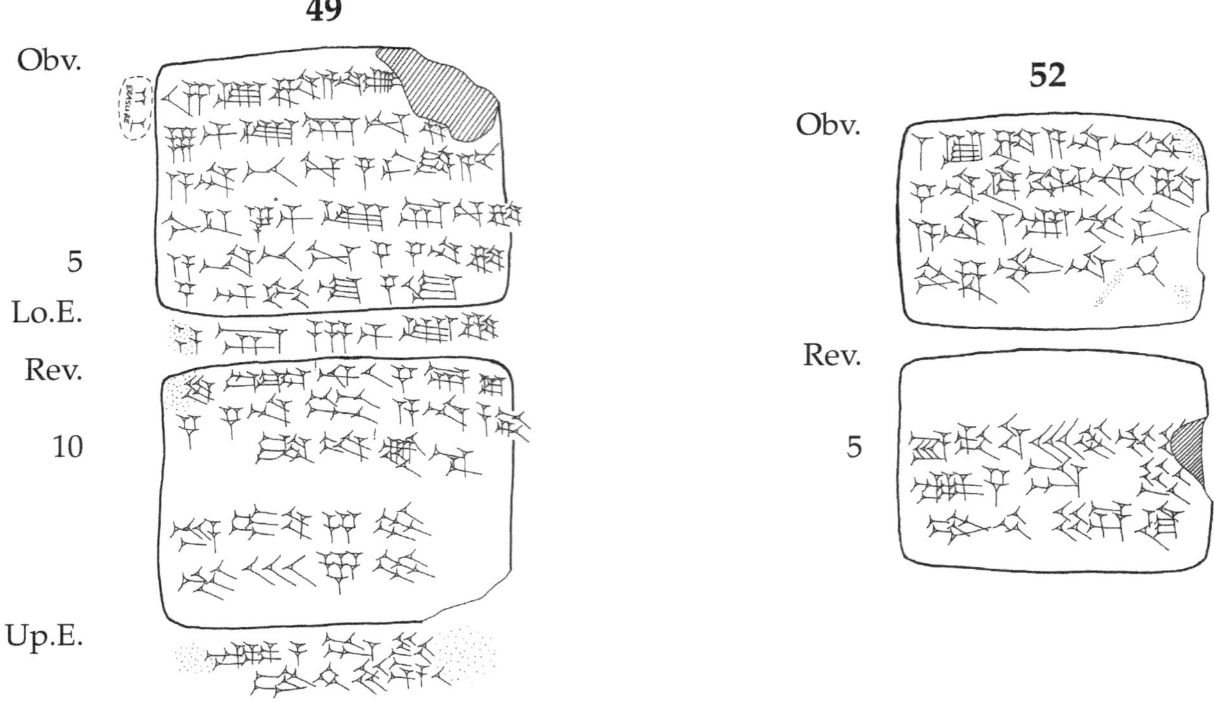
49
Obv.
5
Lo.E.
Rev.
10
Up.E.
52
Obv.
Rev.
5

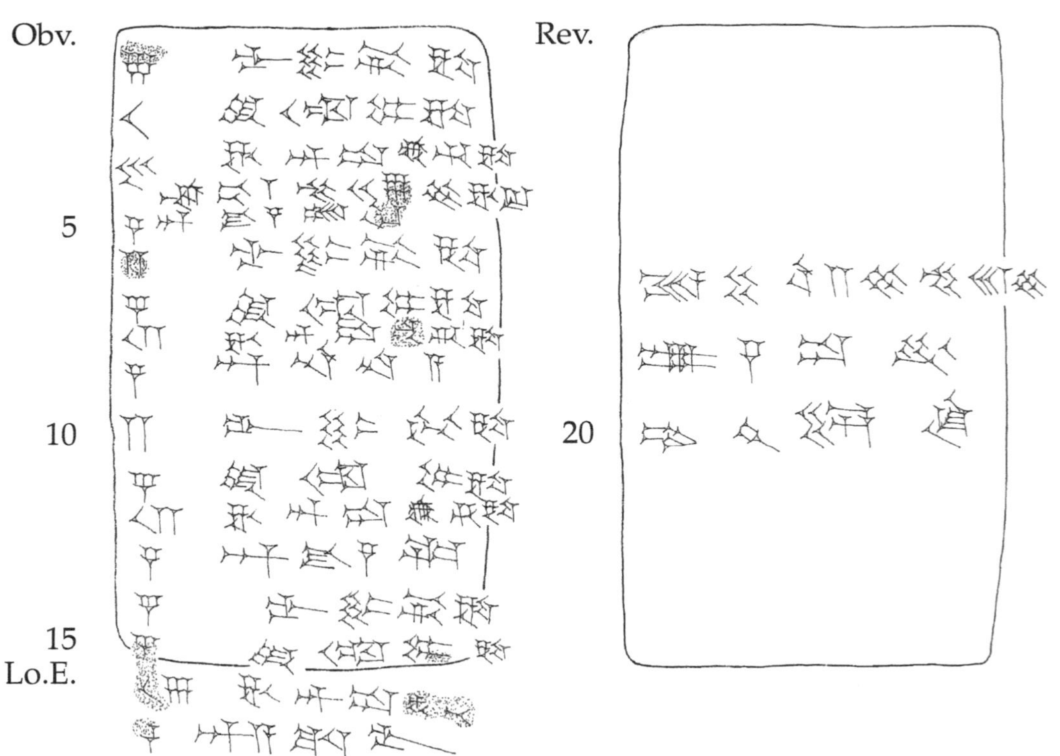
50
Obv.
5
10
15
Lo.E.
Rev.
20

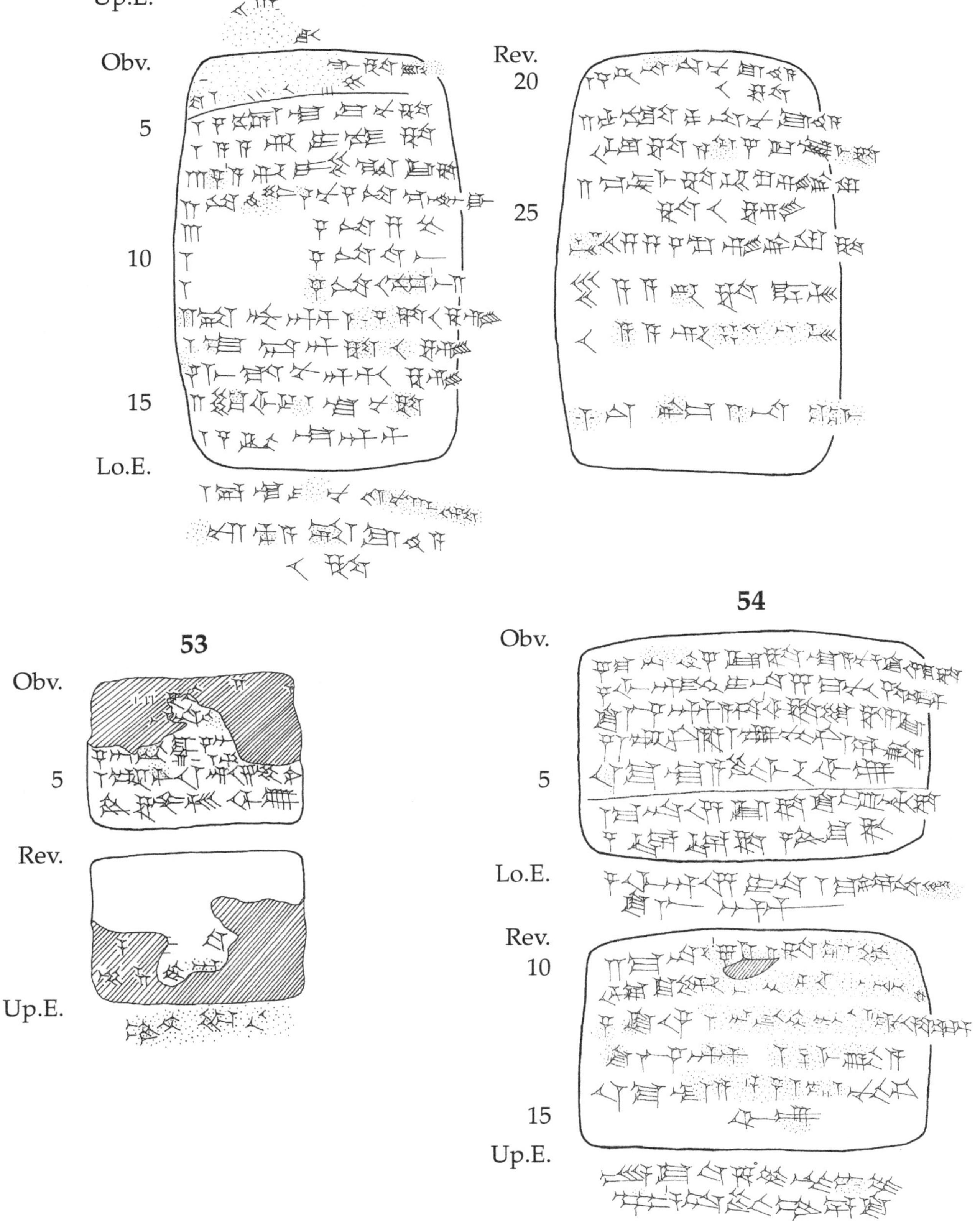
51
Up.E.
Obv.
Lo.E.
Rev.
53
Obv.
Rev.
Up.E.
54
Obv.
Lo.E.
Rev.
Up.E.

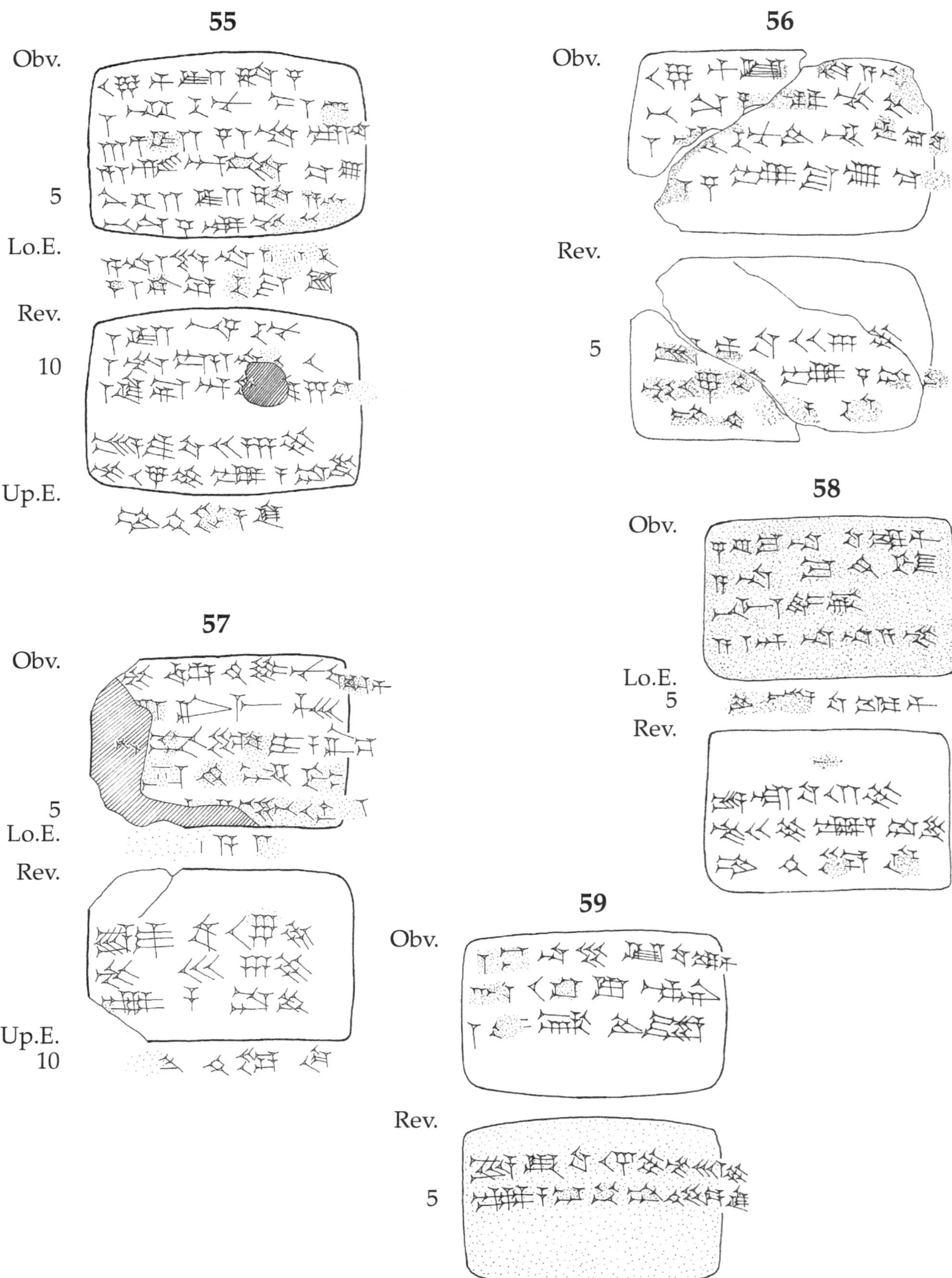
55
Obv.
Lo.E.
Rev.
Up.E.
56
Obv.
Rev.
57
Obv.
Lo.E.
Rev.
Up.E.
58
Obv.
Lo.E.
Rev.
59
Obv.
Rev.

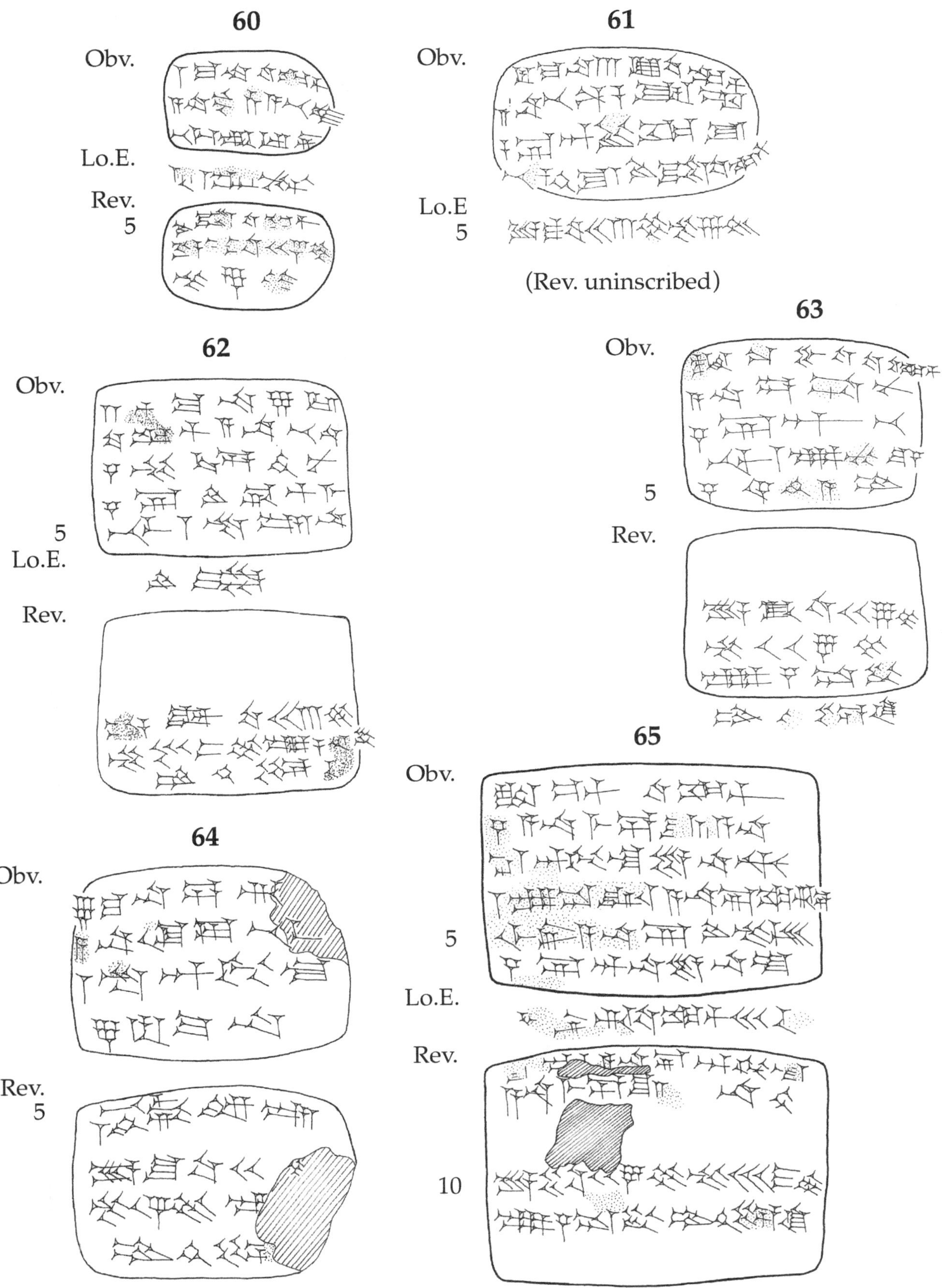
60
Obv.
Lo.E.
Rev.
5
61
Obv.
Lo.E
5
(Rev. uninscribed)
62
Obv.
5
Lo.E.
Rev.
63
Obv.
5
Rev.
64
Obv.
Rev.
5
65
Obv.
5
Lo.E.
Rev.
10

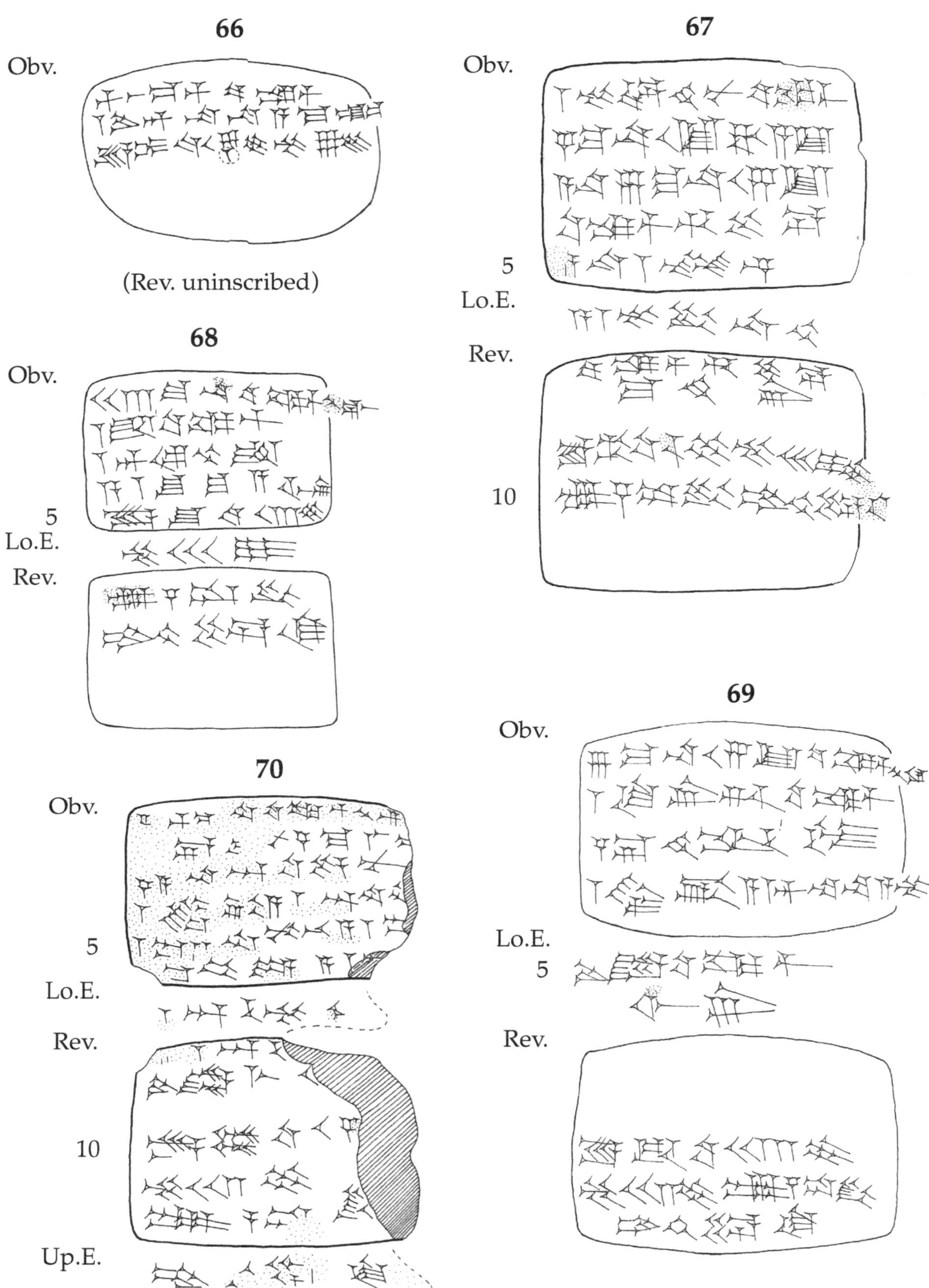
66
Obv.
(Rev. uninscribed)
67
Obv.
5
Lo.E.
Rev.
10
68
Obv.
5
Lo.E.
Rev.
69
Obv.
Lo.E.
5
Rev.
70
Obv.
5
Lo.E.
Rev.
10
Up.E.

71

Obv.

5

Lo.E.

10

Rev.

15

Up.E.

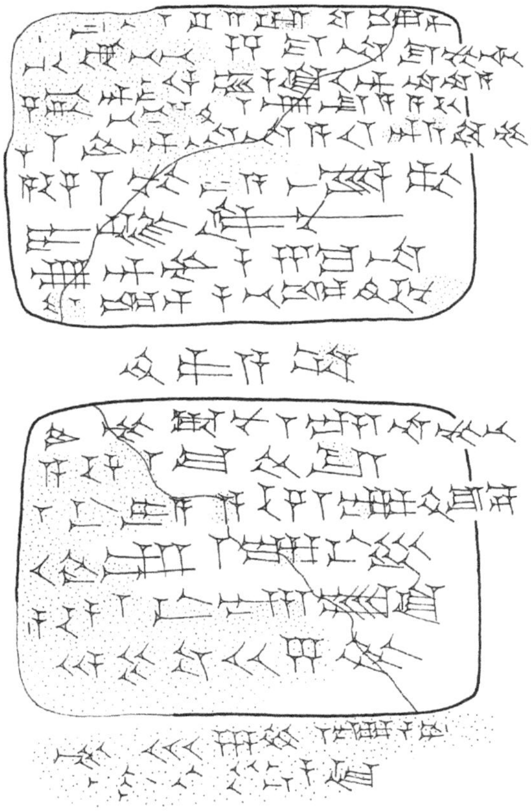

72

Obv.

Rev.

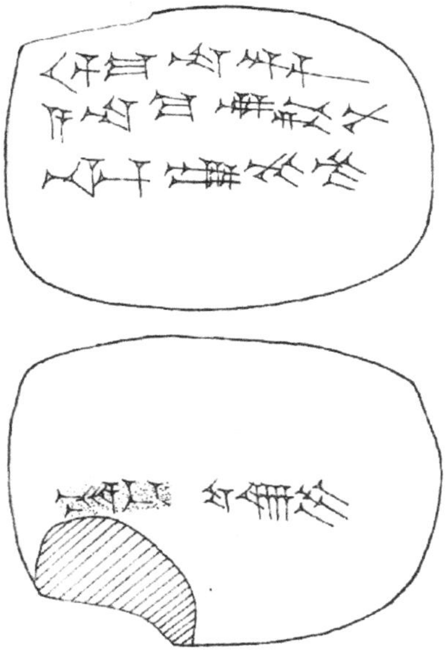

73

Obv.

Lo.E.

Rev.

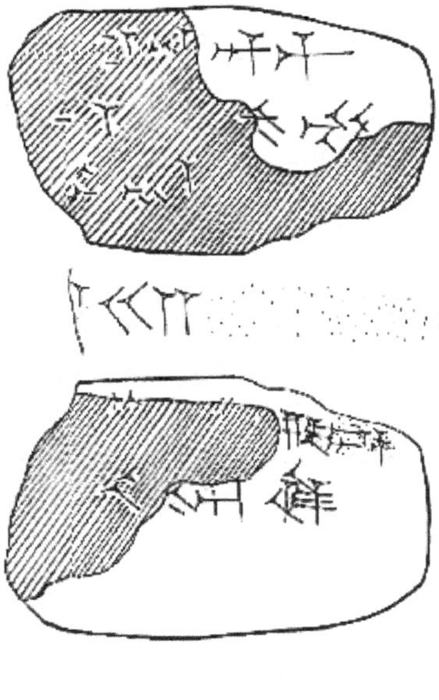

5

74

Obv.

Lo.E.

5

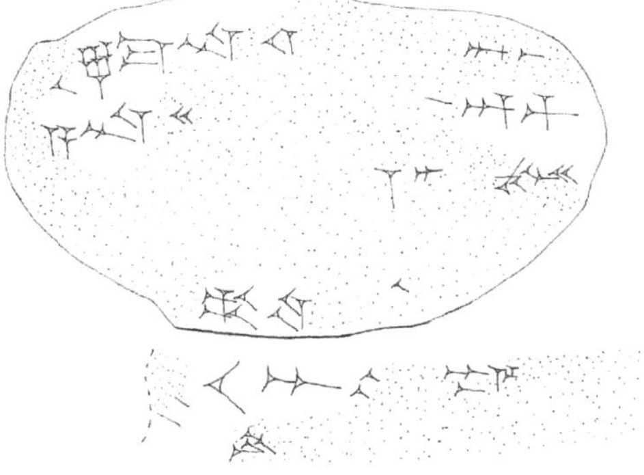

(Rev. uninscribed)

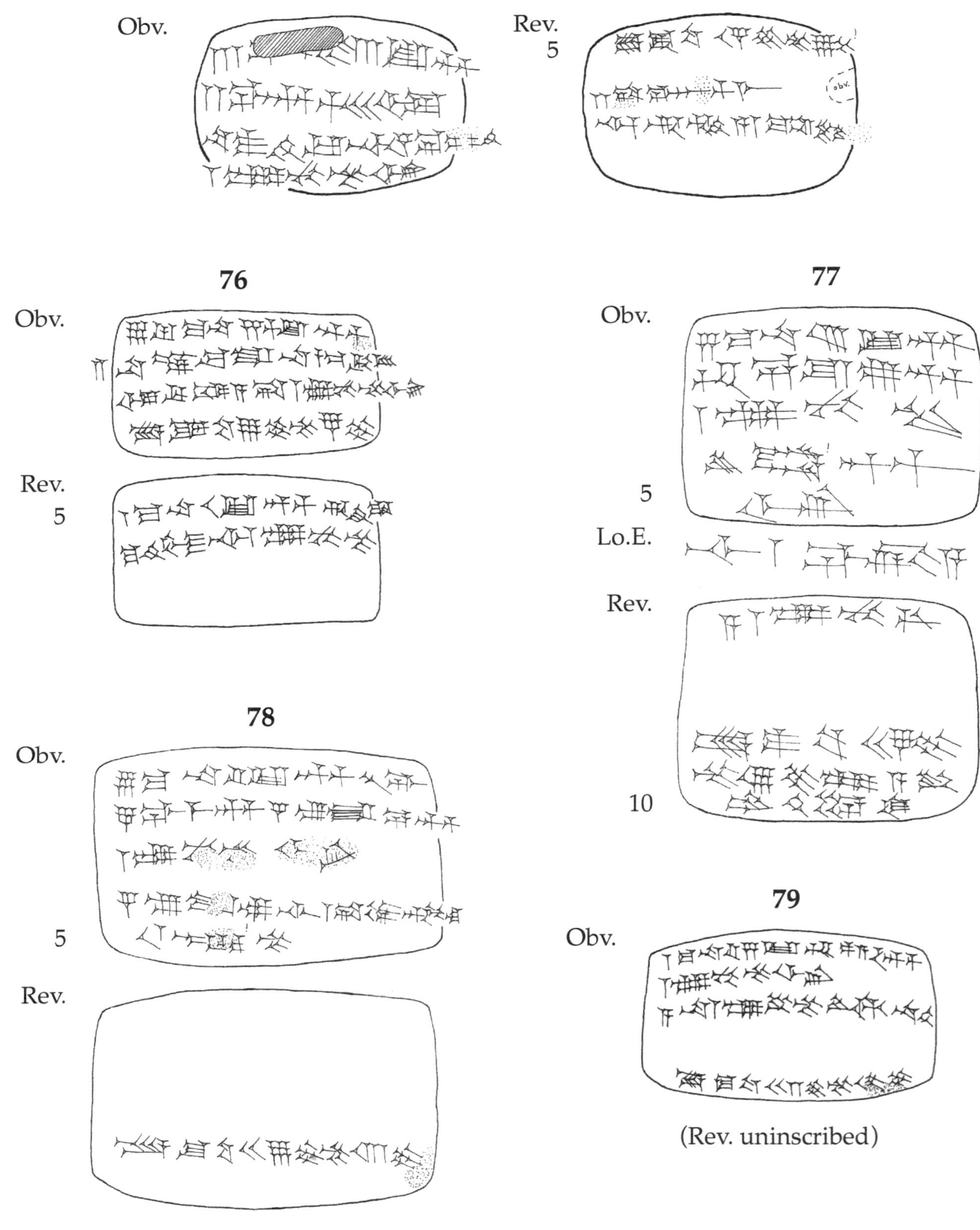
75
Obv.
Rev.
76
Obv.
Rev.
77
Obv.
Lo.E.
Rev.
78
Obv.
Rev.
79
Obv.
(Rev. uninscribed)

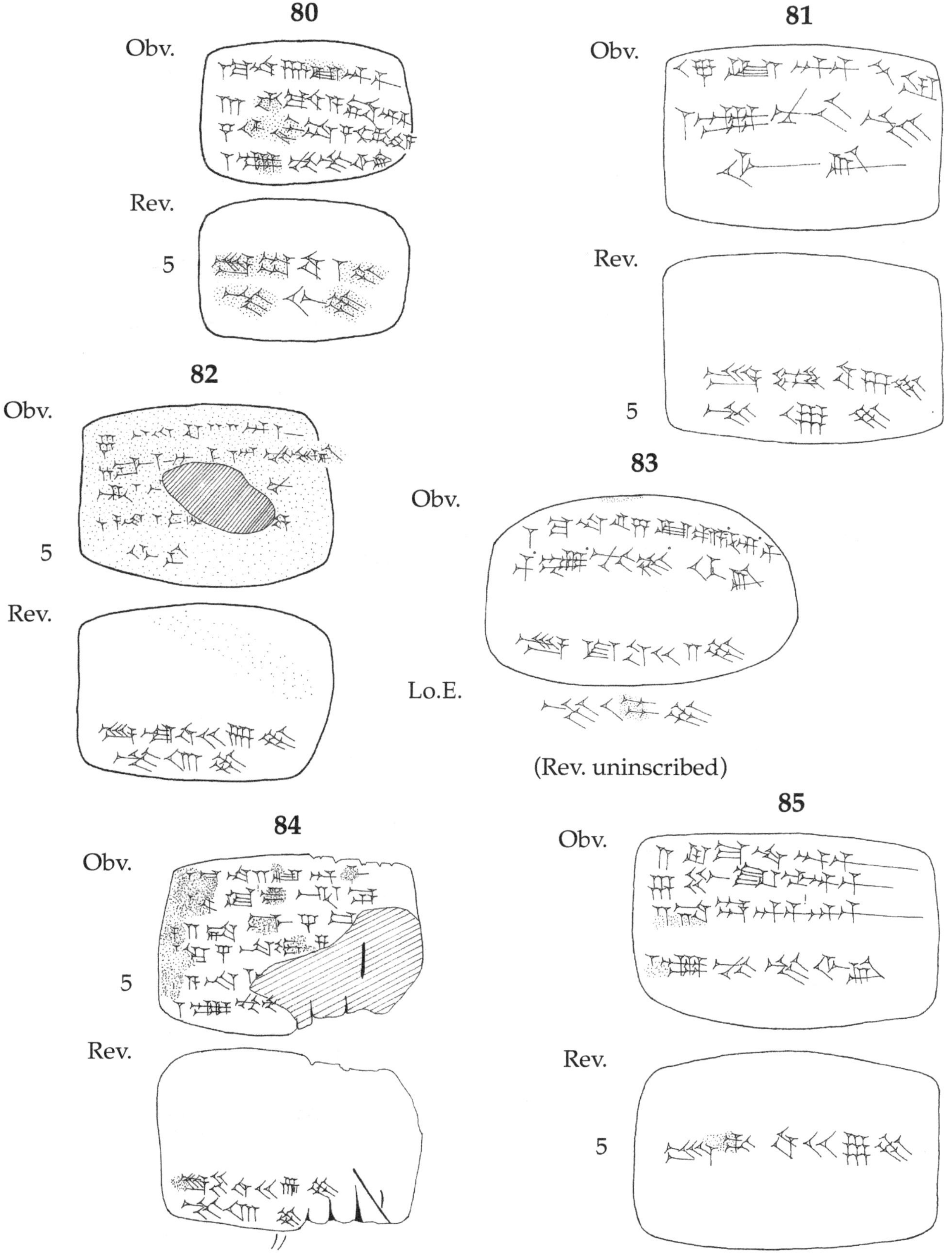
80
Obv.
Rev.
81
Obv.
Rev.
82
Obv.
Rev.
83
Obv.
Lo.E.
(Rev. uninscribed)
84
Obv.
Rev.
85
Obv.
Rev.

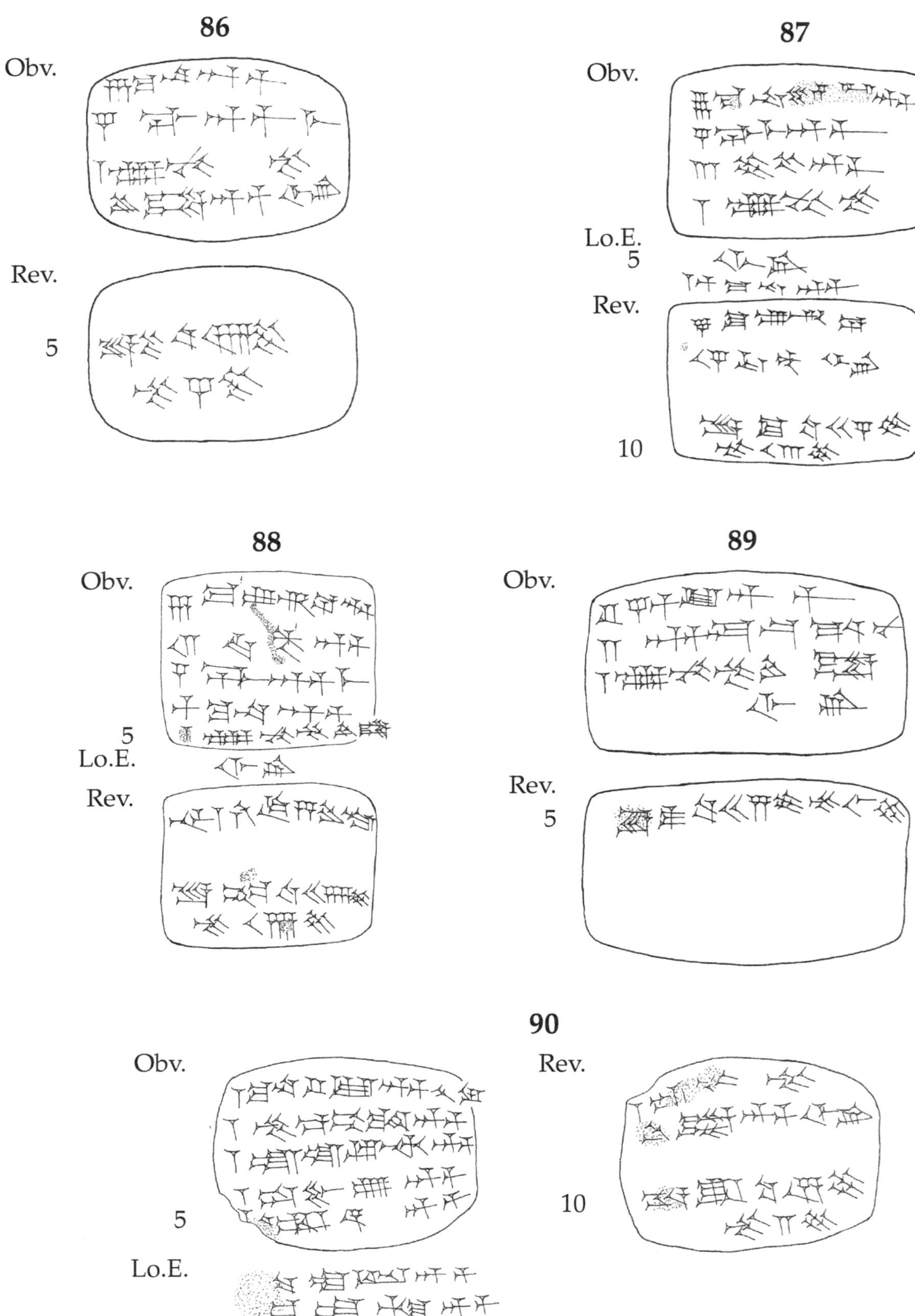
86
Obv.
Rev.
87
Obv.
Lo.E.
Rev.
88
Obv.
Lo.E.
Rev.
89
Obv.
Rev.
90
Obv.
Rev.
Lo.E.

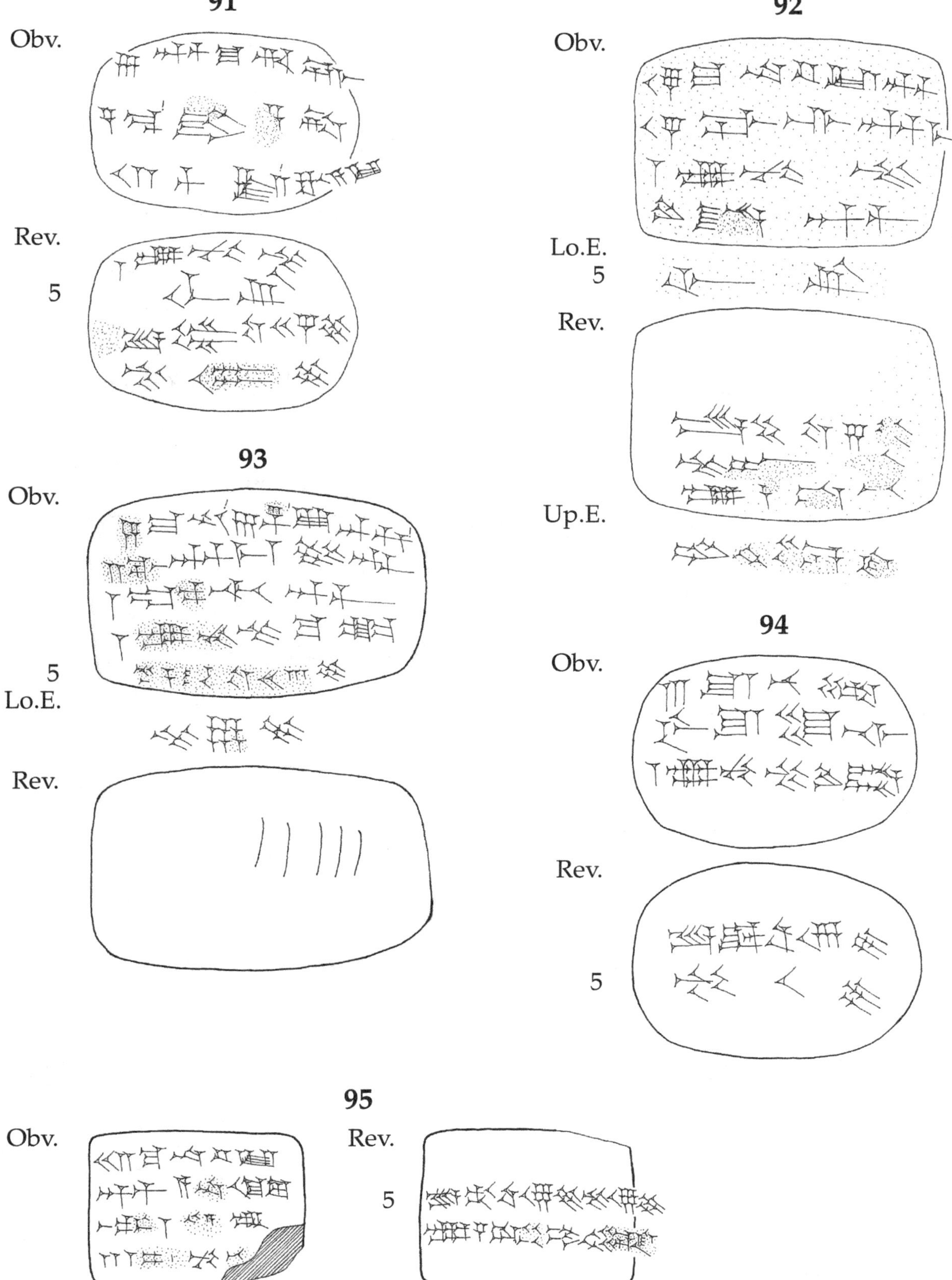
91
Obv.
Rev.
92
Obv.
Lo.E.
Rev.
Up.E.
93
Obv.
Lo.E.
Rev.
94
Obv.
Rev.
95
Obv.
Rev.

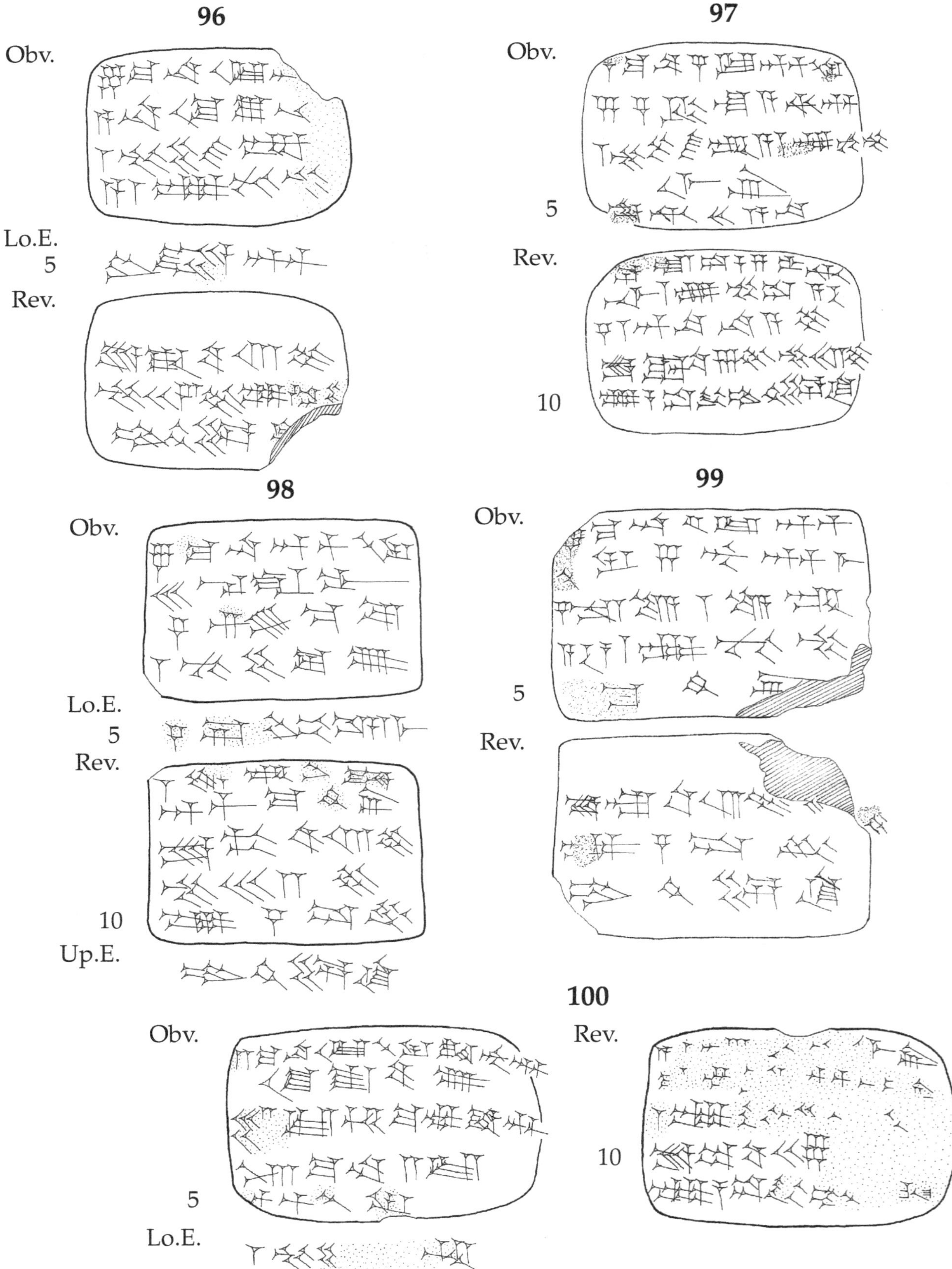
96
Obv.
Lo.E.
Rev.
97
Obv.
Rev.
98
Obv.
Lo.E.
Rev.
Up.E.
99
Obv.
Rev.
100
Obv.
Lo.E.
Rev.

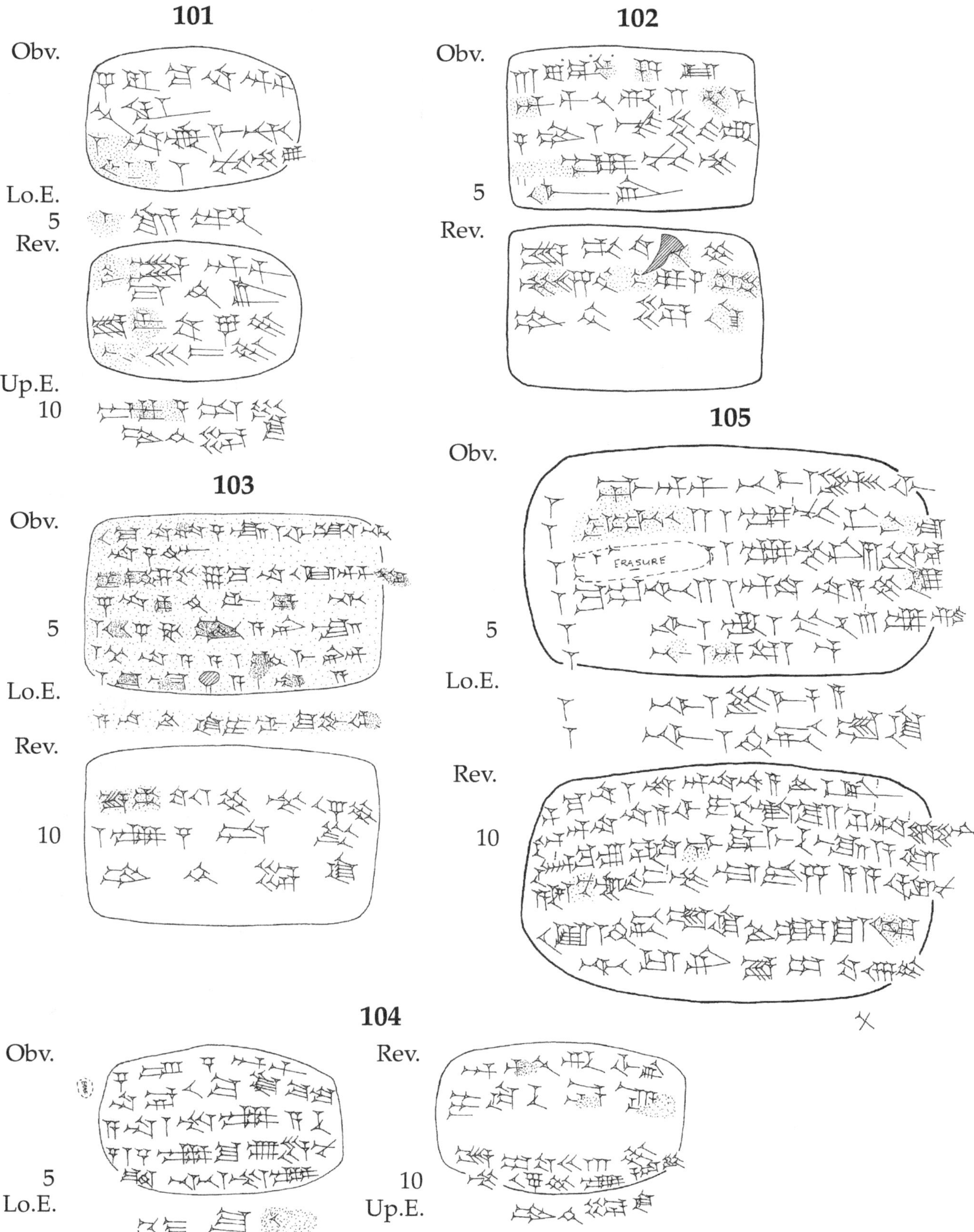
101
Obv.
Lo.E.
Rev.
Up.E.
102
Obv.
Rev.
103
Obv.
Lo.E.
Rev.
105
Obv.
ERASURE
Lo.E.
Rev.
104
Obv.
Lo.E.
Rev.
Up.E.

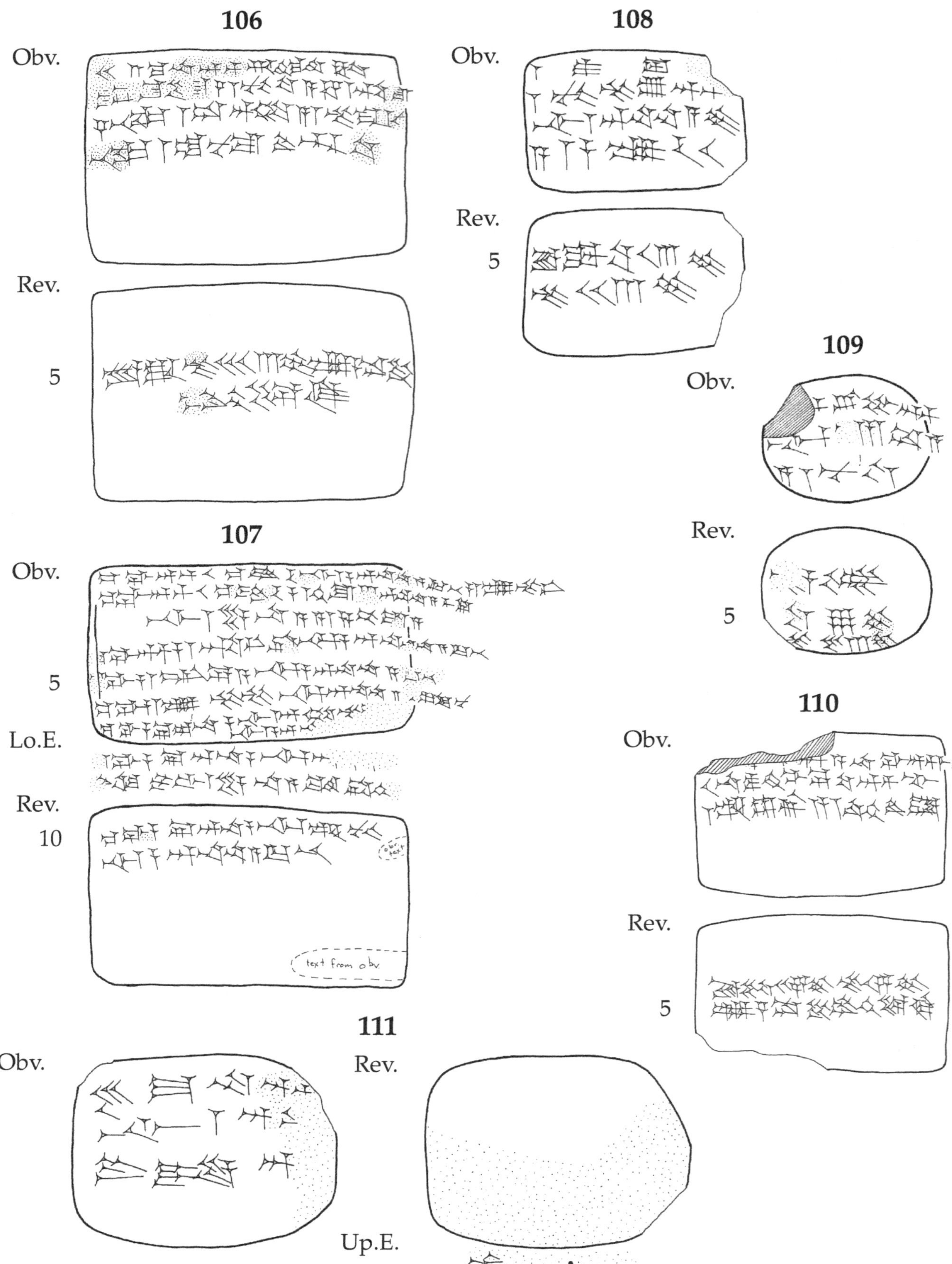
106
Obv.
Rev.
5
108
Obv.
Rev.
5
109
Obv.
Rev.
5
107
Obv.
5
Lo.E.
Rev.
10
text from obv.
110
Obv.
Rev.
5
111
Obv.
Rev.
Up.E.

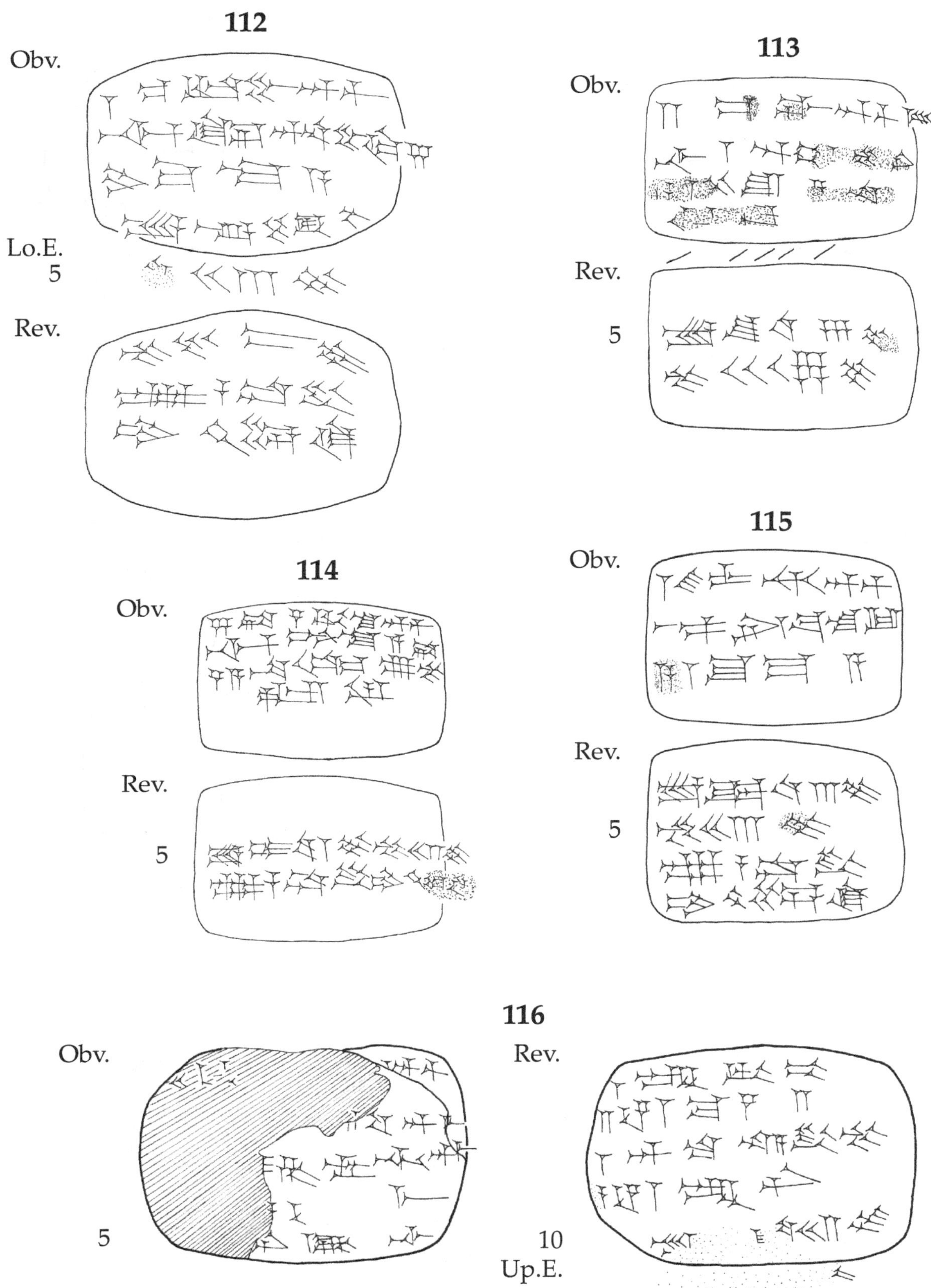
112
Obv.
Lo.E.
Rev.
113
Obv.
Rev.
114
Obv.
Rev.
115
Obv.
Rev.
116
Obv.
Rev.
Up.E.

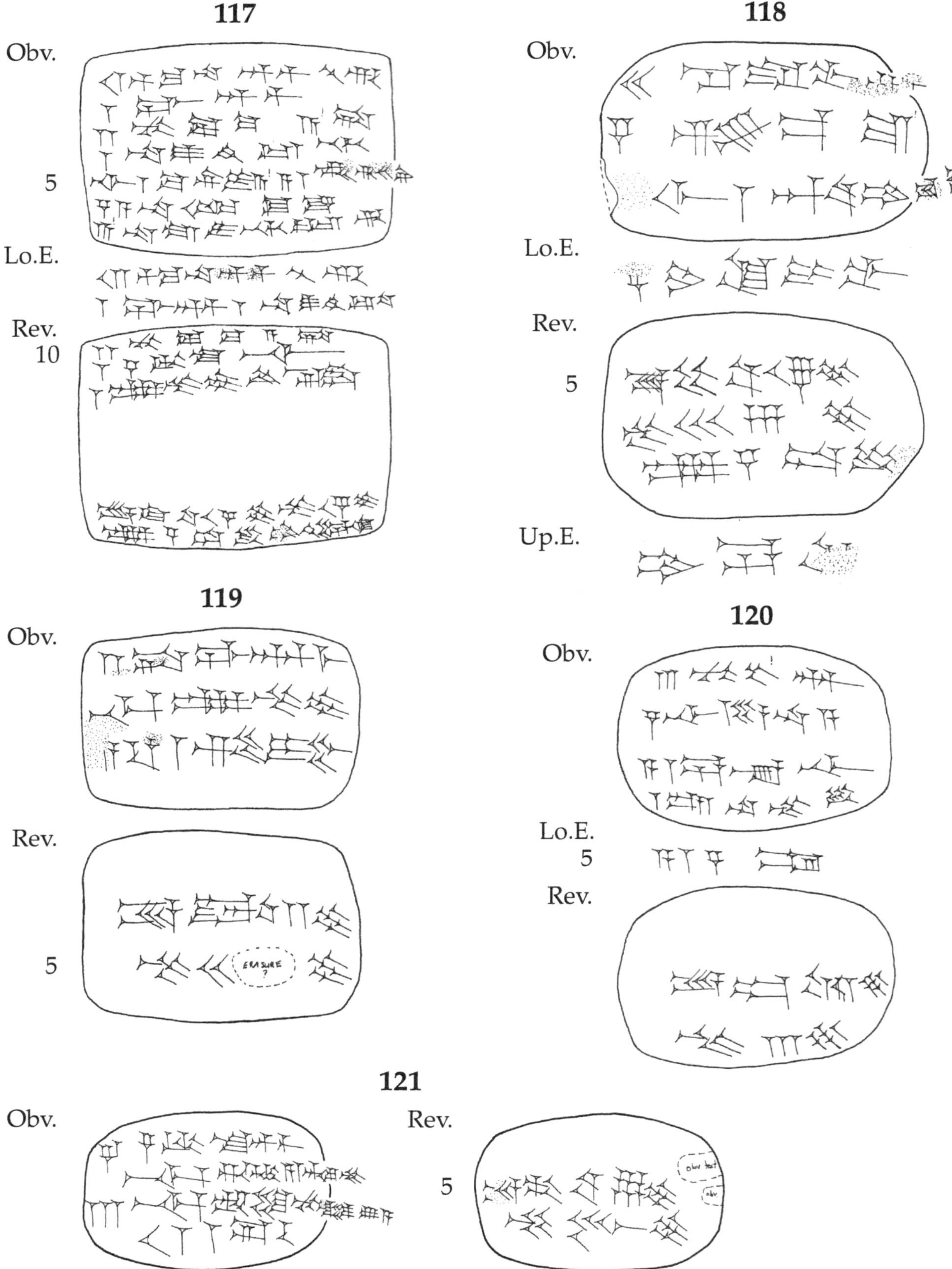
117
Obv.
5
Lo.E.
Rev.
10
118
Obv.
Lo.E.
Rev.
5
Up.E.
119
Obv.
Rev.
5
ERASURE ?
120
Obv.
Lo.E.
5
Rev.
121
Obv.
Rev.
5
obv. text
obv.

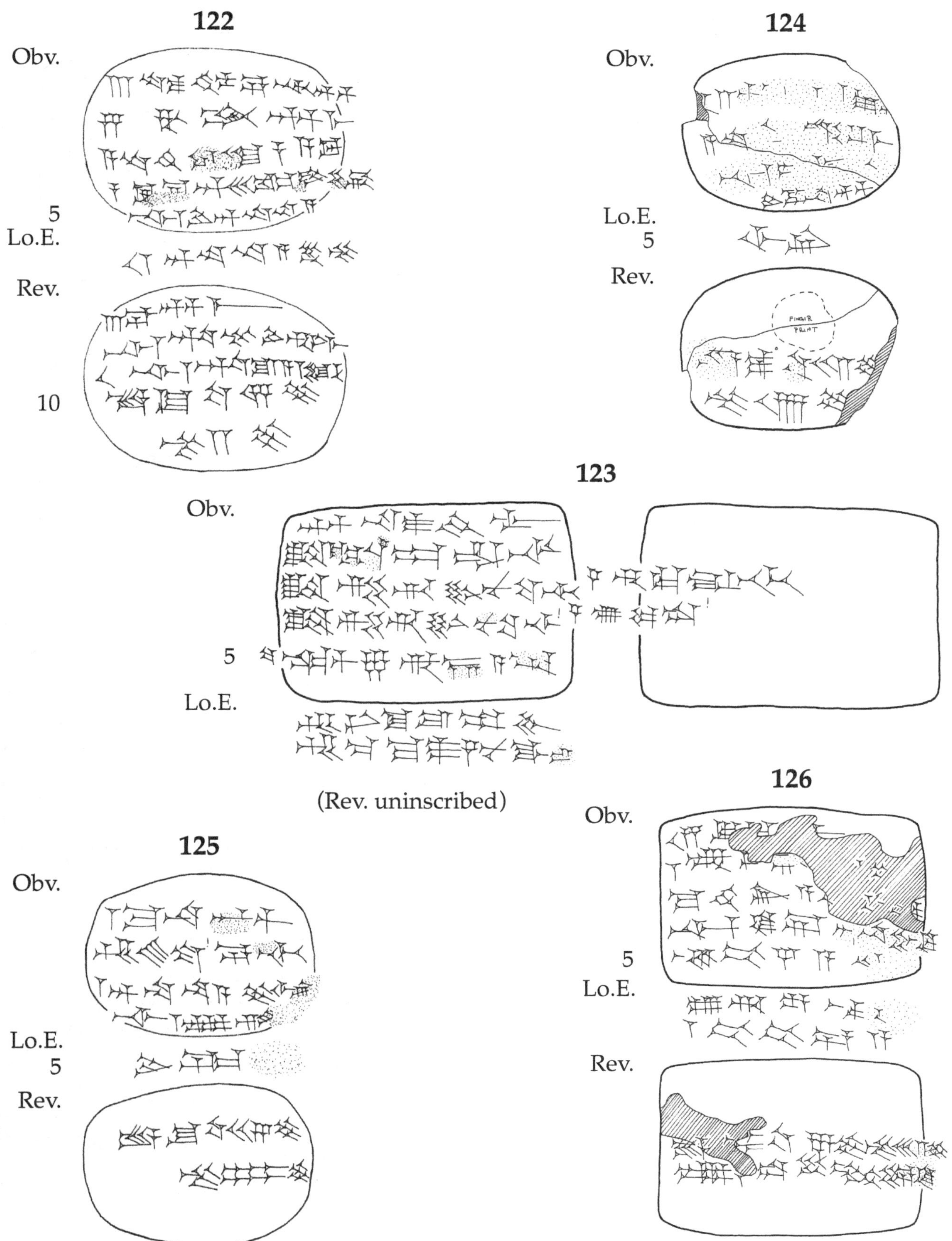
122
Obv.
5
Lo.E.
Rev.
10
124
Obv.
Lo.E.
5
Rev.
123
Obv.
5
Lo.E.
(Rev. uninscribed)
125
Obv.
Lo.E.
5
Rev.
126
Obv.
5
Lo.E.
Rev.

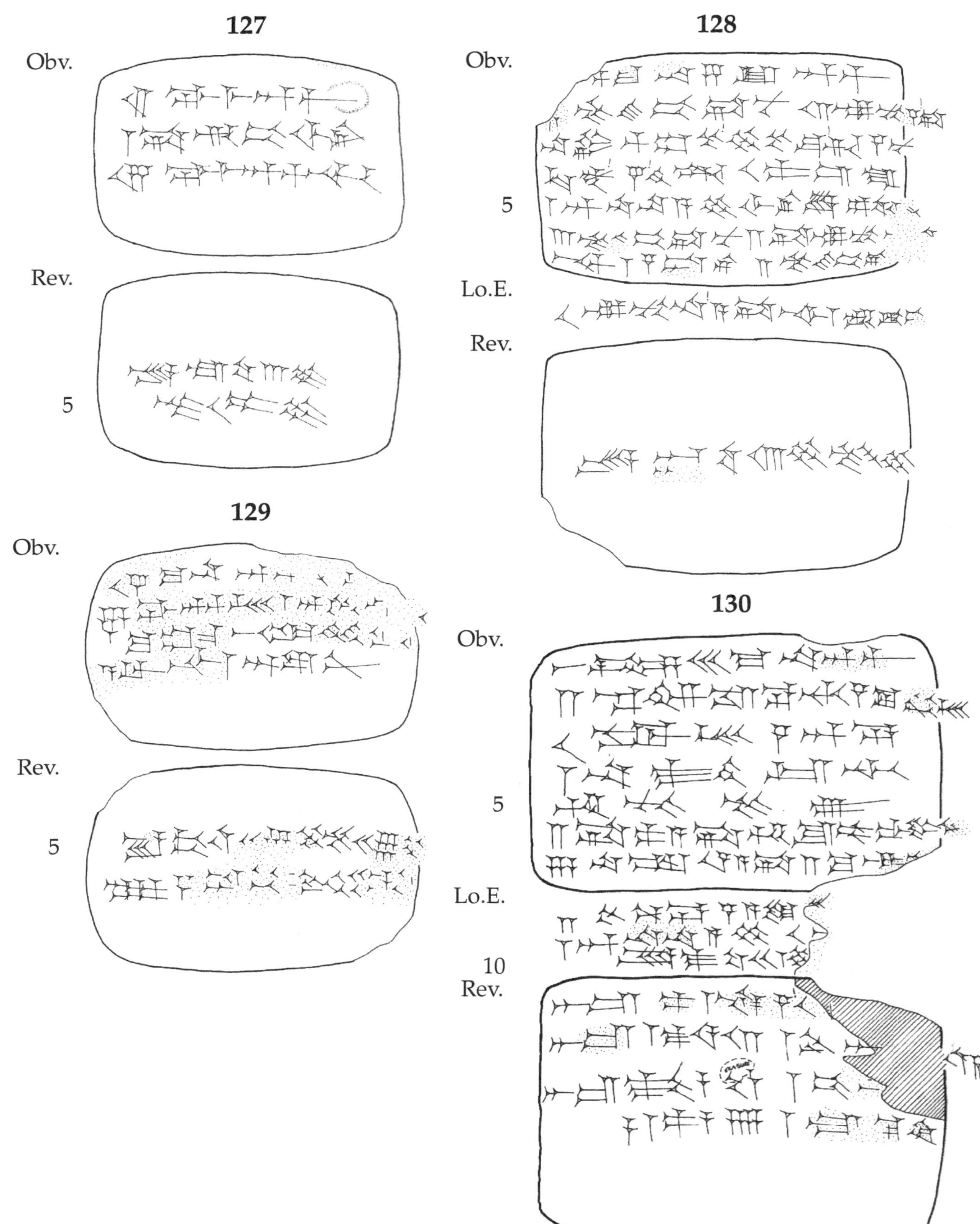
127
Obv.
Rev.
128
Obv.
Lo.E.
Rev.
129
Obv.
Rev.
130
Obv.
Lo.E.
Rev.

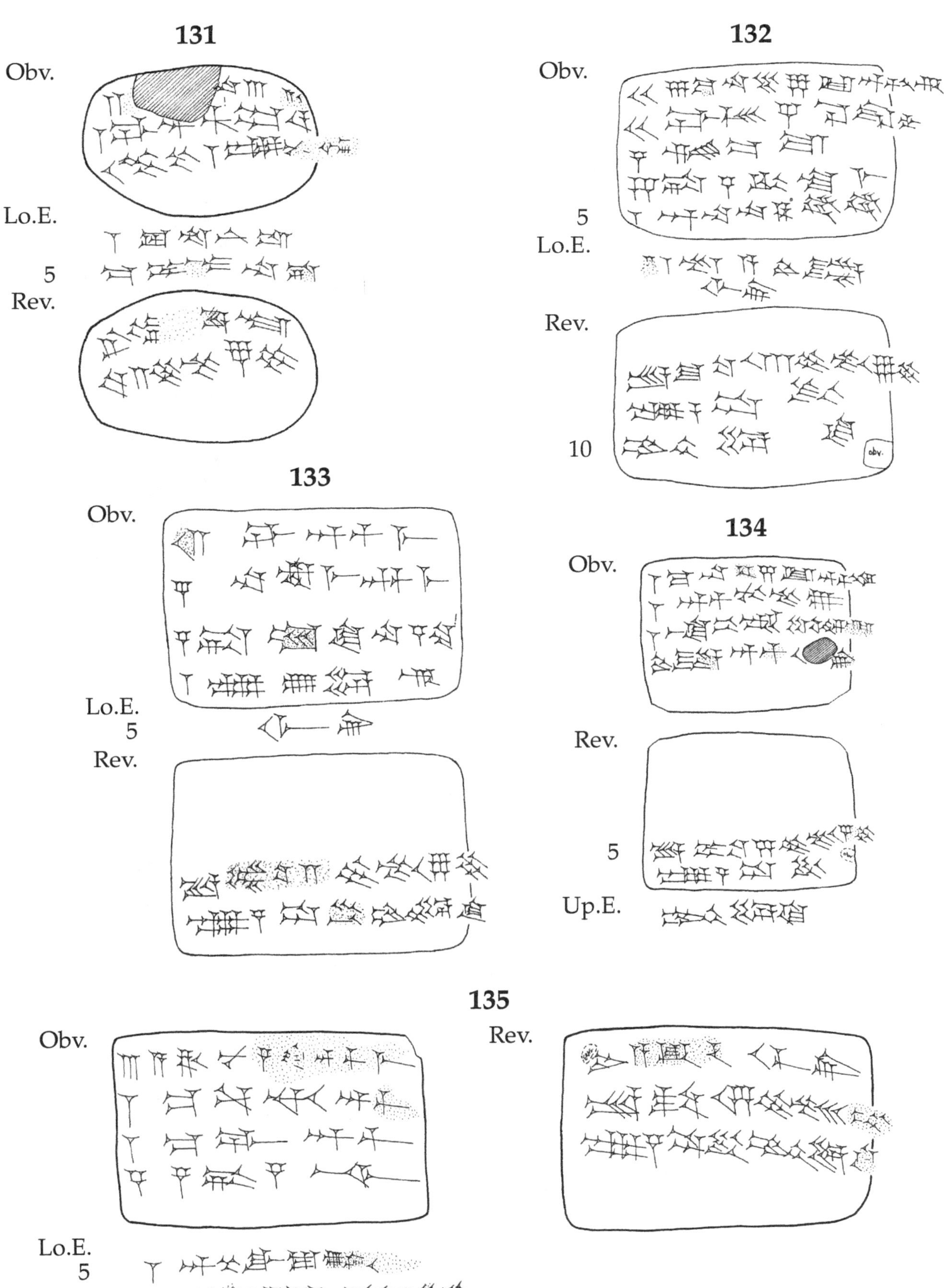
131
Obv.
Lo.E.
5
Rev.
132
Obv.
5
Lo.E.
Rev.
10
obv.
133
Obv.
Lo.E.
5
Rev.
134
Obv.
Rev.
5
Up.E.
135
Obv.
Rev.
Lo.E.
5

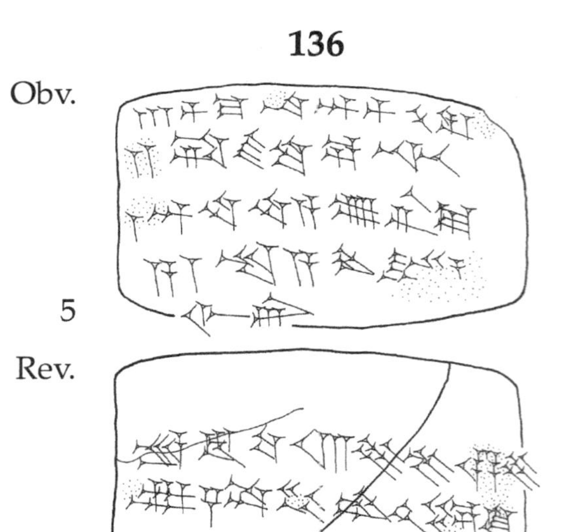
136
Obv.
Rev.

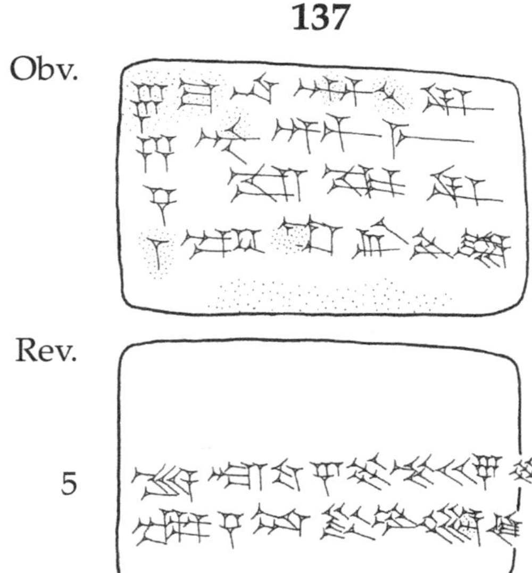
137
Obv.
Rev.

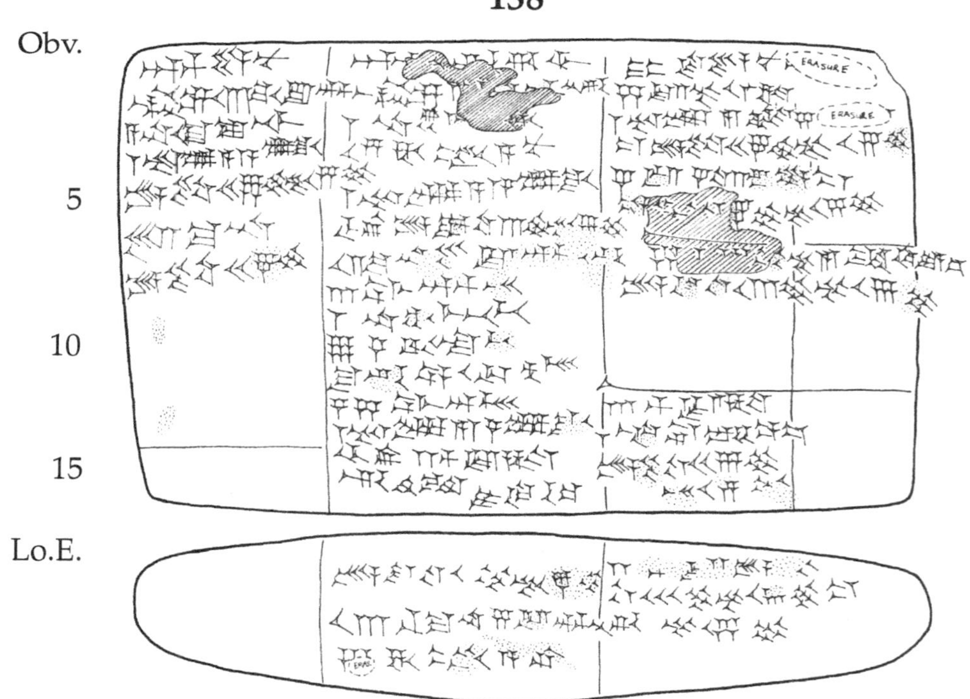
138
Obv.
ERASURE
ERASURE
Lo.E.

139

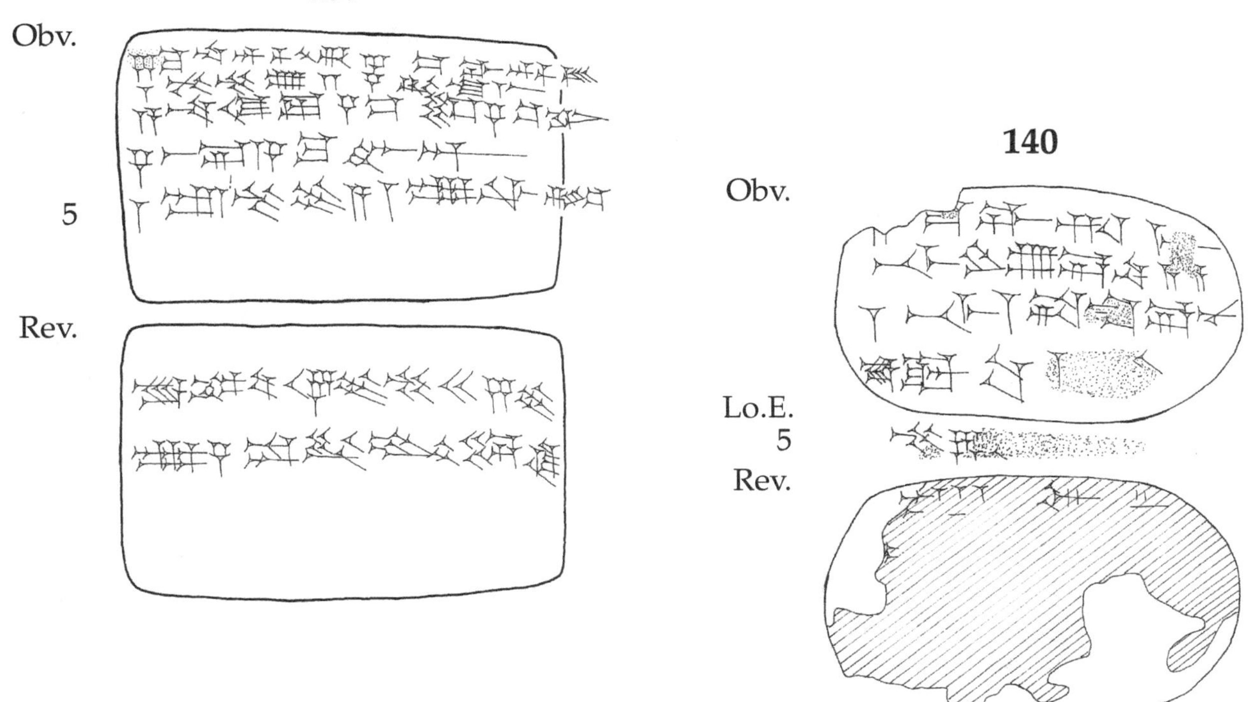

138

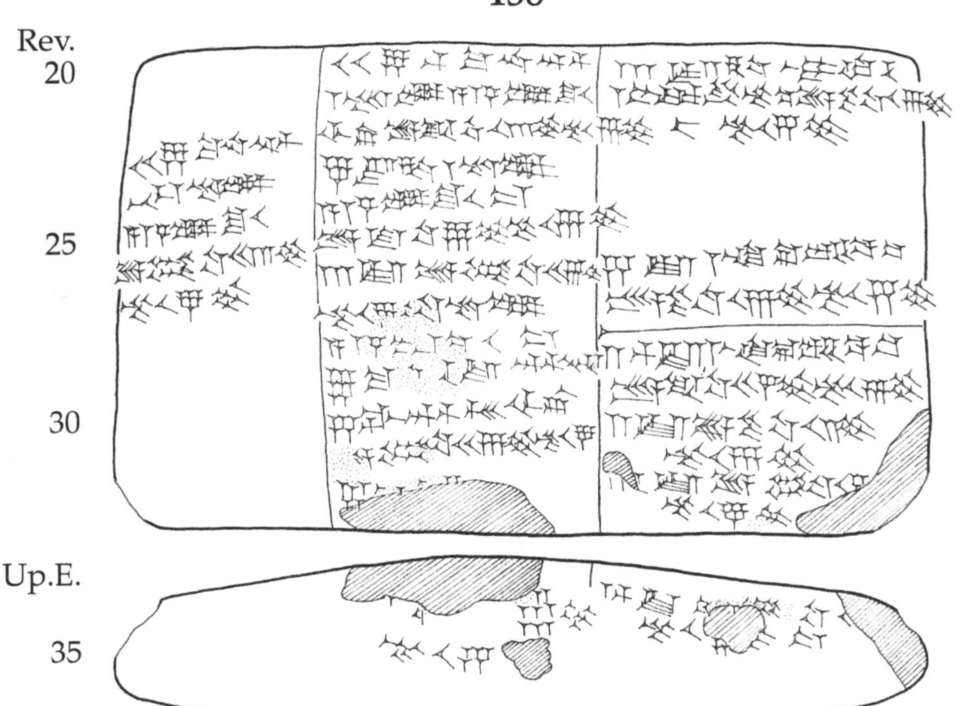

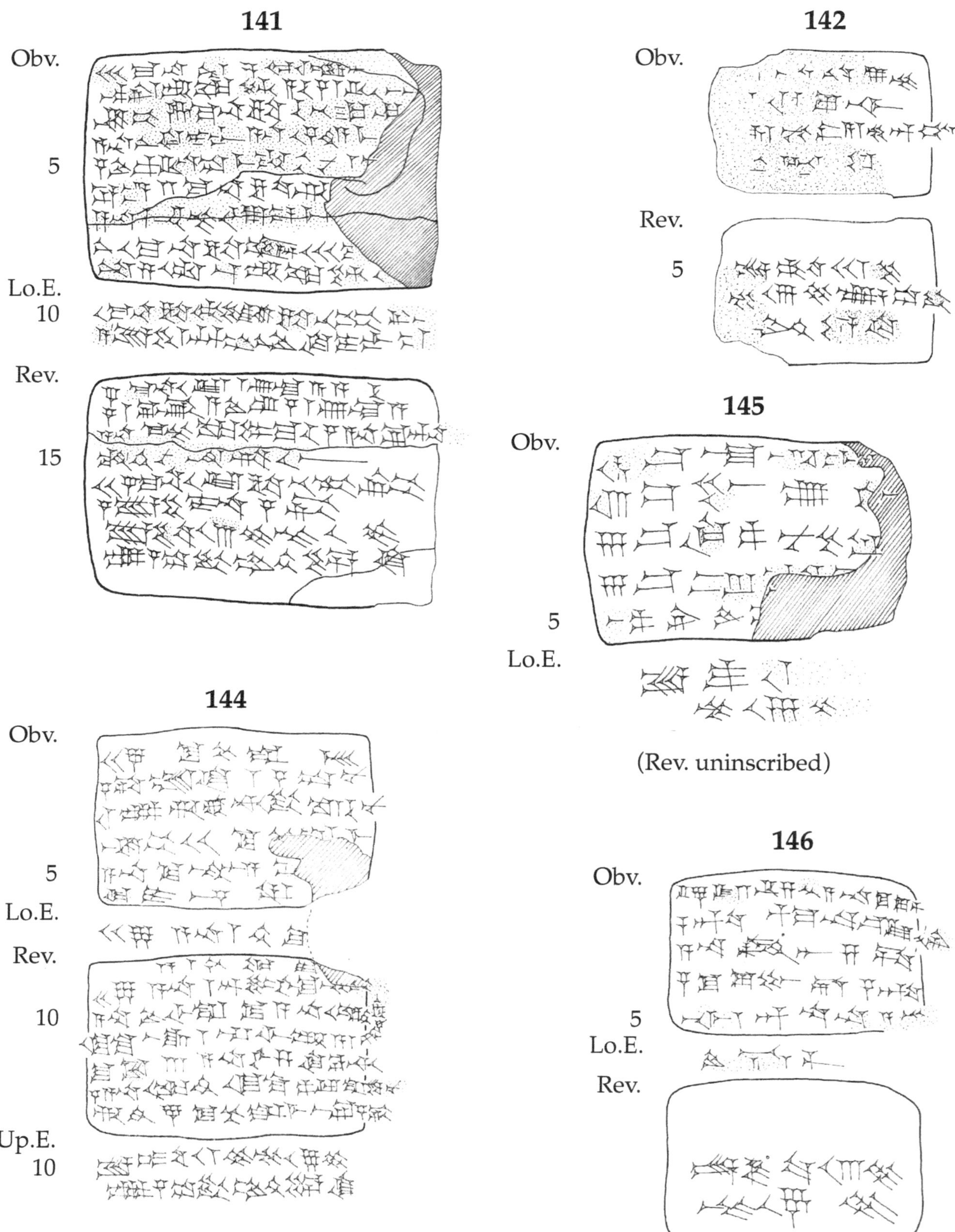
141
Obv.
Lo.E.
Rev.
142
Obv.
Rev.
145
Obv.
Lo.E.
(Rev. uninscribed)
144
Obv.
Lo.E.
Rev.
Up.E.
146
Obv.
Lo.E.
Rev.

143

Obv.

(Rev. uninscribed)

148

Obv.

Lo.E.

Rev.

147

Obv.

Rev.

150

Obv.

Lo.E.

Rev.

Up.E.

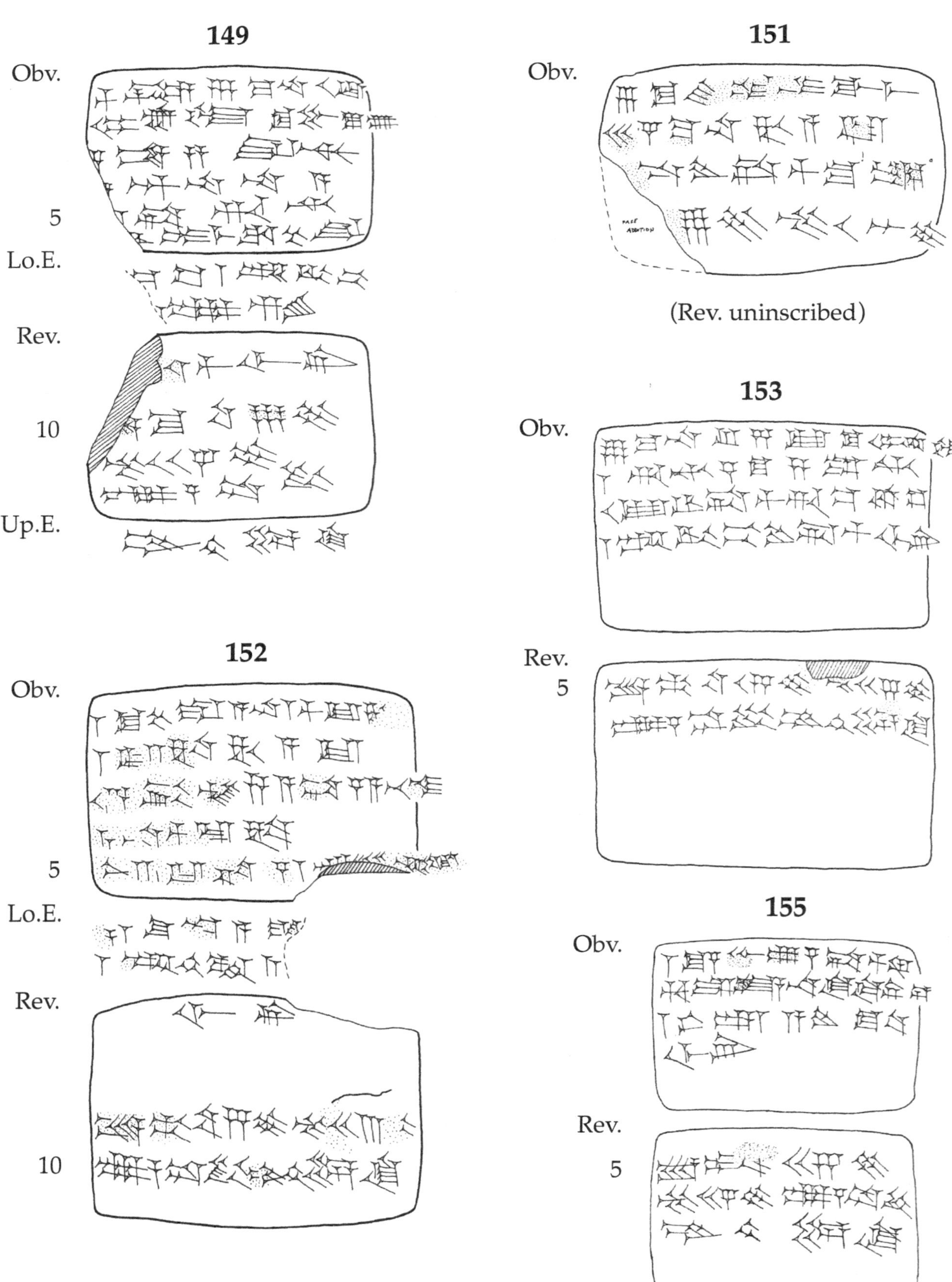
149
Obv.
Lo.E.
Rev.
Up.E.
151
Obv.
(Rev. uninscribed)
153
Obv.
Rev.
152
Obv.
Lo.E.
Rev.
155
Obv.
Rev.

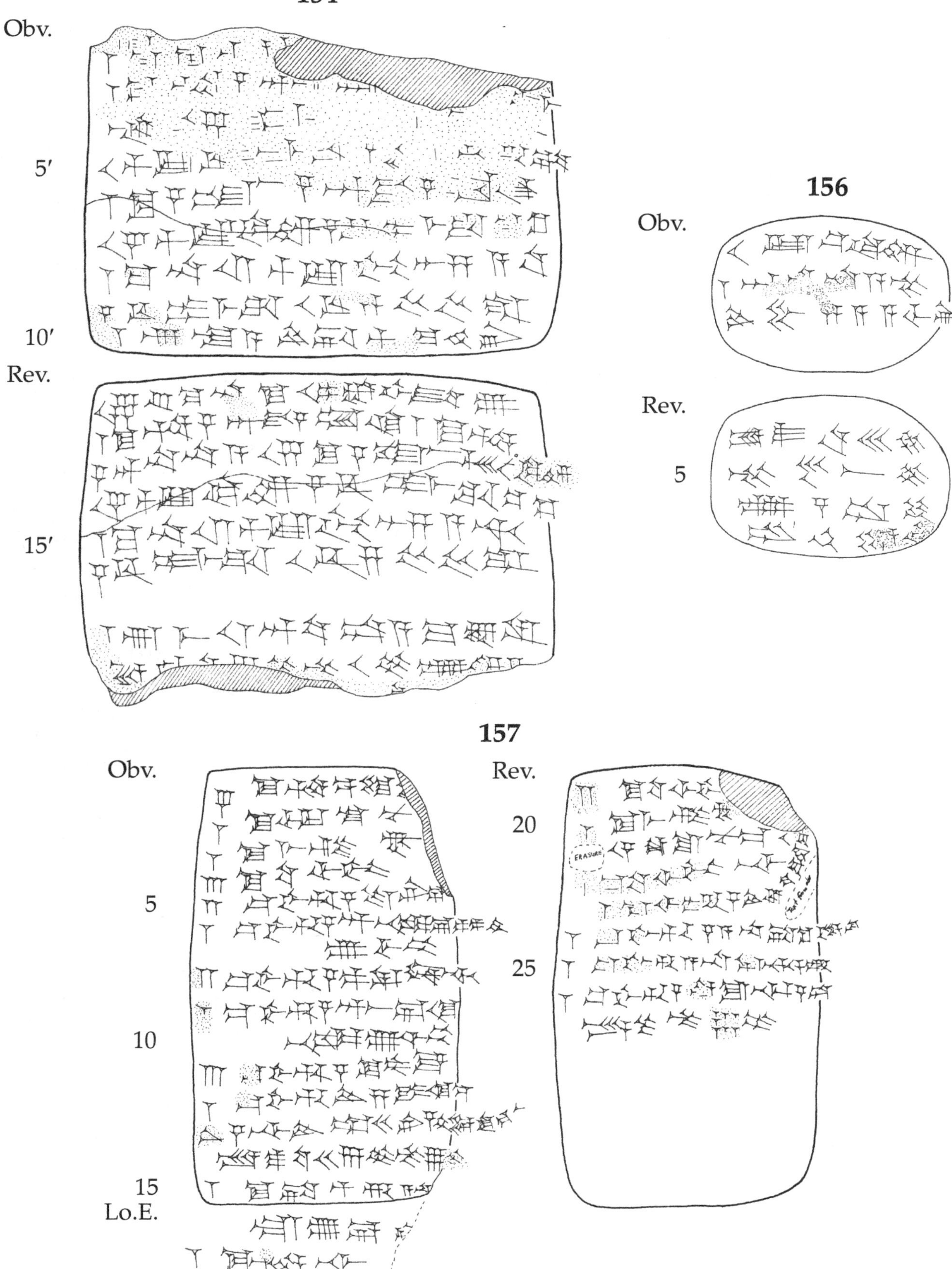
154
Obv.
5′
10′
Rev.
15′
156
Obv.
Rev.
5
157
Obv.
5
10
15
Lo.E.
Rev.
20
25
ERASURE

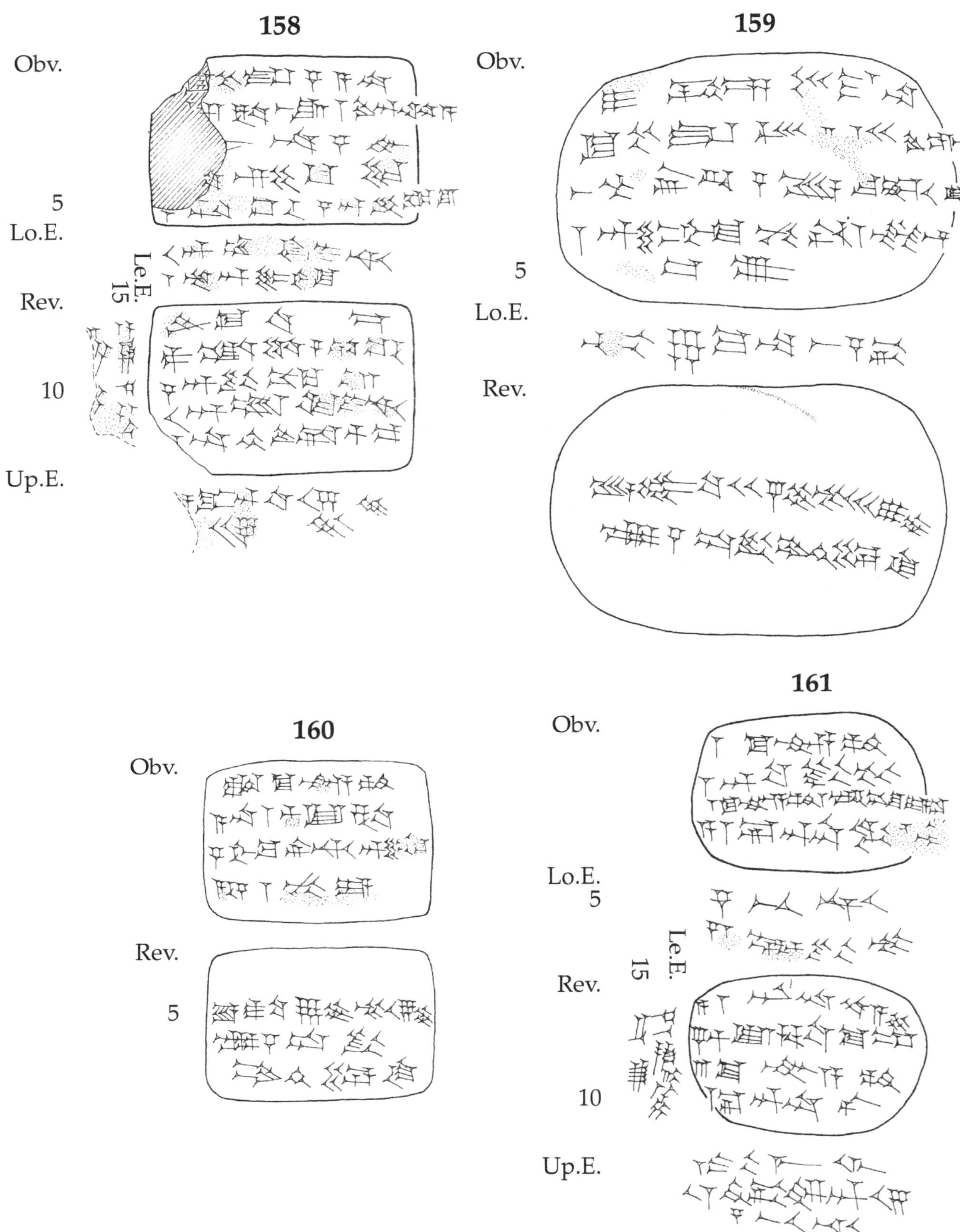
158
Obv.
Lo.E.
Le.E.
Rev.
Up.E.
159
Obv.
Lo.E.
Rev.
160
Obv.
Rev.
161
Obv.
Lo.E.
Le.E.
Rev.
Up.E.

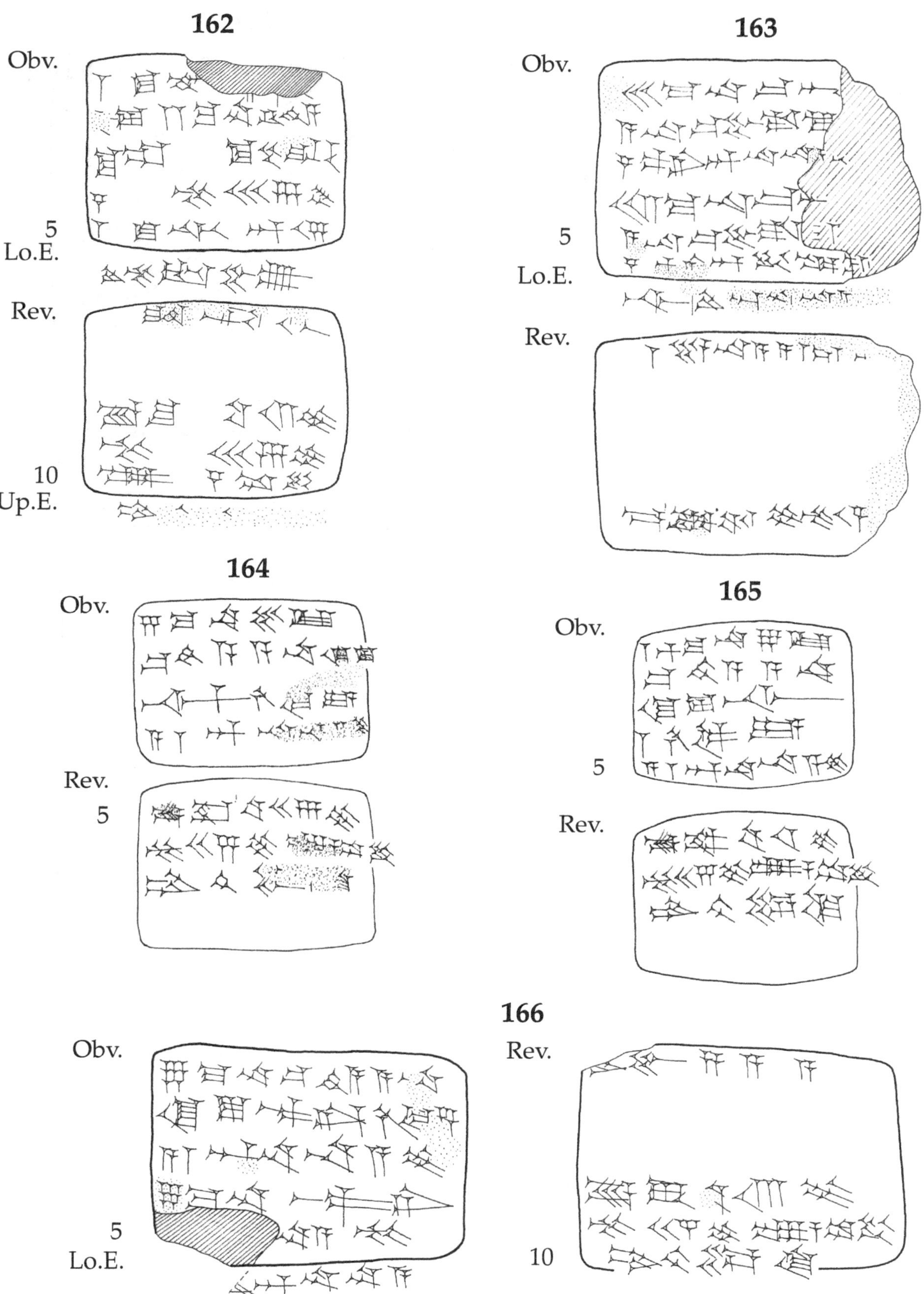
162
Obv.
Lo.E.
Rev.
Up.E.
163
Obv.
Lo.E.
Rev.
164
Obv.
Rev.
165
Obv.
Rev.
166
Obv.
Lo.E.
Rev.

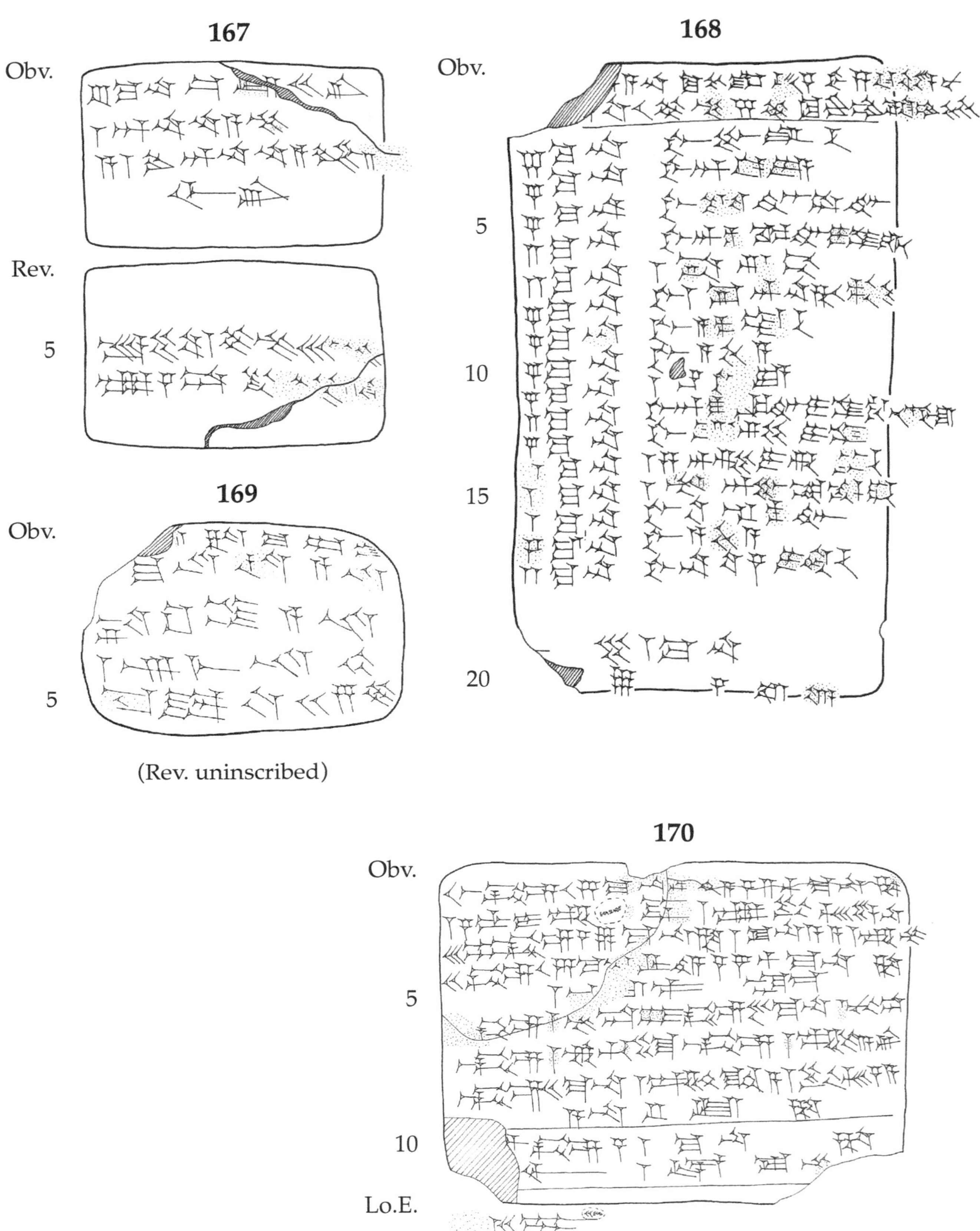
167
Obv.
Rev.
168
Obv.
169
Obv.
(Rev. uninscribed)
170
Obv.
Lo.E.

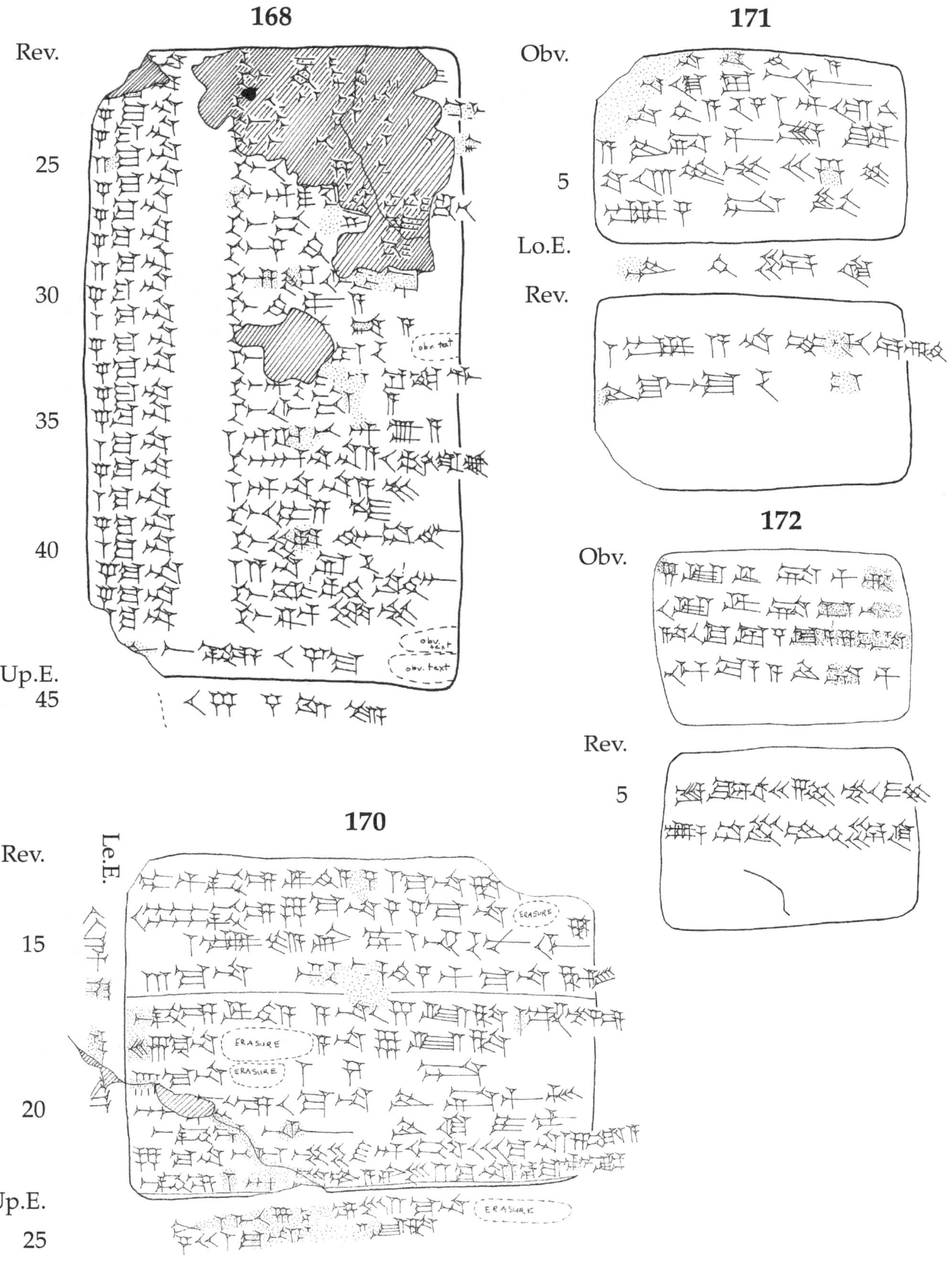
168
Rev.
obv. text
obv. text
obv. text
Up.E.
171
Obv.
Lo.E.
Rev.
172
Obv.
Rev.
170
Rev.
Le.E.
ERASURE
ERASURE
ERASURE
Up.E.
ERASURE

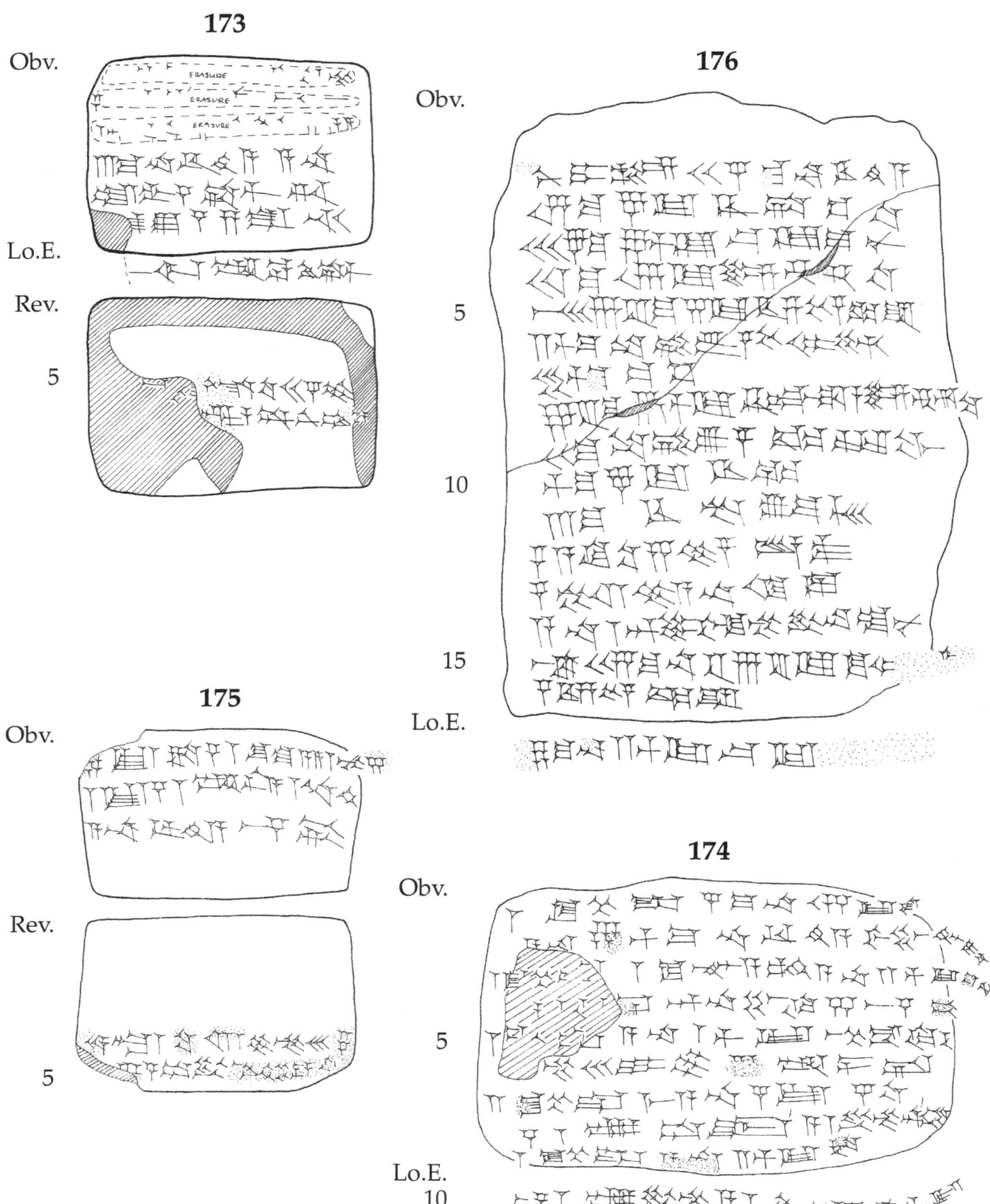
173
Obv.
ERASURE
ERASURE
ERASURE
Lo.E.
Rev.
5
176
Obv.
5
10
15
Lo.E.
175
Obv.
Rev.
5
174
Obv.
5
Lo.E.
10

176

Rev.

177

Obv.

Lo.E.

Rev.

Up.E.

174

Rev.

ERASURE

obv

obv.

Up.E.

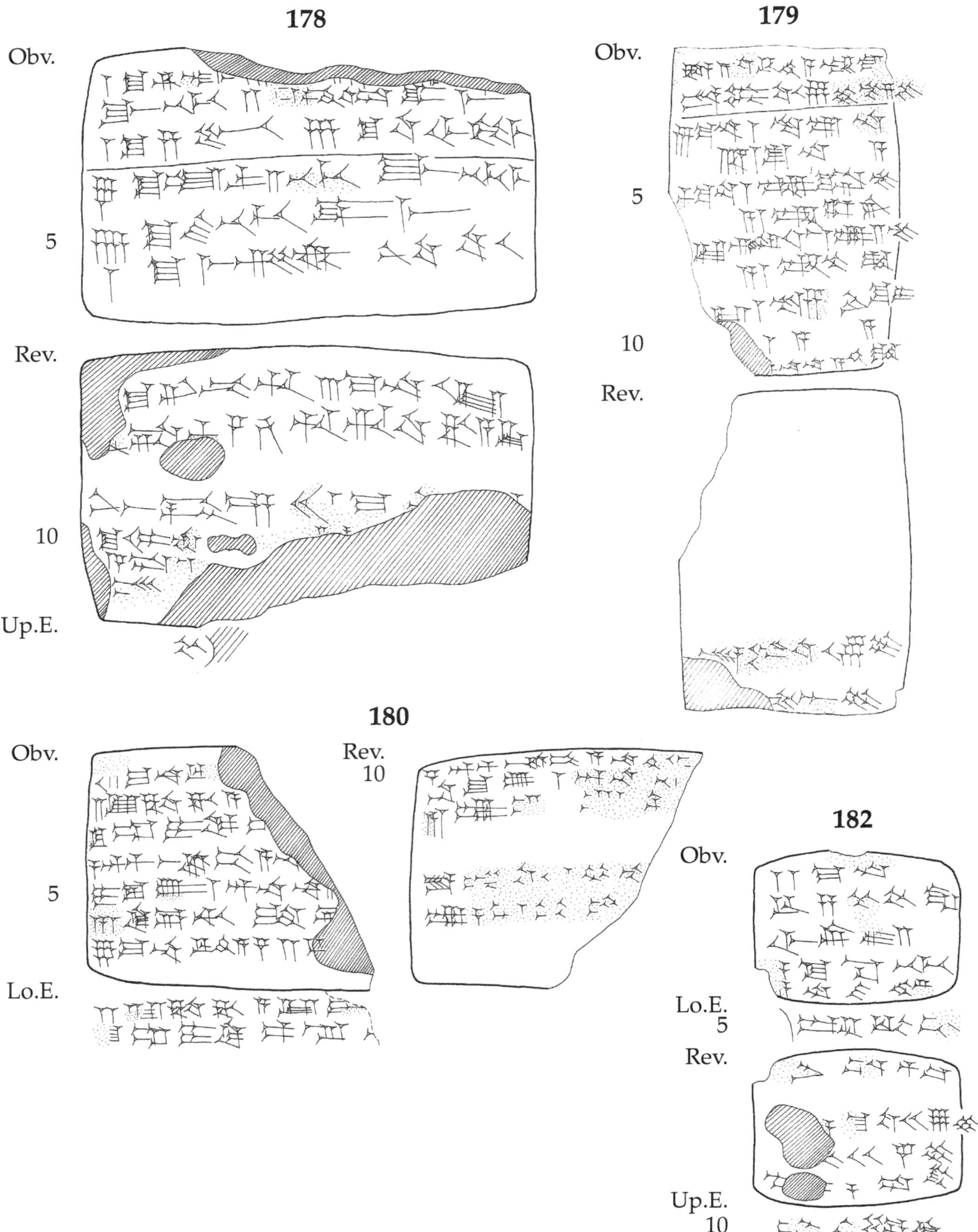
178
Obv.
5
Rev.
10
Up.E.
179
Obv.
5
10
Rev.
180
Obv.
5
Lo.E.
Rev.
10
182
Obv.
Lo.E.
5
Rev.
Up.E.
10

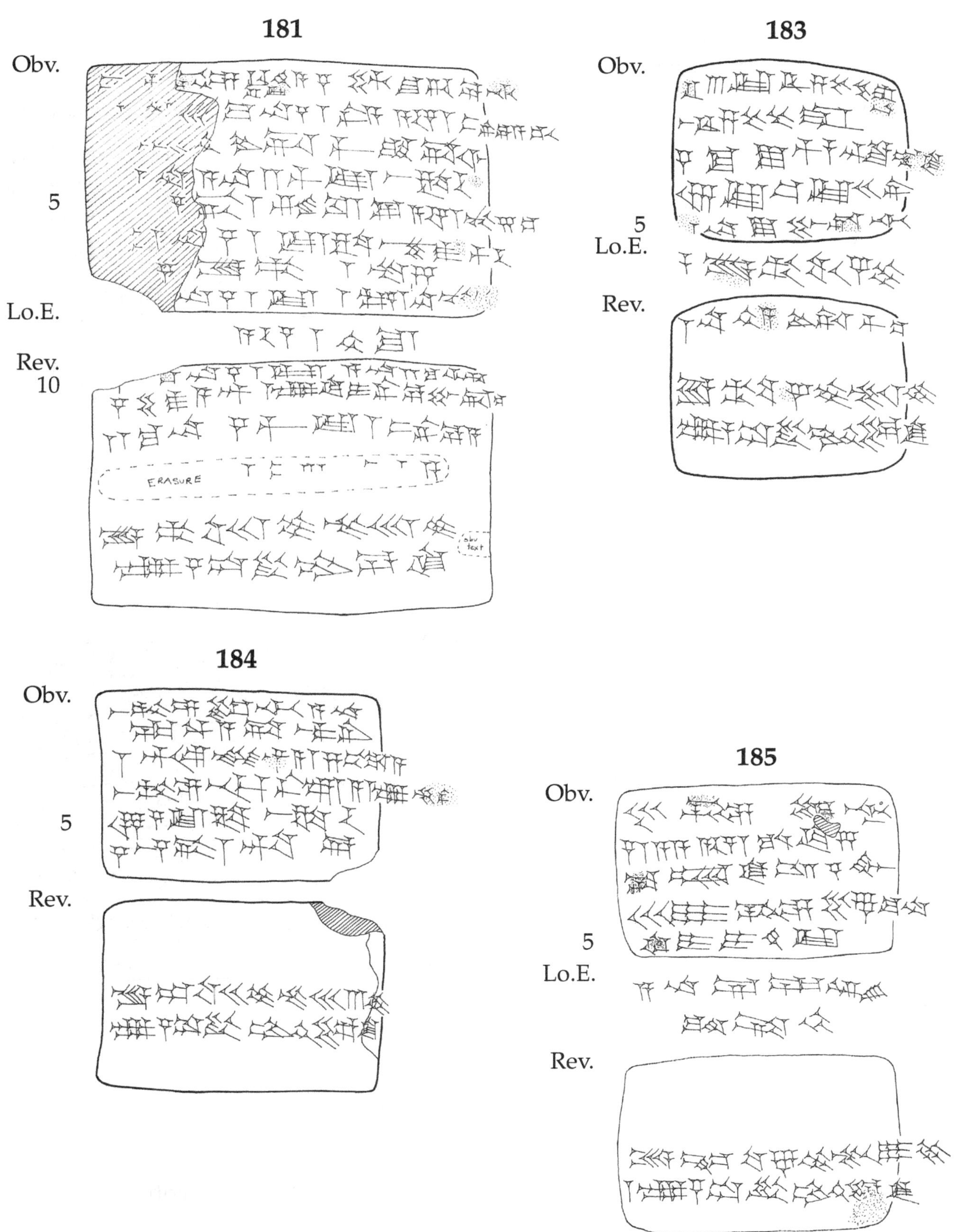
181
Obv.
Lo.E.
Rev.
ERASURE
obv text
183
Obv.
Lo.E.
Rev.
184
Obv.
Rev.
185
Obv.
Lo.E.
Rev.

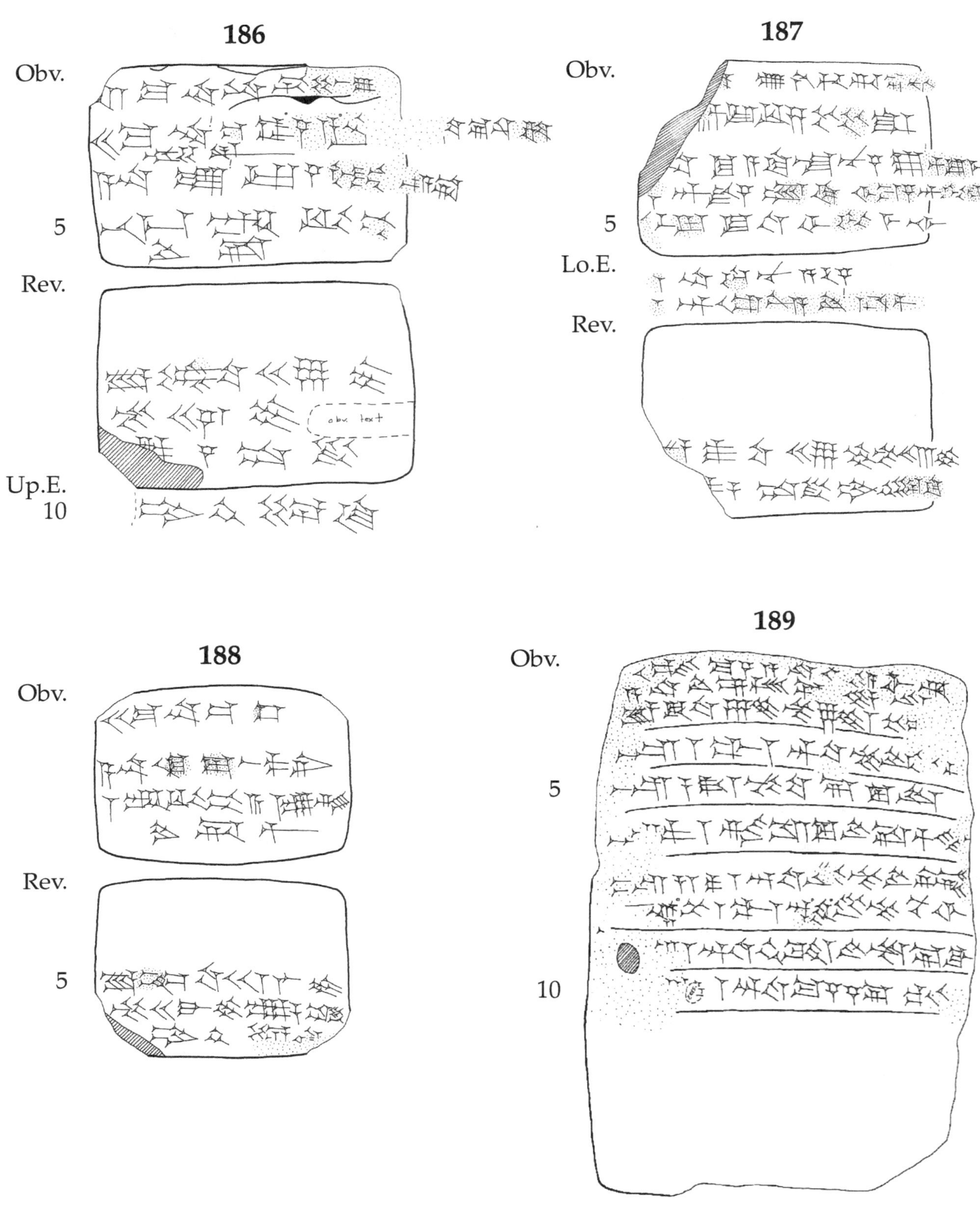

(Rev. uninscribed)

190

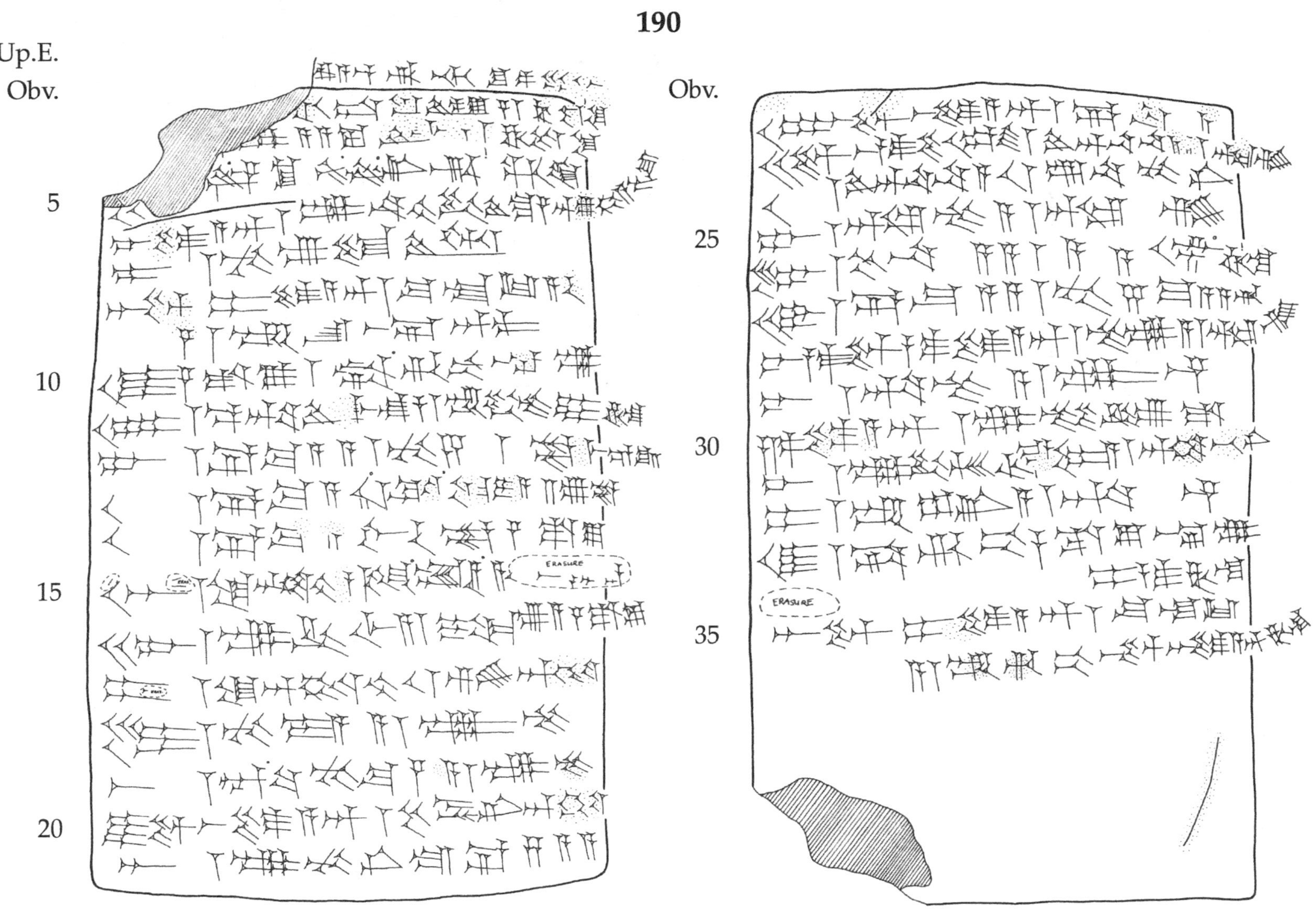

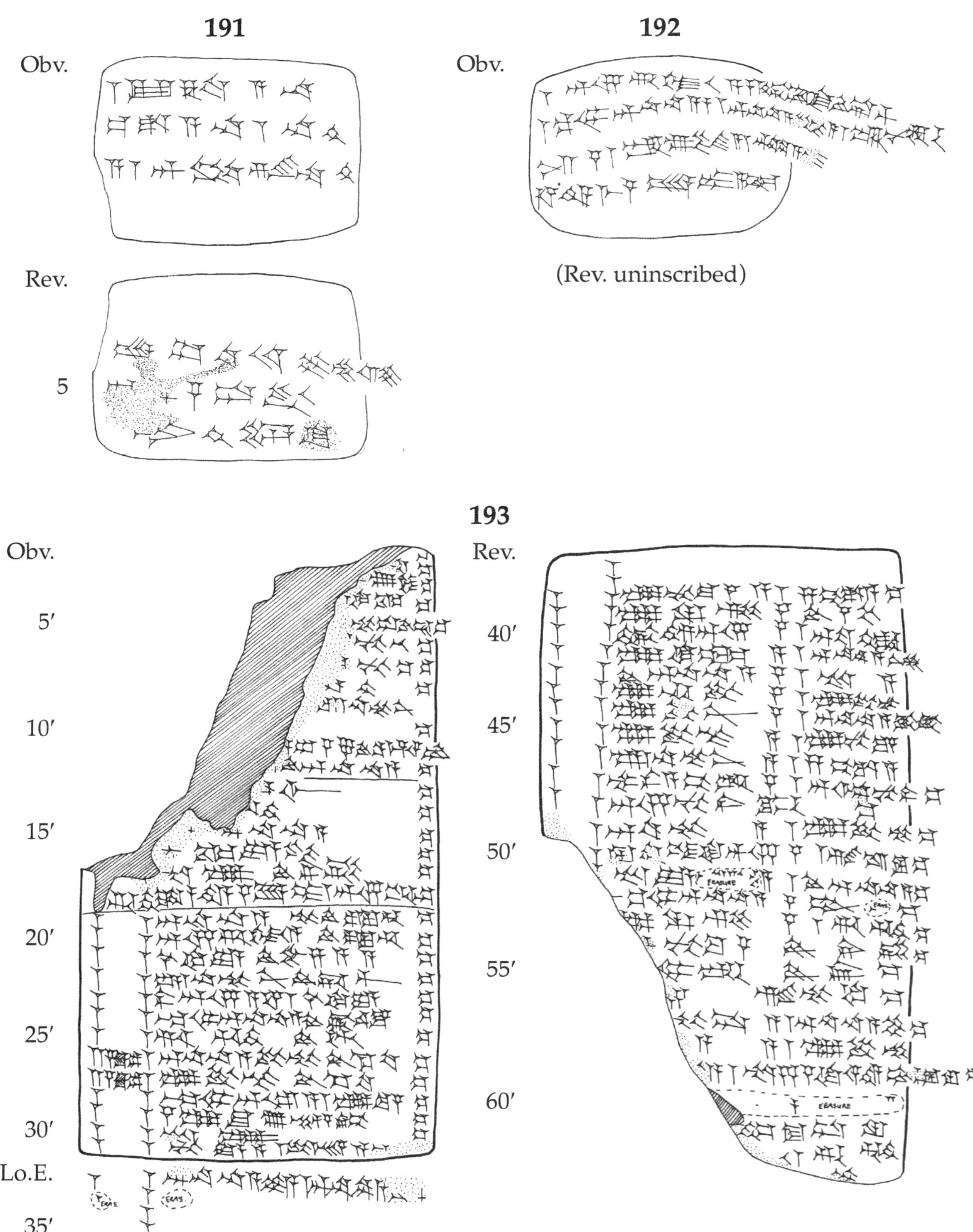
191
Obv.
Rev.
192
Obv.
(Rev. uninscribed)
193
Obv.
Rev.
Lo.E.
ERASURE
ERASURE

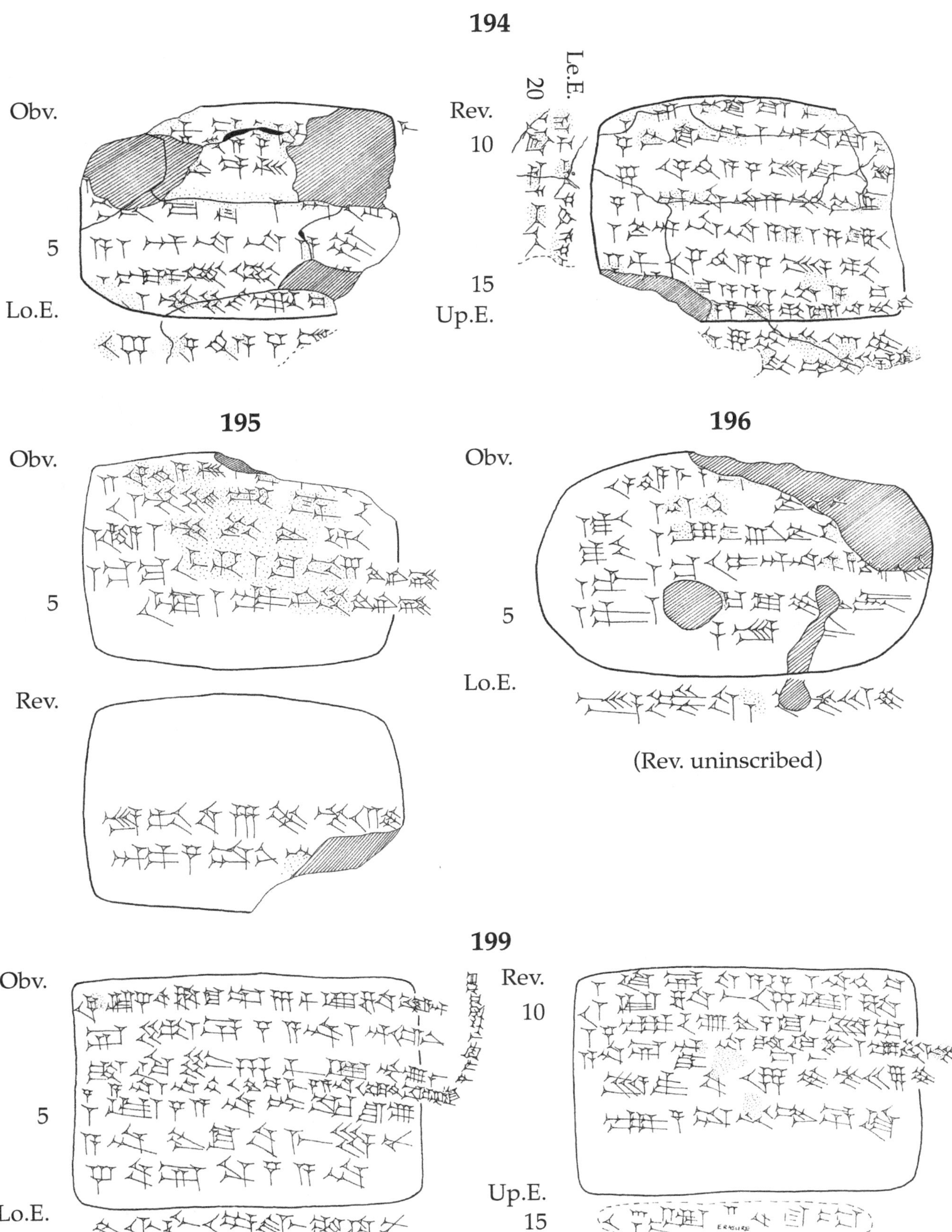
194
Obv.
5
Lo.E.
Rev.
10
15
Up.E.
Le.E.
20
195
Obv.
5
Rev.
196
Obv.
5
Lo.E.
(Rev. uninscribed)
199
Obv.
5
Lo.E.
Rev.
10
Up.E.
15
ERASURE

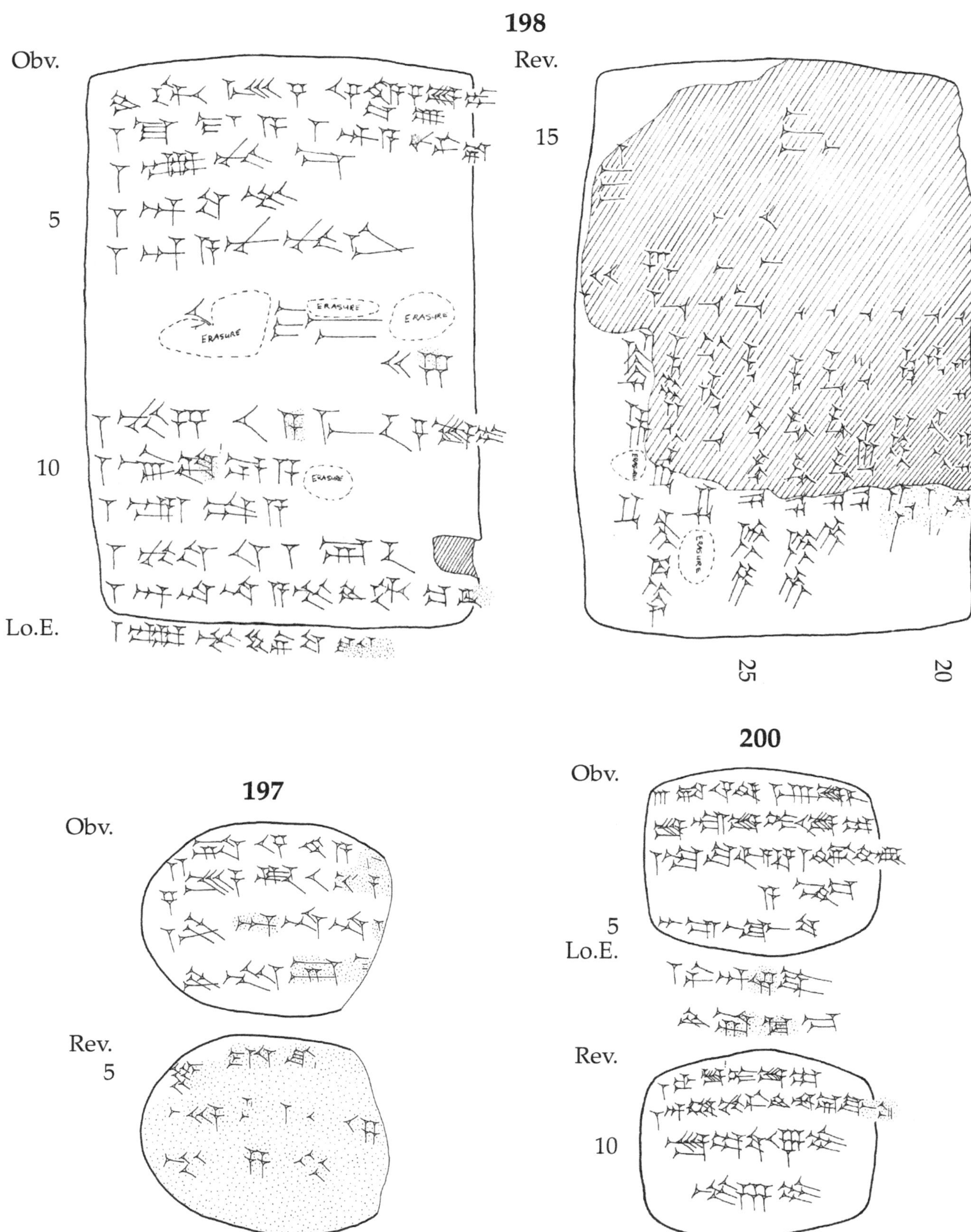
198
Obv.
Rev.
5
10
15
20
25
Lo.E.
ERASURE
ERASURE
ERASURE
ERASURE
ERASURE
ERASURE
197
Obv.
Rev.
5
200
Obv.
5
Lo.E.
Rev.
10

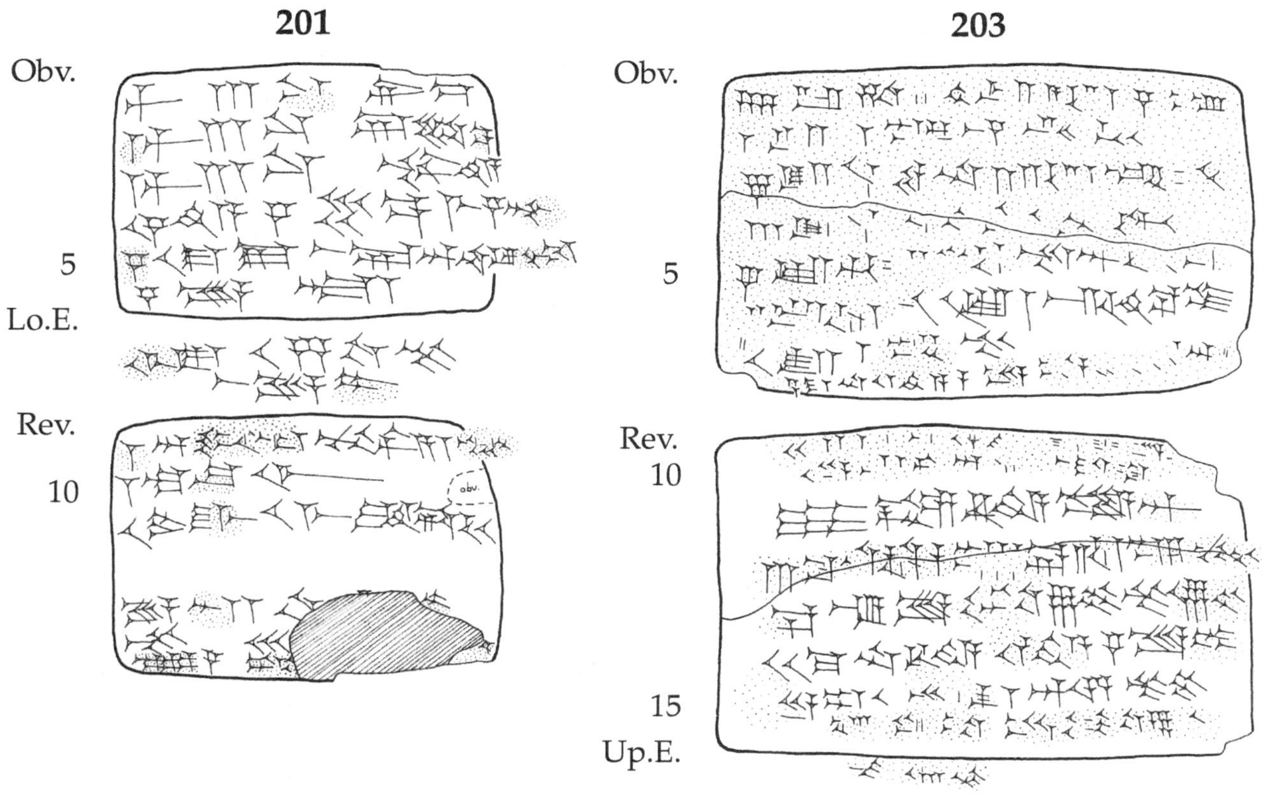
201
Obv.
5
Lo.E.
Rev.
10
obv.
203
Obv.
5
Rev.
10
15
Up.E.

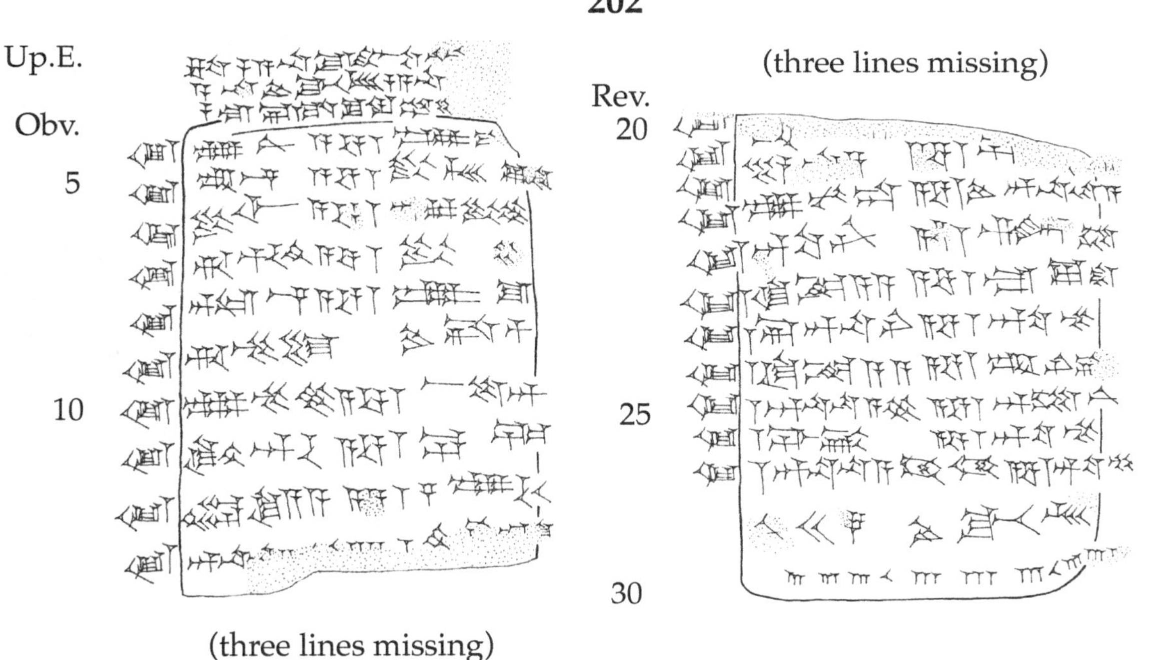
202
Up.E.
Obv.
5
10
(three lines missing)
(three lines missing)
Rev.
20
25
30

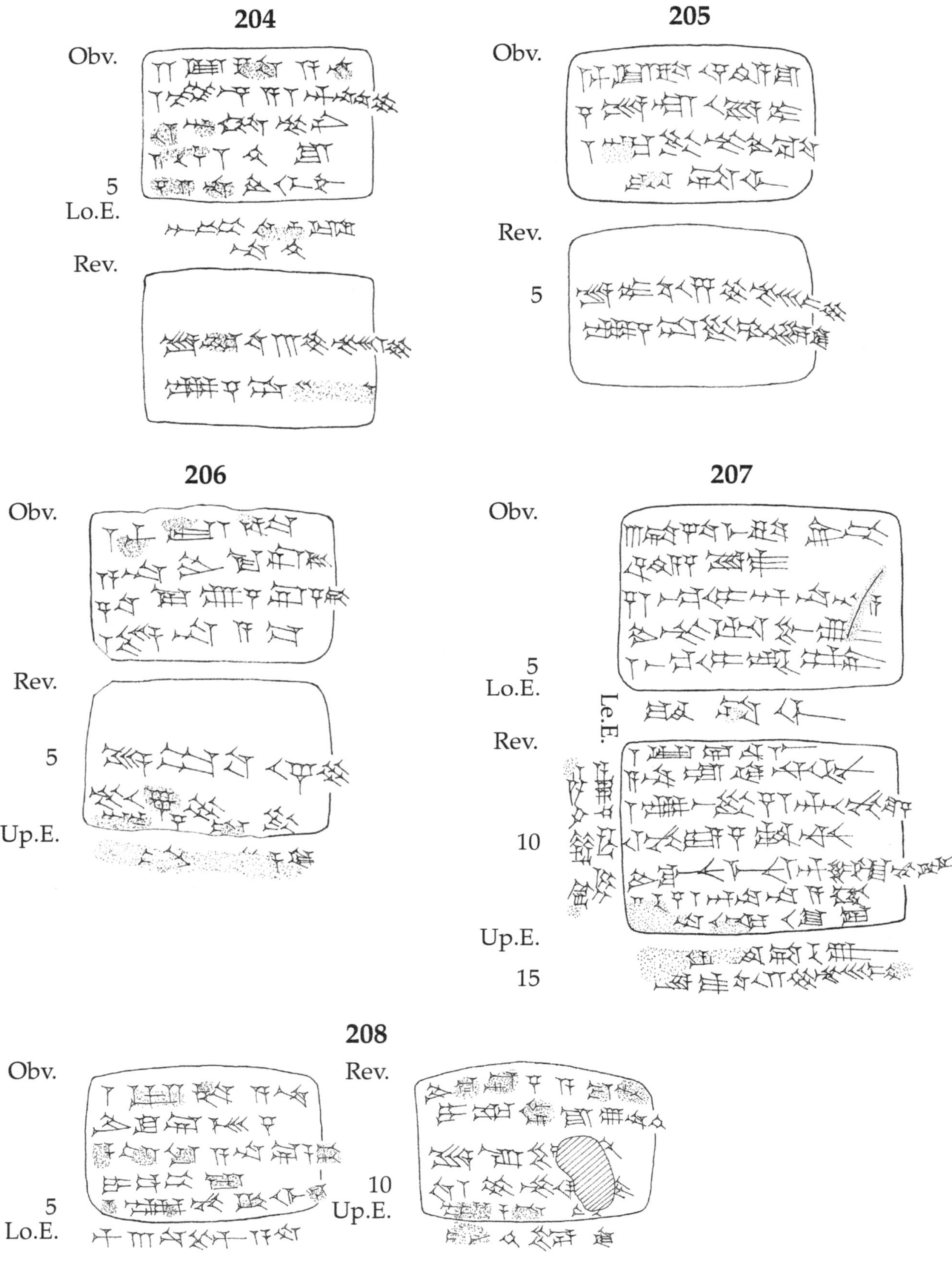
204
Obv.
5
Lo.E.
Rev.
205
Obv.
Rev.
5
206
Obv.
Rev.
5
Up.E.
207
Obv.
5
Lo.E.
Le.E.
Rev.
10
Up.E.
15
208
Obv.
5
Lo.E.
Rev.
10
Up.E.

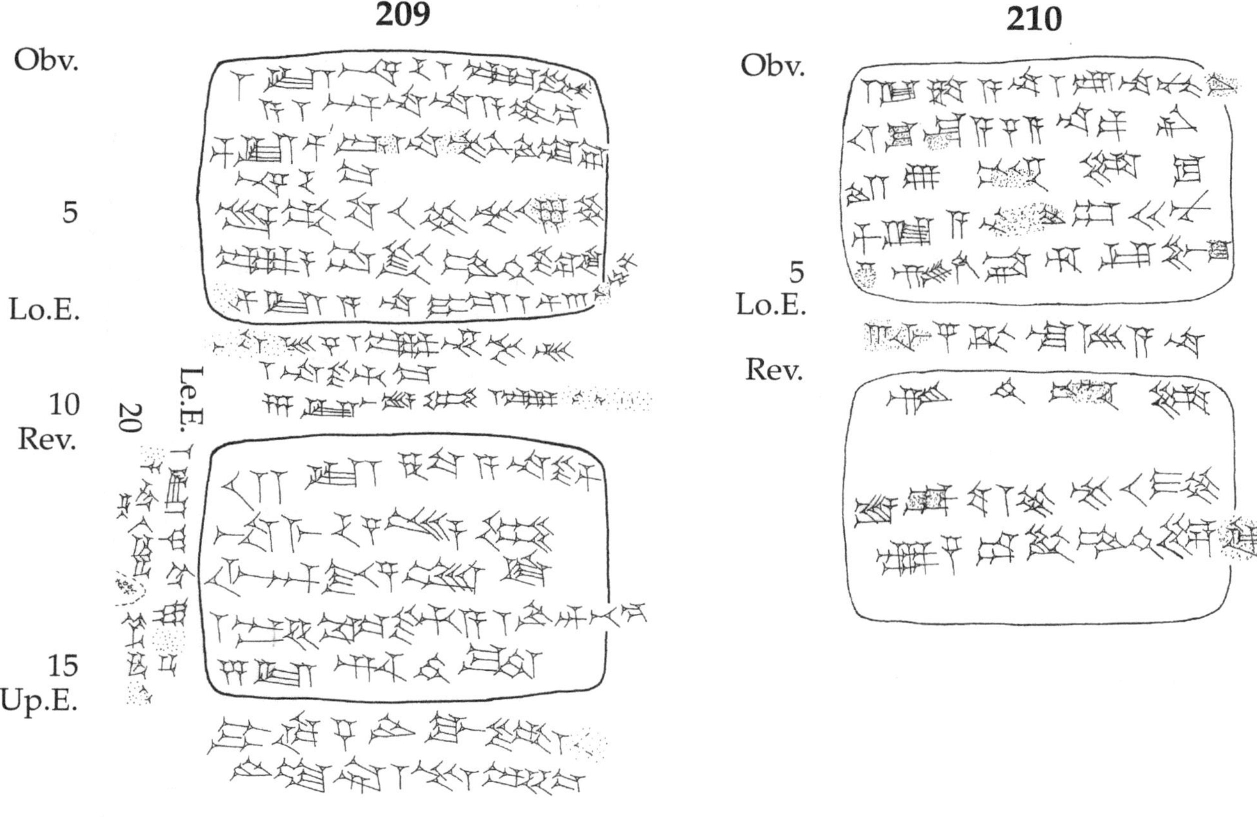

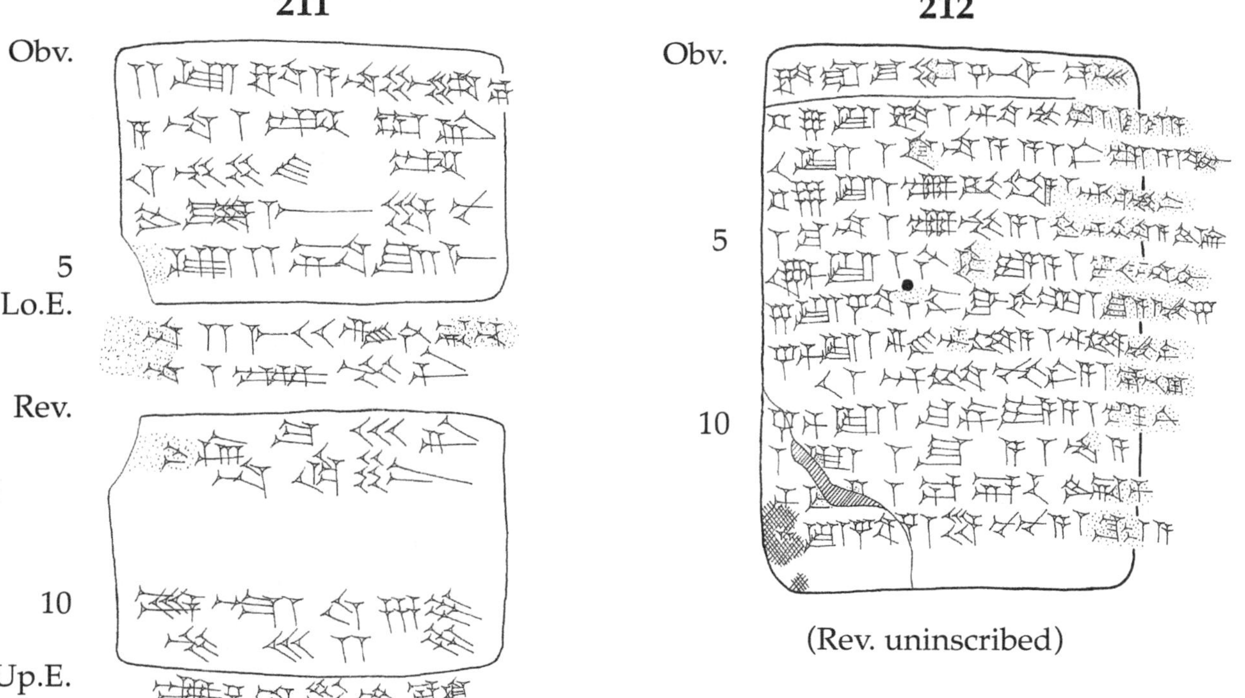

(Rev. uninscribed)

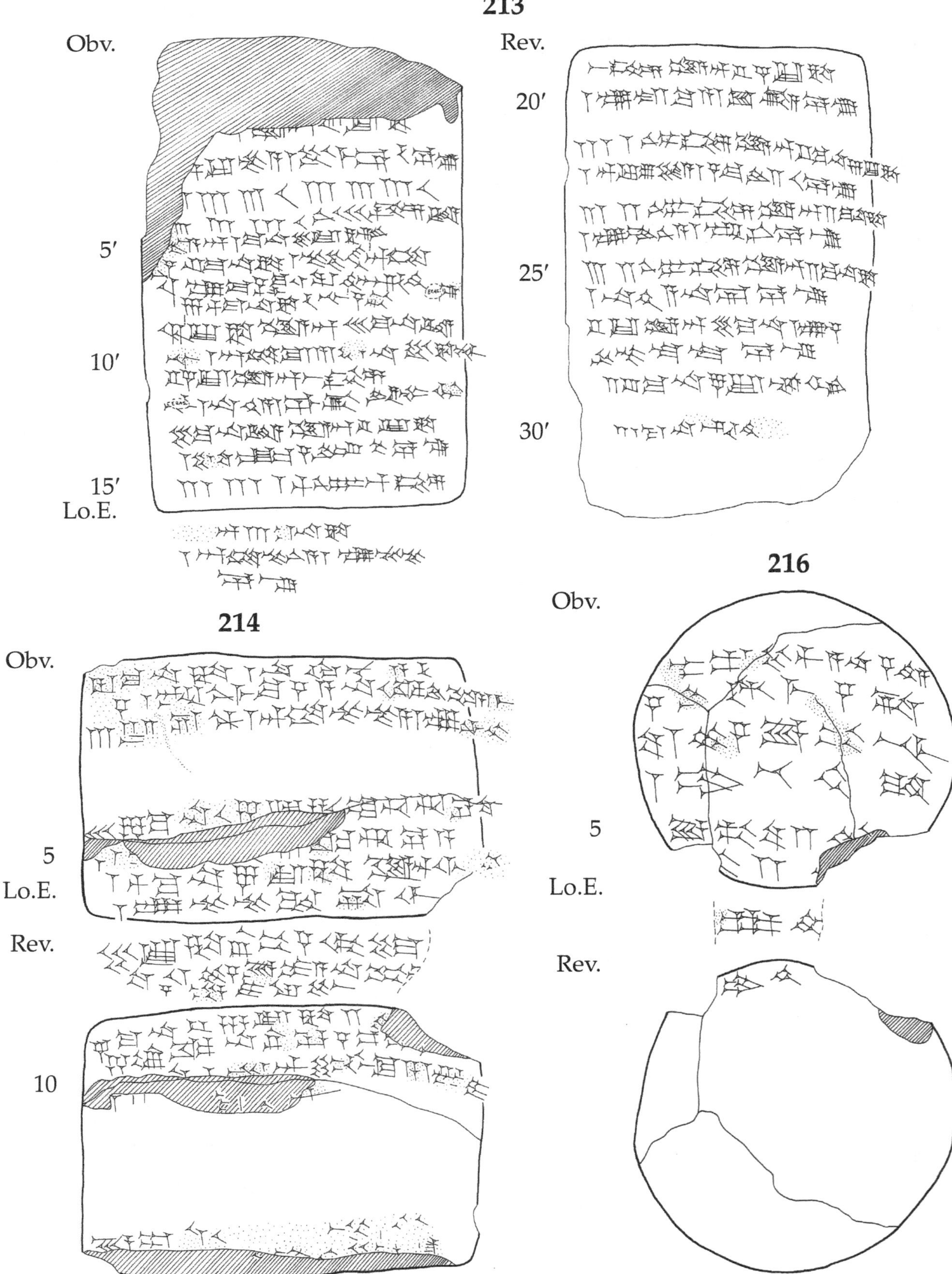
213
Obv.
Rev.
20′
5′
25′
10′
30′
15′
Lo.E.
216
214
Obv.
Obv.
5
5
Lo.E.
Lo.E.
Rev.
Rev.
10

215

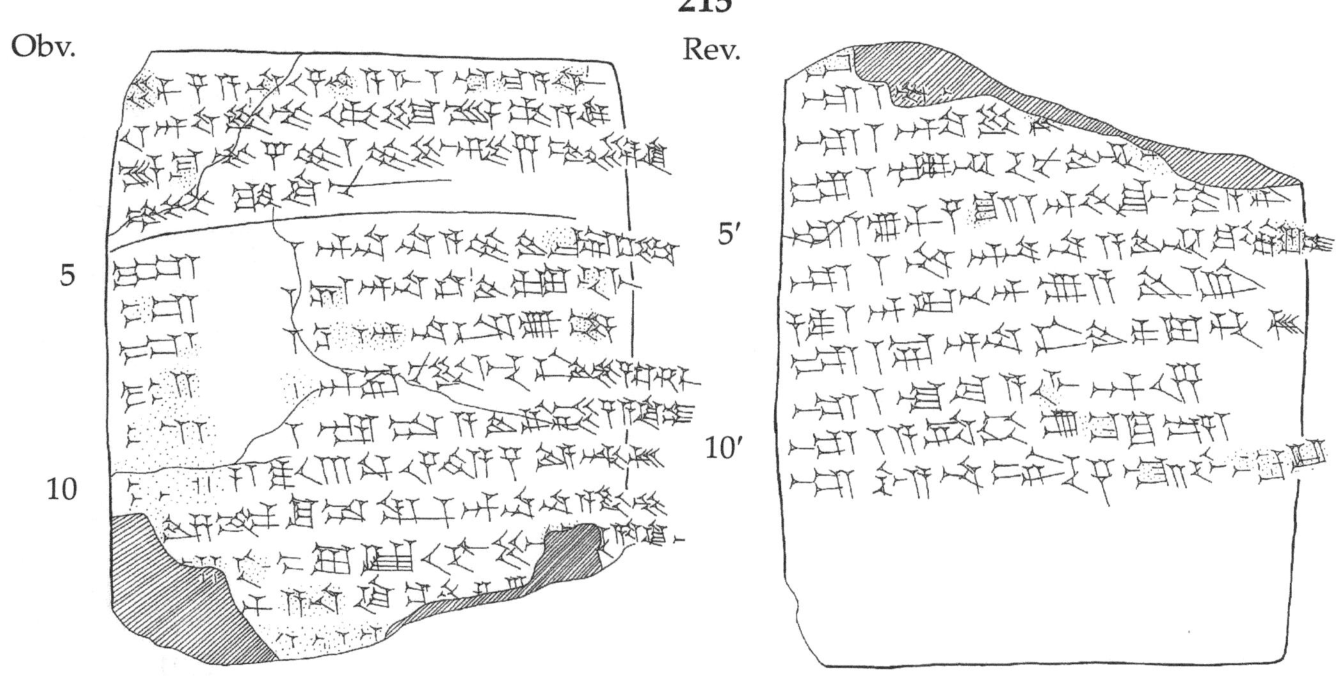

217

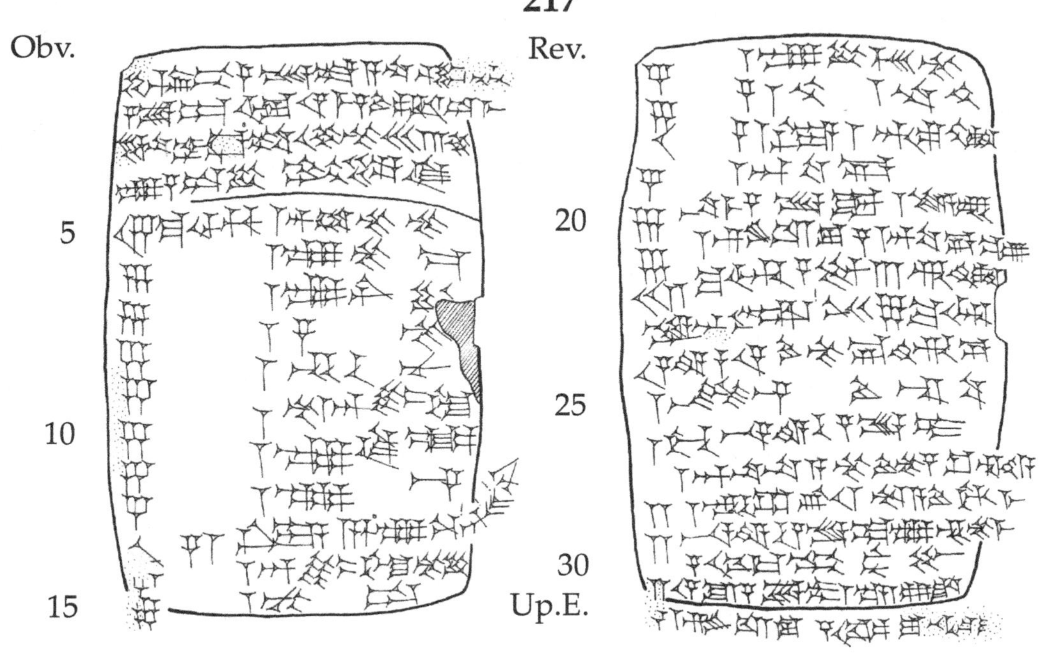

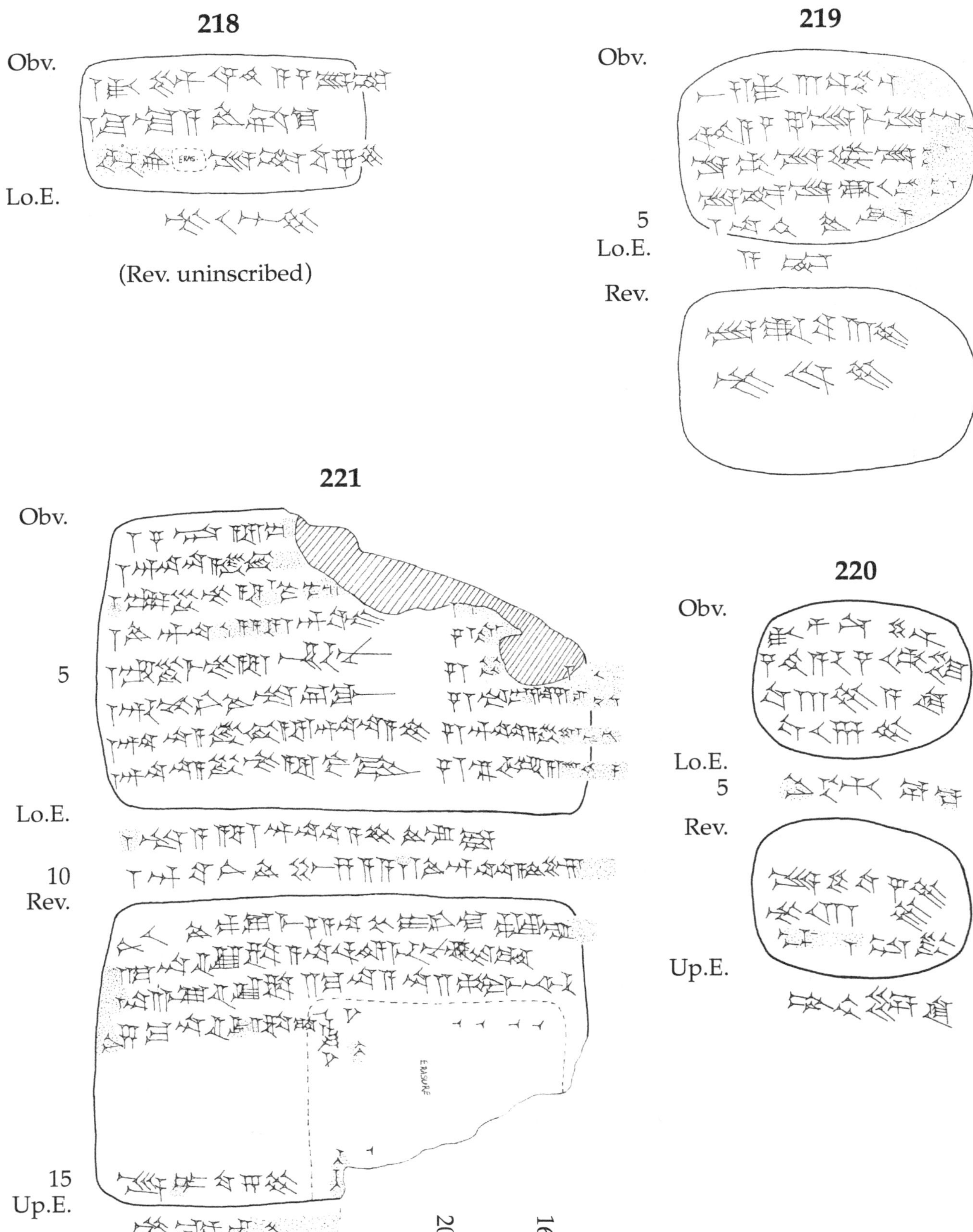
218
Obv.
ERAS.
Lo.E.
(Rev. uninscribed)
219
Obv.
Lo.E.
Rev.
221
Obv.
Lo.E.
Rev.
ERASURE
Up.E.
220
Obv.
Lo.E.
Rev.
Up.E.

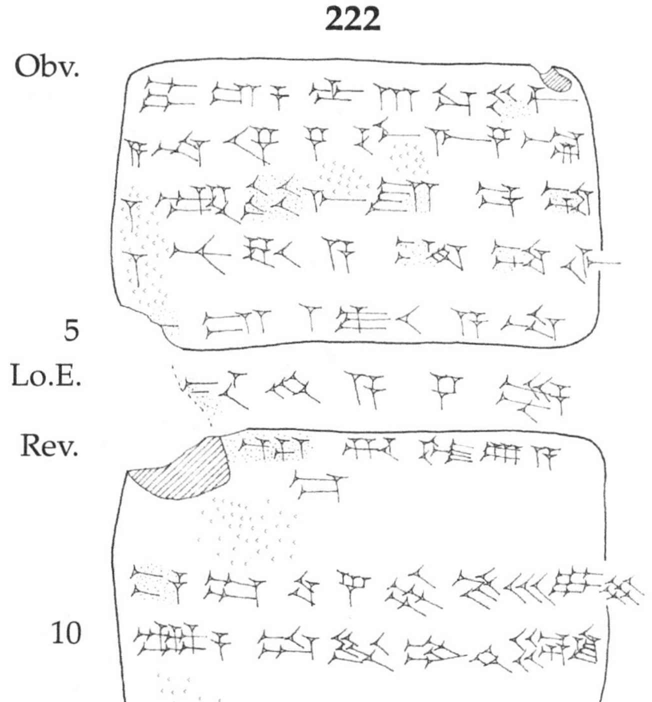
222
Obv.
5
Lo.E.
Rev.
10

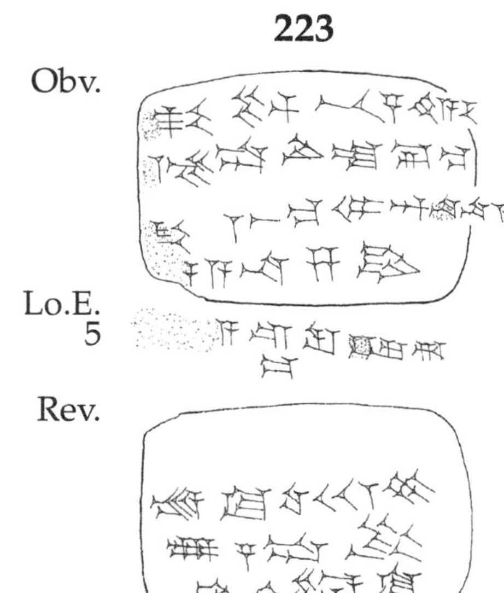
223
Obv.
Lo.E.
5
Rev.

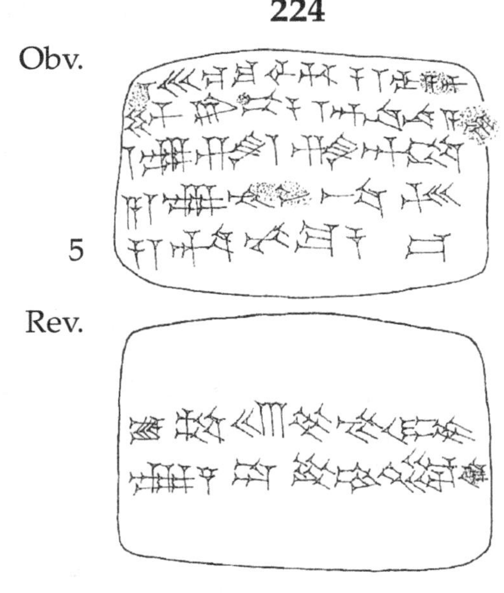
224
Obv.
5
Rev.

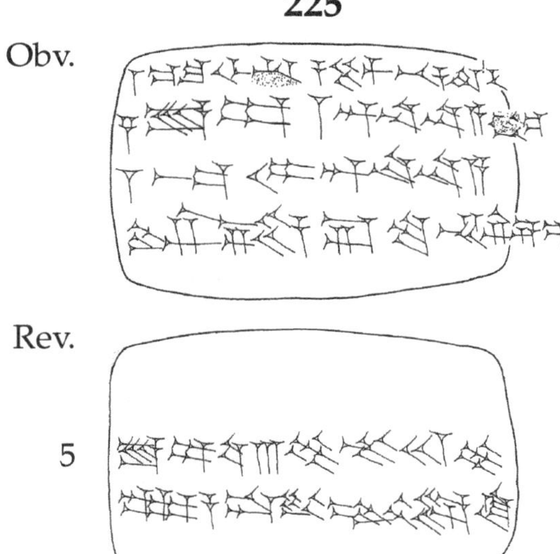
225
Obv.
Rev.
5

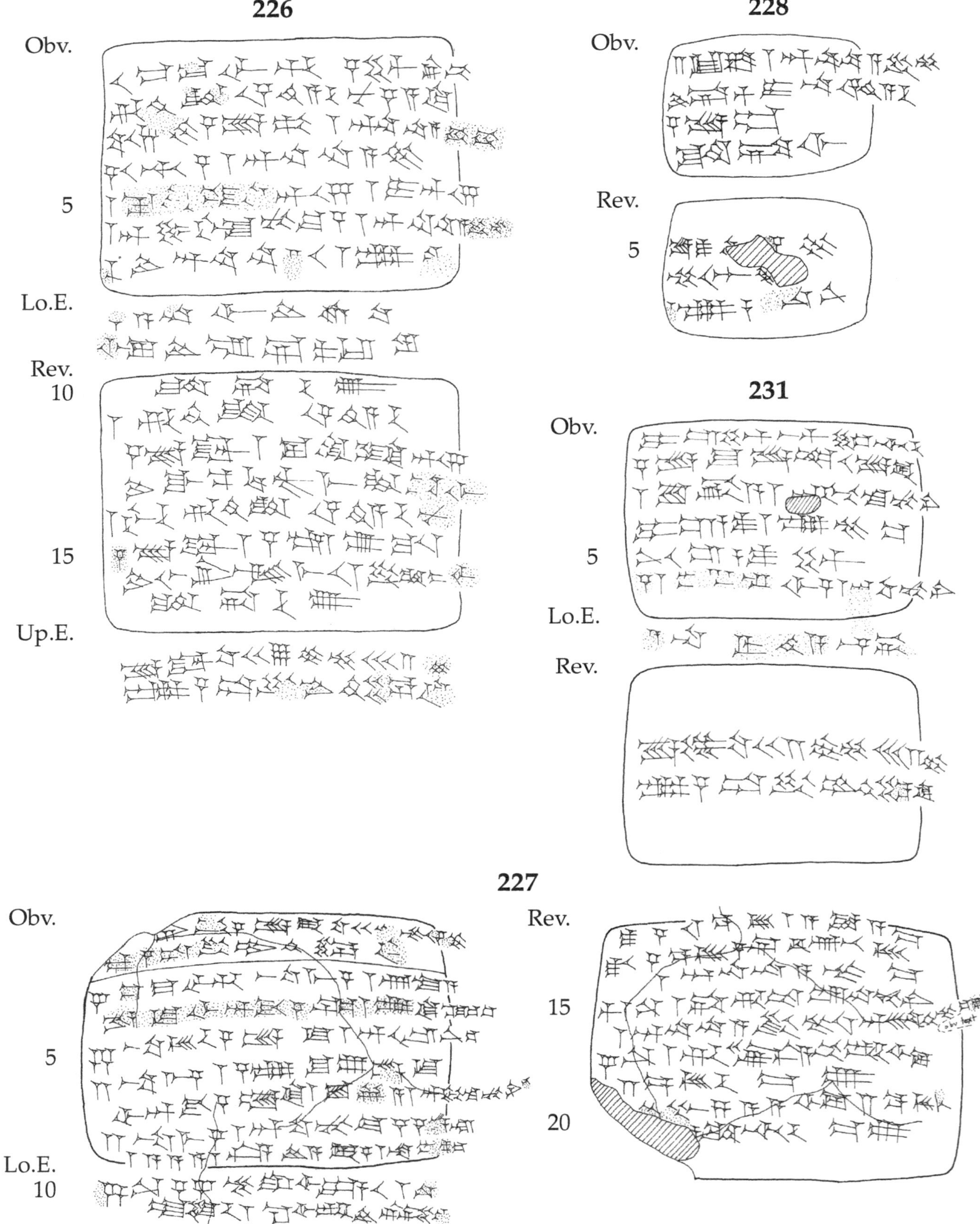
226
Obv.
Lo.E.
Rev.
Up.E.
228
Obv.
Rev.
231
Obv.
Lo.E.
Rev.
227
Obv.
Lo.E.
Rev.

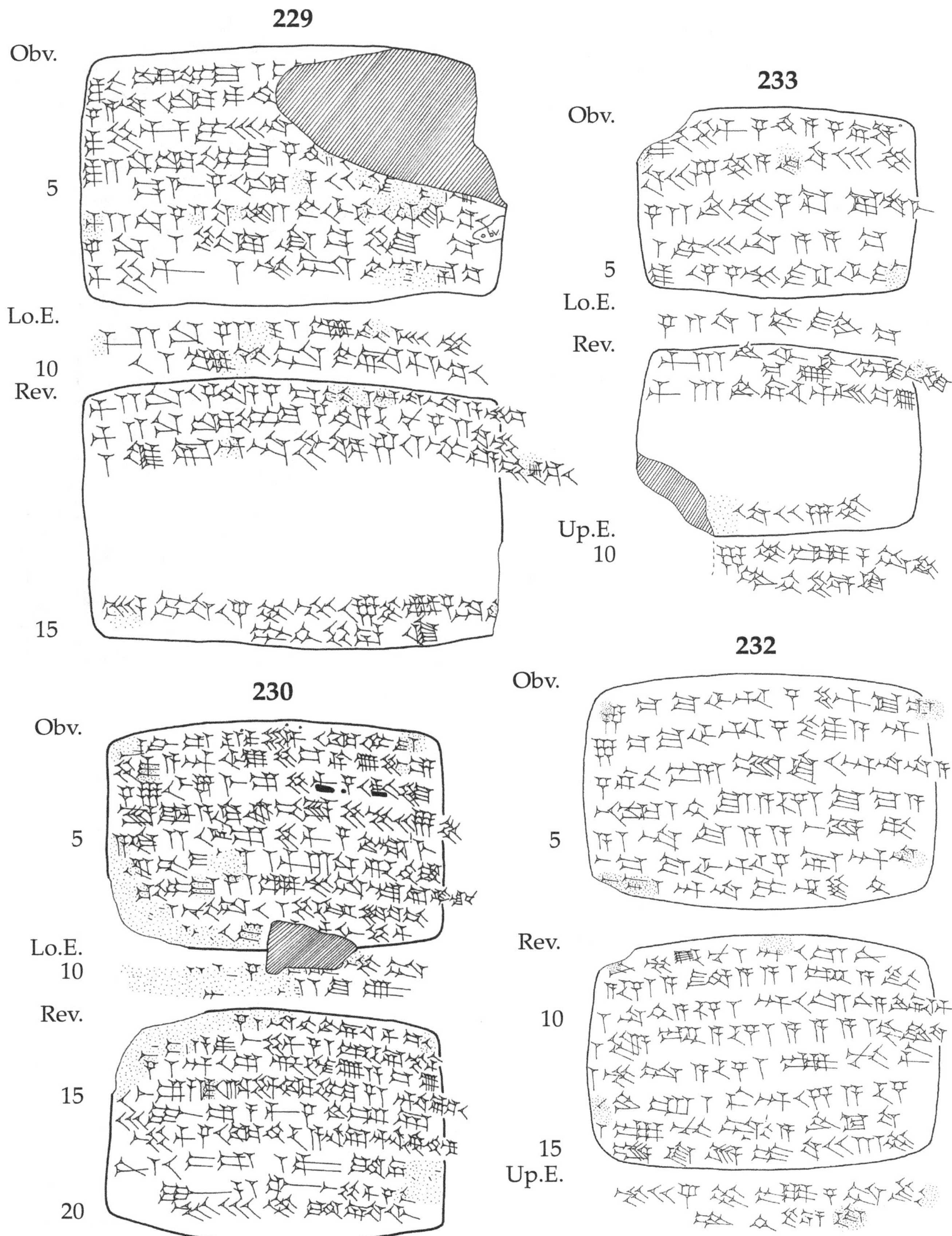
229
Obv.
Lo.E.
Rev.
233
Obv.
Lo.E.
Rev.
Up.E.
230
Obv.
Lo.E.
Rev.
232
Obv.
Rev.
Up.E.

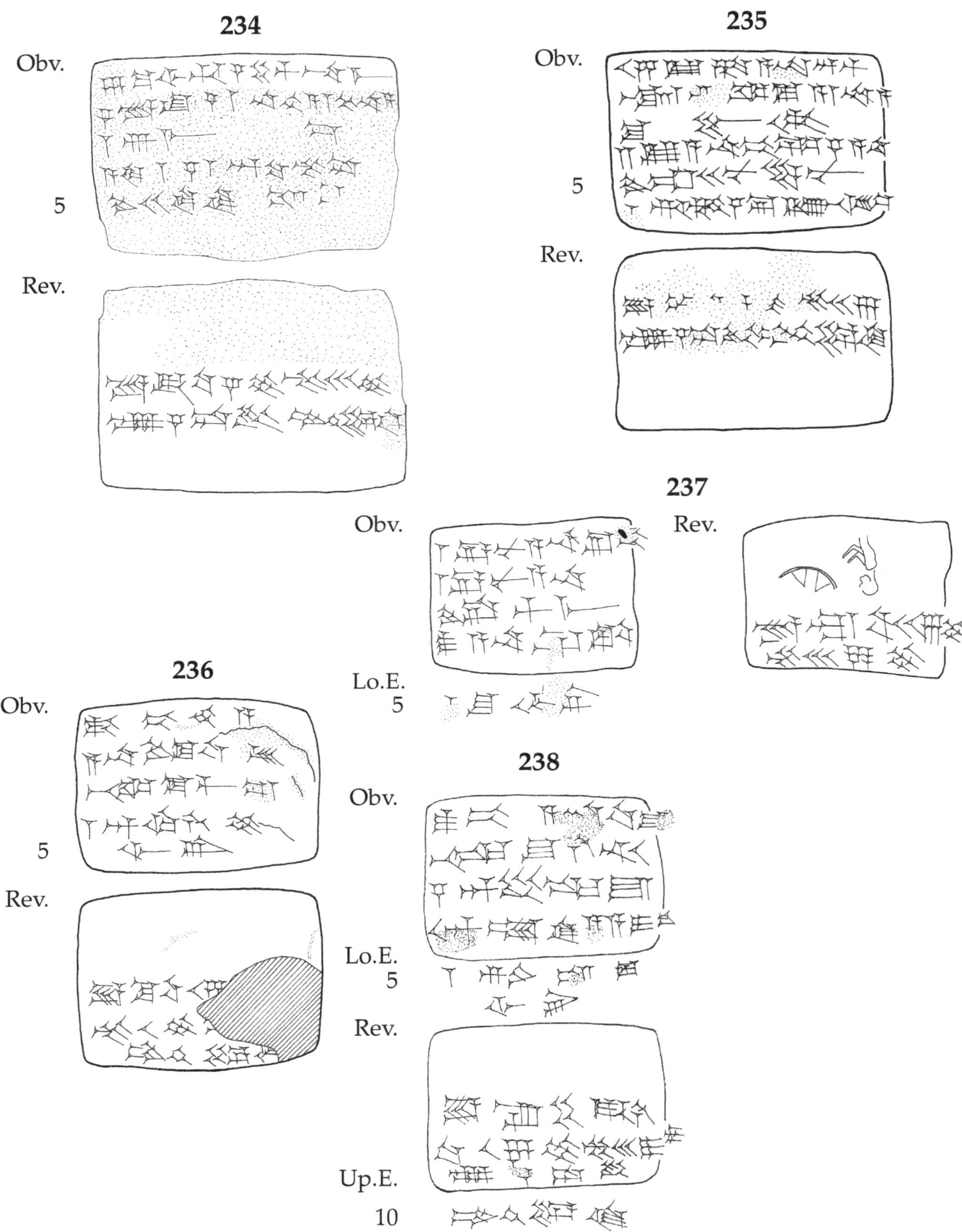
234
Obv.
Rev.
235
Obv.
Rev.
237
Obv.
Rev.
Lo.E.
236
Obv.
Rev.
238
Obv.
Lo.E.
Rev.
Up.E.

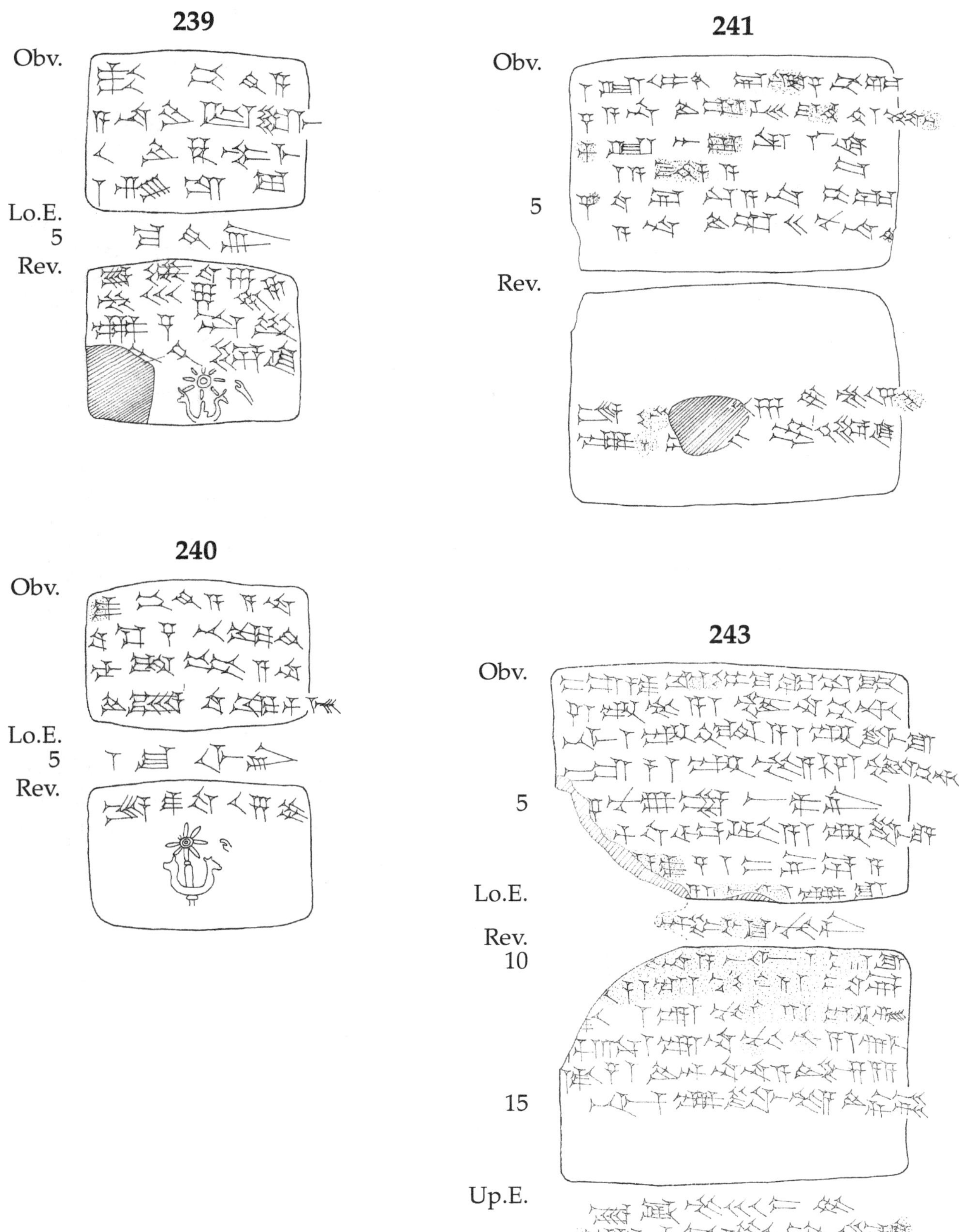
239
Obv.
Lo.E.
Rev.
241
Obv.
Rev.
240
Obv.
Lo.E.
Rev.
243
Obv.
Lo.E.
Rev.
Up.E.

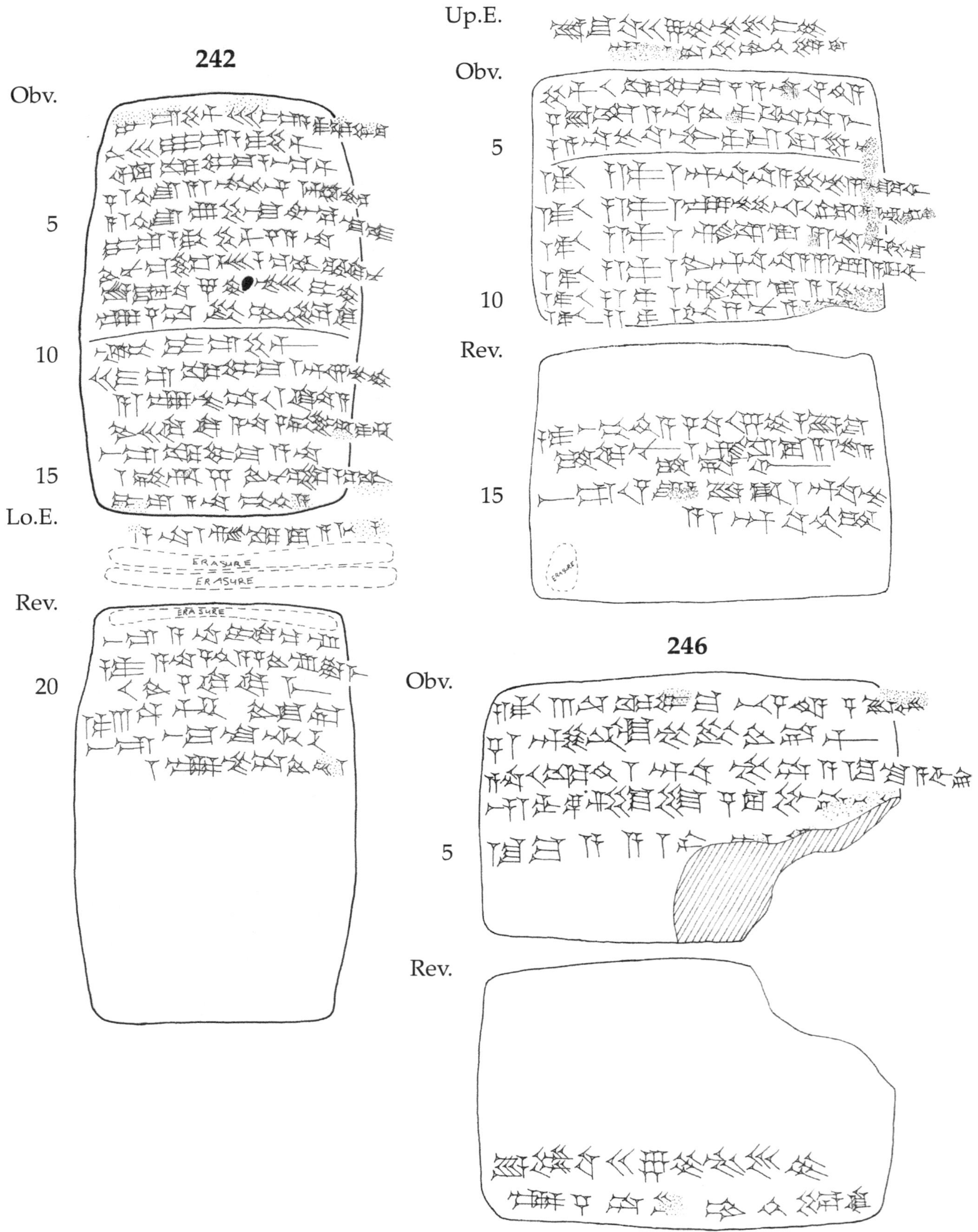
242
Obv.
Lo.E.
ERASURE
ERASURE
Rev.
ERASURE
244
Up.E.
Obv.
Rev.
ERASURE
246
Obv.
Rev.

245

Obv.

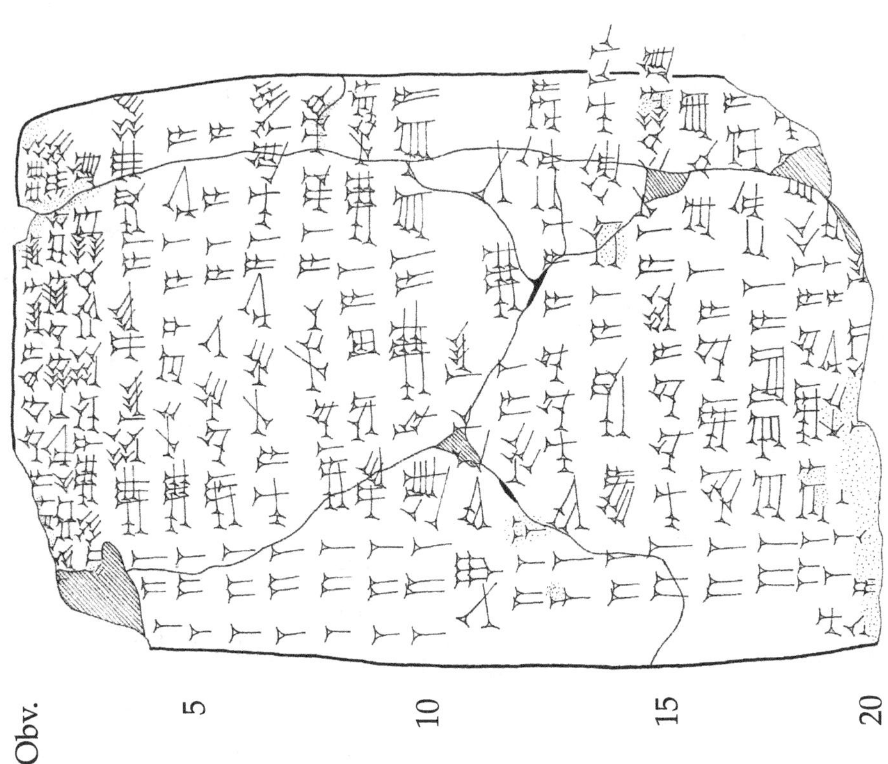

Rev.

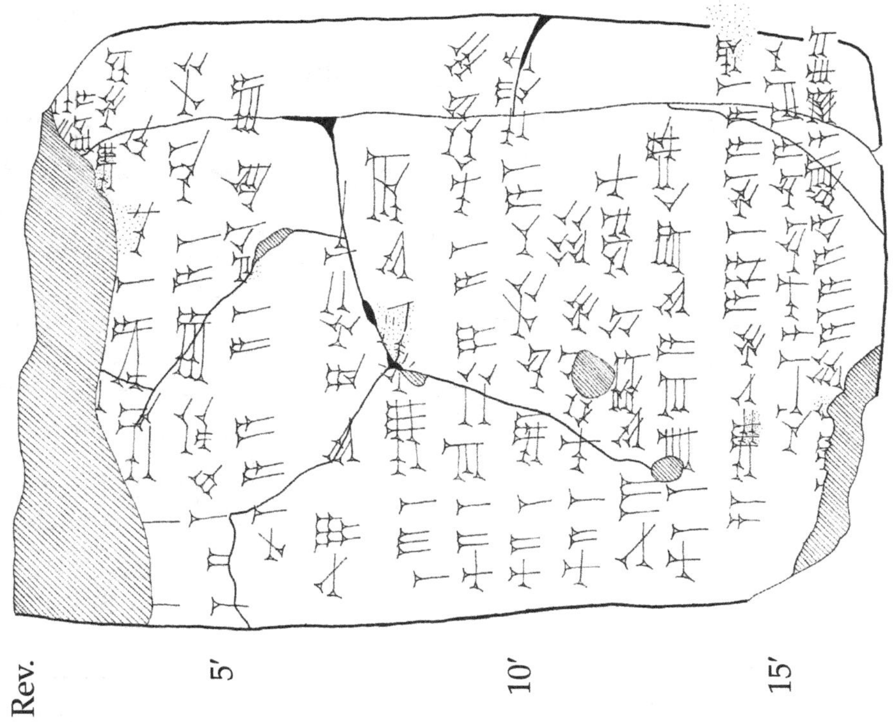

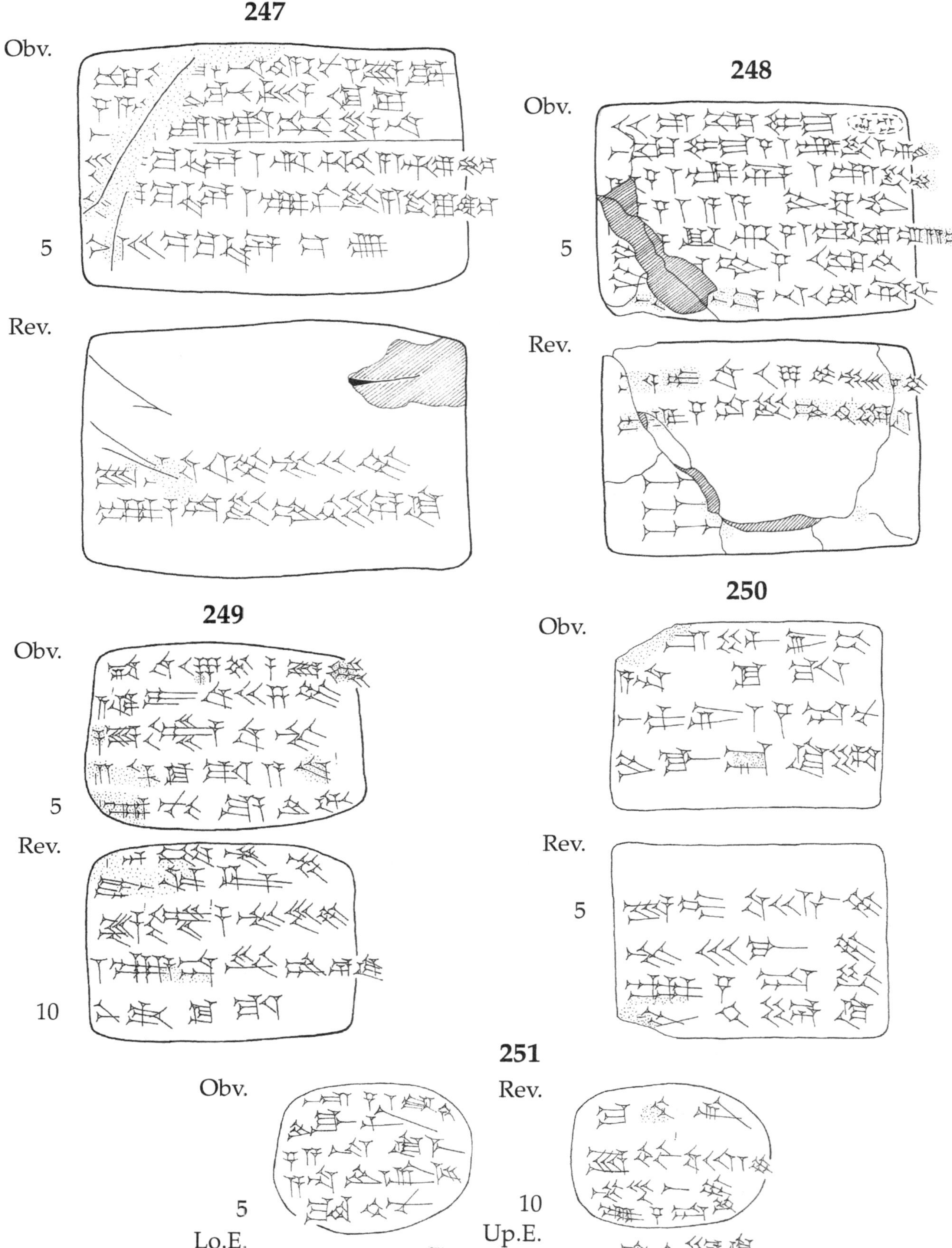
247
Obv.
Rev.
248
Obv.
Rev.
249
Obv.
Rev.
250
Obv.
Rev.
251
Obv.
Lo.E.
Rev.
Up.E.

252

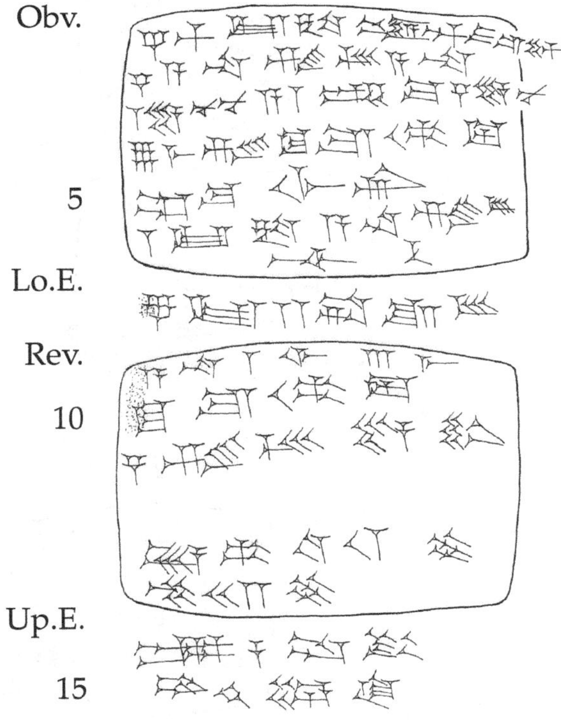

253

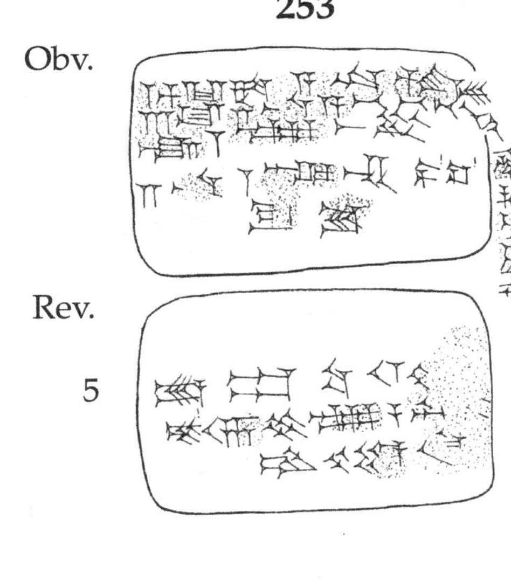

254

Obv.

Lo.E.

Rev.

255

Obv.

Lo.E.

Rev.

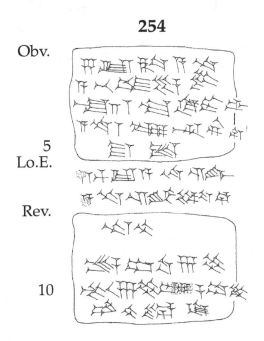

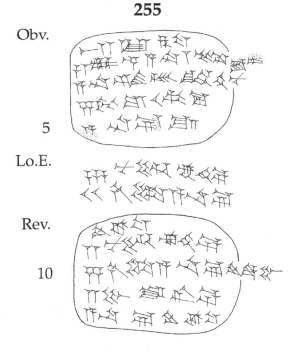

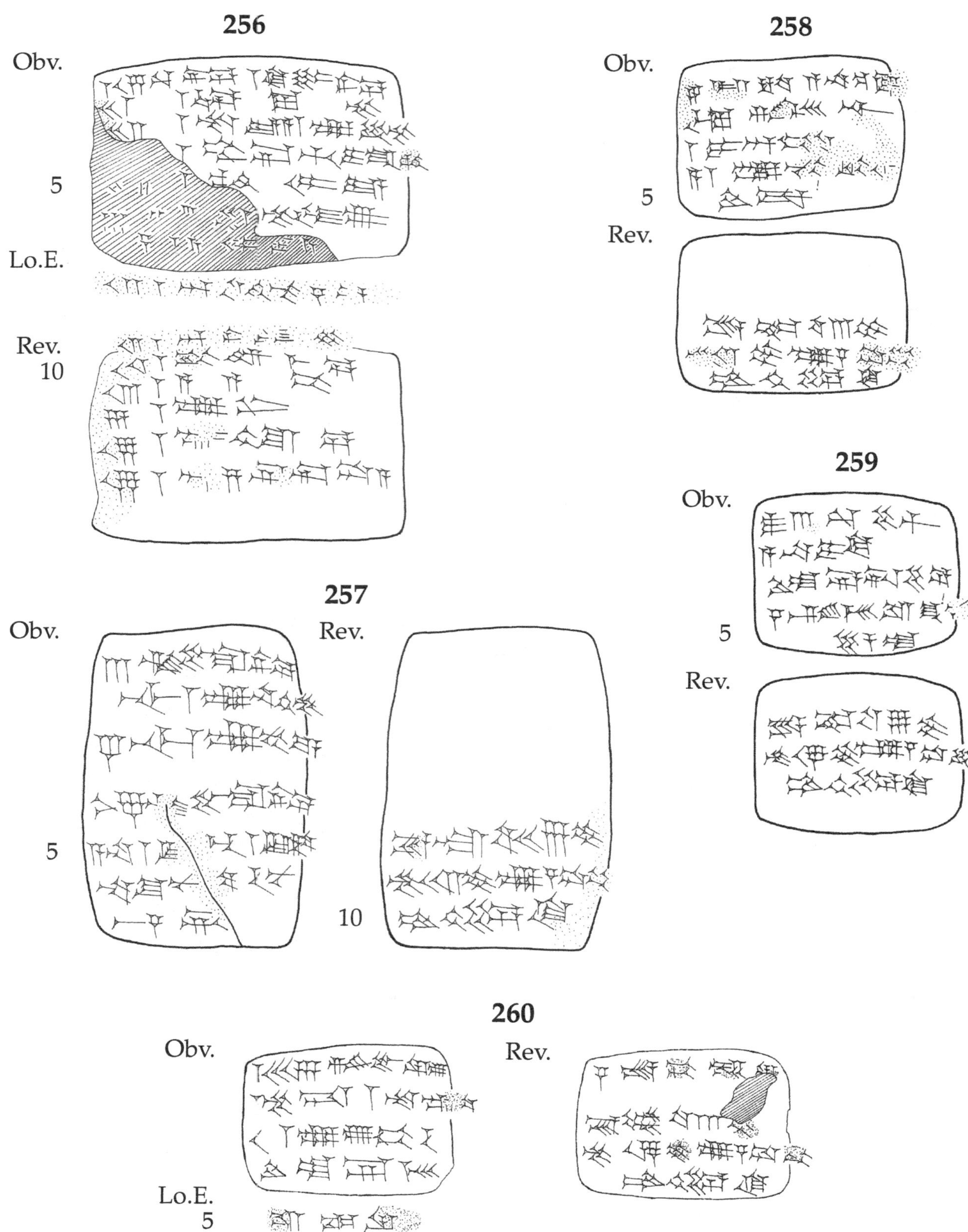
256
Obv.
Lo.E.
Rev.
258
Obv.
Rev.
259
Obv.
Rev.
257
Obv.
Rev.
260
Obv.
Rev.
Lo.E.

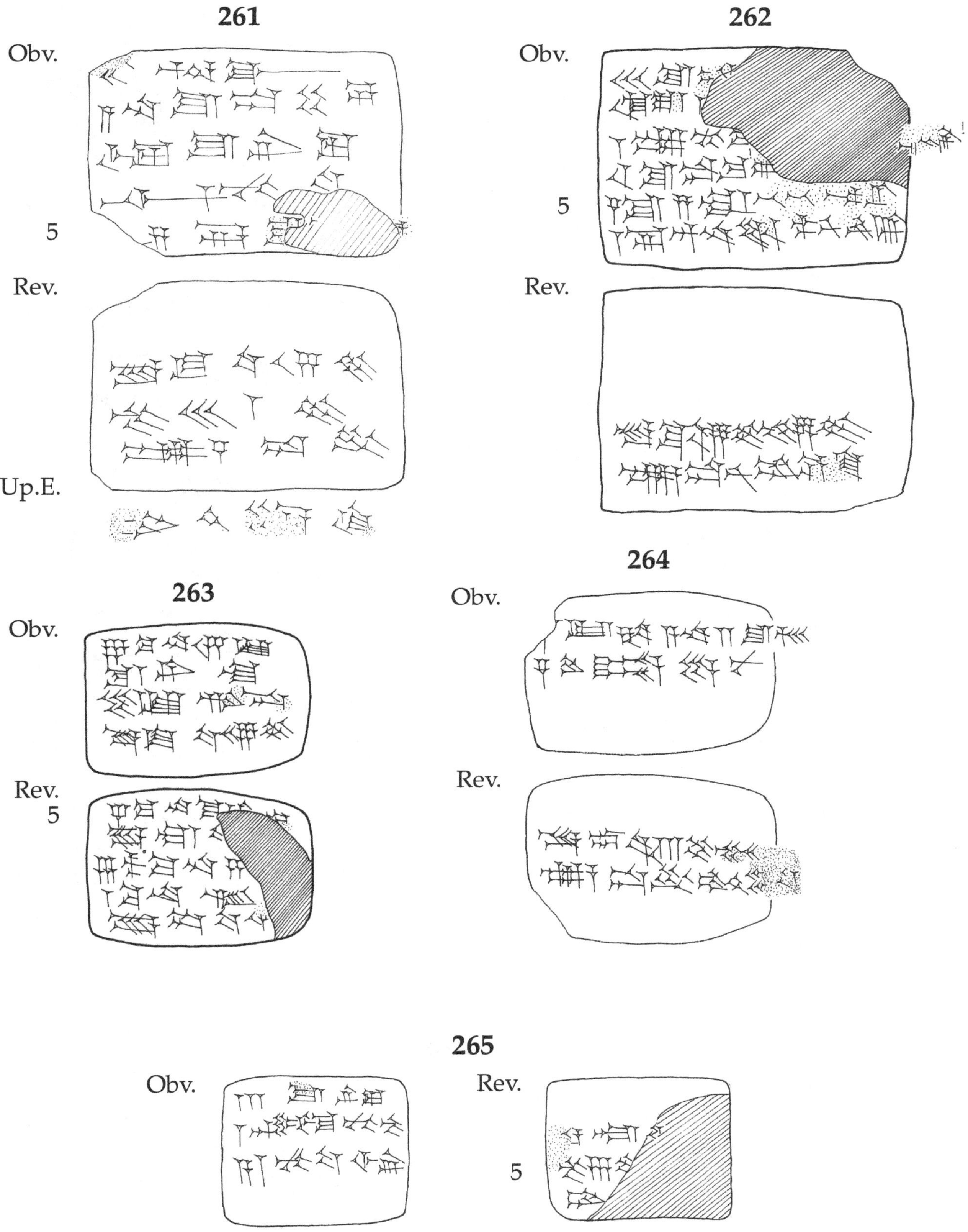

261
Obv.
5
Rev.
Up.E.
262
Obv.
5
Rev.
263
Obv.
Rev.
5
264
Obv.
Rev.
265
Obv.
Rev.
5

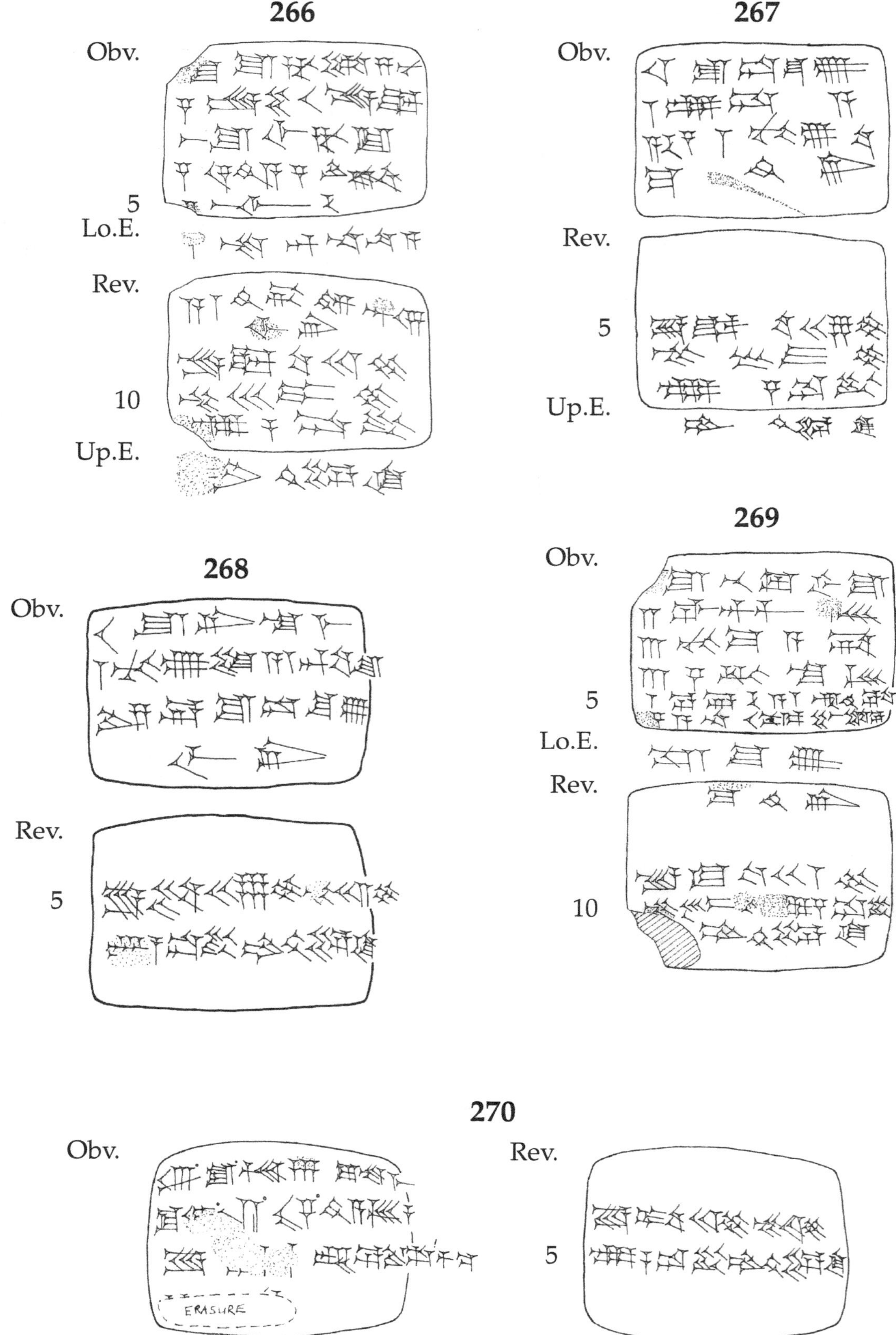
266
Obv.
Lo.E.
Rev.
Up.E.
267
Obv.
Rev.
Up.E.
268
Obv.
Rev.
269
Obv.
Lo.E.
Rev.
270
Obv.
ERASURE
Rev.

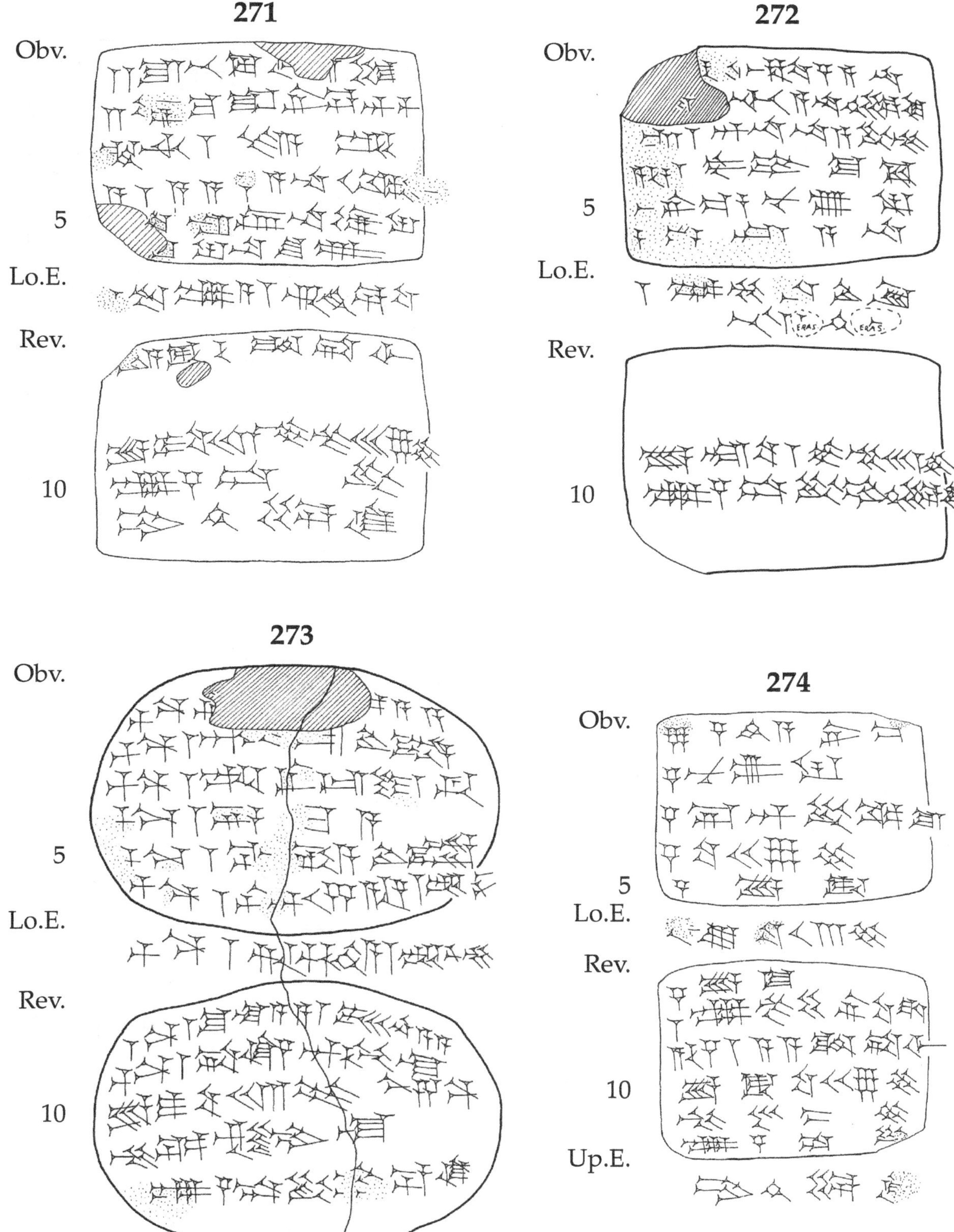
271
Obv.
Lo.E.
Rev.
272
Obv.
Lo.E.
ERAS
ERAS
Rev.
273
Obv.
Lo.E.
Rev.
274
Obv.
Lo.E.
Rev.
Up.E.

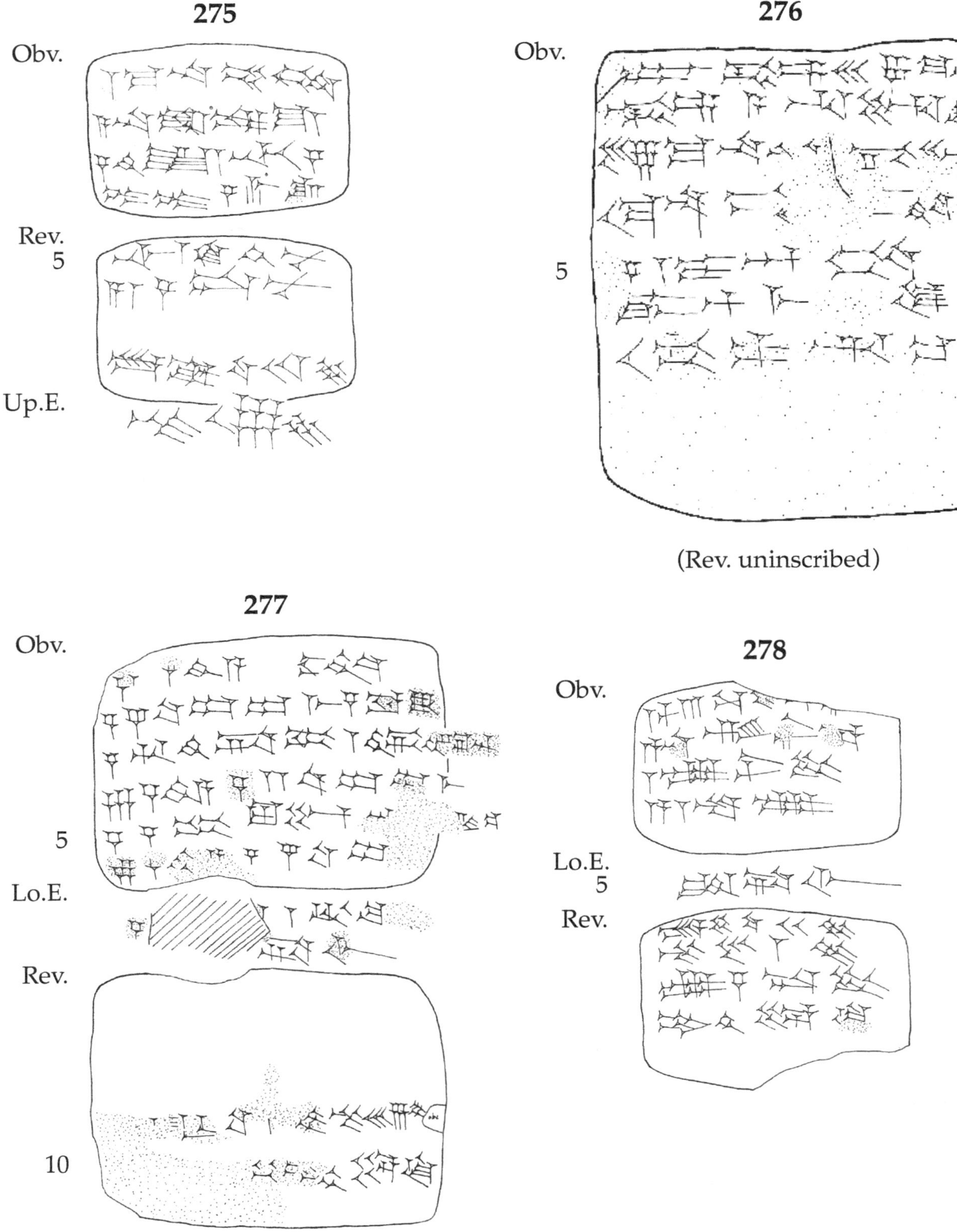
275
Obv.
Rev.
Up.E.
276
Obv.
(Rev. uninscribed)
277
Obv.
Lo.E.
Rev.
278
Obv.
Lo.E.
Rev.

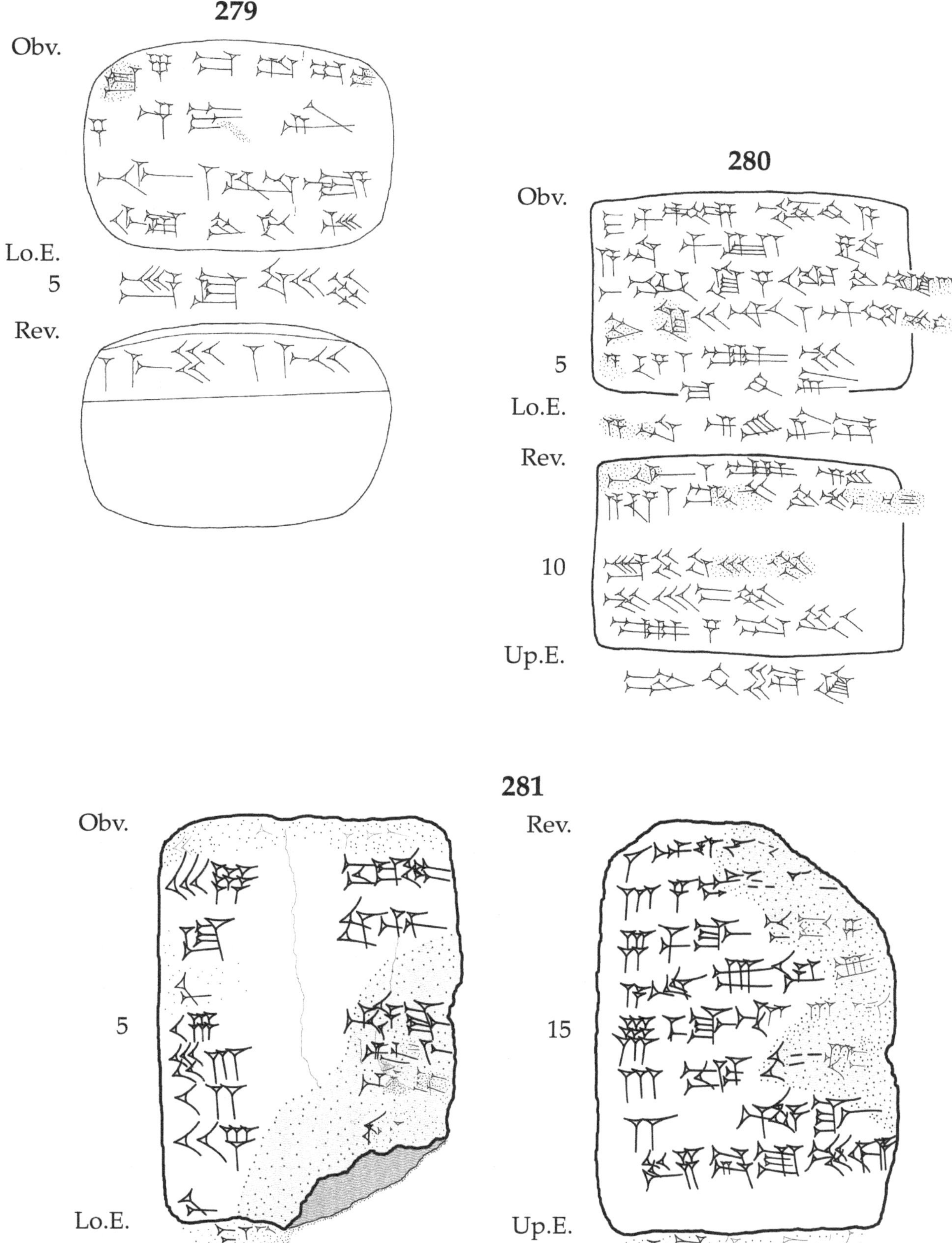
279
Obv.
Lo.E.
Rev.
280
Obv.
Lo.E.
Rev.
Up.E.
281
Obv.
Lo.E.
Rev.
Up.E.

282

Obv.

Lo.E.

Rev.

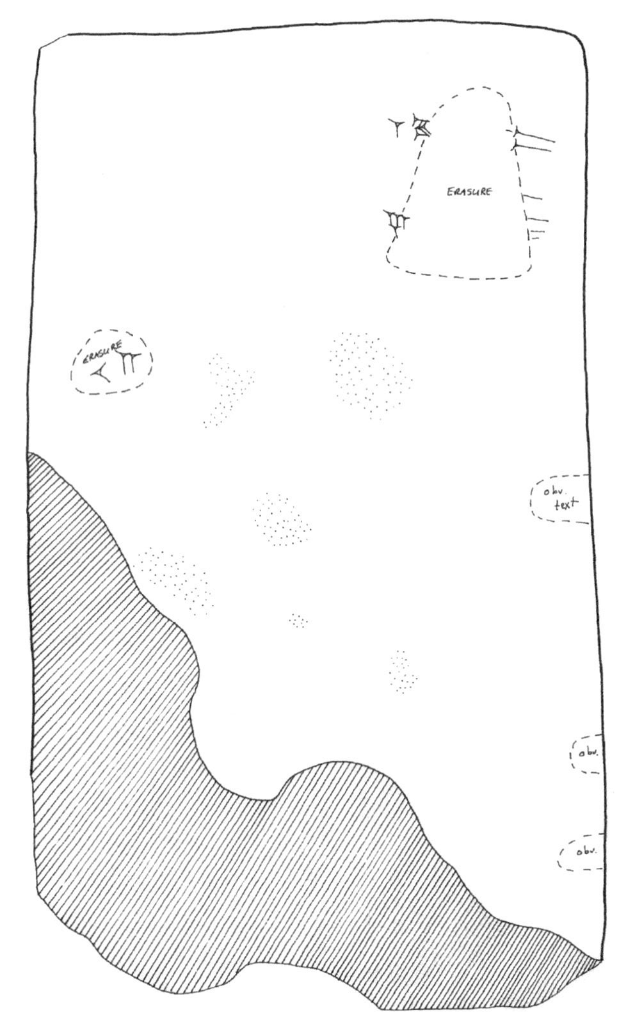

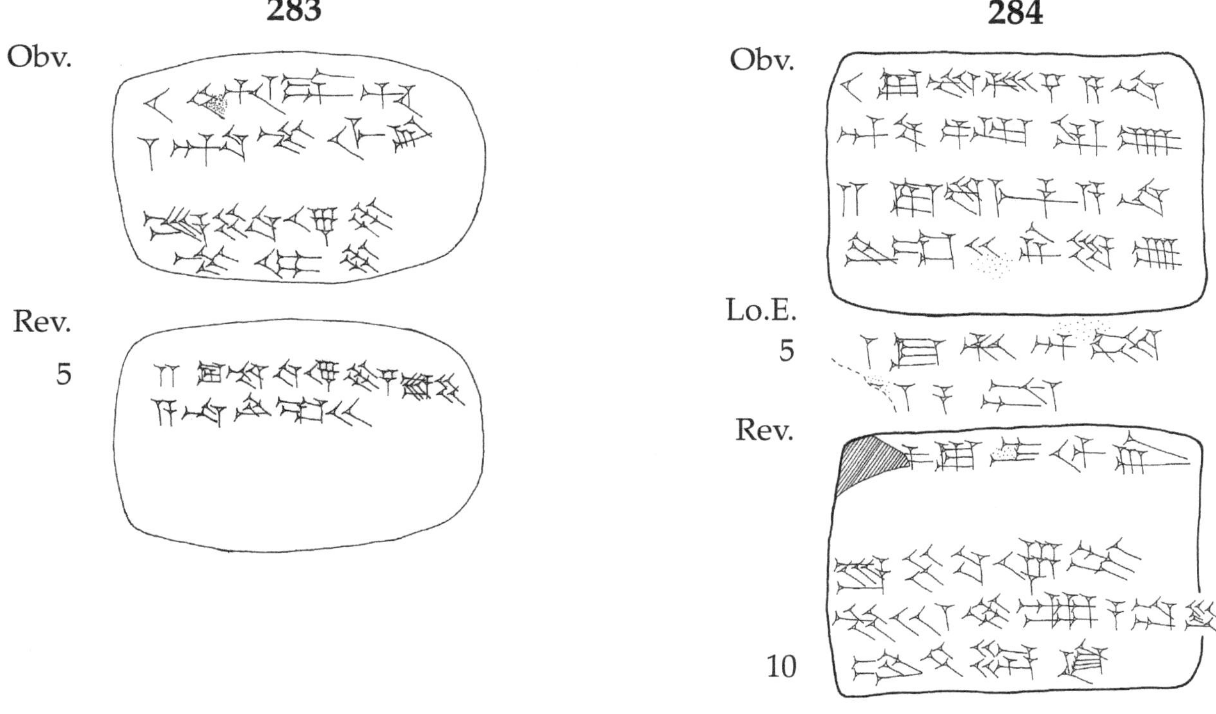
283
Obv.
Rev.
284
Obv.
Lo.E.
Rev.

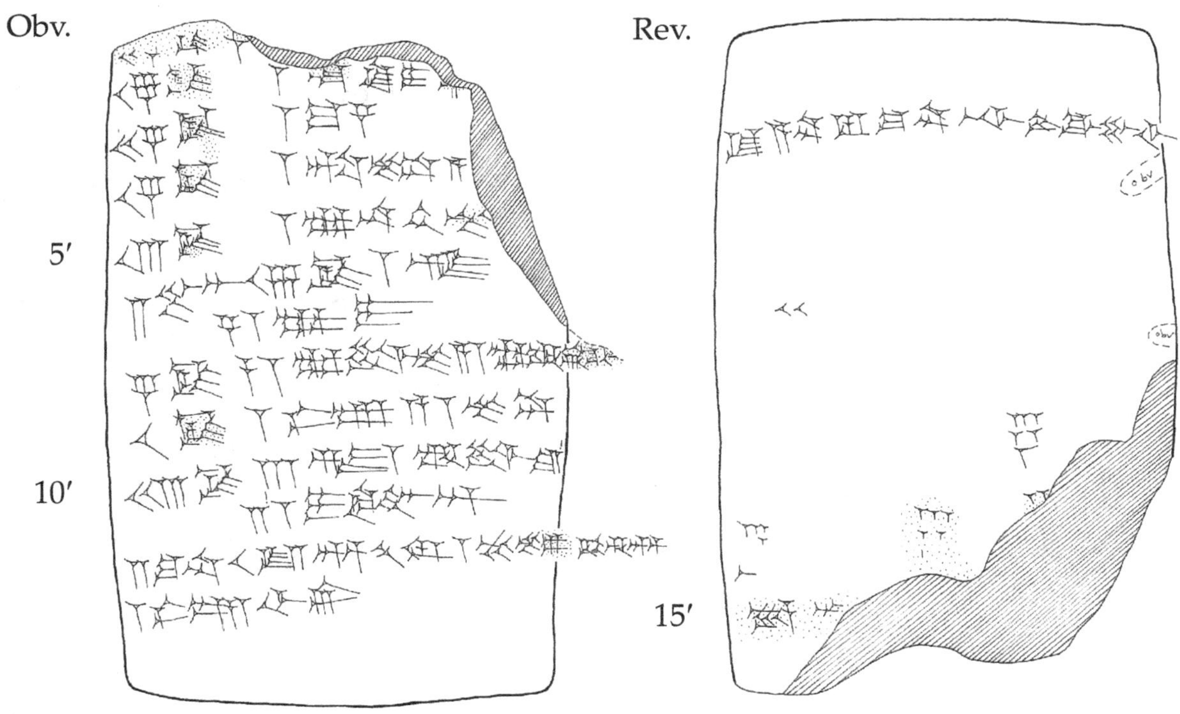
285
Obv.
Rev.

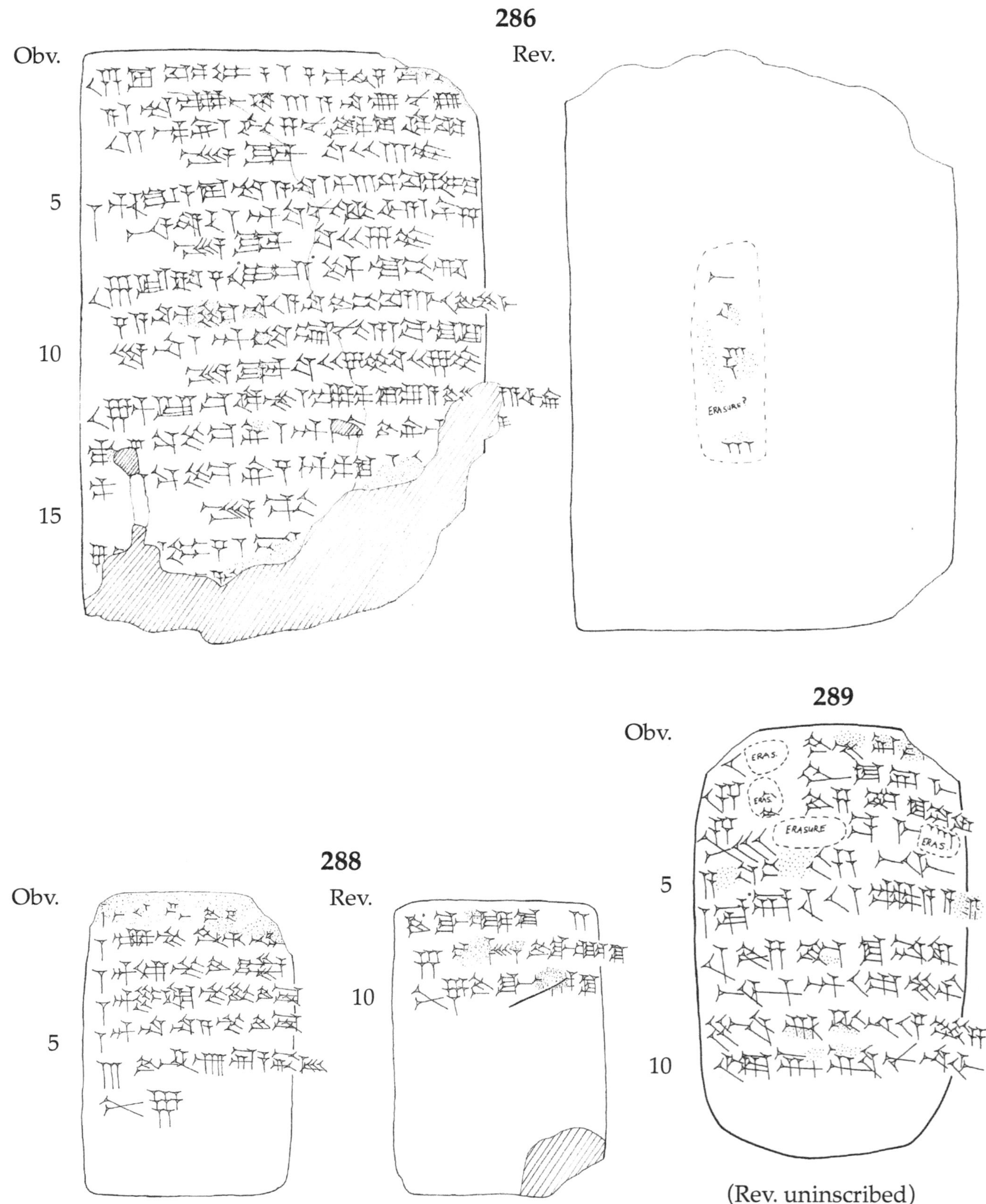

(Rev. uninscribed)

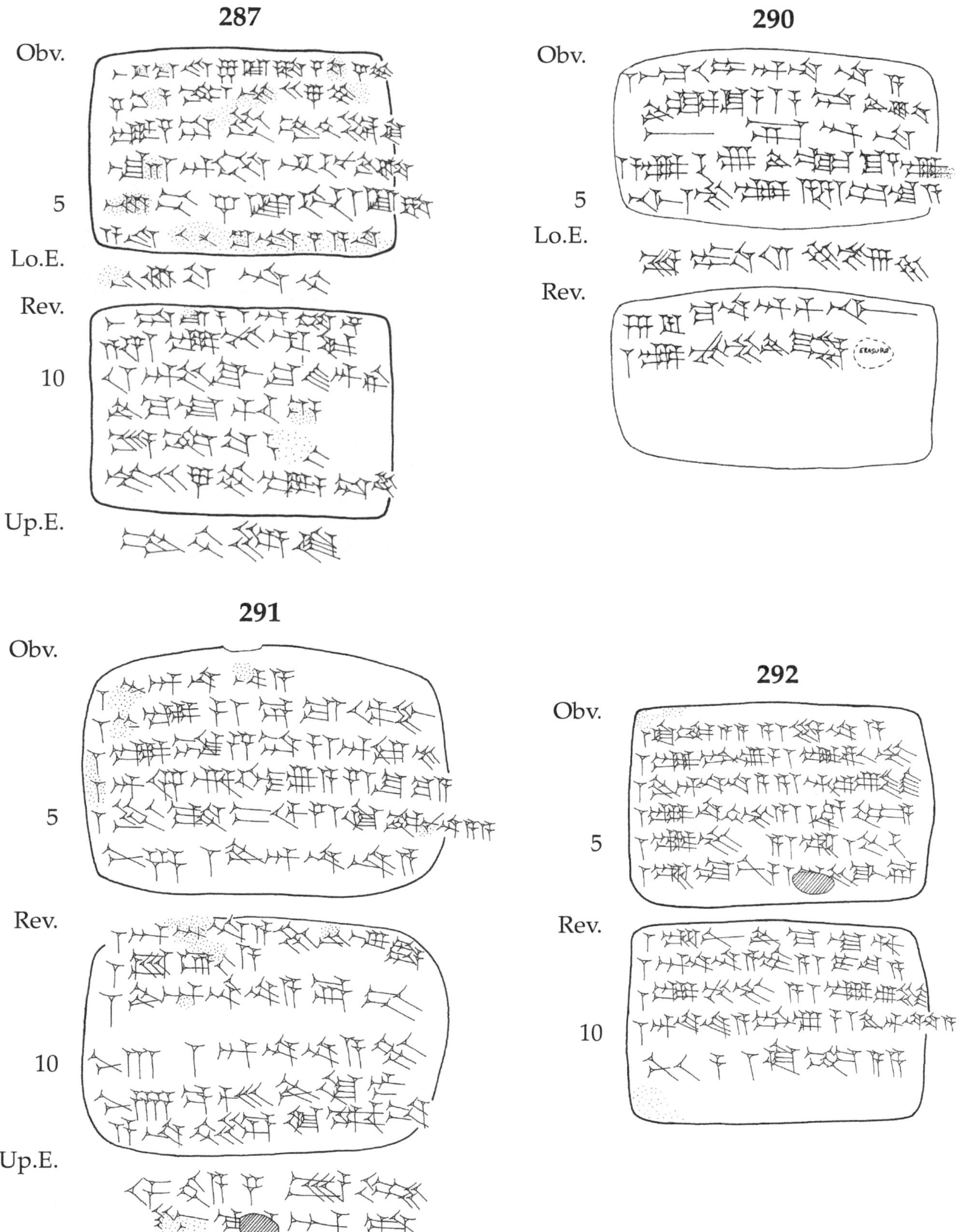
287
Obv.
Lo.E.
Rev.
Up.E.
290
Obv.
Lo.E.
Rev.
ERASURE
291
Obv.
Rev.
Up.E.
292
Obv.
Rev.

296

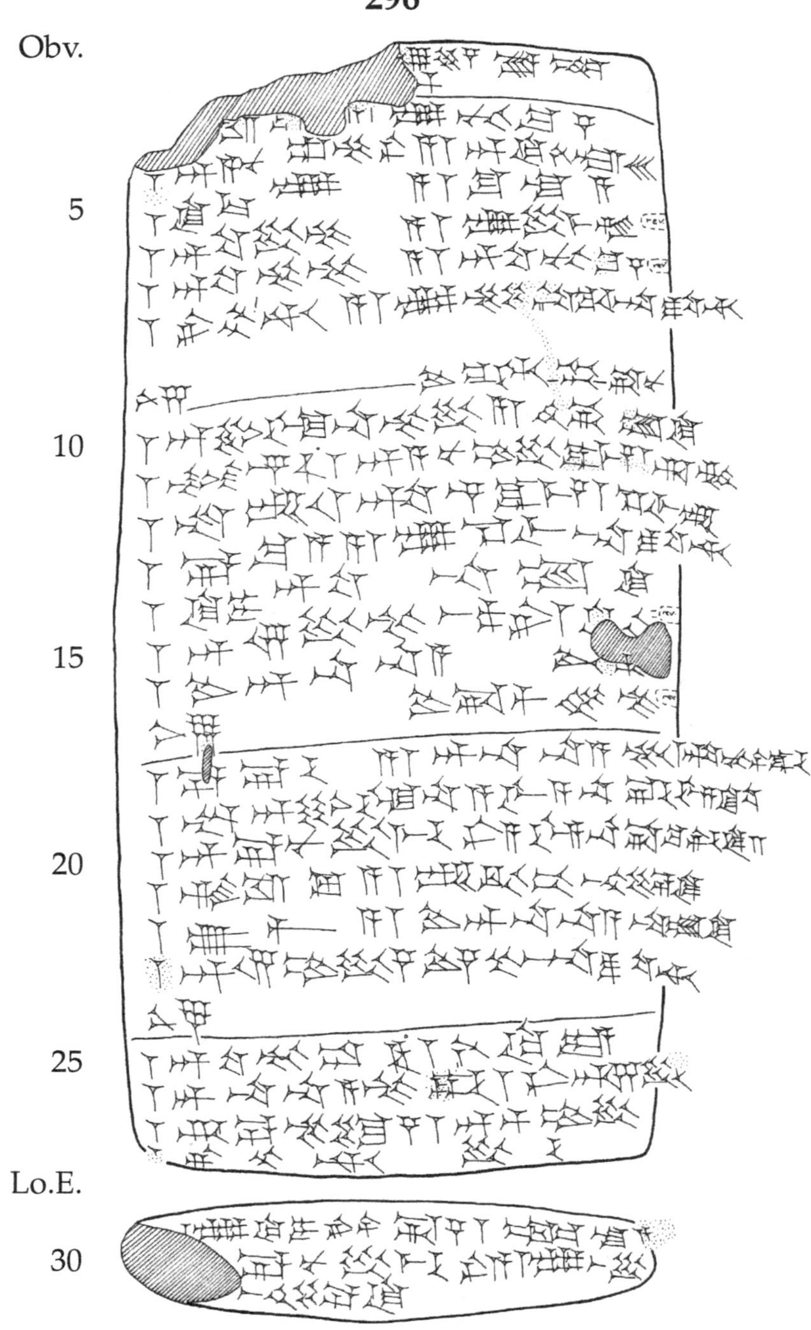

296

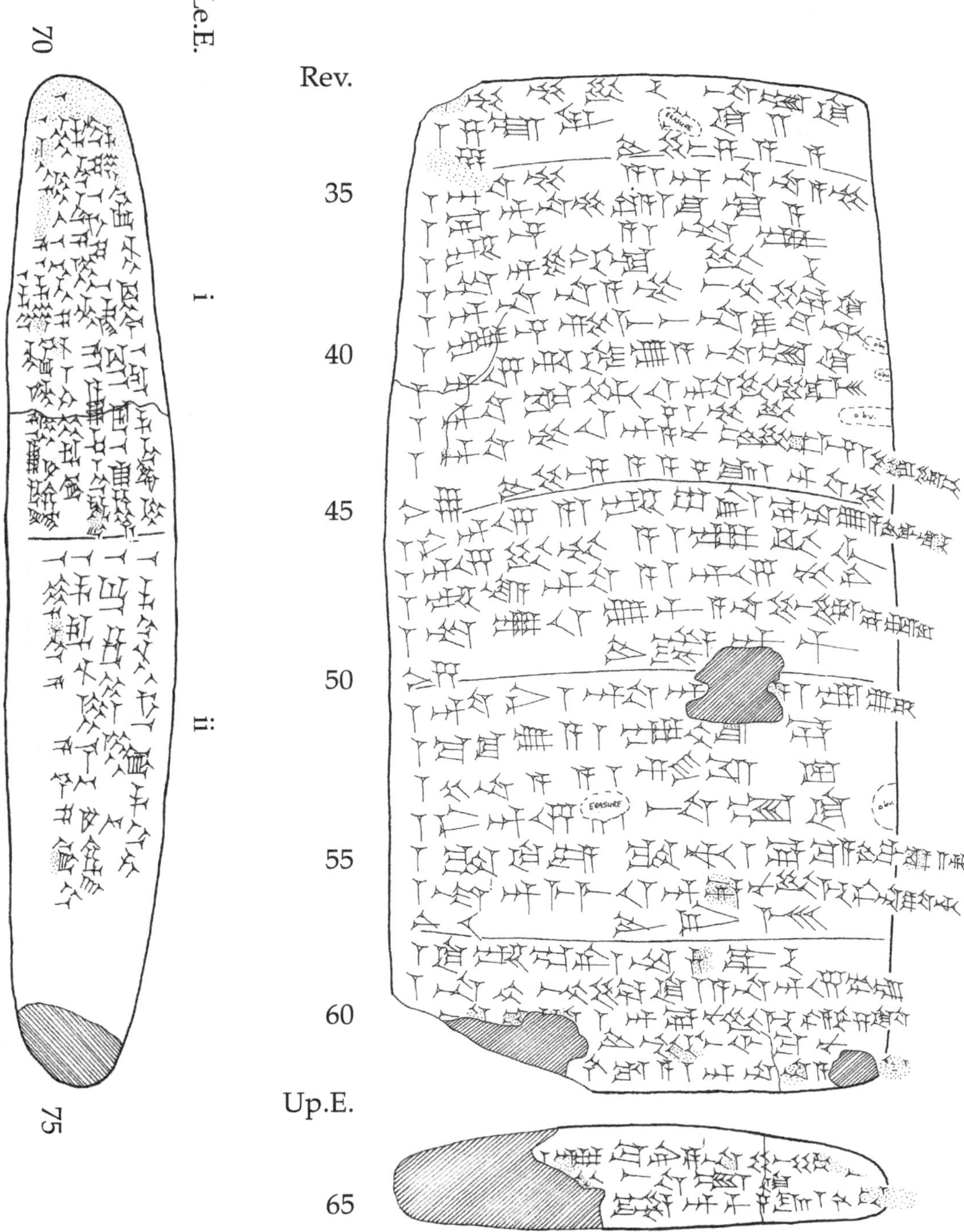

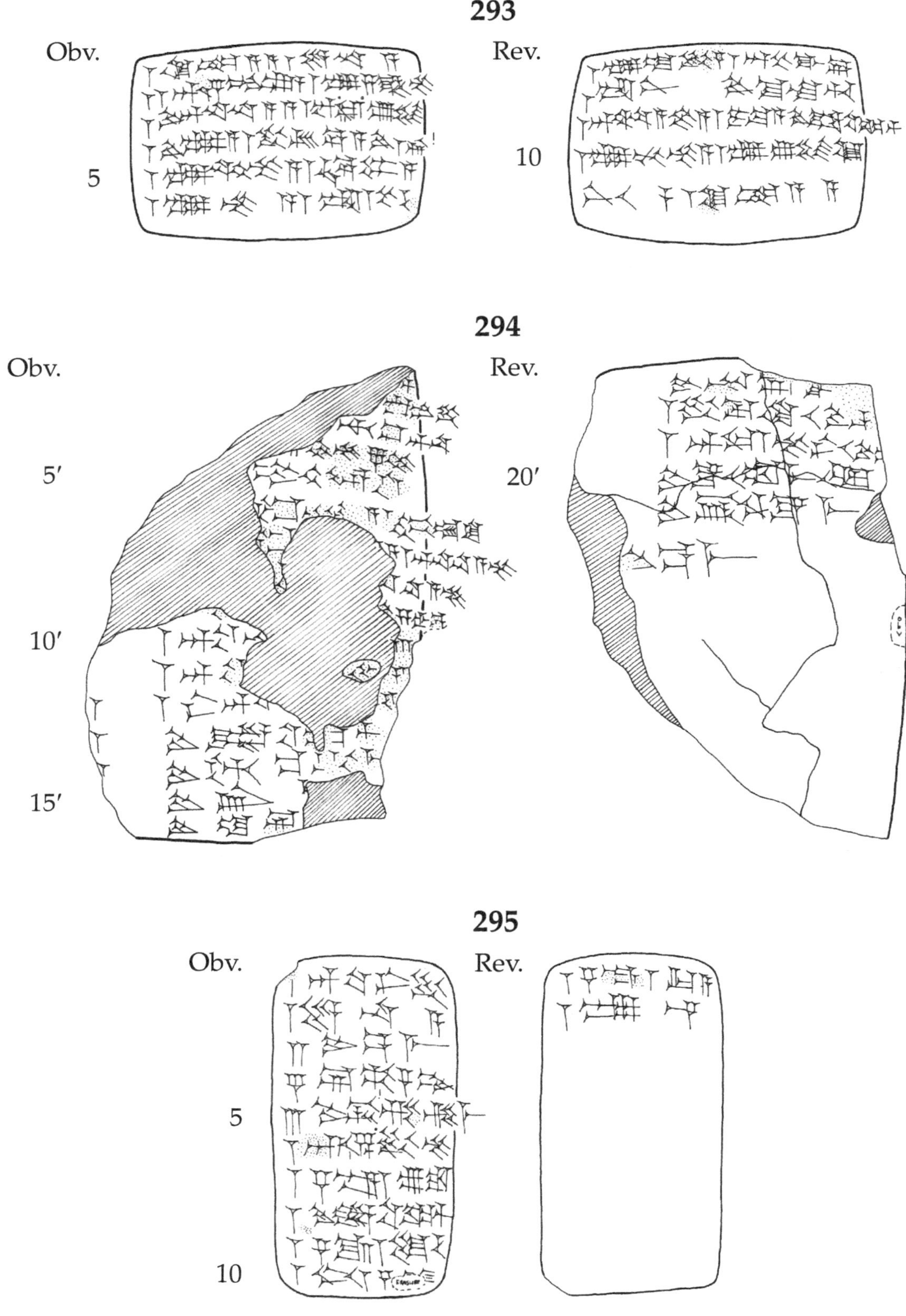
293
Obv.
Rev.
5
10
294
Obv.
Rev.
5′
20′
10′
15′
295
Obv.
Rev.
5
10

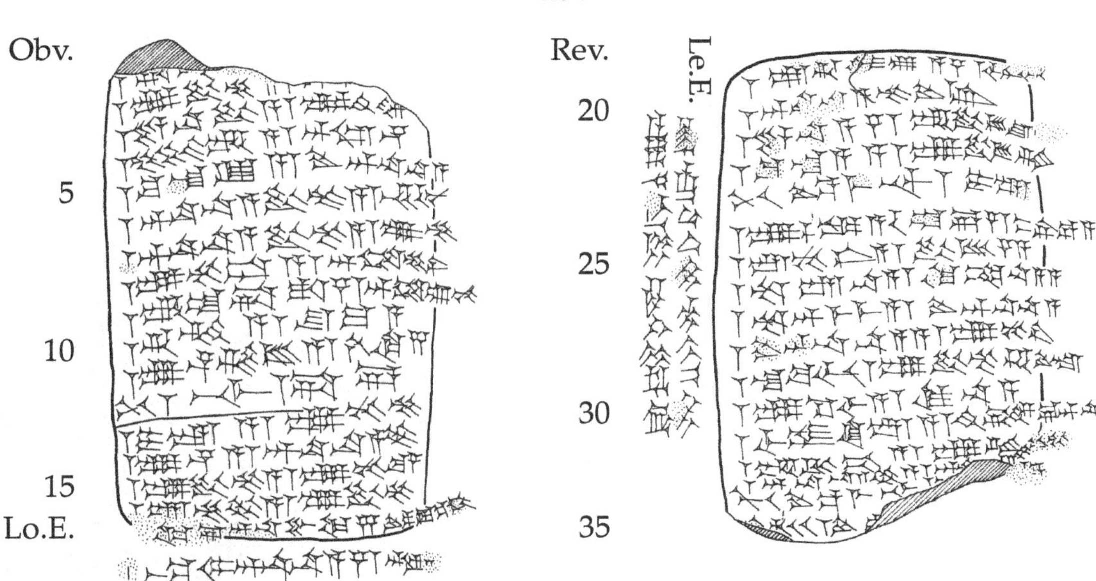

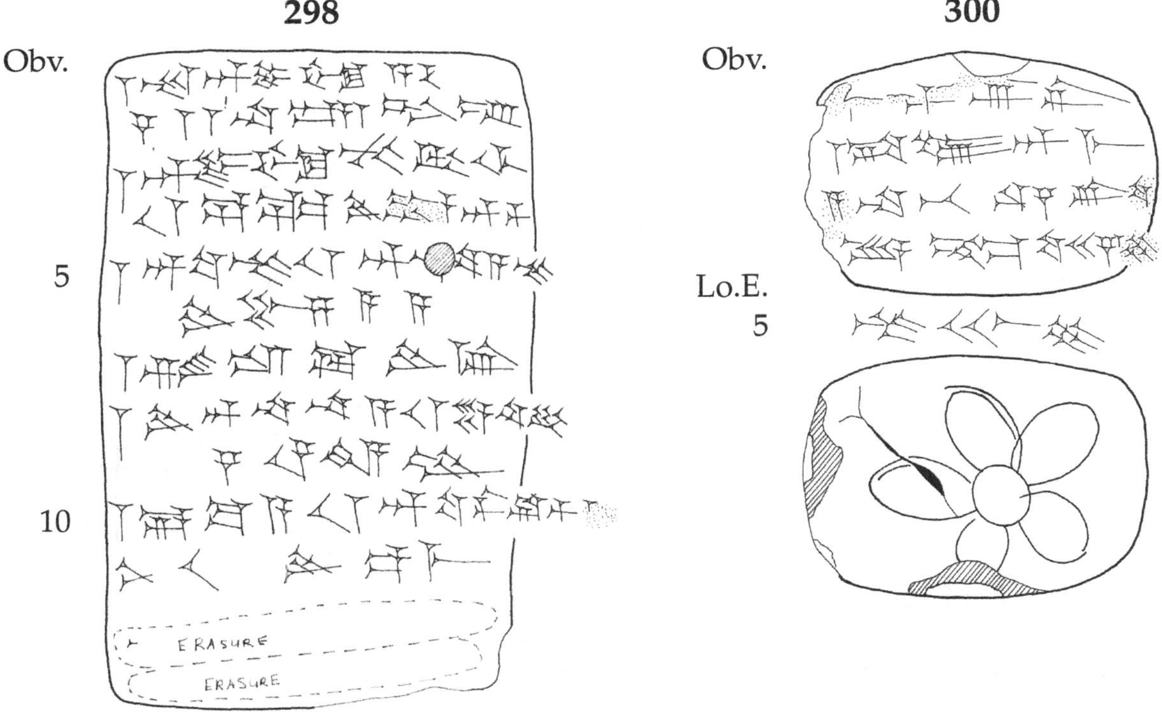

(Rev. uninscribed)

299

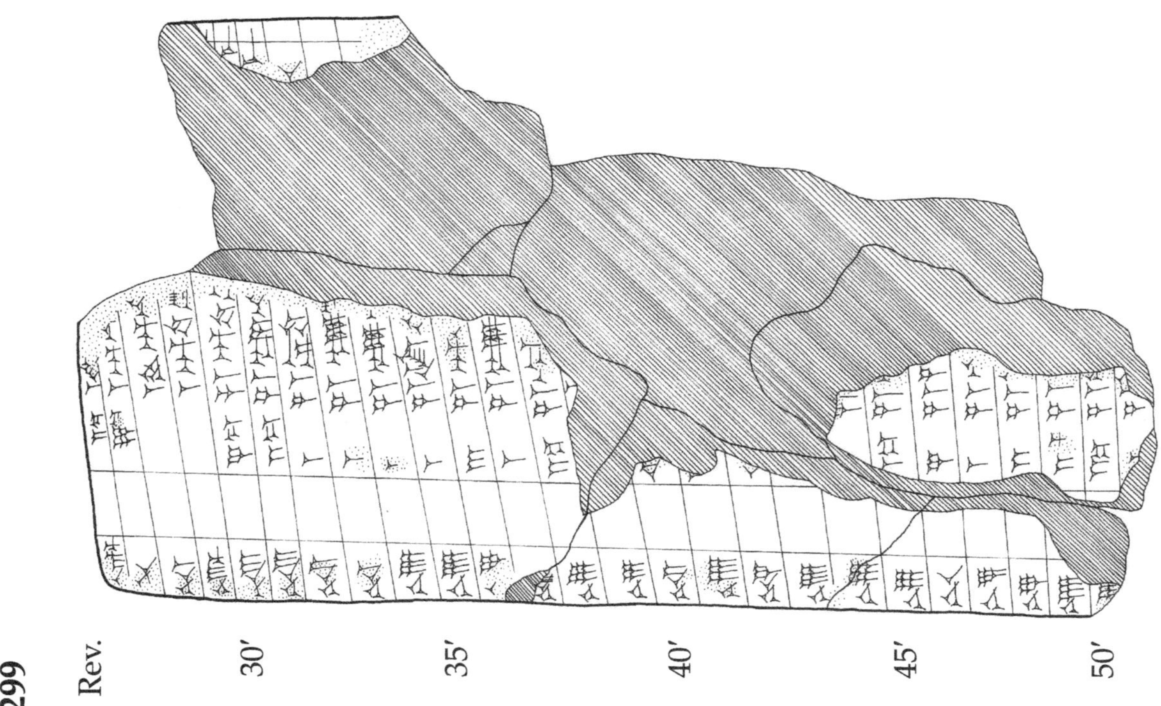

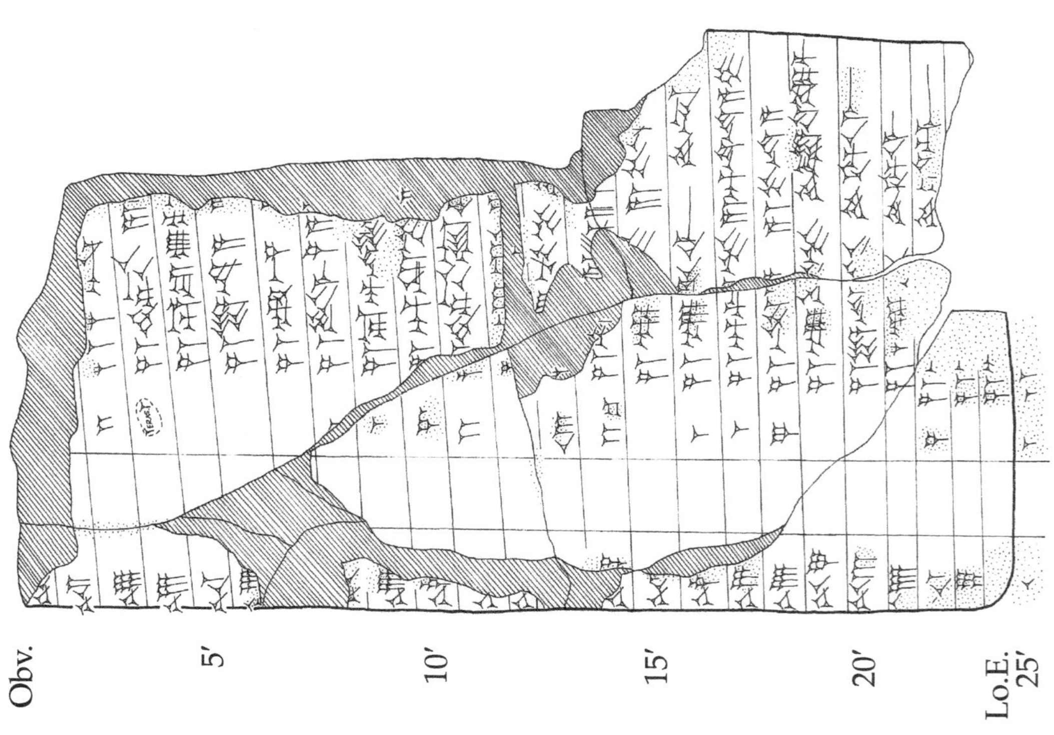

301

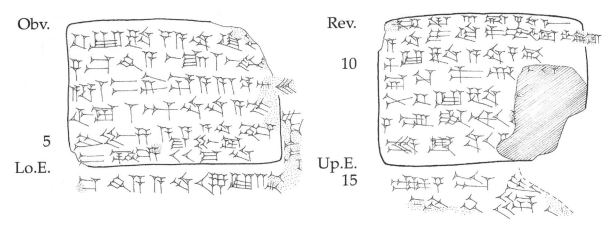

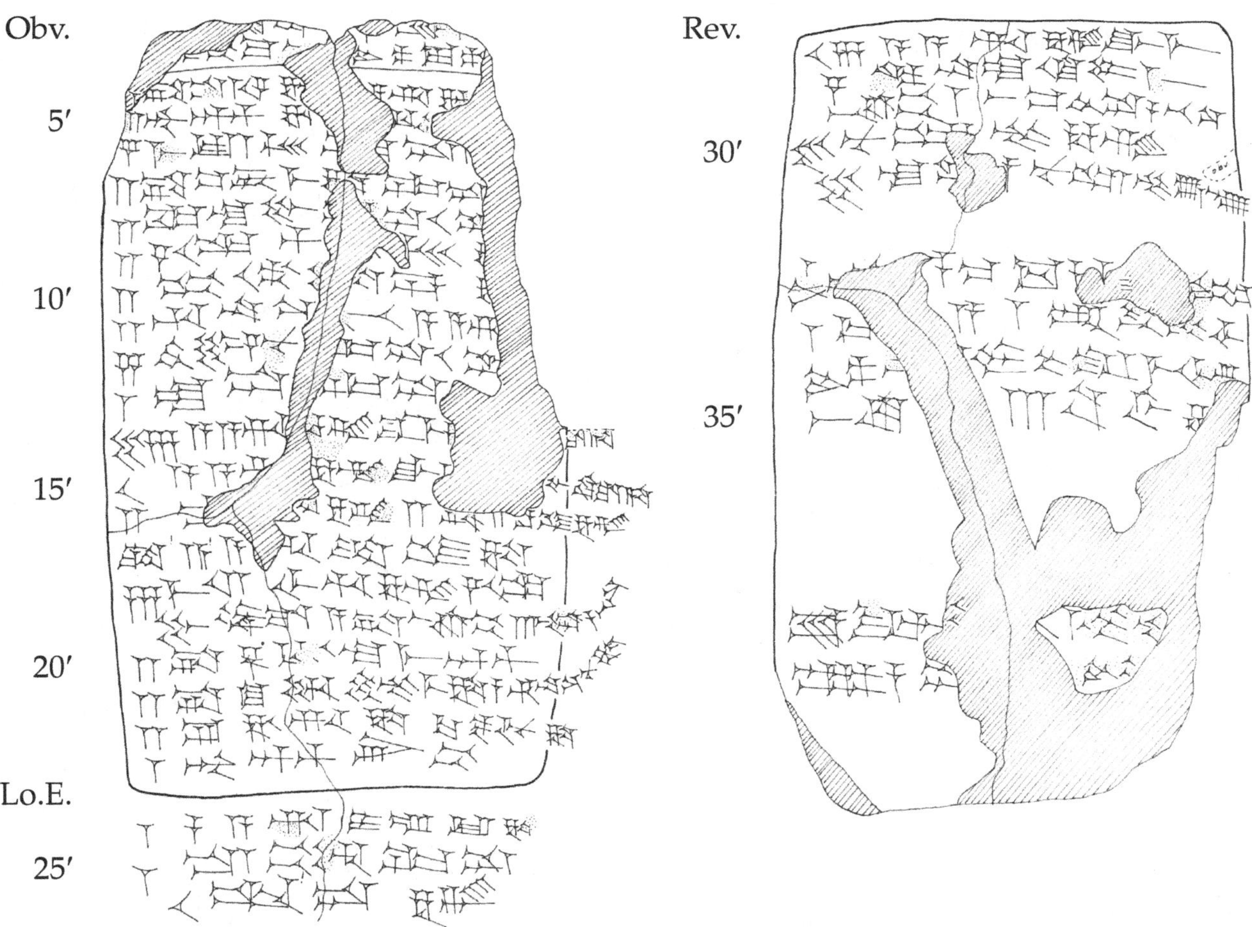

302

Obv.

5

Lo.E.

Rev.

10

Up.E.

15

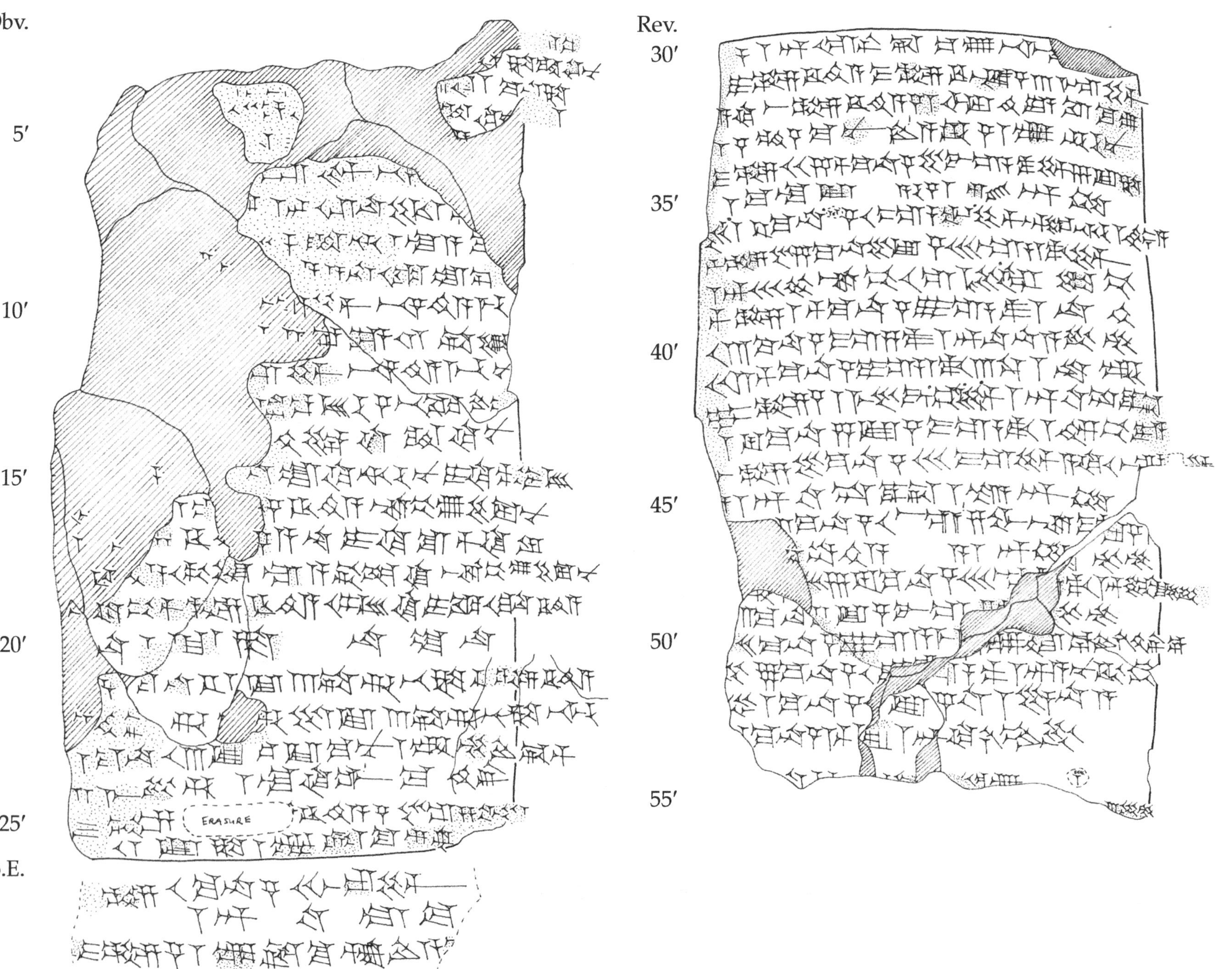
303
Obv.
Rev.
Lo.E.
ERASURE

304

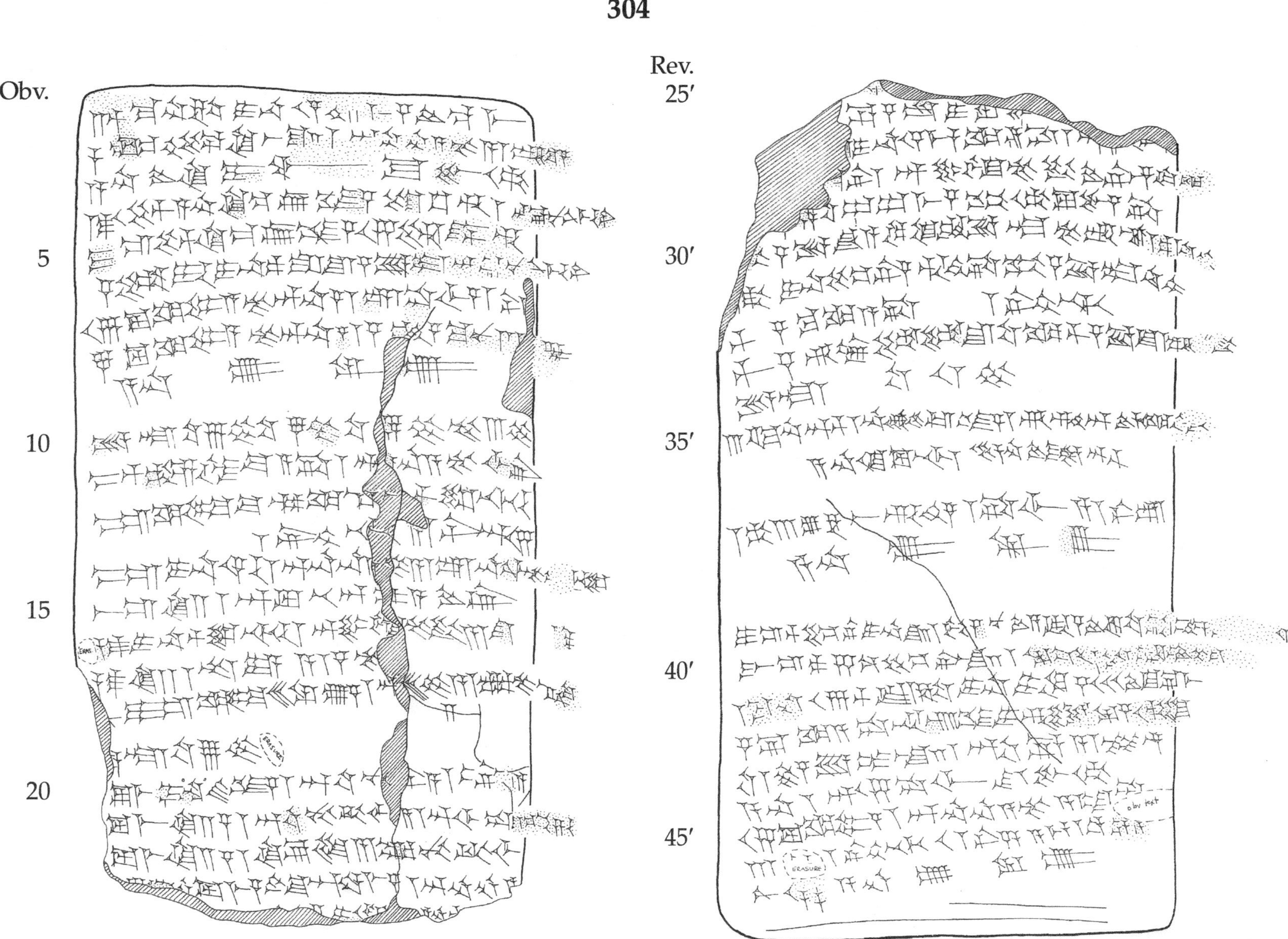

305

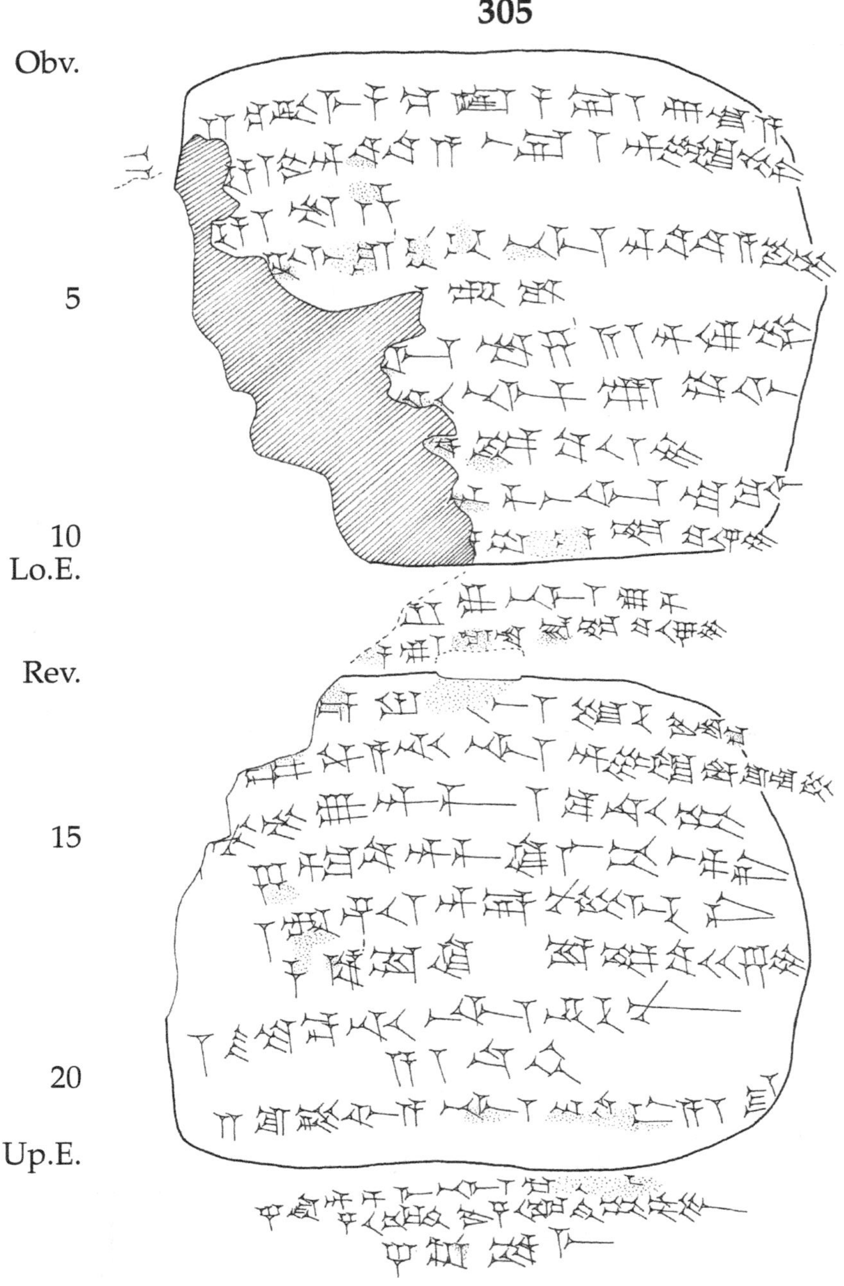

306

Obv.

(Rev. uninscribed)

307

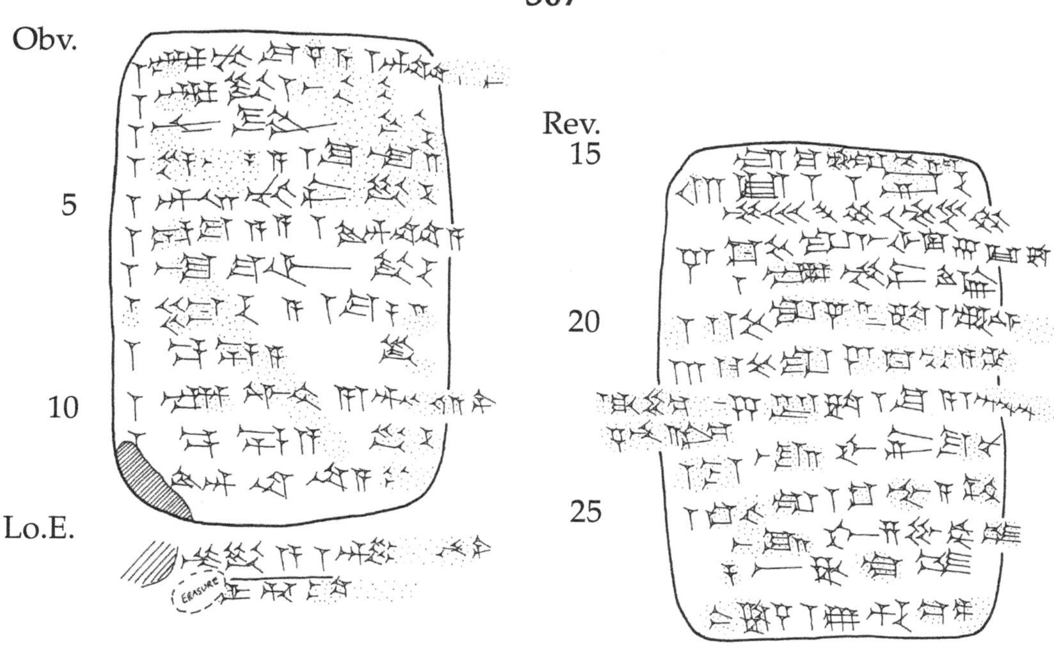

308

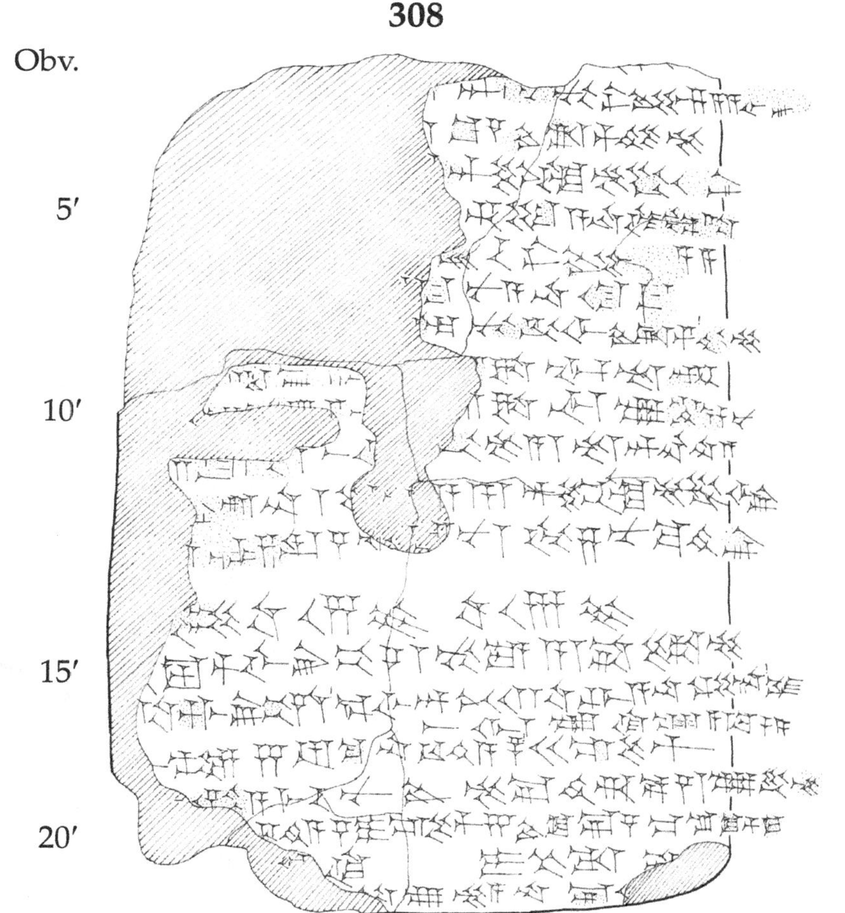

308

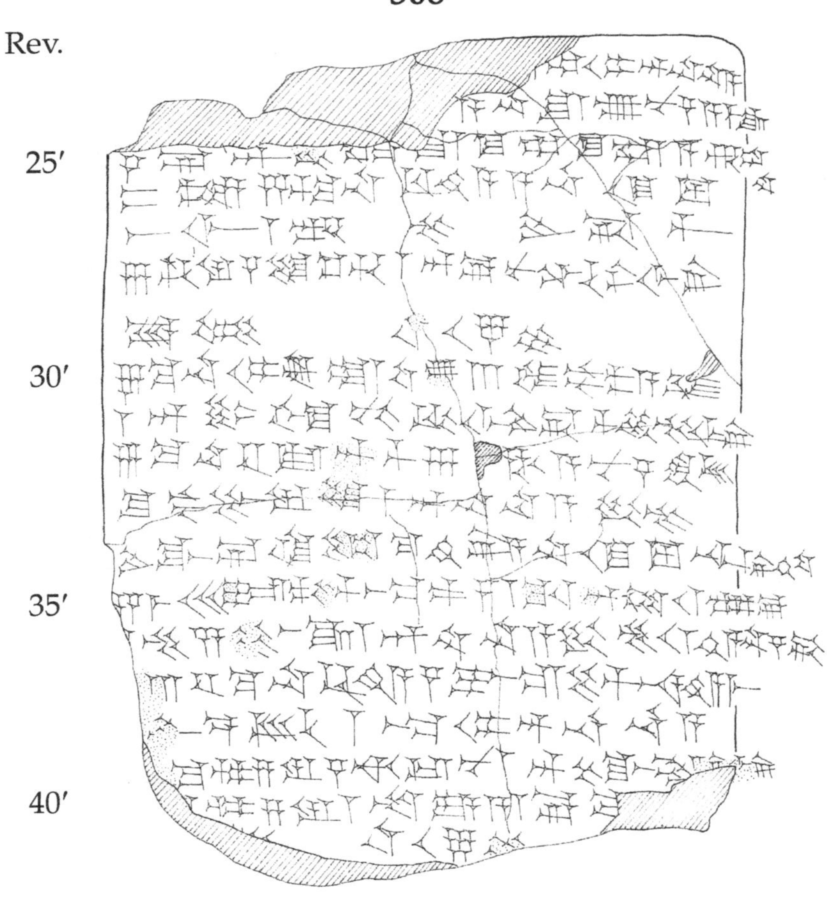
Rev.
25′
30′
35′
40′

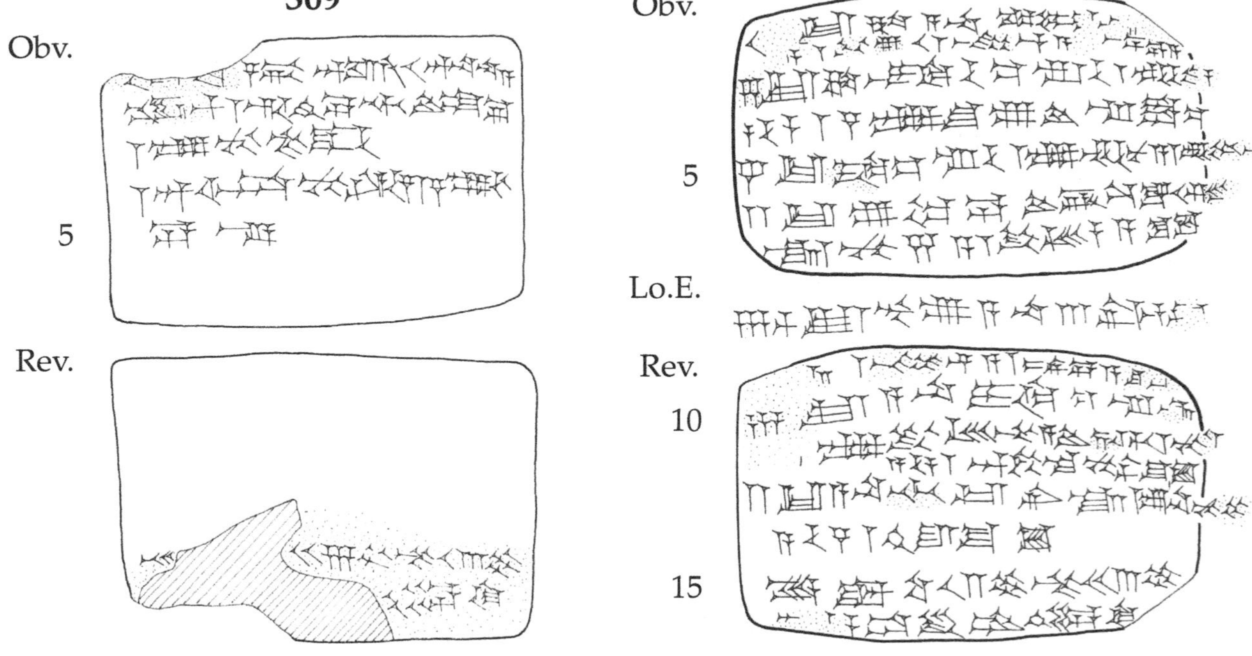
309
Obv.
5
Rev.
310
Obv.
5
Lo.E.
Rev.
10
15

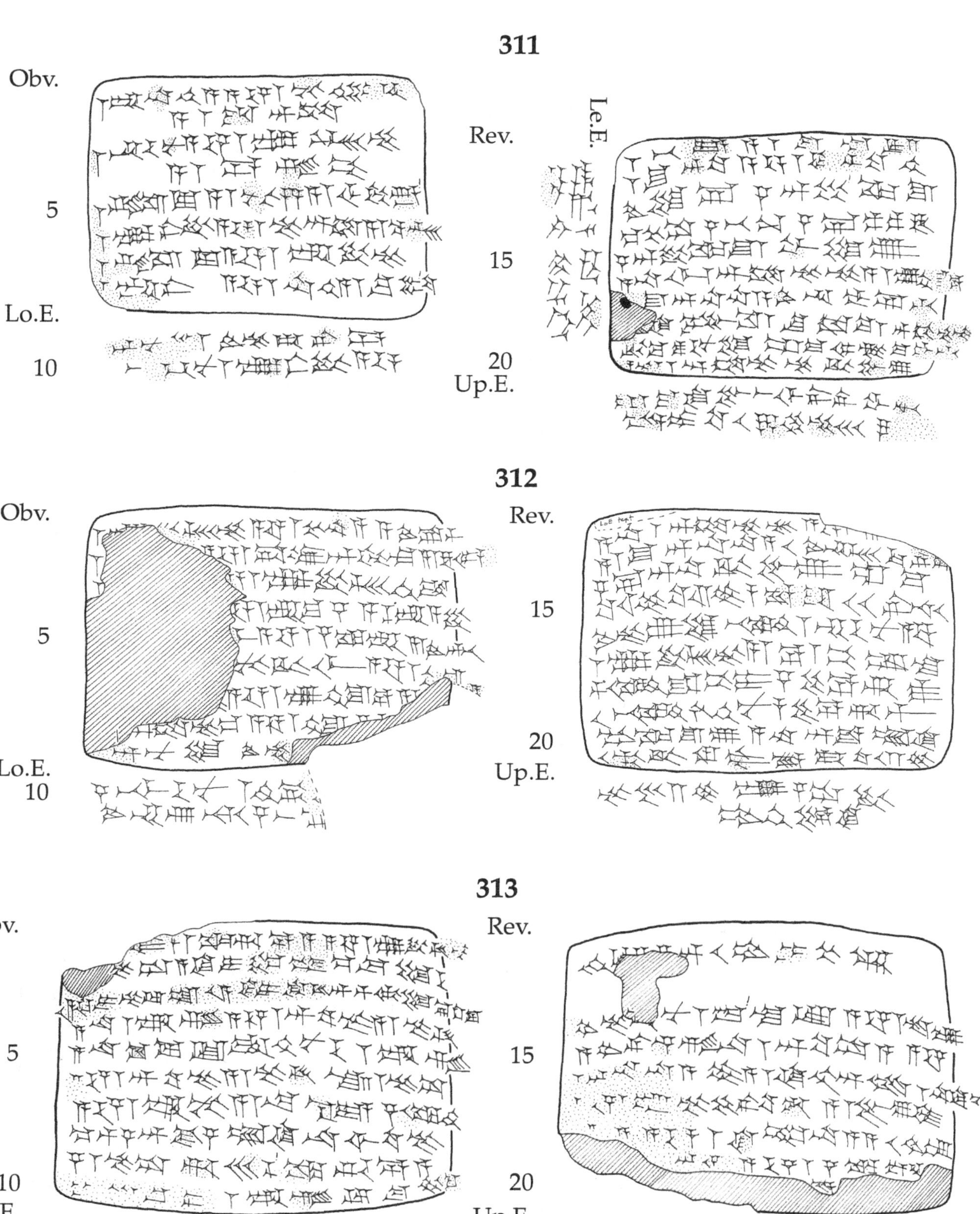
311
Obv.
Lo.E.
Rev.
Le.E.
Up.E.
312
Obv.
Lo.E.
Rev.
Up.E.
313
Obv.
Lo.E.
Rev.
Up.E.

314

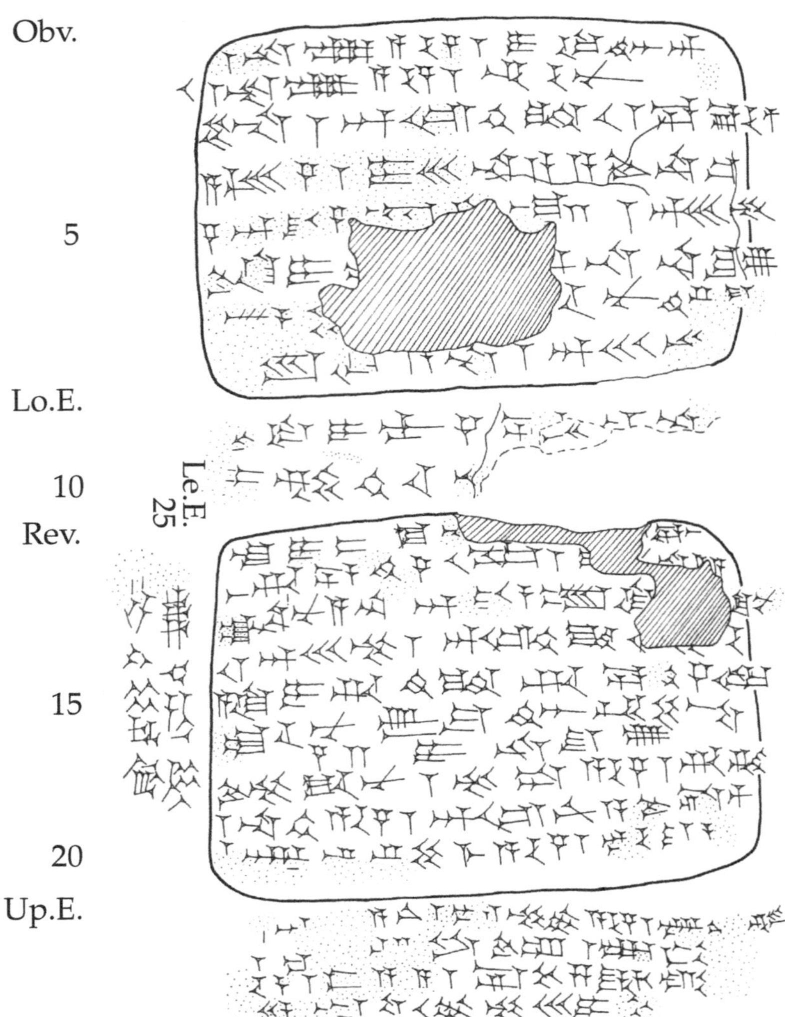

315

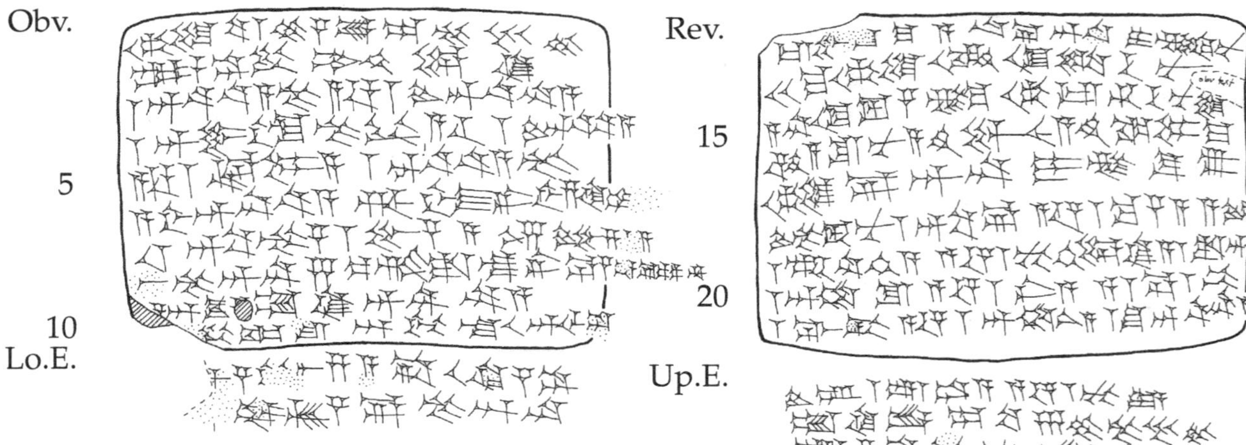

13

Up.E.

237

Rev.

239

Rev.

240

Rev.

300

Rev.